CRIMINAL JUSTICE ILLUMINATED

# Law Enforcement in the United States

## Second Edition

**James A. Conser, PhD, CPP**
Professor, Criminal Justice Department
Youngstown State University
Youngstown, Ohio

**Gregory D. Russell, JD, PhD**
Associate Professor and Director, Criminology Program
Arkansas State University
Jonesboro, Arkansas

**Rebecca Paynich, PhD**
Assistant Professor of Criminal Justice
Curry College
Milton, Massachusetts

**Terry E. Gingerich, PhD**
Assistant Professor
Department of Criminal Justice
Western Oregon University
Monmouth, Oregon

**JONES AND BARTLETT PUBLISHERS**
*Sudbury, Massachusetts*
BOSTON     TORONTO     LONDON     SINGAPORE

**World Headquarters**
Jones and Bartlett Publishers
40 Tall Pine Drive
Sudbury, MA 01776
978-443-5000
info@jbpub.com
www.jbpub.com

Jones and Bartlett Publishers Canada
2406 Nikanna Road
Mississauga, ON L5C 2W6
Canada

Jones and Bartlett Publishers International
Barb House, Barb Mews
London W6 7PA
United Kingdom

Copyright © 2005 by Jones and Bartlett Publishers, Inc.

Cover Image: © Will Dickey, *The Florida Times*/AP Photo

ISBN: 0-7637-8352-8

All rights reserved. No part of the material protected by this copyright notice may be reproduced or utilized in any form, electronic or mechanical, including photocopying, recording, or any information storage or retrieval system, without written permission from the copyright owner.

**Production Credits**
Publisher: Kimberly Brophy
Acquisitions Editor: Chambers Moore
V.P., Production and Design: Anne Spencer
Production Editor: Susan Schultz
Director of Marketing: Alisha Weisman
V.P., Manufacturing and Inventory Control: Therese Bräuer
Composition: Auburn Associates, Inc.
Photo Research: Kimberly Potvin
Cover Design: Anne Spencer
Printing and Binding: Malloy, Inc.
Cover Printing: Malloy, Inc.

**Library of Congress Cataloging-in-Publication Data**

Conser, James A. (James Andrew), 1948-
  Law enforcement in the United States / James A. Conser, Gregory D. Russell, Rebecca Paynich.— 2nd ed.
     p. cm.
  ISBN 0-7637-8352-8 (hardcover)
  1. Law enforcement—United States. 2. Police—United States. I. Russell, Gregory D. II. Paynich, Rebecca. III. Title.
  HV8138.C6445 2005
  363.2'3'0973—dc22

                    2005001703

Printed in the United States of America
08 07 06 05    10 9 8 7 6 5 4 3 2

ACC Library Services
Austin, Texas

# Contents

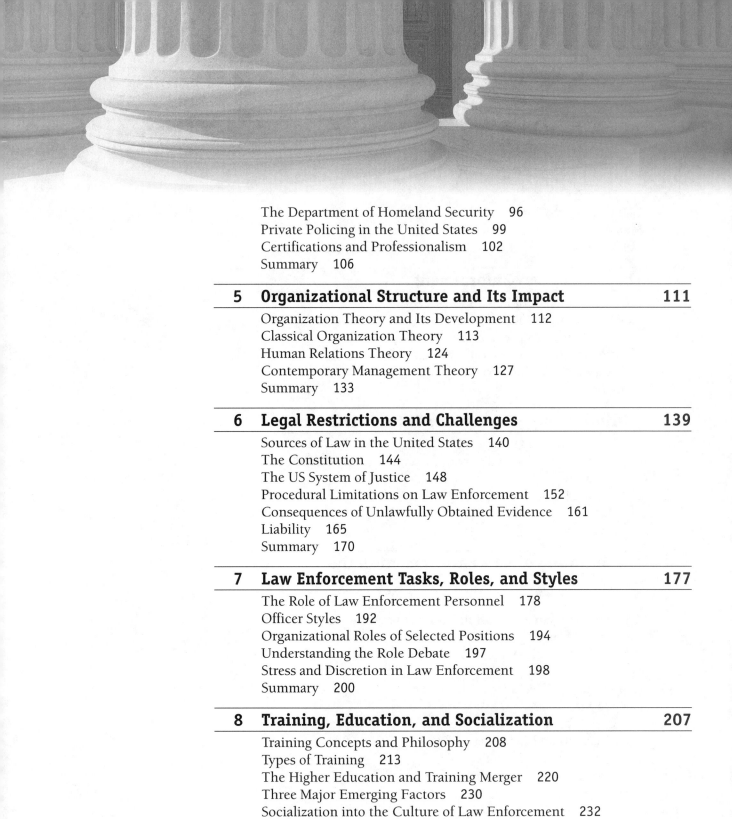

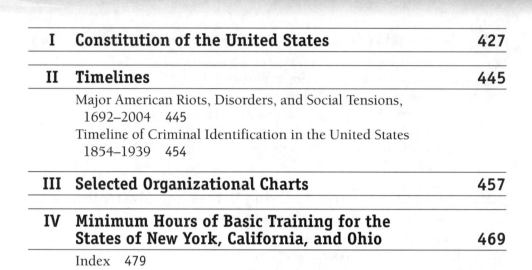

*To the law enforcement officers, fire fighters, EMS providers, and all other public servants who lost their lives in the attacks of September 11, 2001.*  **Dedication**

American law enforcement, at all levels, has undergone tremendous change in the past 40 years. Indeed, it has undergone dynamic change in the past 10 years alone, some as a result of the terrorist attacks of September 11, 2001; some as a result of dramatic technological improvements; and some as a result of political and social pressures on law enforcement to become more engaged with the public.

# Preface

This text is designed to help students of the criminal justice system understand the birth, emergence, and current status of American law enforcement by examining the social, political, institutional, and cultural forces that have shaped this social institution. Law enforcement has undergone three major stages since its formal inception in the United States. First, its creation during the "political era" of American governance—a period characterized by corruption, violence, and political cronyism, and one in which law enforcement was largely the arm of a given political party. Second, the progressive reform movement's reaction to that legacy and the creation of an infant civil service system which, by the 1930s and 1940s, gave at least the hint of some professional demeanor and the absence of political influence. Third, and finally, the reaction to the recommendations of a presidential commission report issued in 1967, many of which have taken nearly 40 years to come to fruition, ushered in what many call the "community era"— one characterized by community policing, problem-oriented policing, and policy driven by community demands rather than the demands of those in command of law enforcement. The latter focus is, of course, largely irrelevant to federal law enforcement agencies, and can be only marginally relevant to state law enforcement agencies. Hence, there is a divide between discourse in those sectors of law enforcement and in those that include municipal police and sheriff's departments. The events of 9/11 have radically altered federal agencies, while the effects on local enforcement are less clear, but no less certain.

To appreciate the organizational challenges that the future holds, it is essential to understand the history of organizational evolution; the creation, maintenance, and transmission of organizational culture across time; and how law enforcement officers see their role—that is, *their perspective on their role* rather than the perspective of others. In short, reform of any sort—structural reform or reform created through policy directive—requires the support and assistance of the officers and agents whose task it is to carry out organizational policy.

Hence, we offer the student a glimpse into not only the historical imperatives that helped shape law enforcement, but also the institutional dynamics, the social movements, and political events that have driven law enforcement to its current status. Law enforcement was not created instantaneously—it evolved in response to a multitude of forces. To illustrate the importance of studying

history, personnel policy, legal concerns, and policy directions, we would like to present two cases which offer, we believe, two starkly contrasting challenges to law enforcement in 2005 and beyond.

In the mid-1990s, a new chief of police took command of the relatively small department in Marysville, California, a small community of about 12,000 citizens roughly 45 minutes north of Sacramento. A young sergeant, fresh from a community policing institute, asked his new chief for some freedom in conducting an exercise that would test the problem-solving theories he had been taught. The chief, a graduate of the prestigious California Command College, agreed. The sergeant had noted that one town park no longer attracted children and parents. Rather, he learned, it had been taken over by prostitutes and drug dealers. His strategy was to first rid the park of these parasites, and then revitalize the park. He could not know what would happen, but he believed it would be good.

At first, he parked his patrol unit at the park from 3 p.m. until midnight every day of the week and made certain someone else was there on the weekends. Then, as the routines of citizens in the area began to change, he coaxed local business leaders, service clubs, churches, and community volunteers to contribute time, money, and material to clean up the park, eliminate underbrush and low hanging limbs, plant new, smaller flowering shrubs, re-pave the parking lot, and install new playground equipment. Then, he hosted (with his chief and fellow officers) a party to celebrate the reopening of the park. Calls for service had dipped considerably in that area, and neighbors had gotten to know one another. But something more happened. They started conveying information to him about drug houses in the immediate vicinity.

He took action to observe these premises and with the help of the drug task force, closed several of them, jailing the offenders. He then helped the city seize the properties under the California Safe Streets Act and, again with volunteer help, rehabilitated the houses and sold them to qualified, low-income buyers, thus increasing the number of homeowners in the area—a key to neighborhood stability.

In short, he used both the tactics of community policing and problem-oriented policing *in concert with traditional law enforcement* tactics. Understanding the relationship of these three concepts is imperative for the future.

Our second case examines the darker side of law enforcement, but one that unfortunately is all too real. This story of alleged corruption and illegal deeds highlights not only the degree of the problem in American law enforcement, but also that the manner in which hiring, promotion, and discipline are exercised can affect the future of an organization.

In April of 2003, Chief David Brame of the Tacoma, Washington Police Department, killed his estranged wife Chrystal Brame in front of the couple's young children, an 8-year-old girl and a 5-year-old boy. The episode culminated a series of organizational blunders that proved to have serious consequences.

When Brame had originally applied to be an officer in the department, he was given a psychological test. He failed the exam but was permitted to take it again. He failed again, but was nonetheless hired. Early in his career, a female coworker alleged that he had raped her after a dinner engagement one night. Even though another officer came forward to say that Brame confessed the rape to him, that confession was never used in any disciplinary proceedings because Brame had not been read his rights before he confessed. Later, his wife filed for divorce, alleging that he had been abusing her for years. The divorce papers were obtained by an amateur journalist and placed on the Web. Soon thereafter, the commercial press picked up on the story.

We are left to wonder how this man became chief. The allegations of rape and the confession were widely known, yet he was promoted. The promotion was made by the City Manager, whose wife had earlier been accused of serious insurance fraud. When her case was being investigated, David Brame was chief of detectives and many later suspected that he had helped her in some fashion. The scandals associated with David Brame resulted in the entire Tacoma Police Department being investigated by the FBI for corruption.

While these two cases are widely divergent in their organizational concerns, they are nonetheless related. Hence, the *system* of law enforcement must be seen for what it is—an interlocked set of institutional structures, behaviors, and conditions, all responding to the external environment and its demands; hence, our choice to view law enforcement from a systems perspective.

In closing, a word about conducting further research. Throughout the text, we have provided a number of Web addresses where readers can find more information on the topics covered herein. Occasionally, a Web site changes its address or becomes temporarily unavailable. If the Web addresses cited in this text are not found, try them again later—perhaps even on another day. If you still cannot locate the site, use your search engine. Simply enter a few key words related to the topic of the original site. You may find the site you were originally looking for, or an alternative site that may serve the same purpose. There is a wealth of criminal justice information on the Internet and more is being added daily.

## Acknowledgments

We would like to express our gratitude to Susette Talarico of the University of Georgia and Professor Lawrence Travis of the University of Cincinnati, who, during the development of this project, reviewed the first edition of the text. Their comments and suggestions were extremely helpful.

Jim Conser wishes to acknowledge his wife, Linda, who has supported him through various projects and endeavors for over 35 years. She helped to instill honesty and integrity in their three daughters and now influences their two grandsons.

Gregory Russell would like to thank his wife and colleague, Ellen Lemley, for her constant support, friendship, and love; his fellow authors for their attention to detail, and particularly Becki and Terry for taking on the task of the major revision of the first edition; and finally Chambers Moore and the staff at Jones and Bartlett for their support and Herculean efforts to get the text out in time.

Rebecca Paynich wishes to express her gratitude to her loving husband, Jason, who provided emotional and editorial support throughout the process, and to her son, Spencer, whose intellectual curiosity motivates her to continually seek knowledge in every arena.

Terry Gingerich wishes to thank his children, Matthew, Peter, Ethan, Annemarie, and April and his grandchildren, Chad and Troy, for their love and support.

# The Field of Law Enforcement

## Learning Objectives

As a person interested in the field of law enforcement, you need to understand that it is not a simple field of study. There are many forces in today's society that influence the operation of law enforcement agencies. This chapter introduces you to the field and the complex set of factors that influence today's agencies. It reviews several approaches to viewing the law enforcement function in the United States. After studying this chapter, you should be able to:

- Define and explain the concepts of law enforcement and policing.
- Define and explain the concept of social control.
- Describe four basic perspectives of the police function.
- Understand how to apply the systems perspective to policing.

## Chapter Outline

## Key Terms Used in This Chapter

| | |
|---|---|
| law enforcement | full enforcement |
| police powers | zero tolerance |
| policing | public policy perspective |
| policing officials | proactive |
| social control | systems theory |
| socialization | global perspective |
| legal perspective | Vienna Convention on Consular |
| discretion | Relations |
| selective enforcement | diplomatic immunity |

## ■ The Basic Concept of Law Enforcement

In a democratic society, as in all modern societies, the enforcement of the law is a vital function. Without some type of law enforcement, a society would eventually cease to exist. Generally speaking, the function called **law enforcement** is a society's formal attempt to obtain compliance with the established rules, regulations, and laws of that society. Without law enforcement, American society as we know it would probably succumb to social disorder and chaos.

The United States is a representative democracy, which places great emphasis on the protection of individual freedoms and liberties. As such, its institutions must reflect those principles upon which the country was founded. Because the United States is predominately an open and free society—in the political sense, with freedom to disagree from region to region, state to state, city to city, about how to design law enforcement, direct it, and develop policy—it is common to have disagreements about how to enforce the law. It also may appear "popular" to question the actions of law enforcement officials, as is commonly done in the mass media. Historically, our country's citizens have often questioned the actions of government officials. As citizens, we may not always agree with what happens on the street, in police stations, in courtrooms, in jails, and in prisons. However, people in the United States possess the freedom to criticize and protest governmental actions because of the structure in which our criminal justice system is placed. That structure and the Constitution may occasionally appear to be in conflict with one another, but that may be evidence that the system works. The debate over civil liberties and national security that has emerged since the 9/11 terrorist attacks on the United States is another example of our principles at work. Inevitably, such issues include the question, How can the law enforcement community function to preserve the civil liberties and freedoms that are cherished and protected by the Constitution? Should we attempt to balance between our constitutional rights and safety, or must the latter be subject to the first?

Our purpose in this book is to assist you in answering these questions by becoming more informed about the field of law enforcement so that you have an understanding and appreciation for its objectives and activities. Such a background is necessary for you to develop informed opinions about the field, rather than opinions based on limited knowledge and experience. Everyone has opinions; some are more informed than others. "Educated persons" have informed opinions and can describe why they believe certain things. They have a foundation (facts and evidence) for their arguments and reasons for doing things, for making choices, and for advocating changes. Society needs informed, knowledgeable citizens that understand the field of law enforcement and its impact on social behavior.

Law enforcement is one means of formally supervising human behavior that ensures that laws and regulations of a society are followed, that there is a certain amount of security and stability in society. The enforcement of law in all of its forms (statutes, regulations, administrative codes, ordinances, zoning laws, etc.) is legally authorized by the concept of **police powers**, which is the government's lawful authority to enact regulations and laws related to health, safety, welfare, and morals. Police powers are carried out by the various levels of government in the United States, including the establishment and regulation of water and sewer systems, highway and transportation systems, fire protection, monetary regulatory systems, health and medical systems, park and recreation areas, general assistance to the economically deprived, and food processing. In short, police powers provide the authority for law enforcement officials to act.

The process of law enforcement is a formal one sanctioned in the United States by the people (voters) through their elected governmental bodies. Of the three branches of government in the United States, the law enforcement function is the responsibility of the executive branch. Executive branch officials include the President of the United States at the federal level, governors at the state level, and mayors at the local level. These officials and their representatives use their governmental authority in the appointment of law enforcement officials and establishing the philosophies and general policies under which they will operate. The other branches of government also affect the abilities of law enforcement officials to perform their jobs. The legislative branch provides the statutory authority under which law enforcement officials operate. This authority includes the lawful right to use different levels of force to achieve law enforcement goals and objectives. It is the authorized use of this force that sets law enforcement officials apart from other occupations. Of course, the legislative branch is formally responsible for defining behavior that is to be considered criminal in a particular jurisdiction. The judicial branch of government reviews the actions of law enforcement officials according to the established rules of constitutional law, civil law, criminal procedure, and evidence. This review normally occurs during judicial proceedings such as initial hearings, preliminary hearings, suppression of evidence hearings, and trials (civil and criminal). **Figure 1-1** summarizes the role of the three branches of government in the law enforcement function of the United States.

## ■ Law Enforcement and Policing

The concept of law enforcement encompasses all levels (federal, state, and local) of the executive branch of government. It includes agencies that enforce adminis-

| Branch | *Legislative* | *Executive* | *Judicial* |
|---|---|---|---|
| Offices or Titles | Congress<br>Legislatures<br>Boards<br>Councils | President<br>Governors<br>Trustees<br>Mayors | Courts<br>Justices<br>Judges<br>Magistrates |
| Law Enforcement Role | Enacts statutes, codes, ordinances and resolutions<br>Establishes policy | Enforces legislative enactments<br>Operates law enforcement agencies<br>Initiates criminal prosecutions<br>Establishes agency procedure/ rules | Reviews enforcement actions<br>Adjudicates legal disputes<br>Tries criminal cases<br>Issues orders and sanctions |

**Figure 1-1** The government's involvement in law enforcement.

trative codes and regulations (rules of agencies) and criminal laws related to the health, safety, and welfare of the people. A broad spectrum of officials with titles such as inspector, compliance officer, deputy, special agent, trooper, auditor, investigator, ranger, marshal, constable, or police officer can be found in law enforcement agencies. These officials may be employees of agencies that inspect the food supply (Department of Agriculture) and places of employment (Occupational Safety and Health Administration), investigate the causes of fires (State Fire Marshal), protect abused and neglected children (County Children Services), investigate airplane accidents (Federal Aviation Administration), conduct audits of government expenditures (State Auditor's Office), investigate criminal complaints (federal, state, and local law enforcement), and/or apprehend offenders (any agency with arrest authority).

The term **policing**, on the other hand, refers to a subset of law enforcement that applies to the process of regulating the general health, safety, welfare, and morals of society when it relates to criminal behavior. The policing function in the United States is primarily observed through the operations of the criminal justice system in the prevention, detection, investigation, and prosecution of crime. The personnel affiliated with such agencies who are engaged in policing functions also can be referred to as law enforcement personnel. However, in the United States, **policing officials** are a unique group of law enforcement officials because they are armed and are authorized to use coercive and physical force under certain conditions when carrying out their duties. They are non-military, armed, governmental personnel who are granted the authority to prevent, detect, investigate, and prosecute criminal behavior and to apprehend alleged offenders. **Figure 1-2** illustrates the policing agencies as a subset of the law enforcement community.

The focus of this text is on the policing agencies of the law enforcement community as identified in Figure 1-2. However it must be understood that the entire law enforcement community is quite extensive. The term law enforcement also is used to describe one of the major functions within policing agencies. Policing agencies normally have other functions besides "enforcing the law." In fact, the local policing agency personnel normally spend less than 20–30% of their time engaged in crime-related law enforcement functions (Greene and Klockars 1991, 279). Most of their time is spent on prevention, general public service, and order maintenance functions. This relationship is depicted in **Figure 1-3**. Today's professional policing officials often do not want to emphasize their law enforcement functions; they prefer to be thought of for their service, especially their public safety functions which do not involve enforcement activities.

Some states add to the confusion of terms by using the phrase "peace officer" to refer to an entire class of policing officials who generally are authorized by statutory law to make arrests and serve warrants. A sample of such statutory language for the state of Ohio is reprinted in **Figure 1-4**. Notice that the state has 19 different types of peace officers. (It is also interesting to note that for definitional purposes in Ohio, "sheriffs" and "state troopers" are not peace officers. However, there are other statutes that describe their authority as "law enforcement officers.")

As a student of the policing function, you should know that the terminology associated with police officials and their agency affiliations are important and occasionally confusing. Several terms (police powers, law enforcement, policing officials, and peace officer) have been used

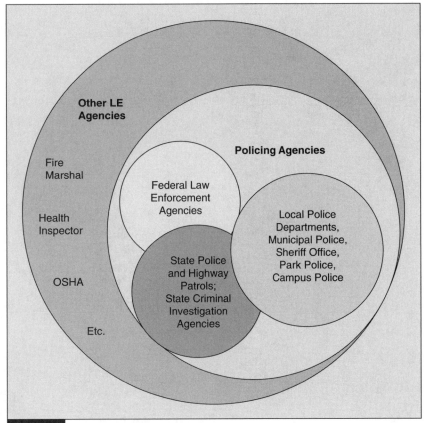

**Figure 1-2** The law enforcement community.

above and may appear to be very similar. But, it is important to know that titles in the law enforcement field are important, and if you are going to be an informed person, and possibly a future criminal justice professional, you should know the different titles that distinguish policing officials. At the federal level, such officials are usually referred to as "agents" or "special agents," although members of the US Marshal's Office are called "deputy marshals." At the state level they may be called "troopers," "state police officers," and/or "agents." At the local level, members of the county sheriff's office are "deputies" or "deputy sheriffs," and members of municipal and village police departments are called "police officers." The terms "constable" and "marshal" may be used in some jurisdictions at the local level, particularly in townships and villages. Members of federal and state forestry, park, or wildlife divisions may have the title of "ranger" or "warden." It does get confusing, but personnel in the law enforcement field do make these distinctions for reasons of courtesy, respect, and clarification of responsibilities. An analogy might be that most of us drive vehicles, but some insist on referring to their vehicles by name—Explorer, Cougar, Grand AM, Civic, Corvette, Jetta, Tacoma, and so on. Not all vehicles are created equal, and some people want you to know that! In this same vein, policing officials are of different types and serve different jurisdictions. All policing officials are law enforcement officers, but not all law enforcement officers are called "police." It is possible that you may encounter some policing officials who are very sensitive about their titles. If you plan to become an employee in the criminal justice field or plan to interview for

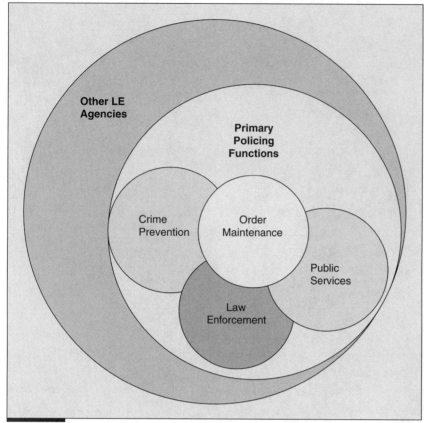

**Figure 1-3** Primary policing functions in the law enforcement environment.

a law enforcement position, it is recommended that you pay attention to titles and job classifications.

Law enforcement personnel occupy unique positions in American society. They act with the authority of the state, meaning that they have been entrusted with the lawful right to enforce the law. Few people in the United States are given the authority (under certain carefully defined conditions) to use coercive force to carry out that duty. Some of these officials are uniformed (and therefore easily visible), and others are not. Regardless of the title or whether they wear a uniform or not, police officials in our society serve in a formal **social control** capacity. Social control is the process whereby a society encourages or enforces compliance with social norms, customs, and laws. There are various viewpoints regarding how limited or extensive this social control function should be. Let us examine in greater depth some of the aspects of the concept of social control.

## ■ Law Enforcement as Social Control

Law enforcement is a societal function necessary for internal stability and security. Through the process of law enforcement, society exercises a form of social control, which impacts the control of behavior, deviant or otherwise. Every society has social control mechanisms because they serve as a means of **socialization**, the process of teaching the culture and norms of the society to its members.

Social control mechanisms are either formal or informal. Formal mechanisms generally refer to the units of the governing authority of the country. Formal social control units in the United States include the executive, legislative, and judicial components of the governmental structure at all levels of government. Informal mechanisms include the family, peers, religious organizations, significant others, and so on. **Figure 1-5** depicts a simplified version of selected social control mechanisms.

Social control mechanisms are not as simple to classify as Figure 1-5 might indicate. For example, where should education be placed? The educational process can be considered a formal control mechanism because it is often supported through government (tax supported) institutions. What you learn in school, however, is not simply the formal curriculum (geography, principles of democracy, math, psychology), but many other things as well (social skills, teamwork, manners, customs, and so on). Thus, it would fit equally well as an informal mechanism.

**"Peace officer" means:**

(1) A deputy sheriff, marshal, deputy marshal, member of the organized police department of a township or municipal corporation, member of a township police district or joint township police district police force, member of a police force employed by a metropolitan housing authority . . . or township constable, who is commissioned and employed as a peace officer by a political subdivision of this state or by a metropolitan housing authority, . . .;

(2) A police officer who is employed by a railroad company and appointed and commissioned by the governor . . .,

(3) Employees of the department of taxation engaged in the enforcement of Chapter 5743 of the Revised Code and designated by the tax commissioner for peace officer training for purposes of the delegation of investigation powers under section 5743.45 of the Revised Code;

(4) An undercover drug agent;

(5) Enforcement agents of the department of public safety . . . ;

(6) An employee of the department of natural resources who is a natural resources law enforcement staff officer . . . , a park officer . . . , a forest officer . . . , a preserve officer . . . , a wildlife officer . . . , or a state watercraft officer . . . ;

(7) An employee of a park district who is designated pursuant to section 511.232 [511.23.2] or 1545.13 of the Revised Code;

(8) An employee of a conservancy district who is designated pursuant to section 6101.75 of the Revised Code;

(9) A police officer who is employed by a hospital that employs and maintains its own proprietary police department or security department, and who is appointed and commissioned by the governor . . . ;

(10) Veterans' homes police officers designated under section 5907.02 of the Revised Code;

(11) A police officer who is employed by a qualified nonprofit corporation police department . . . ;

(12) A state university law enforcement officer . . . or a person serving as a state university law enforcement officer on a permanent basis on June 19, 1978, . . . ;

(13) A special police officer employed by the department of mental health . . . or the department of mental retardation and developmental disabilities . . . ;

(14) A member of a campus police department appointed under section 1713.50 of the Revised Code;

(15) A member of a police force employed by a regional transit authority . . . ;

(16) Investigators appointed by the auditor of state . . . engaged in the enforcement of Chapter 117. . . ;

(17) A special police officer designated by the superintendent of the state highway patrol . . . or a person who was serving as a special police officer . . . on a permanent basis on October 21, 1997, . . . ;

(18) A special police officer employed by a port authority . . . or a person serving as a special police officer employed by a port authority on a permanent basis on May 17, 2000, . . . ;

(19) A special police officer employed by a municipal corporation . . . who is employed on a permanent basis on or after the effective date of this amendment at a municipal airport, or other municipal air navigation facility, that has scheduled operations, as defined in section 119.3 of Title 14 of the Code of Federal Regulations, 14 C.F.R. 119.3, as amended, and that is required to be under a security program and is governed by aviation security rules of the transportation security administration of the United States department of transportation as provided in Parts 1542. and 1544. of Title 49 of the Code of Federal Regulations, as amended.

*Source:* Section 109.71(A) of the Ohio Revised Code, 2004.

**Figure 1-4** The definition of peace officer in Ohio.

The social control mechanisms of a society do not exist in a vacuum. Social, economic, and political influences impact social control. These influences cause shifts in attitudes and values over time. They can cause a society to become more conservative or more liberal in its approach to controlling behavior. Social

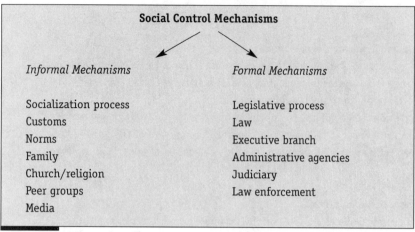

**Figure 1-5** Social control mechanisms.

influences come mainly from the interaction between people and groups and include forces such as customs, values and religion. Economic influences refer to resources (employment, income, and inflation) and the distribution of goods and services (transportation systems and businesses). Political factors refer to the policy-making process (elections, legislative actions, lobbying) and its related institutions (Congress, legislatures, and city councils). As such, these factors relate to the quest for power and the right to influence others, which is one of the major objectives of politics. **Figure 1-6** identifies a number of examples of these influences upon society.

As with the placement of formal and informal social control mechanisms, the influencing factors are not easily categorized into social, economic, or political ones. For example, the factor of "poverty" is purposely listed in all three categories. Is poverty a social condition? Is it an economic one? What influence do politics and public policy have on poverty? Some people could persuasively argue each of these positions, and there is some validity to each. Likewise, "terrorism" was listed under political influences, but doesn't it also influence social and economic issues?

Social control issues raise several questions for law enforcement. How much of a role should policing have on the social control function in society? Should there be greater emphasis placed on formal control mechanisms, that is, the government's influence on controlling behavior? Or should the informal control mechanism be emphasized for guiding and influencing behavior? Ultimately, the question becomes one of how much influence the police should have on controlling people's behavior. A person who believes that the police should not have much of a role in controlling societal behavior would probably believe that there should be greater emphasis placed on the informal mechanisms (e.g., family, church, peer group). One who believes the police should play an active role in controlling social behavior may emphasize tough policing measures to control behavior and greater use of the courts and formal punishments to influence behavior. Let us examine four common perspectives (viewpoints) to social control and their impact on policing in the United States. These perspectives are important because they reflect the di-

| Social | Economic | Political |
|---|---|---|
| Fads/trends | Inflation/recession | Major parties/elections |
| Social movements | Unemployment | Party in power |
| Morality | Welfare | Wars/conflicts |
| Religion | Interest rates | Arms race |
| Poverty | Poverty | Poverty |
| Homelessness | Energy costs | Congress |
| Race relations | Consumer confidence | Patriotism |
| Abortion debate | National debt | Government regulation |
| Crime | Crime control costs | Government policy |
| Mass media | Credit rate | Foreign relations |
| Entertainment | Advertising | Foreign aid |
|  | Imports/exports | Terrorism |

**Figure 1-6** Influences upon social control.

versity of ideas and beliefs of how our government agencies should function. They reflect how citizens view crime and influence government policies related to preventing and controlling criminal behavior.

## ■ Four Perspectives to Law Enforcement

There are several ways to view the world in which we live. Some people take a narrow viewpoint of certain issues, while others take a broader approach in perceiving situations or issues. For example, in a verbal description about the design of a building, the architect may have one mental image or perspective, the builder another, and the prospective resident yet another. The architect may be concerned about how the building "fits" into the landscape or with the surrounding buildings. The builder is possibly thinking about cost and what types of materials are to be used. The resident is concerned about the location of internal features, the size of rooms, utilities costs, and how soon it can be built. Each viewpoint is valid in and of itself, but the focus of the discussion can become very confusing if the three persons do not attempt to see the other person's approach to the building. In this example, a comprehensive set of blueprints and architectural drawings could help each person better perceive the others' concerns. In the following discussion, various approaches to viewing the field of law enforcement are presented. If a person is an advocate of one of these approaches and is discussing law enforcement with a person who holds a different viewpoint, there could be confusion or heated debate over whose position is best. The purpose here is to increase your understanding of each approach to help you reduce confusion and conflict over issues in policing. Sometimes situations are improved when one can see the other person's point of view and compromises can be worked out (or at least there can be better communications about the topic or issue). It must be remembered that these approaches are not totally independent of one another; occasionally some aspects overlap with other perspectives. It is also possible that a person can hold one perspective on a particular issue and a different perspective on another issue.

### The Legal Perspective

One common approach to policing is that "the law is the law." **The legal perspective** is an approach that views behavior from a rule-based philosophy, in that the law is paramount, and it is the guide for behavior that everyone must follow. Strong advocates of crime control and severe punishment for infractions often adopt this perspective. While there is merit in holding the law in high regard, one must be careful to evaluate a particular law's purpose and whether it is too restrictive. The legalistic approach is evident when someone says, "there should be a law against that." The person is implying that making the behavior a crime will stop people from doing it or at least allow the authorities to intervene.

Most people in the United States obey the majority of laws. Indeed, less than 6% of the population account for nearly all crime in the United States. Of course, we cannot know who breaks the law when a crime is not reported (which happens, on average, nearly 50% of the time) or when there is no suspect to arrest (which happens almost as often, depending upon the type of crime). But evidence suggests that most of these crimes are committed by multiple offenders who will eventually be caught unless they "age out" and stop offending. Hence, we can say the vast majority of men, and nearly all women, obey the law. This probably occurs for two reasons: (1) the majority of laws are deemed appropriate, and/or (2) most people respect the law. But, it is known that not everyone believes all the laws are appropriate. There also are different levels of legality. For example, gambling is generally against the law, but certain types may not be (e.g., bingo, horse racing, and lotteries), and some people believe that all forms of gambling should be legal. Some believe that crimes related to certain sexual actions (e.g., prostitution and having sex with children) should not be against the law. Others believe that the law should enforce traditional sexual morality. As any society becomes more diverse in terms of ethnic (national origin), racial, religious, and social backgrounds, agreement on what should be legal and illegal diminishes. This lack of agreement leads to many problems for policy makers as well as law enforcement officials. Too many laws against too many behaviors can reduce respect for the law.

In this perspective, policing officials are placed in awkward positions since they have sworn to enforce the laws of the nation and the state. They know that if they strictly enforce the law, many people would be arrested or given summonses. Therefore, these officials must evaluate behavior in terms of "the letter-of-the-law" and "the spirit-of-the-law." If the letter-of-the-law is adhered to, then any violation of law results in official intervention by the police. If the spirit-of-the-law is followed, degrees of seriousness may be considered. Some laws may not be enforced at all, and some people who non-flagrantly violate the law may be handled informally (e.g., verbal reprimand, warnings, or no intervention at all).

This evaluative process leads to the use of **discretion** and **selective enforcement**. Discretion is the process of making a choice among appropriate alternative courses of action. Although most state codes do not give peace officers the lawful right to use discretion, it has been professionally and judicially acknowledged. The police simply cannot enforce every law that has been enacted. Selective enforcement refers to enforcing those laws deemed appropriate to the situation or related to the priorities of the agency and the community. The opposite of selective enforcement is **full enforcement** which is enforcing all laws all the time, which, again, is not possible. One major drawback of the legal perspective is the belief that simply passing and enforcing criminal laws can solve most social control problems. A type of full enforcement when directed toward certain problems, such as gang, drug, or traffic offenses, is called **zero tolerance**. It is exemplified when officers use every violation for justification to intervene in situations. It often occurs for targeted problem areas or types of offenses within a jurisdiction. The empirical evidence, to date, fails to support this approach except in limited and rare circumstances (e.g., "hot spot" enforcement with directed patrols) (Mazerolle et al. 2000).

## The Public Policy Perspective

**Public policy**, broadly defined, is made up of the rules and regulations legislative bodies and agencies choose to establish. For example, if drug abuse or spouse abuse requires regulation, a city council or state legislature may pass a law or an ordinance regarding domestic violence and drug dealing. At the same time, a bill might be passed to provide counseling for those charged with spousal abuse or drug use. Both of these actions are examples of public policy developed to address societal problems (Cochran and Malone 1995). This approach is similar to the legal approach just discussed; however, greater emphasis is placed on the political process and on internal agency operations in the public policy approach.

Policy also is established in administrative organizations such as law enforcement agencies. A departmental policy regarding citizen complaints might set out the procedure for reviewing a complaint and detail the possible alternative solutions. Policy can also be made simply by consistently doing something in a particular way. For example, some police departments may tend to avoid domestic violence arrests or ignore concealed weapons found on citizens who have no criminal record. In both cases, a policy has been constructed and followed, even if it is not written.

Using a public policy approach to study law enforcement is important for a number of reasons. First, as the field of law enforcement evolves and becomes more **proactive** in community problems, more policy will be made at the department level. (A proactive response to problems is one that anticipates potential problems and tries to prevent the worst consequences from occurring.) Second, law enforcement managers may need legislative assistance in enacting policy because of current legal restrictions or because they lack the proper authority to enact the needed policy. Therefore, it is important to understand the political nature of the policy-making process and the importance of defending or justifying a policy in an appropriate manner.

Formal policy making at the agency level is a function of the executive team. The chief of police, sheriff, or department head is generally the final authority on policy. Policy cannot be made without considering internal procedure and management, legal and political influences, and community expectations. Internal management issues might include union reactions, current contract language, and officer morale or resistance. Community expectations might emanate from meetings held with civic groups or from public meetings on selected issues (e.g., curfew enforcement, treatment of juveniles, or rumors of a growing gang influence). Political influences can relate to local politics and the campaign promises of elected officials who have some influence over the department's budget. Other forces that impact policy development and evaluation are pending litigation over the actions taken by officers and severe fiscal problems that may cause layoffs or a cut in agency services (Gilmour and Halley 1994). Issues related to political concerns and their impact on law enforcement agencies are discussed in later chapters.

Establishing policy within an agency is a three-step process. The first step is the identification of needs for policy. This often becomes apparent when things do not function properly or serious problems have developed, such as an officer who used deadly force when not authorized to do so. However, identification of policy needs also occurs during agency evaluations and review of existing policies when compared to model (suggested) policy. The professional literature and associations often publish the experiences of other agencies in terms of policy.

The second step involves implementation or putting the policy into action. Obviously, this relates to how the written word is translated into practice through the persons affected. This means that policy must be properly interpreted, conveyed, and practiced by the agency's personnel. This often involves meetings and training sessions to explain the policy, its rationale, and significance. Policy implementation is a complex interaction of organizational and environmental variables, and frequently policies fail not because they were bad policies, but because they were poorly implemented. This is particularly true in the justice system inasmuch as there are so many different institutions with an interest in policy outcomes (Lemley and Russell 2002).

The third step in establishing policy is evaluation. In the current law enforcement environment, it is critical to evaluate the effectiveness of all law enforcement policies to ensure that improvements have actually occurred. This can be evaluated through periodic assessment of officer performance, critical incidents, threatened litigation, selected agency measures, and current vulnerability. For example, the policy under Tennessee law prior to 1985 permitted police officers to fire upon fleeing suspects regardless of the threat the suspect posed to officers or others. In *Tennessee v. Garner* (471 US 1), the United States Supreme Court struck down the policy, setting a common law "defense of self or others" when facing an "imminent threat" as the new standard. Subsequent analysis demonstrated that these changes caused the Memphis Police Department to substantially alter its behavior in regard to officer-involved shootings (Sparger and Giacopassi 1992). It should be noted that the evaluation process also leads to the identification of weaknesses and needs for future policy; therefore, the process becomes cyclical and permits continuous updating of policy. Thus, each aspect of policymaking—identification, implementation, and evaluation—must be understood for an agency to function effectively as we enter the next century (Fischer 1995). **Figure 1-7** summarizes the policy-making process.

## The Systems Perspective

Law enforcement can also be viewed from the viewpoint of **systems theory**. This approach views the entire context (environment) in which an issue exists by analyzing all the forces or influences impacting on it. In other words, law enforcement or a particular agency is perceived by analyzing all the influences upon it from the en-

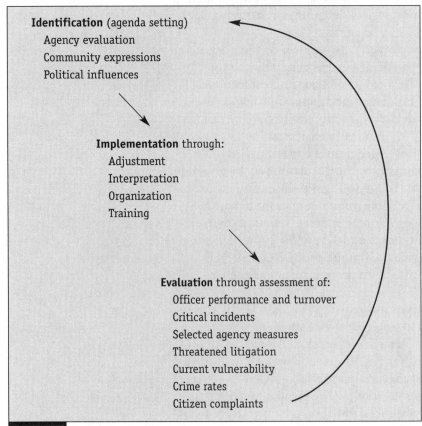

**Identification** (agenda setting)
   Agency evaluation
   Community expressions
   Political influences

**Implementation** through:
   Adjustment
   Interpretation
   Organization
   Training

**Evaluation** through assessment of:
   Officer performance and turnover
   Critical incidents
   Selected agency measures
   Threatened litigation
   Current vulnerability
   Crime rates
   Citizen complaints

**Figure 1-7** The public policy-making process and cycle.

vironment in which it operates. Systems theory is more easily understood if one understands the concept of subsystems. As an example, let us consider a person sitting at home in an air-conditioned room. If the focus of discussion is on the person's body, we could use systems theory to examine the situation this way. The body itself is made up of subsystems—the nervous subsystem, the respiratory subsystem, the cardiovascular subsystem, the skeletal subsystem, and the digestive subsystem. When all of the subsystems function properly, the body as a whole functions well. But, if something affects one subsystem, it can impact the others. If some external force frightens the person, say a bolt of lightning striking the tree outside the room, various subsystems can be affected. Fright causes the heart to beat faster, breathing may become shallow and rapid, digestive juices are released by the nervous system, and the stomach may become upset. Or, the sudden jolt and noise may additionally cause the body to jump or swing around quickly, bumping into a table and breaking a finger bone, causing pain. The subsystems are interconnected, and their functions impact the others. In organization theory, the "biological model" is often employed to compare organizational functioning with that of a biological system such as the ecosystem or the human body. In this regard, internal and external influences are all considered, producing a much more robust and complete view of organizational functioning in the real world.

In this example, the systems theory approach would describe the person's body and the immediate surroundings of the room and house as the "environment." This approach attempts to consider the forces or influences of the environment and their impact upon the entity or issue being considered. Taking a systems perspective to the earlier discussion of social control and its influences (Figures 1-4 and 1-5) would mean viewing each factor as having a possible impact on the others as well as an impact on social control. In other words, the various types of social control and the different types of social, economic, and political influences that impact it are interrelated. The best symbol to illustrate the systems approach is that of the atom. The nucleus becomes the issue being considered (e.g., the concept of social control or the police agency as an organization). The orbiting electrons and their paths become the factors that influence the issue being discussed. So **Figure 1-8** could be a systems approach illustration of the concept of social control with its various influence subsystems, and **Figure 1-9** is a systems representation of a law enforcement agency in today's society with its various subsystems. All of the subsystems interrelate and influence each other. When applying this model to policing, try to think of the illustrations as three-dimensional.

Viewing law enforcement from a systems perspective is important because it ensures that we consider the impact and influence of other environmental forces in our society. It assists in understanding the impact and possible implications of decisions and to anticipate their impact on other subsystems. We say that in a systems approach, "everything affects everything else." It is a view that makes one consider issues that otherwise might be overlooked. For example, what if a neo-Nazi or Ku Klux Klan group seeks a permit to hold a rally in a city? City officials must consider all the implications (forces) and outcomes (effects) to the decision. These questions should be considered regarding this matter:

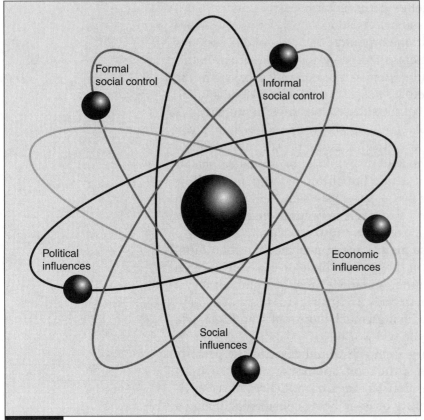

**Figure 1-8** The systems theory applied to social control.

- If denied, might the group have standing to sue the agency for a breach of constitutional rights of freedom of expression?
- Is the city willing and financially capable of fighting the matter in court?
- If the permit is granted, will the rally be orderly or will there be opposition groups present seeking a confrontation?
- Might people get injured and need medical attention?
- Will your officers have to work overtime to provide necessary security?
- Will the budget of the department permit overtime to be used?
- Does your city policy require such groups to have insurance coverage for any damages that may be incurred as a direct result of the rally?
- Does the permit require the group to pay overtime to the officer providing security to the group?
- Will the group provide any security of its own?
- What are the public media ramifications?
- Who protects the rest of the city when most of your officers are protecting the rally?
- Can you enlist the assistance (mutual aid) of state and neighboring law enforcement agencies? If so, what formal process must be undertaken to do so?

In short, the systems approach assists in analyzing issues from a broader perspective, one in which the agency is just one entity (subsystem) among many in the total environment. In this example, the total environment includes several city officials such as the mayor, law director or prosecutor, council members, the fire department, ambulance/medical services, and the city services director.

## The Global Perspective (or Extended Systems Approach)

The **global perspective** is an extension of the systems approach. In addition to recognizing the immediate environmental influences, it gives significant recognition to world events and the international influences upon the agency. The instability of a government can cause problems for other countries. Many great societies and nations have risen and fallen during the last 3,000 years. During the twentieth century, for example, many government officials in powerful countries have lost their right to govern. Some lost that right as a result of war (e.g., World Wars I and II, the war in Vietnam), and some as a result of internal conflict and unrest (e.g., East Germany and the former Union of Soviet Socialist Republics during the early 1990s). Changes continue to occur in the trouble spots around the world. Events in the Middle East, Africa, East Asia, and Korea are a constant threat to regional and even world peace. The terrorist attacks of the 1990s and of post-9/11 are changing the way people and governments view the world. Over $1.5 billion was spent on security and law enforcement protection at the 2004 Olympic Games in Greece. The 2003–2004 Iraq War and the security struggle that followed drew the world's attention to terrorism and the effects of overthrowing a harsh dictator. The international and national divide over disagreements about the actions of the United States in Iraq will continue for years. According to the National Defense Council Foundation, during 1995 there were 71 "little wars" across the globe, which was double the tally of 1989. In 2002 the number

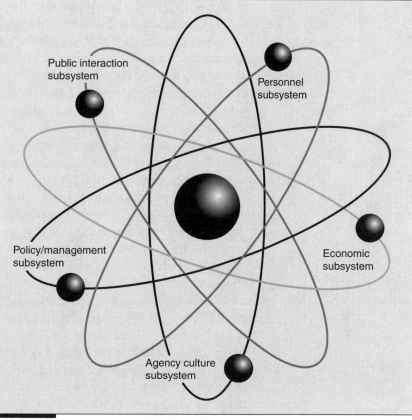

**Figure 1-9** Systems approach applied to law enforcement agencies.

of conflicts had dropped to 53. However, in 2003 the Foundation discontinued their "world conflict list" because "terrorist organizations disregard boundaries, hence solely counting state to state conflicts, or internal state conflicts leaves the total count incomplete and/or inaccurate" (National Defense Council Foundation 2004). According to the State Department, in 1999 there were 1,649 US law enforcement personnel permanently assigned overseas for crime fighting, intelligence, liaison, and training purposes. That number has risen since 9/11 but exact numbers are not made public. Today, several large city police departments in the United States have officers overseas for gathering intelligence related to investigative and counter-terrorism activities. As of January 7, 2004, 413 FBI personnel were assigned overseas, over 200 of whom are permanently assigned (Hulon 2004). As of 2002, the US Treasury Department had over 640 law enforcement personnel assigned overseas (Lawson 2002). The recently created Department of Homeland Security also maintains an overseas presence.

One may ask, "What do the world events in other countries have to do with policing in the United States?" The answer is, "A great deal, depending on where you are." The United States, as a prosperous world leader, is often called upon to provide military and humanitarian aid to those in need. Although the country's success to date places it in this position, continuing this role in the future may become more challenging. The opportunity exists to assist many people in their struggles to survive and to relieve their pain and suffering. Realizing these goals, however, reduces the resources available for American needs of all types, including the enhancement of public safety. For example, whenever the National Guard or Reserves is activated in the United States, police departments are adversely affected since officers are often members of these forces. The call-up of thousands of military reservists during the second Iraq War created staffing hardships for many law enforcement agencies in the United States. A call-up of the magnitude experienced in 2003–2004 cost many agencies dearly. By law, agencies cannot replace personnel called to active duty, and if they fill the spot temporarily, the agencies pay for training knowing (as does the temporary officer) that when the other officer returns, the temporary officer is out of a job. When you consider that more than 50% of agencies in the United States have fewer than 50 officers to cover three shifts over 7 days, losing even one person, let alone two, is devastating.

The global approach is very similar to the systems perspective in that it views the situation in terms of outside forces and environmental impact. The major difference between the two is that the global approach places primary focus on the international influences on the field of policing. In the systems approach, the amount of influence from international issues is much less. The federal law enforcement community, without doubt, is more involved and concerned with the global approach than are local police. However, this approach is important to all US law enforcement officials because they must be alert for possible trouble in the United States because of situations in foreign countries. Terrorist activities are no longer confined to other countries, as witnessed by the 9/11 attacks in the United States, which killed about 3,000 people. Immediately following the attacks, many US agencies assigned additional personnel to protect Muslim neighborhoods, businesses, and mosques. Other examples of international incidents include the bombing of Pan Am flight 103 returning to the United States from Europe in 1988, killing 270, and the 1993 bombing of the World Trade Center in New York City that killed six and injured more than a 1,000.

These kinds of events have increased the cautionary measures law enforcement must take to protect national security and local public safety. For example, since 9/11, the Transportation Security Agency has replaced private screeners at airports, the Department of Homeland Security was created, and the number of FBI/state/local joint terrorism task forces has risen from 34 to 84. During the 2002 Winter Olympics held in Salt Lake City, millions of dollars were spent for additional security equipment and law enforcement personnel because of the threat of another terrorist incident.

The global approach to social control realizes that law enforcement is a global challenge and is impacted by global events. While most law enforcement personnel in the United States are probably not affected greatly by global events, more have been affected in the last decade than in previous decades since the world wars. The professional law enforcement officer understands the importance of world events and their possible impact on policing here.

The global approach to law enforcement and social control realizes that law enforcement is a global challenge and is impacted by global events. While most police officers in the United States are probably not affected greatly by global events, more have been affected in the last decade than in previous decades since the world wars. However, the professional law enforcement officer understands the importance of world events and their possible impact on policing in this country. There were 40 million international visitors to the United States in 2003 (which was down from 50.9 million in 2000) and, unfortunately, some of them have contact with law enforcement and criminal justice officials in their official capacities. The top ten cities for overseas visitors are listed in **Table 1-1** along with their market share of the visitors and the approximate number of visitors to the city.

Officers in larger cities also often have contact with persons possessing (and claiming to possess) **diplomatic immunity**. Diplomatic immunity means that the person enjoys certain privileges and immunities from the laws of the United States and its political subdivisions. The legal basis for diplomatic immunity and other issues relating to consular affairs stems from a multilateral agreement entitled **Vienna Convention on Consular Relations** (VCCR), which was completed in 1963. The provisions of the VCCR became effective in the United States in December of 1969. Currently, over 165 different countries are party to the VCCR. The provisions related to actions by law enforcement officials in the United States are summarized in **Table 1-2**. While some people have difficulty understanding why members of the foreign diplomatic corps should not be subject to our country's laws, we must remember that US diplomats abroad also enjoy diplomatic immunity from the laws of other countries. It should be remembered that most diplomats enjoy their assignments in the United States and seldom are a problem for public law enforcement. Diplomats are not immune from their home country's laws, and generally, they do not want to be sent home for what is considered serious criminal behavior in the United States.

The VCCR also affects every local, state, and federal law enforcement agency and every US citizen that travels abroad. Other provisions of the treaty address the duties and responsibilities of law enforcement agencies when a foreign national is detained or arrested. In short, persons who are not citizens, including foreign visitors, legal permanent aliens, and illegal aliens, have the right to have their consulate notified of their detention or arrest. These treaties also give con-

**Table 1-1** — Overseas* Visitors to Select US Cities and Hawaiian Islands in 2003

| 2003 Rank | City | 2003 Market Share | 2003 Visitation (000) |
|---|---|---|---|
| 1 | New York City | 22.1% | 3,984 |
| 2 | Los Angeles | 11.8% | 2,127 |
| 3 | Miami | 11.5% | 2,073 |
| 4 | Orlando | 9.8% | 1,767 |
| 5 | San Francisco | 9.4% | 1,694 |
| 6 | Honolulu | 9.0% | 1,622 |
| 7 | Las Vegas | 7.2% | 1,298 |
| 8 | Washington, DC | 4.8% | 865 |
| 9 | Chicago | 4.3% | 775 |
| 10 | Boston | 4.2% | 757 |

*Source:* US Department of Commerce, Office of Travel and Tourism Industries, 2004.
*Excludes Canada and Mexico.

## Table 1-2 Diplomatic and Consular Privileges and Immunities from Criminal Jurisdiction

**Summary of Law Enforcement Aspects**

| Category | May be arrested or detained | Residence may be entered subject to ordinary procedures | May be issued traffic citation | May be subpoenaed as witness | May be prosecuted | Recognized family member |
|---|---|---|---|---|---|---|
| **Diplomatic** | | | | | | |
| Diplomatic agent | No[a] | No | Yes | No | No | Same as sponsor (full immunity and inviolability). |
| Member of administrative and technical staff | No[a] | No | Yes | No | No | Same as sponsor (full immunity and inviolability). |
| Service staff | Yes | Yes | Yes | Yes | Yes | No immunity or inviolability.[b] |
| **Consular** | | | | | | |
| Career consular officers | Yes, if for a felony and pursuant to a warrant.[b] | Yes[d] | Yes | No—for official acts. Testimony may not be compelled in any case. | No—for official acts. Otherwise, yes.[b] | No immunity or inviolability.[b] |
| Honorary consular officers | Yes | Yes | Yes | No—for official acts. Yes, in all other cases. | No—for official acts. Otherwise, yes. | No immunity or inviolability. |
| Consular employees | Yes[b] | Yes | Yes | No—for official acts. Yes, in all other cases. | No—for official acts. Otherwise, yes.[b] | No immunity or inviolability.[b] |
| **International organizations** | | | | | | |
| International organizations staff[c] | Yes[c] | Yes[c] | Yes | No—for official acts. Yes, in all other cases. | No—for official acts. Otherwise, yes.[c] | No immunity or inviolability. |
| Diplomatic-level staff of missions to international organizations | No[a] | No | Yes | No | No | Same as sponsor (full immunity and inviolability). |
| Support staff of missions to international organizations | Yes | Yes | Yes | No—for official acts. Yes, in all other cases. | No—for official acts. Otherwise, yes. | No immunity or inviolability. |

[a]Reasonable constraints, however, may be applied in emergency circumstances involving self-defense, public safety, or the prevention of serious criminal acts.

[b]This table presents general rules. Particularly in the cases indicated, the employees of certain foreign countries may enjoy higher levels of privileges and immunities on the basis of special bilateral agreements.

[c]A small number of senior officers is entitled to be treated identically to "diplomatic agents."

[d]Note that consular residences are sometimes located within the official consular premises. In such cases, only the official office space is protected from police entry.

*Source:* US Department of State: http://www.state.gov/m/ds/immunities/c9127.htm.

sular officers the right to have access to their citizens in these situations. Criminal justice officials are obligated by law to comply with the provisions of the VCCR. The US State Department provides publications and training materials on such matters. Failure to comply can cause an "international incident" over a person's detention or arrest. One summary of the requirements pertaining to foreign nationals provides the following six guidelines (US Department of State 2003, 3):

1. When foreign nationals are arrested or detained, they must be advised of the right to have their consular officials notified. (See examples in the From Concept to Practice sidebar.)

2. In some cases, the nearest consular officials must be notified of the arrest or detention of a foreign national, regardless of the national's wishes.

3. Consular officials are entitled to access to their nationals in detention, and are entitled to provide consular assistance.

4. When a government official becomes aware of the death of a foreign national, consular officials must be notified.

5. When a guardianship or trusteeship is being considered with respect to a foreign national who is a minor or incompetent, consular officials must be notified.

6. When a foreign ship or aircraft wrecks or crashes, consular officials must be notified.

## From Concept to Practice

### Suggested Statements to Arrested or Detained Foreign Nationals

*Statement 1: For All Foreign Nationals Except Those From List Countries[1]*

As a non-US citizen who is being arrested or detained, you are entitled to have us notify your country's consular officers here in the United States of your situation. You are also entitled to communicate with your consular officers. A consular officer may be able to help you obtain legal representation, and may contact your family and visit you in detention, among other things. If you want us to notify your consular officers, you can request this notification now, or at any time in the future. Do you want us to notify your consular officers at this time?

### Suggested Statements to Arrested or Detained Foreign Nationals

*Statement 2: For All Foreign Nationals From List Countries[1]*

Because of your nationality, we are required to notify your country's consular officers here in the United States that you have been arrested or detained. We will do this as soon as possible. In addition, you are also entitled to communicate with your consular officers. You are not required to accept their assistance but your consular officers may be able to help you obtain legal representation, and may contact your family and visit you in detention, among other things.

[1]Some countries are on a "mandatory notification" list and some are not. The State Department can provide these statements in multiple foreign languages.

*Source:* US Department of State (June 2004), Consular Notification and Access Reference Card: Instructions for Arrests and Detentions of Foreign Nationals. Washington, DC: US Department of State.

## ■ The Approach of this Text

The field of law enforcement is one component of the process of social control. The focus of this text is on crime-related law enforcement services provided by those agencies commonly referred to as the police. The approach taken in our presentation is primarily the systems approach, which encompasses all the forces or influences in society that impact policing. Among those influences are issues related to politics, public policy, social trends, international events, and national issues. The text describes the background of the field of policing: where it has been, where it is now, and where future challenges remain. Basic elements of management and organizational principles are also included.

The systems approach to policing recognizes the significant involvement of government and public policy makers in setting goals and objectives for law en-

---

### From Concept to Practice

**SPANISH**
**Statement 1: When Consular Notification is at the Foreign National's Option**

Como no es ciudadano de los Estados Unidos, al ser arrestado o detenido tiene derecho a pedirnos que notifiquemos a los representantes consulares de su país aquí en los Estados Unidos, si lo desea. Entre otras cosas, un funcionario consular de su país puede ayudarle a obtener asesoramiento legal, ponerse en contacto con su familia y visitarle en la cárcel. Si Ud desea que notifiquemos a los funcionarios consulares de su país, puede solicitarlo ahora o en cualquier oportunidad en el futuro. Después de que se haya notificado a los funcionarios de su país, ellos podrán llamarle o visitarle. ¿Desea que notifiquemos a los funcionarios consulares de su país?

|  |  |
|:---:|:---:|
| SÍ | NO |
| YES | NO |

(Sírvase poner un círculo alrededor de Sí o No.)

Signature/Firma:

Date/Fecha:

**Statement 2: When Consular Notification is Mandatory**

Debido a su nacionalidad, estamos obligados a notificar a los representantes consulares de su país aquí en los Estados Unidos que Used ha sido arrestado o detenido. Después de notificar a sus funcionarios consulares, ellos podrán llamarle o visitarle. Usted no está obligado a aceptar su ayuda, pero ellos pueden ayudarle a obtener asesoramiento legal, ponerse en contacto con su familia y visitarle en la cárcel, entre otras cosas. Notificaremos a los funcionarios consulares de su país tan pronto como sea posible.

*Source:* U.S. Department of State (June 2004), Consular Notification and Access Instructions for Arrests and Detentions of Foreign Nationals. Washington, DC: US Department of State.

forcement. By taking a systems perspective to policing, the text incorporates selected aspects from the other perspectives of law enforcement. In the systems approach, it is understood that sometimes the other perspectives have merit in certain situations. Sometimes public policy issues are very important to the issues being discussed. Sometimes an officer must have a global perspective to understand the "big picture" of the events that he or she is managing. Whatever the situation, professional law enforcement personnel must understand the power and influence of their office. They make policy-related decisions and/or carry out policy every day they are on duty. They affect the lives of people they encounter, and they possess some of the most powerful discretion of any person working in the criminal justice system.

The chapters that follow should be viewed from a systems perspective. For example, the history of policing influences present-day mindsets. It has an effect on public policy, it helps shape our culture. Law enforcement was first formed during the emergence of political influence in the administration of governmental affairs. Police from the 1830s to the early 1900s were brutal, untrained, and politically controlled. In reaction to that, policing organizations became more professional and more separated from communities. This produced its own set of problems in the 1960s. The result was the reform movement now known as the "community era," which involved community policing, problem-oriented policing, and similar themes. These changes influenced the design of organizations and their relationship with the surrounding environment. Those structures and external political forces influence the selection and training of law enforcement personnel and help to further influence the internal cultures of organizations. History, culture, and politics influence our legal mechanisms that place limitations on the policing community. All of the social, economic, and political forces within our complex society affect the type of policing services delivered to the public. These forces shape the future challenges and influence the professionalism of law enforcement personnel. Everything affects everything else; nothing is simple in today's society. This may sound either too simplistic or horribly complex. But organizations are not isolated from financial crises (e.g., loss of a major employer in the community), political events (e.g., a police shooting and subsequent calls for reform), or social change (e.g., patterns of migration and immigration). The list of potential sources of influence is endless, requiring the United States to have a global and systemic perspective.

## ■ Summary

This chapter introduced you to the field of law enforcement. It described law enforcement as one of the formal processes of social control, which means that it is one of society's attempts to obtain compliance with the law. The common term "policing" is defined as one form of law enforcement that emphasizes the prevention, detection, investigation, and prosecution of crime as well as providing numerous services to society. Policing officials are distinguished from other law enforcement officials by the fact that they are non-military government personnel who are armed and may use coercive and physical force under certain conditions. Since policing is a form of social control, the differences between formal (government sponsored) and informal control mechanisms have been presented here as well. Of particular concern are the many influences upon social control, which have been presented as social, economic, and political factors. These factors influence the police function in every community within the country.

The chapter described the various perspectives to law enforcement in a social control context. The four approaches—legal, public policy, systems, and global—have each been presented and applied to the field of law enforcement. The legal approach emphasizes the enforcement of the law; however, since full enforcement is not possible, discretion and selected enforcement becomes prevalent. The public policy approach emphasizes the process of developing and implementing policy. Policies can have consequent effects on the delivery of police services to the community. The systems approach recognizes the importance of all the environmental influences in society, including international influences. The global approach is an extension of the systems perspective; however it places greater emphasis and priority on international events and influence. Although global issues are very important, they do not yet dominate the daily operation of the 17,000-plus law enforcement agencies in the United States.

The recognition and identification of the multiple influences upon social control is vital to providing effective policing to a complex, democratic society. While there is some overlap among the four approaches to policing, the differences are significant. The legal approach recognizes the formal and informal influence of law and sanctions on members of society. The public policy approach emphasizes the systematic approach to policing (among other things) through the governmental policy-making process. The systems approach attempts to understand how the environmental forces of politics, law, community, and economics effect policing. The global perspective emphasizes the larger impact of world events on the law enforcement function. While each approach has merit, the focus of this text is primarily from a systems approach, which, in essence, recognizes the impact and contribution of all the other approaches as they relate to one another.

# QUESTIONS FOR REVIEW

1. Using the concepts described in this chapter, what does the following statement mean? "All police officials are law enforcement officials but not all law enforcement officials are police officials."

2. How does policing relate to the concept of social control? Which is the broader concept?

3. Using the four perspectives (approaches) to the law enforcement function presented in this chapter, identify the similarities and differences among them.

4. Using the systems approach to policing, what are two social factors, two economic factors, and two political factors that influence policing at your local level of government?

5. What is the significance of the Vienna Convention on Consular Relations?

# SUGGESTED ACTIVITIES

1. Using three different dictionaries, look up the definitions for the terms law enforcement, policing, and discretion. Write them down on three note cards and be sure to note the source used. In the classroom, share your definitions with two other members of the class. Compare the definitions and describe how they are similar or dissimilar to the descriptions used in this text.

2. Ask students who are not in your class to describe what contact they have had with law enforcement officers and what they thought of the experience. Listen closely to what terms they use to describe the officers and write down their version of the experience. Determine whether you consider the experience to be a positive or negative one and why; write down reasons for your assessment.

3. Contact a local health inspector, fire inspector, fire (arson) investigator, or a building inspector and ask them if they consider themselves a "law enforcement" official. After they answer, ask if they consider themselves a "police officer." Ask them to explain their responses.

4. Using the Internet, conduct searches using three different search engines (e.g., Google, Infoseek, Yahoo, Hotbot, etc.) on the terms law enforcement, policing, and police, and compare the total number of categories, pages, or sites found. Browse some of the sites. Then conduct a search for a specific agency (use quotation marks when using phrases such as "Phoenix Police Department" or "Federal Bureau of Investigation").

5. In groups, develop lists of external influences and internal influences that might affect law enforcement operations and policy. Distinguish between social, political, institutional, and economic effects. How should an organization respond to these conditions and events?

# ■ Chapter Glossary

**discretion**    the process of making a choice among appropriate alternative courses of action.

**full enforcement**    enforcing all laws all of the time.

**global approach**    an extension of the systems approach that in addition to recognizing the immediate environmental influences gives significant recognition to world events and the international influences upon the agency.

**law enforcement**    a society's formal attempt to obtain compliance with the established rules, regulations, and law of that society.

**legal perspective**    an approach that views behavior from a rule-based philosophy, in that the law is paramount, and it is the guide for behavior which everyone must follow.

**policing**    refers to the process of regulating the general health, safety, welfare, and morals of society.

**policing officials**    a special group of nonmilitary, law enforcement officials who are armed and authorized to use coercive and physical force under certain conditions when carrying out their duties to prevent, detect, investigate, and prosecute criminal behavior.

**proactive**    a response that anticipates the direction of problems and tries to prevent the worst consequences from occurring.

**public policy perspective**    a viewpoint that emphasizes the rules and regulations that legislative bodies and agencies choose to establish for social control.

**selective enforcement**    refers to enforcing those laws deemed appropriate to the situation or related to the priorities of the agency and the community.

**social control**    the processes whereby a society encourages or enforces compliance with social norms, customs, and law.

**socialization**    the process of teaching the culture and norms of the society to its members.

**systems theory or systems approach**    an approach that views the entire context (environment) in which an issue exists by analyzing all of the forces or influences impacting on it.

**Vienna Convention on Consular Relations** (VCCR)    a multilateral agreement among nations of the world that establishes the legal basis for diplomatic immunity and other issues relating to consular affairs.

**zero tolerance**    a type of full enforcement usually directed toward certain problems, such as gang, drug, or traffic offenses; it is exemplified when officers use every violation for justification to intervene in situations.

# ■ Chapter References

Cochran, Charles L. and Eloise F. Malone (1995). *Public Policy: Perspectives and Choices*. New York: McGraw-Hill.

Fischer, Frank (1995). *Evaluating Public Policy*. Chicago: Nelson-Hall.

Fyfe, James J. (2004). Stops, Frisks, Searches, and the Constitution. *Criminology and Public Policy* 3 (July, 3):379–398.

Gilmour, Robert S. and Alexis A. Halley (1994). *Who Makes Public Policy*. Chatham, N.J: Chatham House.

Gould, Jon B. and Stephen D. Mastrofski. Suspect Searches: Assessing Police Behavior under the US Constitution. *Criminology and Public Policy* 3 (July, 3):315–362.

Greene, Jack R. and Carl B. Klockars. "What Police Do" in Klockars, Carl B. and Stephen D. Mastrofski (eds.) (1991). *Thinking About Police*, 2nd edition. New York: McGraw-Hill.

Harcourt, Bernard E., (2004). Unconstitutional Police Searches and Collective Responsibility. *Criminology and Public Policy* 3 (July, 3):363–378.

Hulon, Willie T. (2004). "Facilitating an Enhanced Information Sharing Network That Links Law Enforcement and Homeland Security for Federal, State and Local Governments." Testimony before the House Government Reform Subcommittee On Technology, Information Policy, Intergovernmental Relations and the Census, July 13.

Lawson, Kenneth (2002). "Rightsizing The US Presence Abroad." Testimony before The Subcommittee on National Security, Veterans Affairs and International Relations, May 1.

Lemley, Ellen C. and Gregory D. Russell (2002). Implementing Restorative Justice by Groping Along: A Case Study in Program Evolutionary Implementation. *Justice System Journal,* 23(2):157–190.

Mazerolle, Lorraine Green, Justin Ready, William Terrill, and Elin Waring (2000). Problem Oriented Policing in Public Housing: The Jersey City Evaluation. *Justice Quarterly*, 17 (March, 1):129–158.

National Defense Council Foundation (2004). http://www.ndcf.org/.

Sparger, Jerry R. and David J. Giacopassi (1992). Memphis Revisited: A Reexamination of Police Shootings After the Garner Decision *Justice Quarterly*, 9 (June, 2):211–225.

US Department of Commerce, ITA, Office of Travel & Tourism Industries. http://tinet.ita.doc.gov/view/f-2003-04-001/index.html?ti_cart_cookie=20040809.212426.25216.

US Department of State (June 2004). Consular Notification and Access Reference Card: Instructions for Arrests and Detentions of Foreign Nationals. Washington, DC: US Department of State.

US Department of State (2003). Consular Notification and Access: Instructions for Federal, State, and Local Law Enforcement and Other Officials Regarding Foreign Nationals in the United States and the Rights of Consular Officials to Assist Them. Washington, DC: US Department of State.

US Department of State (2004). Diplomatic and Consular Privileges and Immunities From Criminal Jurisdiction (chart). http://www.state.gov/m/ds/immunities/c9127.htm.

# A Brief History of Early Law Enforcement

## 2

The history and evolution of policing are important to an overall understanding of the law enforcement profession. Current trends and policies are often a reflection of historic occurrences. After studying this chapter, you should be able to:

- State three reasons why the study of history is important to a professional in the criminal justice system.
- Discuss the contributions of various civilizations and societies to the history of law enforcement.
- Describe the significance of the establishment of the Vigiles in the Roman Empire under Augustus.
- Identify the contributions to policing made by the French from the Middle Ages to the early 1800s.
- Describe the social and economic background of the Metropolitan Police in England in 1829.

## Chapter Outline

    I.  The Significance of History

   II.  Contributions to Law and Law Enforcement from Selected Ancient Civilizations

      A.  Babylon

      B.  Egypt

      C.  The Greeks in Egypt

      D.  The Hebrews

      E.  The Greeks

      F.  The Romans

## Key Terms Used in This Chapter

| | |
|---|---|
| Code of Hammurabi | Police Judiciaire |
| lex talionis | tything (or tithing) system |
| feudalism | hundred |
| Mosaic Law | shire |
| Laws of the Twelve Tables | reeve |
| Praetorian Guards | peace guilds |
| Urban Cohort | praepostus |
| Vigiles | vicecomes |
| frankpledge | Courts of Leet |
| constable | Magna Carta |
| sergeant | Statute of Winchester |
| Commune juree | An Act for Improving the Police |
| Lieutenant of Police |    in and near the Metropolis |
| Surete | |

# ■ The Significance of History

This chapter focuses on the history and evolution of law enforcement and its impact on current policing practices. History is an interpretation of the significance of important events of a society. Because this chapter is a limited presentation, you are encouraged to consult additional sources regarding the history of policing, including those in the references and selected sites on the Internet. Let us begin this section by discussing three reasons for studying history.

First, history is the aggregate of past events. To be more specific, it is a record or narrative description of past events, occurrences that provide the foundation for contemporary society. From an evolutionally perspective, history provides us with a heritage, evident in our customs, culture, and monuments. Consequently, we study the past to better understand current times and our reactions to these times.

Recent history can be referred to as "current events" or those things that have just occurred. The "recent past" includes the last few years of our lives. For some, history is what occurred before they were born, and since it has not been experienced and because memories are limited, we need to study it. To illustrate the significance of history, we need to look no further than the evening news and issues of constitutional controversies. The history and evolution of the United States is strongly tied to the Declaration of Independence, the Constitution, and the Bill of Rights. Moreover, we cannot fully understand current controversies in public policy if we do not know the foundation upon which they are based. For example, think of the statement, "We don't need another Vietnam." Unless you have an understanding of the "what," "how," and "why" of the Vietnam Conflict (it was not an official "war"), you cannot appreciate the context, issues, or implications of what is being discussed.

Today, there is a professional responsibility placed on law enforcement officers to study history. For example, without an understanding of history it would be impossible to effectively respond to the attacks of September 11, 2001. Let's take this example one step further. Think of yourself, for the moment, as one of the hundreds of federal, state, and local agents assigned to investigate the attacks of September 11. Your usefulness as an investigator would be greatly impaired without a broad understanding of Middle Eastern history, the history of terrorism, or contemporary American history. Think of your embarrassment if you were attending an investigative briefing given by a counter-terrorist expert and you had no clue who she was talking about when she discussed Yasser Arafat, or what she was talking about when she mentioned the Mossad. There may have been a time when the average police officer did not need an in-depth understanding of historical events beyond his or her beat. That luxury is now over. It is imperative given the current political climate that law enforcement officers acquire at least a basic understanding (past and present) of our enemies, both at home and abroad. As the 9-11 Commission report states: "The enemy is not just 'terrorism,' some generic evil. This vagueness blurs the strategy. The catastrophic threat at this moment in history is more specific. It is the threat posed by Islamist terrorism—especially the al-Qaida network, its affiliates, and its ideology" (National Commission 2004, 362).

The second reason for studying history is to help us understand and identify the social, economic, and political forces that have and continue to shape American society. We are a culturally diverse nation blessed with many ethnic groups, each with their own subset of cultural histories. Consequently, our history is replete with the social, economic, and political influences fashioned by immigration, urbanization, and industrialization. Interspersed within these forces have been the tempering influences of revolution, slavery, civil war, world wars, depression, cold wars, and the challenge of securing civil rights for every citizen. Throughout our history, law enforcement officers have had ever-increasing parts to play in this titanic mix. Sometimes they have been part of the problem, yet at other times they have been part of the solution. As you study the history of law enforcement, try to place yourself in the time period being discussed; think about what was occurring in society in terms of the economy, politics, and social concerns.

The third major reason for studying history is that criminal justice professionals need to understand the history of their field. "Knowing from whence you came" is part of being a professional. Only then can you make informed decisions based on the realization that others have made similar decisions before you. It is this frame of reference that gives meaning to George Santayana's (1905) famous quotation: "Those who cannot remember the past are condemned to repeat it." Many misquote this statement by saying that history repeats itself, which is not the true basis of the quote. History sometimes repeats itself because people fail to remember events and merely react according to human nature instead of knowledge. Future decisions can be more effective by making the proper analogy to previous events and analysis of similar forces in the environment. Professionals in the criminal justice system must have an understanding and a "sense" of history so that they do not repeat mistakes. However, it should also be understood that sometimes it is desirable to repeat history. This is especially true when thinking about success. We want our public policies and programs to be successful. By reviewing history, we can identify practices and procedures that "worked," hopefully for the purposes of repeating those successes. This is one reason for conducting and reviewing research in the criminal justice field.

## ■ Contributions to Law and Law Enforcement from Selected Ancient Civilizations

Across the thousands of years of ancient civilizations, laws and methods of enforcing them were created. Each in its own way and time was a response to political, social, and economic conditions. In this section, we briefly review the contributions to law and law enforcement of five ancient civilizations: Babylon, Egypt, the Hebrews, the Greeks, and the Romans. Of course, other ancient civilizations existed and thrived as well; the ones described here are generally considered the most significant to policing in the United States.

### Babylon

Babylonian civilization spanned from the eighteenth century BC until the sixth century BC in the ancient lands of Mesopotamia, the fertile plain between the Tigris and Euphrates rivers, in what today is Iraq. It is sometimes called the "cradle of civilization." A long secession of rulers presided over the region, noted for its diverse agriculture and urban trading centers. Over time the region prospered and merchants became more powerful as they collected wealth from trading and banking. Yet, the king's power was absolute, maintained through a system of authority that included dividing land into sections and then placing noblemen in charge of the sections. They held the land at the will of the king and, in return, they paid him tribute and military service. The nobility, in general, were the king's counselors, assistants in government, governors, judges, and military officers. Society below the king and the nobility consisted of the common people, the artisans and tradesmen, and slaves. None of these groups played any role in government or public life (Goodspeed 1904; Brandon 1970; Grun 1991).

One of the most important Babylonian rulers was King Hammurabi, who reigned from about 1728 to 1686 BC. Under his leadership, Babylonian civilization reached the zenith of its cultural development and political power. King Hammurabi is primarily remembered for his extensive legal code. The **Code of Hammurabi** contained some 282 regulations and evidenced a sense of justice built on personal responsibility and accountability (refer to **Figure 2-1**). Historian

Mitchel Roth (2005, 4–5) observes that although Hammurabi "is often credited with conceiving the first law code," archaeologists now believe that "he borrowed extensively from [the law codes of] earlier rulers." Nevertheless, he was astute enough to assemble a collection of both civil and criminal laws that were, in the words of Roth (2005, 5), "more complex and comprehensive than any law code previously attempted." The code included the forms of punishment, fines, or obligations for offenders, although fines were not paid to the state. The code was more advanced than tribal custom in that it recognized no blood feud, private retaliation, or marriage by capture. One of its main legal principles was **lex talionis**, or the law of retaliation. The death penalty was frequently awarded for offenses against the state and criminal negligence. The Code's provision went far beyond offenses; it essentially addressed all aspects of family, social, and business life as well as property transactions (Gadd 1971).

The principal source of the Code of Hammurabi is the stone monument made of black basalt on which the code is inscribed. Part of the code on the lower portion of the monument was erased by an Elamite king who captured the stele around 1200 BC. The stone was discovered in 1901 and is preserved in the Louvre in Paris. For a translation of the Code of Hammurabi, log on to the website at http://duhaime.org/Law_museum/hamm1.aspx. For another view of the stone monument, log on to this website: http://www.abu.nb.ca/ecm/photo/vhamurab.gif.

There are a number of excellent sites on the World Wide Web related to the history of legal codes, history, and philosophy. Examples include the following: the University of Chicago's D'Angelo Law Library at http://www.lib.uchicago.edu/e/law/history.html, the Avalon Project at Yale Law School: http://www.yale.edu/lawweb/avalon/avalon.htm, and the Ancient World Web at: http://julen.net/ancient/Law_and_Philosophy/. Other sites can be located by using the search terms "legal history," "ancient codes," and "history of law."

**Figure 2-1** Historical Legal Codes on the World Wide Web.

Why is the Code of Hammurabi important to us today? The answer is simple. It sets a benchmark from which to measure the progress of civil society. As Roth (2005, 6) states, "By codifying both criminal and civil laws and creating specific penalties for breaking these tenets, for the first time in recorded history a connection was established between crime and its punishment."

## Egypt

When we think of ancient Egypt, we think of the great pyramids at Giza, the Sphinx, the pyramid complexes at Saqqara and Memphis, the temples of Luxor and Karnak, and the Valley of the Kings. We are awed by their sheer size, majesty, and complexity. We also think of the long procession of Egyptian dynasties and their pharaohs, remembering that most of this history occurred 2,000 years before the birth of Christ. What we seldom ponder is the day-to-day lives of the people who built these great monuments. Certainly, nothing of this magnitude and majesty could have been built without a significant degree of social stability, advanced mathematical and engineering skills, law, and public administration—in other words, government.

Historians Zaky Iskander and Alexander Badawy (1965, 28) tell us that as early as the First Dynasty (3200–2980 BC), Egypt had acquired "a highly developed system of centralized government" supported and directed by written laws and a corps of public servants. There was also "a vast middle-class" of skilled craftsmen, which included painters, mason, scribes, and sculptors. By the Second Dynasty (2980–2778 BC), there is ample evidence that most citizens of Egypt enjoyed a comfortable lifestyle measured in abundant quantities of the necessities of life, which were celebrated with wine, beer, and song. Furthermore, they had developed three scripts (forms of writing): *hieroglyphic*, a cursive known as *hieratic*, and later, a simplification of the hieratic know as *demotic*, which served to transcribe the popular tongue. They also had advanced knowledge of, among other things, crop irrigation, seafaring shipbuilding, surgery and medicine, and as we now marvel, a sophisticated knowledge of engineering and architecture.

As Egypt continued to prosper during the "pyramid building period" (from the Third through the Sixth Dynasty, 2778–2680 BC), we find abundant evidence in the archaeological record indicating "that the government was very powerful and well organized" (Iskander and Badawy 1965, 37). For example, there is mention of prime ministers, ministers of public works, tax collectors, local governors, and "vizirs" who acted as the head of the entire organization of government and at the same time as the "chief of justice and chief archivist of the state" (Iskander and Badawy 1965, 49).

According to Trojan (1986), there is some evidence that internal security officials known as "Judges Commandment of the Police" existed during the Fourth Dynasty (circa 2900 BC) and that Hur Moheb created an organized police force around 1340 BC to protect commerce and ensure safe navigation along the Nile. Trojan also states the following about policing in ancient Egypt:

> *Ramses III (1198–1166 BC) invested the police with much authority in an effort to establish peace and security. He produced laws that dealt severely with criminals and punishment being awarded in public. The most important police units were those responsible for the security of the tombs, where valuables were placed with the dead. The Egyptians claim that they were the first to use dogs for police purposes, using them for guarding property. The police of ancient Egypt were also vested with judicial powers; they not only tried the cases, but they passed judgment and executed the sentences (Trojan 1986, 15).*

The advanced civilizations that existed in the Middle East in ancient times had a tremendous influence on other empires that followed. Brandon states that the debt owed to Egypt by Western civilization is immense:

> *The ancient Greeks, probably the most intelligent race that has ever lived, acknowledged this debt freely. From the time when their merchants began setting up trading posts in Egypt in the seventh and sixth centuries BC they were fascinated by Egypt . . . . Archaic Greek art was clearly influenced by Egyptian sculpture, which at its best has few equals anywhere in the world. The Greeks copied Egyptian medicine and surgery and in many other fields of knowledge looked upon the Egyptian priests as their mentors (Brandon 1970, 127).*

## The Greeks in Egypt

It seems the Greeks were also impressed with other aspects of Egyptian society besides art, medicine, and surgery. After Alexander (356–323 BC) liberated

Egypt from the Persians in 332 BC, he and other Greek rulers that followed adopted a policy of tolerance toward Egyptian civilization, which they held in high regard. This included "paying tribute to their religious and social customs" and affording certain rights to property owners (Iskander and Badawy 1965, 118).

Whether the Greeks found an intact police system of the kind known under the reign of Ramses III is not known. Yet we do know that a developed police system did exist during Greek rule. How much was borrowed from the Egyptian experience is speculation, but Iskander and Badawy (1965) cite a number of factors that suggest the police were very well organized. In fact, law enforcement responsibilities were divided into divisions and sections. A mounted police corps patrolled the desert areas; another guarded the borders; there was a special unit to patrol the canals and river; another unit was responsible for buying goods for the government; and still another unit was responsible for inspecting the harvest on royal lands. Every Egyptian village and town had a police unit, which was commanded by a police chief. In addition to these services, some officers were assigned to tax collection duties while others were assigned special duties in the offices of high officials, including acting as bodyguards. Iskander and Badawy (1965, 155) also state that officers were paid for their services by being given "the gift of a plot of arable land" and/or were paid in "money."

## The Hebrews

Between 1650 and 1300 BC, groups of wandering tribes, the Hebrews (later known as the Israelites), migrated toward and into Egypt. They claimed a common ancestor, Abraham, and shared a common religion, Judaism. Eventually, they left Egypt under the leadership of Moses (about 1250 BC), wandered through the "wilderness" (the Sinai desert) for 40 years, crossed the Jordan River, and established a homeland in Palestine along the northern shores of the Dead Sea. The significance of this to the modern-day world was the development of **Mosaic Law**, meaning "the law of Moses." Besides the biblical Ten Commandments, the Law of Moses is recorded in the Old Testament books of Genesis, Exodus, Leviticus, Numbers, and Deuteronomy. At the heart of Mosaic Law is the covenant between man and God. Historian Mitchel Roth (2005, 6) observes that Mosaic Law was "committed to the elimination of class distinctions," placing it in sharp contrast "with Hammurabi's code by repudiating the notion of a rich man's law by applying a uniform moral standard applicable to all people." Under Mosaic Law people abide by the law out of an obligation to a higher authority (God) and not to an earthly ruler. It is from this Hebrew foundation and its principles that Judaism and Christianity evolved. The impact of these religions throughout subsequent history and upon social customs, laws, and moral beliefs is referred to as the "Judeo-Christian influence." Its influence, codified in the Ten Commandments, forms the "foundation of law systems throughout much of the Western world" (Roth 2005, 6).

From about 1050 BC to 930 BC, the Kingdom of Israel was a major power in the Middle East. King David established the national capital at Jerusalem, built up an army, and made its influence felt throughout the region. Under King Solomon, alliances were established with other powers in the region, including Phoenicia and Egypt (Brandon 1970, 127).

## The Greeks

The tribes of the eastern Mediterranean area expanded their trade and commerce into other nearby regions, including that of Asia Minor (Turkey), the Aegean Sea, and into the Balkan Peninsula. The influence of the Egyptians, the Assyrians, the Phoenicians, and the Hittites upon the Greeks allowed them to gain great power and influence of their own by 1500 BC. The Greek conquest of the Aegean area occurred between 1500 and 1200 BC. Their influence declined shortly thereafter because of invading groups (barbarians) from the north. Greeks migrated back toward their homelands, where they prospered in limited geographical colonies called city-states (*poleis* or *polis* in Greek).

Each city-state was an independent, close-knit entity that formed its own political and social life. It was in these self-contained city-states that the principle of democracy, "the rule of the people," was born (Breasted 1916, 300). The early city-states were ruled originally by aristocrats who had accumulated great wealth and, therefore, were able to rule as a king would. As their influence grew weaker, they used unjust and despotic methods to maintain their positions. One of the major complaints of the people about this time was that only the ruler knew all the laws. Consequently, the people began demanding that the laws be written. According to Goodspeed (1904, 100), the Greek custom became one of commissioning "the best man in the state, to whom all power was given that he might prepare, publish and administer a code of law which should be binding upon the people." One such lawgiver, Draco, was appointed around 624 BC in Athens. He codified the oral law and customs of the land. Unfortunately, the law of Draco was considered very harsh and punitive, some saying it was "written in blood." Subsequently, another lawgiver, Solon, modified the law and was responsible for giving political power to all citizens of the state. Because of this, Solon is known as the "Founder of the Athenian Democracy" (Goodspeed 1904, 109–110).

Interestingly, it was the age of tyrants, which originally meant a high office held by a ruler not of aristocratic lineage, that led to the development of a more democratic society. One such tyrant, Pisistratus of Athens, was known for looking after the rights of the people, curbing the nobles, giving great attention to public works like harbor improvements, state buildings, and temples, and cultivating art, music, and literature (Breasted 1916, 317). He expanded the basic principles of political rights of the masses established by Solon. It is also in this time period that Homer's poems were first written, and other cultural advances in the theater prospered.

During the early fifth century BC, many of the larger Greek city-states banded together to successfully ward off invasions by the Persians. This led to a stronger Greek influence in the Aegean Sea area. Following the defeat of the Persians, Athens and Sparta became the more predominate city-states and soon began to rival each other. Sparta represented the tradition of military might and limited privileges to citizens, and Athens represented the seeds of democracy and culture (Breasted 1916, 347). Unfortunately, this rivalry and domination of other cities and lands saw some curtailments in democracy. Citizenship was no longer granted to foreigners, and people with legal disputes were forced to travel to Athens to present their case to the citizen juries; this was a great inconvenience to the people of the Athenian Empire. Also, meetings of representatives from all states of the Empire were discontinued. Athens was being viewed as increasingly dictatorial and was losing favor of people outside her immediate borders.

By 404 BC, following a 27-year war with Sparta, the Athenian Empire had crumbled; democracy had failed to overcome the fragmented nature of the Athenian Empire and to unite the Greek world. In conquered lands, Sparta set up a form of government known as oligarchy (a term meaning "rule of a few") which consisted of the upper class or nobility supported by military force (Breasted 1916, 400–401). The Spartan rule of the area, however, came to an end with a military defeat in 371 BC. As the Athenian Empire was crumbling the Macedonians to the north were gaining power. Alexander of Macedonia was thirteen (around 343 BC) when he studied under the great philosopher Aristotle. Alexander was twenty when he became King of Macedonia. He believed that the Greeks should submit to his leadership, but they did not. He militarily conquered the major Greek city-states and small empires and set out to the east to establish his own empire. Persia, Phoenicia, and Egypt fell to Alexander's armies before he turned 26. During the following six years (circa 323 BC), he conquered the lands of today's Iran, India, and parts of China. He died shortly thereafter at the age of 33. Although his empire was maintained for some time by his heirs, other communities of the region (e.g., the Greek city-states) were beginning to regain their identity and history, and others (e.g., the Romans) were gaining power and expanding their borders (Breasted 1916, 430–438).

## The Romans

Rome, founded between 800–750 BC, was first ruled by aristocratic kings. From 500 to 133 BC, the government of Rome experienced great change. People gradually secured the right to have laws published, the power to elect magistrates, and the establishment of a republican form of government. Around 450 BC, the **Laws of the Twelve Tables** became the foundation of the early Roman legal system. These laws were inscribed upon twelve tablets of brass set up for public inspection on the walls of the Temple of Jupiter. Although only fragmentary portions of the laws remain, it is known that they were a collection of Roman maxims of universal application from which formal law later developed. The Twelve Tables were like crude chapters of procedures of conduct (see **Figure 2-2**).

Later, during the reign of Augustus (28 BC–AD 14), a new system of government was instituted. The army was the key to Roman control and influence. It was responsible for internal security and for the defense of its borders and frontiers, which extended to England (Brandon 1970, 127). Internal social control under Augustus, however, took on a new look. The city of Rome at this time had a population of over 1.25 million people, which included large numbers of slaves and indentured servants from conquered lands. The city was built largely of wood and brick, and buildings were close to one another, causing major problems when fires broke out. Moreover, there was a constant fear of insurrection because of social class distinction, limited civil rights for non-citizens, and discrimination against non-Romans. Crime in the streets was rampant. There was no efficient law enforcement agency or street lighting system; gangs controlled

Table I

1. If a man call another to law, he shall go. If he go not, they shall witness it; then he shall be seized.
2. If he flee or evade, lay hands on him as he goes.
6. If they settle the matter, let it be told.
7. If they settle not, they shall join issue in the assembly or in the Forum before midday, then they shall plead and prove, both being present.

Table II

3. He who needs a witness shall within three days go to his house and notify him.

Table VIII

2. If a man has broken the limb of another and does not settle with him, let there be retaliation.
3. If a man with fist or club breaks the bone of another, he is liable to penalty, of 300 (pence) if done to a free man, 150 if done to a slave.
12. If by night a man have done a theft, and (the owner) kills him, let him be (as if) killed by law.

Table X

1. A dead man you shall not bury or burn within the city.
4. Women shall not tear their faces, nor make excessive lamentation for the dead.

*Source:* Albert Kocourek and John H. Wigmore (1915). *Sources of Ancient and Primitive Law.* Boston: Little, Brown, and Company, 465–468. Also visit the site: http://members.aol.com/pilgrimjon/private/ LEX/12tables.html.

**Figure 2-2** Selected sections of the Laws of the Twelve Tables.

**Excubitorem**—the substation located in the districts; it housed the Vigiles and the equipment needed to fight fire. It also had cells for prisoners.

**Karcerarius**—the Vigile assigned to jailor duty.

**Quae-stionarius**—the interrogator and/or torturer.

**Sebaciarii**—believed to be the plain clothes men or early form of detective.

**Saint Sebastian**—Patron Saint of the police; was an officer in the Vigiles.

*Source:* Martin A. Kelly, "The First Urban Policeman," *Journal of Police Science and Administration*, (March 1973, 58–59).

**Figure 2-3** Terms associated with the Vigiles of Rome.

large areas of the city (Kelly 1973, 56–60).

In an attempt to address these threatening conditions, Augustus established the **Praetorian Guards** as his personal bodyguards (the privileged corps) and the **Urban Cohort** as protectors of the peace throughout Rome. Both were military units and part of the regular army under the control of the emperor. Around 14 BC, and in partial response to political opposition, he appointed a force of freedmen called **Vigiles**, or night watchers, to act as Rome's first fire-fighting unit. The Vigiles eventually numbered about 9,000 and were divided into seven cohorts (districts). Besides their fire-related duties, they were eventually assigned policing duties of making arrests for theft, burglary, assault, capturing runaway slaves, and serving as guards at the public baths. **Figure 2-3** lists terms associated with the Vigiles.

Historians often cite the Vigiles as the first large civilian unit in a metropolitan setting used for law enforcement and social control purposes, overlooking the Egyptian experience with policing (refer to the previous sections of this chapter). Yet, importantly, the Vigiles were the first known public safety unit appointed to serve both the fire-fighting and policing needs of a city. Because of Augustus' creation of the Vigiles, he is referred by some as the "Father of Policing." Some historians claim that policing did not see an equivalent force in history until the establishment of city agencies in nineteenth century Europe (Kelly 1973, 56, 60).

As we conclude this section about social control in selected ancient civilizations, it may be appropriate to ask, What caused great countries or empires to decline? Of course, we must rely on researcher interpretation to answer such a question. One researcher's recent list of reasons points to aspects of social control. Jim Black's (1994) book, *When Nations Die*, identifies ten warning signs of social decline, according to his analysis of history:

1. A crisis in lawlessness
2. A loss of economic discipline
3. Rising bureaucracy
4. Declining level of education
5. Weakening of cultural foundations
6. Lack of respect for traditions
7. Increasing materialism
8. Rising immorality
9. Devaluing of human life
10. Decay of religious beliefs

When one reviews and reflects upon this list of warning signals, the relationship among social, economic, and political factors and their impact upon social control (and policing) becomes profound. The authors of this text are not claiming that Black's warning signs are totally accurate or that they totally agree with his interpretation. However, the warning signs do reflect a type of systems approach in viewing society and the concept of social control. Today, several of the warnings signs are mentioned often in various forums debating issues such as crime, violence, morality, religion, and culture.

## ◼ The French Police

After the fall of the Roman Empire, the next major developments in policing occurred during the Middle Ages in France. During the eighth century, the whole area of Gaul (an area that today encompasses most of Western Europe, including France, Belgium, western Switzerland, and parts of the Netherlands and Germany) was united by Charlemagne, who consolidated power into a centralized government and required all free men to take an oath of fidelity to him. This oath is sometimes referred to as a **frankpledge**, which is a system of social control supported by oath to obey the law of the land. Charlemagne divided his staff of servants into areas of service, one of which was the position of **constable**, or count of the stable, an important position of trust (Seignobos 1932, 58–59).

By the ninth century, the area of Gaul was again fragmented into large centers of authority, each consisting of a king and his subjects. **Feudalism**, the practice of providing basic needs to those under a leader's control or subject to a leader's authority, was established as a system of social life. Under this arrangement in France, the king or lord placed trusted agents in every village, known as mayors, who policed the village with the aid of armed **sergeants**.

> *"The mayors of towns . . . exercised all the powers enjoyed by the town, dispensing justice, both civil and criminal, levying taxation, controlling public order, leading the militia composed of the burgesses, providing for the defense of the walls, and keeping the treasure, the archives and the keys to the town gates"* (Seignobos 1932, 126).

By the twelfth century, many towns had formed a mutual defense association known as **commune juree**, where an oath formed a bond between a large number of men of equal status for the defense of a collective interest (Seignobos 1932, 103–126).

France's first efforts to establish a centralized police force occurred during the reign of Louis XIV. In 1666, he appointed a council under the direction of Jean-Baptiste Colbert to develop a plan for police organization and administration. The edicts of the council (1666–1667) established police powers and procedures, restricted the private ownership of arms, and created the **Lieutenant of Police** for the City of Paris. According to Arnold (1979, 14–15), the Lieutenant of Police was granted seven distinct areas of authority by Louis XIV:

1. The security of Paris, including repression of civil disorders, making arrests, and surveillance of foreigners.
2. The cleaning and lighting of streets, fire fighting and prevention, and flood control.
3. Regulating and upgrading the moral behavior of the citizens.
4. Regulating social affairs in matters of abandoned children, unfaithful wives, organization of hospitals, and inspection of prisons and jails.
5. Assuring adequate food supplies for the city.
6. Protecting the city in times of epidemics and general maintenance of health conditions.
7. Regulating the economy; this included surveillance of worker's associations and policing the marketplace.

Louis XIV later set up Lieutenants-General of Police in all the principal cities of France. The idea of a royal police continued for over 100 years until the French people's growing distrust of the monarchy and its government led to the French Revolution of 1789. Power was transferred from the king to the Assembly, which reorganized the government based on the uniformity of institutions and not obedience to the king. The monarchy, however, was retained, with Louis XVI on the throne. Every region became autonomous, having an elected administration with the power of maintaining order, policing its own area, and even collecting taxes. This manner of decentralized power was adopted from the new government formed in the United States following its independence from England. Conflict between the monarchy and the Assembly, however, led to the revolution of 1792 and years of civil strife. The Committee of General Security was responsible for police power, and centralization of the police became a primary issue. In 1796, the Ministry of General Police was established for the "execution of the laws relative to the police, security, and general tranquility of the Republic" (Arnold 1979, 23–24).

With Napoleon Bonaparte's rise to power in 1799, the police system of France became an integral part of his regime. His initial Minister of General Police was Joseph Fouche. Fouche maintained an elaborate intelligence system that kept the Emperor well informed (Arnold 1979, 33–35, 161). Also, during the reign of Napoleon, a former convict, Eugene Francois Vidocq, became the head of a small detective unit of the Paris police. He staffed his unit with former criminals, under the philosophy that "it takes a thief to catch a thief," and paid them according to their performance (see **Figures 2-4** and **2-5** for additional information about Vidocq's legacy). Vidocq developed an elaborate system of informants and intelligence-gathering networks that became the established procedures for the entire criminal division (the **Surete**, which in 1913 became the **Police Judiciaire**) (Holden 1992, 26). France has undergone a number of changes in the form of governmental structure since Napoleon, but the centralization of the police has remained a major feature of most of these governmental reforms.

# The British Experience

## Early History

As mentioned earlier, the Roman Empire once stretched to England, and by the beginning of the fifth century, London had a population of about 20,000. During much of its early history, parts of England were occupied by other groups as well. Social control in early England was an individual and group responsibility.

Historically, Eugene Francois Vidocq's legendary crime-solving reputation was lauded in Poe's *Murders in the Rue Morgue* and in Herman Melville's *Moby Dick*. The fugitive in Charles Dickens' *Great Expectations* is also inspired by Vidocq's real-life exploits. As a fugitive from French justice he first offered his services as a police spy and informer, later becoming a master of disguise who was so successful at catching criminals that, in 1811, he was named the first chief of the Surete. In time he directed a force of 28 detectives, all of whom were also former criminals.

Eugene Francois Vidocq is considered by historians and those in law enforcement to be the father of modern criminal investigation. Vidocq's accomplishments and contributions to law enforcement were many. He introduced record keeping (i.e., a card index system) and criminalistics, introduced the science of ballistics, was the first to make plaster-of-paris casts of foot/shoe impressions, was a master of disguise and surveillance, held patents on indelible ink and unalterable bond paper, and founded the first modern detective agency and credit bureau, Le Bureau des Renseignements. After resigning from the Surete, he published *Memoires de Vidocq* (1828), a book which became a best-seller in Europe and firmly established Eugene Francios Vidocq as the world's greatest detective.

Vidocq's regard for his fellow man also was legendary. He was a philanthropist who also helped the poor and abandoned of Paris; at the same time that he was pursuing the guilty, he was also freeing the innocent.

*Source:* The Vidocq Society, 1998. Used by permission.

**Figure 2-4** Eugene Francois Vidocq.

Known as the **tything (or tithing) system**, it consisted of a group of ten families (normally an extended family) living in close proximity to each other to provide self-protection and security. If an infraction of the common law happened, members of the tything were expected to raise the "hue and cry" prompting others to come to their aid. A territory containing ten tythings was called a **hundred**, and several hundreds covered an area called a **shire**. Using today's terms, a tything would be a village, a hundred a township, and a shire a county. The chief law enforcement officer or magistrate of the shire was called a **reeve**. It was from this early terminology that the word "sheriff" (shire-reeve) originated (Lee 1971, 3–7)

The shire-reeve was responsible for conducting annual inspections of the tythings and court proceedings. By the end of the tenth century, **Peace Guilds** had become popular as a local means of social control. These guilds were private, voluntary associations, arranged in 10 groups under 10 headmen, one of whom acted as a chief and treasurer. The guilds were mutual assurance societies. The contributions made to them went toward apprehension of offenders.

Following the Norman conquest of 1066, some traditional titles of positions associated with the tything system changed. The headman of the tything be-

One of the most unusual crime-solving organizations in the world meets in the historic area of Philadelphia next to Independence Hall. The Vidocq Society is named in honor of Eugene Francois Vidocq, the brilliant 18th century French detective who founded the Surete. Vidocq Society Members ("V.S.M.s") and their guests draw upon years of forensic skills used each day at work to evaluate, investigate, and endeavor to solve unsolved crimes, particularly murder. When requested, members participate in the investigation and prosecution of the person or persons who are eventually charged with the murder. Members are motivated purely by public service. They are forensic professionals who eagerly donate centuries of deductive and scientific talent for the common good. The Vidocq Society credo is "Veritas Veritatum." The phrase, in Latin, means "Truth Begets Truth." The Vidocq Society was founded in Philadelphia in 1990 by world-renowned sculptor and forensic reconstructionist Frank Bender; internationally-known forensic psychologist and crime "profiler" Richard Walter, M.A.; and Bill Fleisher, a former Philadelphia Police Officer and then FBI Special Agent who later became the Assistant Special Agent in Charge of the US Customs Service in Philadelphia.

Vidocq Society membership represents 17 states and 11 foreign countries. It is a rare privilege and has been bestowed upon less than 150 men and women; new members must be sponsored by existing members. Most members are employed in public service by federal, state and local law enforcement—either behind badges or at prosecutors' tables. Some Vidocqians consult regularly with federal, state, or local law enforcement; attorneys in private practice and entrepreneurs are also members.

A long-unsolved homicide or disappearance is usually the centerpiece of each Vidocq Society meeting. The crime and its evidence are disclosed to members and invited guests, with an eye towards rekindling or refocusing the investigation. The presenter of a cold-case murder or disappearance at a Vidocq Society luncheon could be a law enforcement professional who has investigated the murder over the years and continues to carry it on his caseload, a Vidocq Society member, or a private investigator hired by the murder victim's family. The spirited, synergistic question-and-answer period that follows each formal case presentation becomes a collaborative effort that involves members and invited guests in the search for a solution to a previously unsolved crime. If substantial interest is shown by Vidocq Society members following the case presentation, a "working group" is assembled (an investigative team of Vidocq Society members and volunteers that is tailored to advance that specific investigation).

Additional information about the Vidocq Society can be found on the world wide web at: http://www.vidocq.org.

*Source:* The Vidocq Society. 1999. Used by permission.

**Figure 2-5** The Vidocq Society.

came the **praepostus**, and the shire-reeve was replaced by **vicecomes** who went on the circuit to hold court (known as the police courts). The Normans also established a feudalistic form of social control. By the twelfth century, **Courts of Leet** (local police courts) had been instituted as a substitute for the sheriff's courts. They became so popular that the sheriff eventually "ceased to trouble the village communities with his annual visit of inspection" (Lee 1971, 6–17).

During the 1100s, kings of England continued the slow process of judicial reforms, yet these measures did not satisfy a growing sense of injustice in England's feudal society. In 1215, King John, who had succeeding in alienating every segment of English society due to his ineptness, was forced by a number of barons to sign the **Magna Carta** (Latin, meaning "the great charter"). This profoundly important document, today considered a foundational statement of democratic principles, limited the power of the king and granted the citizens of England certain guarantees, including a church free from domination by the monarchy, reforms to the justice system, making it more equitable, and greater political liberties and rights for citizens. For example, Section 20 of the document rebukes the alleged abuses by officials in rendering justice and penalties: "We will not make men justiciaries, constables, sheriffs or bailiffs, unless they understand the law of the land, and are well disposed to observe it" (Lee 1971, 20).

The importance of the Magna Carta can not be overstated, not only to the citizens of England, when it was signed in 1215, but to all peoples who would subsequently come to live under a democratic form of government. As Roth (2005, 36), observes, "It was a turning point in legal history." Its powerful concepts of due process, justice, and the restraint of unchecked government serve as "one of the foundations of modern democracy," evidenced in the fact that the framers would turn to the Magna Carta for ".... basic principles that would be incorporated in the American Constitution 500 years later . . ." (Roth 2005, 36).

During the reign of Edward I, the **Statute of Winchester** (1285) was enacted in response to increasing incidents of crime brought on by the urbanization of English society. According to Roth (2005, 36) it was "one of the most important pieces of criminal justice legislation to come out of the Middle Ages. . . ." It created, as Historian Melville Lee (1971) observes, a policing system that continued for nearly 500 years. Among other things, it provided for:

- A "watch and ward" system of protection (a night watch system made up of all eligible males who took turns serving on the watch).
- A duty to inform others of offenses and offenders (the "hue and cry").
- The arming of all males aged 15 to 60 to defend the kingdom and to maintain order.
- The removal of brush and most trees 200 feet on each side of the king's highway (to prevent surprise attacks from robbers) (Lee 1971, 24–28).

Consequently, it added new meaning to the French word "frankpledge," which the English had adopted into their language. As Lee (1971, 20) observes, by the end of twelfth century the term "frankpledge" meant recognition of the responsibility of every citizen to take his part in the duty of maintaining peace in the state, or the liability that all men share to render police services when called upon to do so.

## The 1700s and 1800s

The watch system served the English people well until the 1700s, when numerous social, economic, and political circumstances combined to change the character of English society. As the century progressed, England became less and less an agrarian country. The advent of international trade and commerce, the discovery of new lands, the expansion of the British Empire, and war with Spain and France changed England's posture in the world. At home, religious protests and calls for social reform, and civil war within its Empire, created a social environment wherein unpaid, unskilled watchmen were no longer effective agents of social control.

These challenges were compounded by the Industrial Revolution, which brought increased urbanization and a new social class—factory workers and miners. Working conditions in the new factories and mines were often harsh, unsafe, and unhealthy. Following their men in an exodus from the farms of rural England, women and children also entered the workforce in large numbers. They, too, faced a harsh and unsafe working environment. Moreover, living conditions in the new industrial centers, like Manchester, Liverpool, and London, were crowed, unsafe, and unsanitary. These conditions produced a myriad of social problems, including an increase in crime and riots, which were becoming common. The Riots Acts of 1715 made rioting a felonious act and extended powers of the Justices of the Peace. Yet, new laws would not address the underlying social problems of the period. In 1736, Parliament enacted a law allowing London's city council to raise monies for all police purposes, and constables were empowered to make arrests (Lee 1971, 147–151).

In 1746, Henry Fielding, an English writer, playwright, journalist, and lawyer, was appointed magistrate of the Bow Street Magistrates Court, which was located in a particular crime ridden and rowdy section of London. Beyond his accomplished writing abilities and his sense of justice from the bench, he is noted for his research and insights into crime and police reform. He authored one of the first treatises on police reform in 1751, *Enquiry into the Causes of the Late Increase of Robbers*, which addressed the social context of crime. He also established a police office (the Bow Street Police Office) as part of his court. He staffed the office by hiring six constables who were charged with responding to criminal incidents and with apprehending known thieves. These officers, who were very successful at their duties, became know as the Bow Street Runners. They were paid for their services from the fines levied against wrongdoers. Fielding supported the idea of a 24-hour patrol by officers and even recommended horse patrols for the city. Some have called him the "Father of the Police of London." His brother, John Fielding, who succeeded him as magistrate of the Bow Street court, continued the police reform movement. Specific foot patrol officers were assigned in 1782, a horse patrol was added in 1805, and a dismounted horse patrol was established in 1821 (Tobias 1979, 44–52). (For additional information about Henry and John Fielding and Victorian Era policing see the Devon and Cornwall Constabulary website at http://www.devon-cornwall.police.uk/v3/about/history/vicpolice/intro.htm.)

Patrick Colquhoun, a Middlesex magistrate, was another police reformer of this time. He published several works about policing, *Treatise On the Police of the Metropolis* (1796), *The Commerce and Policing of the Thames River* (1800), and *Treatise on the Functions and Duties of the Constable* in 1803 (Lee 1991, 177, 218–219). These reform efforts informed the public of alternatives to the antiquated watch and parish constable systems that served the city. Within the next two decades, police reform was to occur on a much larger scale.

The concepts of police reform advocated by Henry and John Fielding and Patrick Colquhoun would become a reality under the leadership of a young chief secretary for Ireland by the name of Robert Peel (1788–1850). From 1812 through 1818, Peel governed Ireland. His posting occurred during a period marked by civil disorders, increasing crime, and religious conflict. Shortly after passage of the Peace Preservation Act of 1814, he was able to establish a new form of policing—the Royal Irish Constabulary. The Constabulary was a civil (as opposed to military) police force designed to assist in reducing crime and disorder (Stead 1985, 62). Consequently, by the time Peel was selected Home Secretary of England in 1821, he had gained valuable experience with reforming the police. By 1829, five distinct classes of police officers existed in the London area:

1. Parochial Constables, elected annually in parish or townships, serving gratuitously.

2. Their substitutes for deputies serving for a wage voluntarily paid by the principals.

3. Salaried Bow Street officers and patrols charged with the suppression of highwaymen and footpads.

4. Stipendiary police constables attached to the public officers established under the "Middlesex Justices Act."

5. Stipendiary Water-Police attached to the Thames Office, as established by act of Parliament in 1789 (Lee 1971, 177).

In 1829, Sir Robert Peel, in his role as home secretary, introduced a bill to create a "new police." **An Act for Improving the Police in and near the Metropolis** established a centralized police force for the metropolitan London area. According to Roth (2005, 104), "Peel had originally hoped to create a nationwide police force, but to his constituency this suggested oppression and totalitarianism." Consequently, he settled on a more focused mission in London. Two co-commissioners were appointed to help Peel, Charles Rowan, a former military colonel, and Richard Mayne, an attorney. The new management team recruited and trained over 1,000 new officers, who would report for duty in the new Metropolitan Police Department. The force they created was, "A preventative rather than reactive force; it replaced the ages-old night watch with professional, paid, full-time officers" (Roth 2005, 104). Early decisions made about the force included:

- The force would function on a 24-hour basis.
- Officers would wear a uniform and a top hat.
- Officers would carry no weapons beyond a truncheon.
- Officers would carry a small staff with a crown on one end to symbolize the royal authority (Tobias 1979, 44–46).

Based on the *First Instructions* issued by Rowan and Mayne (and approved by Sir Robert Peel), historians have devised various listings of what is known as "Peel's Principles," or "Principles of Peelian Reform." **Figure 2-6** shows two different lists derived from the many versions of the list. The wording has been modernized somewhat.

The New Police did not *replace* the existing classes of peace officers mentioned earlier; it was an addition to them. But by 1839, following a number of select committees to establish the English police system, especially in London, most of the other police forces in London had been "absorbed" into the New Police. Although the new force was not popular at first (because of the fear of centralized police authority), it eventually won wide public support and became one model of municipal police forces worldwide (Emsley 1991), especially in the United States. Peel's influence earned him the recognition as "Father of Modern Municipal Policing."

## ■ Summary

This chapter presented an overview of nearly 3,800 years of the history of policing. We have reviewed selected examples of social control and law enforcement from the Babylonian to the British Empires. The chapter emphasized the evolutionary nature of law enforcement, pointing out that social control methods evolve and change in response to social, political, and economic circumstances and conditions. In most ancient civilizations, with the exception of the Egyptians, the policing function was carried out by the military and the elite forces of the aristocracy. This would start to change in the Roman Empire; law enforcement by civilians became an important feature of social control. In the seventeenth through

Version 1—General Principles

1. Prevention of crime is the basic mission of the police.
2. Police must have full respect of the citizenry.
3. A citizen's respect for the law develops respect for the police.
4. Cooperation of the public decreases as the use of force increases.
5. Police must render impartial enforcement of the law.
6. Physical force is used only as a last resort.
7. The police are the public and the public are the police.
8. Police represent the law.
9. The absence of crime and disorder is the test of police efficiency.

Version 2—Organization Principles
1. Police must be stable, efficient, and organized along military lines.
2. Police must be under government control.
3. The efficiency of the police should be judged by the absence or presence of crime.
4. Distribution of crime information is essential.
5. The police should be deployed by time and area.
6. Qualities such as the command of temper, a quiet determined manner and so on are indispensable to police officers.
7. Good appearance commands respect.
8. Efficiency is premised on securing and training the proper persons.
9. Public security demands that every police officer be given a number.
10. Police headquarters should be centrally located and easily accessible to the people.
11. Police officers should be hired on a probationary basis.
12. Police records are necessary to the correct distribution of police strength.

*Source:* Reprinted with permission from J.A. Conser and G.G. Frissora, *Peel's Principles Revisited*. Paper presented at the annual conference of the Midwestern Criminal Justice Association, Chicago, 15 September, 1994.

**Figure 2-6** Peel's Principles of Policing.

nineteenth centuries, France and England developed the fundamental outlines of the policing systems that are in place today.

History is the study of past events and all the surrounding elements of those events. It provides the foundation for modern society to stand on; it is studied in order to better understand current times and our reactions to current events. History can help us understand and identify the social, economic, and political forces that have been and are shaping our society. Criminal justice professionals need to understand the history of their field. "Knowing from whence you came" is a keystone of any professional. An understanding of history helps us make informed decisions based on the realization that others have made similar decisions before us. It is this frame of reference that gives meaning to George Santayana's (1905) famous quotation: "Those who cannot remember the past are condemned to repeat it."

## QUESTIONS FOR REVIEW

1. What are three reasons why the study of history is important to the field of criminal justice?
2. Describe the organizational structure of Egyptian policing and the degree of authority vested to them. How advanced do you think they were in comparison to the London police department of 1829?
3. What was unique about the establishment of the Vigiles in ancient Rome? What social and political forces affected their creation?
4. What were the key contributions made by the French to the field of policing from the Middle Ages to the early 1800s?
5. What were the reasons for establishing the Metropolitan Police of London in 1829? Who were some of the early police reformers in England during the 1700s and 1800s?

## SUGGESTED ACTIVITIES

1. Select a country or region of the world and research its history of social control. Identify, if possible, early forms of policing. Try to identify the social, political, and economic conditions of the period.
2. Check your library's holdings (possibly on microfilm) of old newspapers of England (e.g., *The Times* of London) and find some of the debate in daily newspapers at the time of the introduction to create the "New Police" in London. Look for letters to the editor and editorials on the subject of the New Police.
3. Using the Internet, check out the home page of the New Scotland Yard (London Metropolitan Police Department) at **http://www.met.police.uk/**. Click on the "History" icon and select "History A-Z," where you can read about the early years of the London policing.

## ■ Chapter Glossary

**An Act for Improving the Police in and near the Metropolis** introduced and enacted during the term of Sir Robert Peel, Home Secretary of England, in 1829 which establish a centralized police force for the metropolitan London area.

**Code of Hammurabi** the legal code of ancient Babylon, about 1750 BC Codified under King Hammurabi; contained some 282 statutes and evidenced a sense of justice built on personal responsibility and accountability.

**Commune juree** twelfth century French mutual defense association where an oath formed a bond between a large number of men of equal status for the defense of a collective interest.

**constable** an important position of trust in France during the Middle Ages; count of the stable.

**Courts of Leet**   (local police courts) instituted as a substitute for the sheriff's courts.

**feudalism**   the practice of providing the living needs of those under a leader's control or subject to a leader's authority.

**frankpledge system**   a form of social control where all free men took an oath of fidelity to the king; introduced in France during the reign of Charlemagne, later adopted by the English.

**hundred**   a collection of ten tythings.

**Laws of the Twelve Tables**   a set of twelve brass tablets describing proper conduct that became the foundation of the Roman Empire's legal system (about 450 BC).

**lex talionis**   the law of retaliation.

**Lieutenant of Police**   established by the edicts of the council in France (1666–1667) for the city of Paris.

**Magna Carta**   the great charter of England signed by King John in 1215; it granted certain guarantees toward a fairer justice system and rights to the people.

**Mosaic Law**   the law of Moses as found in the Old Testament books of Exodus, Leviticus, Numbers, and Deuteronomy.

**peace guilds**   tenth century England; local means of social control; private and voluntary associations, arranged in ten groups under ten headmen; mutual assurance societies.

**praepostus**   the title of the headman of the English tything following the Norman conquest of 1066.

**Praetorian Guards**   personal bodyguards of Caesar Augustus; an elite military unit.

**reeve**   the chief law enforcement official and magistrate of the shire in the English tything system (known as the shire-reeve or later as the sheriff).

**sergeant**   armed police assistants to early French village mayors.

**shire**   a geographical area roughly equivalent to a county.

**Statute of Winchester**   (1285) enacted during the reign of Edward I; it created a policing system that continued for nearly 500 years.

**Surete**   the criminal division of the Paris Police (which in 1913 became the **Police Judiciaire**).

**tything (or tithing) system**   early English system of social control.

**Urban Cohort**   Roman military units used as protectors of the peace throughout Rome.

**vicecomes**   title change of the shire-reeve following the Norman conquest of 1066; responsible for going on the circuit to hold court (known as the police courts).

**Vigiles**   a civilian force of freedmen created by Emperor Augustus around 14 BC to act as night watchers; was the city's first fire-fighting unit and police unit.

# Chapter References

Arnonld, Eric A. Jr. (1979). *Fouche, Napoleon, and the General Police*. Washington, DC: University Press of America.

Black, Jim (1994). *When Nations Die*. Wheaton, IL: Tyndale House.

Brandon, S.G.F. (ed.) (1970). *Ancient Empires*. New York: Newsweek.

Breasted, James Henry (1916). *The Conquest of Civilization*. New York: Harper & Brothers Publishers.

Conser, J.A. and G.G. Frissora. *Peel's Principles Revisited*. Paper presented at the annual conference of the Midwestern Criminal Justice Association, Chicago, IL. September, 1994.

Cottrell, Leonare (1970). "Gift of the Nile." In Brandon (ed.) (1970). *Ancient Empires*. New York: Newsweek, 13.

Emsley, Clive (1991). *The English Police: A Political and Social History*. New York: St. Martin's Press.

Gadd, Cyril John (1971). "Code of Hammurabi." In Benton, W. (publisher). *Encyclopaedia Britannica*, 11, 41–43.

Goodspeed, George S. (1904). *A History of the Ancient World*. New York: Charles Scribner's Sons.

Grun, Bernard (1991). *The Timetables of History: The New Third Revised Edition*. New York: Simon & Schuster.

Holden, Richard N. (1992). *Law Enforcement: An Introduction*. Englewood Cliffs, NJ: Prentice Hall.

Iskander, Zaky and Alexander Badawy (1965). *Brief History of Ancient Egypt*. Cairo, Egypt: Madkour Press.

Kelly, Martin A. (1973, March). "The First Urban Policeman." *Journal of Police Science and Administration*, 1(1):56–60.

Kocourek, Albert and John H. Wigmore (1915). *Sources of Ancient and Primitive Law*. Boston: Little, Brown, and Company.

Lee, W.L. Melville (1971, originally published in 1901). *History of Police in England*. Montclair, NJ: Patterson Smith.

National Commission on Terrorist Attacks Upon the United States (2004). "The 9/11 Commission Report." Authorized Edition. New York: W.W. Norton & Co.

Roth, Mitchel P. (2005). *Crime and Punishment: A History of the Criminal Justice System*. Belmont, CA: Thomson Wadsworth.

Santayana, George (1905). *The Life of Reason* Volume 1. New York: Charles Scribner's Sons.

Seignobos, Charles (1932). *The Evolution of the French People*, translated by Catherine Alison Phillips. New York: Alfred A. Knopf.

Stead, Philip John (1985). *The Police of Britain*. New York: MacMillan.

Tobias, J.J. (1979). *Crime and Police in England, 1700–1900*. New York: St. Martin's Press.

Trojan, Carol (1986). "Egypt: Evolution of a Modern Police State." *CJ International*, 2(1):15.

# The Evolution of Law Enforcement in the United States

## 3

### Learning Objectives

The American experience with the law enforcement function reflects our social, economic, and political heritage. Law enforcement in the United States has a rich and interesting history. Chapter 2 briefly examined part of the rich heritage of the English methods that influenced American policing. This chapter describes how that influence, along with other social, economic, and political factors, has shaped American policing efforts. You should understand that the United States has had a violent past and a history of questioning the authority of government. Policing actions, legislation, and reform often follow societal events that call for change. After studying this chapter, you should be able to:

- Describe the characteristics of the colonial night-watch system.
- Describe how the combined forces of religion, family, and community influenced colonial America.
- Describe the duties of the position of federal marshal.
- Describe how immigration, industrialization, and urbanization influenced the development of American policing in the 1800s.
- Identify the impact on policing of legal and social customs in the United States before and following the Civil War.
- Explain the "Progressive Movement" and its implications for American law enforcement.
- Identify the major American reformers of law enforcement from the 1890s to the 1930s, and discuss their contributions.
- Discuss the evolution of state police.
- Assess the importance of presidential commissions on evaluating law enforcement issues in the United States since 1965.

## Chapter Outline

I. Colonial America
   A. Regional Differences: New England, Pennsylvania, and Virginia
   B. Slavery and Slave Patrols
   C. Urbanization: The Night-Watch, Constables, and Sheriffs
   D. The British Military
   E. Appointment of Federal Marshals

II. Early to Mid-1800s
   A. Establishment of Police Departments
   B. Vigilantism and Private Detection

III. The Civil War and Its Aftermath

IV. Early Reforms and Reformers 1890s to 1930s
   A. Reform and the Progressive Movement
   B. The Birth of Professional Associations
   C. The Emergence of Professionalism
   D. Crime Commissions

V. The Evolution of State Police

VI. Post-World War II Developments
   A. A Changing Society
   B. Presidential Commissions and LEAA
   C. The 1980s and 1990s

VII. Summary

## Key Terms Used in This Chapter

rattlewatch
wardens
slave patrols
vigilantism
"Jim Crow"
Black Codes
Plessy v. Ferguson
Progressive Movement
National Commission on Law
   Observance and Enforcement
International Association of
   Chiefs of Police
Police Benevolent Associations

Fraternal Order of Police
Lola Greene Baldwin
Alice Stebbins Wells
International Association of
   Women Police
President's Commission on Law
   Enforcement and
   Administration of Justice
Law Enforcement Assistance
   Administration
Omnibus Crime Control and
   Safe Streets Act of 1968

# ■ Colonial America

Beginning in 1585, with the founding of the first colony on Roanoke Island, successive groups of settlers from Germany, Holland, Scandinavia, and Great Britain began new lives along North America's eastern seaboard. The British would lead this migration in both numbers and influence. In fact, they would become the dominant presence in North America and would have the most influence in establishing, among other things, a common language, social norms, and political institutions, including the new institutions of criminal justice. As historian Samuel Walker (1998, 14) explains, "American criminal justice begins with the first European colonists," especially the English, who introduced "criminal codes, law enforcement agencies, courts, and various modes of punishments."

The colonization of America, which lasted for more than 150 years, is one of the great sagas of human history. Between 1607 and 1733, a kaleidoscope of social, political, and economic forces, turned by the hands of time and geography, led to the founding of thirteen American colonies. While variations in time and place make generalizations difficult, there were important similarities in the early characteristics of colonies. For example, according to historian James Cox (2003, 1), American colonies "were autocratic and theocratic, with a patriarchal system of justice: magistrates and religious leaders, sometimes one and the same, made the laws, and the burden of obeying them fell on the less exalted—the tradesmen, soldiers, farmers, servants, slaves, and the young." While harsh and undemocratic by today's standards, these arrangements met little resistance. It was a time, as Walker (1998) observes, when crime and sin were seen as one aberration; when social control rested within three closely connected institutions, the church, the family, and the community; and when obedience to authority, especially the church and the male head of the household, was paramount.

By 1770 over two million people of European heritage lived in the thirteen colonies. Yet not all who arrived came willingly. Between 1718 and 1776, England shipped (a practice called transportation) approximately 30,000 convicts to the colonies. While life in the colonies was difficult, it was better than a London prison cell. The young, and mostly male, convicts traded prison for a four- to seven-year contract of hard labor as indentured servants. In doing so, they became America's first source of low-cost labor, many destined for tobacco plantations in Virginia and Maryland. By 1680, the supply of convict labor began to decline. However, it was quickly replaced by even larger numbers of another source of low-cost labor—African slaves.

# ■ Regional Differences: New England, Pennsylvania, and Virginia

Historian Mitchel Roth (2005, 50) observes that from their rudimentary beginnings, the agencies of criminal justice were local creations "resembling those of England, Holland, Spain, and France" depending on the colonists' country of origin. Its development took on a very local (if not regional) character in response to particular social problems, political circumstances, and/or economic enterprise. Consequently, an early visitor to colonial America would note regional

By reviewing the histories of several selected law enforcement agencies, you will be able to identify various similarities and differences.

**Federal Agencies**
Bureau of Alcohol, Tobacco and Firearms
http://www.atf.gov/about/atfhistory.htm
U.S. Coast Guard
http://www.uscg.mil/hq/g-cp/history/h_index.html

**Southern Region**
New Orleans, LA P.D.
http://www.nopdonline.com/history.htm
http://www.nopd.com/
Houston, TX P.D.
http://www.ci.houston.tx.us/hpd/history.htm
Winston-Salem, NC P.D.
http://www.ci.winston-salem.nc.us/psc/

**Northeastern Region**
New York City, NY P.D. 1845–1890
http://www.nycpolicemuseum.org/html/museum-map.html
Portsmouth, NH P.D.
http://www.cityofportsmouth.com/police/depart-history.htm
Westborough, MA P.D
http://www.westboroughma.com/index.htm

**Midwestern Region**
Pennsylvania State Police
http://www.psp.state.pa.us/psp/cwp/browse.asp?A=100
http://www.psp-hemc.org/history.htm
Xenia, OH P.D.
http://www.ci.xenia.oh.us/police/pdhistory.html
Detroit, MI P.D.
www.detnews.com/history/police/police.htm

**Western Region**
Bakersfield, CA P.D.
http://www.bakersfieldcity.us/police/Chiefs/index.htm
Phoenix, AZ P.D.
http://phoenix.gov/POLICE/histor1.html
Los Angeles County Sheriff's Office
http://www.lasd.org/aboutlasd/history.html

Also see:
http://www.questia.com/popularSearches/law_enforcement_history_u_s.jsp and http://www.stungunresources.com/america_enforcement_history_in_law.html for additional links and sites regarding the history of law enforcement around the world.

**Figure 3-1** Selected histories of law enforcement agencies found on the World Wide Web.

differences in the mechanisms of social control as he traveled through the villages of New England then south through Pennsylvania and Maryland and on to the plantations of Virginia and the Carolinas. **Figure 3-1** identifies several informative sites on the World Wide Web that contain histories of selected agencies. You should review some of these, and reflect upon the time period and the evolution of law enforcement.

An early visitor to a New England village would find scant evidence of an organized system of social control. While a county sheriff or constable may have provided an image of justice, they were essentially appointed armatures that performed very little law enforcement as we understand it today. Social circumstances had not yet produced the political will for a more robust law enforcement presence. In many ways, this can be attributed to the ". . . high level of homogeneity and consensus on basic values that prevailed in American communities at that time" (Walker 1998, 2). Consensus and obedience to authority were common. In fact, as Walker (1998, 15) notes, obedience to authority was an accepted condition of daily life offered "first to God, then to the clergy, and finally to the male head of the household." Lesser violations of community norms or church doctrine—swearing, for example—were attended to quickly by the voice of public criticism. If the violation was more serious—for example failing to observe the Sabbath—the offender would be made to suffer the spectacle of public shaming, which included being placed in the stocks, being flogged or branded, or even being banished from the community. Only in the rare case of committing rape or murder was a person put to death (Roth 2005; Cox 2003; Walker 1998).

However, public order in the villages of New England was generally easy to maintain. This can be attributed to a simple fact: The villages of New England were homogeneous communities where shared assumptions of proper conduct were common, were predatory crimes were uncommon, and where the informal influences of church, family, and community were the primary forces of social control. There was little need for the formal agencies of social control that we know today. The church, the family, and the community (formalized in the town meeting) were all that was generally necessary to maintain social order (Roth 2005; Cox 2003; Walker 1998).

In many ways colonial Pennsylvania was much like New England. A visitor would also find a strong religious influence and general consensus on community values. Yet there was a difference. In 1682, the Quakers (the Society of Friends), under the leadership of William Penn, introduced a very different and more tolerant philosophy of Christian teaching and political thought. For example, the Quakers believed that every individual was blessed with certain religious and civil rights, rights that were granted by their creator, not the crown. Therefore, it was the duty of government, in the opinion of Quakers, to protect these rights, rights that were spelled out in Penn's *Frame of Government*, a document also known as *The Great Law or Body of Laws*. In a prophetic announcement, Penn assured the settlers of Pennsylvania that, "You shall be governed by the laws of your own making . . ." (Wallace and O'Brien 1995, 1).

William Penn had introduced elements of a political philosophy that would find great appeal and meaning in America's future. In less than one hundred years the core principles enumerated in Penn's *Frame of Government* would reappear in the Constitution of a new nation. It was a philosophy based on the rule of law, a principle that would come to guide American justice. Yet, for many, it was a hopeful but hollow promise, conflicting with the realities of the American experience, especially those individuals held in bondage.

Unlike Pennsylvania and New England, which were founded primarily by family units for religious reasons, Virginia was established as a business venture. Moreover, its early settlers, according to historian Mitchel Roth (2005, 52), were a loose "assortment of gentlemen, servants, and vagrants" attracted by the opportunities of business. Religion, in the form of the Church of England, although important, played a lesser role in Virginia than it had in New England or Pennsylvania. Moreover, the southern colonies quickly developed an economy based on the cultivation of a single crop—tobacco. Unfortunately, tobacco farming was both labor-intensive and required a large labor force, which according to Roth (2005), was initially satisfied by indentured servants. However, a new source of cheap labor would soon emerge to replace this uncertain workforce—slavery.

## ■ Slavery and Slave Patrols

By the late seventeenth century the institution of slavery had become a dominant presence in southern colonies. The introduction of large numbers of African slaves would eventually lead to a general fear of slave revolts and "insurrection, real or imagined" among white plantation owners and settlers (Roth 2005, 55). Consequently, in 1705, Virginia passed the first slave codes, in an attempt to regulate and control the behavior of this growing population of bondsman. South Carolina followed suit in 1740 when it established a basic slave law. These laws were intended to protect people from runaway slaves, inhibit insurrection, and authorize the recapture of slaves. The law also created an enforcement mechanism, the **slave patrols**. Slave patrols had the right to visit every plantation and to search all "Negro-houses for offensive weapons and ammunition." The infliction of corporal punishment was also permitted if any slave was found to have left his owner's property without permission (Wood 1984, 123–124).

According to Walker (1998, 23), "Charleston, South Carolina and New Orleans both established slave patrols systems that preceded northern city police departments by many decades." By 1837, the Charleston slave patrol, which included about 100 officers, was possibly the country's largest single police force at that time (Wintersmith 1974, 19–21). This is not to suggest that northern colonies were havens for African-American slaves or freemen. In 1702 New York passed an Act for Regulating Slaves. This was followed in 1703 by a law in Massachusetts that "forbade Indians, Negroes, and mulatto slaves and servants from being away from their homes after 9:00 PM, unless on a specific errand for their master" (Walker 1998, 24).

Historian Sally Hadden (2001) observes that early slave patrols were semiorganized groups of volunteers who worked at the behest of an individual plantation owner or a local group of slave masters. However, the early volunteer patrols were erratic and proved ineffective, thus prompting the legislatures of Virginia, North Carolina, and South Carolina to replace voluntarily patrols "with colony-sanctioned authority figures who would monitor slave movement and behavior" (Hadden 2001, 38). This created an institution of government (the hundreds of slave-patrols that operated throughout the South) that was specifically designed to regulate the activities of a class of "citizens" based on the explicit criteria of race.

Social, political, and economic forces had coalesced in the colonies, especially the southern colonies, to create a two-headed monster—slavery and the apparatus to maintain it. This would have grave ramifications for the future development of southern law enforcement, not to mention the nation as a whole. Hadden (2001) believes that as conditions in the South changed between the late eighteenth and mid-nineteenth centuries, many slave patrollers moved to employment in city police departments, bringing a culture and practice of racism with them. Some historians even maintain that the slave patrols of the South were America's first modern-style police forces (Williams and Murphy 1990, 3).

## ■ Urbanization: Night-Watch, Constables, and Sheriffs

This chapter so far has briefly reviewed some of the social, political, and economic forces that coalesced, and sometimes collided, to form the early structures and nature of American law enforcement. It was just the beginning. As the nation grew these forces became even more apparent. For example, cities like Boston, New York, and Philadelphia would soon grow too large and diverse to be effectively controlled by the informal influences of church, family, and community. Their size and diversity weighed against the influences that had prevailed during earlier times in smaller villages and towns. Urbanization, accelerated in years to come by immigration and industrialization, would lead to and compound the problems of social order in America (Walker 1998). Consequently, the historical study of American law enforcement is a selected study of government's ineffective response to social problems, tempered by the ever-present dynamics of political and economic calculation.

The remainder of this chapter will take a brief chronological look at some of the most important evolutionary developments affecting law enforcement as the nation grew.

The night-watch system is the earliest manifestation of organized law enforcement in America. A night watchman's "duties included walking rounds crying the time of night and the state of weather in a moderate tone" (Roth 2005, 64). First introduced in Boston in 1631, the concept would soon be introduced to other cities. Service as a night watchman or constable (as was the case in some cities) was an obligation of the adult males of the community. Although some communities experimented with paid constables, most colonists relied on volunteers to staff their law enforcement offices well into the 1700s (Johnson 1981, 5). Some variations existed, however. For example, in New Amsterdam (later named New York when the British took over the city), a group of citizens equipped with rattles to warn of their watchful presence was referred to as the **rattlewatch**. In 1658 New Amsterdam appointed eight paid watchmen to replace the volunteers, but it was not until 1693 that the mayor appointed the first uniformed police officer.

Night watchmen and constables, appointed or elected in villages and cities, were assigned a number of duties. For example, Joshua Pratt, the constable in Plymouth, Massachusetts in 1634, was the sealer of weights and measures, surveyor of land, jailer, and an announcer of marriages (Whitehouse 1973, 88). County governments copied the English precedent of appointing sheriffs as their primary law enforcement officials. These sheriffs, like their British counterparts, were appointed through the political system (usually the colonial governor's office) and were not elected. In some locations, sheriffs had oversight responsibilities for constables, who performed much of the day-to-day law enforcement activity. Despite their official status, early sheriffs and constables were essentially untrained amateurs who ". . . played a relatively minor role in maintaining law and order" (Walker 1998, 13).

During the 1700s, policing in most colonial cities changed little, although Johnson (1981, 6–7) notes that the reliance on volunteer watchmen was becoming strained:

> By the middle of the eighteenth century the colonists faced a dilemma, which some residents felt they could no longer ignore. The towns had become large enough to need reliable police, but their best citizens habitually refused this duty and the men who did serve were not as effective as they needed to be. Circumstances, not incompetence, dictated this ineffectiveness. Watchmen who worked all day at other jobs could hardly stay awake, let alone maintain order at night. Some cities did pay their watchmen, but not enough to allow someone to earn his

*living by law enforcement. The idea of citizen participation in polic-
ing was breaking down, and something was needed to replace it.*

According to Walker (1998, 27), "Philadelphia had so much trouble finding people to serve that a special law was passed in 1712 fining anyone who refused to serve." Yet many people simply paid the fine rather than serve. In 1749, the city of Philadelphia was permitted to levy a tax and appoint **wardens** with the authority to hire watchmen as needed. Only those interested in working on the watch for pay applied to the wardens, and watchmen could now be dismissed for inefficiency (Johnson 1981, 7).

## ■ The British Military

Another peacekeeping mechanism loomed over colonial America—the British military. Its presence became an increasing factor, as massive social and political discontent grew stronger toward the latter part of the 1700s. This military presence extended to the frontier in the Ohio Valley and Lake Erie during the French and Indian War (1756–1763). From 1765 through the end of the Revolutionary War (1783), the colonies faced several riots and disturbances, economic depression, and an ever-increasing imperial policy of Britain. In many cases of mob violence, especially in important coastal cities, like Boston, New York, and Baltimore, the duties of public safety were given to British military forces. However, many citizens were resentful and hostile when it came to the British. In fact, resistance to British intervention, which culminated in incidences like the Boston Massacre and other seminal events, led to the American Revolution (Roth 2005, 78). Following the Revolutionary War, policing was turned back over to civilians. Nevertheless, America still lacked effective police services as it began its great experiment with democracy (Walker 1998, 45–46; Roth 2005, 78).

## ■ Appointment of Federal Marshals

On the national level, the British military had provided a certain level of social control and protection. Its cross-colony emphasis was on the borders and in those areas where discontent, insurrection, and rebellious behavior were fermenting among the colonists. In 1789, thirteen years after the American Revolution, the Congress of the newly formed United States began to take over this function. The first federal law enforcement position, the federal marshal, was created.

George Washington appointed the first marshals following authorization by the Judiciary Act of 1789. They were to support the federal courts and to carry out all lawful orders issued by judges, Congress, or the president. Throughout their early years, they were assigned to enforce unpopular federal laws, which included collection of taxes on whiskey. A marshal served papers on distillers in western Pennsylvania in 1794. Before the incident ended, 13,000 state militiamen had to be summoned to put down what is known as the Whiskey Rebellion (Jackson 1989). The job of a marshal had its shortcomings and situations could turn dangerous when it was not expected. The Web page of the US Marshal Service describes many such incidents (see **Figure 3-2**).

Some of the duties of marshals seemed to work at cross-purposes, duties rooted in the social chasm that would eventually bring the country to war again. For example, marshals enforced the law banning African slave trade following its passage in 1819 and later carried out the Fugitive Slave Law of 1850 (which required the return of runaway slaves to their owners). Marshals were often met with local resistance, and sometimes their efforts were less than successful. Also, before the Civil War, marshals tracked down counterfeiters (since the Secret Service did not exist until 1865). Marshals may be best remembered for their efforts to bring some justice to the Wild West. Marshals pursued Billy the Kid, Jesse James, and Butch Cassidy. Marshals such as Heck Thomas, Chris Madsen, and Uncle Billy Tilghman patrolled the Oklahoma Territory. It also appears that Wyatt Earp had an overstated reputation and instead may have used the law as a way to make money and avenge his brother's murder (Jackson 1989). Today, as part of the Department of Justice, marshals' responsibilities include: ensuring federal court security; protecting federal witnesses; transporting prisoners; executing court orders; capturing fugitives; and seizing, managing, and disposing of federally seized property (US Marshals Service 1994).

On January 11, 1794, Robert Forsyth, U.S. Marshal for the District of Georgia, was shot and killed while attempting to serve civil papers. He was the first civilian official of the United States government and the first of as many as 400 marshals killed in the line of duty over the past 200 years. He was shot while trying to serve civil process on Beverly Allen.

Marshal Forsyth may have expected trouble. He took two of his deputies with him to Mrs. Dixon's house in Augusta, Georgia on January 11, 1794, because the Allen brothers, Beverly and William, had reportedly been seen there.

The forty-year-old Forsyth, a veteran of the Revolutionary War, knew how to take care of himself, but in the four years he had served the new federal government as the first marshal in the District of Georgia he had experienced little, if any, difficulty or resistance.

Most of his work had consisted of routine administrative duties in support of the federal court. His search for the Allen brothers was no different. The marshal merely wanted to serve them with some court papers in a civil suit. Nonetheless, Forsyth took the precaution, for whatever reason, of taking two of his deputies with him. When the three officers entered Mrs. Dixon's house, they found the Allens talking with friends. Wishing to spare the brothers embarrassment, Forsyth asked to speak to them privately outside. Instead of following the marshal, however, the brothers ran up to the second floor and darted into the nearest room, bolting the door behind them. While they waited for Forsyth and his deputies to come after them, Beverly Allen loaded, primed, and cocked his pistol.

Forsyth and his deputies went after the brothers. Hearing their approach, Beverly Allen aimed his pistol toward the door and squeezed the trigger. Before the sound of the gunshot could echo off the walls, the ball splintered through the wooden door and struck Forsyth fair in the head. He was dead before his body hit the floor, the first of 400 or more marshals killed performing their duties.

*Source:* U.S. Marshal's Service, http://www.usmarshals.gov/history/forsyth/in_line_of_duty.htm.

**Figure 3-2** First marshal killed in the line of duty.

# Early to Mid-1800s

According to historian Samuel Walker (1998, 37), "The American Revolution had a major impact on criminal justice, speeding up the process of reform and accentuating the differences between American and English law." Additionally, there were many social and political uncertainties in the unsettled American society such as economic depression, continued debates over slavery, waves of immigrants, Indian skirmishes on the frontier, vigilantism, anti-immigrant/anti-Catholic sentiment, racial disturbances, and the like. American cities were poised for police reform, and they began establishing police departments that extended beyond night watches.

## Establishment of Police Departments

Historian Mitchel Roth (2005, 121) observes that the decades from 1820–1850, sometimes referred to as the Jacksonian period (in reference to President Andrew Jackson), was "a period when Americans first perceived crime as a threat to the order and security of the Republic." The general decline in law and order was attributed to "the declining authority of the church and family" (Roth 2005, 121). Which, as historian Samuel Walker (1998) notes, was tied to the destabilizing influences of immigration, urbanization, and industrialization. Leaders in large cities along the nation's eastern seaboard "groped for ways to maintain order in cities that were increasingly divided by ethnic, religion, lifestyle, and social class (Walker 1998, 49). Their solution was the creation of institutions of criminal justice, including the modern police, whose major charge was preventative patrol.

During the 1830s to 1860s, larger cities established paid police forces. Many of these departments were structured, in part, after the Metropolitan Police of London that had been formed a few years earlier. Major American cities such as Philadelphia, Boston, and New York have interesting histories as to the emergence of a unified, 24-hour, police operation. Each had a social, economic, or political situation that caused reorganization and reform in the police department. In Philadelphia, Stephen Girard, a wealthy philanthropist, left a large sum of money to the city to establish a competent police force. It became one of the first American police forces to offer an organized metropolitan service. It consisted of 24 daytime police officers and 120 night watchmen. In Boston, an assault on the publisher William Lloyd Garrison, because of his anti-slavery writings, and the Broad Street Riot of 1837 led to police reform. Marshal Francis Tukey was hired to establish a competent and efficient police force. In New York (1844), because of rivalries that existed among the three separate components of the police force, it was reorganized as a unified department modeled after the Metropolitan Police of London (LEAA 1976, 17–18).

Historian Roger Lane (1967) notes that because early police departments simply absorbed the hapless bureaucracy and personnel that already existed, the process of change was painfully slow and uneven. This was complicated by the fact that in some cities there was uncertainty on how to structure the police and a reluctance to adequately fund the agency after it was formed (Walker 1998, 52). Yet, it was an effort that eventually led to better-defined and more coherent organizations. Moreover, as departments struggled in their organizational efforts, they exchanged information and ideas, which helped to increase "standardization among cities, symbolized by the almost universal adoption of uniform blue" (Lane 1967, 1).

## Vigilantism and Private Detectives

Another form of policing, **vigilantism**, appeared more frequently during the late-1790s through the mid-1870s. Especially where law enforcement officials or agencies did not exist or were ineffective, citizens took control. For example, in 1767, South Carolina citizens organized the South Carolina Regulators in an attempt to defend themselves against criminals and Indian attacks. It was one of the easiest vigilante organizations, lasting until 1769, when legislators passed the Circuit Court Act authorizing sheriffs, jails, and circuit courts (Walker 1998, 36). Originally, the philosophy of vigilantism was based on self-preservation and self-protection. It was a form of vigilance, often encouraged and supported by the best of citizens. According to one source, vigilance committees were first organized to patrol towns in California by citizen volunteers. Most members were honest men who were forced to collective action to protect their communities (LEAA 1976, 19). Yet there was a darker side to vigilante action in California. According to historian Michelle Jolly (2003, 1), "widespread theft and arson, largely unchecked by the courts, provoked the formation of extralegal organizations to stamp out crime. One of these, the [San Francisco] Vigilance Committee of 1851, involved seven hundred European and American merchants who hanged four men and exiled many others, mostly Australians, from the city on pain of death."

Vigilance committees had different names (e.g., regulators, committees, and vigilantes) and spread to other states, particularly Arizona, Montana, Colorado, and Nevada. Such vigilance committees were common until formal policing methods and agencies developed in those areas (Bopp and Schultz 1972, 50–51).

Along with the vigilante movement, the private police (detective) field was forming. Private industry and the railroads needed to protect their assets from criminals and disgruntled employees and competitors. An early private protection agency was founded by Allan Pinkerton in 1855. Known as Pinkerton's North West Police Agency, its initial task was to investigate criminal activity against railroads. Earlier, in 1850, Henry Wells and William Fargo established the American Express Company, which was a freight service company. They had to provide their own protection as they transported goods and valuables, including payrolls. Their security personnel were known as "shotgun riders" (Green and Fisher 1987, 11). (Chapter 4 describes the private police movement in the United States in greater detail.)

## ■ The Civil War and Its Aftermath

At the time of the Civil War in the United States, racism and discrimination were common in states beyond the South. Every new state admitted to the union after 1819 restricted voting to whites only. Several northern and western states prohibited black testimony in court if whites were a party to the proceeding. Even where blacks were totally free, some states maintained "**Jim Crow**" laws and practices that separated the races and discriminated against blacks. The term "Jim Crow" is believed to have originated around 1830 when it was first used in a minstrel show that mocked the mannerisms of blacks. Eventually, the term became a racial slur used to describe stereotypical images of black inferiority. One eminent historian, C. Vann Woodward has been cited by Williams and Murphy (1990, 5–6) regarding this practice: "One of the strangest things about Jim Crow was that the system was born in the North and reached an advanced age before moving South in force."

Following the Civil War and during the Reconstruction Period in the South, states began to enact laws that specifically spelled out the rights and responsibilities of the newly freed slaves. The laws, known as the **Black Codes**, were eventually enacted by every former confederate state. According to Foner (1988, 203), the entire complex of Black Codes was enforced ". . . by a police apparatus and judicial system in which blacks enjoyed virtually no voice whatever. Whites staffed urban police forces as well as state militias, intended, as a Mississippi white put it in 1865, to 'keep good order and discipline amongst the Negro population.'" During this time period, whites victimized blacks with nearly total immunity. When whites were prosecuted, their sentences were less harsh than for blacks committing the same offense. After the Civil War, the federal government reacted by passing the Civil Rights Act of 1866, which specified the rights of citizens regardless of race. It also allowed for lawsuits against persons who deprived a citizen of a civil right. This law led Congress to adopt the Fourteenth Amendment to the Constitution, which provided "equal protection" under the law. The Fifteenth Amendment, enacted shortly thereafter, addressed the voting rights of blacks. The Civil Rights Act of 1875 outlawed the exclusion of blacks from hotels, theaters, railroads, and other public accommodations (Williams and Murphy 1990, 7).

With the guarantee of the right to vote, politicians courted blacks. Moreover, the political system responded by appointing blacks to police departments. Selma, Alabama hired black officers in 1867; Houston, Texas in 1870; Galveston, Texas in 1870; Jackson, Mississippi in 1871; Chicago in 1872, Columbia and Charleston, South Carolina in 1873; and Philadelphia in 1874. The city of New Orleans, by 1870, had 177 black officers, and three of the five police board members were black. Although agencies were appointing blacks, it did not mean that they were equal to their white counterparts. In many cities, blacks were restricted in making arrests and may not have been permitted to arrest whites. Some cities refused to put the officers in uniform, having them wear plain clothes instead. Other cities assigned them to black areas and even marked the cruisers "Negro Police" (Williams and Murphy 1990, 7).

The Supreme Court added to this disparity in treatment and authority by deciding *Plessy v. Ferguson* (1896), stating that the doctrine of "separate but equal" was constitutional and that states could enact laws that allowed segregation in public accommodations. Some cities began firing black officers after the court decision. Even New Orleans dropped to only five black officers by 1900 and did not appoint another black officer until 1950 (Williams and Murphy 1990, 9). **Figure 3-3** identifies the dates of the appointments of black and female officers (discussed below in this text) in selected cities in the United States.

## ■ Early Reforms and Reformers, 1890s to 1930s

Policing from the end of the Civil War to the early 1900s witnessed many improvements in operations and organization across the country. For example, historian Roger Lane (1967, 201) notes that in Boston:

> *Applicants were forbidden to offer petitions or otherwise attempt to use political influence. Promotions were granted only after examination. Prospective sergeants were tested on the police rules and infantry drill; lieutenants and captains were required in addition to answer questions on infantry tactics, state law, city ordinances, police reports, and police records.*

Yet these and other improvements were stymied and subverted to a great extent in many cities by corrupt partisan politics. Appointments and terms of office for regular uniformed officers were often made on an annual basis by elected officials bent on political advantage and personal gain. The concept of efficient government was only beginning to attract vocal advocates. Consequently, corrupt "political machines" heavily influenced the selection of officers and the management of police departments. According to Walker (1998, 61), New York City many have been the worst example, a place where "corruption was not only rampant but, according to some historians, was the principle activity of the police."

**Wichita, KS**

[Frank] Burt is credited with hiring Sam Jones, the first black police officer on the Wichita Police Department. Sam Jones came to Wichita in 1874, was the first black to attend school there, played in Wichita's first Negro band, and in 1894 was elected constable, becoming the first of his race voted to county office. He worked as a lather, printer, fireman, soldier and in the Spanish American War reached the rank of Major. He later became the Deputy State Fire Marshal. Historic Wichita, Inc. named Jones history consultant in 1952, and he was still busy two days before his death at the age of 93 in 1960.

*Source*: http://www.wichita.gov/CityOffices/Police/History/1890s.htm.

**New York, NY**

In 1911, Samuel J. Battle became the first African-American police officer in New York City, and in 1920, Lawon R. Bruce became the first African-American NYPD policewoman.

*Source:* http://www.lowermanhattan.info/news/museum_honors_nypd_s_27751.asp.

**Massillon, OH**

In 1955, the Massillon Police Department had hired its first black police officer, Lemie Gibson, under Chief Switter's administration.

On August 9, 1980, the first female police officer for the city of Massillon, Pam Whitmyer, was hired onto the department. History was again made with the hiring of Sylvia Simms as the first black female police officer.

*Source:* http://www.massillonohio.com/police/history.html.

**Figure 3-3** Selected appointments of black police officers and female officers.

The prevalence of corruption and its inevitable path to inefficiency prompted angry calls for government reform. Beginning in the 1890s, a procession of reformers would lead this charge; first among them was the Reverend Charles Parkhurst, who denounced corruption within the New York City Police Department (NYPD). Parkhurst's crusade galvanized the city and the state, focusing great attention on the problem. However, by the end of the 1890s, little had changed within the NYPD, and "corruption, inefficiency, and brutality continued for decades" (Walker 1998, 65). It would take a concerted effort to produce real change; reforms that would slowly emerge through the efforts of many progressive citizens outside policing, and, eventually, professionals within the law enforcement community.

## Reform and the Progressive Movement

Efforts to initiate reform in policing coincided with the **Progressive Movement**. In the words of Fogelson (1977, 44):

> This [Progressive] movement, which began at the turn of the century and thrived for the next two decades, sought to shore up the position of the upper middle and upper classes by reforming the courts, schools and other urban institutions. It attempted to reorganize their structure, upgrade their personnel, and redefine their function in ways that would . . . destroy the system of machine politics which had developed in the mid- and late-nineteenth century. Police reform subsequently gathered momentum as part of the so-called war on crime.

Well-known figures of the day took part in the movement, including Theodore Roosevelt, who became Police Commissioner of New York City (see **Figure 3-4**).

## The Birth of Professional Associations

Reform also came from the police administrators themselves, who established the National Chiefs of Police Union in 1893. The National Chiefs of Police Union changed its name to the **International Association of Chiefs of Police** (IACP) in 1902. The original purpose of the association was to provide mutual assistance and cooperation in arresting and detaining persons known to have committed a crime. Some of the issues addressed in early meetings of the association would continue to be concerns for decades (see **Figure 3-5**).

The IACP addressed other issues such as civil service standards, arresting persons on the basis of telegrams, adopting a police telegraph code, and adopting a uniform system of identification of criminals. Early reformers within the group included Major Richard Sylvester, Superintendent of the District of Columbia Police, Chief William S. Seavey of Omaha, Superintendent Robert McLaughrey of Chicago, Chief W.C. Davis of Memphis, Chief Roger O'Mara of Pittsburgh, Chief L. Harrigan of St. Louis, and Chief Harvey O. Carr of Grand Rapids (Dilworth 1976, 3–6; Walker 1977, 48). The IACP's annual conventions allowed police executives from across the country and around the world to exchange ideas and keep current on the latest technology and legal developments.

Police executives were not alone in reforming policing. **Police benevolent associations** began to appear as early as 1867, when the city of St. Louis, Missouri organized the Police Relief Association to assist disabled officers and widows of officers. Their appearance and gradual spread to police departments across the country (e.g., Cleveland in 1881 and Denver

During his three years as police commissioner of New York City (1895–1897), Roosevelt gained international acclaim for his reforms. He pioneered a bicycle squad, a telephonic communications system, and training for new recruits. He routed out corrupt elements within the department and instituted promotion based on merit rather than on politics. Later, he enthusiastically supported the Pennsylvania State Constabulary (State Police) and, in 1908, as president, he organized the Bureau of Investigation in the Department of Justice, the forerunner of the FBI.

*Source:* Law Enforcement Assistance Administration (LEAA) (1976). *Two Hundred Years of American Criminal Justice.* Washington, DC: U.S. Department of Justice, p. 20.

**Figure 3-4** Police Commissioner Theodore Roosevelt.

in 1883) marked an important milestone in American policing—the self-consciousness of the rank-and-file police officer. Through these organizations, officers organized and advanced their collective interests. Memberships also performed charitable work in their respective cities (Kuechler 2003). By the 1890s, as rank-and-file police officers started to see police work as a career, members began turning their attention to political and labor issues. Consequently, many associations took on a fraternal character (Walker 1977, 48–49). This coincided, in the early 1900s, with the rise of big business and trade unionism and the accompanying labor strikes affected police forces. In 1915, two Pittsburgh patrol officers founded the **Fraternal Order of Police** as a social benevolent association that included all ranks in the police organization. The early involvement by officer associations led to attempts to unionize some departments in larger cities. In 1919, such an attempt led to the Boston Police Strike, which had national ramifications in that it curtailed police unionization efforts for nearly 40 years (refer to Chapter 8 for a more detailed discussion of the unionization movement).

Chief Benjamin Murphy of Jersey City, New Jersey addressed the 12th annual convention (1905) of the IACP about a system adopted in his department some ten years earlier.

It is one of the standing rules of force . . . we have what we term a statement. This statement is typewritten and is furnished to each station house. Just as soon as a person is arrested on the charge of having committed a felony, rape, robbery, burglary, murder, etc., it is the duty of the superior officer present to bring that defendant into a room. This statement is picked up and read to him in the presence of the arresting officer, and, if possible, some other witness. The statement reads in this way: I am John Brown, a sergeant of police. I am going to ask you some questions concerning the crime for which you are arrested. You are arrested for _____ on _____ street a short time ago. You may answer these questions or not just as you please, but what you do say will be taken down in writing and used at your trial. It must be a free, voluntary statement. Do you understand that?"

Source: Reprinted with permission from Donald C. Dilworth (ed.). *The Blue and The Brass: American Policing 1890–1910*, p. 66. Gaithersburg, MD: International Association of Chiefs of Police, 1976.

**Figure 3-5** Flashback to 1905: the "Rights" warning.

## The Emergence of Professionalism

From 1905 to 1914, over 10.5 million immigrants from southern and eastern Europe entered the United States. Urbanization became a major problem; police departments were strained in their efforts to keep order. Communities were turning to their police departments to assist in all types of issues emerging from an ever more diverse and complex society. Women officers were needed to assist with problems related to women and juveniles. In 1908, according to historian Gloria Myers (1995, 1) the City of Portland, Oregon hired **Lola Greene Baldwin**, a forty-eight-year-old social worker, "to perform police service" as a "police detective," thus becoming America's first policewoman. Baldwin was an effective and energetic police officer during her sixteen-year career, gaining international recognition for her pioneering work with women and children. Among her many accomplishments, she helped to organize the "municipal policewomen's division, juvenile, morals, and domestic relations courts, a citizens vice commission, a state institution for sexually delinquent girls, a city venereal detention hospital for prostitutes, and pushed a variety of state and local protection legislation for women and children" (Myers 1995, 3). Baldwin was a member of a small but important

The International Association of Women Police was originally organized in 1915 as the International Association of Policewomen. The International Association of Chiefs of Police lent their support to the newly formed organization by helping to draft the original constitution and outline the association's objectives. The charter was adopted and was incorporated in Washington, DC in 1926.

Unfortunately, in 1932, the International Policewomen's Association became a "depression casualty." Not having had a chance to be fully implemented, the programs set into motion by the Association went by the wayside. However, its programs and ideals remained only temporarily dormant. Mrs. Wells lived to see the rebirth of the organization.

In 1956, at a meeting of the Women Peace Officers of California in San Diego, California, the association was reorganized and recognized as the International Association of Police Women. Several years later the organization changed its name to the International Association of Women Police (IAWP). Under the direction of Dr. Lois Higgins, its newly elected president, IAWP began to change and grow. Dr. Higgins, a thirty-year member of the Chicago Police Department, held the position of IAWP president for eight years and then served twelve more years as its executive director.

Speaking at the first biannual meeting of the IAWP held at Purdue University in 1957, Dr. Higgins commented, "The advent of women into [police] departments brought into existence the crime prevention and juvenile bureaus. . . . These women brought a social viewpoint into police work."

The IAWP, through its constitution and activities, promoted separate women's bureaus. Many women felt this was their only opportunity for advancement within the department. Before 1969, women were never assigned to patrol, and many did not even own a uniform. Their duties were still restricted to those performed in the early 1900s by Mrs. Wells.

Though IAWP membership remained small through the 1960s, the IAWP began to hold annual three-day conferences in 1963. Attendance at the conferences was minimal. In 1973, by general membership vote, the clause [. . . to encourage] was deleted from the IAWP constitution in the section that dealt with "the establishment of women's bureaus in police departments. . . ." IAWP began working toward promoting the assignment of women officers into other areas of law enforcement within police departments.

While originally established primarily for women officers, IAWP members recognized that cohesiveness, professionalism, and communication must exist between men and women in all aspects of the criminal justice system. Therefore, in 1976, IAWP began actively recruiting male officers to join its ranks as active IAWP members.

*Source:* International Association of Women Police (2004). "Past & Present, 1915–today." http://www.iawp.org/history/pastpresent.htm.

**Figure 3-6** International Association of Women Police.

group of early police professionals. In 1910, **Alice Stebbins Wells** became the first policewoman with full police powers in the city of Los Angeles. She became a national advocate of women in policing, and helped organize and was the first president of the International Association of Policewomen in 1915 (today known as the **International Association of Women Police**, see **Figure 3-6**). By the end of World War I, over 200 US cities had policewomen on their police forces, frequently operating out of separate "women's bureaus."

World War I added more tensions and strain to US society. Many male police officers left their departments to serve in the war effort. In some parts of the country, women and older volunteers helped supplement the existing resources. When the "troops" returned, the number of women in policing actually decreased. Other events that affected the number of women in law enforcement included the start of the era of Prohibition (1919–1933) and, in 1920, the granting of the right to vote to women.

During this era of early reform, August Vollmer (Chief of Berkeley, California from 1905–1932) and Superintendent Richard Sylvester (Washington, DC and President of IACP from 1901–1915) were staunch advocates of police professionalism. They encouraged greater use of science and technology and less political interference from elected and non-elected officials. They were helped in these reform efforts by an emerging body of literature on police administration. Scholars like Leonhard F. Fuld (1909), who wrote *Police Administration*, and Raymond B. Fosdick (1920), who wrote *American Police Systems*, advocated the idea of reforming policing through the introduction of strong management, centralization, and administrative efficiency. Each of these seminal books gained wide readership in police reform circles helping to usher in the concept of professional policing. However, efficient administration was not the only topic being discussed. Progressive police leaders were also turning to a new body of literature that sought to improve the art of investigation. For example, Charles W. Fricke's 1930 book on *Criminal Investigation* gained wide use within detective units. (See **Figure 3-7** for the major contributions of August Vollmer.)

## Crime Commissions

In the latter part of the 1920s, several state and local commissions began looking into corrupt and inefficient police practices and the related issues of the administration of criminal justice. Four of these investigations are important because they had a significant influence on police reform in their respective locations. Included in the list is the Cleveland Survey of 1922, the Chicago Crime Survey of 1926, and the Missouri Crime Survey of 1926. These city and state investigations were followed in 1929 by a national investigation, when President Hoover appointed Attorney General George W. Wickersham to chair the **National Commission on Law Observance and Enforcement** (commonly referred to as the Wickersham Commission). The country was facing a surging crime problem, private detectives and crime prevention activities were mounting, the public was fearful of lawlessness, and some people advocated a reduction in civil liberties in the name of safety (Fogelson 1977, 120). The Wickersham Commission undertook the first national study of the criminal justice system in the

Recognition:  America's Greatest Cop
Father of Modern Police Science
Dean of American Law Enforcement

August Vollmer served the city of Berkeley, California for 27 years, first being elected town marshal in 1905 and then as police chief until his retirement. In 1907, he was elected president of the California Police Chiefs Association, and by 1922 he had ascended to the presidency of the International Association of Chiefs of Police.

He was a strong advocate of college educated police officers. He established one of the first police training schools in the United States and initiated the first college-level law enforcement courses at San Jose State College in 1916. He became a full professor of police administration at the University of Chicago (in 1929 while on leave from Berkeley P.D.) which was followed with an appointment as Professor of Police Administration at the University of California at Berkeley. He served as the Police Consultant to the National Law Observance and Enforcement Commission and was the primary author of its *Report on Police* (1929–1931). He was instrumental in many other state and national professional associations. He acted as a consultant to over 75 police departments throughout the world during his career. He promoted police professionalism through his many writings which included books, articles, reports, and correspondence with academic and police leaders throughout the country.

Vollmer was an ardent innovator and advocate of the use of technology. He instituted bicycle patrols (1905), a red light recall system (1906), police records and modus operandi systems (1906), motorcycle patrol (1913), automobile patrol service (1914); installed a fingerprint system, handwriting system, and deception detection system (1921); and installed the first aluminum street signs (1924).

He believed in stringent recruit standards, emphasized ethical conduct, and advocated freedom from political interference. At times his views were unpopular with contemporaries. He considered crime prevention a priority, opposed capital punishment, supported decriminalization of victimless crime, and advocated probation for the first-time offenders.

Plagued by ill health in his later years, he ended his own life on 4 November 1955.

*Source:* Data from Gene E. Carte and Elaine H. Carte (1975). *Police Reform in the United States.* Berkeley: University of California Press; p. 125–128. D.E.J. MacNamara, August Vollmer, in *The Encyclopedia of Police Science*, Second Edition, W. Bailey, ed., 1955. Garland Publishing, Inc., New York, NY; and *Biographical Sketch*, August Vollmer Papers, BANC MSS C-B 403, The Bancroft Library, University of California, Berkeley.

**Figure 3-7** The contributions of August Vollmer (b. 1876–d. 1955).

United States. Vollmer was placed in charge of surveying and reporting the findings regarding the police community. Publication Number 14, *Report on Police*, was released in 1931. Its ten major conclusions were as follows:

1. The corrupting influence of politics should be removed from the police organization.

2. The head of the department should be selected at large for competence, a leader, preferably a man of considerable police experience, and removable from office only after preferment of charges and a public hearing.

3. Patrolmen should be able to rate a "B" on the Alpha test, be able-bodied and of good character, weigh 150 pounds, measure 5 feet 9 inches tall, and be between 21 and 31 years of age. The chief for good and sufficient reasons could disregard these requirements.

4. Salaries should permit decent living standards, adequate housing, eight hours of work, one day off weekly, annual vacation, fair sick leave with pay, just accident and death benefits when in performance of duty, and reasonable pension provisions on an actuarial basis.

5. Adequate training for recruits, officers, and those already on the roll is imperative.

6. The communication system should provide for call boxes, telephones, recall system, and (in appropriate circumstances) teletype and radio.

7. Records should be complete, adequate, but as simple as possible. They should be used to secure administrative control of investigations and of department units in the interest of efficiency.

8. A crime-prevention unit should be established if circumstances warrant this action, and qualified women police should be engaged to handle juvenile delinquents and women's cases.

9. State police forces should be established in states where rural protection of this character is required.

10. State bureaus of criminal investigation and information should be established in every state (National Commission on Law Observance and Enforcement 1931, 140).

Some of these points were adopted immediately, for a variety of reasons in many jurisdictions, but not nationally. However, the United States was in the midst of a depression; the political machines were stronger than originally thought. Municipal authority was more diffused than centralized, and the public did not believe that there would be any effect on the crime and morality problem of the day (and even less on their underlying causes) (Fogelson 1977, 134–136). The recommendations did set the groundwork for a later generation of reform efforts.

## ■ The Evolution of State Police

The changing social environment of the early decades of the twentieth century in the United States included urbanization, industrialization, rising immigration, governmental regulation, and a rising crime problem. State governments often found themselves with no agency to enforce state laws. Only Texas and Massachusetts had created state agencies prior to the twentieth century. The Texas

Rangers were officially formed in 1835, originally to protect the frontier life of American settlers, primarily from Indian raids. Although Massachusetts created its first state agency in 1865 to focus on vice laws (which some concluded was directed toward Irish Catholics), the force was abolished in 1875 because of the lack of public acceptance (Johnson 1981, 157–158).

Pennsylvania led the reform efforts to create a modern state police force. Rural crime and violence in the industrial union movement (especially in the coal fields) led Governor Samuel Pennypacker to encourage legislative creation of the Pennsylvania Constabulary, which was modeled after the Philippine Constabulary (a para-military structure). Between 1908 and 1923, fourteen states (mostly in the northern industrial regions) established similar organizations. After the decline of labor strife and reduced immigration during the war years, state police turned more toward rural policing and traffic enforcement. During the 1930s, eight more states added "state police" forces, while eighteen established highway patrols whose authority was limited by law to traffic matters. State involvement in policing also included setting up communication systems and bureaus of criminal identification. By 1934, twenty-four states had bureaus of criminal identification. Also by the early 1930s, telephone systems and two-way radios were sufficiently developed to permit more modern police practices. State troopers generally enjoyed good reputations, and across the United States they became elite law enforcement officers (Johnson 1981, 158–164).

# Post-World War II Developments

## A Changing Society

Following the Second World War, policing in the United States continued its march toward professionalism. Historian Samuel Walker (1977, 167) summarized this period best, stating, "From the 1940s through the early 1960s police reform continued along the lines that were already well established. Police professionalism was defined almost exclusively in terms of managerial efficiency, and administrators sought to refine techniques that would further strengthen their hand in commanding and controlling rank-and-file patrolmen." These efforts were lead by a new generation of reformers who were better educated than earlier counterparts, had distinguished service records, held positions of public influence, and spoke out and debated issues. Some of these individuals were responsible for spearheading the movement for improved training and for creating police science and criminology programs in colleges and universities. They wrote books and authored articles about the police profession; they began to establish a systematic body of knowledge about the field. When the relatively tranquil 1950s turned into the tumultuous 1960s, people and political leaders were more prone to listen and search for answers (conditions necessary for serious reform). It is not possible to list everyone who had some impact on this wave of reform efforts. **Figure 3-8** identifies some major reformers; you may wish to seek out other sources that detail their accomplishments. Some of these individuals will be mentioned in other chapters of this text as well.

*Orlando Winfield Wilson* (1900–1972)

O.W. Wilson is best known for authoring several major texts in the police field, especially *Police Administration*, which was first published in 1950 and became the unofficial "bible" for police managers (and students). In 1921, he began his police career as a patrolman in Berkeley, California. He served as chief in Fullerton, California and later in Wichita, Kansas. He taught at Harvard and in 1939 became Professor of Police Administration at the University of California at Berkeley, replacing August Vollmer, who retired. He served with the military and also assisted in reorganizing the police forces in Europe following WWII. He served as Superintendent of the Chicago Police Department from 1960–1967.

*Vivian Anderson Leonard* (1898–1984)

V.A. Leonard joined the Berkeley Police Department in 1925. He went on to earn a BA and MA in colleges in Texas and a Ph.D. from Ohio State in 1949. He served as Superintendent of the Records and Identification Division of the Ft. Worth Police Department from 1934–1939. From 1941 to 1963, he was affiliated with Washington State University and became a full professor of Police Science and Administration. He authored *Police Organization and Management* in 1950, as well as seven other texts: *Police Communications Systems, Police Records Systems, The Police of the Twentieth Century, The Police, Police Personnel Administration, Criminal Investigation and Identification,* and *Police Crime Prevention*. He was active in several national organizations, was a founder of what later became the Academy of Criminal Justice Sciences, and was founder of Alpha Phi Sigma (the national criminal justice honor society).

*John Edgar Hoover* (1895–1972)

Born and educated in Washington, DC, Hoover spent his career there as well. During WWI, he worked as a special assistant on counterespionage activities to the U.S. Attorney General. In 1924, at age 29, he was appointed Director of the FBI following a major reorganization. He reformed the agency into a highly effective and efficient organization. By the 1930s, the agency was a modern crime-fighting organization that was aggressively pursuing major criminals throughout the United States. He adopted modern crime lab technology (in addition to fingerprinting), detailed criminal records and statistics, and later computerization (the National Crime Information Center). The National Police Academy was established to help train state and local managers in the latest methods and techniques. Under Hoover's leadership, the FBI became one of the most effective and respected law enforcement agencies in the world. Unfortunately, some of Hoover's methods and constitutional rights abuses tarnished his latter years of service. He served as director until his death in 1972.

*William H. Parker* (1902–1966)

Parker is best known for his professional leadership of the Los Angeles Police Department from 1950 to 1966. During that time, he took the agency to national and international prominence by demanding excellence and efficiency, and by projecting a positive public image. He began his career in LA in 1927 and rose through the ranks. During WWII, he served in the US Army and was highly decorated, receiving the American Purple Heart, the French Croix de Guerre with Silver Star, and the Italian Star of Solidarity. He served under Colonel O.W. Wilson and assisted in the reorganization of European police forces following the war. As Chief of LA, he demanded that highly qualified personnel be employed and that they receive only the best training. He reorganized the department and modernized the agency in terms of procedures, buildings, and equipment.

**Figure 3-8** Selected reformers of the 1950s–1970s.

During the 1950s and early 1960s, police departments across the country successfully completed the marriage of three technologies—the telephone, the patrol car, and the two-way radio. This arrangement led to an overarching strategy in policing—rapid response to calls for service. There were, of course, exceptions; some larger cities maintained foot and mounted patrols, nevertheless the die was cast. The tacit relationship between police officer and citizen had changed forever. Rapid mobility and effective communications, coupled with the promise that the police would attempt to solve any problem, created a new dynamic—short duration (impersonal, but professional) intervention and enforcement strategies.

The country, however, was changing. Rural parts of the United States were mostly white, generally prosperous, and relatively free of crime. At the same time, urban life was becoming more chaotic, fast-paced, and burdened with increasing racial/ethnic tensions. Black migration from the rural south increased during the 1940s as workers moved north to fill wartime factory jobs. Conversely, during the 1950s and 1960s, there was an exodus of whites from the inner city. Investment capital followed as they fled to the new suburbs that would come to ring the old cities of their parents and grandparents. Social service agencies and institutions were ill-prepared to serve the needs of those who would be caught in hopeless blight of inner city decay. Moreover, the United States was becoming a violent country. Roth (2005, 293) notes that, "no era in American history was marked by the murder of as many public figures as the 1960s. Leaders as diverse as Martin Luther King Jr., John F. Kennedy, Medgar Evers, Robert F. Kennedy, and Malcom X were silenced by assassin's bullets."

Domestic troubles were compounded by the ever-increasing involvement of the United States in foreign affairs (the Korean Conflict, the "cold war," the Cuban missile crisis, and Vietnam). The baby-boom generation began questioning the country's social and political direction—questions that often went unanswered by government. People of all ages across the country began to engage in civil protest.

From the mid-1950s through the 1960s, political protest, racial unrest, and demands for racial equality sparked violent incidents and major riots in cities across the United States. The police, who now prided themselves as professionals, were put to the test. In nationally televised incident after incident (e.g., school desegregation in Alabama, civil rights marches, riots in major cities, and the "police riot" of the Democratic National convention in 1968), it became apparent to many citizens, and a growing number of progressive police managers, that there was still a great divide between the rhetoric of professionalism and actual professionalism. Samuel Walker (1998, 181) summarized these feeling best when he observed, ". . . never before had the day-to-day operations of the police and prisons been as seriously challenged; and never before had there been such a pervasive sense that something was fundamentally wrong with the criminal justice system." Bob Dylan, a popular songwriter and singer of the period, captured the nation's mode best in the lyrics of a best-selling song titled "Times They are a Changing." This would certainly be true for American policing.

## Presidential Commissions and LEAA

Social unrest and crime conditions were so severe that in 1965, President Johnson declared a "war on crime" and appointed the **President's Commission on Law Enforcement and Administration of Justice**. Officially charged to investigate the causes of crime, the commission was quite broad in its analysis. The summary report, *The Challenge of Crime in a Free Society,* was issued in 1967. Nine supplemental reports also were published: *The Police, The Courts, Corrections, Juvenile Delinquency and Youth Crime, Organized Crime, Assessment of Crime, Narcotics and Drug Abuse, Drunkenness,* and *Science and Technology.* These reports provide interesting reading, since each elaborates on the conditions found in the criminal justice system during the mid-1960s. Each report as well as the summary report contained numerous recommendations for improvement of the policing system, some of which have never been implemented or adopted as public policy.

After the publication of the president's Crime Commission's findings, Congress created the **Law Enforcement Assistance Administration** (LEAA) to assist government agencies at all levels of government to implement some of the recommendations set forth by the commission. The enabling legislation was the **Omnibus Crime Control and Safe Streets Act of 1968**, commonly referred to as the "Safe Streets Act" or the "Crime Control Act" of 1968. LEAA provided billions of dollars of assistance to the criminal justice community until its funding was removed in 1980.

During the late 1960s and through the 1970s, various presidents established major commissions that focused on perceived serious problems or a specific series of incidents:

— Commission on Civil Disorders, 1968

— Commission on Causes and Prevention of Violence, 1969

— Commission on Campus Unrest, 1970

— Commission on Civil Rights, 1970

— Commission on Obscenity and Pornography, 1970

— Commission on Marihuana and Drug Abuse, 1972

— National Advisory Commission on Criminal Justice Standards and Goals, 1973

— Commission on Gambling, 1976

— Commission on Disorders and Terrorism, 1976

— Commission on Private Security, 1976

— Commission on Organized Crime, 1976

National commissions were not used much during the 1980s and 1990s for crime-related issues. They have become more popular on the state and municipal level, primarily to investigate allegations of police corruption and abuse.

## The 1980s and 1990s

Since the late 1970s, policing in the United States has continued to undergo reform and scrutiny. According to police historian Samuel Walker (1992, 26–28), the police have been "caught between old problems and new ideas." Old problems include the crime rates (down in the 1980s, then rising until the last several years) and varying types of crime (drug offenses, drive-by shootings, domestic violence, juvenile crime) that upset the community. The new ideas have included problem-oriented policing, community policing, neighborhood crime prevention programming, and other enhanced community efforts. However, added to this puzzle are problems associated with police corruption and abuse, rising fear of international and domestic terrorism, the application of military technology to civilian public safety and law enforcement, and the availability of economic resources.

The many issues, debates, and trends in policing of the last two decades are incorporated throughout the rest of this text. They include organizational issues (Chapter 5); legal restrictions (Chapter 6); functions, roles, and styles (Chapter 7); training (Chapter 8); personnel issues (Chapter 9); crime, theory, and strategies (Chapter 10); technological applications (Chapter 11); and general future directions (Chapters 12). Each of the following chapters contains selected historical and current descriptions of the status of policing in the United States and the many challenges it faces.

# ■ Summary

During America's colonial period, volunteer watchmen provided communal security. Gradually, however, as cities grew more populated and diverse law enforcement services were shifted to full-time, paid police forces, forces that remained inefficient and unprofessional for years. The founding of a new nation created the need for federal law enforcement, which was first performed by federal marshals. In many regions of the country, vigilantism, which often had a dark side, augmented or even replaced established police departments with their own brand of justice. Private security agencies arose in areas where law enforcement was ineffective or did not exist. A bright spot in the evolution of law enforcement was the creation of state police agencies. First used in Texas, they gradually evolved into highly professional state highway patrols and state investigative agencies.

The early stages of professional policing can be traced to the Progressive Reform Movement, the collective work of civic-minded citizens, early scholars of police administration, and visionary leaders within the law enforcement community. The goal of creating a police profession moved one step closer with the founding of the International Association of Chiefs of Police (IACP). It took another step forward when rank-and-file officers began to establish associations like the Fraternal Order of Police and the International Association of Women Police, organizations that emerged to address concerns of the working officers. Following the lead of city and state investigations conducted in the 1920s, the Wickersham Commission issued the first national study of the criminal justice system in 1931. Its recommendations became the basis for future reform. Following the Second World War, United States law enforcement started to bend, shaped by social and political forces that included increasing urbanization and crime, general social disorder, racial and gender discrimination, changing technology, and the quest for professional status.

Still, there are lingering problems from (1) the evolution of policing during the "political" period (which lasted from around the 1828 federal elections to the early twentieth century), (2) police enforcement of Black Codes and Jim Crow laws, and (3) the effects of the professionalization movement. Because of the "political" era in policing (the Progressive Reform Movement's efforts to "get politics out of management"), police developed a cultural history of the use of violence toward citizens, given that citizens felt that police officers were nothing but political instruments and therefore held no legitimacy. Coupled with the enforcement of clearly discriminatory codes aimed at African-American citizens, a climate of conflict between police and the African-American community was solidified within policing and within the communities of citizens who were targets of police actions. Finally, the professionalization movement isolated policing from the general community, largely assuring the inability to fix the conflict with the African-American community, and generating a general isolation with the entire society—a "we" versus "them" culture that we see today. These conditions are one of the major obstacles to police reform in the year 2005 and beyond.

## QUESTIONS FOR REVIEW

1. What was the night-watch system of protection during the colonial period and what were its characteristics?

2. How was colonial America influenced by religion, the family, and community norms?

3. What historical development led to the creation of the position of federal marshal? What were the marshal's duties?

4. How did immigration, industrialization, and urbanization affect the development of American policing in the 1800s?

5. What were the legal and social customs in America prior to and following the Civil War and how did they impact policing?

6. What was the "Progressive Movement," and how did it impact American policing in the early 1900s?

7. What were the names and contributions of at least three major American reformers of law enforcement of the period from the 1890s to the 1930s?

8. How did the functions of state police evolve?

9. What was the major commission that reviewed and reported on law enforcement issues in the mid-1960s? What were its findings?

## SUGGESTED ACTIVITIES

1. Select a state in the United States and write a letter to its attorney general asking how law enforcement agencies at the state level are structured and organized.

2. At your local library or police department, locate a history of the police department. Summarize your findings in class.

3. Secure a copy of one of the commission studies mentioned in this chapter and write a brief (3-page) summary of its major findings and recommendations.

4. On the World Wide Web, log on to the address http://www.fbi.gov and click on the "history" icon to read "A Short History of the Federal Bureau of Investigation."

## ■ Chapter Glossary

**Alice Stebbins Wells**   was the second policewoman employed in the United States. Hired by the City of Los Angeles in 1910, Officer Wells gained international recognition for her work advocating for policewomen. She helped found the International Association of Women Police.

**Black Codes**   laws that specifically spelled out the rights and responsibilities of the newly freed slaves and were enacted in southern states after the Civil War.

**Fraternal Order of Police**    formed in 1915 by two Pittsburgh patrol officers as a social benevolent association that included all ranks in the police organization.

**International Association of Chiefs of Police** (IACP)    Originally the National Chiefs of Police Union; established in 1893 to organize cooperative efforts among police departments.

**International Association of Women Police**    originally organized as the International Association of Policewomen in 1915; it advocated and advanced the employing of more women in law enforcement.

**"Jim Crow"**    law practices and formal sanctions established primarily in the northern states, which continued to separate the races (segregation).

**Law Enforcement Assistance Administration** (LEAA)    a federal agency created in 1968 to assist government agencies at all levels of government to implement some of the recommendations set forth by the president's commission.

**Lola Greene Baldwin**    was the first policewoman employed in the United States. Hired by the City of Portland, Oregon in 1908, Officer Baldwin gained international recognition for her work advocating for policewomen, the rights of children, and the rights of women.

**National Commission on Law Observance and Enforcement**    appointed by President Hoover in 1929 to survey the criminal justice system and causes of crime in the United States; commonly referred to as the Wickersham Commission.

**Omnibus Crime Control and Safe Streets Act of 1968**    the enabling legislation for the LEAA; commonly referred to as the "Safe Streets Act" or the "Crime Control Act" of 1968.

*Plessy v. Ferguson*    the Supreme Court decision in 1896 that sanctioned the doctrine of "separate but equal"; the decision focused on segregation in public accommodations.

**police benevolent associations**    organizations formed to assist injured or disabled officers and widows of officers. Through these organizations, officers organized and advanced their collective interests.

**President's Commission on Law Enforcement and Administration of Justice**    commission appointed by President Johnson in 1965 to investigate the causes of crime and the condition of the criminal justice system.

**Progressive Movement**    a movement in the United States, beginning at the turn of the century and thriving for the next two decades, that attempted to reform the courts, schools and other urban institutions by reorganizing their structures, upgrading personnel, and redefining their functions.

**rattlewatch**    in colonial New Amsterdam (New York City), a group of citizens equipped with rattles to warn of their watchful presence; a form of night-watch.

**slave patrols**    an early form of American police (1740s) created to protect persons from runaway slaves and to inhibit insurrection or other irregularities.

**vigilantism**    a form of policing in America appearing during the late 1790s through the mid-1800s; originally, the philosophy of vigilantism was premised on self-preservation and self-protection.

**wardens** early supervisors of night watchmen established in the city of Philadelphia in 1749.

# ■ Chapter References

Alex, Nicholas (1969). *Black in Blue: A Study of Negro Policemen*. New York: Appleton-Century Crofts;

Bopp, William J. and Donald O. Schultz (1972). *Principles of American Law Enforcement and Criminal Justice*. Springfield, IL: Charles C. Thomas.

Cox, James A. (2003). Bilboes, Brands, and Branks: Colonial Crimes and Punishment. *The Journal of the Colonial Williamsburg Foundation*, Spring 2003.

Dilworth, Donald C. (ed.) (1976). *The Blue and the Brass: American Policing 1890–1910*. Gaithersburg, MD: International Association of Chiefs of Police.

Eldefonso, Edward, Alan Coffey, and Richard Grace (1982). *Principles of Law Enforcement, 3rd Edition*. New York: Wiley.

Fogelson, Robert M. (1977). *Big-City Police*. Cambridge, MA: Harvard University Press.

Foner, E.F. (1988). *Reconstruction: America's Unfinished Revolution: 1863-1877*. New York: Harper and Row.

Fosdick, Raymond B. (1920). *American Police Systems*. New York: The Century Company.

Fricke, Charles W. (1930). *Criminal Investigation*. Los Angeles, CA: O.W. Smith Law Books.

Fuld, Leonhard F. (1909). *Police Administration*, reprint edition, Montclair, NJ: Patterson Smith, 1971.

Green, Gion and Robert Fisher (1987). *Introduction to Security*, 4th Edition. Boston: Butterworths.

Hadden, Sally E. (2001). *Slave Patrols: Law and Violence in Virginia and the Carolinas*. Cambridge, MA: Harvard University Press.

Jackson, Donald Dale (April 1989). Take the oath, put on the badge and do the job. *Smithsonian*, Vol. 20, No. 1:114–25.

Johnson, David R. (1981).*American Law Enforcement: A History*. St. Louis, MO: Forum Press.

Jolly, Michelle (2003). Sex, Vigilantism, and San Francisco in 1856. *Common-place: The Interactive Journal of Early American Life*, Vol. 3, No. 4, July. (Available online at http://www.common-place.org).

Kuechler, Lori S. (2003). *The Portland Police Sunshine Division: An Early History*. Portland, OR: Sunshine Division, Inc.

Lane, Rodger (1971). *Policing the City: Boston, 1822–1885*. New York, NY: Atheneum Press.

Law Enforcement Assistance Administration (1976).*Two Hundred Years of American Criminal Justice*. Washington, DC: US Department of Justice.

Myers, Gloria E. (1995). *A Municipal Mother: Portland's Lola Greene Baldwin, America's First Policewoman*. Corvallis, OR: Oregon State University Press.

National Commission on the Causes and Prevention of Violence (1968). *Rights in Conflict: The Chicago Police Riot*. New York, NY: New American Library, Inc.

National Commission on Law Observance and Enforcement (1931). *Report on Police*. Washington, DC: US Government Printing Office.

Roth, Mitchel (2005). *Crime and Punishment: A History of the Criminal Justice System*. Belmont, CA: Thomson Wadsworth.

Strecher, V.G. (1971). *The Environment of Law Enforcement: A Community Relations Guide*. Englewood Cliffs, New Jersey: Prentice Hall.

Thayer, George (1967). *The Farther Shores of Politics: The American Political Fringe Today*. New York: Simon and Schuster.

Trojanowicz, Robert and Samuel Dixon (1974). *Criminal Justice and the Community*. Englewood Cliffs, New Jersey: Prentice Hall.

Trojanowicz, Trojanowicz, and Moss (1975). *Community Based Crime Prevention*. Englewood Cliffs, New Jersey: Prentice Hall.

US Marshals Service (May 1994). *The United States Marshals Service: Past and Present*. US Marshals Service, Publication Number 3.

Walker, Samuel (1998). *Popular Justice: A History of American Criminal Justice*. New York, NY: Oxford University Press.

Walker, Samuel (1992). *Police in America: An Introduction*. New York, NY: McGraw Hill.

Walker, Samuel (1977). *A Critical History of Police Reform*. Lexington, MA: Lexington Books.

Wallace, Paul A.W. and James P. O'Brien (1995). "William Penn in Pennsylvania," a document retrieved on October 3, 2004, from the Pennsylvania Historical and Museum Commission web page (www.dep.state.us/dep/PA_Env-Her/William_Penn.htm).

Whitehouse, Jack E. (March 1973). Historical Perspectives on the Police Community Service Function. *Journal of Police Science and Administration*, Vol. 1, No. 1.

Williams, Hubert and Patrick V. Murphy (1990). The Evolving Strategy of Police: A Minority View. *Perspectives on Policing*, No. 13. Washington, DC: National Institute of Justice and Harvard University.

Wintersmith, Robert F. (1974). *Police and the Black Community*. Lexington, MA: Lexington Books.

Wood, B. (1984). *Slavery in Colonial Georgia*. Athens, GA: University of Georgia Press.

# Public and Private Law Enforcement in the United States

**4**

## Learning Objectives

In Chapter 3, you learned about the evolution of policing in the United States. This chapter presents the governmental framework for the authority and existence of law enforcement agencies. It also describes the type and number of agencies that operate in the country. The private sector law enforcement community is described here as well; it has several common references such as private policing, private security, and loss prevention. After studying this chapter, you should be able to:

- Understand how policing fits in the governmental structure of the United States.

- Explain the basic principles of US government such as federalism, checks and balances, three branches of government, implied powers doctrine, and judicial review.

- Describe what is meant by "political subdivision."

- Cite the approximate number of law enforcement agencies and the number of law enforcement personnel in the United States.

- Distinguish between "specific police authority" and "general police authority" and be able to give examples of each.

- List the major federal law enforcement agencies and their organizational placement in the federal government structure.

- Summarize the purpose and extent of private policing in the United States.

## Key Terms Used in This Chapter

| | |
|---|---|
| federalism | specific police authority |
| checks and balances (or | general police authority |
|   separation of powers) | implied powers doctrine (or the |
| judicial review |   necessary and proper clause) |
| political subdivisions | private police/security |
| concurrent or overlapping | |
|   jurisdiction | |

# ■ The US Governmental Framework Applied to Policing

The agencies responsible for criminal law enforcement in the United States vary significantly in size, scope of responsibility, and authority. The model of law enforcement that has evolved in the United States can be referred to as a "fragmented system" since there is no "national police force." The country's law enforcement community is decentralized—made up of many independently organized agencies. In comparison, some countries (e.g., France and Italy) utilize a "centralized system" of law enforcement, in which all agencies' policies and procedures are controlled by a national or governmental headquarters (Hunter 1990).

## Basic Organizing Principles

A review of basic organizing principles of US government is appropriate in examining the authority of US law enforcement agencies. By ratifying the Constitution, the American colonies adopted a form of representative democracy known as **federalism**. This established a "dual system" of government made up of the federal and state systems. The authority, powers, and limitations of the federal government were framed in the Constitution and the Bill of Rights (reprinted in Appendix I for reference). The Tenth Amendment (also referred to as the "state rights amendment") clearly indicated that there would be a sharing of power in the United States: "The powers not delegated to the United States by the Constitution, nor prohibited by it to the states, are reserved to the states respectively, or to the people." Thus, the states were permitted to establish their own governmental structures as long as they did not violate or interfere with the federal Constitution. This permitted the formation of various state structures that could deviate somewhat from the federal system (see **Figure 4-1**).

When a conflict of laws (between state and federal law) exists, the federal judicial system may be asked to clarify and interpret the law in order to resolve the conflict. Such conflicts fall under the "supremacy clause" of Article IV of the United States Constitution, which states:

> *This Constitution, and laws of the United States which shall be made in pursuance thereof . . . shall be the supreme law of the land; and the judges in every state shall be bound thereby, any thing in the constitution or laws of any state to the contrary notwithstanding.*

Throughout the federal and state governments, there is a system of **checks and balances**. By establishing three branches of government—executive, legislative, and judicial—the United States Constitution provided a mechanism to prevent any one branch from becoming too powerful. This principle is also referred to as **separation of powers**. Once the legislative branch enacts legislation, it is the responsibility of the executive branch to enforce it. The judiciary supervises judicial proceedings, including trials, and through the process of **judicial review**, rules on the constitutionality of laws enacted by the legislative branch and procedures used by the executive branch in enforcing laws.

## Multiple Jurisdictions

The framework outlined above has led to many geographical jurisdictions, not just those of the federal and state governments. Although the federal level of government maintains a single national jurisdiction, the states have created **political subdivisions**. The most common names for these political subdivisions include: county, municipality or city, village, borough, and township. However, park districts, school districts, public colleges and universities, and port authorities can also be subdivisions of states. Political subdivisions may have the authority to establish law enforcement agencies if the legislative body that created the subdivision granted such authority. As a result, often more than one law enforcement agency can have jurisdiction over the same geographical

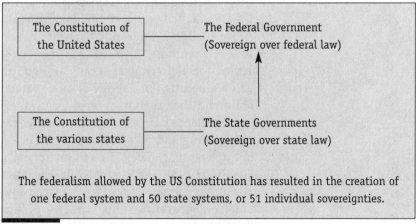

**Figure 4-1** The federalism concept in the United States.

territory. For example, township police officers have police authority within their township, but so do members of a county sheriff's department of the county wherein the township lies. Additionally, state law enforcement agencies would have jurisdiction within both the county and the township. Based on this example, the possible complications and conflicts over jurisdiction become evident. When this situation exists, it is referred to as **concurrent** or **overlapping jurisdiction**. Usually, when agencies have overlapping jurisdiction, there is an understanding (perhaps formal, but usually informal) as to which agency is the "primary" responding agency and which is the "secondary" or "supportive" agency.

## Executive Authority

Every law enforcement agency has a chief executive official. The most common title is "police chief." Other titles include "sheriff," "director," "superintendent," "colonel," "commissioner," "marshal," or "chief constable." Whatever the title of the chief executive, the position has the authority and responsibility to guide the organization and direct its members. Duties include establishing and enforcing policy, managing the budget, recommending personnel for employment and for dismissal, scheduling resources, addressing community concerns, and evaluating the overall daily performance of the agency. In addition to these responsibilities, the agency's chief executive official reports and is accountable to another jurisdictional official or board. The law normally describes how the chief executive is appointed. For example, in many large cities in the United States, the mayor appoints the police chief. In some cases, however, the chief is promoted from within the agency and occupies the position regardless of who is mayor. In some jurisdictions, a board of three or more members chooses the chief executive. Once appointed, the chief executive official may occupy the position until retirement, be removed by a new mayor for cause, or be removed at any time. Any action for removal depends on the appointment authority within the jurisdiction and the specific law related to removal or dismissal. (See Chapter 9 for additional information about personnel issues and civil service systems.)

## Statistical Profiles and Functions

How many law enforcement agencies are there in the United States? Although this is a straightforward question, it is extremely difficult to answer. Because of the fragmented nature of the governmental system, no one agency or office is responsible for maintaining accurate lists of information on the US law enforcement community. Also, the accuracy of state statistics regarding their agencies varies. Smaller agencies "come and go" at the deliberation of executive and legislative boards. An agency can be formed in one community and abolished in another during the same week. Central registries of this activity are rare, although some reliable data are maintained by state regulatory agencies responsible for the training and certification of officers. Thus, any count of the number of law enforcement agencies is an estimate and not an exact figure.

Since 1987, the Bureau of Justice Statistics in the Office of Justice Programs within the United States Department of Justice has been collecting data from law enforcement agencies under the Law Enforcement Management and Administrative Statistics (LEMAS) program. This program conducts surveys of the law enforcement community every three years. Because the survey consists of several thousand questionnaires and considerable amounts of data, there is some time delay in reporting the results. The data reported in this chapter were the most recent available when the text was updated but Web sites of the Bureau of Justice Statistics, Office of Justice Programs (part of the US Department of Justice) should be consulted as well; the latest reports can be found at: http://www.ojp.usdoj.gov/bjs/whtsnw2.htm. Additional information on law enforcement personnel can be found in the annual publication of the Uniform Crime Reports, located on the World Wide Web at: http://www.fbi.gov/ucr/ucr.htm.

## Local Agencies

Table 4-1 summarizes the number of state and local law enforcement agencies, employees, and operating expenses at the various levels of government by type of agency.

Obviously, of the 17,784 state and local agencies, the large majority (over 13,000) are the general policing agencies that include the municipal, village, town, and township departments in the United States. These agencies employ over 471,000 full- and part-time sworn officers and over 160,000 full- and part-time civilians. When the local agencies' totals are added to the state primary agencies and the special jurisdictions, it yields 708,000 sworn officers and over 311,000 civilians in full-time positions. These numbers have been growing at a rate of about 3% every three years, so in 2003 there should have been approximately 729,000 full-time sworn officers and 320,000 full-time civilians at the state and local levels. The largest local level police department in the country is New York City, with over 53,774 personnel, of which over 37,240 are sworn. FBI data for 2002 or the indi-

| Table 4-1 | Employment by State and Local Law Enforcement Agencies in the United States, 2000 | | | | | | |
|---|---|---|---|---|---|---|---|
| | | Number of employees | | | | | |
| | | Full-time | | | Part-time | | |
| Type of agency | Number of agencies | Total | Sworn | Civilian | Total | Sworn | Civilian |
| Local police[a] | 13,289 | 568,995 | 443,550 | 125,445 | 62,594 | 27,741 | 34,853 |
| Sheriff | 3,070 | 293,823 | 164,711 | 129,112 | 22,737 | 10,300 | 12,437 |
| Primary state | 49 | 87,028 | 56,348 | 30,680 | 817 | 95 | 722 |
| Special jurisdiction[b] | 1,376 | 69,650 | 43,413 | 26,237 | 13,583 | 4,667 | 8,916 |
| Total | 17,784 | 1,019,496 | 708,022 | 311,474 | 99,731 | 42,803 | 56,928 |

[a]Includes Texas County Constables and consolidated police-sheriff agencies.

[b]The special police category includes both state-level and local-level agencies.

*Source:* Adapted from Reaves, Brian (2002). *Census of State and Local Law Enforcement Agencies, 2000*. Washington, DC: US Department of Justice.

vidual city Web sites indicated the following staffing levels (full-time sworn officers) for other major US cities:

| | | | |
|---|---|---|---|
| Chicago | 13,705 | Detroit | 4,006 |
| Los Angeles | 9,600 | Washington, DC | 3,600 |
| Philadelphia | 6931 | Baltimore | 3,316 |
| Houston | 5,360 | Dallas | 2,977 |

A more revealing finding from the LEMAS data is the relationship between the number of agencies and size of agency in terms of sworn personnel. **Table 4-2** lists the breakdown of local agencies by number of sworn personnel. Notice that 27.4% of the agencies have fewer than five sworn officers, 46.5% employ less than 10, and about 89% employ fewer than 50 officers. Notice that there are over 676 agencies that employ only one officer. Of all the local police departments in the United States, only 4.6%, or 582 departments, employ 100 or more officers. It is noteworthy that since 1993, the number of "one officer" agencies dropped approximately 20%. This may be indicative of the realization that there is a certain level of effectiveness and efficiency in order to staff an agency. The issue of agency consolidation and/or merger is a controversial one in the United States because of the desire for home rule. See **Figure 4-2** for some "what if" statements regarding the impact of possible consolidation based on a minimum number of officers.

Although there are many small agencies in the United States employing small numbers of officers, 60.7% of all full-time sworn officers at the local level are employed in agencies with 100 or more sworn employees. These sworn officers

**Table 4-2** — **Local Police Departments and Total Full-Time Sworn Personnel by Agency Size, 2000**

| Total number of full-time officers in agency by size* | Number | Percentage | Cumulated percentage |
|---|---|---|---|
| **1,000 or more** | 47 | 0.4 | 100 |
| **500–999** | 37 | 0.3 | 99.6 |
| **250–499** | 103 | 0.8 | 99.3 |
| **100–249** | 395 | 3.1 | 98.5 |
| **50–99** | 807 | 6.4 | 95.4 |
| **25–49** | 1,683 | 13.3 | 89.0 |
| **10–24** | 3,700 | 29.2 | 75.7 |
| **5–9** | 3,085 | 24.4 | 46.5 |
| **2–4** | 2,133 | 16.8 | 22.1 |
| **1** | 676 | 5.3 | 5.3 |
| **Total** | 12,666 | 100 | 100 |

*Total full-time officer appointments only per agency.

*Source:* Adapted from Matthew J. Hickman and Brian Reaves (2003). *Local Police Departments, 2000*. Washington, DC: US Department of Justice, p. 2.

are employed in only 567 agencies, or 4.5% of all local agencies. This means that there is an inverse relationship between the number of agencies and the number of persons employed by those agencies. That is, of the over 12,600 agencies, the largest number of agencies (over 12,000) employ about 40% of the local officers, while a small number of agencies (about 567) employ over 60% of all local police officers in the United States. In other words, less than 5% of the local agencies in the country account for 60% of all sworn officers employed full-time.

What if the United States undertook an agency consolidation effort? Based on recent data, if a federal law were enacted to require a minimum of 10 full-time officers in an agency in order to exist, how many agencies would be affected? At least 5,894 agencies would be affected (about 46.5% of all local agencies). If the law were to require a minimum of 25 full-time officers, 9,594 agencies would be affected (about 75.7% of all local agencies). If the law required a minimum of 50 full-time officers, 11,277 agencies would be affected (about 89% of all local agencies). Not all of the effected agencies would be eliminated. They could consolidate or merge with other small agencies to form new ones or they could merge with larger existing agencies. The point is that the vast majority of jurisdictions in the United States has small law enforcement agencies providing services to their communities.

**Figure 4-2** What if agencies had to be a minimum size?

Local law enforcement, the uniformed officer on the beat, is what most Americans observe on a daily basis. It is the local police who respond to general street crime and most of the traffic accidents. Local police authority is general in scope. They can enforce the general criminal code of the state plus appropriate county or city ordinances. They are also responsible for initiating federal charges in many jurisdictions. However, such situations are usually referred to federal authorities or investigated jointly. Nearly all local police departments have primary responsibility for investigating at least some types of crimes occurring in their jurisdiction. All departments in jurisdictions with a population of 250,000 or more have primary responsibility for investigating homicides and other violent crimes such as rape, robbery, or assault. Nearly all departments serving a population of 10,000 or more have primary responsibility for homicide investigation, but 11% of those serving a population of 2,500 to 9,999 and 30% of those serving fewer than 2,500 residents report that they do not have primary responsibility for such investigations. In jurisdictions under 2,500 in population, about one in seven local police departments do not have primary responsibility for the investigation of any violent crimes. The size of agencies does have some relationship to their primary function and responsibilities (Reaves 1996, 9–13). The major functions carried out by law enforcement agencies are also discussed in Chapter 7.

## Sheriff's Departments

One unique type of local agency is the county sheriff's department. The LEMAS survey treats these departments as a separate category and for the year 2000 identified 3,070 such agencies (Hickman and Reaves 2003). The sheriff's departments in the United States are predominately operated by county governments, and most are small in terms of the number of employees. Nearly 62.5% of them employ fewer than 25 sworn officers each, and 32.5% (998 agencies) employ fewer than 10 officers (see **Table 4-3**). Of all the sheriff's departments, 64% of the full-time sworn personnel work in the 323 agencies (or 10.5% of all sheriffs' departments) that employ 100 or more full-time sworn personnel.

| Table 4-3 | Sheriff's Departments by Number of Sworn Personnel, 2000 | | | |
|---|---|---|---|---|
| Number of full-time sworn personnel in agency | Agencies | | Full-time sworn personnel | |
| | Number | Percentage | Number | Percentage |
| 1,000 or more | 12 | 0.4 | 28,817 | 17.5 |
| 500–999 | 27 | 0.9 | 18,152 | 11.0 |
| 250–499 | 78 | 2.5 | 27,274 | 16.6 |
| 100–249 | 206 | 6.7 | 31,170 | 18.9 |
| 50–99 | 311 | 10.1 | 21,586 | 13.1 |
| 25–49 | 515 | 16.8 | 17,758 | 10.8 |
| 10–24 | 923 | 30.1 | 14,391 | 8.7 |
| 5–9 | 658 | 21.4 | 4,518 | 2.7 |
| 2–4 | 315 | 10.3 | 1,020 | 0.6 |
| 1 | 25 | 0.8 | 25 | * |
| Total | 3,070 | 100 | 164,711 | 100 |

*Less than 0.5%.

*Source:* Adapted from Hickman, Matthew J. and Brian Reaves (2003). *Local Police Departments, 2000*. Washington, DC: US Department of Justice, p. 8.

Unlike local agencies, sheriff's departments often have primary responsibilities for jail operations and court-related duties. Generally speaking, about 80% of the sheriff's departments have jail operations responsibilities; over 98% serve the civil process of the local county court systems, 98% have criminal investigative responsibilities, and nearly 95% provided court security (Reaves and Hickman 2001, 6-7). Some counties (in Delaware, Georgia, Hawaii, Illinois, Maryland, Missouri, New York, Pennsylvania, and Virginia) have a county police department as well as a county sheriff's department. Where this occurs, the sheriff's department of that county usually has no police patrol or criminal investigation responsibilities. These police departments operate much like municipal police departments.

The ten largest county sheriff's offices in the United States, based on their full-time sworn personnel, are the following (Reaves and Hickman 2001, 2):

| | | | |
|---|---|---|---|
| Los Angeles County (CA) | 8,107 | Hillsborough County (FL) | 1,889 |
| Cook County (IL) | 5,768 | Jefferson Parish (LA) | 1,449 |
| Harris County (TX) | 2,648 | Orange County (CA) | 1,361 |
| Broward County (FL) | 2,419 | San Bernardino County (CA) | 1,341 |
| San Diego County (CA) | 1,999 | Sacramento County (CA) | 1,339 |

## State Agencies

Every state except Hawaii has at least one state-level policing agency. Usually, this major agency is known as the "state police," "state patrol," or "department of public safety." Other state agencies exist, however, and may have responsibilities for specific areas of enforcement such as alcoholic beverage control, fish and wildlife protection, parks protection, health care fraud, and environmental crimes. As with other governmental levels, the jurisdiction and authority of state agencies depend on legislative mandate. The terms used to describe and distinguish police authority are **specific police authority** and **general police authority**. As the terms imply, agencies with limited or specifically stated responsibilities (such as highway patrols) possess specific police authority. Those with policing authority over a broad range of criminal offenses or those that can enforce any statutory laws possess general police authority (see **Figure 4-3**). For example, in Ohio, the state highway patrol is authorized to exercise specific police authority to (a) enforce the traffic code on all roads and highways of the state, (b) enforce the criminal code on state property, (c) investigate accidents and incidents involving aircraft, and (d) protect the governor and other dignitaries. Therefore, the Ohio Highway Patrol does not have jurisdiction over common criminal offenses such as robbery, burglary, and murder unless committed on state property. Local or county agencies, which have general police authority, must investigate those offenses. In contrast, in Pennsylvania (and in most states with a "state police" agency), the state police are authorized to exercise general police authority to investigate any criminal offense anywhere in the state.

**Table 4-4** lists each primary state agency in the United States and gives information about the number of full-time employees, the number of sworn officers, and the percentage of total personnel that are sworn. The estimated state population for 2002 is also listed, as well as the number of sworn employees per 10,000 residents. This last figure is used for comparison purposes; however, remember to consider the primary responsibility of the agency (traffic and/or general policing) when making such comparisons. For example, Ohio has 1.4 officers in the highway patrol per 10,000 population, while Pennsylvania has 4.8 officers in its state police per 10,000 population. The two are not directly comparable because of the differences in primary responsibilities.

Of the 49 primary state law enforcement agencies, 37 (75.5%) have more than 500 full-time officers; 19 (38.7%) have more than 1,000 officers. The ratio of full-time officers per 10,000 population ranged from 1.0 (Florida Highway Patrol) to 8.1 (Vermont Department of Public Safety). The major functions performed by state policing agencies included the following:

- Accident investigation and traffic enforcement

| Agencies with Specific Police Authority | Agencies with General Police Authority |
|---|---|
| Highway Patrols | State Police |
| Environmental Enforcement Units | County Police |
| Bureau of Liquor Control | Municipal Police |
| Fish & Wildlife | County Sheriff's Depts. (most) |
| State Narcotics Units | Townships/Villages (most) |

*The concept of specific and general police authority applies to all levels of policing, not just state agencies.

**Figure 4-3** Specific versus general police authority.*

**Table 4-4** Number of Full-Time Employees per 10,000 Residents in Primary State Law Enforcement Agencies, 2002

| Name of state agency | Full-time employees | | | State population | Officers per 10,000 residents |
| | Total | Sworn officers | | | |
| | | Number | Percentage | | |
| --- | --- | --- | --- | --- | --- |
| Alabama Department of Public Safety | 1,248 | 631 | 50.5 | 3,930,746 | 1.6 |
| Alaska State Troopers | 585 | 341 | 58.3 | 642,955 | 5.3 |
| Arizona Department of Public Safety | 1,894 | 1,090 | 57.6 | 5,443,984 | 2.0 |
| Arkansas State Police | 829 | 502 | 60.5 | 2,710,079 | 1.9 |
| California Highway Patrol | 10,317 | 6,847 | 66.4 | 30,685,929 | 2.2 |
| Colorado State Patrol | 962 | 712 | 74.0 | 4,403,008 | 1.6 |
| Connecticut State Police | 1,793 | 1,248 | 69.6 | 3,374,179 | 3.7 |
| Delaware State Police | 859 | 625 | 72.8 | 807,385 | 7.7 |
| Florida Highway Patrol | 2,126 | 1,637 | 76.9 | 16,401,847 | 1.0 |
| Georgia State Police | 1,384 | 872 | 63.0 | 7,226,657 | 1.2 |
| Idaho State Police | 330 | 250 | 75.8 | 1,311,796 | 1.9 |
| Illinois State Police | 3,840 | 2,136 | 55.6 | 12,542,030 | 1.7 |
| Indiana State Police | 1,916 | 1,230 | 64.2 | 6,049,242 | 2.0 |
| Iowa State Patrol | 894 | 619 | 69.2 | 2,916,660 | 2.1 |
| Kansas Highway Patrol | 811 | 526 | 64.9 | 2,691,202 | 2.0 |
| Kentucky State Police | 1,681 | 941 | 59.0 | 4,068,895 | 2.3 |
| Louisiana State Police | 1,607 | 1,009 | 62.8 | 4,356,611 | 2.3 |
| Maine State Police | 478 | 327 | 68.4 | 1,291,698 | 2.5 |
| Maryland State Police | 2,356 | 1,578 | 67.0 | 5,291,592 | 3.0 |
| Massachusetts State Police | 2,742 | 2,354 | 85.8 | 6,268,238 | 3.8 |
| Michigan State Police | 2,956 | 2,035 | 68.8 | 9,976,197 | 2.0 |
| Minnesota State Patrol | 796 | 525 | 66.0 | 4,895,720 | 1.1 |
| Mississippi Highway Safety Patrol | 1,016 | 530 | 52.2 | 2,426,944 | 2.2 |
| Missouri State Highway Patrol | 2,167 | 1,075 | 49.6 | 5,604,305 | 1.9 |
| Montana Highway Patrol | 270 | 205 | 75.9 | 909,453 | 2.3 |
| Nebraska State Patrol | 670 | 485 | 72.4 | 1,719,618 | 2.8 |
| Nevada Highway Patrol | 1,249 | 715 | 57.2 | 2,173,591 | 3.3 |
| New Hampshire State Police | 400 | 284 | 71.0 | 925,055 | 3.1 |

| Table 4-4 | Number of Full-Time Employees per 10,000 Residents in Primary State Law Enforcement Agencies, 2002, continued | | | | |

| Name of state agency | Full-time employees | Sworn officers | | State population | Officers per 10,000 residents |
| | Total | Number | Percentage | | |
|---|---|---|---|---|---|
| New Jersey State Police | 3,982 | 2,735 | 68.7 | 8,331,239 | 3.3 |
| New Mexico State Police | 714 | 576 | 80.7 | 1,851,009 | 3.1 |
| New York State Police | 5,443 | 4,553 | 83.6 | 16,675,972 | 2.7 |
| North Carolina State Highway Patrol | 1,804 | 1,368 | 75.8 | 8,313,727 | 1.6 |
| North Dakota Highway Patrol | 187 | 126 | 67.4 | 608,703 | 2.1 |
| Ohio State Highway Patrol | 2,638 | 1,526 | 57.8 | 10,878,422 | 1.4 |
| Oklahoma Highway Patrol | 1,451 | 852 | 58.7 | 3,493,714 | 2.4 |
| Oregon State Police | 1,160 | 753 | 64.9 | 3,492,816 | 2.2 |
| Pennsylvania State Police | 5,859 | 4,140 | 70.7 | 8,590,601 | 4.8 |
| Rhode Island State Police | 257 | 211 | 82.1 | 1,063,557 | 2.0 |
| South Carolina Highway Patrol | 1,092 | 883 | 80.9 | 3,735,856 | 2.4 |
| South Dakota Highway Patrol | 221 | 145 | 65.6 | 747,844 | 1.9 |
| Tennessee Department of Safety | 1,831 | 910 | 49.7 | 5,787,364 | 1.6 |
| Texas Department of Public Safety | 7,480 | 3,031 | 40.5 | 21,670,261 | 1.4 |
| Utah Highway Patrol | 458 | 427 | 93.2 | 2,315,689 | 1.8 |
| Vermont Department of Public Safety | 474 | 295 | 62.2 | 364,545 | 8.1 |
| Virginia State Police | 2,466 | 1,817 | 73.7 | 7,292,082 | 2.5 |
| Washington State Patrol | 2,034 | 1,105 | 54.3 | 6,064,698 | 1.8 |
| West Virginia State Police | 938 | 583 | 62.2 | 1,790,599 | 3.3 |
| Wisconsin State Patrol | 709 | 529 | 74.6 | 4,849,982 | 1.1 |
| Wyoming Highway Patrol | 320 | 172 | 53.8 | 496,899 | 3.5 |

*Source:* Data compiled from the FBI (2003). *Crime in the United States, 2002.* Washington, DC: US Department of Justice for number of officers and estimated population; for Arkansas, correspondence.

■ Patrol and first response
■ Communications and dispatch
■ Narcotics/vice enforcement and training academy operations
■ Homeland Security-related activities

- Fingerprint processing
- Death investigation
- Property and violent crime (rape, robbery, serious assault) investigation
- Ballistics/laboratory testing and search/rescue operations

## Special Law Enforcement Agencies

The 2000 LEMAS survey identified 1,376 special police agencies at both the state and local agency levels. Such agencies employed 69,650 full-time personnel, of which over 43,413 were sworn officers (see Table 4-1). These special police agencies constitute about 7.7% of all local and state agencies in the United States. This category of agency is very difficult to describe because of the variety of special law enforcement agencies. Such agencies usually have names that describe their uniqueness, such as transit police, park district, alcohol beverage control, metropolitan housing authority, campus police, port authority, or airport police. Officers working in such special law enforcement agencies may possess general police authority only within the geographical limitations of their jurisdiction. Some of these agencies possess specific police authority over a large geographical area (for example, a state liquor control agent has authority throughout a state, but only over liquor-related offenses and regulations).

Of all the special law enforcement agencies, approximately 50% are college/university (campus) law enforcement agencies. The findings of a 1995 survey of campus police agencies clearly indicate that as size of campus enrollment decreases, the percentage of campuses using officers with arrest authority and on armed patrol also generally decreases. The survey verified that sworn and armed officers were more likely to be found at institutions under public rather than private control (Reaves 1996). **Table 4-5** summarizes the breakdown of these special law enforcement agencies by type of jurisdiction and the number of full-time officers employed in each category in the year 2000.

## ■ The Federal Agencies and Their Responsibilities

Currently the executive branch of the US federal government consists of 15 departments and 62 independent agencies. The executive branch is primarily responsible for national security, homeland security, public safety, and the delivery of most national services. Criminal law enforcement responsibility at the federal level in the United States is shared among approximately 60 agencies. These agencies have been created by Congress under the authority of the **implied powers doctrine** or the **necessary and proper clause** of Article I, Section 8 (Paragraph 18) of the United States Constitution, which states:

> *[Congress shall have power . . . ] To make all laws which shall be necessary and proper for carrying into execution the foregoing powers, and all other powers vested by this Constitution in the Government of the United States, or in any Department or Officer thereof.*

"Foregoing powers" refers to the powers of Congress specifically enumerated in the first 17 paragraphs of Section 8 (see Appendix I of this text). These powers in-

| Table 4-5 | Special Law Enforcement Agencies, State and Local Jurisdictions by Type And Number of Full-Time Sworn Personnel, June 2000 | |
|---|---|---|

| Type of special jurisdiction | Agencies | Full-time sworn personnel |
|---|---|---|
| **Total** | 1,376 | 43,413 |
| **Government buildings/facilities** | | |
| 4-year college/university | 467 | 9,308 |
| Public school district | 162 | 3,219 |
| 2-year college/university | 222 | 2,011 |
| State capitol/government buildings | 21 | 1,121 |
| Medical school/facility | 42 | 978 |
| Public housing | 14 | 673 |
| Other | 6 | 274 |
| **Conservation laws/parks/recreation** | | |
| Fish and wildlife | 66 | 7,935 |
| Parks and recreational areas | 80 | 3,218 |
| Waterways and boating | 13 | 477 |
| Environmental laws | 3 | 377 |
| Forest resources | 5 | 283 |
| Sanitation laws | 2 | 169 |
| Water resources | 5 | 118 |
| **Criminal investigations** | | |
| County/city | 62 | 1,838 |
| State bureau | 8 | 692 |
| Arson | 31 | 490 |
| **Transportation systems/facilities** | | |
| Mass transit system/railroad | 21 | 2,627 |
| Airports | 87 | 2,462 |
| Transportation centers—multiple types | 5 | 1,697 |
| Port facilities | 17 | 940 |
| Commercial vehicle enforcement | 3 | 440 |
| Roadways, bridges, tunnels | 5 | 234 |
| **Special enforcement** | | |
| Alcohol enforcement | 17 | 1,287 |
| Agricultural | 3 | 272 |
| Gaming/racing laws | 6 | 204 |
| Drug enforcement | 2 | 65 |
| Business regulation | 1 | 4 |

*Source:* Reprinted from Reaves, Brian A. and Matthew Hickman (2003). *Census of State and Local Law Enforcement Agencies, 2000.* Washington, DC: Bureau of Justice Statistics, US Department of Justice, table 14, p. 12.

clude the right to lay and collect taxes and duties, provide for the general welfare, regulate commerce with foreign nations and among the states, establish a uniform rule of naturalization, coin money and provide for the punishment of counterfeiting, establish post offices and roads, declare war, and raise and support armies and a navy. These specific powers and others of the Constitution are important because they provide the federal authority under which law enforcement agencies are created and operated by the federal government. Generally, when Congress enacts a criminal offense or law enforcement responsibility, it specifically designates which agency is responsible for its enforcement. **Figure 4-4** lists major federal agencies with some type of enforcement responsibility. They are listed according to the department in which they are found in the federal government's organizational structure.

The extent of federal law enforcement is very broad and diverse as is evident from Figure 4-4. There are many opportunities existing for employment in the federal sector. As of June 2002, federal agencies employed about 93,000 full-time personnel authorized to make arrests and carry firearms, according to a Bureau of Justice Statistics (BJS) survey. Compared with June 2000, employment of such personnel increased by about 6%. The data gathered by the Bureau of Justice Statistics represented 67 agencies, and the numbers do not reflect the changes brought about by the creation of the Department of Homeland Security (Reaves and Bauer 2003). The major federal agencies with primary criminal investigative responsibilities in terms of size (number of agents) are listed in **Table 4-6** (Reaves and Bauer 2003). They are the most commonly thought of agencies when one mentions federal agents with law enforcement responsibilities.

The federal law enforcement community is very fragmented in terms of jurisdictional authority. Each agency has specific authority by statute. The primary duties for federal officers include criminal investigation (40%), police response and patrol (22%), corrections (18%), non-criminal investigation and inspection (14%), court operations (4%), and security and protection (1%). In terms of gender and racial composition, women accounted for 14.8% of federal officers in 2002. Minority representation was 32.4% in 2002, up from 30.5% in 1998. Hispanic or Latino officers comprised 16.8% of officers in 2002, and African American or black officers, 11.7%. Prior to the creation of the Department of Homeland Security in November of 2002, the Department of Justice employed 58% of all federal law enforcement personnel and the Treasury Department employed 23%. Currently, the Department of Homeland Security employs 38% and the Justice Department 37% (Reaves and Bauer 2003). Agencies with 500 or more officers employed about 87,000, or 93%, of the federal officers covered by the Bureau of Justice Statistics' 2002 survey. The number of officers, special agents, or investigators that is reported here is probably less than the current strength because most agencies have increased the number of personnel since September 11, 2001. Several hundred more law enforcement personnel were authorized in the 2003 and 2004 budget allocations of the federal government.

The following sections contain a brief description of several of the major law enforcement agencies of the federal government including the Department of Homeland Security.

**Department of Agriculture**
Forest Service*
Office of Inspector General*

**Department of Commerce**
Bureau of Export Administration
National Institute of Standards and Technology*
National Oceanic & Atmospheric Administration
Office of Inspector General

**Department of Defense**
Criminal Investigation Command, Army*
Defense Investigative Service
Intelligence and Security Command, Army*
Military Police Corps, Army*
Naval Investigative Service, Navy*
Office of Security Police, Air Force*
Office of Special Investigations, Air Force*
Office of Inspector General*

**Department of Education**
Office of Inspector General*

**Department of Health and Human Services**
Food & Drug Administration, Office of Criminal
   Investigation*
National Institutes of Health, Police*
Office of Inspector General*

**Department of Homeland Security**
Animal and Health Inspection Service
Federal Air Marshals*
Federal Emergency Management Agency
Federal Protective Service*
Transportation Security Administration
US Citizenship and Immigration Service*
US Coast Guard, Intelligence & Law Enforcement Branch
US Customs and Border Protection Agency*
US Secret Service*
White House Police, Secret Service*

**Department of Housing and Urban Development**
Office of Inspector General*

**Department of Interior**
Bureau of Land Management
Bureau of Reclamation*
Bureau of Indian Affairs*
National Park Police*
Office of Inspector General*
US Fish and Wildlife Service*

**Department of Justice**
Bureau of Alcohol, Tobacco, Firearms and Explosives*
Federal Bureau of Prisons*
Drug Enforcement Administration*
Federal Bureau of Investigation*

Office of Inspector General*
US Marshals Service*

**Department of Labor**
Office of Labor-Management Standards
Office of Inspector General*

**Department of State**
Bureau of Diplomatic Security*
Office of Inspector General*

**Department of Transportation**
Federal Aviation Administration Police
Office of Inspector General*

**Department of the Treasury**
Criminal Investigation Division, Internal Revenue Service
   (IRS)*
Inspection Service, Internal Revenue Service
Office of Inspector General*
Bureau of Engraving and Printing, Police*

**Department of Veterans Affairs**
Office of Inspector General*
Veterans Health Administration*

**Independent Agencies**
Administrative Office of the US Courts, Federal Corrections &
   Supervision Division*
Amtrak Police*
Civil Aeronautics Board
Environmental Protection Agency
   Office of Inspector General*
   Office of Criminal Enforcement*
Federal Communications Commission
Federal Maritime Commission
Federal Trade Commission
General Services Administration
   Office of Inspector General*
Interstate Commerce Commission
Government Printing Office, Police*
Library of Congress, Police*
National Aeronautics and Space Administration
   Office of Inspector General*
Office of Personnel Management
   Compliance and Investigations Group
   Office of Inspector General
Securities and Exchange Commission
Smithsonian Institution, National Zoological Park Police*
Social Security Admin., Office of Inspector General*
Tennessee Valley Authority, Public Safety Service*
US Postal Service, Postal Inspection Service*
US Capitol Police*
US Supreme Court Police

*Authority to carry firearms and make arrests.
*Sources:* Adapted from Donald A. Torres (1985). *Handbook of Federal Police and Investigation Agencies*. Westport, Connecticut: Greenwood Press; and Reaves, Brian A. (1998). *Federal Law Enforcement Officers, 1996*. Washington, DC: US Department of Justice; Reaves, Brian A. and Lynn M. Bauer (2003). *Federal Law Enforcement Officers, 2002*. Washington, DC: Bureau of Justice Statistics, US Department of Justice, and US Department of Homeland Security. www.dhs.gov.

**Figure 4-4** Major federal law enforcement agencies.

**Table 4-6** Federal Agencies Employing 100 or More Full-Time Personnel With Arrest and Firearm Authority as of June 2002

| Agency | Number of full-time personnel |
|---|---|
| Immigration and Naturalization Service | 19,101 |
| Federal Bureau of Prisons | 14,305 |
| US Customs Service | 11,634 |
| Federal Bureau of Investigation | 11,248 |
| US Secret Service | 4,256 |
| Administrative Office of the US Courts | 4,050 |
| Drug Enforcement Administration | 4,020 |
| US Postal Inspection Service | 3,135 |
| Internal Revenue Service, Criminal Investigation Division | 2,855 |
| US Marshals Service | 2,646 |
| Bureau of Alcohol, Tobacco, and Firearms | 2,335 |
| National Park Service | 2,139 |
| Veterans Health Administration | 1,605 |
| US Capitol Police | 1,225 |
| US Fish and Wildlife Service, Division of Law Enforcement | 772 |
| General Services Administration, Federal Protective Service | 744 |
| USDA Forest Service, Law Enforcement and Investigations | 658 |
| Bureau of Diplomatic Security, Diplomatic Security Service | 592 |
| US Mint | 375 |
| Bureau of Indian Affairs | 334 |
| Amtrak | 327 |
| Pentagon Force Protection Agency | 327 |
| Bureau of Land Management | 235 |
| Environmental Protection Agency | 220 |
| Department of Energy, Transportation Safeguards Division | 212 |
| Tennessee Valley Authority | 197 |
| Bureau of Engraving and Printing | 195 |
| Food and Drug Administration | 162 |
| National Marine Fisheries Service | 137 |
| Library of Congress | 127 |

Notes: US Courts total includes probation officers.

National Park Service includes 1,549 Park Rangers and 590 US Park Officers.

Listing does not include Inspector General Offices.

*Source:* Reaves, Brian A. and Lynn M. Bauer (2003). *Federal Law Enforcement Officers, 2002.* Washington, DC: Bureau of Justice Statistics, US Department of Justice.

# The Federal Bureau of Investigation

The FBI is part of the Department of Justice. The Bureau has approximately 11,248 special agents who are responsible for criminal investigation and the enforcement of more than 200 categories of federal crimes including bank fraud, embezzlement, kidnapping, and civil rights violations. It also has concurrent jurisdiction with the Drug Enforcement Administration (DEA) over drug offenses under the Controlled Substances Act. Since the September 11, 2001 terrorist attacks on the United States, the FBI has undergone major internal reorganization, which modified the priorities of the agency to the following (FBI 2004a):

1. Protect the United States from terrorist attack.
2. Protect the United States against foreign intelligence operations and espionage.
3. Protect the United States against cyber-based attacks and high-technology crimes.
4. Combat public corruption at all levels.
5. Protect civil rights.
6. Combat transnational and national criminal organizations and enterprises.
7. Combat major white-collar crime.
8. Combat significant violent crime.
9. Support federal, state, county, municipal, and international partners.
10. Upgrade technology to successfully perform the FBI's mission.

The mission of the FBI is to protect and defend the United States against terrorist and foreign intelligence threats, to uphold and enforce the criminal laws of the United States, and to provide leadership and criminal justice services to federal, state, municipal, and international agencies and partners. To accomplish this mission, in fiscal year 2003, the FBI received a total of $4.298 billion, including $540.28 million in net program increases to enhance counterterrorism, counterintelligence, cybercrime, information technology, security, forensics, training, and criminal investigation programs. Besides the more than 11,000 special agents, the FBI also employs over 15,900 support personnel in its 56 field offices and 400 satellite offices in the United States and its 45 Legal Attaché offices around the world (FBI 2004b).

# The Drug Enforcement Agency

The DEA is also part of the Department of Justice and its 4,000-plus special agents investigate major narcotics violators, enforce regulations governing the manufacture and dispensing of controlled substances, and perform other functions to prevent and control drug trafficking. The DEA's budget for fiscal year 2003 was about $1.9 billion. The agency's primary responsibilities include the following (DEA 2004):

- Investigation and preparation for the prosecution of major violators of controlled substance laws operating at interstate and international levels.
- Investigation and preparation for prosecution of criminals and drug gangs who perpetrate violence in our communities and terrorize citizens through fear and intimidation.
- Management of a national drug intelligence program in cooperation with federal, state, local, and foreign officials to collect, analyze, and disseminate strategic and operational drug intelligence information.

- Seizure and forfeiture of assets derived from, traceable to, or intended to be used for illicit drug trafficking.
- Enforcement of the provisions of the Controlled Substances Act as they pertain to the manufacture, distribution, and dispensing of legally produced controlled substances.
- Coordination and cooperation with federal, state, and local law enforcement officials on mutual drug enforcement efforts and enhancement of such efforts through exploitation of potential interstate and international investigations beyond local or limited federal jurisdictions and resources.
- Coordination and cooperation with federal, state, and local agencies, and with foreign governments, in programs designed to reduce the availability of illicit abuse-type drugs on the United States market through non-enforcement methods such as crop eradication, crop substitution, and training of foreign officials.
- Responsibility, under the policy guidance of the Secretary of State and US Ambassadors, for all programs associated with drug law enforcement counterparts in foreign countries.
- Liaison with the United Nations, Interpol, and other organizations on matters relating to international drug control programs.

## The US Marshals Service

The Marshals Service is part of the Department of Justice. The responsibilities of its 2,646 marshals and deputy marshals include the receiving, custody, and transporting of all persons arrested by federal agencies; fugitive matters concerning escaped federal prisoners, probation and parole violators, persons under DEA warrants and defendants released on bond; managing the Federal Witness Security and Federal Asset Seizure and Forfeiture Programs; and security for Federal judicial facilities and personnel (Reaves and Bauer 2003). The Marshals Service is the oldest federal law enforcement agency; its authority was established in 1789. For nearly 75 years, it was the primary enforcement agency of the federal government. The Director, Deputy Director, and 94 US Marshals—appointed by the President or the Attorney General—direct the activities of 95 district offices and personnel stationed at more than 350 locations throughout the 50 states, Guam, the Northern Mariana Islands, Puerto Rico, and the Virgin Islands. The Marshals Service is involved in virtually every federal law enforcement initiative because of its responsibilities. The service operates the Justice Prisoner and Alien Transportation System (JPATS) for transporting prisoners and criminal aliens. JPATS is one of the largest transporters of prisoners in the world, handling hundreds of requests every day to move prisoners between judicial districts, correctional institutions, and foreign countries. On average, more than 270,000 prisoner and alien movements a year are completed by JPATS via coordinated air and ground systems. Since 1983, the Marshals Service has maintained the "15 Most Wanted" fugitives list that is a high-profile list of the most dangerous career criminals in the United States. Of the 167 individuals who have appeared on the list, 159 have been captured. Each year approximately 34,000 federal felons are apprehended because of investigations carried out by deputy marshals. The Marshals Service arrests more federal fugitives than all other law enforcement agencies combined. During fiscal year 2002, Marshals Service-sponsored task forces arrested more than 27,000 state and local fugitives wanted on felony charges and the service successfully completed 334 extraditions from around the globe (US Marshals Service 2004).

## The Internal Revenue Service

The IRS's Criminal Investigation Division (Department of the Treasury) has 2,855 special agents charged with enforcing the nation's tax laws. The IRS is the only federal agency that can investigate potential criminal violations of the Internal Revenue Code. IRS special agents lend their financial investigative expertise to money laundering and narcotics investigations conducted in conjunction with other law enforcement agencies at the local, state, and federal levels. Operations and investigations are carried out through six regional offices, 35 field offices, and 10 fraud detection centers (Reaves and Bauer 2003).

## The Bureau of Alcohol, Tobacco, Firearms, and Explosives

The ATF has about 2,335 agents and officers who enforce federal laws related to alcohol, tobacco, firearms, explosives, and arson. In 2003 ATF became a Justice Department agency and its name was changed to include the word "explosives" (Reaves and Bauer 2003). Although established in 1972 as a separate agency within the Treasury Department, many of its tax-related enforcement responsibilities have been carried out since 1789. ATF provides investigative support to the nation's state and local partners through the National Integrated Ballistic Information Network (NIBIN), that provides for the nationwide installation and networking of automated ballistic imaging equipment. The Comprehensive Crime Gun Tracing Initiative, created in 2001, provides nationwide firearms tracing capability. In fiscal year 2002, the ATF's National Tracing Center conducted over 240,000 trace requests of crime guns. ATF maintains four National Response Teams (NRT) comprising highly trained and well-equipped special agents, forensic chemists, and professional support staff that can be deployed within 24 hours to major explosion and fire scenes anywhere in the United States. The ATF International Response Team participates with the Diplomatic Security Service of the US Department of State to provide technical and investigative assistance at international explosive and fire incidents. There are 36 ATF trained explosives detection canine teams deployed with state, local, and other federal law enforcement agencies and 48 ATF trained and certified accelerant detection canine teams deployed with state and local fire and police departments. To date, ATF has trained over 310 international law enforcement organization's explosives detection canine teams worldwide. ATF maintains three national laboratory facilities in Maryland, Georgia, and California. ATF provides funding and instructor training for a key prevention program called Gang Resistance Education And Training (GREAT). GREAT is a life skills competency program designed to provide middle-school children the ability to avoid gangs, resist conflict, make responsible decisions, and develop a positive relationship with the law enforcement community. In fiscal year 2002, ATF provided funding to 228 law enforcement agencies and 1,163 officers were certified to instruct in the GREAT program, providing GREAT instruction to 364,701 students (ATF 2004).

## The US Postal Inspection Service

The US Post Office is an independent federal agency with about 3,135 postal inspectors and police officers. They are responsible for criminal investigations covering more than 200 Federal statutes related to the postal system. They also provide security for postal facilities, employees and assets, and escort high-value mail shipments (Reaves and Bauer 2003). It is one of our country's oldest federal law enforcement agencies, founded by Benjamin Franklin. The United States Postal Inspection Service "has a long, proud, and successful history of fighting criminals who attack our nation's postal system and misuse it to defraud, endanger, or otherwise threaten the American public" (US Postal Service 2004). The Postal Inspection Service operates four forensic crime laboratories. They are staffed with forensic scientists and technical specialists who assist inspectors in analyzing evidentiary material needed for identifying and tracing criminal suspects and in providing expert testimony for cases brought to trial.

Federal employment is often a goal of many students pursuing criminal justice degrees. It is evident that the number of agencies involved in the law enforcement function is considerably large. Many of the agencies with investigative and criminal responsibilities often require three years of full-time experience (not necessarily in law enforcement) before being considered for an armed agent or investigative position. Persons graduating from college may want to consider seeking employment with other federal agencies and then transferring to one of the major policing agencies after gaining the necessary experience. **Figure 4-5** describes one of the lesser known but very important federal agencies.

# ■ The Department of Homeland Security

Following the terrorist attacks of September 11, 2001, considerable discussion ensued about the complexity and number of federal agencies involved in intelligence gathering and national security. One result of these debates was Public Law 107-296, signed on November 25, 2002, which established the Department of Homeland Security effective January 24, 2003. This is an executive department agency within the executive branch composed of the following directorates (Office of Personnel Management 2003):

- Office of the Secretary
- Directorate for Border and Transportation Security
- Directorate for Emergency Preparedness and Response
- Directorate for Information Analysis and Infrastructure Protection
- Directorate for Management
- Directorate for Science and Technology

In addition to the five directorates, several other agencies were either folded into the new department or are being created. They include:

- United States Coast Guard
- United States Secret Service

The federal agency responsible for providing security for federal buildings and grounds nationwide is the Federal Protective Service, which until its transfer to the Department of Homeland Security was part of the General Services Administration. Its personnel design security features and programs at federal facilities. Sixty-nine percent of its 732 officers provide police response and patrol services to over one million tenants and daily visitors to all federally owned facilities. The FPS also contracts for security protection at many buildings, and the US Marshals Service additionally provides security at federal courthouses. Its Web site identifies the following responsibilities and initiatives:

Responsibilities:

- Providing a visible uniformed police presence.
- Management and oversight of 10,000 armed contract security guards.
- Responding to criminal incidents and emergencies with full law enforcement authority.
- Authority to detain and arrest individuals and seize goods or vehicles.
- Participation in national and local Federal Anti-terrorism Task Forces.
- Specialized response capabilities—Canine and Weapons of Mass Destruction Teams.
- Providing protection during demonstrations, protests, and acts of civil unrest.
- Investigating criminal incidents.
- Continuous monitoring of building alarms/emergencies through four FPS MegaCenters.
- Conducting building vulnerability and security assessments.
- Implementating appropriate security threat countermeasures.
- Purchasing/installing/monitoring security equipment and enhancements to designated buildings.
- Protection support for special events: Olympics, Kentucky Derby, and Presidential Inaugurals.
- Presenting formal crime prevention/security awareness presentations to the federal population.
- Conducting background suitability determinations and adjudications for contract security guards and GSA daycare workers.
- Providing Federal Emergency Management Agency (FEMA) support.

New Initiatives:

- Deployment of additional weapons capabilities needed to respond to an increased threat.
- Increased participation in the FBI Joint Terrorism Task Force operations nationwide.
- Improved intelligence gathering and sharing capability.
- Expansion of the national MegaCenter alarm monitoring and dispatch operations to all DHS components.
- Resurgence of the government-wide role of the Federal Interagency Security Committee.
- Extending FPS Physical Security Academy training to other ICE components.

*Source:* US Immigration and Customs Enforcement (2004). "Federal Protective Service (FPS)." http://www.ice.gov/graphics/fps/.

**Figure 4-5** Why consider a career with the federal protective service?

— Bureau of Citizenship and Immigration Services
— Office of State and Local Government Coordination
— Office of Private Sector Liaison

## Immigration and Customs Enforcement

The US Immigration and Customs Enforcement (ICE) includes the enforcement and investigation components of the Immigration and Naturalization Service, Customs, the Federal Air Marshals Service, and the Federal Protective Services. The Department of Homeland Security absorbed the former Immigration and Naturalization Service from the Department of Justice and the US Customs Service from the Department of Treasury. The primary function of ICE is the enforcement and investigation of the nation's immigration, customs, and air piracy laws. The mission of the Federal Air Marshal Service is "to be responsible for and protect air security and promote public confidence in our nation's civil aviation system through the effective deployment of Federal Air Marshals in order to detect, deter and defeat hostile acts targeting US air carriers, airports, passengers, and crews" (US Immigration and Custom Enforcement 2004). The Federal Protective Service is described in Figure 4-5.

## Customs and Border Protection Agency

The newly restructured Customs and Border Protection Agency within the Department of Homeland Security includes the former Border Patrol, part of the former Immigration and Naturalization Service, Customs, and Agricultural Quarantine Inspectors. The Border Patrol consists of:

- officers, numbering about 9,830, who detect and prevent smuggling and illegal entry of non-documented persons into the United States at the ports of entry and along/nearby the 8,000 miles of US boundaries
- immigration inspectors, numbering about 4,529, who oversee incoming tourists and those with visas to enter the country
- criminal investigators and immigration agents, numbering about 2,139, who are responsible for investigating crimes under INS jurisdiction and 2,603 officers with detention and deportation duties (Reaves and Bauer 2003)

The US Customs Service (formerly part of the Department of the Treasury) consists of about 11,634 officers. Of these, about 8,167 are inspectors and 3,467 are criminal investigators who interdict and seize contraband, process persons, vehicles, and items at more than 300 ports of entry, and administer certain navigational laws (Reaves and Bauer 2003). The Customs Service has an extensive air, land, and marine interdiction force as well as an investigations component supported by its own intelligence branch. The Customs Service investigates violations of more than 400 laws related to customs, drugs, export control, and revenue fraud. It is the second oldest enforcement agency of the country, founded on July 31, 1789. For nearly 125 years, it funded virtually the entire US government, and paid for the nation's early growth and infrastructure.

## The US Secret Service

The Secret Service was formerly part of the Department of the Treasury. The agency has about 4,256 special agents and officers who have investigation and enforcement duties primarily related to counterfeiting, financial crimes, computer fraud, and threats against dignitaries. The Secret Service is well known for protecting the president and vice president and their immediate families. The Uniformed Division provides protection for the White House complex and other presidential offices, the main treasury building and annex, and foreign diplomatic missions. The Secret Service was created originally in 1865 to combat counterfeiting, but it became the general investigative and law enforcement arm of the federal government until 1908 when Congress restricted its authority.

The Department of Homeland Security is undergoing transition, and it is expected that some reorganization may occur over the next few years. Its creation was the largest reorganization effort of the federal government in nearly 50 years. It combined, in whole or in part, 22 agencies and included over 170,000 existing employees. Students in the field of criminal justice should attempt to keep abreast of the ongoing changes to the department and the many opportunities that will exist in terms of career pursuits. The department's home page can be found at http://www.dhs.gov/dhspublic/.

## Private Policing in the United States

An interesting and often overlooked police-related field is the **private police/ security** profession. It does not have a single title—it has been referred to as "private security," "private policing," "loss prevention," "loss control," "assets protection," and even "risk management." The field encompasses dozens of job titles extending from the uniformed guard at financial and retail establishments to corporate security directors of international companies. It includes private detectives, hospital security personnel, railroad police, nuclear power plant SWAT team members, armored car officers, computer security specialists, access control specialists, electronic technicians, occupational health/safety personnel, fire safety experts, contingency/disaster management planners, and security and crime prevention consultants. Regardless of titles and terms, the field consists primarily of proprietary and contract security personnel. Proprietary security personnel are those who are employed directly by the entity they serve and protect. Contract security personnel are those who are employed by a security services company that contracts security services to others.

The field has many professional associations, the largest one (in terms of individual memberships) being ASIS International (formerly known as the American Society for Industrial Security, but its evolution now encompasses all aspects of the security/loss prevention/assets protection arena). Founded in 1955, today ASIS International has a worldwide membership of over 33,000. It is headquartered in Alexandria, Virginia and has an extensive Web site (www.asisonline.org/). Another influential association is the National Association of Security Companies (NASCO), which is also based in Alexandria, Virginia.

The exact number of security personnel in the United States is difficult to determine because there is no central reporting mechanism to collect such data. According to research, private security is now clearly the nation's primary protective resource, outspending public law enforcement by 73% and employing two times the workforce. The study estimated 1990 annual expenditures for private security at $52 billion and employment of 1.5 million persons. Public law enforcement in that year cost $30 billion and had a workforce of 600,000. In 2002, public policing expenditures were about $69.8 billion for about 800,000 full-time law enforcement officers. If the above trends hold true, then private sector expenditures for protections of all types would exceed $100 billion and employ about two million persons. Private security is a growth industry, with estimates ranging from 8% to 15% per year, depending on which aspect of the field is being considered. One of the fastest growing components is the manufacture, distribution, and installation of security equipment and technology. Historically, the growth rate for private security services is double that of the public sector (Cunningham, et al. 1991) and that was prior to the 9/11 attacks. The uniformed private security component alone is about a $12 billion industry and, according to the US Bureau of Labor Statistics, the demand for private officers is likely to grow faster than average for all occupations through 2010 (Sutherland 2003).

The security field, however, is much broader than the uniformed officers, alarm systems, locks, and security equipment areas. Additionally there are numerous types of supervisory positions—on the local, regional and national levels. Think about it: How do multinational corporations, such as IBM, Citicorp, General Motors, Microsoft, Toyota, and Wal-Mart protect their personnel, facilities, and other assets? There is significant opportunity in the private sector. Consider the following career areas (ASIS International, nd):

| | | |
|---|---|---|
| Construction | Government | Pharmaceutical |
| Corporate | Operations | Retail |
| Credit Card | Healthcare | Security Consulting |
| Educational | Hi-Tech Industry | Security Training |
| Institutions | Information Systems | Special Event |
| Entertainment | Insurance | Anti-Terrorism |
| Executive Protection | Lodging | Transportation |
| Financial Institutions | Manufacturing | Utilities |
| Gaming/Wagering | Nuclear | |

What is the earning power of positions in the private policing field? Annual salaries range from $17,000 to over $100,000 depending on the position and type of business in which one is employed. Obviously the higher salaries are for the "directors" or "chiefs" of security or loss prevention, and the lowest is for uniformed positions.

## Authority and Regulation of Private Police

The authority of private police is primarily dependent upon the law of the state in which the person is employed. Generally, they have no more authority than private citizens, although even that varies from state to state. Many states have enacted specific statutes regulating and delimiting the authority of private persons employed in a security or protective capacity. One study identified 43 states as having statutes regulating security guards with the other seven not doing so. The study only addressed provisions that related to employees of security agencies (Maahs and Hemmens 1998, 124). States may permit the carrying of weapons, the right to detain and arrest, and the right to search persons. State law may address actions ranging from the arrest of shoplifters (in mercantile statutes) to the use of deadly force. The focus of most state regulation is to license certain types of security-related activity such as carrying a firearm, private detective services, security guard services, and alarm installation services (see Figure 4-6).

There are no federal regulations setting standards for the private security field regarding the training and qualifications of officers. In Ohio, only armed, licensed officers must successfully complete a minimum of 20 hours of firearms-related training. If not armed and/or working in a proprietary (as opposed to a contract—for hire—officer) capacity, there is no state requirement of any training. In some states such as California, Florida, and Oklahoma, unarmed security officers must complete 40 hours of training. In 30 other states there are no specific training requirements. Approximately 22 states require officers to be put through a federal background check (Sutherland 2003). In about 22 states they do not have to be licensed and in 16 states there are no state background checks required (Hall 2003). Therefore, private businesses with their own security force and private security companies that provide contract officer services often take it upon themselves to train their own officers. Many establish education and training requirements for employment and even provide annual training to officers.

Based on a recent research, at least 47 states regulate some aspect of private security services:

- 33 states regulate private investigators.
- 47 states regulate contract security and guard services.
- 32 states disqualify the hiring of felons.
- only 2 states have a minimum educational level (8th grade).
- 19 states set the minimum age for employment at age 18; seven states set it at age 21; one at age 22; and seven set the age at 25.
- 16 states require a minimal level of training for armed personnel in security.
- 8 states regulate alarm system contractors.

*Sources:* Charles Buikema and Frank Horvath (1984) and Jeffrey R. Maahs and Craig Hemmens (1998).

**Figure 4-6** What do states regulate in the security field?

Because of the variations among the states, and the reluctance of Congress to set any national standards, professional associations like the National Association of Security Companies (NASCO) and ASIS International are placing greater efforts on influencing state legislatures (Sutherland 2003). ASIS International has a standing Commission on Guidelines which has recommended several for the field, one of which is the Private Security Officer Selection and Training Guideline (see **Figure 4-7** for other guidelines). Other guideline projects are being planned.

Case law (the court's previous decisions) is extremely important within states as to how the law applies to private police. For example, in *Bowman v. State* (1983), an Indiana court ruled that *Miranda* warnings (informing those arrested of their rights) did not have to be given by private police, since they were not involved in "state action" (Hess and Wrobleski 1992, 100). Generally, US constitutional protections only apply to governmental actions, not those of private citizens. In 1921, the United States Supreme Court clearly stated in *Burdeau v. McDowell* (1921) that the Fourth Amendment gives protection against unlawful searches and seizures conducted by governmental agencies. The court held that the Constitution does not protect persons against arrests, searches, and seizures conducted by private parties (including private security personnel). However, the courts also have indicated that if there is a close relationship or a state connection to the actions of the security

The Commission on Guidelines of ASIS International has developed or is developing the following guidelines. The current status of each can be reviewed at their Web site: www.asisonline.org/guidelines/guidelines.htm.

Business Continuity Guideline
Chief Security Officer Guideline
General Security Risk Assessment Guideline
Private Security Officer Selection and Training Guideline
Protecting Information Guideline
Threat Advisory System Response Guideline
Workplace Violence Prevention and Response
Conducting Investigations
Security Countermeasures

*Source:* ASIS International, www.asisonline.org/guidelines/guidelines.htm.

**Figure 4-7** Security-related guidelines.

officer, a review based upon constitutional considerations may be required. In other words, if private security personnel are acting at the request of governmental agents, their actions may be governed by constitutional restrictions (*People v. Selinski* 1979; Euller 1980).

## ■ Certifications and Professionalism

We noted above that there is very limited regulation of the security industry. Since the 1970s the security field has been attempting to improve its image and overall professionalism. One effort that has achieved some success and national recognition is the certification efforts of various national organizations. The ASIS International awarded its first Certified Protection Professional designation in the fall of 1977. Recently, the organization added two other certifications: the Physical Security Professional and the Professional Security Investigator. The eligibility criteria for each certification are displayed in **Table 4-7** (ASIS, http://www.asisonline.org/certification/eligibility.xml).

The National Association of Security Companies (NASCO) consists of 15 large security services providers in the United States and it articulates their mission as being "dedicated to promoting and sustaining professional integrity and competence throughout every aspect of the private security business," (NASCO 2004). It has published a number of position papers on the following topics:

— Digital Electronic Fingerprinting Process
— Statement on Private Security Officer Training
— Statement on Privatization
— Statement on Disabled Persons in the Security Industry
— Security Officer Code of Ethics
— Security Company Code of Ethics

Contents of these papers can be reviewed on their Web site at: http://www.nasco.org/nasco/position-papers.asp. As you can see by the last two items above, there are codes of ethics articulated for the "security officer" and the "security company." A code of ethics is one aspect of improving professionalism in the field. ASIS International also supports a code of ethics for its members, as illustrated in **Figure 4-8**.

### Public and Private Police Relationships

Both the public and private police fields exist for specific purposes or reasons. Public law enforcement is usually responsible for the enforcement of criminal behavior by investigating crime and apprehending offenders. As such, it is reactive in nature and usually responds upon receiving a complaint from a citizen or company. Private policing, on the other hand, has traditionally been focused on prevention of crime, accidents, injuries, and loss of resources, and the detection of crime or emergency situations. Private security extends beyond crime and policing and into areas of loss reduction, safety, hygiene, and risk management.

| Table 4-7 | ASIS International Certifications |

| Certification | Criteria for Eligibility | | | |
| | Experience* | Education* | National Exam | Other |
| --- | --- | --- | --- | --- |
| Certified Protection Professional (CPP) | 9 years of security experience, at least 3 years of which shall have been in responsible charge of a security function; **OR** | An earned Bachelor's Degree or higher from an accredited institution of higher education and 7 years of security experience, at least 3 years of which shall have been in responsible charge of a security function. | Yes | No convictions for any criminal offense that would reflect negatively on the security profession, ASIS, or the CPP program. |
| Physical Security Professional (PSP) | 5 years of experience in the physical security field. | A high school diploma or GED equivalent. | Yes | No convictions for any criminal offense that would reflect negatively on the security profession, ASIS, or the PSP program. |
| Professional Certified Investigator (PCI) | 5 years of investigations experience, with at least two (2) years in case management. | A high school diploma or GED equivalent. | Yes | No convictions for any criminal offense that would reflect negatively on the security profession, ASIS, or the PCI program. |

*Source:* ASIS, http://www.asisonline.org/certification/pci/pcieligibility.xml.

*For exact definitions of terms see: http://www.asisonline.org/certification/eligibility.xml.

**Preamble**

Aware that the quality of professional security activity ultimately depends upon the willingness of practitioners to observe special standards of conduct and to manifest good faith in professional relationships, the American Society for Industrial Security adopts the following Code of Ethics and mandates its conscientious observance as a binding condition of membership in or affiliation with the society.

**Code of Ethics**

I. A member shall perform professional duties in accordance with the law and highest moral principles.

II. A member shall observe the precepts of truthfulness, honesty, and integrity.

III. A member shall be faithful and diligent in discharging professional responsibilities.

IV. A member shall be competent in discharging professional responsibilities.

V. A member shall safeguard confidential information and exercise due care to prevent its improper disclosure.

VI. A member shall not maliciously injure the professional reputation or practice of colleagues.

*Source:* ASIS International, used with permission.

**Figure 4-8** American Society for Industrial Security—code of ethics.

There are areas of obvious conflict and concern in which it appears that public and private police are responsible for the same thing, such as protecting areas open to the public (e.g., supermarkets, banks, bus terminals, etc.). When uniformed private officers are involved, they are "supplementing" the public agency's responsibility. Public agencies do not have enough personnel to permanently assign officers to private establishments to provide protection. Private officers also "complement" public agency responsibility in that the public officers have limited authority on totally private property and may not even provide the services that the private officers perform. These services include private employment background checks, armored car services, private detective work, alarm installation and monitoring, initially investigating suspected financial crimes, and protecting trade secrets or sensitive corporate information and data.

The general relationship between private and public officers varies from place to place. Some communities have worked hard to promote a clear understanding of the roles of each entity. In other places, visible conflict may exist. This may be the case even though some estimates categorize 20% of the security personnel in the United States as off-duty public officers working a second job. In fact, both groups are needed. The public cannot afford to employ all the security personnel at its expense, and clearly much of what private security involves is not a public responsibility.

Since the terrorist attacks of 9/11, greater emphasis and concern regarding the relationships between public law enforcement and private policing entities has occurred. Several cities are including local private security and loss prevention personnel in their overall emergency planning strategies. One unique program has actually been in operation since 1990. The Atlanta Police Department has implemented a technique called Communications Network (COMNET); it is a continuous link between private sector security providers and the department. It is a two-way, VHF radio network, established to provide quick and efficient communications between the security providers and the department. The city recognizes that private security officers can often serve as the first line of notification for the police department since they are visible, trained, and strategically posted on property throughout the city. Today, COMNET links over 150 member sites that include campus police departments, federal agencies, the downtown improvement district, corporate and hotel security departments, retail loss prevention departments, and property management companies (Atlanta Police Department 2004: http://www.atlantapd.org/). The city of Dallas has implemented the Downtown Emergency Response Team (DERT) to implement its emergency plan. The details of any major crisis can be announced over a local AM radio station dedicated to emergency announcements. Key groups are updated throughout the incident. Once an incident is reported, other groups such as the Downtown Improvement District (DID) can put an emergency call on the organization's email-based text-messaging system that can reach DERT's members via emails and by text message to mobile devices—cell phones, PDAs, and pagers. Property managers, security directors, and engineers in all of the downtown buildings are kept informed of the incident, which helps coordinate resources in both the public and private sectors. DERT was actually envisioned prior to 9/11, but the attacks brought greater interest and cooperation from the downtown community to get organized for major incidents or catastrophes. Dallas has had a history of public police and security cooperation. For example, the Law Enforcement and Private Security (LEAPS) program began in 1995 and has been operated by the Dallas Police Department. It has over 125 local law enforcement and corporate members and holds monthly meetings to share information. One major function of the LEAPS is to coordinate issues and problems related to law enforcement and security (Anderson 2004).

With approximately 85% of the nation's infrastructure protected by private security personnel, there needs to be greater cooperation between public and private policing efforts. In 2004, a national policy summit was undertaken through the cooperative efforts of the International Association of Chiefs of Police and the Office of Community Oriented Policing Services (COPS) of the Department of Justice. The summit participants undertook their tasks in six working groups and produced five policy recommendations. According to the report of the proceedings of the summit, the first four recommendations are national-level and long-term in scope. The fifth recommendation relates to local and regional efforts that could begin immediately. The policy recommendations are:

1. Leaders of the major law enforcement and private security organizations should make a formal commitment to cooperation.
2. The Department of Homeland Security and/or Department of Justice should fund research and training on relevant legislation, private security, and law enforcement—private security cooperation.
3. The Department of Homeland Security and/or Department of Justice should create an advisory council composed of nationally prominent law enforcement and private security professionals to oversee the day-to-day implementation issues of law enforcement—private security partnerships.
4. The Department of Homeland Security and/or Department of Justice, along with relevant membership organizations, should convene key practitioners to move this agenda forward in the future.
5. Local partnerships should set priorities and address key problems as identified by the summit. Examples of local and regional activities that can and should be undertaken immediately include the following:
   - Improve joint response to critical incidents.
   - Coordinate infrastructure protection.

- Improve communications and data interoperability.
- Bolster information and intelligence sharing.
- Prevent and investigate high-tech crime.
- Devise responses to workplace violence.

If the United States is going to be a safe nation, secure in its infrastructure and institutions, the public law enforcement sector must initiate cooperative initiatives with private security and assets protection agencies and their personnel who work diligently every day to prevent crime and to protect property, visitors, and employees.

## ■ Summary

The public law enforcement community of the United States consists of nearly 17,000 separate agencies employing over 800,000 personnel. Those agencies are found throughout the political subdivisions of each state and of the federal government. Consequently, the law enforcement system of the United States is fragmented and non-standardized. Each agency operates within its own jurisdiction; each agency has its own chief executive official; and each agency operates within its own rules and regulations. Some of these agencies possess general police authority, while others are restricted to specific police authority such as offenses related to the traffic code, fish and wildlife, or narcotics.

In 2002, public policing expenditures were about $69.8 billion. It is estimated that the private policing sector today expends about $100 billion and employs about two million persons. Although the authority of private police is usually the same as private individuals, they serve the private sector by supplementing and complementing local public policing efforts. They provide protection for private property that cannot be provided by local public police. The major focus of private policing is on the prevention and detection of crime rather than the investigation of crime and the apprehension of offenders. The events of September 11, 2001 have had a significant effect on both the public and private sectors of law enforcement and security. Greater focus has been placed on prevention, intelligence sharing, and public-private partnerships. The future holds many opportunities for personnel in both sectors.

## QUESTIONS FOR REVIEW

1. In what branch of US governmental structure is law enforcement found? Why is this the case?

2. Define the following terms or principles of government: federalism, checks and balances, three branches of government, implied powers doctrine, and judicial review.

3. What is meant by a "political subdivision" of a state? Name at least four such subdivisions.

4. Approximately how many law enforcement agencies are there in the United States? How many persons do they employ?

5. Compare and contrast "specific police authority" and "general police authority."

6. Identify the major federal law enforcement agencies with investigative and criminal responsibilities and their organizational placement (major department) in the federal government structure.

7. Explain the major reorganization of law enforcement agencies at the federal level brought about by the creation of the Department of Homeland Security.

8. Explain the purpose and extent of private policing in the United States.

## SUGGESTED ACTIVITIES

1. Obtain accurate figures regarding how many sworn police officers your state has. You may want to log on to the Bureau of Justice Statistics at http://www.ojp.usdoj.gov/bjs/ to review additional data, analyses, graphs and updated statistics about law enforcement and criminal justice issues in the United States.

2. Identify the various law enforcement agencies in your state or a neighboring state. Based on information in this chapter, determine whether they possess specific or general police authority.

3. Select one local, state, and federal agency and search the World Wide Web for sites that contain information about each one. Compile a three-page report on what you found.

4. Check your state laws on the regulation and licensing of private security and private investigators. You may need to call or write to a licensing board for the criteria and requirements for licensing. Check the World Wide Web for such information as well.

5. Search the World Wide Web for selected federal law enforcement agencies and write an agency profile on one of the agencies not described in this text.

6. Using the Internet, log on to http://www.asisonline.org and navigate the site to review the scope of the private security and loss prevention field.

7. Log onto the NAPO Web site (http://www.nasco.org/nasco/position-papers.asp) and compare the similarities and differences between the officer's and company's codes of ethics, and then compare both of them to the ASIS Code of Ethics printed in this chapter.

## ■ Chapter Glossary

**checks and balances** (or **separation of powers**)  a mechanism for preventing any one branch of government (executive, legislative, or judicial) from becoming too powerful.

**concurrent** or **overlapping jurisdiction**  when two or more law enforcement agencies, often from different levels of government, have jurisdiction (the right and authority), or are empowered to respond to and investigate criminal complaints in a given geographical area.

**federalism**  a form of representative democracy establishing a "dual system" of government made up of the federal and state systems.

**general police authority**  police responsibility extends to most any criminal offense committed within the jurisdiction.

**implied powers doctrine** (or the **necessary and proper clause**)  Article I, Section 8 (Paragraph 18) of the United States Constitution, which grants Congress the right to enact laws in order to properly carry out the specific rights of Congress enumerated in the Constitution.

**judicial review**  the authority of the courts to review cases from lower courts and rule on constitutionality of laws.

**political subdivisions**  jurisdictions or entities created by the state that possess authority and control over local matters. The most common names for these political subdivisions include: county, municipality or city, village, borough, and township.

**private police/security**  a policing-related field found in the private sector that is referred to as "private security," "private policing," "loss prevention," "loss control," "assets protection," and even "risk management"; the field emphasizes prevention and detection of crime and safety hazards.

**specific police authority**  police responsibility and the right to investigate limited by law to certain matters.

## ■ Chapter References

Anderson, Teresa (2004). "Dallas Gets DERT on Downtown." www.securitymanagement.com/library/001652.html.

ASIS International (2004a). ASIS Guidelines Update. *ASIS Dynamics*, July/August, 8.

ASIS International (2004b). "Code of Ethics." http://www.asisonline.org/membership/resources/code-ofethics.xml.

ASIS International (nd). "Career Opportunities in Security," Alexandria, VA: ASIS International.

ATF (2004). "2004 Bureau of Alcohol, Tobacco, Firearms and Explosives (ATF)" http://www.atf.gov/about/snap2004.htm.

Buikema, Charles and Frank Horvath (1984). Security Regulation—A State-by-State Update. *Security Management*, January 1984, Vol. 28, No. 1:39–43.

*Burdeau v. McDowell*. 256 US 475 (1921).

Cunningham, William C., John J. Struchs, and Clifford W. Van Meter (1991). *Private Security: Patterns and Trends*. Washington, DC: National Institute of Justice.

Customs and Border Protection (2004). *Customs and Border Protection Today*, Vol 2, No. 9, September 2004, http://www.cbp.gov/xp/CustomsToday/2004/Sep/.

DEA (2004). "DEA Mission Statement." http://www.usdoj.gov/dea/agency/mission.htm.

Euller, Stephen (1980). Private Security in the Courtroom: The Exclusionary Rule Applies. *Security Management, March 1980*. Vol. 24, No. 3:38–40.

FBI (2004a). "FBI Priorities." http://www.fbi.gov/priorities/priorities.htm.

FBI (2004b). "FBI Headquarters." http://www.fbi.gov/hq/area.htm.

FBI (2003). *Crime in the United States, 2002*. Washington, DC: US Department of Justice.

Hall, Mimi (2003). Private Security Guards: Homeland defense's weak link. *USA Today*, January 23, pp. 1A and 6A.

Hess, Karen M. and Henry M. Wrobleski (1992). *Introduction to Private Security, Third Edition*. St. Paul, Minnesota: West Publishing Co.

Hickman, Matthew J. and Brian Reaves (2003). *Local Police Departments, 2000*. Washington DC: US Department of Justice.

Hunter, Ronald D. (Fall 1990). Three Models of Policing. *Police Studies*, Vol. 13, No. 3:118–123.

IACP/COPS (2004). *National Policy Summit: Building Private Security/Public Policing Partnerships to Prevent and Respond to Terrorism and Public Disorder*. Ohlhausen Research, Inc., http://www.cops.usdoj.gov/mime/open.pdf?Item=1355.

Lindgren, Sue A. (1997). *Justice Expenditures and Employment Extracts, 1992: Data from the Annual General Finance and Employment Surveys*. Washington, DC: US Department of Justice.

Maahs, Jeffrey R. and Craig Hemmens (1998). Guarding the Public: A Statutory Analysis of State Regulation of Security Guards. *Journal of Crime and Justice*, Vol. XXI, No. 1., pp. 119–134.

NASCO (2004). "Mission Statement." http://www.nasco.org/nasco/mission-summary.asp.

Office of Personnel Management (July 2003). *Federal Civilian Workforce Statistics Employment and Trends as of March 2003*. Washington, DC: United States Office Of Personnel Management.

*People v. Zelinski*. 594 P.2d 1000 (1979).

Reaves, Brian A. (1998). *Federal Law Enforcement Officers, 1996*. Washington, DC: US Department of Justice.

Reaves, Brian A. (December 1996). Campus Law Enforcement Agencies, 1995. Washington, DC: US Department of Justice.

Reaves, Brian A. and Lynn M. Bauer (2003). *Federal Law Enforcement Officers, 2002*. Washington, DC: Bureau of Justice Statistics, US Department of Justice.

Reaves, Brian A. and Matthew Hickman (2003). *Census of State and Local Law Enforcement Agencies, 2000*. Washington, DC: Bureau of Justice Statistics, US Department of Justice.

Reaves, Brian A. and Matthew J. Hickman (2001). *Sheriffs' Offices 1999*, Washington, DC: Bureau of Justice Statistics, US Department of Justice.

Reaves, Brian and Pheny Z. Smith (1996). *Sheriffs' Departments, 1993*. Washington DC: US Department of Justice.

Reaves, Brian A. and Pheny Z. Smith (1995). *Law Enforcement Management and Administrative Statistics, 1993: Data for Individual State and Local Agencies with 100 or More Officers*. Washington, DC: US Department of Justice.

Sutherland, Randy (2003). "Pushing for Better Private Security Officers." http://securitysolutions.com/mag/security_pushing_better_private/.

US Immigration and Custom Enforcement (2004). "Federal Air Marshal Service." http://www.ice.gov/graphics/fams/index.htm.

US Marshals Service (2004). "Major Responsibilities of the US Marshals Service." http://www.usdoj.gov/marshals/duties/index.html.

US Postal Service (2004). "Who We Are." http://www.usps.com/websites/depart/inspect/missmore.htm.

# Organizational Structure and Its Impact

**5**

## Learning Objectives

This chapter addresses the questions of how organizational structure relates to the effectiveness of the police and the ability to meet the challenges from society. By studying and understanding these ideas you will be able to:

- State why law enforcement agencies are nationally organized in similar ways.
- Identify the reasons why traditional organizational structure is now questioned.
- Describe the newer organizational strategies being implemented nationally.
- Explain the benefits that can be derived from organizational change.
- Identify the importance of the patrol officer and supervisor in contemporary law enforcement management approaches.
- Define the benefits and limits of both traditional and contemporary law enforcement organizational designs.

## Chapter Outline

IV. Contemporary Management Theory

V. Summary

## Key Terms Used in This Chapter

organization theory

organization behavior

human relations/humanistic

human resource

classical organization theory

rationalization

hierarchy

bureaucracy

scientific management

span of control

unity of command

organize by function

organize by product

dominance of an idea

structuring by authority

task force

stable environment

dynamic environment

goal displacement

trained incapacity

organizational dysfunction

organize by time

organize by place

organize by clientele

motivation

leadership

motivators

hygiene factors/maintainers

satisfaction

stress

job enrichment

traits

contingent leadership

systems theory

contingency theory

matrix organization

problem-oriented policing

team policing

flat design/flat organization

## ■ Organization Theory, Its Development, and Its Impact on Law Enforcement

Law enforcement agencies are, above all else, organizations. In law enforcement, as in all other areas of government, questions about size, function, and role are directly related to how law enforcement agencies are organized and the reasons for a particular form of organization. Another word for organization is organizational arrangement—how the various pieces of the organization relate to one another, what function they play, and the goals they seek. We organize to do work, and the nature of the work determines how best to organize. For example, a fast food restaurant is typically organized in a production line fashion in order to get orders out fast. Every person has a specialized job and the work (order taking and processing) is passed from one specialist to the next. Efficiency is the goal or value sought in that organizational arrangement. Similarly, law enforcement organizations are organized around their work. After discussing some general concepts of organization theory, we will address the challenges facing law enforcement in the early twenty-first century as the work begins to change.

This chapter introduces students to law enforcement organizational structure. It proceeds from the assumption that students are prepared to discard preconceived notions of how an organization should be structured. Accordingly, this chapter invites the student to consider multiple options of organization. As this material is read and pondered, memories of organizational experiences should be called upon for examples. Every one of us has been in organizations, even if we did not think of them as such. The Girl Scouts and Boy Scouts, churches, political parties, schools, our employment location, fraternities and sororities, the military, colleges, universities, and even neighborhood watch groups provide examples of organizations. Each is slightly different, and they are different for a reason. The student should examine those differences as we discuss law enforcement organizations which also differ greatly.

Generally, there are two fields of theory and practice of which law enforcement students should be aware. First is **organization theory**, which is a body of research and practice that looks at organizational arrangements in a structural sense, much like a map. The subjects of organization theory include how an organization should be structured, how tasks should be divided, how personnel should be assigned to those tasks, and the level of control or supervision over their work. The second field of study and practice is **organization behavior**, which examines how people act within an organization. This field includes motivation, leadership, group dynamics, and organizational change and development. Subfields include the **human relations** and **human resource** movements. The former addresses the needs of individuals in an organization, while the latter views the individual as an organizational asset. Both are treated here in the context of human relations theory as a single topic. Each of these sub-fields and topics will be examined in turn, together with their importance to law enforcement personnel.

Organizations have been a part of social life from the beginning of recorded history. The Romans, for example, had very complex bureaucracies before the birth of Christ, and the Greeks before the Romans. Still, very little theory about organization design survived. There is evidence that thought was given to the problem of how to organize. Aristotle, for instance, wrote in 360 BC of some organizational issues influenced by culture. Even earlier, the Chinese philosopher Sun Tzu, in his classic work *The Art of War*, discussed the need for hierarchy in organizing armies (see **Figure 5-1**). An early Muslim scholar, Abu Yusuf, discussed the administrative problems of Islamic government, including finance and criminal justice (Shafritz and Ott 1992). What emerged from these early efforts are scattered general ideas about the organization of large entities. Heavy duty, "industrial strength" organization theory really did not arrive until the advent of the industrial revolution.

## ■ Classical Organization Theory

Throughout most of the early history of the United States, the postal department was the largest government organization. As a highly decentralized organization, little thought was given to its structure. Moreover, from the earliest days of the nation there was virtually no permanent army or navy. The nation was

Sun Tzu said:

The art of war is of vital importance to the state. It is a matter of life and death, a road either to safety or to ruin. Hence under no circumstances can it be neglected.

The art of war is governed by five constant factors, all of which need to be taken into account. They are: the Moral Law; Heaven; Earth; the Commander; Method and discipline.

The *Moral Law* causes the people to be in complete accord with their ruler, so that they will follow him regardless of their lives, undismayed by any danger.

*Heaven* signifies night and day, cold and heat, times and seasons.

*Earth* comprises distances, great and small; danger and security; open ground and narrow passes; the chances of life and death.

The *Commander* stands for the virtues of wisdom, sincerity, benevolence, courage, and strictness.

By *Method and discipline* are to be understood the marshaling of the army in proper subdivisions, the gradation of rank among the officers, the maintenance of roads by which supplies may reach the army, and the control of military expenditure.

These five factors should be familiar to every general. He who knows them will be victorious; he who knows them not will fail.

*Source:* Clavell, James (ed.) (1983). *The Art of War by Sun Tzu*. New York: Delacorte Press, 9–10.

**Figure 5-1** *The Art of War by Sun Tzu.*

largely agricultural as well. Accordingly, there was little experience with permanent, large scale organizations anywhere, in the United States. Indeed, the first law enforcement organizations were created at a time in our nation's history when little thought was given to organizing an enterprise of any sort—public or private. Moreover, it just happens that formal law enforcement formed at a time when local governments (cities, towns, and counties) were generally run by political parties for the benefit of the party members.

In the election of 1828, Andrew Jackson was elected president and he came to office in 1829 with a unique perspective on government in a democracy. He argued that elections should be employed not only to elect officials, but to fire those who worked for the loser. In short, "To the victor belong the spoils," a system that came to be called the "spoils system." If you wanted a job as a police officer, you joined the party, and voted and donated a portion of your salary to the party. In return, the party took care of you. Because there was no training and the only criteria for selection was party support, police were little more than political hacks. This is not a particularly pretty picture, but it is essentially correct. Because they were known to be nothing but politicians, they employed violence and brutality to maintain order—if they did anything. Teddy Roosevelt, a newly appointed Commissioner of Police in the early 1900s, set out one day to see where his officers were. He found them in bars (drunk), in alleys (gambling), and in houses of ill repute. He quit in frustration after trying to bring some semblance of order to what was essentially a uniformed mob (Knott and Miller 1987; Walker 1998). This system of political patronage was partially responsible for the development of civil service systems (see **Figure 5-2**).

In the late 1800s a movement, a "progressive reform" movement, rose in the Midwest as a political backlash to the political machines that had come to dominate local and state government. One of the concerns carried out by this movement was the improvement of public works. The objective was to hire by merit, train people for specialized jobs, promote by merit (not by who you knew), and discipline by rule. If the earlier period can properly be called the "political" era in policing, the emerging era in the 1900s was the "professional" era—one in which law enforcement came to look more and more like a profession with standards for performance and training.

At the head of the charge for professionalization were some of the most important leaders in law enforcement, including August Vollmer, O.W. Wilson, and V.A. Leonard. The influence of organization science, particularly in the case of Vollmer, who was one of the first presidents of the IACP, presented the first major change in law enforcement management. Vollmer was a fan of Frederick Taylor and his notion of "scientific management." Vollmer adopted Taylor's ideas from beginning to end. Vollmer's leadership, teaching, and writing influenced others who in turn adopted Taylorism and other aspects of what came to be called "classical organization theory," or sometimes, just "orthodoxy."

The creation of police departments, schools, sanitation districts, fire departments, and prisons required greater attention to the organization and management of large-scale organizations. The models for organizational design were necessarily drawn from the military model, the Roman Catholic Church, or the newly emerging economic model (mass production lines). **Figure 5-3** illustrates a typical organizational chart for a large agency and **Figure 5-4** explains the rationale for "interpreting" the meaning of the lines connecting the boxes and the relationships that can be determined by such charts. (Also, see Appendix III of the text for additional organizational charts for selected agencies.)

In the next sections, we discuss the development of classical organization theory and its direct impact on law enforcement. We describe how, particularly in local law enforcement, it produced organizational culture, structure, and goals that in the minds of some were not wholly consistent with major law enforcement policy shifts of the twenty-first century (notably community policing and problem oriented policing). We also discuss the conflicts, possible solutions, and misconceptions associated with organization science.

When the United States began as a nation, the process of hiring for government positions was generally political. There was no standing army or navy and very little in the way of administrative agencies. There were not many jobs. As the nation grew, it became clear to some that only the elite were serving in government either by election or appointment. These were generally white males with money and education. They were the same citizens who controlled the new states as well as the new federal government. In the 1820s General Andrew Jackson ran for the presidency and vowed that "the common man" should run government. He also vowed that if elected the person being elected should take only friends into office. For him, this was democracy. Whoever wins the election should run the entire government. It was said, "To the victor belong the spoils. . . ." Hence, it came to be called the spoils system. By the 1880s, as cities grew and city services expanded to police, fire, road, and sanitation services, nearly every city was run by one party. Some cities were democratic while other were republican. But if you did not work for that party, you could not get a job (and sometimes, services). When President Garfield was assassinated by a job seeker who did not get a job in 1881, Congress passed a major civil service bill in 1883. As the use of civil service merit hiring grew, political machines died. However, civil service also places employees beyond political control, which makes government respond more slowly. Political hiring and merit hiring both have benefits and detriments.

**Figure 5-2** The spoils system and civil service.

## Max Weber

The evolution of early organization practices led several theorists to develop highly articulated theories about organization design. Max Weber, writing in the late 1800s (but not published in English before 1922), suggested that organizations represented the natural trend in society toward what he called **rationalization**. Drawing upon early theory and his observations about world social development, Weber concluded that the essential aspect of organization was **hierarchy** represented by the emergence of **bureaucracy**. This meant a division of labor, clear

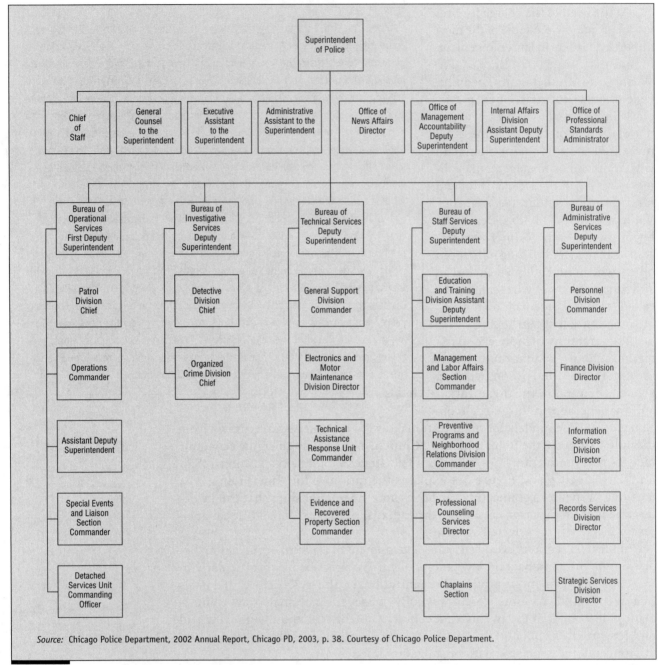

Source: Chicago Police Department, 2002 Annual Report, Chicago PD, 2003, p. 38. Courtesy of Chicago Police Department.

**Figure 5-3** Typical traditional organizational chart design.

lines of authority, specialization and communication between superior and subordinate, a single unifying authority at the top of the hierarchy producing a clear chain of command, and, most important, hiring and promotion based upon merit and productivity, not personality or politics (Gortner, Mahler, and Nicholson 1987). Weber was a social scientist (sociology by trade) and examined what he saw as emerging patterns of behavior in society. He neither recommended nor dismissed organizations so designed. Rather, he argued that society was getting progressively more "rational"—that is, choices made on the basis of criteria, not on the basis of charisma (personal power), or tradition ("this is how we have always done it"). That society generally was becoming rational held certain effects for public organizations, including law enforcement. Rules and criteria would replace personality and habit. This single condition would lead to a trend to remove direct political influence from law enforcement organizations, and hence remove public contact from public organizations. There were other theorists, however, who had far greater direct impact on police organizations, and none was more important than Frederick Winslow Taylor.

## Frederick Winslow Taylor

Another theorist of the same era, Taylor, examined both the way people work (job design) and the way the organization is structured. His **Scientific Management** Theory centered on understanding the work to be done

A table of organization is a chart that shows the positions in an organization and the prescribed interaction between those positions. Each little box on such a chart represents a position or a category of positions. Height on the page is a measure of status. Vertical lines represent the interaction of superiors and subordinates. Horizontal lines represent the interaction of equals.

Any table of organization resembles any other in representing the structure of the organization to consist of positions and interactions. Positions are identified by activity and status. The title of the position on the chart ordinarily identifies its activity. Its distance from the bottom or the top of the chart measures its status. The lines that are drawn between positions indicate prescribed (or occasionally observed) interaction with other positions. Most tables of organization emphasize interaction between superiors and direct subordinates. They minimize or omit interaction between equals and between widely separated positions.

It is sometimes objected that the table of organization does not tell us how an organization works, only how it is *supposed* to work. Informal interaction accounts for part of the discrepancy, but there are other reasons, too, such as the tendency for information to lag behind the small social changes that occur continuously and the tendency for desirable conditions to be hopefully included as facts. . . . Nevertheless, the table of organization always tells us a great deal, and it is doubtful whether we can talk sensibly about a particular organization without it.

*Source:* Adapted from Caplow, Theodore (1964). *Principles of Organization*. New York: Harcourt, Brace & World, 50–62.

**Figure 5-4** Reading a traditional organizational chart.

by breaking it down into its smallest parts (which he called "therbligs"). By understanding the work better, you could scientifically train a worker to do exactly what the job required. He also developed the organizational idea of a planning staff to give management direction (Fry 1989). These notions, together with those of Weber, gave organizations a model for structuring work. Define the job, train to the tasks of that job, hire the best trained, promote on the same basis, and have a strong and clear hierarchy—all of which were consistent with the themes of the progressive reform movement and Vollmer's call for professionalization. Taylor's purpose was to directly link skill and productivity to pay. He reasoned that if skill was in place and properly applied, productivity should follow. Hence, the notion of "job design" contributed to organization theory as well as the nature of organizational arrangement concerns. The fact that Vollmer and other leading executives and the emerging field of police science regarded Taylor's scientific management so highly would deeply impact the structuring and managing of law enforcement organizations for three generations, well into the 1970s.

## Luther Gulick

In the period of the late 1930s, other organization theorists added to the growing body of thought. The most famous, Luther Gulick, a trusted advisor to then

President Franklin Roosevelt, noted that there were limits to the ways work could be divided. He argued that effective communications were essential, and that the **span of control**—the number of employees supervised—should be small. This meant that no single individual should control more than a few people (three to seven). Further, the notion of **unity of command** should apply from the top of an organization to the bottom. This meant that every individual should report to only one individual in the organization, and the line of authority (or chain of command) was traceable from any person to the top of the organization.

Most interestingly, he started the debate over whether you should organize by function or organize by product (both defined later in this chapter), a concept very important to current designs for law enforcement organizations. Finally, he noted that you could also control an organization either by **dominance of an idea** or by **structuring authority** (Shafritz and Ott 1992). Dominance of an idea meant that a set of values (such as a mission statement or agency goals) could dominate the management of an organization and direct its activities. Structuring by authority was simply the use of hierarchical authority to impose management's desires by orders and supervision. The primary problems in organizations are control and coordination (Marsden et al. 1994). The cause of these concerns is the need to direct members of the organization toward policy goals set by the organization, not individuals. Complex organizations, those that carry out many tasks with ambiguous processes, are particularly in need of controlling and directly organizing members. Law enforcement is no different, and we need look no farther than use of force questions to understand management's need to control and coordinate. Thus, while structuring by authority is important, so are values, ideas, mission statements, and policies and procedures—dominance by ideas.

## Classical Theory Applied to Policing

The body of concepts and philosophy from Weber, Taylor, and Gulick, among others, is frequently called **classical organization theory** (see **Figure 5-5**). It took hold in policing for three major reasons. The first was political reform. Prior to the early 1900s, police forces were quite political, and hiring was politically influenced as positions of rank such as captain were literally bought and sold (Knott and Miller 1987). The so-called spoils system of politics controlled government.

The Progressive Reform Movement of the late 1800s and early 1900s sought to end these abuses, in part by advocating reliance on a civil service system. This system employed objective testing for employment and promotion. However, reformers also wanted to maintain some political accountability. In a democracy, there should be some way to control government agencies and maintain political accountability. An organization run much as Weber and Taylor suggested would theoretically achieve these competing goals. Political control would come from carefully designing the jobs to be performed and the manner of performance. A single executive, merit hiring, and promotion would ensure that the most qualified would be employed and be responsible to one person.

One executive
Unity of command
Chain of command
Short span of control
Merit hire (qualifications)
Scientifically designed jobs
Merit promotion (performance)
Division of labor and specialization
Line and staff functions defined by position

**Figure 5-5** Tenets of classical organization theory.

The second reason for the hold that classical theory had on policing was the use of the paramilitary model of command which fit well in a classic hierarchy. Third, the effort to professionalize law enforcement reinforced the importance of merit and, therefore, hierarchy. The professionalization movement, as noted earlier, was the focus of teaching and writing on law enforcement management; hence the influence of the likes of Vollmer and Leonard.

Classical writers in organization theory often referred to their observations as the "principles of scientific management." These principles were applied to law enforcement agencies throughout the United States just at the time professionalization and political reform were taking hold. Accordingly, most existing police departments tend to emulate the traditional hierarchical model of an organization. The organizational chart in Figure 5-3 is an example of what resulted from the application of traditional organization theory. The trademarks of classic organizations included distinct levels, the differentiation between units (specialization), progressive promotion from within based upon merit, and a single line of authority from top to bottom. The following sections examine some of the ways in which classical principles were applied to policing organizations, and these are followed by a discussion of more contemporary designs.

## Organization by Product and Function

When Luther Gulick observed that an enterprise could organize by function or by product, he concluded that the most effective means was to organize by function (Gulick 1937). A function is a narrow job orientation. This was the prevailing belief in most government agencies, and, as Figure 5-3 demonstrates, this became the accepted organization method in police agencies. In early application, **organization by product** was ignored in law enforcement agencies. Organization by product means that all officers needed to produce a result, such as drug arrests. Organization by product is more of an end result focus, rather than a task focus. This would include patrol, investigation, clerical, non-sworn officers, and other support staff throughout the agency. **Organization by function** is characterized by grouping employees together according to the major functions that they performed. The number of functions grew as administrative and service demands grew. A listing of typical functions serviced by police agencies is indicated in **Figure 5-6**.

The most obvious function associated with law enforcement is patrol. In an agency that was organized solely by function, patrol units would be unrelated to other units except by chain of command (see Chapter 7 for a detailed discussion of patrol). In some departments, specialized patrol teams using helicopters, bicycles, motorcycles, boats, or horses may be organized as separate units or deployed as part of the general patrol unit. In larger departments, there may be traffic units that are separate from general patrol. Others may have specialized patrol functions such as park patrol, harbor or river patrol, or border patrol. In each case, the method or design of organization is related to function. The organization of each department is re-

| | |
|---|---|
| Criminal investigation | |
| Personnel | Budgetary control |
| Criminal identification | Purchasing |
| Communications | Crime prevention |
| Traffic regulation and control | Transportation |
| Planning | Property control |
| Police records | Follow-up control |
| Statistical operations | Jail administration |
| Supply | Public relations |
| Criminalistics | Intelligence |
| Patrol | Internal affairs |
| | Community relations |

**Figure 5-6** Functional activities.

lated to the variety of functions identified by that department. Many functions, such as general patrol, are common to nearly all departments while others, such as harbor patrol or school patrol, are employed in only a few places. **Figure 5-7** identifies the typical line and staff functions within policing agencies.

Similarly, while all law enforcement agencies perform investigations, most have designated investigators or detectives, but the use of personnel is defined by local circumstances. There is usually a separate detective bureau or investigations unit. In larger agencies, these may be further broken down into heavily specialized investigative units (e.g., burglary, robber, sex crimes, and homicide squads). Sometimes specialized units are given the name **task force**, though technically, a task force is really a temporary organizational unit that is created for a limited purpose. Examples are organized crime task forces or narcotics task forces, which may be inter-agency units (e.g., composed of members from several different law enforcement agencies).

Still other departments create permanent units and give them a title that conveys permanency, such as an organized crime unit. The most common such units specialize in organized crime, narcotics, auto theft, vice (gambling and prostitution), crimes against women (rape and domestic violence), gangs, and white collar crime. Newer problems have introduced new functional demands such as environmental crime, terrorism, computer (cyber) crime, and growing levels of official corruption. Whether these are given specialized status or not depends solely upon the need and priorities of the agency, which accounts for the wide variation in organizational applications across the country. For example, white collar crime is more likely in communities with high concentrations of banking, insurance, or securities activities. Environmental crimes are more likely in communities with industrial facilities using toxic materials, agricultural facilities, and concentrations of transportation such as railroads and major truck routes.

Other organizational functions are relatively similar from agency to agency such as records, personnel, and purchasing. In larger agencies, these are usually separate offices or units. In smaller agencies, functions are frequently combined. For example, criminalistics may be part of the investigations unit, while crime prevention, public relations, and community relations may be combined into one unit. The organization principle, however, is generally the same—personnel functions determine organizational placement.

There are both benefits and limitations to this organizational principle. Beneficially, the organi-

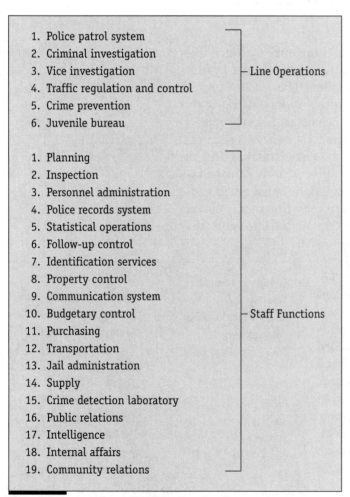

1. Police patrol system
2. Criminal investigation
3. Vice investigation
4. Traffic regulation and control
5. Crime prevention
6. Juvenile bureau

— Line Operations

1. Planning
2. Inspection
3. Personnel administration
4. Police records system
5. Statistical operations
6. Follow-up control
7. Identification services
8. Property control
9. Communication system
10. Budgetary control
11. Purchasing
12. Transportation
13. Jail administration
14. Supply
15. Crime detection laboratory
16. Public relations
17. Intelligence
18. Internal affairs
19. Community relations

— Staff Functions

**Figure 5-7** Common line and staff functions in police agencies.

zational chart indicates who to contact for a given question or problem. Another benefit is the clarity it brings to the organization. Individual duties and responsibilities are more easily defined, making it simpler to train and integrate new personnel. Politically and administratively, this approach produces clear accountability and also encourages an organizational identification or esprit de corp. For the administrator and legislative policy-maker, it makes budgeting decisions much easier. In short, organization by function is a classical organizational model because divisions are based upon specialization of task.

The classical model, as useful as it is, has its limitations (Franz and Jones 1987). The problems induced by this traditional form of organization are as numerous as the benefits. The impact of benefits and limitations varies according to the environment in which the organization operates. Obviously, a police department in a town of 20,000 people surrounded by farm land operates in a different environment than does one in a city of 800,000 that is surrounded by urban sprawl. Similarly, budget and economic conditions, social upheavals, and changing population patterns alter an organization's environment. Issues related to rural crime are mentioned in **Figure 5-8**.

In a **stable environment**, traditional structures are able to predict future needs and demands and rationally plan for those needs. For example, if you can reasonably predict the amount of crime you expect to see in an area over a certain period of time, you can plan patrol and investigation staffing to meet those needs. You can determine your deployment needs by shift, by area, and by day. But, in a turbulent and chaotic environment, a condition that organization theorists refer to as a **dynamic environment**, the situation is different. It is more difficult to

- Compared with urban area, little is known about rural crime or rural policing. It appears, however, that crime is less frequent in rural areas, and that "community policing," to which many urban departments now aspire, has been a long-standing practice in rural police agencies.
- While the terms "rural" and "urban" are used frequently in everyday language, there are no precise meanings of these terms upon which everyone can agree. Despite this, it is clear that the idea of rural is useful.
- Differences between rural and urban cultures have implication for rural crime and rural policing. For example, both rural and urban areas have pockets of extreme poverty, but the effects of poverty on crime are different in the two areas.
- Differences across rural areas are large and vary by region of the country, across counties within a state, and sometimes even within a county. For example, illegal immigrants may be a concern in the Southwest, vandalism in the Midwest, and the smuggling of tobacco and liquor in areas along the Canadian border. Thus, national policies uniformly covering rural areas may be a mistake, unless those policies can be tailored to fit local needs.
- There are contradictions across studies that need to be explained. For example, some authors report that homicide is higher in rural areas, while others (including UCR data) suggest the opposite. It is unclear whether these differences are the product of sampling, the definitions used, or regional variations.
- Studying these issues across rural areas and between urban and rural areas is useful in the same way that studies of crime across countries tell us much about larger patterns and suggest what works and what does not work in policing and crime prevention.

*Source:* Weisheit, Ralph, David Falcone, and L. Edward Wells (1994). Rural Crime and Rural Policing, *Research in Brief*. Washington, DC: US Department of Justice, National Institute of Justice.

**Figure 5-8** Rural crime and policing.

predict adequately the demands that will be placed on an organization. Surprises are more frequent, and in this environment, results are more unpredictable if things are done the way they "always were." The organization and its members feel as if they are in chaos. Classical organizational models assume stable conditions—a constant supply of raw resources, for example, to make steel. These models do not do well in turbulent times.

Herbert Simon also recognized that one of the primary functions of an organization is to make decisions, but he argued that organizations and decision makers are "bounded" by limitations of time, money, knowledge, and other resources (Fry 1989). Classical or traditional organizational structures are designed to limit the amount of information that flows to the top decision-making levels. These limitations mean that organizations make decisions with imperfect knowledge. In a stable environment, this is not fatal to organizational decisions, but in a turbulent or dynamic environment, the consequences may be quite negative.

Conditions for law enforcement, in 2005, are changing. Concentrated pockets of violent crime are increasing even while much traditional crime is decreasing. The emergence of crack and designer drugs, proliferation of automatic weapons, escalation of drive-by shootings, threats of terror attacks, and increased juvenile violence have changed the environment for law enforcement. Cities are growing ever more diverse; many neighborhoods are physically deteriorating and becoming highly transient. Conditions such as these are the perfect pre-conditions for increases in violent crime (Short 1997). These conditions are not suitable to rigid organizations. The major limitations of traditional organization structure, then, relate to the process of decision making and response to environmental change.

Another limitation of classical organization theory is **goal displacement**. Those who work in the organization learn to focus on rules rather than service or product. Similarly, members of the organization are likely to respond to requests for assistance with phrases like "it's not in my job description." This is called **trained incapacity** because people are trained not only what to do, but what not to do, even if it makes sense to do it. The result of these limitations, called **organizational dysfunctions**, is that organizations are not inclined to be imaginative or innovative. They will not use information about the environment properly and are inclined to rigidity. Retreating to "the book" serves to further isolate the organization from its clients, which in the case of policing is the public. Structure and rule rigidity prevent flexibility. All of these problems suggest that law enforcement may need to reassess its current approach to organizational design. This holds important implications for the patrol officer. In classical organizations, patrol officers are at the bottom of the structure. Their role, more or less, is to follow orders within a narrow range and engage in a limited set of predefined tasks. In alternative organizational formulations, the role of patrol officers would change dramatically.

For example, many law enforcement agencies recognized some of the limitations of classical organization structure relatively early in the development of modern policing. Many also realized the limitations built into the organization by function approach. Minor changes in organizational principles resulted. These included the **organize by time** and **organize by place** (or area) approaches (Wilson 1950). For example, many law enforcement agencies are inherently spread out over large distances, which require time to cover. A specific example is the state highway patrol. Such agencies may be divided into relatively self-contained units called posts, regions, or districts. Similarly, municipal police agencies may cover vast amounts of territory and hundreds of thousands or millions of people. Usually, these agencies are divided into precincts, which may have not only patrol and investigation but other organic specialized units such as Special Weapons and Tactics (SWAT) teams. The typical arrangement is for each such precinct to include all of the line functions (refer to Figure 5-7) and some of the staff functions (such as records, jail administration, and community relations, for example) in one unit. In this arrangement, a department is organized by area and divided into precincts, while each precinct is organized by function. Another kind of organizational approach is to **organize by clientele** (Leonard and Moore 1987). A relatively common example of this approach is the creation of juvenile units. Similarly, state highway patrol agencies normally have a special unit assigned to truck safety.

Each of these organizational approaches can temporarily address some of the limitations of classical hierarchy, but they have their own built-in limitations since each approach is similar to organization by function. In order to understand the reasons why policing is changing and how it is changing structurally, it is important to understand these prior forms of organization. These examples represent the cumulative effects of merit service, professionalization of law enforcement, and specialization. For the period from the 1880s to the 1920s, the mission of law enforcement agencies was relatively clear. Patrol, much of it on foot, was the primary function. Crimes were largely theft and personal assaults, and keeping the peace primarily explained law enforcement's mission. Poor communication, little training, and limited education among officers required close supervision and, therefore, a very short span of control. Law enforcement organizations were thus shaped by the social and environmental forces that surrounded them. While the problems of control and command were largely settled by the 1960s, the external conditions—crime, city structure, economic stability—were largely stable. The impression was that traditional law enforcement, and hence traditional structures, were working.

By the late 1960s, that perspective was dispelled. A significant increase in crime, riots, demonstrations, and other disorder left the impression that society was falling apart and law enforcement could not seem to react to or correct these conditions. In 1966 a presidential commission was appointed to study both the increase in crime and the incapacity of the criminal justice system to respond effectively. The reports of this commission, published largely in 1967, argued for a number of things regarding policing: better education and training, a closer connection to the community, and more research on policing.

Research on policing produced several organizational effects. First, it became clear that random patrol did not prevent crime (Kelling et al. 1974). Similarly, the process of investigation came into question for its overall effectiveness (Chaiken et al. 1975). Subsequent research showed that focused patrols (e.g., focusing on identified "hot spots") did work. Research also found that patrol had a role in investigations and that certain techniques of investigation improved the process. The impact of these and other findings called into question the traditional role of specialization, hierarchy, and command decision making. This propelled the discussion of community policing and problem-oriented policing as both a product and structural fix to law enforcement's perceived problems (Skogan and Roth 2004).

Organizations are structured as a response to different task demands made by society and by the environment surrounding the organization (Zhao 1996). If either changes, the organization must change. This is why so many private sector organizations are altering their business structures. Each kind of organizational design has certain benefits, but each also has limits. Organizations that fail to accommodate changes in demand will invariably falter. Attempts at more flexible organizational approaches began to appear as a consequence of the need to adapt to rapidly changing conditions.

# ■ Human Relations Theory

Another set of researchers and practitioners in organizations looked beyond the mere structure of an organization for ways to make organizations more efficient and effective. These theorists examined the impact of individuals and small groups on organizations. Experiments in industrial psychology led theorists as early as the 1930s to examine how human beings worked in organizations. The collected body of research and concepts associated with this approach is called the Human Relations Theory of management, or the "Humanistic Theory" of management. The basic tenets of this perspective are listed in **Figure 5-9**.

Despite more than 60 years of efforts, only the past 30 years produced real change in organization theory and in organizations themselves. For law enforcement agencies, we can generally reduce these to two major areas: motivation and leadership. **Motivation** is a broad field of study, which focuses on why people want to work (Conser 1979; Katzell and Thompson 1990). The field of **leadership** is closely related and focuses on how management is able to get organizations to follow a defined path. Line and staff employees frequently see both concepts differently than do leaders or managers in an organization. This chapter attempts no detailed analysis of these very complex concepts; we leave that for a course on human resources or organizational behavior. However, it is important for the entry-level officer to be aware of the issues in these areas and how they are developing. The trends hold important implications for patrol officers and supervisors.

Needs and desires of employees matter
Group dynamics affect productivity
Job satisfaction
Three-way communications
Participative decision making
Motivation is a complex concept
Leadership styles matter

**Figure 5-9** Tenets of human relations theory.

## Motivation

Researchers addressing motivation focused on human needs and found that while some aspects of work motivate people (**motivators**), others only prevent dissatisfaction (so called **hygiene factors** or **maintainers**) (Herzberg 1968). These researchers also found that motivation is the product of a calculated process in which individuals arrive at the probabilities of acquiring certain needs (Campbell, Dunnette, Lawler, and Weick 1970). The central thrust of the Motivation-Hygiene Theory is that people in organizations have two general drives related to their performance. The first is motivation. People are motivated to perform tasks if three conditions exist: (1) they believe that rewards are tied to performance, (2) they value the rewards, and (3) performance is thought to be achievable. Motivation is enhanced if people are permitted to participate in the setting of organizational goals, are given interesting tasks, and are permitted to participate in deciding how to perform those tasks. Together this means people can be motivated in an organization if they see clear, achievable goals which they value and to which there is a clear path (Rainey 1993).

The second distinct drive is **satisfaction**, or the degree to which employees feel satisfied with their work and rewards for that work. Motivation is a response to the expectation of future rewards. Satisfaction is a response to past rewards. They are also distinct in that satisfaction is related to turnover and absenteeism. More importantly, satisfaction improves as participation in decision making increases (Wagner 1994; Lawler 1986). These are important factors for both leaders and subordinates to understand. For law enforcement organizations, the known sources of motivation and satisfaction pose a problem. The single most common reward (motivator) is monetary compensation and promotion (Ledford 1995). In civil service systems, these two are tied together in a way they are not tied together in private business. That is, pay for performance is common in business, while pay for longevity (length of tenure) is common in civil service systems such as law enforcement. Moreover, law enforcement agency pay is set by legislative bodies, not by managers, and promotion is largely controlled by civil service rules. Hence, managers in law enforcement are left to find other means to motivate officers including special training, special assignments, shift assignment, and over-time consideration.

In order to do this, however, they need information. Patrol officers, supervisors, and staff must communicate the level of morale in the agency to managers in order to permit effective decisions. You will recall that traditional hierarchical organization structures restrict effective communication. One solution is to use an alternate organizational structure. An additional solution is for law enforcement managers to adopt leadership approaches which seek out information and participation in decision making.

Alternative motivators are numerous. One is the degree to which leaders listen to subordinates and communicate reasons for actions. Others include job definition, temporary job assignments, reassignments, and the creation of task forces or teams. Jobs can be redefined to permit subordinates to focus on areas of their own interest. Thus, reassignment of patrol officers to community service programs, such as DARE, is normally within the authority of managers, but does not involve pay or promotion.

Task force and team approaches also address satisfaction. As temporary assignments outside of the normal hierarchy, these approaches overcome the limitations of classical structure and permit employees to take advantage of specialized skills and interests. More importantly, they encourage cooperative decision making. Employees who are given active input into their roles are more motivated and more satisfied (Russell and MacLachlan 1999).

Issues of motivation and satisfaction are also important due to the high levels of job burnout and **stress** in law enforcement. Sources of stress are organization practices, criminal justice system practices, public attitudes, and factors intrinsic to the job including danger, differential social treatment, and unusual working hours. These combine to create personal, social, and family difficulties for officers. Not all stress is negative, of course. It may make officers cautious in dangerous situations or work harder when the stakes are exciting. Negative stress may cause officers to react to outside stimuli in ways that are not positive (Gaines 1993). Strategies such as exercise can be employed to avoid debilitating stress. Also, officers need to feel free to communicate personal problems to their superiors who, in turn, must reduce the role that the organization plays in creating stress. Participative decision making and the use of **job enrichment** (discussed in detail later in this chapter) to increase levels of motivation and satisfaction will have a beneficial effect. Finally, fellow officers must discuss problems and solutions with one another.

## Leadership

Theories about leadership demonstrate the close relationship that exists between organization structure, motivation, and leader behavior. Initially, theories of leadership focused on **traits** that "good" leaders have. But, this is a very limited view since it implies that certain people are born to be leaders and others are not, which is untrue. The more likely possibility is that leaders are people who can use certain skills to obtain information and act in an appropriate way depending upon circumstances. This **contingent leadership** model suggests everyone can learn to be a leader and employ learned skills where conditions permit. More importantly, it does not limit leadership to only top positions in an organization. Rather, it implies that patrol officers and supervisors are leaders and can learn skills to become more effective at leading. Research demonstrated that the most effective leaders were those who employ teams, show a high level of concern for people as well as a high level of concern for results, and are able to show others in the organization how to achieve goals (Hersey, Blanchard, and Johnson 1996; Rainey 1991).

This leadership approach produced high performance, high satisfaction, and high levels of motivation. Some argue that this is why community policing is particularly suited to law enforcement organizations, as both a salve for community relations problems and to organizational problems as well (Langworthy and Travis 2003). However, we think that is an incorrect read of the theory. As Hersey, Blanchard, and Johnson make clear, we do not yet have solid empirical evidence that any of the theories of leadership work. We have some evidence that they all work if certain conditions exist. Some organizations simply are not mature enough to avoid orthodox management styles and hence, are really not ready to transform their decision-making systems (1996). Recent evidence suggests that even after extensive efforts of implementation of community policing and problem-oriented policing, there is little evidence of attitudinal or behavioral change among line officers (Gingerich and Russell 2005).

Clearly, patrol officers are equally important in developing good leadership. Training for leadership roles begins at the patrol level as the use of task forces, teams, community policing, and similar concepts requires leadership at the lowest levels of the organization. Leaders in teams and task forces learn to invite participation and cooperation and discover that every member of the group can lead and can teach others or learn from others. This produces the so-called "learning organization."

Leadership roles may only be temporary. This is very different from a definition of leadership that is dependent upon position in the organization. Top managers must be leaders, yes, but all officers must exercise leadership. Because diverse skills, backgrounds, and knowledge increase leadership resources in the organization, patrol officers can contribute dramatically to the leadership of the department.

The key is seeing leadership not as controlling or commanding, but rather as assisting, helping, guiding, facilitating, and contributing knowledge to others. Traditional "authority" is produced not by demand, but instead by demonstrating an ability to command an organization's resources. Command, therefore, is not obtained merely by giving orders.

# ■ Contemporary Management Theory

As the previous discussion suggests, the classical paramilitary hierarchy employed in most law enforcement agencies is not very adaptive to rapidly changing conditions. It is also clear from other chapters in this book that environmental conditions surrounding law enforcement are changing rapidly. Further, classical organization structures do not enhance motivation, increase satisfaction, or reduce stress. Yet, law enforcement organizations are faced with emerging demands from their communities, complex social problems related to crime, shifting crime patterns, shrinking budgets, terror threats, and slipping morale.

These internal and external environmental forces play a unique role in contemporary management perspectives. Two particular theoretical approaches that are concerned with environmental and situational conditions are the **systems theory** and **contingency theory**. Systems theory was described in some detail in Chapter 1, where we stated that it views the entire context (environment) in which an issue exists by analyzing all the forces or influences impacting it. When focused on organizational and management issues in the law enforcement field, it is particularly interested in analyzing all the influences from the environment that affect the agency. Such influences in the environment have been identified by Stojkovic, Kalinich, and Klofas (2003, 47) as including legal, political, cultural, economic, demographic, ecological, and technological forces. See **Figure 5-10** for a brief explanation and examples of each of these environmental forces. This approach emphasizes that administrators and managers need to consider the influence and affect of these multiple forces upon the agency and its operations.

The contingency theory perspective is one that recognizes multiple factors within the organization; it is an attempt to identify which factors are most relevant and what their impact is. Organizations are viewed as open systems and much of the systems approach is accepted by contingency advocates. However, contingency theorists maintain that they cannot rely on any one theoretical approach to address all issues because of the differences in organizations and situations. Decisions are "dependent upon" and "subject to" the evaluation and interaction

| Forces | Description | Examples |
|---|---|---|
| Legal | The various types of law and lawful authority of the federal, state, and local governments | Statutes, administrative code, agency policies, and case law |
| Political | The quest for influence by individuals, groups, and governmental actions | Interest groups, the electorate, unions, professional associations |
| Cultural | The collective norms, values, mores, behaviors, and expectations of a society or group | Male/female roles, ethnic identity and customs, morality |
| Economic | The financial resources of a community and an agency | Budget, tax base, employment and business conditions |
| Demographic | The characteristics of the population—federal, state, and local levels | Population statistics by age, race, ethnicity, sex, educational level |
| Ecological | Climate, geological, and geographical conditions and related patterns | Weather, rivers, coastline, tourism, agriculture, industrial base |
| Technological | The practical application of any science or tool to common endeavors | Communications, computerization, vehicle video, forensic science |

*Source:* Adapted from Stojkovic, Stan, David Kalinich, and John Klofas (2003). *Criminal Justice Organizations: Administration and Management*, Third Edition. Belmont, CA: Wadsworth/Thompson Learning, chapter 3.

**Figure 5-10** Environmental forces—systems theory perspective.

of several factors; the primary ones being (a) organizational size, (b) technology, (c) environment, and (d) life cycle stage.

In our modern society, the application of classical hierarchy is not very adept at satisfying employees. Low employee satisfaction levels produce burnout, stress, and high rates of turnover. Law enforcement officers who are burned out or who are operating under stress are likely to make poor decisions and work with a low degree of effectiveness. Costs to the organization are both financial and performance related. Turnover is costly because organizations have tremendous investments in employees. The cost of training replacements is significant, and the loss of experienced officers is damaging from a performance perspective. Indeed, the greater the experience of the lost employee, the greater the cost to the organization in terms of performance. For each of these reasons, law enforcement agencies find themselves questioning the current practice of organizing by hierarchy (Roberg and Kuykendall 1997; Langworthy and Travis 2003; and Greene 2004).

The first approach to take advantage of multiple talents in a given project or operation was the use of **matrix organization (Figure 5-11)** (Swanson, Territo, and Taylor 1993). In this approach, a number of personnel are assigned to a given problem regardless of their permanent duty assignment. In this manner, the organization is able to take advantage of the best personnel for a given problem without permanent structural changes. However, it is very difficult to manage day-to-day operations and achieve accountability in matrix organizations. In many respects, this is not very different from task force operations, because typically a task force takes 100% of an employee's time. A matrix assignment involves only part of an employee's time. Hence, an officer could be involved in two or three matrix-based projects at one time.

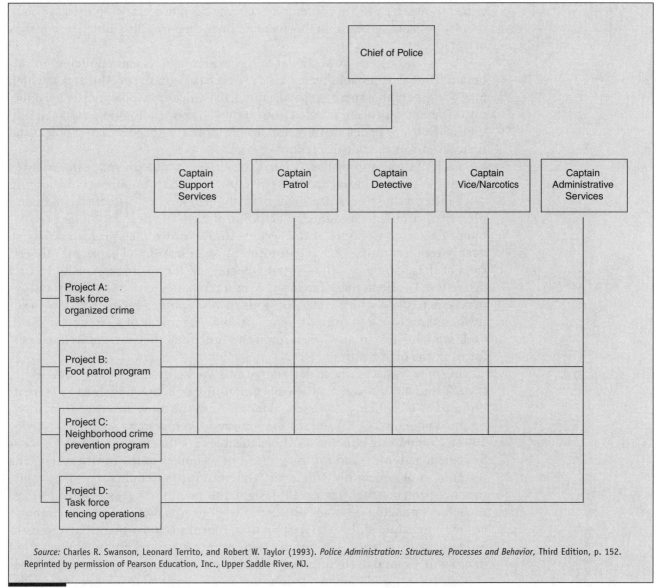

*Source:* Charles R. Swanson, Leonard Territo, and Robert W. Taylor (1993). *Police Administration: Structures, Processes and Behavior,* Third Edition, p. 152. Reprinted by permission of Pearson Education, Inc., Upper Saddle River, NJ.

**Figure 5-11** Matrix organization applied to a law enforcement agency.

A variation of this form is **problem-oriented policing**, where efforts are organized around a particular problem (Goldstein 1990). This means that whole operations are mounted against a particular problem. Participant officers may be temporarily or partially assigned to the problem. This is a form of organization by product, but it may be considered a team design, depending upon the specific situation. For example, in Santa Rosa, California, the police department detailed all patrol officers to spend some of their time working on community problem solving. To do so, all officers in a given beat (all shifts) would meet periodically to discuss problems and solutions. For beat operations they reported to their beat sergeant. For community policing operations they reported to a community policing sergeant. In this manner, their time was distributed by a matrix orientation.

An organizational form similar to the matrix form is **team policing**. In this organizational approach, teams are created based upon specific areas, which may be a geographic area or a specific problem (similar to problem-oriented policing). Team members are selected from various line operations and assigned full-time to the team. Teams are fully responsible for the assigned area or problem and typically are given wide discretion.

Each of these approaches (matrix, task force, problem, and team-oriented policing) is very similar from the perspective of an organization theorist. They differ only in organizational permanence, level of discretion, and complexity of problems assigned. The point of each of these methods is an attempt to overcome some of the serious limitations of classical hierarchy so deeply representative of law enforcement organizations. For patrol officers, each of these methods offers varying degrees of increased responsibility and discretion. In effect, these models give more freedom to patrol officers and supervisors to use a wider variety of skills in attempting a broader variety of solutions than those permitted by traditional organizational structure. Still, each model is essentially based upon the functions that each individual performs in the organization.

In some respects, these determinations are being made independently of the effort to move toward the use of community policing models as a theory or philosophy of policing. In practical terms, both the move toward community-oriented policing (COP) and the move away from hierarchy are linked (Bayley 1994). Community policing redefines the roles of officers, the targets of law enforcement activities, and the assignment of resources in the organization. The result is an organization with a very different focus than before. Many argue that traditional structures are ill designed to meet the needs of this new approach. As policing becomes broader in its concerns, with a focus on employees with multiple skills, the narrow design of traditional hierarchy ceases to hold relevance. Hence, law enforcement agencies are redefining management in order to respond to environmental challenges to the organization, to advances in organization, and human relations theory, and respond to the developing theory of community policing (Greene, Bergman, and McLaughlin 1994). Evidence suggests that COP might improve officer satisfaction and motivation, though there is insufficient evidence to be certain (Wilkinson and Rosenbaum 1994). However, we do know that research generally supports the notion that participation improves performance and satisfaction levels (Wagner 1994; Russell and MacLachlan 1999).

What should modern law enforcement organizations look like, and how should they work to meet each of the challenges and satisfy the needs of community policing? In terms of look, modern organizations are developing very "flat" structures (**Figure 5-12**). These are called **flat designs** or **flat organizations** because there are very few levels of hierarchy. Compare Figure 5-3 with Figure 5-12. The most obvious differences between the two designs are, first, the number of levels of organization and, second, the number of units that report to any one per-

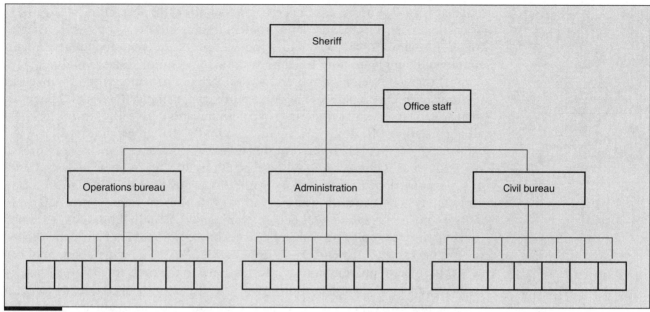

**Figure 5-12** Sample of a flat organizational design.

son or office above. The so-called span of control is much broader in a flat organization structure.

This form of organization improves communications within organizations as management obtains information with fewer "filters." That is, information is less likely to be "sanitized," a process by which only good information percolates to the top. Most people hate to be the bearer of bad news, and multiple levels increase the probability that negative information will be blocked. Similarly, orders, instructions, and goals are more easily communicated to lower levels in a flat organization.

In flat organizations, accountability for actions becomes more certain. Previously, it was thought that accountability was best achieved with someone looking over an employee's shoulder at all times. That required a good deal of looking and many people to do it. Hence, large bureaucracies grew to satisfy the need for accountability. We now know, however, that bureaucracy actually allows individuals to escape personal accountability. Responsibility can be pushed to lower or higher levels, thereby avoiding responsibility. In flat organizations, however, accountability is very localized and forces individuals to take personal responsibility for performance.

Flat organizations also respond to the need for new ways to motivate and satisfy employees. In flat organizations, the possibility of job enrichment is greater. Job enrichment is a process where employees are given more discretion, flexibility, and authority for performance of assigned duties. Employees are given freedom to determine how best to carry out their tasks. This doesn't mean more work. It means more responsibility for deciding how to do tasks and how to achieve goals set by management. This approach produces both higher levels of motivation and higher levels of job satisfaction.

Flat forms of organizational design also offer the possibility of organizational flexibility, fluidity, and rapid problem response. More resources are directly under the control of management, and fewer people are required for agreement. Employees are given more freedom in how to accomplish tasks and management is thereby freed to set goals and evaluate performance without a need to micromanage. As employees are given more responsibility, their skill inventory increases; coupled with the increase in communications, this leads to greater overall organizational flexibility to respond to rapidly changing conditions.

An agency that is organized in this manner will reduce the costs of bureaucracy. Previously, one role for mid-level positions was information analysis. In flat organizations, there is less need for organizational positions dedicated to acquiring and analyzing information. These positions will be merged into patrol and other delivery positions, which will become "enlarged." Rapidly improving computing, communications, and data analysis technologies make this not only possible but necessary. Each employee, from patrol officer to deputy chief, now has access to tremendous amounts of information and the tools for analysis, thereby reducing the need for supervision.

The negative aspects of flat organizations are few, but significant. First, this form of organization relies heavily upon a well-trained and educated work force. This includes training in and commitment to basic organizational values and goals. Among these would be the mission statement of the organization and the values in the Constitution of the United States and the state in which the agency is located. Training and education become the basis for decision making that is decentralized.

A second drawback is the likelihood that divisions or groupings of employees will not be headed by individuals of the same "rank," though they may report to the same superior. In a flat organization, where cooperative decision making at lower levels combines with job enrichment to produce new forms of motivation and satisfaction, rank holds a reduced role. This reduction in rank influence will have negative consequences in the short run, until the correct "rank mix" is established. A third drawback is related to recruitment. Flat designs require the ability to recruit and retain individuals who have the desire and skill to become "self-starters." But, the available talent pool is shrinking for every employer in terms of skills and education (Clark 1998).

To summarize the modern perspective: In order to motivate and satisfy employees, avoid burnout, and remain flexible, law enforcement leaders and their organizations must innovate. Law enforcement agencies cannot avoid the imposed hierarchy of civil service, but can employ alternative structures to avoid the limitations of classical structure and gain the benefits of modern managerial approaches. The field must invite job enrichment, cooperative and decentralized decision making, and organizational flattening. Each of these changes is essential to the effective implementation of community policing. To get effective, efficient, satisfied, and motivated employees, organizations must be redesigned. Entry-level officers and veterans alike must accommodate themselves to the implications of these changes and the demands they will make. **Figure 5-13** summarizes the tenets of modern management theory.

Systems perspective
Broad discretion
Situational analysis
Open communications
Value adherence and ethics
Participative decision making
Cooperative decision making
Team and matrix assignments
Flat organizational structure

**Figure 5-13** Tenets of modern management theory.

# ■ Summary

In this chapter we briefly reviewed the development of organizational theory typically applied to law enforcement organizations for the better part of the past 100 years. In most respects, we found that traditional or classical structures dominate law enforcement. We examined the benefits of that organizational approach as well as the problems inherent with that approach. We found that in a rapidly changing world, traditional structures suffer. However, structures operate better when they allow lower-level employees to make decisions and participate in leading organizations.

We also examined some of the ways in which law enforcement organizations may be able to take advantage of this new organizational form, including task groups, teams, and matrix organizations. In each case, the effort increases the span of control, increases individual officer responsibility, and invites innovation and participation in problem solving. We also found that motivation achieves higher levels in this design where management sets clear goals and permits small teams to determine how to achieve those goals. Leadership in such an organization arises from all levels of an organization. Hence, patrol officers must see themselves as leaders and followers. Rather than being passive receivers of orders, developing forms of policing theory and organizational principles place patrol officers in the role of leader and decision-maker. While adhering to the command structure that is important for political accountability in a democracy, officers must understand the direction of their organizations as we continue through the twenty-first century, even though the police function seemingly has changed little in the past 25 years (Gaines and Cordner 1999).

## QUESTIONS FOR REVIEW

1. What were the historical causes of current (traditional) law enforcement?
2. What are the limitations and benefits of the traditional or classical organizational structure?
3. What are the benefits and limitations of modern organizational approaches?
4. What motivates employees?
5. What seems to cause stress?
6. What is leadership, and who are leaders?
7. What are the basic characteristics and beliefs of contemporary (modern) management organization theory?

## SUGGESTED ACTIVITIES

1. Obtain the organizational chart for a local law enforcement agency. Compare your chart with other students' charts and identify the ways in which they are similar and the ways in which they differ.
2. Scan local print media and contact law enforcement agencies and community groups for information about how your community has changed in the past 5, 10, and 15 years. When has the most change occurred? What are the challenges that seem to be most pressing?
3. Develop a list of future challenges not yet present, but that seem likely to happen in the near future, which will cause law enforcement problems. These may be variations on current problems or entirely new problems.
4. Most readers of this text have experimented with tale-telling in circles. Start a story and whisper it to your neighbor. By the time it gets back to you, it is not recognizable. This illustrates how information is slow and inaccurate when it must pass through multiple layers of bureaucracy. Hence, decisions may be based upon faulty or only partial information. In a dynamic environment, it is expected that information will change rapidly.
5. Using your Internet browser, find at least one World Wide Web page for a police department and locate its organizational chart. How would you classify it? Can you find a non-traditional chart?

## ■ Chapter Glossary

**bureaucracy**    term used to describe large complex organizations that have several layers of supervisors representing the largest portion of the hierarchy; tend to be characterized as closed systems with significant division of labor, and predicated on a routine demand for services.

**classical organization theory**    the body of theory from Weber, Taylor, and Gulick, among others, which relied upon hierarchy, merit hiring, small spans of control, and a single command authority.

**contingency theory**   theoretical perspective that recognizes multiple factors within the organization; it is an attempt to identify which factors are most relevant and what their impact is. This perspective recognizes that one cannot rely on any one theoretical approach to address all issues because of the differences in organizations and situations.

**contingent leadership**   a theory of leadership that suggests that everyone can learn to be a leader depending upon the circumstances and the abilities of that person in that situation.

**dominance of an idea**   managing an organization by mission statements, values, and goals.

**dynamic environment**   a changing environment; a condition that prevents predicting future problems or needs with certainty, and one which produces constantly changing organizational challenges.

**flat design/flat organization**   an organizational design that limits the number of levels of an organization, increases the span of control, increases individual responsibility for performance, relies upon teams and task groups, increases communications flows, and increases individual discretion for judgment.

**goal displacement**   a behavior of employees who work in the organization and learn to focus on rules rather than service.

**hierarchy**   a form of organizational structure that includes a division of labor, clear lines of authority between superior and subordinate, and a single unifying authority at the top of the hierarchy.

**human relations/humanistic**   a theory of management that focuses on the needs of the individual and assumes that these matter in terms of organizational performance.

**human resource**   a theory of management that looks at individuals as an organizational asset and recommends organization based on their needs and talents.

**hygiene factors/maintainers**   aspects of a job that will maintain satisfaction, but which do not motivate greater performance.

**job enrichment**   a process where jobs are given more discretion, flexibility, and authority for performance of assigned duties so that employees have freedom to determine how best to carry out their tasks.

**leadership**   a field of study closely related to motivation that focuses on what makes people able to get organizations to follow a path set by management.

**matrix organization**   a number of personnel are assigned to use a portion of their time for a given problem regardless of their permanent duty location.

**motivation**   a broad field of study that focuses on what makes people want to work.

**motivators**   those things that can increase motivation.

**organization behavior**   a body of research that examines organizations in the micro or small group and individual levels.

**organization theory**   the body of research that explores the ways in which people organize themselves to do work.

**organizational dysfunction**   problems inherent in the design of an organization.

**organize by clientele**   structuring an organization according to the people to be served or targeted by organizational activities.

**organize by function**   characterized by grouping employees together according to the major functions or tasks that they performed.

**organize by place**   structuring according to the location of tasks; precincts are an example.

**organize by product**   structuring an organization according to what people are producing or making; an outcome-centered means of organization.

**organize by time**   structuring an organization according to the time it takes to carry out tasks; shifts, for example, are organizing structures based on time

**problem-oriented policing**   an organizing method where teams of officers are organized around a particular problem.

**rationalization**   the process by which Weber felt society was organizing itself; a social system using rules and criteria as the basis for all judgments.

**satisfaction**   happiness with one's job, workplace, and performance.

**scientific management**   a theory of work organization that held that if you understand and analyze a job by breaking it down into its smallest parts, you can train workers to the exact task without wasting time or effort.

**span of control**   the number of individuals that one person directly supervises or who otherwise directly report to that person.

**stable environment**   the conditions of an organization that do not change and therefore permit the organization to predict future needs and demands and rationally plan for those needs.

**stress**   positive stress is concern that makes people focus on doing a good job; negative stress is uncontrolled concern that leads people to develop personal, social, and work-related problems that lead to mistakes, burnout, early retirement or intervention, or each of these.

**structuring by authority**   the use of hierarchical authority to impose management's desires by orders and supervision.

**systems theory**   theoretical perspective that views the entire context (environment) in which an issue exists by analyzing all the forces or influences impacting it. When focused on organizational and management issues, it is particularly interested in analyzing all the influences from the environment that affect the organization.

**task force**   a temporary organizational division that is created for a limited purpose.

**team policing**   an organizational approach in which teams are created based upon specific areas which may be geographic or problem-oriented in nature.

**trained incapacity**   a behavior that results when employees are trained not only what to do, but what not to do, and thus refuse to go beyond the limited role of their predefined jobs.

traits    aspects of a person once thought to be related to leadership.

**unity of command**    one person is in command of an organization, and all individuals report to only one person who can then trace a line of command to the single unifying command at the top.

## ■ Chapter References

Bayley, David H. (1994). *Police for the Future*. New York: Oxford University Press.

Campbell, J.P., M.D. Dunnette, E.E. Lawler, and K. Weick (1970). *Expectancy Theory*. New York: McGraw-Hill.

Caplow, Theodore (1964). *Principles of Organization*. New York: Harcourt, Brace & World, 50–62.

Chaiken, Jan, Peter Greenwood, and Joan Petersilia. (1975). The Criminal Investigation Process, in *Police Operations: Analysis and Evaluation* (1996) Cincinnati: Anderson Publishing, 161–184.

Clark, Jacob R. (1998). Is Anybody Out There? Stiff Competition for Recruits Fuels Agencies' Personnel Woes. *Law Enforcement News* 24, no. 488 (April 30, p. 1).

Clavell, James (ed.)(1983). *The Art of War by Sun Tzu*. New York: Delacorte Press.

Chicago Police Department (2003). 2002 Annual Report, Chicago PD, p. 38.

Conser, James A. (1979). Motivational Theory Applied to Law Enforcement Agencies. *Journal of Police Science and Administration* 7(3):285–91.

Franz, V. and D.M. Jones (1987). Perceptions of Organizational Performance in Suburban Police Departments: A Critique of the Military Model. *Journal of Police Science and Administration* 15(2):153–61.

Fry, Brian R. (1989). *Mastering Public Administration: From Max Weber to Dwight Waldo*. Chatham, NJ: Chatham House.

Gaines, Larry K. (1993). Coping with the Job: Stress in Police Work, in *Critical Issues in Policing: Contemporary Readings*, Second Edition, edited by Roger G. Dunham and Geoffrey P. Alpert. Prospect Heights, IL: Waveland, 535–550.

Gaines, Larry K. and Gary W. Cordner (1999). The Function of the Police, in *Policing Perspectives*, edited by Larry K. Gaines and Gary W. Cordner. Los Angeles, CA: Roxbury Publishing Co, 1–2.

Gingerich, Terry E. and Gregory D. Russell (2005). "Accreditation and Community Policing: Are They Neutral, Hostile, or Synergistic? An Empirical Test Among Street Cops and Management Cops," unpublished manuscript currently under review.

Goldstein, Herman (1990). *Problem-Oriented Policing*. New York: McGraw-Hill.

Gortner, Harold F., Julianne Mahler, and Jeanne Bell Nicholson (1987). *Organization Theory: A Public Perspective*. Chicago: The Dorsey Press.

Greene, Jack R. (2004). Community Policing and Police Organizations, in *Community Policing: Can it Work*, by Wesley G. Skogan, Belmont, CA: Thompson/Wadsworth, 30–54.

Greene, Jack R., William T. Bergman, and Edward J. McLaughlin (1994). Implementing Community Policing: Cultural and Structural Change in Police Organizations, in *The Challenge of Community Policing: Testing the Promises*, edited by Dennis P. Rosenbaum. Thousand Oaks, CA: Sage Publications, 92–109.

Gulick, Luther (1937). Notes on the theory of organizations, in *Papers on the Science of Administration*, edited by Luther Gulick and Lyndall F. Urwick. New York: Institute of Public Administration, 3–13.

Hersey, Paul, Kenneth H. Blanchard, and Dewey E. Johnson (1996). *Management of Organizational Behavior: Utilizing Human Resources*, Seventh Edition. Upper Saddle River, NJ: Prentice Hall.

Herzberg, Frederick (1968). One More Time: How Do You Motivate Employees? *Harvard Business Review* 46(1):36–44.

Katzell, Raymond A. and Donna E. Thompson (1990). Work Motivation: Theory and Practice. *American Psychologist* 45(2):144–153.

Kelling, George E, Tony Pate, Duane Dieckman, and Charles E. Brown (1974). The Kansas City Preventative Patrol Experiment, in *Police Operations: Analysis and Evaluation 1996* Cincinnati: Anderson Publishing, 71–104.

Knott, Jack H. and Gary J. Miller (1987). *Reforming Bureaucracy: The Politics of Institutional Choice*. Englewood Cliffs, NJ: Prentice Hall.

Langworthy, Robert H. and Lawrence F. Travis (2003). *Policing in America: A Balance of Forces,* Third Edition. Upper Saddle River, NJ: Prentice Hall.

Lawler, Edward E. (1986). *High Involvement Management.* San Francisco: Jossey-Bass.

Ledford, Gerald E., Jr. (1995). Pay as an organization development issue. *Newsletter of the Organizational Development and Change Division. Academy of Management,* Summer.

Leonard, V.A. and Harry W. Moore (1987). *Police Organization and Management,* Seventh Edition. Mineoloa, NY: Foundation Press.

Marsden, Peter V., Cynthia R. Cook, and Arne L. Kallenberg (1994). Organizational Structures. *American Behavioral Scientist,* 37:539–563.

Rainey, Hal G. (1991). *Understanding and Managing Public Organizations.* San Francisco: Jossey-Bass.

Rainey, Hal G. (1993). Work Motivation, in *Handbook of Organization Behavior,* edited by Robert T. Golembiewski. New York: Marcel Dekker, 19–39.

Roberg, Roy R. and Jack Kuykendall (1997). *Police Management,* Second Edition. Los Angeles: Roxbury Publishing Co.

Rosenbaum, Dennis P. and Deanna L. Wilkinson (2004). Can Police Adapt? Tracking the Effects of Organizational Reform Over Six Years in Wesley G. Skogan, in *Community Policing: Can it Work?* Belmont, CA: Thompson/Wadsworth, 79–108.

Russell, Gregory D. and Susan MacLachlan (1999). Community Policing, Decentralized Decision Making, and Employee Satisfaction. *Journal of Crime and Justice,* 22(2):33–54.

Shafritz, Jay M. and J. Steven Ott (1992). *Classics of Organization Theory,* Third Edition. Pacific Grove, CA: Brooks Cole.

Short, James F., Jr. (1997). *Poverty, Ethnicity, and Violent Crime.* Boulder, CO: Westview Press.

Skogan, Wesley G. and Jeffrey Roth (2004). Introduction in *Community Policing: Can it Work?* by Wesley G. Skogan. Belmont, CA: Thompson/Wadsworth, xvii-xxxiv.

Stojkovic, Stan, David Kalinich, and John Klofas (2003). *Criminal Justice Organizations: Administration and Management,* Third Edition. Belmont, CA: Thomson/Wadsworth Learning.

Swanson, Charles R., Leonard Territo, and Robert W. Taylor (1993). *Police Administration: Structures, Processes and Behavior,* Third Edition. New York: Macmillan Publishing, Co.

Wagner, John A. III (1994). Participation's Effects on Performance and Satisfaction: A Reconsideration of Research Evidence. *Academy of Management Review* 19(2):312–30.

Walker, Samuel (1998). *Popular Justice: A History of American Criminal Justice.* New York: Oxford University Press.

Weisheit, Ralph, David Falcone, and L. Edward Wells (1994). Rural Crime and Rural Policing. *Research in Brief.* Washington, DC: US Department of Justice, National Institute of Justice.

Wilkinson, Deanna L. and Dennis P. Rosenbaum (1994). The Effects of Organizational Structure on Community Policing: A Comparison of Two Cities, in *The Challenge of Community Policing: Testing the Promises,* edited by Dennis P. Rosenbaum. Thousand Oaks, CA: Sage Publications, 110–126.

Wilson, O.W. (1950). *Police Administration.* New York: McGraw-Hill.

Wilson, Woodrow (1887). The Study of Administration. *Political Science Quarterly,* June:197–222.

Zhao, Jihong (1996). *Why Police Organizations Change: A Study of Community-Oriented Policing.* Washington, DC: Police Executive Research Forum.

# Legal Restrictions and Challenges

**6**

Law enforcement is obviously involved with the law and the courts. The degree of that involvement and the resulting number of limitations placed on law enforcement is not so obvious. In order to briefly examine those limitations, this chapter starts with *where* law comes from, *how* it affects law enforcement, and *why* it matters to law enforcement officials. After studying this chapter, you will be able to:

- Identify the broad variety of legal restrictions on law enforcement and state the reasons for those limitations.
- Describe the structure of the system of justice in the United States and explain the relationship between state and federal courts.
- State the basic principles of the criminal law.
- Determine the relationship between the principles of criminal law to officers' decisions.
- Summarize the basic procedural limitations on law enforcement officers and explain why these restrictions exist.
- Understand the rule of law and how it both restricts and protects officers.
- Identify the basic sources of legal threats to the officer on a personal and professional basis.

## Chapter Outline

I. Sources of Law in the United States
   A. Common Law
   B. Criminal and Civil Law
   C. Statutory and Code Law
   D. The Constitution

## Key Terms Used in This Chapter

| | |
|---|---|
| common law | preliminary hearing |
| precedent | probable cause |
| stare decisis | suppression |
| civil law | self-defense |
| criminal law | search |
| felony | warrant requirement |
| misdemeanor | seizure |
| statutory law | stop and frisk |
| model penal code | exigent circumstances |
| rap sheet | plain view doctrine |
| constitutional law | exclusionary rule |
| administrative law | custodial interrogation |
| delegation of authority | fruit of the poisonous tree |
| minimum administrative due | *respondeat superior* |
|   process | principal |
| writ of certiorari | agent |
| writ of habeas corpus | |

## ■ Sources of Law in the United States

Law in the United States is derived from several sources. These sources became more numerous as the nation grew and became more complex, both socially and economically. Law enforcement personnel must understand the sources of law because they are also the sources of authority for their decisions and actions. The first part of this chapter provides an overview of these sources.

## Common Law

The first source of law that traditionally involved law enforcement was the **common law**. Derived from England, this body of legal rules developed over a period of several hundred years. English judges were frequently faced with problems, or cases, for which there were no legal guidelines. Nevertheless, courts needed to reach decisions in an attempt to resolve these problems. Acting under the authority of the king, courts developed legal rules to settle these cases.

These decisions, over time, were relied upon by other judges with similar problems and came to be called **precedent**. Courts would draw upon these older cases to help decide new ones. In effect, the old cases gave the judges guidance. The act of applying and relying upon precedent was called **stare decisis**. This meant that prior decisions should be followed if the facts of the case at issue were similar to the prior case. The courts could construct new rules only if the case to be decided was unlike prior cases. Gradually, this body of law developed and was called the common law.

## Criminal and Civil Law

The common law included both **civil law** and **criminal law**. Criminal law and civil law are distinctive areas of the law. Generally speaking, crimes are offenses against the public (or the state), while civil violations are violations against individuals. While individuals are frequently victims in criminal offenses such as assault, rape, or murder, the law considers the public at large to be the victim. The theory is that a society must have order and must protect its members. If the rules of that order are violated and a crime is committed, it is society that is offended. This perspective has governed American law for over 200 years, but as we see elsewhere in this book, emerging theories of victims' rights and restorative justice are challenging this long held assumption.

In criminal cases, the state is represented by the prosecutor (or district attorney) who initiates the criminal charge (a process described below). In civil cases, each side is represented by private counsel, and complaining party (or counsel) must file a complaint alleging a civil violation. A violation of a criminal statute can result in jail or prison time. Civil cases can only result in money damages or orders compelling parties to do or not do something. One does not go to jail or prison for a civil violation (generally speaking); however, if a court order is ignored or violated, one could be jailed for contempt of court. That is not a crime. Similarly, those who are ordered to pay child support and fail to do so despite the ability to pay may similarly be jailed. In both cases, civil actions could result in being jailed, but only because a court order was ignored or violated. That is different than a criminal case.

Civil law includes contracts, torts, property, and civil procedure. A tort is a civil injury to a person or a person's property. Examples of a tort include cutting down a tree belonging to another or damaging a person's car by reckless driving. Torts may be intentional or negligent (described below). It is important to understand, however, that an action by someone may create both a criminal act and a tort. For example, suppose two people get into an argument and one strikes the other. The person who struck the victim committed an assault and battery (discussed below). The state could charge that person with assault and battery and, if convicted, jail him or her. That would be a criminal charge.

Additionally, the person who was struck could file a civil complaint alleging the tort of assault and battery, an intentional tort, and seek damages from the assailant. In the O.J. Simpson case, the family of Ronald Goldman, one of the two victims Simpson is alleged to have killed, sued O.J. Simpson. While Simpson was tried for murder when the State of California brought criminal charges and was found innocent by a jury, he nevertheless was required to defend a civil action alleging a wrongful death. Eventually, he lost that tort litigation and owed the family of Ron Goldman millions of dollars in damages awarded in the lawsuit. Essentially, a wrongful death alleges that a person (i.e., Ron Goldman) was killed due to the unlawful actions of the defendant (i.e., O.J. Simpson) and that the defendant is liable for damages resulting from the death. Thus, the same act resulted in criminal charges and civil complaints.

Common law courts created the **felonies** of murder, suicide, manslaughter, burglary, arson, robbery, larceny, rape, sodomy, and mayhem. These offenses generally carried a possible sentence of more than a year in prison. These same courts gradually developed a set of **misdemeanor** crimes including assault, battery, false imprisonment, libel, perjury, corrupting morals, and disturbing the peace. These offenses were generally punishable by a sentence of less than a year in prison. Many states in the United States, particularly on the East Coast, relied and continue to rely heavily on the common law definitions of these crimes.

## Statutory and Code Law

As the nation grew, the complexity of life and changing social norms outstripped the ability of the courts to respond. The creation of common law took centuries and required centuries to evolve, but the changes that came with expansion and industrialization required a more rapid adjustment; so reformers used legislative efforts to create new laws. Legislative bodies such as the Congress of the United States and state legislatures passed formal laws that adopted common law definitions of some crimes. These legislatures also created new crimes. Laws that are passed by a legislative body are called statutes and are compiled into a coded (numbered) collection of laws (often referred to as the "state code"). When a law is passed by a legislative body, it becomes **statutory law**. It is assigned a number and placed into the state's code. The process of numbering statutes is called codification. All laws of a given type are placed in one section of the code making it easy to find. For example, each state has a Penal Code or Criminal Code, and all crimes in that state are organized in that section of the code, usually called a "Title" (e.g., Title 29). Also, statutes can be related to one another and cross-referenced by the numbering system. This process of adding new social rules to the criminal law greatly increased the number and kinds of things for which a person could be punished. Today, with state and federal jurisdictions included, every person in the United States is subject to thousands of laws for which they can be criminally prosecuted. It is important to locate statutes and cases for research and reference purposes. **Figure 6-1** will assist in an initial understanding of how to read statutory and case references.

Criminal justice students are frequently confronted with footnotes that refer to a case or a statute. How would you find these cases or statutes if you wanted to see the original? The citation attached to each case or statute is the key to finding the original. But what do they mean?

**Looking up a statute      42 USC 1981**

The statute noted here is described later in this chapter. Where would you find the original? In citing a statute, common practice requires the *first* number to be the volume or *title* of the code in which this section is found. The second number is the number given to that section of the title. Sections are always in consecutive order (e.g., 1981, 1982, 1983, etc.). The letters in the middle are an abbreviation for the name of the code. The way to read this statute citation is **Title 42, United States Code, section 1981**. Once you know that, all you need to do is find a copy of the Federal Code in the library. Locate the volume labeled 42 (this title may be split into several volumes due to its size). Flip through the pages to section 1981. You will notice that after a code section, there is a long list of what are called *annotations*. These are brief (usually short paragraphs) summaries of cases which interpreted that section. This is a good way to see what this section means.

**State codes**

The various state codes vary considerably in format and numbering. For example, 13-1105 ARS is the shorthand citation for the Arizona Revised Statute, Title 13, Section 1105 which is the criminal code section for first-degree murder.

In Ohio, RC § 2907.04 is the Ohio Revised Code section for unlawful sexual conduct with minor. RCW 9A.40.020 refers to the Revised Code of Washington for its statute on kidnapping in the first degree. One can find all the state codes by searching the World Wide Web, especially at http://www.findlaw.com/11stategov/indexcode.html.

**Looking up a case      *Rizzo v. Goode* 423 U.S. 362, (1976)**

The case name is that assigned by the court issuing the opinion. Case names carry the name of *two* of the parties to the case. There may be more, but this is the official title of the case. The *first* number is the volume of the *reporter* in which the case is found. Reporters literally report cases. In this case, U.S. is read as United States Reports, which is the official reporter for the United States Supreme Court. Volumes are in consecutive order. Every time a case is decided by the Supreme Court, it is placed in the reporter. Cases are placed in consecutive order based upon the date they are decided. Cases appearing in Volume 422, therefore, were merely announced before this case. The second number is the *page* number of the volume in question. Hence, this case citation is read as **Rizzo versus Goode, volume 423 of the United States Reports, at page 362**. The date, 1976, is used as a reference point only. The volume and page numbers are critical. One set of reference books, called *Shepard's Citations*, permits you to take the volume and page number of this case (or any case) and look up *the citations of every case that cited this case*. This is how legal research is done. The same process works for statutes and code sections.

**Figure 6-1** Reading code and case citations.

## The Model Penal Code

Many crimes have been standardized into the **model penal code** (MPC) which was adopted by many states. The MPC was written by the American Law Institute, which is supported by the legal community and sought to bring consistency to issues of law common in all states. If each state adopted the same code and each used the same definitions for each crime, confusion and inequity would decrease. Despite these efforts, however, even states adopting the MPC have changed major portions of that code. What is either legal or a minor offense in one state may well be illegal or a very serious offense in another. For example, in Georgia, breaking into an unattached garage is felony burglary; in Ohio it is criminal trespass, a misdemeanor. Similarly, possession of a small amount of marijuana may be trivial in one state such as Ohio or California, but very serious in Mississippi. While "common law" crimes are basically illegal in all states, the punishment for any one of them may not be the same in all states. This causes confusion for law enforcement. It also makes it very difficult to keep records that communicate useable information on offenders. A computerized **rap sheet**, which is a record of an individual's offenses, will usually not describe in detail the nature of a crime in the state from which the conviction was noted. This can cause a problem if, for example, the defendant can be charged with enhanced penalties or a higher level of offense based upon a prior offense. For example, in many states a conviction for petty theft (misdemeanor theft) may elevate a subsequent petty theft to the felony level of grand theft merely on the basis of a prior theft offense. However, unless the title of the prior crime is clear, it could be overlooked. The same is true for registered sex offenders, or morals offenses. In some states, people accused of urinating in public at a party or outside of a bar were frequently charged with "indecent exposure." Unfortunately, that offense is now seen as a "sex" offense requiring offenders to register as "sex offenders," a result that surely was not intended.

## ■ The Constitution

Another source of law that significantly influences law enforcement is the Constitution of the United States (see Appendix I). The body of law that has evolved around the Constitution is called, quite simply, **constitutional law**. The Constitution is the "supreme law of the land" (*Marbury v. Madison*, 1 Cranch 137, 1803). This means that no state law may contradict the US Constitution. A constitution plays a specific role in our system of law and politics. Theoretically, it is a grant of power from the people to the government. That means that the power of government is limited by the terms of the grant (the Constitution).

The Constitution is a contract. Political theorists describe it as a social contract. If you buy a car and you obtain a loan, you agree to pay a certain amount of money each month. The loan company cannot change the terms of that agreement and make you pay more. In the same way, the Constitution is a limited grant of authority. However, the government (both state and federal) can use every bit of that authority until it is revoked or altered by amending the Constitution.

The first portion of the United States Constitution sets out, in very broad terms, the powers of Congress, the president, and the federal judiciary. The Constitution specifically created a Supreme Court, but it left the size of the court to be determined by Congress. The size of the Supreme Court has varied from four members to its current size of nine.

### The Bill of Rights

While the Constitution itself is a limited grant of authority, there are also specific limitations on the use of that authority. We call these the Bill of Rights. Generally, people think of these as the first ten amendments to the Constitution. Actually, only the first eight are truly rights. The ninth and tenth amendments attempt to clarify the meaning of limited federal authority and the retention of state roles. The actual meaning of these last two amendments remains the subject of great debate among scholars in constitutional law. The federal constitution, specifically the Bill of Rights, tends to play more of a restrictive role on law enforcement. The amendments we call the Bill of Rights have been repeatedly interpreted by the Supreme Court of the United States. It is these amendments that are most troublesome for law enforcement, since theoretically officers must follow the court's pronouncements or risk losing a case or being sued or both (see Appendix I for the Bill of Rights). We will see later in this chapter, however, that the assumption that officers in fact heed the law is not always a good one.

Originally, the Bill of Rights did not apply to the states. When the Constitution was reported out from the Constitutional Convention in 1787 for ratification by the 13 former colonies, there was no Bill of Rights. During the debate over approval (ratification) of the Constitution, concern was expressed in many states over the potential power of a centralized government. This concern resulted in the adoption of a Bill of Rights that was attached to the Constitution in 1791. These amendments sought to limit the power of the federal government. They were not intended to apply to the states. The Supreme Court held in 1833 that the Bill of Rights was only a limitation upon the power of the national government (*Barron v. Mayor and City Council of Baltimore*, 7 Pet. 243, 1833). Until the Civil War, this was the understanding of the role of the Bill of Rights.

## The Fourteenth Amendment

The Fourteenth Amendment was adopted in 1868, after the Civil War, and was forced on the secessionist states (the southern states that tried to leave the union) as part of the terms to end the war. This amendment was designed to restrict the states in their operations and power, an action that seemed necessary after the Civil War. However, it was nearly 80 years before the Fourteenth Amendment was interpreted by the Supreme Court as protecting individual rights from encroachment by the states. Beginning in the mid-1940s, the Supreme Court held that portions of the Bill of Rights were incorporated into the Fourteenth Amendment (see **Figure 6-2**). This meant certain rights found in the Bill of Rights were considered to be part of that amendment and, therefore, applicable to the states.

Many restrictions of state power in the area of criminal procedure have resulted from this incorporation approach. For example, a search of one's belongings and a seizure of evidence are restricted by the Fourth Amendment. The Constitution governs the daily activities of law enforcement because it directly limits how officers perform their duties. Because law enforcement officers take an oath to uphold the Constitution of the United States, they are also restricted by their duty as officers of the Constitution.

## Administrative Law

Another source of law that affects law enforcement comes from what is known as **administrative law**. This body of law is relatively recent and in-

Section 1. All persons born or naturalized in the United States and subject to the jurisdiction thereof, are citizens of the United States and of the State wherein they reside. No State shall make or enforce any law which shall abridge the privileges or immunities of citizens of the United States; nor shall any State deprive any person of life, liberty, or property, without due process of law; nor deny to any person within its jurisdiction the equal protection of the laws.

**Figure 6-2** Section 1 of Amendment XIV to the Constitution of the United States.

cludes court-made law, agency rules, and statutory law. It had its beginnings with the creation of the civil service and state regulation of the economy in the 1880s. The purpose of administrative law is to guide the process of administrative officers in government agencies and guard against arbitrary decisions. Essentially, administrative law flows from one central principle, the rule of law, which seeks to remove arbitrariness from decision making (Carter and Harrington 1991). An arbitrary decision is one that has no clear objective criteria from which to judge each event. If a decision is made without clear criteria, the possibility is very high that the decision rule will differ from case to case. That is, different standards could be used for different people, which is obviously unfair. This means that decisions of administrative officers must meet, and be based upon, criteria or standards that are applied to each case in the same manner. This area of law impacts law enforcement because, among many other things, it deals with the procedure for hiring, promoting, and disciplining law enforcement officers (see **Figure 6-3**).

Actions of an administrative officer (such as a chief of police) must be based upon statutory authority, which is delegated to that administrative officer. This is called **delegation of authority**. It means that a legislative body gave authority to make laws or administrative rules in a certain area to a specific administrative officer or agency. The reasons for the need for administrative law are twofold: (1) legislatures cannot plan all possible alternative situations within a given law, and (2) administrative agencies must have some freedom to make rules based upon their experience but guided by the law. This is guided discretion. Rules must be adopted in a public manner and generally must be supported with facts. In other words, not only must decisions be free of arbitrariness, but so must rules. For example, a state statute may give chiefs of police authority to make "all necessary rules and regulations for the orderly management" of their department. Relying upon standards of the profession and known training standards, a chief might promulgate (or write) rules that govern procedures for citizen complaints, review of disciplinary actions, job functions, and the like. These are known as the "Policy and Procedures Manual," but they are not the same from department to department. That is because the chief was given discretion to draw rules which are merely guided by some standard principles. Hence, the rules are not arbitrary, nor is their application. The rule making process must produce written regulations (oral regulations are not enforceable).

Additionally, rules must be applied to everyone in the same manner. Exceptions cannot be made. If there are "exceptions," they are based on the rules and, therefore, are not really exceptions. In fact, many administrators make exceptions. It is important to understand that once exceptions are made, it is difficult to argue that you treat everyone the same. More importantly, because true "exceptions" are outside of the rules, you cannot distinguish between one exception and another. For example, suppose a chief of police has three rookie police officers, each of whom

| | |
|---|---|
| State training curriculum | State labor relation procedures |
| Mandated selection criteria | OSHA-type safety regulations |
| Civil service testing procedures | Personnel appeals boards |
| Police insignia and uniform standards | Vehicle/equipment bidding procedures |
| Promotion procedures and criteria | Licensing/certification provisions |

**Figure 6-3** Examples of administrative law affecting policing.

has violated similar, but minor, rules during their field training. Assuming the violations are similar, the chief generally would be required to treat all three similarly.

A decision must be based upon standards or criteria found in the rules, and facts must support the decision. This is the process designed to prevent biased decisions from being made and insures due process. It ensures that two people with similar facts or problems will be treated in the same manner. Law enforcement officers should also know that this process protects them. If you follow policy, you will generally be safe.

Parties that are affected by a rule or its potential enforcement must be given an opportunity to challenge any potential adverse decision before it is made. This is usually called an opportunity for an administrative hearing coupled with "notice." Notice means simply being informed of what the substance of the claim involves and the time and place set for the hearing. An administrative hearing does not mean a trial, or even face-to-face discussion. It means that an administrative officer is preparing to make a decision, and that the time and place of the decision is given to the affected parties. It also means the affected parties are entitled to know the position of the administrative officer and may respond before a decision is reached on the merits of the issue. Finally, some process of appeal is essential.

Together, all of these requirements are generally called **minimum administrative due process**. Due process essentially requires fundamental fairness. In the area of administrative law this usually means notice of the nature of a pending administrative action, an opportunity to respond, and the basis of the proposed action. This is a constitutional standard applied to ensure that government does not treat people unfairly or arbitrarily. **Figure 6-4** contains a section from the Federal Administrative Procedures Act that describes certain rights of individuals who suffer legal wrong because of federal agency actions.

Other examples of administrative law are those which comprise the process of hiring, training, promoting, deploying, and disciplining personnel. These are sometimes called

### § 702. *Right of Review*

A person suffering legal wrong because of agency action, or adversely affected or aggrieved by agency action within the meaning of a relevant statute, is entitled to judicial review thereof. An action in a court of the United States seeking relief other than money damages and stating in a claim that an agency or an officer or employee thereof acted or failed to act in an official capacity or under color of legal authority shall not be dismissed nor relief therein be denied on the ground that it is against the United States or that the United States is an indispensable party. The United States may be named as a defendant in such action and a judgment or decree may be entered against the United States: *Provided,* that any mandatory or injunctive decree shall specify the Federal officer or officers (by name or by title), and their successors in office, personally responsible for compliance. Nothing herein (1) affects other limitations on judicial review or the power or duty of the court to dismiss any action or deny relief on any other appropriate legal or equitable ground; or (2) confers authority to grant relief if any other statute that grants consent to suit expressly or impliedly forbids the relief which is sought.

### § 703. *Form and Venue of Proceedings*

The form of proceeding for judicial review is the special statutory review proceeding relevant to the subject matter in a court specified by statute or, in the absence of inadequacy thereof, any applicable form of legal action, including actions for declaratory judgments or writs or prohibitory or mandatory injunction or habeas corpus, in a court of competent jurisdiction. If no special statutory review proceeding in applicable, the action for judicial review may be brought against the United States, the agency by its official title, or the appropriate officer. Except to the extent that prior, adequate, and exclusive opportunity for judicial review is provided by law, agency action is subject to judicial review in civil or criminal proceedings for judicial enforcement.

*Source:* Federal Administrative Procedures Act, 5 U.S.C. §702 and 703, 2004.

**Figure 6-4** Review of federal agency actions.

personnel policies and some of these issues are covered in detail in Chapter 9 of this text. For example, what authority does a chief of police have in prohibiting officers under her command from speaking to the press or city council? What limitations are there for assigning personnel to various duties? What actions are required in order to fairly terminate someone's employment? These and other similar matters are the subject of administrative law.

It is clear that each of these sources of law affects law enforcement in many ways. Because law enforcement must respond to all of these areas of law, the environment for law enforcement is growing more and more complex. Law enforcement officers of the past rarely had to worry about such matters. US law continues to evolve, and law enforcement must be alert to these developments.

## ■ The US System of Justice

The US system of justice is frequently called a "dual system of justice" because there are two parallel systems of courts. The state court system is typically made up of three levels of courts: trial, appellate, and supreme courts. The federal system is generally designed along the same pattern (see **Figure 6-5**). Both systems have special types of trial courts, but these courts differ in their jurisdictions (the types of cases a court can hear). Geographical jurisdiction (also called venue) means the courts can hear only cases occurring in their city, county, state, or district. Some federal courts, such as the US Supreme Court, have no geographical limits and theoretically may hear a case originating anywhere in the United States or its territories so long as it is on appeal (the original jurisdiction of the Supreme Court is very limited). Other jurisdictional factors involve the seriousness of the case. If a case is civil but involves a small amount of money, jurisdiction may be restricted to a municipal court. The same is frequently true for misdemeanor offenses in criminal codes, which is an example of jurisdiction based upon the substance of the case. This provides the difference between subject matter jurisdiction (the type of case), and geographical jurisdiction (an area such as a county or city). Municipal courts, for example, rarely have subject matter jurisdiction to try felony cases, but a county trial court such as the Superior Court in California does have subject matter jurisdiction of felony trials. Similarly, the courts in Greene County, Arkansas do not usually have jurisdiction over crimes that occurred in Craighead County, Arkansas (unless venue is moved for reasons of fairness to the defendant).

### Federal Courts

Generally speaking (though not always), federal courts cannot hear cases based upon state law, and state courts

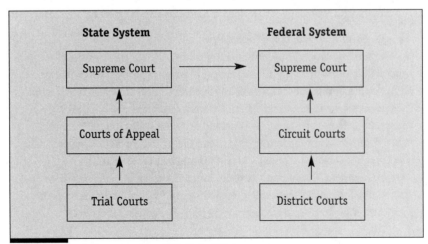

**Figure 6-5** The dual court system of the United States.

cannot hear cases based upon federal law. For example, the federal system employs bankruptcy courts for the special function of trying cases of economic bankruptcy. No state court can hear a bankruptcy claim. In the same manner, a federal trial court such as the Federal District Court cannot hear a case based upon a state's criminal law. State courts can interpret the United States Constitution, but the federal judiciary has the final word on this interpretation. State supreme courts have the final say in the interpretation of state law so long as it does not involve a federal constitutional question. Law enforcement officers at the state and local government level rarely have contact with federal criminal courts, unless working cases involving federal agents that go to trial (this occurs today with some of the cases developed by federal task forces that include state and local law enforcement personnel).

Sometimes a federal court will hear a case that could have been tried in a state court, but which was removed to federal court because the parties live in different states. This is called diversity of jurisdiction and is provided for in the federal code, which sets out the jurisdiction of the federal courts. Basically, the code provides that if two or more parties live in different states, the action may be heard in a federal district court using state law (where the event occurred). This is intended to provide a neutral forum. It attempts to avoid the advantage one party might have just because he or she is from that state.

## Federal Courts and State Crimes

There are only two ways that a state criminal case can be heard by a federal court. First, a defendant might appeal an issue such as the constitutionality of an ordinance or state law. Initially, a state trial court adjudicates such a claim. Regardless of the results of such a ruling, the losing side has the right to appeal. Appeals go to the state court of appeals. Similarly, the court of appeals has the authority to rule on the issue. Again, the losing side may then seek an appeal to that state's highest court. (In most states the highest court is called the Supreme Court. However, in New York the Supreme Court is the trial court and the Court of Appeals is the highest court. The names of courts usually indicate their level, but not always.)

In most states, the Supreme Court of that state can refuse an appeal at its discretion. Whether refused or heard, however, the losing side may still ask the Supreme Court of the United States to hear the case when it involves a federal question which was heard by the highest court in that state. This is done by petitioning the Supreme Court to issue a **writ of certiorari**, which is an order requiring the lower court to give the Supreme Court the record for review. Taking a case to the US Supreme Court is rare, however. Millions of cases, both criminal and civil, are filed in the United States each year, yet only about 5,000 appeals are filed with the Supreme Court each year, and, in a given year, the Supreme Court generally hears only about 100 of those cases. Because state courts are usually bound by *stare decisis* on constitutional issues, they will rarely contradict a rule that the Supreme Court of the United States previously announced as one that would invite a rebuke from the United States Supreme Court.

A second method by which a state criminal case can be heard in a federal court is less rare, but still not very frequent. If a prisoner exhausts all traditional appeals after conviction (as discussed above), there is usually little that can be done. However, if the law upon which he or she was convicted is later challenged or if there is new evidence that was not known at the time of trial, the prisoner may seek a federal **writ of habeas corpus**. This is an order requiring the person who is holding the prisoner, such as a warden or sheriff, to show cause why the prisoner should not be released. It is not truly a criminal case at this stage, but rather a civil case based upon federal law. If the court issues the writ, the prisoner must be released. The state may appeal to the US Court of Appeals or, if need be, the Supreme Court of the United States.

Efforts to secure writs of habeas corpus are not very successful and have generated a good deal of dispute. There is a growing debate over the use of such methods to stall death penalty executions, for example. Still, courts are reluctant to see innocent people punished, and the justice system must assume that errors can be made in any human decision process.

## State Courts

States divide trial responsibility between courts of general jurisdiction and those of limited jurisdiction. The former are generally organized along county boundaries. Some general jurisdiction courts are called common pleas or superior courts. These courts typically hear serious misdemeanors and all felonies as well as large civil law suits. Lower state trial courts such as district, municipal or county courts generally have jurisdiction over traffic cases and misdemeanors as well as uncomplicated civil lawsuits such as small claims. Boundaries of courts with limited jurisdiction are usually within one county but encompass only a portion of that county. Some of these lower courts also have the power to hear the beginning of a felony case, called a **preliminary hearing**. This is a hearing to determine if there is sufficient evidence (probable cause) to send the case to the district attorney or grand jury for further prosecution.

### Trial Courts

Law enforcement officers who go to court will spend most of their time in state trial courts. When an officer makes an arrest, contact with the local court is initiated. Arrests may be the result of either officer discretion or a warrant for arrest previously issued by a court. Officer discretion arrests occur when an officer determines that **probable cause** exists to arrest. Probable cause is not always easy to define, but one US Supreme Court decision described it this way:

> *Probable cause exists where the facts and circumstances within the [arresting officers'] knowledge and of which they had reasonably trustworthy information [are] sufficient in themselves to warrant a [person] of reasonable caution in the belief that an offense has been or is being committed [by the person to be arrested]. Brinegar v. US 338 US 160, 175-176 (1949).*

A determination to arrest may be subject to review first by the officer's supervisor. After the officer submits a report justifying the action, a formal approval or disapproval is noted by the supervisor. In practice, many who are arrested are released at the discretion of the officer and his or her supervisor. Written reports reflect the justification for the action.

Those who study the relationship between law enforcement and the courts notice certain behaviors which reflect the experience of working with one another. For example, even though probable cause may exist, an experienced officer, detective, or supervisor may know that there is insufficient evidence to satisfy the judge or district attorney likely to handle the case. Hence, the officers may decide to dispose of the matter at their level. Sometimes officers release a suspect because of assistance the suspect gave on a co-suspect or on another case. It is also possible that on further investigation the case looked different or another suspect emerged. Finally, officers could "look the other way" in order to develop a confidential informant (CI) for future use, though typically superiors must be informed if this is the case.

In many cases, officer discretion will prevail. However, it is also possible that an assistant district attorney (ADA) or assistant prosecutor will review the reports and initial charges and make an independent determination whether or not to proceed with the charge. Frequently, officers confer with an ADA in order to get advice on cases. Once a charge is made, it may also be reviewed by a court in a probable cause hearing (for misdemeanors) or a preliminary hearing (for felonies). In each case, the purpose of the hearing is to determine whether there is probable cause to proceed with the charge. At any stage of the proceedings, a court has the authority to dismiss a case with or without prejudice. If it is dismissed with prejudice, the charge cannot be re-filed at a later date regardless of the evidence then available. If it is dismissed without prejudice, the charge may be re-filed.

Arrest warrants are issued by an officer of the court after a probable cause hearing as the result of an indictment by a grand jury, or by the issuance of a prosecutor's information. In each case, the investigating officers must present testimony to justify issuance. The process varies slightly from state to state.If a charge is formally approved and moves to the warrant stage, the next step is either a dismissal, a plea, or a trial. If there is a plea to the charges, it may involve what is called a plea bargain. Typically this involves a discussion involving defense counsel, the prosecutor, and a judge. Law enforcement officers are frequently involved in plea discussions and should be prepared to make their case. It is possible that other participants in plea discussions will include probation officers, psychologists, and social workers.

The object of the prosecution is to obtain a guilty plea. One way to obtain that is to either agree to the potential sentence of a defendant or reduce the charge to a lesser included offense. In either case, the potential sentence of a defendant appears to be reduced. This induces defendants to plead guilty, avoid a trial, and presumably avoid a tougher sentence. The actual sentence may be determined by statute so that the only real "bargaining" concerns the level of offense. But, a sentence discussion may also include a fine, restitution to be paid to a victim, probation terms, and time to be served.

The process of plea bargaining produces heated debate in the public. Some argue that it saves time and money because it eliminates trials. If the incentive were eliminated, defendants might decide to try their case since they could not receive a worse sentence for doing so. In effect, there would be nothing to lose by going to trial. Since only about 5% or less of all cases go to trial, even a slight increase in trials would overwhelm the already over-burdened justice system. Not only would more officers spend their time waiting in courthouse hallways to testify, we would need to add more clerk and court personnel. Further, more citizens would have their lives disrupted for jury service. The cost in additional judges and prosecutors (who would not be available for other duties) would be tremendous. Others argue that deals should not be made with criminals, and the cost should be absorbed by the current system.

Still others argue there really is no plea bargain process at all. Some who have studied several courts across the United States suggest that sentencing outcomes do not differ much regardless of the use of plea bargaining. Rather, each court house seems to have a "going rate" for each kind of offense considering the record of the defendant. In this view, the "bargaining" is really a process of further identifying what the correct charge should be (Nardulli, Flemming, and Eisenstien 1988; Eisenstein, Flemming, and Nardulli 1988).

If there is no plea in the case or if it is not dismissed, the case will go to trial. Before a trial begins, and in some states during trial, hearings may occur which determine the admissibility of evidence. These are called **suppression** hearings. Evidence may be suppressed because of the manner in which it was seized, because it was not presented to the other side during pre-trial discovery, or because of some legal restriction on its use (such as forcing a priest to testify about a parishioner).

### Appellate Courts

While lower trial courts may rule on matters such as the admission of evidence or the constitutionality of a law, it is the state courts of appeals that settle disputes of law by interpreting state law or the state and federal constitutions. Consequently, these courts have a large impact on law enforcement, though officers rarely attend the oral arguments before such courts. These courts hear criminal and civil appeals. These same courts hear appeals from lower courts involving civil service cases and related disputes, including law enforcement hiring and discipline. Because lower courts are required to follow the precedents of the appeals courts, appellate decisions shape behavior in the courts below.

## ■ Procedural Limitations on Law Enforcement

The substantive criminal law is carefully defined by statute. Unfortunately, the procedural restrictions on law enforcement are not so clear. They are unclear because they are based upon relatively vague constitutional provisions such as due process and unreasonable searches and seizures. We will consider only an overview of procedural limitations here, but the restrictions are considerable. Among the most significant are without question those applying to searches and seizures. For both, law enforcement is bound by the Fourth Amendment to the Constitution of the United States and the interpretations that have been made of its language:

> *The right of the people to be secure in their persons, houses, papers, and effects, against unreasonable searches and seizures, shall not be*

*violated, and no warrants shall issue, but upon probable cause, supported by oath or affirmation, and particularly describing the place to be searched, and the persons or things to be seized.*

A **search** is generally defined as the invasion, by an agent of the state, of an area which a person believes is protected or private. That is an area in which it is reasonable for a person to have an expectation of privacy, and those expectations change depending upon where you are. You obviously have a higher expectation of privacy in your own home than you do walking down a public street, even though you have some expectation of privacy there (e.g., the expectation that you will be left alone if you are doing nothing wrong). That belief will be upheld and a search negated by a court if the ". . . person exhibited an actual (subjective) expectation of privacy, and . . . the expectation is one that society is prepared to recognize as 'reasonable'," (*Katz v. US*, 389 US 347, 361; 1967).

A **seizure** is generally defined as a "meaningful interference with the possessory interests of the suspect," (*US v. Jacobsen*, 466 US 109, 113; 1984). The Fourth Amendment applies to searches and seizures of evidence in the same way it applies to arrests. A search or seizure of evidence or persons without a warrant is presumed to be unreasonable. **Figure 6-6** depicts a sample form for a search warrant affidavit and the warrant itself. An officer seeking a search warrant must produce facts in the affidavit which is sworn to in the presence of a judge. The facts must support a conclusion that there is probable cause to believe that evidence of a crime, or a person, will be found in the location names. The affidavit and the warrant, pursuant to constitutional command must "specifically" identify the things or persons to be searched or seized. That specification is the limit of the warrant. Once the items or persons are found the search must end. If evidence turned up in the process of executing the warrant, additional warrant authority must be sought to continue the search. A search can be of a person or a person's property. Similarly, a seizure may be of property, but it may also be of a person. The latter are called arrests. After arrest, suspects are questioned, and this behavior is limited by the fifth and sixth amendments.

The general rule of searches and seizures holds that without a warrant, any search or seizure is presumed to be unconstitutional (see *Payton v. New York*, 445 US 573; 1980 and *Chimel v. California*, 395 US 752; 1969). The Fourth Amendment does not require a warrant; it only prohibits a search or seizure that is "unreasonable." The Supreme Court of the United States firmly established the doctrine that absence of a warrant raises the presumption that the search or seizure in question is unreasonable and, therefore, unconstitutional. It is also generally required that before serving a warrant, officers must "knock and announce" their intentions of serving a search or arrest warrant at a premises (Cerullo and Means 2004). The court also created many exceptions to this doctrine, which serve to rebut the presumption of unreasonableness. In effect, the court made these exceptions statements of reasonableness. If any of the recognized exceptional circumstances apply, the search or seizure is considered reasonable. The ability to understand search and seizure limits on law enforcement, therefore, depends upon one's knowledge of the exceptions to the warrant rule.

**STATE OF CALIFORNIA – COUNTY OF BUTTE**
**SEARCH WARRANT AND AFFIDAVIT**
**(Affidavit)**

_____, being sworn, says that on the basis of the information contained within this
(Name of Affiant)

Search Warrant and Affidavit and the attached and incorporated Statement of Probable Cause, he/she has probable cause to believe and does believe that the property described below is lawfully seizable pursuant to Penal Code Section 1524, as indicated below, and is now located at the locations set forth below. Wherefore, affiant requests that this Search Warrant be issued.

_____, NIGHT SEARCH REQUESTED:     YES [  ]   NO [  ]
(Signature of Affiant)

**(SEARCH WARRANT)**

THE PEOPLE OF THE STATE OF CALIFORNIA TO ANY SHERIFF, POLICEMAN OR PEACE OFFICER IN THE COUNTY OF BUTTE: proof by affidavit having been made before me by _____
(Name of Affiant)

that there is probable cause to believe that the property described herein may be found at the locations set forth herein and that it is lawfully seizable pursuant to Penal Code Section 1524 as indicated below by "x" in that it:

_____ was stolen or embezzled.

_____ was used the means of committing a felony.

_____ is possessed by a person with the intent to use it as means of committing a public offense or is possessed by another to whom he or she may have delivered it for the purpose of concealing it or preventing its discovery.

_____tends to show that a felony has been committed or that a particular person has committed a felony.

_____tends to show that sexual exploitation of a child, in violation of P.C. Section 311.3 has occurred or is occurring.

**YOU ARE THEREFORE COMMANDED TO SEARCH:**

**FOR THE FOLLOWING PROPERTY:**

**AND TO SEIZE IT IF FOUND** and bring it forthwith before me, or this court, at the courthouse of this court. This Search Warrant and incorporated Affidavit was sworn to and subscribed before me this _____ day of _____, _____, at _____ A.M./P.M. Wherefore, I find probable cause for the issuance of this Search Warrant and do issue it.

_____, NIGHT SEARCH APPROVED:     YES [  ]   NO [  ]
(Signature of Magistrate)

Courtesy of Sheriff Scott A. Mackenzie, Butte County Sheriff's Office, Oroville, California, 1999.

**Figure 6-6** Sample search warrant and affidavit.

## Arrest of the Person

The Supreme Court traditionally interpreted arrest to mean any substantial limit upon the ability of a person to freely come and go. Recently that same court revised that principle: "An arrest requires either physical force. . . , or, where that is absent, submission to the assertion of authority . . . ." (*California v. Hodari D.*, 499 US 621, 1991). When is a warrantless arrest an "unreasonable" seizure under the Fourth Amendment? Generally speaking, the following rules have emerged. An arrest is reasonable if one of the following is true:

1. The offense was committed in the presence of an officer.
2. The offense is a felony, and the officer has probable cause to believe the defendant committed it.
3. The offense, though a misdemeanor, is one of violence, and the officer has probable cause to believe that the defendant committed the offense (the test is most applicable to domestic violence cases, for example). This applies whether or not the offense was committed in the presence of the officer.

Each of these exceptions relies upon the establishment of "probable cause." It is certainly easier to establish probable cause if the officer sees the defendant assault someone or commit some other offense. Otherwise, law enforcement officers must rely upon their training, education, and experience to determine if probable cause is present and sufficient to justify a warrantless arrest.

If the case falls outside these exceptions, then law enforcement officials must seek the issuance of an arrest warrant based upon the evidence available. This typically requires a "neutral magistrate" (typically a judge or in some states a clerk of courts) to determine whether sufficient evidence exists for a warrant to issue. The same standard of probable cause used for warrantless arrests applies for the issuance of a warrant.

The reason for the general **warrant requirement** is to reduce the likelihood of arbitrary arrests. The reason for the exceptions to the warrant requirement is the belief that in those circumstances set forth above, arrest without a warrant is "reasonable" within the meaning of the Fourth Amendment. For example, it makes sense that if a crime is committed in front of an officer, it would frustrate the meaning of justice in a civil society to delay arrest. Similar rationales are used by courts in the other circumstances. However, it is still good practice to obtain a warrant if there is time to do so. The risk of being wrong is not worth mere convenience.

## Search and Seizure

There are also a multitude of circumstances that are clearly law enforcement initiated stops, but which may or may not reach the status of being full arrests. These require careful study by law enforcement. While the restrictions on the seizure or arrest of an individual are relatively clear, the restrictions that cover a search of a person or his property and seizure of that property are less clear. It is frequently the case that stops, searches, and seizures are closely related in the field.

However, as in arrest, there are various specific exceptions that permit law enforcement officers to engage in searches for evidence, and the seizure thereof, without a warrant to do so. One way to think of these exceptions to the warrant rule is to imagine the expectation of privacy as a cave. The deeper law enforcement seeks to go into the cave, the greater the justification it needs. The exceptions to the warrant rule focus on the question of how reasonable the claimed expectation of privacy may be in the particular circumstances of that search. Some of the most important of these exceptions we address next.

## Stop and Frisk

Most of us would expect to have some privacy as we walk along a public street. But our behavior, if not criminal per se, may lead others to conclude that we may be preparing to commit a crime. In *Terry v. Ohio* (392 US 1, 1968), Chief Justice Earl Warren of the United States Supreme Court contemplated a case in which an off duty Cleveland, Ohio police detective saw such activity (**Figure 6-7**). In the holding, the court announced the rule for "**stop and frisk**" cases. While the court permitted a "pat down" of the outer clothing for weapons, a full search of the person was not reasonable in the circumstances. The court recently revisited this issue and focused on a pat down that found not weapons, but crack cocaine. The court found that while an officer could seize something other than a weapon after a stop and frisk pat down, the nature of the item would need to be clear after a mere pat down. In reversing the conviction in this case, the court found that the officer had to manipulate the item through the outer clothing to determine what it might be. That, the court held, was going too far (*Minnesota v. Dickerson*, 506 US 366, 1993). In other words, the item being felt had to be identifiable immediately. Moreover, a *Terry* Search cannot be conducted on a hunch, but only upon facts that can be articulated and produce reasonable suspicion that crime may be afoot, thus justifying a brief stop and inquiry. The pat down is merely for safety of the officers and others, including the subject of the inquiry.

It is also important to keep in mind that police cannot randomly stop you on the street and ask you questions. In order for them to do that there must be some reasonable suspicion that you are engaging in some sort of crime or that you may be a witness to a criminal offense that the officer is investigating. In 2004, the US Supreme Court ruled that under such circumstances failure to give your name when asked can constitutionally lead to an arrest (*Hiibal v. Sixth Judicial District Court of Nevada*, US, 124 S. Ct. 2451, 2004).

## Search Incident to Arrest

Another exception, rarely commented upon but the subject of many Supreme Court cases, is the limit of a search incident to arrest. When a person is lawfully arrested (by warrant or otherwise), law enforcement officers may search the immediate vicinity of the person in order to secure any weapons or evidence within the suspect's reach (*Chimel v. California*, 395 US 752, 1969). This does not include an entire house, or even an entire car or locked baggage in a car. However, officers may conduct a "protective sweep" of a house to search very briefly for more victims or potential

"We merely hold today that where a police officer observes unusual conduct which leads him reasonably to conclude in light of his experience that criminal activity may be afoot and that the persons with whom he is dealing may be armed and presently dangerous, where in the course of investigating this behavior he identifies himself as a policeman and makes reasonable inquiries, and where nothing in the initial stages of the encounter serves to dispel his reasonable fear for his own or others' safety, he is entitled for the protection of himself and others in the area to conduct a carefully limited search of the outer clothing of such persons in an attempt to discover weapons which might be used to assault him." *Terry v. Ohio*, 392 US 1, (1968).

"It remains unclear how many different types of non-arrest detentions might usefully or perhaps must be distinguished for Fourth Amendment purposes. Those detentions of major concern are what is often called 'investigatory stops,' 'investigatory detentions,' 'field stops,' or—memorializing *Terry v. Ohio*—'*Terry* stops.' They are widely assumed to be detentions made in the field for the purposes of gathering further information upon which to base a decision as to whether or not to arrest the suspect. It is similarly assumed that they are and should be effected in situations presenting inadequate grounds for arrest and that they cannot involve either prolonged detention of the suspect or substantial movement of the suspect during the detention."

*Source:* Miller, Frank W., Robert O. Dawson, George E. Dix, Raymond I. Parnas (1991). *The Police Function*, 5th Edition. Westbury, NY: The Foundation Press, Inc., p. 210.

**Figure 6-7** Stop and frisk.

assailants who may pose a threat to the officers if the officers might reasonably expect to find such persons (*Maryland v. Buie*, 494 US 325, 1990). Obviously, people do not hide in cupboards or in drawers, so this is a limited exception, taken by itself.

## Automobile Exception

Officers may also conduct a full search of a vehicle at the time of an arrest or stop if there is probable cause to believe the vehicle contains evidence of a crime. This includes any packages or bags in the car (*Carroll v. United States*, 267 US 132, 1925 and *California v. Acevedo*, 500 US 565, 1991). The theory behind the automobile exception is, first, that cars are mobile and can carry away the evidence they contain. Secondly, automobiles are highly regulated and, therefore, offer a low expectation of privacy. Hence, if a reliable informant suggests that a bag in the trunk contains drugs, the car may be stopped and the trunk searched as well as any bag in the trunk. However, this probable cause would not necessarily transfer to a suitcase in the back seat. Absent probable cause to search an automobile, officers may only search for weapons in the areas immediately within the reach of the occupant(s) (*Adams v. Williams*, 407 US 143, 1972). This is the automobile version of a stop and frisk.

Some commentators refer to this as an **exigent circumstances** search. Exigent circumstances refer to the conditions that create a need for immediate action to prevent the destruction of evidence. But, the Supreme Court made it clear that the automobile exception to the warrant rule is not that simple. For one thing, exigent circumstances cannot create probable cause or even reasonable suspicion. Second, the fact that an automobile is the subject of the search does not create an exigent circumstance. The automobile (or other vehicle) may add to the conditions, but alone it is not enough to create exigent circumstances. The touchstone of the exception is the pre-existence of probable cause. Probable cause may exist before the stop or it may develop in the course of a routine traffic stop. But without probable cause, only a *Terry* type of weapons check is permissible. **Figure 6-8** illustrates the complexity involved in legal issues surrounding automobile searches.

In April of 1999, the US Supreme Court ruled in *Wyoming v. Houghton* (526 US 295, 1999) that when law enforcement officers have probable cause to search a car, they may inspect passengers' belongings found in the car that are capable of concealing the object of the search. This decision triggered debate among civil libertarians who believe the law enforcement community will abuse the ruling. Recent research has confirmed some of those fears. Early on in the court's debate about applying federal standards of search and seizure to the states, many on the court repeated the belief that violations of rights by unconstitutional searches could be remedied with suppression of the evidence. For example, police could be kept in check by being sued for their actions. That reasoning eventually failed, as we will see later in this chapter. But the question the court never thought to ask was what about violations of constitutional rights that never see a courtroom. That is what several researches found in a study reported in the summer of 2004 (Gould and Mastrofski). The researchers engaged in direct observations of more than 100 street searches (*Terry* Searches), recording the evidence

BLACKMUN, J., delivered the opinion of the Court,

Although we have recognized firmly that *the doctrine of stare decisis serves profoundly important purposes* in our legal system, *this Court has overruled a prior case on the comparatively rare occasion when it has bred confusion or been a derelict or led to anomalous results.*

In the case before us, *the police had probable cause to believe that the paper bag in the automobile's trunk contained marijuana.* That probable cause now allows a warrantless search of the paper bag. The facts in the record reveal that *the police did not have probable cause to believe that contraband was hidden in any other part of the automobile and a search of the entire vehicle would have been without probable cause and unreasonable under the Fourth Amendment.*

Our holding today neither extends the Carroll doctrine nor broadens the scope of the permissible automobile search delineated in Carroll, Chambers, and Ross. *It remains a cardinal principle that "searches conducted outside the judicial process, without prior approval by judge or magistrate, are per se unreasonable under the Fourth Amendment subject only to a few specifically established and well-delineated exceptions."* Mincey v. Arizona, 437 US 385, 390 (1978), quoting *Katz v. United States*, 389 US 347, 357 (1967).

Until today, this Court has drawn a curious line between the search of an automobile that coincidentally turns up a container and the search of a container that coincidentally turns up in an automobile. The protections of the Fourth Amendment must not turn on such coincidences. We therefore interpret Carroll as providing one rule to govern all automobile searches. The police may search an automobile and the containers within it where they have probable cause to believe contraband or evidence is contained (emphasis added).

**Figure 6-8** *California v. Acevedo*, 500 US 565 (1991).

which led to the stop and frisk, the actions of the officers, and the results. This information was coded by experienced criminal prosecutors and investigators as either being constitutional or not constitutional. Startlingly, 30% of the searches conducted were found to be unconstitutional. Broken down by type of search, 45.5% of *Terry*-style pat-down searches were unconstitutional, while 19.7% of the full searches were deemed unconstitutional. Even worse, only 18% of the unconstitutional searches resulted in citations or arrests and 84% of all searches were conducted on non-whites.

Areas involving "searches" of vehicles using technological devices are less clear. Currently, it is unclear, for example, if GPS or global positioning system sensors can be attached to vehicles without a warrant. This would enable law enforcement to track a vehicle wherever it went, an important investigative tool. At the moment, the law is unclear as different state supreme courts have rendered different answers and the federal courts have not weighed in. That said, the Supreme Court did strike down a conviction in Oregon for drug cultivation where the police employed a thermal imaging device on a home to literally see through the house—including into the bathroom—in order to gather evidence to obtain search and arrest warrants. Based on this device, it was obvious that the residents of the house were growing large numbers of marijuana plants. The court found that the use of such a device, "not generally in use in the public," violated the expectation of privacy and effectively suppressed all of the evidence (*Kyllo v. United States*, 533 US 27, 2001).

## Administrative Searches

Officers may seize a vehicle when the driver is arrested or the automobile is evidence in a crime, and they may conduct an impoundment (or inventory) search. If personal belongings or automobiles are routinely seized at arrest as a matter of departmental policy, these may be fully searched in order to protect the property of the defendant and to protect officers from claims of property theft, loss or damage. However, there must be some departmental rule or standard practice that supports an impoundment (*South Dakota v. Opperman*, 428 US 364, 1976 and

*Chambers v. Maloney*, 399 US 42, 1970). Any evidence found in the process of such a search may be seized.

## Check Points

Another type of exception is the checkpoint. Checkpoints may be employed in a number of limited circumstances. One example is the sobriety checkpoint. Automobiles may be stopped and the driver directed to answer questions if certain conditions are met. First, the initial stop at a checkpoint must be directed at all vehicles passing the point. Second, the intrusion must be minimal in order to remain "reasonable" under the standards of the Fourth Amendment. Merely stopping each car briefly in order to make limited inquiries is reasonable. Further inquiries, such as field sobriety testing, could be done if and only if the initial contact produced reasonable suspicion to precede further (*Michigan Department of State Police v. Sitz*, 496 US 444, 1990). This type of stop is considered reasonable because the expectation of privacy on public highways is very low, and automobiles are highly regulated. However, random stops are not permissible (*US v. Martinez-Fuerte*, 428 US 543, 1976). However, an investigative or informational checkpoint is valid. If officers stop vehicles coming through an area where a crime has been committed (in this case a vehicular homicide) then a simple inquiry as to whether the driver or passengers saw anything is a reasonable reason to stop vehicles, so long as all are stopped at that point (*Illinois v. Lidster, US*, 2004). However, crime control checkpoints with drug sniffing dogs and visual examination of the interior of the vehicle are not constitutionally permissible (*City of Indianapolis v. Edmond*, 531 US 32, 2000). Still, border patrol checkpoints for citizenship papers are constitutional (*U.S. v. Martinez-Fuerte*, 428 US 543, 1976).

## Airports and Public Transit

Since the events of September 11, 2001, airport security, and the security concerns regarding ports and other public conveyances, have escalated significantly. However, search and seizure law has for a considerable time reflected the dual concerns of privacy expectations and security needs in these locations. The law regarding airports, and, by implication, other public conveyances, has developed into three different types of possible exceptions to the warrant rule. First, administrative searches (based upon the same principles as general administrative searches) may be carried out for passenger screening so long as it is employed as a regulatory scheme to deter hijackers and not for the purpose of criminal investigation (e.g., narcotics trafficking) (*United States v. Davis*, 482 F.2d 893, 9th Circuit, 1973). Second, *Terry* Searches may be conducted so long as the conditions warrant. In the leading case, the search was conducted in the lounge at the boarding gate and the bulge in the passenger's pocket and his nervous demeanor suggested further inquiry was in order. However, the courts have distinguished between passengers about to board and other people in the air terminal (*United States v. Moreno*, 475 F.2d 44, 5th Circuit, 1973 and *United States v. Skipwith*, 482 F.2d 1272, 5th Circuit, 1973). Finally, there are issues of implied and express consent. Generally, passengers must be given the opportunity to avoid a search by refusing to fly. However, if they place their luggage on the conveyer for boarding the implication is that they have consented (*United States v. Pulido-Baquerizo*, 800 F.2d 899, 9th Circuit, 1986).

## Schools

See **Figure 6-9** for the US Supreme Court's key statements concerning school searches and a general rule regarding searches on public school grounds.

## Plain View

Another very important exception is the **plain view doctrine**. Essentially, this holds that an officer may seize evidence of a crime or contraband that falls into the plain view of the officer when the officer otherwise has a right to be at that location. If in the process of investigating one crime, an officer sees what is clearly evidence of another crime, it may be seized (*Coolidge v. New Hampshire*, 403 US 443, 1971). However, the officer may not take any action to "discover" additional evidence beyond those actions necessary to carry out the tasks that originally

To hold that the Fourth Amendment applies to searches conducted by school authorities is only to begin the inquiry into the standards governing such searches. Although the underlying command of the Fourth Amendment is always that searches and seizures be reasonable, what is reasonable depends on the context within which a search takes place. . . . Of course, the Fourth Amendment does not protect subjective expectations of privacy that are unreasonable or otherwise "illegitimate. . . ." To receive the protection of the Fourth Amendment, an expectation of privacy must be one that society is "prepared to recognize as legitimate. . . ."

Although this Court may take notice of the difficulty of maintaining discipline in the public schools today, the situation is not so dire that students in the schools may claim no legitimate expectations of privacy. We have recently recognized that the need to maintain order in a prison is such that prisoners retain no legitimate expectations of privacy in their cells, but it goes almost without saying that "[t]he prisoner and the schoolchild stand in wholly different circumstances, separated by the harsh facts of criminal conviction and incarceration. . . ." Against the child's interest in privacy must be set the substantial interest of teachers and administrators in maintaining discipline in the classroom and on school grounds. Maintaining order in the classroom has never been easy, but in recent years, school disorder has often taken particularly ugly forms: drug use and violent crime in the schools have become major social problems.

How, then, should we strike the balance between the school child's legitimate expectations of privacy and the school's equally legitimate need to maintain an environment in which learning can take place?

The warrant requirement, in particular, is unsuited to the school environment: requiring a teacher to obtain a warrant before searching a child suspected of an infraction of school rules (or of the criminal law) would unduly interfere with the maintenance of the swift and informal disciplinary procedures needed in the schools. Just as we have in other cases dispensed with the warrant requirement when "the burden of obtaining a warrant is likely to frustrate the governmental purpose behind the search," we hold today that school officials need not obtain a warrant before searching a student who is under their authority.

The fundamental command of the Fourth Amendment is that searches and seizures be reasonable, and although "both the concept of probable cause and the requirement of a warrant bear on the reasonableness of a search, . . . in certain limited circumstances neither is required."

Under ordinary circumstances, *a search of a student by a teacher or other school official will be "justified at its inception" when there are reasonable grounds for suspecting that the search will turn up evidence that the student has violated or is violating either the law or the rules of the school. Such a search will be permissible in its scope when the measures adopted are reasonably related to the objectives of the search and not excessively intrusive in light of the age and sex of the student and the nature of the infraction* (emphasis added).

*Source: New Jersey v. T. L. O.*, 469 US 325 (1985).

**Figure 6-9** School searches.

called the officer there (*Arizona v. Hicks*, 480 US 321, 1987). Plain view means plain view, literally right out there for everyone to see (Hunsucker 2003).

## Consent

One exception, which is more a waiver of rights than a true exception, is that of consent. If a person permits a search to occur without a warrant, assuming the consent was freely and intelligently given, he or she cannot later contest the results of the search. The person who gives consent must have some apparent authority to do so so that it can be said the officers reasonably relied upon the apparent authority (*Illinois v. Rodriguez*, 497 US 177, 1990).

# ■ Consequences of Unlawful Searches

The above exceptions (and some others such as abandoned property, open fields, inevitable discovery, etc.) play a particular role in the administration of the Fourth Amendment relative to searches and seizures. However, if no applicable exception exists and no valid warrant was obtained, the search is unreasonable and is therefore unconstitutional.

## The Exclusionary Rule

The punishment for conducting an unreasonable search is suppression of the evidence. This generally means the evidence may not be used against the defendant. The notion of suppression comes from the **exclusionary rule** at the federal level, which dates back to 1914. The rule was extended to the states as a result of fairly flagrant abuse of authority by police officers in Cleveland, Ohio in the case of *Mapp v. Ohio* (367 US 643, 1961). Officers fabricated a story of a fleeing fugitive to burst into a woman's home. When she demanded a warrant, and was shown a piece of paper, she grabbed the paper, placing it inside an article of her clothing. The officers wrestled her to the ground and removed the paper from her blouse. It was not a warrant. Based upon such outrageous conduct the Supreme Court had little trouble suppressing the evidence officers seized from her home (pornography, which today would look like a famous mail order catalogue) and applying the exclusionary rule to the states, hence ending the prosecution of Ms. Mapp.

## Interrogation

The rules that restrict police questioning of a suspect are, in at least one sense, fairly clear. In another, they are not at all clear. However, there are a few basic notions that we can accept. First, a voluntary statement made by a suspect without any questions being asked is always admissible (*Colorado v. Connelly*, 479 US 157, 1986). But, it is much more likely that questions will be asked by an officer. In order for any responses to be admissible in a court (generally speaking), the suspect must be warned not to say anything. These are the famous *Miranda* warnings (**Figure 6-10**).

It is important to remember that these are warnings, not rights in and of themselves. The warnings were developed because of a long history of abuses by governments using torture to obtain confessions. The history of the Fifth Amendment

". . . (W)e hold that when an individual is taken into custody or otherwise deprived of his freedom by the authorities in any significant way and is subjected to questioning, the privilege against self-incrimination is jeopardized. Procedural safeguards must be employed to protect the privilege, and unless other fully effective means are adopted to notify the person of his right of silence and to assure that the exercise of the right will be scrupulously honored, the following measures are required. *He must be warned prior to any questioning that he has the right to remain silent, that anything he says can be used against him in a court of law, that he has the right to the presence of an attorney, and that if he cannot afford an attorney one will be appointed for him prior to any questioning if he so desires. Opportunity to exercise these rights must be afforded to him throughout the interrogation. . . (T)he individual may knowingly and intelligently waive these rights and agree to answer questions or make a statement*" (emphasis added).

*Source: Miranda v. Arizona, 384 U.S. 436, (1966).*

**Figure 6-10** The *Miranda* warnings.

and its prohibition against self-incrimination is based upon historical lessons. Whenever government has the power to compel confessions, it will use it. If there are no limits, then when is one confession valid and another not? In one case, *Brown v. Mississippi* (297 US 278, 1936), the defendants were beaten and whipped until they confessed. The deputies who presided over the beatings openly admitted their acts (see **Figure 6-11**). It is difficult to imagine how a confession obtained in such a manner can be acceptable in a democracy. Most law enforcement officers today have never seen such behavior. But, at one time it was too common a practice, even in this republic.

On first reading this case, most students cannot believe it happened in the United States. Yet it did. If our system is designed to seek justice, coerced confessions work against the system. How can a confession which results from threats or intimidation be trustworthy? If a person confesses but is not guilty, it will permit the truly guilty person to continue victimizing society. We must be certain those whom we punish are the guilty parties. The convenience of law enforcement is not the most important concern. The *Miranda* warnings, therefore, seek to contain government's power and ensure justice. Many in law enforcement do not agree, but the truth is that the mandatory use of the warnings did not cause any loss of effectiveness. Indeed, it is now generally and widely recognized that these and other procedural restrictions on law enforcement forced better training, better procedure, and more professional behavior. As you will see in the chapter regarding training, education, and accreditation, the push for standardized policies and procedures has in fact produced much improved and more effective law enforcement.

The warnings themselves are basic and, while the Supreme Court has permitted some deviation from the written warnings, they should be remembered by all law enforcement officers. It would be a mistake to assume that they are no longer important. Indeed, the court has recently reaffirmed its support of their importance. In a 2004 case, a man was indicted by a federal grand jury. When the officers went to his home to serve the warrant and arrest him, they did not advise him of his *Miranda* rights, despite the attachment of the formal charge which begins the process in which *Miranda* attaches. Instead, they questioned him, eliciting incriminating statements. Later, at the jail house, they read him his rights but used the prior statements to elicit more incriminating statements. The court held that all of his statements must be suppressed and cannot be used at trial (*Fellers v. United States,* US 124 S Ct 1019, 2004). In short, once the "rights attach," by custody or formal charge, the *Miranda* rights must be given. But that

MR. CHIEF JUSTICE HUGHES delivered the opinion of the Court.

The question in this case is whether convictions, which rest solely upon confessions shown to have been extorted by officers of the State by brutality and violence, are consistent with the due process of law required by the Fourteenth Amendment of the Constitution of the United States.

Petitioners were indicted for the murder of one Raymond Stewart, whose death occurred on March 30, 1934. They were indicted on April 4, 1934, and were then arraigned and pleaded not guilty. Counsel were appointed by the court to defend them. Trial was begun the next morning and was concluded on the following day, when they were found guilty and sentenced to death.

Quoting the lower federal court: The crime with which these defendants, all ignorant negroes, are charged, was discovered about one o'clock p.m. on Friday, March 30, 1934. On that night one Dial, a deputy sheriff, accompanied by others, came to the home of Ellington, one of the defendants, and requested him to accompany them to the house of the deceased, and there a number of white men were gathered, who began to accuse the defendant of the crime. Upon his denial they seized him, and with the participation of the deputy they hanged him by a rope to the limb of a tree, and having let him down, they hung him again, and when he was let down the second time, and he still protested his innocence, he was tied to a tree and whipped, and still declining to accede to the demands that he confess, he was finally released and he returned with some difficulty to his home, suffering intense pain and agony. The record of the testimony shows that the signs of the rope on his neck were plainly visible during the so-called trial. A day or two thereafter the said deputy, accompanied by another, returned to the home of the said defendant and arrested him, and departed with the prisoner towards the jail in an adjoining county, but went by a route which led into the State of Alabama; and while on the way, in that State, the deputy stopped and again severely whipped the defendant, declaring that he would continue the whipping until he confessed, and the defendant then agreed to confess to such a statement as the deputy would dictate, and he did so, after which he was delivered to jail.

Further details of the brutal treatment to which these helpless prisoners were subjected need not be pursued. It is sufficient to say that in pertinent respects the transcript reads more like pages torn from some medieval account, than a record made within the confines of a modern civilization which aspires to an enlightened constitutional government. . . . But the freedom of the State in establishing its policy is the freedom of constitutional government and is limited by the requirement of due process of law. Because a State may dispense with a jury trial, it does not follow that it be substituted for the witness stand. The State may not permit an accused to be hurried to conviction under mob domination. . . . And the trial equally is a mere pretense where the state authorities have contrived a conviction resting solely upon confessions obtained by violence. The due process clause requires "that state action, whether through one agency or another, shall be consistent with the fundamental principles of liberty and justice which lie at the base of all our civil and political institutions" (*Hebert v. Louisiana*, 272 U.S. 312, 316). It would be difficult to conceive of methods more revolting to the sense of justice than those taken to procure the confessions of these petitioners, and the use of the confessions thus obtained as the basis for conviction and sentence was a clear denial of due process.

*Source: Brown v. Mississippi, 297 U.S. 278 (1936).*

**Figure 6-11** The privilege against self-incrimination.

is different than the general right to counsel, which may not be interfered once invoked. That is to say, once requested, questioning must stop and none can occur absent the participation and agreement of counsel (Means 2003).

What is interrogation? It is important to understand that failure to administer *Miranda* warnings does not necessarily invalidate statements made by a suspect. The theory of *Miranda* is based upon possible coercion from **custo-**

**dial interrogation**. Custodial interrogation occurs (1) if words or actions which call for some verbal response are (2) made by someone acting on behalf of the state (3) while the suspect is in custody (*Pennsylvania v. Muniz*, 496 US 582, 1990). The person asking questions could be an officer or an informant such as a cell mate.

In order for custody to exist, the suspect must (1) know she is in custody or (2) believe her freedom is significantly curtailed. These rules apply at the point that someone *reasonably* becomes a suspect (*Oregon v. Mathiason*, 429 US 492, 1977). Moreover, whether or not *Miranda* warnings are given, a fully voluntary statement, not in response to questions, is admissible. The courts generally presume a statement is involuntary without *Miranda* warnings. However, this can be rebutted based on circumstances surrounding the statement. The best practice, of course, is to give *Miranda* warnings when a person becomes a suspect. But, those warnings do not prevent questions or inducements to give statements. Nor do they prevent the suspect from waiving the right against self-incrimination. However, if counsel is requested, questioning must stop.

## Fruit of the Poisonous Tree

Sometimes, an officer may make an error and obtain evidence or testimony improperly. What happens if that evidence or testimony leads investigators to other testimony or evidence? That question was addressed by the United States Supreme Court in 1963. The case of *Wong Sun v. United States* (371 US 471, 1963) involved a warrantless invasion of a San Francisco laundry. As a result of information solicited during that illegal search, other potential suspects and locations were identified. The federal officers involved similarly invaded these locations and acquired information and suspects which led to yet another suspect. The question was whether to consider all the evidence tainted. The Supreme Court held that some was. But in some cases, most particularly that of *Wong Sun*, the evidence was admissible. The test was whether or not conditions intervened to "cut" the connection to the "poisonous tree" of the original invasion. In Wong Sun's case, his home was invaded as a result of evidence obtained at one of the earlier bad searches. But, though he was taken into custody, he was later released without charges. He returned voluntarily and made a statement which resulted in his charges and conviction.

In a more recent case, a suspect kidnapped and murdered a 10-year-old girl on Christmas Eve from a community gathering. When he was arrested, he was Mirandized, and he requested counsel. While officers were transporting the suspect, one of the officers (without asking questions) told the defendant he should tell them where the body could be found. He alluded to the sorrow of the family, the time of year, an approaching snow storm, and the need for a Christian burial. The defendant relented and showed them the body. That, of course, was compelling evidence against him. It was also taken from a poisonous tree in that the interrogation was unlawful due to the request for counsel. However, the court reasoned that since the body was found in the search zone of a search team, the evidence was going to be discovered inevitably. Hence, the inevitable discovery exception to the **fruit of the poisonous tree** rule was established (*Nix v. Williams*, 467 US 431, 1984; also, see *Oregon v. Elstad*, 470 US 298, 1985).

# ■ Liability

Liability law is a body of civil law that really is a sub-theme of tort law. Tort law is the body of civil law that defines behaviors for which someone can be held legally and financially responsible. It also defines the methods by which the injured parties are made "whole." Usually, this means money damages, but a verdict or court order may also force or command policy changes in an organization or agency.

## Tort Law

Tort law is a very large area of the law. For our purposes, we are interested in a brief discussion of two major areas of tort law. The first is in the area of so called "common law torts." The second is federal civil rights law. Of the common law torts, those which pose the largest threat to law enforcement, particularly patrol officers, are clearly assault and battery or, in the event an assault goes too far, wrongful death. These usually are described in the law enforcement literature as training and use of excessive force issues. First, we will briefly discuss assault and battery.

The common law tort of assault was the threat to do harm to someone without a privilege to do so. Battery was a non-permitted touching of another resulting in physical harm without privilege to do so. In modern usage, assault merged with battery so that one term is applied to both. Privilege is a defense to both. Law enforcement officers have a privilege to commit what would otherwise be an assault, if force is used to detain or arrest a person. However, excessive force would negate the privilege.

The well known case of the Rodney King arrest in Los Angeles involves this issue. Criminal charges against several officers resulted from the beating they inflicted upon King in a traffic stop. However, tort claims also arose from that incident. If the use of force is more than necessary to affect an arrest, the privilege to commit an assault ends. More problematic for law enforcement officers is the reality that community standards determine when force is too much. Effectively, juries make this decision. While guidelines exist in each state's law, they are merely words. Images and witnesses impact juries in different ways.

Departments have tried to protect themselves by developing rules on excessive force. They have tried to train officers in the appropriate use of force. It is important to know that if departmental operations or training standards are violated resulting in the injury of someone, liability follows. This is true because departmental rules and training, as well as state law and constitutional law decisions, set the appropriate standards of behavior. If standards are violated, liability follows. As noted below, this can be very costly for the individual officer (who is individually liable) as well as for that officer's department and governmental subdivision (e.g., city, township, county). Generally, most departments have adopted some type of "use of force continuum." About 1990, the Federal Law Enforcement Training Center's Use-of-Force Oversight Committee developed a use-of-force continuum model that was consistent with Department of Treasury policies. That model has been used to train federal officers since then.

The model is composed of five color-coded levels of force designed to correspond to officers' perceptions of the level of threat with which they are confronted (see **Figure 6-12**). It describes the progression or de-escalation of force on the basis of the demonstrated level of compliance or resistance from a subject (United States General Accounting Office 1996). Other use of force continuums have been developed and additional examples can be found on the World Wide Web by using search engines.

## Civil Rights

The most significant liability concern for law enforcement, both patrol and supervision, is undoubtedly that which springs from section 1983 of Title 42 of the United States Federal Code (see **Figure 6-13**). Originally part of the post-Civil War reconstruction acts, this section is the basis for horrifying numbers of law suits. Whether or not one agrees with the policy of the statute, it is a reality that has been on the books for over 100 years and is not likely to be changed. We will consider briefly the implications of this act.

Basically, the act provides that anyone acting under the "color of any statute, ordinance, regulation, custom, or usage" and who subjects someone to the deprivation of their constitutional rights is liable to that person for damages. False arrest, false imprisonment, use of excessive force, conduct which fails to meet training standards, failure to obtain medical aid for a suspect, and a hundred other specific events will trigger this statute. The deprivation of any known constitutional right will produce liability (Antieau 1998).

If there is probable cause to arrest or search someone, there is a privilege to violate related rights. In other words, citizens are free from unreasonable searches and seizures, but not from those that are reasonable. Probable cause gives us reasonableness, but the arrest, detention, seizure, or search must be accomplished in a reasonable manner.

Law enforcement officers are limited in the amount of force they may use to effectuate an arrest or search. The amount of force may only be the force reasonably necessary to place a person into custody (see **Figure 6-12**). Deadly force may be used only if the suspect is threatening the safety of the officer or another person. Any law, custom, or rule to the contrary cannot be relied upon by law enforcement officers. In *Tennessee v. Garner* (471 US 1, 1985) the Supreme Court struck down a state statute that permitted the use of deadly force on any fleeing felon. In doing so, it permitted the parents of a dead teenager to sue a police officer and his department despite the fact that he was trained to fire upon unarmed fleeing felons. Improper use of force will result in personal liability.

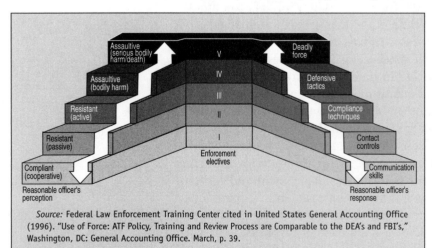

*Source:* Federal Law Enforcement Training Center cited in United States General Accounting Office (1996). "Use of Force: ATF Policy, Training and Review Process are Comparable to the DEA's and FBI's," Washington, DC: General Accounting Office. March, p. 39.

**Figure 6-12** Sample use of force continuum.

Of concern to supervisors and managers is the fact that they can be held liable for the civil rights violations of their subordinates. Essentially, liability may be established if it can be shown that a supervisor or manager "knew or should have known" that the event might happen. Liability of superiors for the actions of subordinates has been based upon poor hiring practices, poor training, failure to discipline, improper assignment, and improper retention, among other things (Russell 1994).

> **42 U.S.C. § 1983. Civil action for deprivation of rights.**
>
> Every person who, under color of any statute, ordinance, regulation, custom, or usage, of any State or Territory or the District of Columbia, subjects, or causes to be subjected, any citizen of the United States or other person within the jurisdiction thereof to the deprivation of any rights, privileges, or immunities secured by the Constitution and laws, shall be liable to the party injured in an action at law, suit in equity, or other proper proceeding for redress. For the purposes of this section, any Act of Congress applicable exclusively to the District of Columbia shall be considered to be a statute of the District of Columbia.

**Figure 6-13** Federal civil rights statute.

In most cases, insurance will not cover an officer's losses resulting from violations of either the civil rights acts generally or those resulting from an unlawful use of force specifically. Officers who violate these rules do so at their own financial peril. These are not negligent events; rather, they are intentional acts. Because most insurance polices will not pay claims for intentional acts, officers risk their own property. Worse, these kinds of debts are not generally subject to bankruptcy proceedings. If law enforcement officers lose, they lose big. As officers of the Constitution to which they take a pledge (see sample oath of office in **Figure 6-14**), they are held to a high standard.

Most insurance policies covering law enforcement will cover only negligent acts. Negligent acts are those which were not intended. Negligent acts happen when a law enforcement officer owes a duty to someone but violates that duty causing an injury. For example, if an officer drives his or her patrol car at excessive speed without emergency display (lights or siren), in most circumstances it would be negligent. Any traffic accident caused would result in liability. The failure to obtain medical treatment for someone in custody where clear signs of illness were ignored could be another source of negligence. In virtually every contact with the public, whether handling people or information, officers have duties set out by law, training, or departmental rules. Failure to perform any such duty is negligence.

We noted before that supervisors and managers may be held liable for civil rights violations of subordinates as well as intentional acts. They may also be held liable for negligent actions of subordinates. The legal theory of *respondeat superior* holds that a principal (supervisor or manager) is liable for the actions of his or her **agent** (subordinate) when those actions are taken in the course of employment. Usually, what an officer does in off-duty time will not create liability for the agency or superiors.

Some commentators suggest that *respondeat superior* is the theory of liability used in civil rights cases. However, it is not. It is important to know the difference. In negligence law, *respondeat superior* makes a superior liable for every act by a subordinate done in the course of employment. In civil rights law, a superior can be liable only if he or she knew or should have known that the act would occur, and the act must be the result of some law, rule, or custom (de-

I, do solemnly swear, that I will support and defend the Constitution of the United States, and the Constitution of the State of California against all enemies, foreign and domestic; that I will bear true faith and allegiance, to the Constitution of the State Of California; that I take this obligation freely, without any mental reservations or purpose of evasion; and that I will well and faithfully discharge the duties, of the office of Police Officer of the City of Anaheim, acting to the best of my ability.

*Source:* Anaheim Police Department (2004). "Police Officer Oath of Office," http://www.anaheim.net/article.asp?id=639.

**Figure 6-14** Typical oath of office.

partmental or individual patterns of behavior). Obviously, this can cover actions which are outside the scope of employment. Most officers drive vehicles too fast from time to time, but no one is hired with the intention of doing acts which violate civil rights by, for example, beating a prisoner. Therefore, civil rights liabilities beyond the offending officer are harder to establish but have a broader reach. In general, the defense to a civil rights claim is that of "qualified immunity."

To establish this the officer sued must show either that (1) the facts alleged do not show a constitutional right was violated or (2) was this right clearly established prior to the event in question so that the officer "knew or should have known" that his or her actions would violate a right. The test is similar for supervisors including chiefs and sheriffs. If a deputy or officer has a known history of violence, and management took no action to ameliorate the problem or end employment, the agency executives, too, may be found liable because they "knew or should have known" that someone under their supervision was a "walking time bomb" (Spector 2002).

The recent shooting death of the wife of the chief of police in Tacoma, Washington may be a prime example of a case in which proper standards were not adhered to. On April 26, 2003 Chief David Brame, who had been chief of the Tacoma, Washington Police Department for about 18 months, fatally shot his estranged wife and himself in front of their two small children. It has been widely alleged that city management knew that he had failed his psychological exams twice when he applied for the force, yet Brame was hired anyway. Moreover, he had been accused of and allegedly admitted to the rape of a coworker some years before. Finally, it has also been alleged that his wife had made numerous complaints about abuse, the alleged reason she left him. Yet he was promoted to chief. The subject of a CBS *48 Hours* inquiry, this series of apparent internal failures points out the importance of maintaining the highest standards in hiring and promotional practices. And it cautions against sweeping things under the rug of the "blue line."

Other areas of tort law that we did not examine are destruction or damage to the property of another, slander, libel, false arrest or imprisonment, and conversion of property all of which arise from common law and state statutes which have codified the common law. These and a number of other torts are important, and deserve discussion at a later date in a separate course. A good policy is to act conservatively since officers have no way of knowing what interpretation a court may place on his or her behavior. For example, a court recently ruled that not only may testimony of a suspect not be used if the suspect is not Mirandized, the officer may be liable under section 1983 for the failure to do so (*Cooper v. Dupnick*, 963 F.2d 1220; 113 S Ct 407, 1992; see also, Ronzio1993), though the Supreme Court of the United States overturned that principle (*Chavez v. Martinez*,

538 US 760, 2003). The point is that it took 10 years for the rule to be changed and in that period of time countless officers were subjected to litigation under the Cooper rule.

Another area of great public concern as well as police executive concern is the problem of the high speed chase to apprehend a suspect. In Memphis, Tennessee in 2004, two West Memphis, Arkansas police officers chased a vehicle from what started as a traffic stop into Memphis, Tennessee and fired upon a moving vehicle. They shot the driver several times as well as the passenger, both of whom were killed. Both officers have been charged with manslaughter and face trial and likely prison time on those charges. Their department no doubt faces serious civil litigation. In *County of Sacramento v. Lewis* (118 S Ct 118, 1998) the Supreme Court set the standard for liability from automobile chases. Essentially, they held that officers could not be held liable under Section 1983 unless the facts of the case produce conclusions that the actions of the officers can be said to "shock the conscience" (Smith 1999). The Memphis case would seem to fit that standard. However, most cases, where injury results from auto collisions, do not fall under that standard. Still, many departments have revisited their policies on pursuit, since they are not only a threat to innocent civilians, but to the officers as well. Injury to officers, damage to equipment, and the possibility of legal action all are costly to departments struggling to keep the budget line healthy (see **Figure 6-15**).

Finally, the entire area of use of force has come under scrutiny regarding use of less-than-lethal (LTL) weapons, or weapons designed to disable but not likely kill suspects. These include 37 mm guns that throw projectiles 70 feet or so, including bean bags and batons, all with the intention of disabling a suspect. Conducted energy weapons like Tasers are also at issue. The questions of liability were brought to a new high in October of 2004 when a 21-year-old college student was killed by a Boston police officer with a gas canister. She was among more than 50,000 people celebrating a Red Sox victory around Fenway Park. She was struck directly in the eye and died a short time later. There is no evidence that she was even engaging in criminal behavior. The point is that she was killed with an LTL weapon. Most likely, we will see liability issues surrounding these weapons in the courts soon (Newbold 2002).

The decision to pursue a motor vehicle is among the most critical made by law enforcement officers. This decision must often be made in tense, uncertain, and rapidly changing circumstances. The department has a duty to enforce the law and apprehend violators of the law. This duty must be exercised in accordance with federal and state law.

Federal courts use the "shocks the conscience" test. This test is used to determine liability under civil rights law. The court must review the actions of law enforcement and determine if the officer purposefully caused harm unrelated to the legitimate object of the arrest. A pursuit with no intent to physically harm a suspect or to worsen their legal plight does not give rise to substantive due process liability. In addition, if officers intentionally seize a vehicle then their actions must be objectively reasonable.

State law requires that officers not recklessly disregard the safety of others in pursuit of a violator but drive with due regard for the safety of all persons. Officers will abide by state and federal requirements. Pursuit is justified only when the necessity of apprehension outweighs the degree of danger created by the pursuit.

Officers are not automatically prohibited from pursuing traffic offenders or misdemeanor suspects. However, officers shall carefully weigh the seriousness of the offense with the hazards of the pursuit. Violation of this policy may expose the officer to criminal and/or civil liability.

(This policy statement is followed by one page of definitions and about five pages of procedures and regulations.)

*Source:* Tulsa Police Department (2003). Vehicle Pursuits. *Procedure*, August 15.

**Figure 6-15** Sample vehicle pursuit policy.

## ■ Summary

This chapter illustrated how law enforcement is limited in a number of major and distinct ways by legal restraints. First, it is limited by how the criminal laws are drawn by legislative authority and interpreted by a multitude of other actors. Second, while arrests may be made, a prosecutor, grand jury, jury, judge, or appeals court may disagree as to the guilt or culpability of the suspect. Third, law enforcement is impacted by constitutional procedural limitations. This covers search and seizure, warrants, arrest, interrogation, and a host of other day-to-day activities. Fourth, agencies are limited by administrative law which orders and restricts the manner in which agencies may manage their own business. Finally, law enforcement is limited by its potential liability in damages for torts and civil rights violations. For these reasons, aspiring law enforcement officers must take to heart their training and education, which, if followed, will generally protect them.

## QUESTIONS FOR REVIEW

1. What are the distinctions between the various sources of law in the United States?
2. What is meant by the "model penal code," and why is it significant?
3. What route is taken in a felony criminal case that has a federal issue when it is tried at the local level and is appealed all the way to the US Supreme Court?
4. What are at least four legal restrictions on law enforcement officers, and what are the general rules associated with each?
5. What is the automobile exception to the warrant requirement?
6. What is meant by the "exclusionary rule?"
7. In an essay format, answer the question, "Why are coerced confessions excluded as evidence?"
8. What role does liability and civil rights play in effecting the performance of law enforcement personnel?

## SUGGESTED ACTIVITIES

1. Examine a case in a local or national news report regarding alleged excessive use of force by a law enforcement officer. Debate the use of force continuum in light of that case. Is the continuum reasonable? Can it be applied with fairness?
2. If you were the chief of police of your local department, what steps would you take to adopt and enforce rules so that you are in compliance with minimum due process requirements?
3. Using your Web browser, go to the home page of the American Bar Association or the United States Courts and locate links to the online versions of case law and code law. Download or print out a case and one statutory code section.

## ■ Chapter Glossary

**administrative law** purpose of administrative law is to guide administrative officers in government agencies and guard against arbitrary decisions.

**agent** a subordinate employee.

**civil law** civil violations are violations against individuals.

**common law** body of legal rules developed over a period of several hundred years by judges acting under the authority of the king.

**constitutional law** the body of law that grew around the Constitution.

**criminal law** crimes that are offenses against the public (or the state).

**custodial interrogation**    occurs (1) if words or actions *which call for some verbal response* by a suspect are (2) made by someone acting on behalf of the state (3) while the suspect is *in custody*.

**delegation of authority**    the process of a legislative body permitting an administrative agency some authority to make rules, both to carry out law and to operate the agency, which have the effect of law; in effect, the legislature permits administrators to make law on behalf of the legislative body.

**exclusionary rule**    the doctrine that prohibits the use of illegally seized evidence in court.

**exigent circumstances**    refers to the conditions that create a need for immediate action to protect the general safety of the public, to prevent the destruction of evidence, or to prevent injury to others.

**felony**    generally a serious crime carrying a penalty of more than one year of incarceration.

**fruit of the poisonous tree**    evidence that was found solely as a result of a prior illegal search or seizure.

**minimum administrative due process**    when someone's rights are affected by an administrative decision, that person must be at least accorded these procedural rights.

**misdemeanor**    generally a less serious crime carrying a penalty of less than one year.

**model penal code**    a "model" criminal code created by the American Law Institute and adopted by many states.

**plain view doctrine**    an officer may seize evidence of a crime or contraband that falls into the plain view of the officer when the officer otherwise has a right to be at that location.

**precedent**    decisions, over time, relied upon by other judges with similar problems.

**preliminary hearing**    a hearing to determine if there is sufficient probable cause to send the case to the district attorney or grand jury for further prosecution.

**principal**    a superior, supervisor, or employer relative to another who serves in a subordinate position.

**probable cause**    exists where "the facts and circumstances within their [arresting officers'] knowledge and of which they had reasonably trustworthy information [are] sufficient in themselves to warrant a man of reasonable caution in the belief that an offense has been or is being committed [by the person to be arrested]."

**rap sheet**    slang term used to describe the list of offenses in a defendant's background, a list usually generated by computer such as the NCIC.

**respondeat superior**    a legal theory which makes a superior or principal liable for any damages caused by a subordinate or agent as a result of any actions taken in the normal course of employment.

**search**   is generally defined as the invasion, by the state, of an area which a person believes is protected or private. That belief will be upheld by a court if the ". . . person exhibited an actual (subjective) expectation of privacy, and . . . the expectation is one that society is prepared to recognize as 'reasonable'."

**seizure**   is generally defined as a "meaningful interference with the possessory interests of the suspect."

**self-defense**   generally permitted where it is necessary to use violence to protect yourself or another from imminent harm.

**stare decisis**   means that prior decisions should stand if the facts are similar.

**statutory law**   created by legislative authority.

**stop and frisk**   in the course of investigating this behavior he identifies himself as a police officer and makes reasonable inquiries, and where nothing in the initial stages of the encounter serves to dispel his reasonable fear for his own or others' safety, he is entitled for the protection of himself and others in the area to conduct a carefully limited search of the outer clothing of such persons in an attempt to discover weapons which might be used to assault him.

**suppression**   a court order ruling that certain evidence may not be used.

**warrant requirement**   the general rule of searches and seizures holds that without a warrant the search or seizure is presumed to be unconstitutional.

**writ of certiorari**   an order requiring a lower court to give the Supreme Court the record of a case for review.

**writ of habeas corpus**   an order requiring the person holding a prisoner to show cause why the prisoner should not be released.

## ■ Chapter References

Antieau, Chester J. (1998). *Federal Civil Rights Acts: Civil Practice,* 2nd Edition. New York: Lawyers Co-operative Publishing.

Associated Press (2003). Woman recounts alleged rape by former chief. *The Olympian*, May 5. http://www.theolympian.com/home/news/20030505/frontpage/4320.shtml.

Carter, Lief H. and Christine B. Harrington (1991). *Administrative Law and Politics: Cases and Comments*. New York: Harper Collins.

Castro, Hector (2004). Tacoma city manager says no heads to roll over Brame slaying-suicide. *Seattle Post-Intelligencer Reporter*, October 13, http://seattlepi.nwsource.com/local/194994_brame13.html.

Cerullo, Rob and Randy Means (2004). US Supreme Court Sharpens Police Drug-Fighting Tools, *The Police Chief*, 710(2, Feb.):10–12.

Eisenstein, James, Roy B. Flemming, and Peter F. Nardulli (1988). *The Contours of Justice: Communities and Their Courts*. Boston: Little, Brown, and Co.

Gould, Jon B. and Stephen D. Mastrofski (2004). Suspect Searches: Assessing Police Behavior under the US Constitution. *Criminology and Public Policy*, 3(3):315–362.

Hunsucker, Keith (2003). Right to Be, Right to See: Practical Fourth Amendment Application for Law Enforcement Officers. *The Police Chief*, 70 (9, Sept.):10–14.

KOMO Staff (2004). More Fallout From David Brame Tragedy. October 12, http://komotv.com/news/story_m.asp?ID=33480.

Means, Randolph B. (2003). Interrogation Law. . . . Reloaded: Two Rights to Counsel. *The Police Chief,* 70(12, Dec.):11–12.

Nardulli, Peter F., Roy B. Flemming, and James Eisenstein (1988). *The Tenor of Justice: Criminal Courts and the Guilty Plea Process.* Urbana, IL: University of Illinois Press.

Newbold, Mark H. (2002). Conducted Energy Weapons and Police Liability. *The Police Chief,* 69(5, May):11–12.

Ronzio, Judith A. (1993). Upping the Ante on *Miranda. The Police Chief,* 60(5, May):10–11.

Russell, Gregory D. (1994). Liability and Criminal Justice Management: Resolving Dilemmas and Meeting Future Challenges. *American Journal of Criminal Justice,* 18(2, Spring):177–98.

Smith, Michael R. (1999). Police Pursuits: The Legal and Policy Implications of *County of Sacramento v. Lewis. Police Quarterly,* 2(3, Sept.):261–282.

Spector, Elliot B. (2002). The Confusing State of "Clearly Established Law." *The Police Chief,* 69(12, Dec.):11.

Tulsa Police Department (2003). Vehicle Pursuits. *Procedure,* August 15.

United States General Accounting Office (1996). "Use of Force: ATF Policy, Training and Review Process are Comparable to the DEA's and FBI's," Washington, DC: General Accounting Office, March, p. 39.

## CASES CITED

*Adams v. Williams,* 407 US 143, 1972

*Arizona v. Hicks,* 480 US 321, 1987

*Barron v. Mayor and City Council of Baltimore,* 7 Pet. 243, 1833

*Brinegar v. United States,* 338 US 160, 175–176, 1949

*Brown v. Mississippi,* 297 US 278, 1936

*California v. Acevedo,* 500 US 565, 1991

*California v. Hodari D.,* 499 US 621, 1991

*Carroll v. United States,* 267 US 132, 1925

*Chambers v. Maloney,* 399 US 42, 1970

*Chavez v. Martinez,* 538 US 760, 2003

*Chimel v. California,* 395 US 752, 1969

*Colorado v. Connelly,* 479 US 157, 1986

*Coolidge v. New Hampshire,* 403 US 443, 1971

*Cooper v. Dupnick,* 963 F.2d 1220; 113 S Ct 407, 1992

*County of Sacramento v. Lewis,* 118 S Ct 118, 1998

*Fellers v. United States,* US 124 S Ct 1019, 2004

*Hiibal v. Sixth Judicial District Court of Nevada,* US, 124 S Ct 2451, 2004

*Illinois v. Lidster,* US, 2004

*Illinois v. Rodriguez,* 497 US 177, 1990

*Indianapolis v. Edmond,* 531 US 32, 2000

*Katz v. United States,* 389 US 347, 361; 1967

*Kyllo v. United States,* 533 US 27, 2001

*Mapp v. Ohio,* 367 US 643, 1961

*Marbury v. Madison,* 1 Cranch 137, 1803

*Maryland v. Buie,* 494 US 325, 1990

*Michigan Department of State Police v. Sitz,* 496 US 444, 1990

*Minnesota v. Dickerson,* 506 US 366, 1993

*Nix v. Williams,* 467 US 431, 1984

*Oregon v. Elstad,* 470 US 298, 1985

*Oregon v. Mathiason,* 429 US 492, 1977

*Payton v. New York,* 445 US 573; 1980

*Pennsylvania v. Muniz,* 496 US 582, 1990

*South Dakota v. Opperman,* 428 US 364, 1976

*Tennessee v. Garner,* 471 US 1, 1985

*Terry v. Ohio,* 392 US 1, 1968

*United States v. Davis,* 482 F. 2d 893, 9th Circuit, 1973

*United States v. Martinez-Fuerte*, 428 US 543, 1976
*United States v. Morena*, 475 F.2d 44, 5th Circuit, 1973
*United States v. Pulido-Baquerizo*, 800 F.2d 899, 9th Circuit, 1986
*United States v. Jacobsen*, 466 US 109, 113; 1984
*United States v. Skipwith*, 482 F.2d 1272, 5th Circuit, 1973
*Wong Sun v. United States*, 371 US 471, 1963
*Wyoming v. Houghton*, 526 US 295, 1999

# Law Enforcement Tasks, Roles, and Styles

**7**

## Learning Objectives

In Chapters 5 and 6 you explored the nature of legal restrictions and organizational issues and how they impact the law enforcement function in the United States. Now we turn our attention to the somewhat complex and occasionally controversial matter of the role of law enforcement in our modern society. After studying this chapter, you should be able to:

- Identify the five basic tasks required of law enforcement personnel in the United States.
- Define the concept of "role."
- Identify eight influences upon role and role perceptions.
- Explain why there is confusion as to what the role of law enforcement is.
- Cite three examples of the research that examines role.
- Distinguish between "role" and "style."
- Identify 11 influences on "law enforcement style."
- Distinguish how the research on role differs from that of style.
- Compare and contrast the basic organizational roles of the Patrol Officer, the Patrol Supervisor, the Detective, and the Chief Executive Officer.
- Describe the four categories of law enforcement stressors.

## Chapter Outline

I. The Role of Law Enforcement Personnel
    A. What is Meant by Role?
    B. What Influences Role and Role Perception?
    C. Concepts, Dilemmas, and Controversies
    D. Research on Role

## Key Terms Used in This Chapter

| | |
|---|---|
| role | sustained order maintenance |
| popular justice | full neighborhood management |
| role conflict | officer styles |
| Project STAR | stress |
| temporal order maintenance | discretion |

# ■ The Role of Law Enforcement Personnel

The **role** of law enforcement personnel in US society is defined by five important tasks. First, the personnel are tasked with protecting life and property. Second, they are tasked with preserving the public peace. Third, they are tasked with preventing crime and terrorist activity. Fourth, they are tasked with detecting and arresting violators of the law. Finally, law enforcement personnel are tasked with enforcing the law. To help accomplish these tasks, they are given wide discretionary authority guided by the rule of law. Certainly, given the magnitude of their mission, they are entrusted with one of the most important and challenging roles in US society.

For those interested in taking up the call, the field offers a direct and rewarding opportunity for individuals to advance the public good. Yet, crime control is a difficult role to play, by definition, and none of these five mandated policing tasks can be entirely achieved. No matter how efficient or professional the personnel are in fulfilling their varied tasks, their situational efforts are at best temporary solutions to chronic social problems. As James Fyfe (2001, 161), a noted policing professional and scholar, observes, the policing personnel are sometimes ". . . called upon to do the impossible or to attempt to provide services they have not been adequately prepared to perform." Because this dilemma is unlikely to change in the near future, "crime control," as Chief Darrel W. Stephens[1] (2003, 31) notes, "remains the central mission of the police, but how it should be accomplished and whether it should be the exclusive focus of police is less clear."

Because of its great importance, the role of the law enforcement personnel is one of the most commonly discussed topics in policing literature. While few advocate discarding any of the mandates mentioned above, scholars, public officials, and law enforcement professionals continually search for ways to make policing more responsive to the public's safety needs. In the larger search for improvement, the reform debate usually centers on the policies and procedures that facilitate aspects of the policing role, not on its core mandates. For example, some researchers have questioned the usefulness of random patrol. They suggest this traditional tactic is not as effective as once believed (Wilson and Kelling 1982). Other researchers suggest a better result could be secured through a more focused or problem-oriented approach to policing (Goldstein 1977; 1979; 1990). Sometimes major events drive the debate. For example, since the terrorist attacks of September 11, 2001 there has been a heightened awareness of the importance of law enforcement's role in protecting society. As one noted author observed, "communities have started looking to their police departments to assume a new role in identifying and countering potential terrorist activity—creating new challenges for police executives and local government managers" (O'Neill 2003).

Because it is one of the most visible and important services of government, most people have a general understanding of the law enforcement role in our society. From a citizen's perspective, it is that omnipresent helping hand ready at our beck and call when nothing else will work or when everything else has failed. From an applied perspective it can be described as three major spheres of simultaneous activity: calls for service, tactical operations to suppress crime, and strategic problem-solving (Sweeney 2003). People have come to expect certain actions from officers when they are summoned. It makes no difference what the officers are asked to accomplish; they are expected to perform these functions decisively, professionally, and courteously. Consequently, officer's performance (the application of role), ranging from the most critical to the most mundane, is scrutinized by the public, the media, and by concerned agencies of government, including the officers themselves.

Building on this general introduction, we will now turn our attention to several related topics, including the concept of role, forces that influence role and role perception, controversies and dilemmas surrounding this role, and, finally, research on role.

This chapter contains some conceptual material that may be difficult to grasp at first. Do not become frustrated if you read some sections and need to read again and contemplate the points being stressed.

---

[1]Darrel W. Stephens is the chief of police of Charlotte-Mecklenburg, North Carolina and has 36 years of law enforcement experience.

## What is Meant by Role?

Instead of relying on any one perspective of what is meant by role, we prefer to define it as a multidimensional concept consisting of expected behaviors performed by a person in a given situation or position for the purpose of achieving certain objectives or goals. In other words, role is a blend of behaviors (what one does), expectations and perceptions (what one thinks should be done), and outcomes (what is to be accomplished). Certainly, in an abstract sense, role is difficult to define in concrete terms; it is a concept, and like all concepts, it must be worked out in the mind. It is not a tangible object that simply exists and can be described.

As a practical matter, we can simply state that each peace officer develops a role perspective based on his or her training, socialization, and experiences within a law enforcement agency. These factors are then accentuated to the degree that performance measures and department values are established, maintained, and reinforced (Nowicki 2003).

The concept of role is very complex and relational (see **Figure 7-1**). Role can be viewed from a social (interpersonal) perspective such as the role of a parent,

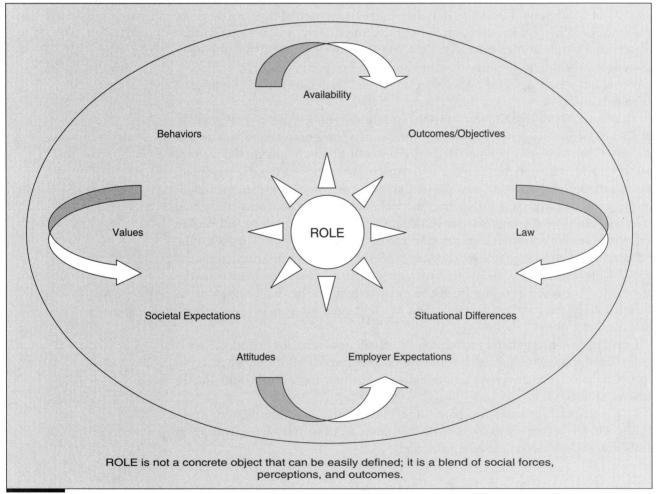

ROLE is not a concrete object that can be easily defined; it is a blend of social forces, perceptions, and outcomes.

**Figure 7-1** The complexity of role.

brother, sister, neighbor. Role, as we have discussed above, can also be viewed from an occupational perspective, such as the role of a doctor, lawyer, judge, teacher, nurse, fire fighter, or police officer. Importantly, social roles and occupational roles often overlap and even influence the way we behave while performing one or the other role. For example, a mother may also have roles as a wife, a sister, a daughter, an aunt, and an employee of an agency or company. In her role as an employee, she also may occupy the role of colleague, confidante, supervisor, detective, and so on. The role component in each of these is actually the *behavior* involved and not the status that the person occupies (e.g., mother, sister, detective). What is achieved (outcome) by way of that behavior is a significant determinant in role performance and is the basis of evaluation by others.

The relational aspects of role include the perspectives, personalities, and perceptions of the persons who are in the process of determining their proper role for a given situation. Interpersonal relationships affect how role is interpreted. Therefore, there are sociological and psychological variables at work during the process of role determination. People interpret their role by viewing others, communicating with others, evaluating their surroundings, and gauging their progress toward a desired objective. This process becomes very dynamic which may cause persons to modify their behavior as they interpret situations while they unfold.

Applying the concept of role to law enforcement is very challenging. The common question is, "What is the role of the police in a democratic society?" The answer depends on who is asked. To some, the role of the policing personnel is *to enforce the law*; to others it is *to prevent crime*, while still others will say it is *to maintain order*. The point is that all of these responses are correct because the role of policing in the United States is multifaceted (remember the five tasks that we introduced in the first paragraph of this chapter) and varies according to place and time and the objective to be accomplished. Notice that all of these responses are actually objectives (often referred to, interchangeably, as outcomes, functions, or tasks) to be accomplished by the various behaviors of officers. Practically speaking, whether one refers to them as functions, outcomes, or tasks, they are still the goals to be accomplished through the behaviors of officers. Over the years, the law enforcement personnel have acquired or were assigned many different functions. The duties of the officers have changed dramatically over the last 150 years (see **Figure 7-2**).

## What Influences Role and Role Perception?

A number of factors, including the democratic process, occupational culture, ethics, socialization, training, availability, technology, and laws combine to influence the role of policing in American society, or an officer's perception of that role. Some factors are more influential than others. Some factors are universal and influence both the institution of policing itself and the individual officer, like technology. Other factors, like ethics, are only apparent when demonstrated in appropriate behavior or the lack thereof. With the exception of ethics (personal character), we make no attempt to order their importance; we simply assert that it is important to have an understanding of how these forces, conditions, products, and mandates influence the role of policing, and an officer's perception of that role.

The local police officer's role has included the following duties:

1820s   cared for common sewers, cared for vaults, and whatever else affected the health, safety, and comfort of the citizens.

1830s   emptied privies, conducted cholera checks.

1850s   removed obstructions from the street, put out fires, tested doors, turned off running water, took drunks home, gathered in stray horses, helped the unemployed find jobs, sheltered the homeless.

1870s   assisted and advised immigrants and strangers, supervised licenses of all types.

1880s   called upon and escorted physicians for patients, inspected tenements and lodging houses for sanitary conditions, tested boiler operators.

1910s   assisted probation officers, were called "welfare" officers, entertained children at Christmas, initiated Junior Police programs, assisted ex-cons to find work, became probation and parole officers.

*Source:* Modified from Law Enforcement Assistance Administration (LEAA) (1976). *Two hundred years of American criminal justice.* Washington, DC: US Department of Justice.

**Figure 7-2** Early police officer duties.

## Democracy

The first influence on the role of law enforcement personnel is democracy itself, or more accurately the democratic process. Since the introduction of policing personnel in the United States, their role has reflected society's prevailing customs, values, and beliefs. For better or worse, law enforcement agencies have taken on a distinct and often local presentation, based on popular social and political demands. Samuel Walker (1998) referred to this phenomenon as "**popular justice**." He observes, "the administration of criminal justice in the United States reflects the highly democratic character of American politics and society" (6). For example, the forces of democracy, marching under the banner of progressive reform, have long since cast out the dark shadows of inefficiency, corruption, and partisan politics, afflictions that characterized policing in the 1800s and well into the early 1900s. A review of Chapter 3 will help make this historical observation more apparent.

Today "popular justice"—the will of the people—is more apparent than at any other time in our history. For example, popular justice is often brought into play through a sequential process that follows a predictable course: unwanted social conditions/events/behaviors give rise to social indignation, which is channeled into political action, which prompts a government response that manifests itself in one (or a combination) of three ways. First, laws are passed in an attempt to control the unwanted behavior. Second, law enforcement organizations introduce new administrative policies to correct an internal problem or to improve an aspect of service. Third, as is more likely to occur, law enforcement agencies respond directly to citizen complaints and develop policies or strategies to address a specific problem. Through these processes, the public defines and redefines the poling mandate.

In the traditional scenarios described above, we see the policing role as dynamic, pushed or pulled into action by an alignment of unwanted social conditions that led to political demands for action. These circumstances repeat themselves over and over again in different locations and for different reasons. Sometimes the conditions and events take on national prominence. For example, advocacy groups like Mothers Against Drunk Drivers (MADD), and victims' rights groups like the National Organization for Victim Assistance and the National Center for Missing and Exploited Children (to name just a few), address national issues of social concern.

Each of these organizations was established when citizens banded together in a common effort to correct a social injustice or to improve the government's response to the plight of victims. However, in the vast majority of cases problems remain a local concern. To correct a specific problem, community leaders, elected officials, citizens' groups, and individual citizens appeal to their local police or sheriff's department for help. Their requests have a direct influence on criminal justice policy and consequently officer behavior. If, on occasion, the problem is not answered in a timely or appropriately manner, political and/or media attention moves the agency into reactive action. Again, even in a reactive mode, we see evidence of democracy at work and the policing role being defined.

## Occupational Culture

Occupational culture also influences role perceptions. In fact, there are three separate cultures operating concurrently within a law enforcement organization. Each culture can be seen as a hidden force that seeks to maintain the status quo. The first force is the omnipresent culture of policing itself. This is a formal force championed and maintained by the mission, traditions, customs, and myths that define the organizations and the profession of policing in general (Selznick 1947). The second force influencing role perceptions is a working culture associated with rank or position. Scholars have suggested that there are two distinct perceptions of one's working role in policing, a management perspective and a street or line officer/agent perspective. On occasion, antagonistic relationships can development between the two perspectives when individuals (usually at the line level) attach themselves to philosophies that are in conflict with the department's mission or goals (Guyot 1979; Reuss-Inni 1984). The third force influencing an individual's perception of role is the subculture of policing. Here role perceptions are established and defined informally, but profoundly, by one's collective peers who have established a parallel set of traditions, customs, and myths that are not always in sync with those of the organization (Crank 1998).

## Ethics

Ethics, or more specifically one's character, has a fundamental influence on role perceptions. No matter what rank or position an officer holds, behavior is still an individual choice. Individual perception and interpretation of expectations are very significant aspects in determining a person's behavior. An officer, for example, will engage in certain behavior because he or she believes it to be the appropriate behavior for that given situation. However, the degree to which officers attach themselves to a value system will have an overarching bearing on all other aspects of behavior, and perceptions of proper behavior, both on and off duty (Pollock 2004).

Edwin Delattre (2002, 15), an eminent scholar of police ethics, summarized this point best when he observed, "The mission of policing can safely be entrusted only to those who grasp what is morally important and who respect integrity. Without this kind of personal character in police, no set of codes or rules or laws can safeguard that mission from the ravages of police misconduct." Therefore, we suggest personal ethics is the most influential determinant of role perceptions in policing.

## Socialization and Training

Just as we expect each officer to possess a moral compass, we also expect him or her to be competent. This brings us to two closely related influences on role and role perceptions—socialization and training. Socialization and training are the primary ways officers learn their role and the craft of policing. Training takes many forms and occurs in a variety of settings. For example, training may take place in classroom instruction, role-playing, field training programs, role-call briefings, and after-action incident debriefings. Training also occurs in a less formal, but equally important, setting when officers' contemplate and/or critique their own actions or omissions. Often these critiques occur in the company of trusted peers and more experienced officers and can be quite candid, informative, and influential.

Training is an important part of the socialization process, yet socialization within a law enforcement agency is more than training: It is the purveyor of culture and the architect of attitudes and behaviors. According to policing scholars, socialization occurs when less experienced officers learn and then mimic the values and behavior patterns of experienced officers (Roberg et al. 2005). David Carter (2002, 398) suggests that, "Formal socialization occurs when specific information is directed toward an individual with the intent of shaping values and belief." Since every officer begins his or her career at the same point, as a rookie on the streets, a common socialization occurs. It produces a universal rite of passage leading to a brotherhood among all officers. As John Van Maanen (1985, 155) observes, "One of the most distinctive characteristics of American police agencies is that virtually everyone in the organization, from station house broom to chief, shares the common experience of having worked the streets as a patrol officer." These experiences are essential if one is to master the craft of policing and fulfill its service role. (See Chapter 8 for additional details about training and socialization issues.)

## Availability and Technology

Two additional factors help define an officer's role—availability and the technologies that make them so available. Samuel Walker (1992) focused on one aspect of this when he stated, "The most important factor shaping the role of the police [from a purely physical perspective] is their twenty-four-hour availability." Because they are readily available, officers are often called upon to perform various tasks. This seems like an obvious statement of reality, and one hardly worth mentioning. However, its is very important when one considers that in the last 50 years four technologies—the automobile, the telephone, the two-way radio, and the computer—have been married under a 24-hour umbrella. Collectively, they facilitate modern policing and accentuate its service role.

## Laws

A final influence on role is the legal provision by which a society lives and prospers. Of course, the legal precepts in the United States are both stable and ever-changing. They are stable in the sense that most of our legal principles are grounded primarily upon British Common Law and the Constitution. The legal provisions are ever-changing, however, in that they are constantly being evaluated, interpreted, expanded, or modified by the legislative and judicial branches of the government. In any case, it is important to remember a seminal concept underlying and guiding the policing role. "Law cannot rule; only men and women, judges and police officers, and human beings in other roles can rule. The rule of law means that decisions taken by these individuals will be determined by a set of general principles that have been established in advance by some authority social group or agent" (Skolnick et al. 2005, 135). Consequently, an officer's reverence for the law, including an organization's administrative and operational policies, is critical in ordering and fulfilling the policing role.

Our presentation of the major influences upon policing role is summarized in **Figure 7-3**.

## Concepts, Dilemmas, and Controversies

The concept of role and its complexities has led to several dilemmas and controversies as far as policing is concerned. One of the major dilemmas is that of definition and context of the concept. For instance, some practitioners and researchers focus on and debate the mission, goals, and values of the law enforcement community. Are those the same as role? Others refer to the functions of law enforcement officers, such as to prevention of crime, to guarantee constitutional rights, to resolve conflict, or to respond to emergencies. Is it any wonder that students of policing become confused when asked, "What is the police role in the United States?" Does the person asking the question want a "conceptual" response that focuses on the definition, or does she want a "functional" response that relates to a process of doing something (behaviors or duties)? Does she want an "outcome" response in terms of what is desired regarding the goal or objective of the role?

---

*Availability*—twenty-four-hour service.

*Democracy* (specifically the democratic process)—the will of the people.

*Occupational culture*—the formal culture of the policing organization, the culture of rank and position, and the informal subculture of policing.

*Ethics*—an officer's value system and character.

*Socialization*—the transfer of values, beliefs, and knowledge from one generation of officers to the next.

*Training*—classroom instruction, role-playing, field training programs, role-call briefings, after-action incident debriefings, and personal critiques.

*Law*—the formal rules, regulations, statutes, ordinances, and court decisions.

*Technology*—innovations and equipment that facilitate officer efficiency.

**Figure 7-3** A summary of the major influences upon the policing role.

Because of the inconsistent use of terms and phrases such as role, mission, objective, function, and task, certain vagueness clouds the quest for role definition. In 1931, August Vollmer stated that the "police were organized to suppress crime, protect life and property, and preserve the peace" (National Commission on Law Observance and Enforcement 1931, 17). This should be considered a functional statement because of the infinitive verb phrases (to suppress . . . [to] protect . . . [to] preserve). A behavioral statement (sometimes called "tasks"), on the other hand, would include such phrases as "officers engage in community policing activities," "officers arrest offenders," "officers engage in preventative patrol," and "officers conduct investigations." Role statements that focus on outcomes usually point to the desired result of a policing activity such as crime prevention, crime suppression, the protection of property, protection of rights, and so on (see **Figure 7-4**).

Therefore, it is very important in any discussion of role to clearly understand the differences in perspective whether one is speaking about the functional, behavioral, or outcome aspects of the job of policing. There are subtle but significant differences in language, and that is part of what leads to confusion over the definition of role.

The following observation might help to explain the confusion and frustration sometimes encountered by officers who experience competing, and sometimes opposite, values and expectations. It is referred to as **role conflict** and was explained this way by James S. Campbell in 1970:

> *Perhaps the most important source of police frustration, and the most severe limitation under which they operate, is the conflicting roles and demands involved in the order-maintenance, community-service, and crime-fighting responsibilities of the police. Here both the individual officer and the police community as a whole find not only inconsistent public expectations and public reactions, but also inner conflict growing out of the interaction of the policeman's values, customs, and traditions with his intimate experience with the criminal element of the population. The policeman lives on the grinding edge of social conflict, without a well-defined, well-understood notion of what he is supposed to be doing there (291).*

| Functional | Behavioral (task example) | Outcomes |
|---|---|---|
| To prevent crime | Community policing activity | Crime suppression |
| To protect life and property | Preventative patrol | Protection of life and propery |
| To detect and arrest violators | Arrest offenders | Bring the accused to justice |
| To preserve the peace | Counsel/warn/advise | Order maintenance |
| To serve the public | Assist motorists | Public service |

**Figure 7-4** Types of role statements.

More recently, Carter and Radelet stated:

> . . . the role conflict has been complicated with the addition of quality-of-life issues as a police responsibility. Certainly, this goes beyond the traditional view of the police as either law officer or peace officer. What is more apparent is the police officer in the role of problem solver. Officers are being asked to be "proactive," that is, to aggressively look for broad solutions to crime, disorder and quality-of-life problems in the community (1999, 118).

While role conflict has been recognized for decades, it is still very prevalent in some (if not all) agencies. The issue is really how officers deal with it rather than whether it exists. It will probably always exist because the various forces influencing it (Figure 7-3) will seldom be in total agreement. Role conflict is one factor that influences the level of stress on officers. (Stress is addressed in greater detail later in the chapter.)

## Research on Role

The quest to define or determine the appropriate role of law enforcement personnel in the United States has been a focus of scholars for many decades. The purpose of this section is to identify several of the major systematic attempts to observe and analyze the role of officers; it is not to report the many statements that appear in the literature of what that role is or is not. The role of officers has always been a subject of concern, as evidenced by the statements of voices from the past, which appear in **Figure 7-5**.

We believe that one of the most comprehensive statements regarding the role and expectations of police is that of James Currant:

> A simple answer to the question as to what the urban policeman does is that he does everything. Cliches abound concerning the fact that the policeman is a combination psychiatrist, medical doctor, lawyer, marriage counselor and crime-stopper. The truth of the matter is that he is all of these things, yet none of them.
>     . . . In broad general terms, it can be said that police deal with virtually every kind of emergency, human problem, and, moreover, appear to spend more of their time dealing with problems not related to crime than with crime-related human problems (1972, 112).

"A policeman's duties are numerous, and he is brought in contact with the very best as well as the very worst element of the community. He is called upon to settle family difficulties; arbitrate differences between neighbors; regulate the ubiquitous small boy; act in the capacity of sanitary officer when contagion stalks about, and perform a thousand other offices that are never made public. . . ."

—Chief D.S. Gaster, New Orleans, 1900

"The police were organized to suppress crime, protect life and property, and preserve the peace. Where they have commanded the respect and receive the support of the people they have had little difficulty in carrying out their duties. Under our form of government and, more especially, due to the attitude of the American people generally, law enforcement agencies are usually held in contempt and law enforcement is one of our national jokes. Crime, despite the magnitude of the problem, is but one of the many difficulties confronting the police."

—National Commission on Law Observance and Enforcement, Report on Police, 1931

*Source:* National Commission on Law Observance and Enforcement, Report on Police (1931). Washington, DC: United States Government Printing Office.

**Figure 7-5** Notable quotes on the role of officers.

Throughout the 1960s and early 1970s, criminal justice scholars attempted to explain the role of officers by examining what they did and how they did it. Some focused on the question of "why police behave the way they do." One text summed up much of these early findings this way:

> *If the police are not sure whether their principal function is to prevent crime or serve the public, the researchers are no more consistent in their conclusions. . . . In truth the ambivalence of the police is built into the very structure of law enforcement by the variety of duties imposed upon police practitioners by the law, custom, and ethical requirements of the society they live in* (Niederhoffer and Blumberg 1976, 64).

The major research efforts of the President's Crime Commission on Law Enforcement and Administration of Justice in the mid-1960s established that the role of the law enforcement officer was not well understood in the United States. **Figure 7-6** clearly depicts a finding that was inconclusive, but exemplifies the complexity of the issues. What is most interesting in these historical sentences is that they appear to coincide with the 1990s explanation of the philosophy of community policing (discussed in more detail in Chapter 10).

One of the most comprehensive research efforts on role was the 3 1/2 year effort of **Project STAR**, which began in 1971. The project involved agencies in four states and attempted to identify appropriate roles for six key positions (police officer, prosecuting attorney, defense attorney, judge, caseworker, and correctional worker) in the criminal justice system. In this study, role was defined as "the personal characteristics and behavior expected in a specific situation of an individual occupying a position" (Smith et al. 1974). Although the project is

---

In the course of inquiring into police activities, the commission encountered many differences of opinion among police administrators as to whether the primary police responsibility of law enforcement is made easier or more difficult by the many duties other than enforcing the law that policeman ordinarily perform. . . . They are services somebody must perform, and policemen being ever present and mobile, are logical candidates. . . . Moreover, it is natural to interpret the police role of "protection" as meaning protection not only against crime but against other hazards, accidents or even discomforts of life. . . .

The community's study of the role of the police should cover additional ground. It should examine whether it is desirable, or possible, for the police to devote more time than they now generally do to protecting the community from social injustices. . . . They are in constant contact with the conditions associated with crime. They see in minute detail situations that need to be and can be corrected. If a park is being badly maintained, if a school playground is locked when it is most needed, if garbage goes uncollected, if a landlord fails to repair or heat his building, perhaps the police could make it their business to inform the municipal authorities of these derelictions. In this way, police would help to represent the community in securing services to which it is entitled.

*Source:* Reprinted from President's Commission on Law Enforcement and Administration of Justice, *The challenge of crime in a free society* (1968). Washington, DC: US Government Printing Office.

**Figure 7-6** The community service role—reflections from the past.

over 30 years old, its findings included excellent discussions and qualitative data related to understanding the concepts associated with the policing role.

The project also identified tasks and performance objectives that were defined respectively as follows (refer to **Figure 7-7**):

> *Task*—an activity to be accomplished within a role that usually involves a sequence of steps and can be measured in relation to time.

> *Performance objectives*—statements of operational behavior required for satisfactory performance of a task, the conditions under which the behavior is usually performed, and the criteria for satisfactory performance.

Within the research, findings indicated that for the position of police officer: a) each role involved the performance of several tasks and b) each task involved the performance of more than one role (Smith et al. 1974, 2). The 13 roles of police officers identified by Project STAR were:

— Assists criminal justice system and other appropriate agency personnel
— Builds respect for law and the criminal justice system
— Provides public assistance
— Seeks and disseminates knowledge and understanding
— Analyzes and communicates information
— Manages cases
— Assists personal and social development

| | |
|---|---|
| Advising | Participating in community relations and education programs |
| Booking and receiving inmates | |
| Collecting and preserving evidence | Participating in trial preparation conferences |
| Communicating | Patrolling and observing |
| Conferring about cases | Preparing reports |
| Contacting families of suspects and clients | Preparing search warrant requests |
| Controlling crowds | Recovering property |
| Defending self and others | Referring |
| Deterring crime | Regulating traffic |
| Engaging in legal research | Responding to offender requests |
| Engaging in professional development | Reviewing case materials |
| Interacting with other agencies | Searching and examining |
| Interviewing | Searching for fugitives |
| Investigating | Testifying as a witness |
| Making arrests | Testing for drug and alcohol use |
| Managing interpersonal conflict | Training |
| Moving inmates | Using and maintaining equipment |

*Source:* Compiled from Smith, Charles P., Donald E. Pehlke, and Charles D. Weller (1974). *Role performance and the criminal justice system, volume II: Detailed performance objectives*. Project STAR. Cincinnati, OH: Anderson Publishing Company and Santa Cruz, CA: Davis Publishing Company, pp. 9–12.

**Figure 7-7** Project STAR's 33 tasks performed by police officers in carrying out the roles of their job.

— Displays objectivity and professional ethics

— Protects rights and dignity of individuals

— Provides humane treatment

— Enforces law impartially

— Enforces law situationally

— Maintains order

To further illustrate the research of Project STAR and the analysis related to each of the identified roles, **Figure 7-8** details the finding for the role labeled "provides public assistance."

In 1973, the National Advisory Commission on Criminal Justice Standards and Goals addressed the issue of officer role in what today is considered one of the seminal studies of American policing—*Report on Police*. The report began by

---

Roles for police officers can be placed into categories; the roles can be described and performance objectives (or outcomes) identified; roles can involve several tasks and each task can relate to more than one role. The relationship among these aspects is illustrated here for the single role of "provides public assistance."

**Role:**

Provides public assistance.

**Role description:**

Treating all needs for assistance, requested by the public or observed, in a serious and helpful manner regardless of the appropriateness of the requests. Providing services or appropriate referrals, including any needed arrangements for special assistance, expeditiously and courteously.

**Performance objectives:**

- To respond courteously and expeditiously to requests for assistance.
- To obtain information about public and private community resources for use in helping people.
- To make referrals to other public and private agencies.
- To take advantage of opportunities to provide assistance based on an assessment that the need exists.

**Tasks:**

- Advising
- Communicating
- Interacting with other agencies
- Interviewing
- Patrolling/observing
- Referring
- Using equipment

*Source:* Derived from Smith, Charles P., Donald E. Pehlke, and Charles D. Weller (1974). *Role performance and the criminal justice system, volume II: Detailed performance objectives*. Project STAR. Cincinnati, OH: Anderson Publishing Company and Santa Cruz, CA: Davis Publishing Company.

**Figure 7-8** Relationship of tasks and performance objectives to role.

defining the "functional police role" concept, which they emphasized is the idea that an agency must prioritize the expectations placed on its officers in terms of serving the community. Because these expectations are so important, the report suggested that they should be put in writing to guide officers' performance. It was expected that the chief executive officer would develop such a policy in consultation with department employees, the community, and government officials. It was suggested that the policy on role be central to other written policies that guide the department. Other recommendations concerning role included the assurance that every officer understand his or her role (Standard 1.5) and that the public as well be informed of the agency's defined policing role (Standard 1.6). Other standards related to role addressed the recognition of the use of force and the use of discretion by officers (National Advisory Commission 1973).

During the 1970s, several scholars published texts that included discussions about the policing role in the United States and how it was multifaceted (Goldstein 1977; Muir 1977, Manning and Van Maanen 1978; Skolnick and Gray 1975; Broderick 1977; Staufenberger 1980). In essence, most agreed that it was a very complex matter to conceptualize and dissect. The role is heavily influenced by officer perceptions of the job, the demands placed upon them by the public, and by legislative enactment. Coupled with this is the need to occasionally use force, the need to often use discretion, and the expectation that the job be carried out under strict constitutional protection of rights and liberties. One researcher put it this way in describing what makes a good officer: "Intellectually, he has to grasp the nature of human suffering. Morally, he has to resolve the contradictions of achieving just ends with coercive means" (Muir 1977, 4).

Another attempt to describe one's policing role was made in 1991, when researchers reviewed the statutory language of all 50 states to determine whether the role of officers was clear or specified. The study indicated that only one state (New York) specifically mentions a service function (assists citizens) as part of the formalized role of officers. Order maintenance and law enforcement were the most prevalent roles indicated in the state codes (Burton, Langworthy, and Barker 1991).

Hoover (1992) classified the policing role in the United States into three models: the **temporal order maintenance** role mainly associated with crime-specific models of policing, the **sustained order maintenance** role associated with problem-oriented policing, and the **full neighborhood management** role linked with community-oriented policing. As community policing tends to expand in its application, roles will become more committed to long-term relationships (full neighborhood management) with citizens as opposed to the short-term involvement (temporal order maintenance) of answering single incident calls or solving short-lived crime-related problems (sustained order maintenance). These models of policing are more directly associated with the strategies of law enforcement that are discussed in Chapter 10.

Essentially, what the literature describes about the policing role in the United States is that it is unsettled, subject to ongoing societal change, and is continually evolving because of the democratic processes that shape and reshape its activities. The role of officers cannot be static; it cannot remain constant because society is always changing. As new problems surface, the local police are called to deal with them because there usually is no other agency "out there" to respond. Consider for example the additional demands placed on law enforcement personnel since the September 11, 2001 terrorist attacks, such as homeland security information sharing, preparation for response to the threat of weapons of mass destruction (WMD), and greater security of the nation's infrastructure.

# ■ Officer Styles

What is sometimes not distinguished in discussions of role is the difference between an officer's role and an officer's style. Simply stated, **officer style** is the manner in which an officer carries out his or her role. It includes the various techniques, mannerisms, vocabulary, body language, and so on, employed by an officer to achieve an objective. An effective law enforcement officer probably will utilize several styles of behavior to accomplish tasks. Officers' styles will reflect their training, role expectation, values, skills, personality, and/or experience. Officers may develop a primary style (the one used most often) and a secondary style or styles (those used as alternatives to the primary style). In short, these styles may be situationally based. For example, officers may be very direct and shout out specific commands to a person they are attempting to control. They may be very soft spoken when addressing children who need comforting, or they may attempt to reason logically and rationally with a couple during a domestic disturbance. So, regardless of the role and tasks being performed, the officer's style (demeanor and manner) becomes the most observable behavior to the public.

## What Influences Style?

As we mentioned in our discussion of role, there are several factors that influence an officer's policing style. In part, style will be dependent on the nature of the complaint, the type of service needed, the environment, the person or persons present, the objective to be achieved, the agency's philosophy and values, and peer pressure. Other elements may influence an officer's style as well, such as the quality of training received, the levels of knowledge, education, and skills possessed, backgrounds of the subjects involved in the encounter, the officer's knowledge of available alternatives, and the officer's experience. However, underlying and guiding all of this is an officer's character, his moral compass. **Figure 7-9** identifies many of the sub-elements of these influencing factors. Without question, style is influenced by a number of critical factors, which collectively, and sometimes individually, determine the quality of officer service rendered.

## Research on Style

Several scholars in recent decades have started to label various types of officer styles. One of the most noted is the work of James Q. Wilson, *The Varieties of Police Behavior*, published in 1968. Wilson identified three predominant policing styles, which can be summarized as follows:

> *Watchman*—emphasis is on maintaining order by invoking "path of least resistance." Officers often ignore minor violations unless their authority is challenged.

*Legalistic*—stresses authority and control mechanisms with emphasis on the letter of the law; generally does not ignore even minor violations.

*Service*—all calls for service are approached in a serious manner regardless of their nature, and alternatives to formal arrest are emphasized.

Wilson's typologies are widely cited, but the important part of his work is that he developed these styles based upon analysis of eight police departments across the country. In essence, his research was an attempt to show that the ways in which officers perform their tasks are influenced by the nature of the community and political systems of that community. His focus was primarily on the predominant style of the organization and its influence upon the officers.

*Nature of the complaint*—criminal, civil; misdemeanor, felony

*Type of service needed*—emergency, public assistance, investigation

*The environment*—rural, suburban, urban; house, apartment, outdoors

*Person or persons present*—one-on-one contact, crowds, rioters

*Goal/objective of contact*—identify offender, arrest, referral

*Agency philosophy and values*—department policies and procedures

*Peer pressure*—expectations of other officers

*Quality of training*—depth of training; sensitivity/cultural skills

*Officer abilities*—communication, evaluation, and empathy skills

*Experience*—skills and insights learned from doing the job

*Character*—a moral compass that guides each decision

All of the above factors, and possibly others, can impact an officer's choice of style in handling contacts with citizens and complainants.

**Figure 7-9** Influences on officer styles.

Several other scholars have contributed to the discussion of style by identifying their own conceptual categories of officer types. The two scholars mentioned here have developed style typologies for individual officers and not the organization. William Muir (1977) categorized four types of officers in his research of coercive power and the policing function:

*Enforcer*—emphasizes legal authority and makes quick decisions as to whether arrest is necessary. Crime control is the major objective.

*Reciprocator*—adopts an extreme helping pose trying to reach a solution in all problems. Attempts accommodation with vice operators and undesirables.

*Avoider*—an officer who attempts to avoid all involvement in situations.

*Professional*—officer understands the complexities of the job and attempts to do the best he or she can, using verbal skills, knowledge, and experience.

Muir's work has influenced others to pursue similar research on the policing styles of officers. Sometimes such research focuses on personality types instead of styles. It should be remembered that, to a large degree, an officer's style is a reflection of his or her personality. Consequently, this line of research reveals the psychological dimension of role development. John J. Broderick (1987) classifies police personalities into four ideal types that reflect officers' values and styles of behavior (Broderick 1987):

*Enforcers*—a high value is placed on social order and peace and low value on individual rights and due process of law; tend to stress need for authority and respect for law.

*Realists*—place low value on both social order and individual rights; tend to be less frustrated than other officers, apparently having found a way to come to terms with a difficult job.

*Idealists*—individual rights and due process of law receive high value; preservation of social order is viewed as a major role; generally suffers from lack of job satisfaction and frustration.

*Optimists*—job seen as people-oriented, placing a high value on individual rights, less emphasis on crime fighting.

Broderick's 1987 book, *Police in a Time of Change,* presented an excellent discussion of the conceptual styles of policing identified by Muir and similar styles developed by other researchers. Broderick mentioned that many of the conceptual styles developed by researchers were similar and overlap each other's categories (see **Table 7-1**). A detailed discussion of each of these research efforts is beyond our purpose here; however, the reader is encouraged to review additional material for more in-depth analysis of officer styles (Coates 1972; White 1972; Brown 1968; Hatting et al. 1983; Walsh 1984).

## ■ Organizational Roles of Selected Positions

Law enforcement organizations consist of many levels (ranks) and positions. Every person working in the organization occupies a position and has certain job functions to perform. These job functions tend to define, within limits, the role of that particular position. Of course, occasionally new job functions (duties) may develop or appear, and they must be assigned to someone to perform. This indicates the fluctuating nature of a person's occupational role when working in an agency whose functions and obligations are not static.

### Table 7-1  A Comparison of Officer Styles From Research

| Researcher | Overlapping or Similar Styles | | | |
|---|---|---|---|---|
| Coates (1972) | Abusive | Community | Task officer | Service |
| White (1972) | Tough cop and Crime fighter | Problem solver | Rule applier | |
| Muir (1977) | Enforcer | Reciprocator | Avoider | Professional |
| Broderick (1977) | Enforcers | Idealists | Realists | Optimists |
| Brown (1981) | Old style and Clean beat Crime fighter | Service style I helper | Service style II avoider | Professional |
| Hatting et al. (1983) | Blue-collar | True blue | Jaded blue | |
| Walsh (1984) | Medium arrest | Low arrest | Zero arrest | High arrest |

*Source:* A minor revision of Table 3 from Broderick, John J. (1987). *Police in a Time of Change,* 2nd Edition. Prospect Heights, IL: Waveland. p. 12. Used with permission.

## Patrol Officers

Patrol officers are the "eyes and ears" and the "backbone" of all municipal, county, and state policing organizations. Patrol forces comprise the largest component of a department. All other units in the organization are designed to directly or indirectly support their operations. Importantly, all local officers and deputy sheriffs began their careers as patrol officers. This is where the craft of policing is learned. Officers usually patrol within assigned beats or districts while in uniform as they tend to the immediate needs of the community. They are usually the first responders to most complaints, which in the vast majority of cases are non-emergency calls for service for both criminal and non-criminal issues. However, calls (and patrol observations) are prioritized by their service nature, with emergencies receiving first attention. In emergencies, officers' temporarily abandon routine calls and redirect their attention to the emergency.

In fulfilling their daily routines and assignments, officers are given wide discretion in deciding enforcement and service activities. Other than making general work assignments, supervision, when it is present, usually comes in the form of review and critique of work preformed, not work in progress. Specifically, most reports and all arrests are reviewed and approved by a sergeant or the watch commander. Only on rare occasions, for example during and following major crimes or incidents, will officers have direct supervision, and this comes more in the form of coordinating efforts than supervision. In terms of doing the work for which a local police agency generally exists, much, if not most of it, is done by patrol officers.

## Detectives (Investigators)

In most departments, a patrol officer at the scene conducts the initial investigation of a crime or incident. If the initial officer can appropriately handle the incident or crime (usually decided by department policy), no further investigation, beyond the continuing work of the initial officer, generally occurs. However, if the incident or crime requires a more intensive investigation (e.g., major burglary, high value theft, fatal accident, etc.), or the initial officer lacks the expertise (e.g., arson, rape, child abuse, homicide, etc.), the report is forwarded to a detective for follow-up or subsequent investigation.

Detectives are officers who have been promoted or assigned to the investigative function on a full-time basis. It should be noted that smaller agencies often do not have full-time investigators so the duties may be assigned as necessary to a patrol officer. In larger agencies, detectives are either appointed by the chief executive or selected through competitive examination. The role of the detective is to conduct follow-up investigation of assigned cases with the objective of developing a case suitable for prosecution of the alleged offender. This may involve crime-scene analysis, evidence collection, photography, interviewing, interrogating, record searches, interpreting crime lab and autopsy reports, preparing reports, preparing affidavits for search and arrest warrants, executing search and arrest warrants, preparing documents for prosecutors, and testifying in court. Investigators spend at great deal of time at their desks using the telephone or computer or evaluating reports, records, and miscellaneous stores of information.

Much of this activity is unfruitful, yet they must continue to probe for elusive answers. From this activity, they glean various bits of information, all of which must be culled for the useful tidbit. Subsequently, their work must be accurately summarized into an investigative report. Unlike television shows, the detective may have a dozen or more active cases being pursued simultaneously. One aspect of investigative work is "managing the case," which means keeping things organized and progressing toward the desired objective of identifying a suspect and prosecuting the guilty offender.

In state and federal agencies where uniformed officers do not exist, the personnel are often all investigators (some agencies refer to them as agents). Their primary function is to investigate specialized crime such as fraud, embezzlement, liquor violations, counterfeiting, homicides, robberies, kidnapping, computer crime, and so on. These investigators may be assigned their cases hours and days after the incident occurred and may not work on some cases unless local agencies request their assistance. In crimes where specialized knowledge or equipment is needed, local agencies often call for the assistance of county, state, and/or federal agents. These cooperative arrangements have helped to improve and professionalize service outcomes (bring the accused to justice) across the country.

## Supervisors

The organizational role of a supervisor is one of coordinating and managing a group of personnel for which he or she is responsible. This means that supervisors are responsible for leading and guiding the work accomplished by the unit. The role of the supervisor includes general assignment of duties or cases, scheduling personnel, answering questions, making decisions, advising others, evaluating and documenting performance, approving leave and vacation requests, and receiving complaints from the public about unit personnel. Supervisors usually hold the rank of sergeant or above unless they are civilian personnel, in which case their title could be supervisor, officer-in-charge (OIC), agent-in-charge (AIC), coordinator, manager, or director. Supervisors are assigned throughout the agency in both operational and staff units.

## Specialized Units

Specialty functions within law enforcement agencies include units such as special weapons and tactics (SWAT), crime prevention, public information, internal affairs, training, personnel, fiscal control, identification, detention services, planning and research, vehicle maintenance, parking control, and so on. Usually, the primary functional role of each of these units can be deduced from their titles. It must be remembered that the roles of personnel will vary according to their assigned unit. The priority tasks performed by many specialists does impact the total functioning of the agency; however, these personnel may not be very visible to the public in carrying out the daily policing role of the agency.

## The Chief Executive Officer

The primary task and role of the chief executive officer of any law enforcement agency is to lead, coordinate, guide, and manage all the units and personnel employed within the agency. This person is responsible for the agency's operation on a daily basis. Law enforcement officials occupying this position may have various titles besides the common Chief of Police. Titles vary from agency to agency and include Sheriff, Commissioner, Director, Superintendent, Colonel, Marshal, and Chief Constable. The chief executive officer's role usually includes determining the mission and goals of the agency and communicating these to the department personnel and the community. Of course, it has long been recommended that the community, the elected officials, and the officers of the department should be involved in determining the mission and goals of the agency (President's Commission 1968).

Chief executive officials are generally either appointed or promoted to that position (the sheriff is usually an elected position, however). Appointed officials generally have little or no job security or specified term of office. For example, "The average length of time in office for 'big-city' chiefs has dropped to 3.5 years. In Houston the average for a 25-year period was calculated to be 2.3 years" (Frankel 1992). The reasons for such short periods include politics (the election of different mayors who appoint the chief), scandals or public incidents that forced resignation, mandatory retirement ages, and personal reasons. However, promoted officials usually occupy positions where a civil service or promotion exam of some type determines who obtains the job. Often these positions have job security or tenure, meaning that the official cannot be removed except for cause. The job may be theirs for the rest of their working career. Systems vary from state to state and often depend on state law and city charter.

## ■ Understanding The Role Debate

How do the concepts discussed in this chapter relate to policing today? Why are the issues of role and styles of concern? Many officers go about their jobs every day and do not express any problems with their role or the various tasks they perform. Others, however, are vocal about the frustrations they have from the job. They make statements like, "I'm a cop, not a social worker!", "I joined this force to enforce the law, not to play games with the neighborhood youth" and "I don't have time to worry about overgrown vacant lots, condemned buildings, and abandoned cars." It is statements like these that provide evidence that some officers do not understand their role in a democratic society. Research clearly shows that enforcement of laws or response to crime-related activities consumes between 20% and 50% of an officer's time (Greene and Klockars 1991). Of course, there are exceptions to this figure in some areas within some cities, but that does not negate the fact that the role of today's officer goes beyond law enforcement. It includes public assistance on many matters, order maintenance, traffic control, and crime prevention.

As discussed in earlier segments of this chapter, the role of officers in the United States is unsettled, subject to ongoing societal change, and is continually evolving. As new problems surface, the local police are called to deal with them because there often is no other agency to respond. Over time, officers have been caretakers of common sewers, lamplighters, the issuers of licenses, health inspectors, housing inspectors, probation officers, parole officers, employment counselors, animal wardens, child welfare agents, and so on. Other social service agencies came into existence because some of the duties became too time-consuming for officers to continue. In the future, other positions (or agencies) may be created to assume some of the non-law enforcement tasks done by officers today. Until that happens, the role of officers is to do whatever society calls upon them to do.

Those who can accept this responsibility can make excellent law enforcement officers. It is the acceptance of this role ambiguity that impacts the officer's style. Those who accept the changing demands of society, who accept the social service requests from the public, who understand the complexity of social disorder and frustration, and who can acknowledge the rights of all persons, should be officers who are accepted by the public. It is this type of officer who exhibits concern for people from all walks of life and learns to treat people with respect and dignity.

So that there is no misunderstanding, an officer can accept this multifaceted role and still be a law enforcer when necessary. Today's role requires the "wearing of many hats" and the willingness to adjust one's demeanor and style as necessary for the tasks at hand. The ability of officers to understand the complexity of their role is the challenge facing them today. In 1977, Herman Goldstein discussed the impact of recognizing the multiple functions of officers and he described one ramification this way:

> . . . in recruiting personnel to be police officers we need individuals who will not only perform well in dealing with serious crime, but will also be capable in many other areas: resolving conflicts, protecting constitutional guarantees, and handling an incredibly wide range of social and personal problems; and most important who will have the ability to shift with ease from performing one of these functions to performing another (42).

## ■ Stress and Discretion in Law Enforcement

Two other concepts are worthy of mention in the overall discussion of the role of policing in today's society. **Stress** and **discretion** are factors that influence the daily lives of many professionals. Both can influence decisions he or she makes and, therefore, both affect behavior. It is not our purpose here to give a detailed analysis of either of these concepts, but we would be remiss not to mention their relationship to issues in this chapter.

### Stress

Stress has been broadly defined as "the body's non-specific response to any demand placed on it" (Selye 1974). Policing is often thought to be a high-stress job compared to other occupations. The conventional wisdom holds that law enforcement personnel face perilous conditions, tedious tasks, and hostile work environments, all of which lead to high stress. Stress, it is thought, produces lower productivity, higher levels of physical and mental illness, suicide, and misconduct. Empirical evidence, however, has been mixed, and there appears to be little evidence that officers are any more stressed than other employees in other occupations, including some with similar jobs characteristics. Still, there is some evidence to support the idea. One stressor common among occupations is the loss of job discretion, which officers face organizationally (Lennings 1997). Hence, the one stressor that appears to have a significant impact in law enforcement is the organizational restrictions on work, including standard operating procedures and legal rulings. Levels of stress do appear to relate to certain negative health outcomes (Golembiewski et al. 1992). Clearly, this is an area of concern and one that will lead to further research.

An excellent treatise and guide for law enforcement managers on the topic of stress, published in 1990, is Ayers and Flanagan's *Preventing Law Enforcement Stress: The Organization's Role*. It divides law enforcement stressors into four categories: (1) those external to the organization, (2) those internal to the organization, (3) those in law enforcement work itself, and (4) those confronting the individual officer. **Figure 7-10** depicts many of the stressors in each of the four categories.

## Discretion

Discretion is not a role. Rather, discretion means that law enforcement officers have wide latitude in choosing which role to assume and which tactics, approaches, or behaviors to employ while acting within a given role. In most respects, officer discretion is an essential component of the job. In fact, discretion is the essence of policing. Discretionary choices are normally made without direct supervision due to the decentralized and distributed nature of patrol and investigative work.

Discretion can be defined as "the use of individual judgment by officers in making decisions as to which of several behavioral responses is appropriate in specific situations" (Cox 1996, 46). According to Sykes, Fox, and Clark (1976, 171), "discretion exists whenever an officer is free to choose from two or more task-relevant alternatives interpretations of the events reported, inferred, or observed in a police-citizen encounter." Therefore, discretion is the process of making a choice among believed appropriate alternative courses of action. Although most state codes do not give officers the specific right to use discretion, it has been professionally and judicially acknowledged. As mentioned in Chap-

External stressors:
- Frustration with the American judicial system
- Lack of consideration by the courts in scheduling officers for court appearances
- The public's lack of support and negative attitudes toward law enforcement
- Negative or distorted media coverage of law enforcement

Internal (agency) stressors:
- Policies and procedures that are offensive to officers
- Poor or inadequate training, career development opportunities
- Poor economic benefits and working conditions
- Excessive paper work
- Inconsistent discipline

Stressors in the work itself:
- The rigors of shift work, especially rotating shifts
- Role conflicts between enforcing the law and serving the community
- Frequent exposure to life's miseries and brutalities
- Fear and dangers of the job
- Work overload

Stressors confronting the individual officer:
- Fears regarding job competence, individual success, and safety
- Necessity to conform
- Necessity to take a second job or to further education
- Altered social status in the community due to attitude changes of others because he or she is now an officer

*Source:* Ayres, Richard M. and George S. Flanagan (1990). *Preventing law enforcement stress: The organization's role.* Washington, DC: US Department of Justice and the National Sheriffs' Association.

**Figure 7-10** Stress factors in policing by category.

ter 1, the police simply cannot enforce every law that has been enacted. They must, instead, use prudent discretion and enforce only those laws that are reasonable to enforce given the totality of the situation and the interest of justice. They must also use prudent discretion in their non-enforcement or service decisions, again basing their professional judgments on the best interests the community and the goals and mission of their department. By way of definition, we might add that selective enforcement refers to enforcing those laws deemed appropriate to the situation or related to the priorities of the agency and the community. The opposite of selective enforcement is full enforcement, which means enforcing all laws all the time—a condition that most Americans simply do not want.

According to Cox (1996), there are a number of factors influencing discretion, such as the law, officer attitude and character, department policy, political expectations, public expectations, the situation/setting, and the occupational culture in which they operate. The process of making decisions involves the evaluation of all of these factors. In other words, the officer must evaluate the "totality of circumstances." (Review Figure 7-1 again—think of all of the interrelated factors mentioned there and compare them to the ones influencing discretion.)

The lack of guidelines in law enforcement agencies gives individual officers the opportunity to inject their own prejudices and legal interpretations into their job performance. This can lead to the abuse of discretion. In making a decision, officers must understand that the decision should be appropriate and defensible. They may be asked to explain their decision in the reporting process or in court. In today's litigious society, decisions made by officers are subject to review by others and can result in suits for damages. This adds to the levels of stress an officer endures in his or her career.

One study found that in responding to disturbances, officers engaged in 13 distinct contact actions (e.g., request separation, physical restraint, or forced dispersal), 17 processing actions (e.g., follow complainant's request, restrain someone, or admonish disputants), and 17 distinct exit actions (e.g., just leave, arrest, or warn alleged offenders). Similar patterns were observed in traffic stops (Bayley 1986). Discretion is a large part of law enforcement and a major issue in law enforcement reform (Brown 1968). It produces the most significant dilemma in policing. Discretion is essential to job performance due to the nature of the work and the geographic dispersal of decision-making officers. Indeed, community policing and various related approaches expect higher levels of discretion. Yet it is also the case that discretion leads to opportunities for misconduct of all sorts. Hence, standard operating procedures, orders, written directives, skill training, incident reviews, and supervisory approval of reports all operate to restrain discretion, reduce the likelihood of misconduct and standardize operations. It is worth noting that, largely due to the high level of inherent danger in such operations, special operations teams operate with very low levels of discretion in tactical terms.

## ■ Summary

This chapter examined the relationships among the concepts of role, tasks, and style. Role was defined as a multidimensional concept consisting of expected behaviors performed by a person in a given situation or position for the purpose of achieving certain objectives or goals. Since there are multiple objectives to policing (public safety, law enforcement, protection of constitutional rights, etc.) there are multiple roles. These roles require the performance of different tasks. Style, on the other hand, referred to how these tasks were carried out—the officers' demeanor, approach, and technique. Since these concepts are inter-related, they are difficult to discuss separately. The many factors or influences upon role determination and the development of one's style compounds the issues. Some of the more relevant research was presented regarding role and style. Additionally, organizational roles of selected positions (assignments) were described. The important factors of stress and discretion were briefly discussed in relation to their general impact on role determination.

So what is the role of the officers in a democratic society? It is essentially what society says it is (defined by the community, not the officer). Since reaching a consensus is extremely difficult and there are so many different communities across this country, there cannot be just one role for law enforcement personnel to perform. There are many roles for officers in our society. What sets policing apart from other occupations in society may be the fact that the state has given officers the authority to use force if necessary to carry out their duties (Klockars 1985; Bittner 1990). The fact that officers have this authority and power must not be forgotten, since we ask individual officers to come to our rescue when needed and do what has to be done to protect us, but society expects them not to use excessive force even when they have to use force. Also, we want our streets to be safe and free from reckless drivers and others who endanger our lives and the lives of our loved ones, but we get upset if we are the ones pulled over and given a citation. No one said the job would be easy!

## QUESTIONS FOR REVIEW

1. List the five basic tasks required of the law enforcement officer in the United States.
2. What is the definition of the concept of "role"?
3. List five influences upon role determination and briefly explain how these factors influence role determination.
4. Describe how the democratic process, occupational culture, ethics, socialization, training, availability, technology, and laws combine to influence the role of policing in American society, or an officer's perception of that role.
5. What is meant by "role conflict"?
6. Compare and contrast the concepts of "officer role" and "officer style."
7. What are the role differences between the positions of the patrol officer and a detective?
8. Why is it difficult to precisely and definitively answer the question, "What is the role of the police in the United States?"

## SUGGESTED ACTIVITIES

1. Engage a law enforcement officer in a discussion of role and seek his or her interpretation of what roles take priority in the agency that employs him or her.
2. Videotape a 15-minute segment of a police action TV show. Then analyze it for role versus style based on the concepts presented in this chapter. Write a brief report of your findings.
3. Read the mission statements of local police departments or find three or four on the World Wide Web and write down the key phrases that relate to the agency's role. Based on their articulated statements, what are the primary roles of the agencies?

## ▪ Chapter Glossary

**discretion**   individual judgment by officers in making decisions as to which of several behavioral responses is appropriate in specific situations.

**full neighborhood management**   a commitment and philosophy of an agency to allow officers to intervene in any problem in a community that requires a response by police officers or other government personnel.

**officer styles**   the manner in which officers carry out their police role; it includes the various techniques, procedures, mannerisms, vocabulary, body language, and so on, that are available to them.

**popular justice**   a term used to describe how police departments have taken on a distinct, and often local, presentation throughout their development, based on popular social and political demands (sometimes referred to as "the will of the people").

**Project STAR**   a comprehensive 3 1/2-year research effort (1971–1974) that involved the federal government and agencies in four states; it attempted to identify appropriate roles for six key positions (police officer, prosecuting attorney, defense attorney, judge, caseworker, and correctional worker) in the criminal justice system.

**role**   a multidimensional concept consisting of expected behaviors performed by a person in a given situation or position for the purpose of achieving certain objectives or goals.

**role conflict**   the confusion and frustration brought on by competing and sometimes opposite values and expectations experienced by officers while performing their job tasks.

**stress**   broadly defined as "the body's nonspecific response to any demand placed on it" (Selye 1994).

**sustained order maintenance**   a phrase referring to intervention by police that has required greater problem-solving analysis and possibly a greater commitment of resources than for short-term intervention.

**temporal order maintenance**   a phrase referring to the short-term intervention by police officers in situations of interpersonal conflict and social disorder.

## ■ Chapter References

Ayres, Richard M. and George S. Flanagan (1990). *Preventing law enforcement stress: The organization's role*. Washington, DC: US Department of Justice and the National Sheriff's Association.

Bittner, Egon (1990). *Aspects of police work*. Boston: Northeastern University Press.

Bayley, David (1986). The tactical choices of police patrol officers. *Journal of Criminal Justice* 14(4):329–348.

Broderick, John J. (1977). *Police in a time of change*. Morristown, NJ: General Learning Press.

Broderick, John J. (1987). *Police in a time of change*, Second Edition. Prospect Heights, IL: Waveland Press, Inc.

Brown, Michael K. (1968). *Working the street: Police discretion and the dilemmas of reform*. New York: Macmillan.

Burton, Velmer S., Jr., Robert H. Langworthy, and Troy A. Barker (1991). *The prescribed role of police in a free society: A national survey of state legal codes*. Paper presented at the annual conference. Chicago: Midwest Criminal Justice Association.

Campbell, James S., Joseph Sahid, and David Stang (1970). *Law and order reconsidered: Report of the task force on law and law enforcement to the National Commission on the Causes and Prevention of Violence*. New York: Bantam Books.

Carter, David L. (2002). *The police and the community*, Seventh Edition. Upper Saddle River, NJ: Prentice Hall

Carter, David L. and Louis A. Radelet (1999). *The police and the community*, Sixth Edition. Upper Saddle River, NJ: Prentice Hall

Coates, Robert B. (1972). *The dimensions of police-citizen interaction: A social psychological analysis*. Ph.D. dissertation. College Park, MD: University of Maryland.

Cox, Steven M. (1996). *Police: Practices-perspectives-problems*. Boston: Allyn and Bacon.

Crank, John P. (1998). *Understanding police culture*. Cincinnati, OH: Anderson Publishing Co.

Currant, James (ed.) (1972). *Police and law enforcement 1973-1974.* Vol. II. New York: AIMS Press, Inc.

Delattre, Edwin J. (2002). *Character and cops: Ethics in policing,* Fourth Edition. Washington, DC: American Enterprise Institute.

Frankel, Bruce (1992), Police chiefs worry about job security. *USA Today,* November 19:10A.

Fyfe, James J. (2001).Good Policing in Roger G. Dunham and Geoffrey P. Alpert (eds.) *Critical issues in policing,* Fourth Edition. Prospects Heights, IL: Waveland Press, Inc.

Goldstein, Herman (1977). *Policing a free society.* Cambridge, MA: Ballinger Publishing Company.

Goldstein, Herman (1979). Improving policing: A problem-oriented approach to improving police service. *Crime and Delinquency* 25:236–258.

Goldstein, Herman (1990). *Problem-oriented policing.* New York: McGraw-Hill.

Golembiewski, Robert T., Michael Lloyd, Katherine Scherb, and Robert F. Munzenrider (1992). Burnout and mental health among police officers. *Journal of Public Administration Research and Theory* 2(4):424–439.

Greene, Jack R. and Carl B. Klockars (1991). What Police Do, in Carl B. Klockars and Stephen D. Mastrofski *Thinking about police: Contemporary readings,* Second Edition. New York: McGraw-Hill.

Guyot, Dorothy (1979). Bending granite: Attempts to change the rank structure of American police departments. *Journal of Police Science and Administration* 7(3):253–284.

Hatting, Steven H., Alan S. Engel, and Philip A. Russo (1983). Shades of blue: Toward an alternative typology of police. *Journal of Police Science and Administration* 11:54–61.

Hoover, Larry (1992). *Police management: Issues and perspectives.* Washington, DC: Police Executive Research Forum.

Klockars, Carl B. (1985). *The idea of police.* Newbury Park, CA: Sage Publications, Inc.

Law Enforcement Assistance Administration (LEAA) (1976). *Two hundred years of American criminal justice.* Washington, DC: US Department of Justice.

Lennings, C.J. (1997). Police and occupationally related violence: A review. *Policing: An International Journal of Police Strategies and Management* 20(3):555–566.

Manning, Peter and John Van Maanen (eds.) (1978). *Policing: A view from the street.* Santa Monica, CA: Goodyear Publishing Company, Inc.

Muir, William K. (1977). *Police: Streetcorner politicians.* Chicago: University of Chicago Press.

National Advisory Commission on Criminal Justice Standards and Goals (1973). *Report on police.* Washington, DC: United States Government Printing Office.

National Commission on Law Observance and Enforcement (1931). *Report on police.* Washington, DC: United States Government Printing Office.

Niederhoffer, Arthur and Abraham Blumberg (1976). *The ambivalent force: Perspectives on the police,* Second Edition. Hinsdale, IL: The Dryden Press.

Nowicki, Dennis E. (2003). Human resource management and development, in William A. Geller and Darrel W. Stephens (eds.) *Local government police management.* Washington, DC: International City/County Management Association.

O'Neill, Robert J. (2003). Foreword, in William A. Geller and Darrel W. Stephens (eds.) *Local government police management.* Washington, DC: International City/County Management Association.

Pollock, Joycelyn M. (2004). *Ethics in criminal justice,* Fourth Edition. Belmont, CA: Thomson/Wadsworth.

President's Commission on Law Enforcement and Administration of Justice (1968). *The challenge of crime in a free society.* New York: Avon Books.

Reuss-Inni, Elizabeth, (1984). *Two cultures of policing: Street cops and management cops.* New Brunswick, CT: Transaction Books.

Roberg, Roy, Kenneth Novak, and Cary Cordner (2005). *Police and society.* Los Angeles: Roxbury Publishing Company.

Selznick, Philip (1947). *TVA and the grass roots: A study in the sociology of formal organizations.* Berkeley: University of California Press.

Selye, Hans (1974). *Stress without distress.* New York: Avon Books.

Skolnick, Jerome H., Malcolm M. Feeley, and Candace McCoy (2005). *Criminal justice: Introductory cases and materials,* Sixth Edition. New York: Foundation Press.

Skolnick, Jerome and Thomas C. Gray (eds.) (1975). *Police in America.* Boston: Little, Brown and Company.

Smith, Charles P., Donald E. Pehlke, and Charles D. Weller (1974). *Role performance and the criminal justice system, Volume II: Detailed performance objectives, Project STAR.* Cincinnati, OH: Anderson Publishing Company and Santa Cruz, CA: Davis Publishing Company.

Staufenberger, Richard (ed.) (1980). *Progress in policing: Essays on change.* Cambridge, MA: Ballinger Publishing Company.

Sweeney, Thomas J. (2003). Patrol, in William A. Geller and Darrel W. Stephens (eds.) *Local Government Police Management*, Fourth Edition, pp. 89–133. Washington, DC: International City/County Management Association.

Sykes, R., J. Fox, and J. Clark (1976). A socio-legal theory of police discretion, in A. Blumberg and E. Niederhoffer (eds.) *The ambivalent force: Perspectives on the police*, Second Edition. Hinsdale, IL: The Dryden Press.

Van Maanen, John (1985). Making rank: Becoming an American police sergeant. *Urban Life* 13:155–176.

Walker, Samuel (1992). *The police in America: An introduction,* Second Edition. New York: McGraw-Hill.

Walker, Samuel (1998). *Popular justice: A history of American criminal justice.* New York: Oxford University Press.

Walsh, Willam F. (1984). *The analysis of the variation in patrol officer felony arrest rates.* Ph.D. dissertation. New York: Fordham University.

White, Susan O. ( 1972). A perspective on police professionalism. *Law and Society Review*, 61–85.

Wilson, James Q. (1968). *The varieties of police behavior: The management of law and order in eight communities.* Cambridge, MA: Harvard University Press.

Wilson, James Q. and George L. Kelling (1982). *Broken Windows,* in the March edition of the *Atlantic Monthly.*

# Training, Education, and Socialization

## 8

Learning Objectives

This chapter addresses the important issues of training, education, and socialization of the police. These concepts and issues have a major impact on both the culture and the performance of law enforcement in the United States. By studying the concepts and principles presented here, you will be able to:

- Understand the relationship of learning, learning domains, and teaching to the concept of education.
- List the seven purposes achieved through the training process.
- Identify and differentiate five types of training commonly found in law enforcement.
- Describe the evolution of thought since the President's Commission of 1967 on the importance of education for police officers.
- Explain the influence that both training and education has had on policing.
- Define the concept of police subculture.
- Explain the negative and positive characteristics of the police subculture.
- Describe the role of training in the socialization of law enforcement officers.

## Chapter Outline

## Key Terms Used in This Chapter

| | |
|---|---|
| on-the-job training (OJT) | citizen police academy |
| education | college academies |
| learning | socialization process |
| learning domains | police subculture |
| mandatory minimum training standards | occupational dimension |
| field training | psychological dimension |
| in-service training | political dimension |
| advanced or specialized training | social dimension |
| continuing education credit | symbolic assailant |
| executive and managerial training | detraining syndrome |

## ■ Training Concepts and Philosophy

The thought of putting untrained people in uniform and expecting them to enforce the law is a foreign concept by modern standards. However, some of today's police officers experienced just that when they entered the field of law enforcement! A survey of 4,000 police departments, conducted by IACP in 1956, found that 85% of all officers received no pre-service training (President's Commission 1967, 138). For most of America's history, police officers learned their duties and acquired necessary skills through **on-the-job training (OJT)**. OJT included the lessons taught by co-workers and supervisors and allowed officers to obtain experience through performing the daily tasks of the job. While some of these lessons were formal, most were informal and guided by the individual experience and attitude of the "teacher." Another term used to describe this early form of training (OJT) was "apprenticeship," which is a term commonly used in the trade and vocational fields. Today, a true apprenticeship program would be more structured and formal than what OJT actually was.

Today, it is readily apparent that the tasks and responsibilities of law enforcement officials are so complex and burdened with liability that the need for training is uncontested. However, even though there is unilateral agreement on the need for training, there is little consensus about the amount, type, and format of training that is necessary for the modern officer. A reflection of this lack of consensus is the great diversity in the level and quality of police training across the country. Access to resources is also important. Some academies have access to and utilize the latest technology available, such as interactive computer assisted learning and virtual reality scenarios, while others are relegated to primarily the lecture and drill format with little or no integration of technology into the classrooms.

As a concept and philosophy, "training" can mean different things to different people. Some hear the term and immediately think of formal physical exercise and skill development as in basic military training. Others think of it as a combination of classroom and field-based learning in preparation for a job. Still others perceive it as extensive college preparation followed by an internship and residency, as in medical training. Many discussions of training just presume that students in criminal justice understand what happens at the police academy and have a common understanding of training concepts.

At the outset of this chapter, permit us to state our philosophical position on a number of concepts. We define **education** as what one has learned. **Learning** can be defined as a process that changes a person's behavior or attitude. It refers to changes that are determined primarily by the individual's interaction with his or her environment (Eson 1972, 58). A person's education is achieved by various means: socialization, experience, academics, training, and so on; it is not limited to the classroom or formal setting. Some in the criminal justice field have insisted on making a distinction between "training" and "education," essentially stating that training inculcates the *how* to do something while education focuses on the *why*. Traditionalists argue that training emphasizes skill and ability development while education emphasizes concepts, theory, and critical thinking. Such simple distinctions are unfortunate because as Saunders (1970, 115) stated, ". . . the best of each will always contain elements of the other." In lieu of distinctions between the concepts, we believe it is more relevant to focus on matters of process and outcomes. The common link between education and training is the process of teaching or instruction which includes a broad range of activities (Conser 1981, 42, 64). In this perspective, both training and education are considered outcomes, and the "teaching-instruction" process becomes the critical focal point. Various instructional methods can then be utilized to structure the desired outcome. The relationship of these outcomes to the learning process is illustrated in **Figure 8-1**.

## Major Purposes of Training

Police training serves a number of organizational purposes. First, it orients the person to his or her new job or position. Second, it indoctrinates the person to identify with the organization and believe in its goals and objectives. Third, it transfers the skills and knowledge necessary to do the job. Fourth, it standardizes procedures and increases efficiency. Fifth, it builds confidence in the person since critical tasks can be practiced and mastered in learning situations. Sixth, it improves safety and helps assure survival. Finally, it yields other benefits such as morale and discipline.

*Source:* A slight modification of Figure 1 in Gronlund, Norman E. (1970). *Stating Behavioral Objectives for Classroom Instruction*. New York: The Macmillan Company, p. 3.

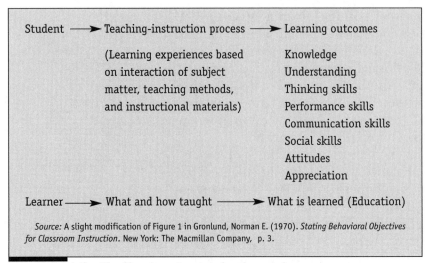

**Figure 8-1** Relationship of learning outcomes to learning experiences.

It is important to appreciate the complexity of these purposes of training. Often, to a new recruit, it seems that one attends the academy to "learn how to do the job." However, the purposes identified above go beyond that simple notion. Recruits must understand the various objectives of the training experience; otherwise, their focus may be very narrow in terms of what is expected of them. They may miss the "bigger picture" of the learning process.

It also can be argued that training is the foundation for the interrelationship (linking together) of conduct, ethics, and discipline, which is graphically illustrated in **Figure 8-2**.

These concepts should be presented in a very positive fashion. For example, people often think of discipline as a negative process. Actually, the root of the word comes from the Latin and Greek concepts for training and instruction. We need to think of the term in relation to a "well disciplined" group of officers (or a self-disciplined individual), referring to those who are well trained and know how to conduct themselves properly and who perform well in critical situations. Training provides the standards by which conduct is measured and judged acceptable. Related to the concepts of conduct and discipline are issues of ethics, morality, societal values, democratic values, and the public interest. These must be discussed and presented in a training context because they are related to the standards just mentioned. The point being made here is that there are very complex relationships that exist be-

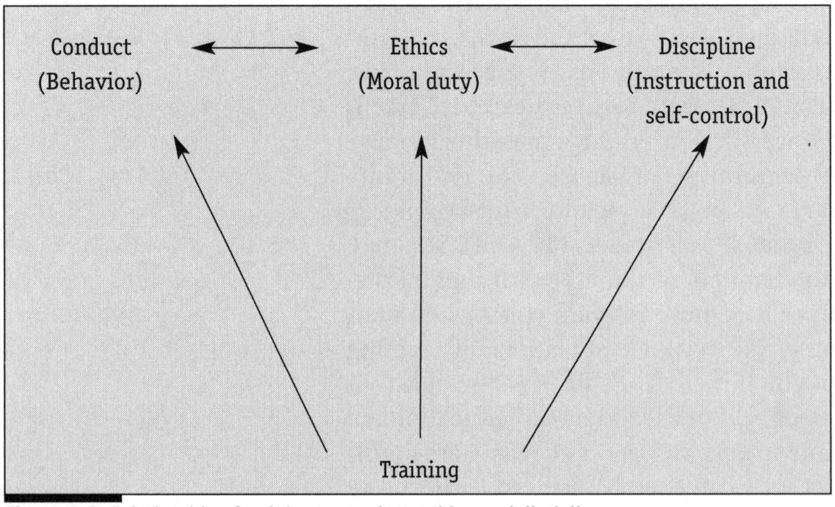

**Figure 8-2** Relationship of training to conduct, ethics, and discipline.

tween these concepts—relationships that are missed or not properly specified when training and education are presented as two distinct processes.

## Learning Domains and Styles

There are three generally accepted levels of learning, called the **learning domains** (Bloom, 1956):

*Cognitive*—refers to acquiring new knowledge, understanding, and thinking skills. Learning in this domain includes remembering the definitions of crimes, translating legal terms so that others can understand them, and evaluating a given situation when given certain facts and making a decision based on the facts and your knowledge of the law. It also would include knowing which methods and techniques to employ in a given situation, such as writing reports or sketching a crime scene.

*Psychomotor*—relates to motor skills and the ability to physically perform a specific behavior. Simple tasks such as learning to walk or ride a bike are examples. Policing examples include properly firing a weapon, conducting a crime scene search, dusting for fingerprints, driving a vehicle at high speeds in a safe manner, and mediating a domestic argument. This domain builds upon the cognitive domain in that one may know "how" to do something but may not be able to actually do it. In law enforcement, skills are learned and practiced so that they become almost automatic (performed without much forethought). Some of the more critical skills relate to self-defense, defensive driving, and radio procedure. It is a general principle of training that during a critical situation, officers revert to the manner in which they learned such skills.

*Affective*—relates to learning that impacts one's values, emotions, and/or attitudes. In policing it relates to "appreciations" and keeping an open, accepting mind to new knowledge. Persons who are "set in their ways" and are not receptive to new ideas or thinking about things differently are difficult to train. If an officer is to properly benefit from training, he or she must be willing to learn; this is a precondition to learning. Examples of the affective domain include listening attentively, accepting differences in race and culture, demonstrating a belief in democratic principles, accepting responsibility for one's own behavior, maintaining good health habits, displaying safety consciousness, and accepting and practicing ethical standards of the law enforcement profession.

Within each domain are different levels of learning; the higher levels become more difficult and complex. For example, in the cognitive domain, six levels are part of the taxonomy:

1. Knowledge: ability to remember previously learned material.
2. Comprehension: ability to grasp the meaning of words and concepts.

3. Application: ability to use learned material in new situations.
4. Analysis: ability to break down material into its component parts so that its structure can be understood.
5. Synthesis: ability to put parts together to form a new whole.
6. Evaluation: ability to judge the value of material for a given purpose.

Notice that "knowledge" and "comprehension" are the lowest levels of cognitive learning whereas "synthesis" and "evaluation" are the higher levels. Often academy training (and even some college-level course work) focuses on the lower levels of these domains; not much time is spent on the higher levels. Unfortunately, success on the street and in complex interpersonal situations often requires one to use higher levels of learning in these domains. Learning how to analyze and synthesize the information gathered during incidents and interpersonal contacts is very important in today's society, especially in multicultural and ethnically diverse population centers, which pose new experiences for officers who have different backgrounds.

Another challenge to instructors is determining the learning styles of students. This refers to how one learns or acquires new information and processes it internally. Each person has their own set of ways by which he or she learns best. Some people learn quite well from lectures, some by visually seeing the material in the form of charts and graphs; others learn from actively doing things. There are several categorizations of learning styles and the terminology varies among them. Some of the common categories include (a) visual, (b) auditory, (c) tactile (small motor movements), and (d)kinesthetic (large motor movements) (Xavier University 2004). Each of us has a preferred learning style. For example, a law enforcement trainee may prefer to visualize the activities carried out on patrol rather than just read about them. She may prefer to actually walk through the activities in order to learn and associate the duties, procedures, and techniques that are being taught. There are several excellent Web sites that discuss learning styles and some offer a free learning style test or inventory:

- http://www.xu.edu/lac/learning_styles.htm
- http://coe.etsu.edu/department/cuai/starlinks/learningstyles.htm
- http://www.ldpride.net/learningstyles.MI.htm

The significance of understanding learning styles is to develop training and education methods that ensure the person learns the material that is being presented. This is one reason why educators and trainers today attempt to incorporate multiple learning style materials into their presentations.

## Methods of Instruction

There are a number of acceptable methods of instruction used in law enforcement training of all types and levels. **Figure 8-3** identifies these methods according to those being taught: a group or an individual.

Of course, this listing of methods does not tell the whole story. We all know that lectures, for example, can be either boring or interesting depending on the instructor's delivery, the content, and the learner's interest. Likewise, computer-aided instruction can be a simple computerized quiz or tutorial program or it can consist of multimedia presentations, interactive decision making, Internet-based assignments, and/or virtual reality scenarios. The method of instruction alone does not ensure successful learning of course objectives. The methods listed in Figure 8-3 are not mutually exclusive and some may involve aspects of others mentioned.

Officers must apply learned concepts to field situations. They must analyze behavior and motives of subjects in evaluating truthfulness of statements. They must gather bits and pieces of information and synthesize them for meaning and development of inferences, probable cause, or other conclusions.

| For groups | For individuals |
|---|---|
| Lectures | Inquiry |
| Field experience | Field experience/practice |
| Field observation | Field observation |
| Case studies | Case studies |
| Field trips | Field trips |
| Demonstrations | Demonstrations |
| Interviews | Interviews |
| Role-playing | Supervised study |
| Seminars | Reading clubs |
| Conferences | Job rotation |
| Discussions | Correspondence courses |
| Debates | Computer-based instruction |
| Distance learning | Distance learning |

*Sources:* Data from A.Z. Gammage (1963). *Police Training in the United States*, p. 206, and Project STAR, *Police Officer Role Training Program* (1974). Washington, DC: National Institute of Justice. p. 75; with current techniques added.

**Figure 8-3** Methods of instruction.

# ■ Types of Training

In law enforcement, there are many different forms or types of training. The average person watching TV shows depicting police or their favorite *Police Academy* movie usually is exposed to only one type, the training of recruits. But, training is an on-going process in an officer's career. Laws change: new ones are added, the Supreme Court may modify existing police procedure that does not conform to constitutional standards, and better ways of accomplishing tasks (most often through new technology) are developed—all require that new information be conveyed to current officers.

Let us review some fundamental descriptions about the various types of training. It must first be mentioned that there is not a single accepted authority that has defined these different types of training. Nor is there consensus necessarily on the terminology used to differentiate one type from another. For example, what is "in-service" training in one agency could be "advanced" training in another.

## Mandatory/Basic/Recruit/Entry-Level Training

The universal training of recruits is a recent development in the United States. Although police academies date back to the early 1900s (see **Figure 8-4**), it was not until the late 1950s and 1960s that most states adopted **mandatory minimum training standards**. In 1959, California and New York established their commissions on Peace Officer Standards and Training (POST) for the purpose of establishing minimum training and selection criteria. All but two states have an office that has legislative authority to establish state minimum standards for law enforcement personnel (Flink 1997, 1). Generally, these offices oversee the certification and/or licensing of peace officers. Although many of these commissions

1895—New York City establishes its School of Pistol practice.

1908—First formal training school established in Berkeley, California by Marshal August Vollmer (initially the program was for in-service training).

1909—New York City instituted its police academy (for in-service and recruits).

1911—City of Detroit's first police training school started.

1916—First university-level police training school created at the University of California at Berkeley.

1918—The first school for policewomen was presented at the University of California at Los Angeles.

1919—Louisville, Kentucky Police School organized.

1924-28—University of Southern California sponsored a series of lectures of LAPD command officers that eventually leads to a full police curriculum in the Department of Public Administration.

1930—San Jose State College initiated its police science program. Students could earn an associate in arts degree and then a bachelor's degree.

1933—The nation's first baccalaureate degree in criminology was approved at the University of California at Berkeley.

1935—The FBI Police Training School, renamed The National Academy, began offering its special course work for state and local officers.

1935—Michigan State College initiated its baccalaureate program and optional 5-year police program.

1936—The Traffic Institute at Northwestern University (Evanston, Illinois) began operation.

1946—The Delinquency Control Institute was established at the University of Southern California.

1951—The Southern Police Institute at the University of Louisville began operation.

1959—The states of New York and California both set up their state minimum standards boards, the Municipal Police Training Council and the Commission on Peace Officer Standards and Training, respectively.

1963—49 two-year institutions in the United States were identified.

1968—The passage of the Omnibus Crime Control and Safe Streets Act authorized the funding of new academic and training programs.

1974—The University of Louisville opened the National Crime Prevention Institute.

*Sources:* Compiled from A.Z. Gammage, *Police Training in the United States* (1963). G.D. Eastman, and J.A. McCain (1981). "Education, professionalism, and law enforcement in historical perspective." *Journal of police science and administration*, Vol. 9, No. 2:119–130, International Association of Chiefs of Police.

**Figure 8-4** Police academy training and college program timeline.

are referred to as POSTs, they may have different agency titles such as "council" or "board," and they may or may not have the terms "peace officer" and "standards" in their title. For example, in Alaska the agency is known as the Alaska Police Standards Council; in Indiana, it is called the Indiana Law Enforcement Training Board; and in Florida it is the Florida Department of Law Enforcement. Provisions vary from state to state; however, the International Association of Directors of Law Enforcement Standards and Training (IADLEST) has published a "Model Minimum State Standards," which provides recommendations for law enforcement agencies on various issues related to training and recruitment. (This document can be found on-line at: http://www.iadlest.org/modelmin.htm.)

The training hours for new recruits vary from jurisdiction to jurisdiction. The state mandatory minimum hours of training is exactly that—a minimum (see Appendix IV at the end of this text for examples of minimum hours of training for the states of New York, California, and Ohio). Many training academies exceed the state minimums, especially academies that service large municipalities and state agencies. Recent data illustrate the variation in the number of "class-room" hours required in selected jurisdictions in the United States (Reaves and Hickman 2004):

| | | | |
|---|---|---|---|
| Albany PD, NY | 884 | Summit County (OH) Sheriff Dept. | 611 |
| Atlanta PD, GA | 1320 | Beaufort County (SC) Sheriff Dept. | 320 |
| Baltimore City PD, MD | 730 | Kent County (MI) Sheriff Dept. | 500 |
| Boston PD, MA | 1040 | Montgomery County Police (MD) | 1680 |
| Chicago PD, IL | 1230 | Massachusetts State Police | 1040 |
| Denver PD, CO | 852 | Texas State Dept. Pub. Safety | 1257 |
| Indianapolis PD, IN | 920 | NC State Highway Patrol | 1200 |
| Los Angeles PD, CA | 1064 | Pennsylvania State Police | 1112 |
| Miami PD, FL | 756 | Utah Highway Patrol | 560 |

Keep in mind that these are 2000 data; the number of mandated hours could be different today because agencies consistently upgrade the hours. Also, these hours do not include field training hours (discussed below). According to the 2000 LEMAS survey, the median number of training hours for municipal police was 720; for sheriff's departments it was 640, and for primary state agencies it was 960. Median field training hours were 520 for municipal agencies and 480 for other types of agencies. Occasionally (and today, more frequently), the question of reciprocity between states and/or municipalities arises because of officers moving to other jurisdictions. This is a difficult question to answer (as is exemplified in **Figure 8-5**) because of the various regulations and rules within and among the various states.

The topics addressed in a basic training academy are numerous, in some schools numbering over 100 (especially when all the "sub-topics" are totaled). Instead of discussing the details of these topics here, see Appendix IV of this text for the condensed listing of subjects and the minimum mandated hours for selected states. Keep in mind that local agency academies may add topics and hours to the state minimums.

Can the police training received in one jurisdiction be transferred to another if an officer changes departments? The answer to this question varies greatly. In some states, departments will not honor or recognize the training hours a person received while working in another jurisdiction within the same state. If a current officer decides to change departments, he or she may have to complete the entire academy training at the new agency. On the other hand, a person may be able to change departments, go to another state, and only have to take the hours necessary to learn that state's criminal code—usually 40 to 80 hours.

Some states require a certified officer from another state to take their state exam before receiving a new certification. If you plan a career in law enforcement and intend to start in one agency and move to another, you should learn about any possible reciprocity before you join the first agency; you may have to attend the academy a second time. Other factors enter into the equation, such as moving from a local to a state agency, or from a local or state agency to a federal agency. In short, portability of training is not consistent.

**Figure 8-5** Training reciprocity between jurisdictions.

Usually persons attending basic academies have been hired by a law enforcement agency; however, a recent trend in some states allows "students" to pay their own way through the academy whether sponsored by an agency or not. Where this is permitted, the student can attend the academy, graduate, and seek employment with an agency in that state that recognizes the training. Additionally, 23 states permit colleges to conduct some or all of the entry-level law enforcement training (Flink 1997, 113). Although this is a significant number, the training usually must be regulated or meet the specific guidelines and standards of the state office that certifies the training.

Once a person is employed by an agency, even during the attendance of a basic academy, he or she is said to be "on probation," which usually includes one's attendance at the basic academy. The probationary period may extend from 6 to 24 months, but one year is the norm. For most officers, the probationary period represents the only time during which the department can terminate an employee without cause (Gaines and Forester 1983), although this is an overstatement in today's litigious society. Chapter 9 discusses the probation period as part of the selection process.

## Field Training

**Field training** consists of "formalized, actual on-the-job instruction by specially selected and trained personnel called Field Training Officers (FTOs). Field training (generally combined with periodic evaluation of the recruit's performance) usually occurs immediately after the recruit completes the classroom portion of basic training" (McCampbell 1986, 2). A 1997 survey of state regulatory commissions found that only seven states mandated field training for entry-level personnel as part of state standards (Flink 1997, 89). Of course, local agencies are normally responsible for this type of training. One of the most noted formalized field training programs was established in 1972 in the San Jose, California Police Department and has been a model for many departments. (See **Figure 8-6** for an overview of the San Jose Program, as originally implemented.)

Most field training programs commence after the recruit has completed the basic academy (which normally is 10–15 weeks in duration). Then the recruit is assigned to an FTO, or to several of them, for a number of weeks. Some field training programs last up to a year. The FTO is responsible for evaluating the recruit during the field training period. The evaluations usually are formal and very detailed and may occur on a daily or weekly basis. If any weaknesses are found in the recruit's performance, they must undergo remedial training. If successful, the recruit can move on to a solo assignment. The officer must continue to perform successfully during this solo phase or he can be assigned for remedial training. During this intensive evaluation period, the department also determines whether the officer should be terminated. Successful completion of the field training leads to permanent employment status. Of course, variations to this sequence may occur since not all jurisdictions are alike in their operation of field training programs. Hughes et al. (1996) found that probation officers spent an average of 125 days with an FTO and that the top three typical duties of an FTO were "teaching by example," "mending weaknesses," and "allowing the probationer to take initiative." In California, effective January 1, 1999, every peace officer who is required to complete the regular basic training course must also complete an approved field training program. The FTO program, at a minimum, must include

**Phase I**

Weeks 1–16
Academy and in-agency classroom and range training.

*Successful academy performance leads to Phase II. Failure at the Academy leads to dismissal.*

**Phase II**

Weeks 17–18
Assigned to primary FTO. No evaluations.

Weeks 19–28
Daily observation reports by FTOs with weekly evaluation reports by supervisors.

Weeks 29–30
Daily and weekly reports continue, but primary FTO rides in plain clothes with recruit.

*During Phase II, recruit is assigned to initial FTO, then to two other FTOs on different shifts. Then back to initial FTO. Recruit receives a District Evaluation after completing assignment with each FTO.*

*At completion of Phase II, successful recruit goes to Phase III. Otherwise, recruit may receive remedial training or be dismissed.*

**Phase III**

Weeks 31–36
Recruit works a solo beat outside the training district. Supervisors evaluate biweekly.

Weeks 37–40
Recruit continues solo beat. Supervisors evaluate monthly.

Weeks 41–44
Recruit continues solo beat. Ten Month Review Board meets to recommend retention, remedial training, or dismissal.

Weeks 45–52
Reserved for remedial training if needed. Special board meets to review the performance of recruits with deficiencies.

*Recruit begins solo assignment and initial biweekly evaluations followed by monthly ones.*

*At ten month review, recruit is certified to continue in Phase III or is recommended for remedial training.*

*At completion of Phase III, recruit becomes certified as a permanent employee or has Phase III extended. The option of dismissal still exists.*

*Source:* Adapted from M.S. McCampbell (1986). Field training for police officers: State of the art. *Research in Brief.* Washington, DC: National Institute of Justice.

**Figure 8-6** San Jose Academy and original field training model.

10 weeks of training; the criteria for structured training, remediation, and evaluation; daily trainee evaluations, and criteria for the selection and training of field training officers and program administrators. As of June 1999, over 400 programs had been approved (O'Brien 1999).

Not all departments have formal FTO programs; however, most departments do have some type of orientation or "break-in" period that involves others. In the Metro Nashville Police Department, after graduation from the academy, rookie officers are oriented and evaluated by "Master Patrol Officers" for a period of six months. They ride with one MPO for two months, then ride with another MPO, in another area of the city, for another two months. Following a rotation to a third MPO, the MPOs and Patrol Supervisors hold a meeting to decide whether to keep the officer, extend probation, or terminate the rookie's employment.

## In-service Training

During a police officer's career, ongoing training is necessary to keep up with changes in the criminal law and procedures. **In-service training** (sometimes called "refresher") is the phrase used to refer to training received by officers following their recruit training. It is usually done at the department's facilities, and may be during regular tours of duty (while on-duty). The form of in-service training may vary from "roll-call" training sessions (held just prior to or after a tour of duty) to ones several hours in length. The subject matter of in-service training normally is related to the general assignments of most officers, or officers of a particular unit. Common material covered in such sessions includes legal updates in criminal procedure, new or modifications to standard operating procedures, the proper use of new equipment or weapons, and utilization of new forms or means of incident reporting. Some in-service sessions are used as "refreshers" that include updated material on topics originally covered at recruit school. In the pre-recruit academy years of policing, in-service training served as the primary means of upgrading personnel.

In-service training may be mandated by state law or regulations. By 1997, 33 states required such training for law enforcement personnel (Flink 1997, 77). Such training may include firearms re-qualification, an additional minimum number of hours, or other types of training. The time frame for such training may be annually or up to 48 months.

## Advanced/Specialized

**Advanced** or **specialized training** refers to those sessions that address specialty topics or material that is an extension or a more enhanced version of what was received at basic academies. Such training allows officers to specialize in selected areas of the field. For example, general recruit training covers traffic accident investigation and crime scene processing, but advanced training is available to allow officers to become traffic accident specialists and crime scene technicians. The length of advanced/specialty courses can range from 1 day to 3 weeks, although some courses at special institutes may be from one to nine months in length. The following listing is a portion of the 90 different courses offered at the Ohio Peace Officer Training Academy in London, Ohio which is the state's advanced training center for local law enforcement (for a course catalog, visit their Web page at http://www.ag.state.oh.us/online_publications/pota/index.htm):

| | |
|---|---|
| Infant/Child Death Investigation | Dealing with the Suicidal |
| Dignitary Protection | Incident Command System |
| Evidence Technician I and II | Basic Instructor Training |
| Bloodstain Evidence | Drug Impaired Detection |
| Internet Investigation I and II | Advanced Hostage Negotiations |
| Death Investigation | Financial Investigative Techniques |
| Chemical Agents | Surveillance Photography and |
| Trip Wires and Explosive | Videography |
| Devices | Traffic Accident Reconstruction |

In addition to specialized institutes and periodic training courses offered by professional associations, most states have some type of advanced training facility that offers specialized course work. Colleges and universities also routinely offer specialized courses for police personnel, and many of the courses carry **continuing education credit**. Such credit may be awarded in the form of hours or units, which usually apply to any state or local requirement where training hours are required each year.

## Executive and Managerial Training

Another type of training, sometimes called **executive and managerial**, focuses on administrative decision making or supervision issues and skills. Courses in this type of training address subjects such as leadership, motivation, budgeting, first-line supervision, FTO program development and administration, media relations, public speaking, and communication skills. Some states require promoted officers to attend a managerial or supervisor's course as a condition of promotion; however, usually there is no such requirement to do so. **Figure 8-7** is an illustration of a course description of the line supervision course in the state of Florida.

A California-based program is rather unique to the field; it is known as the California Law Enforcement Command College. Originally, it was a 24-month program consisting of 10 workshops and independent study projects. It has evolved into a 12-month, 7-session program. Its faculty consists of university professors and consultants who are recognized for their expertise. The Command College curriculum is designed "to provide a leadership course with a futures perspective to prepare law enforcement leaders of today for the future" (California Commission on POST 2000). Attendees must be employed in a management position in a California law enforcement agency. The objectives of the program are to help these individuals develop strategies and methods for managing the complex issues facing law enforcement today and in the future. A "futures research" orientation is a fundamental component to the program. Each participant must complete an independent study project that will contribute to the body of knowledge of law enforcement through information sharing. The Command College has its own Web site at http://www.commandcollege.com/. **Figure 8-8** identifies the session sequence and content of the Command College Program.

## Citizen Police Academy

In recent years, **citizen police academies** have begun appearing in many jurisdictions. This academy usually is a means of establishing a liaison and dialogue with the community. The format varies, but such a program can consist of one evening a week for 8–10 weeks. The course is open to residents of the jurisdiction and covers many of the same topics as taught in a regular police academy. The sessions are

Tailored to the new supervisor, this course will assist the student with understanding the transition from operations to management responsibilities. It will also provide the experienced supervisor with the additional knowledge, skills, and attributes to function effectively in this significant role. Topics include: communications and semantics, management theory, elements of supervision, organization theory, reporting and records, human relations, planning practices, staff work requirements, considerations in policy development and enforcement, budgeting practices, performance appraisal techniques, staffing and assignment of personnel, community relations, civil liability, methods of developing personnel and proper use of discipline.

*Source:* Tallahassee Community College. http://www.tcc.fl.edu/dept/ptlea/adv_special/index.asp.

**Figure 8-7** Line supervision course.

**Sessions**

1. Defining the Future

   A conceptual roadmap for studying the future and the role of a leader will be introduced. Using the STEEP futures forecasting scanning model (social, technological, environmental, economic, and political), the student will learn techniques to identify faint signals and emerging issues that may be important to the future of California law enforcement.

2. Enhanced leadership

   The session will focus on the various leadership theories and how they relate to the students personally as leaders. Self-assessment instruments, facets of self-mastery, and the creative decision making will be instrumental in identifying their role as a leader today and in the future.

3. Social and political issues

   Forecasting methods and the importance of scenario writing will be covered in this workshop. Today's faint signals and emerging trends as they relate to social issues, the first element of STEEP, will be discussed. The potential impact of these social issues on the student's agency and his/her role as a leader will be explored.

4. Technological and environmental issues

   This session will include discussions on broad-based technological and environmental issues. Students will be required to research cutting edge technology and environmental issues, share information, and assess the impact on law enforcement leadership.

5. Futures forecasting and economic issues

   This session will explore multiple forecasts of economic and political issues. In-depth discussion will be conducted concerning the impact of these issues on law enforcement. Students will create alternative scenarios and define probable futures.

6. Futures planning tools

   This session will provide a "tool box" that includes strategic planning skills, transition management systems, and evaluation components. Emphasis is placed on expanding the student's knowledge of resources that enhance leadership roles and strategies for mitigating the impact of change on the agency.

7. Politics of change

   This session provides an overview of the program and study results. Chief and city manager panels discuss pratical application of change strategies. The session concludes with graduation ceremonies.

*Source:* Reprinted with permission from Center for Leadership Development, State of California Commission on Peace Officer Standards and Training (2000), *The Law Enforcement Command College.*

**Figure 8-8** California Command College program.

taught by members of the local police department who speak on their areas of expertise. The course is designed to give an overview of the department's policies and procedures. The course also can provide a forum for the participants to offer suggestions and provide input regarding the operations of the agency. Some citizens' academies provide simulations so participants can learn what it is like to approach suspects, patrol in a cruiser, and fire a weapon. Firearms training is an option in some academies. One of the objectives of the citizen police academy is to achieve a greater public awareness and understanding of the agency's role in the community through the educational aspects of the program. The Metropolitan Nashville (Tennessee) Police Department maintains a citizen police academy on the World Wide Web that includes considerable information about the department. Participants can log on, study the information presented about the department, and take a 25-question test, the successful completion of which allows the participant to print out a certificate of completion.

# ■ The Higher Education and Training Merger

Since the early 1900s, professionals in the field of policing have been advocating college education for officers. However, the standard educational requirement for most local (3 out of 4) and state (2 out of 3) agencies in the United States is a high school diploma or GED. The 2000 LEMAS survey of agencies of 100 or more sworn personnel found that about 25% of local agencies required some college; 10% required a degree, and only 2% required a baccalaureate degree. Of the 49 state agencies, approximately one-third required some college; 12% required an associate degree, and 2% required a baccalaureate degree at the time of appointment (Reaves and Hickman 2004, v). Two states, Minnesota and Wisconsin, reported that law enforcement personnel were required by state standards to possess a minimum of an associate degree (however, in Wisconsin, an officer has up to 5 years to complete the associate degree after appointment).

In 1967, the President's Commission on Law Enforcement and Administration of Justice (1967b, 109–110) recommended that "the ultimate aim of all police departments should be that all personnel with general enforcement powers have baccalaureate degrees," and "police departments should take immediate steps to establish a minimum requirement of a baccalaureate degree for all supervisory and executive positions." Later, in 1973, the National Advisory Commission on Criminal Justice Standards and Goals stated in Standard 15.1 that every police agency should, no later than:

— 1975, require as a condition of initial employment the completion of at least 2 years of college education.

— 1978, require as a condition of initial employment the completion of at least 3 years of college education.

— 1982, require as a condition of initial employment the completion of at least 4 years of college education.

A study published by the Police Executive Research Forum (PERF) in 1989 reported on the state of education in the police field (Carter et al. 1989). It found that 55% of all police officers in the study had completed two years of college, as compared to 15% in 1970. The study's recommendations included (Ayers 1990, 17):

- All law enforcement agencies should develop long-range plans for requiring a college degree as a minimum criterion for promotion and employment by 1995.
- Effective immediately, all candidates for promotion to management and command ranks should be required to have baccalaureate degrees.
- Effective immediately, all candidates for promotion to first-line and supervisory positions should have a minimum of 60 college credits.
- The federal government should develop a program to provide financial aid to in-service officers to help further their educations.

Obviously, these time periods have come and gone and the requirement of a college education—even 2 years of college—has not yet become a requirement in most agencies. In 1967, the President's Commission reported that only 70% of the police agencies in the United States minimally required a high school diploma as a condition of employment, although the median educational level for all police officers in the country was 12.4 years. By 1988 (in a survey of 531 law enforcement agencies with 100 or more sworn officers or serving a population of 50,000 or more) the average educational level of officers was 13.6 years (Carter and Sapp 1992). Although the minimum educational requirements for entry into the field are not increasing significantly, the competition for the jobs is.

Persons possessing only a high school level education are competing with baccalaureate and master's degreed applicants. Colleges and universities are graduating thousands of criminal justice majors annually in the United States, and many are seeking employment in the policing field. According to the US Census Bureau, "Americans are more educated than ever." Approximately 52% of Americans have had at least some college or more, and about 27% have earned a bachelor's degree. Given these figures about the general population's education level, do citizens want officers whose educational levels are below average?

There are plenty of educational programs at the college level today and there is ample opportunity for interested persons to attend college. That wasn't always the case. By the early 1960s, only about 60 educational programs existed nationally. With the creation of the Law Enforcement Education Program (LEEP) as part of the Law Enforcement Assistance Administration of the late 1960s and early 1970s, by 1977 there were over 750 programs (Hoover 1983). Although exact data are not available, it is estimated that there are about 1,000 criminal justice education programs in the United States today. There has been ample debate over the type and quality of educational programming in the United States, and little consensus exits on curricular matters. In 1998, the Academy of Criminal Justice Sciences adopted a set of "Standards for Criminal Justice Education Programs," which are voluntary guidelines and recommendations. They generally address content areas, qualification of faculty, facilities, student-to-faculty ratios, and so on.

Recently, Tulsa, Oklahoma became the largest city in the nation and the only city in that state to require a baccalaureate degree for new recruits, effective January 1998. Prior to that, in 1981 the agency required 108 semester credit hours of college. Chief Palmer stated that officers with college degrees "come to you a little bit more mature, they're a little more aware of diversity issues, and they're more prone to use their minds to problem-solve than one that doesn't have that type of background. . . . What I've seen here is that there's a world of difference between a high school graduate and a college graduate in regard to skill levels and the handling of people" (Men & Women of Letters 1997, 1). Of the city's 794 officers, 73% have baccalaureate degrees, and another 20% have 60 hours or more of college; 40 officers have master's degrees, three have law degrees, and one has a Ph.D.

## Research on Law Enforcement and Higher Education

Essentially, empirical studies examining education levels of police officers to date can be divided into two broad categories: behavioral measures (arrest rates, citizen complaints, commendations, etc.), and attitudinal measures (job satisfaction, receptivity to innovation, etc.). However, research within each of these categories has yielded inconsistent and often conflicting results. For example, when examining education and police management, Withal (1985) argued that "[f]ormal schooling and varied experience offer police chiefs no guarantee of effectiveness." However, Krimmell and Lindenmouth (2001), in contrast to Withal, found that not only was education an important factor in predicting leadership success, but that there were significant differences between police chiefs with a background that included some college and those police chiefs who only possessed a high school diploma on 35 different performance and leadership indicators.

In his review of the literature, Hayeslip (1989) argued that officers with higher education have higher motivation, are better able to utilize innovative techniques, display clearer thinking, have a better understanding of the world of policing, and the necessity of education given the role of police. Kenney and Cordner (1996) offer that:

> ... among the presumed advantages of this preference include the assumption that college-educated officers will have a better understanding of the police role in general, of the importance of the police in society, and an improved sensitivity to the problems and differences in the communities they police. In addition, proponents of college-educated officers argue that the ability to communicate, exercise discretion, and analyze problems can only be enhanced. Unfortunately, the evidence to support these assumptions is inconclusive at best (53).

Penegor and Peak (1992) suggest that inconsistencies in research linking education and job performance are most likely due to differences in how variables are measured. In a meta-analysis of five empirical studies examining policing and job performance, Hunter, Schmidt, and Jackson (1982), concluded that all five studies had significant findings consistently in the positive direction between education and police performance, and that the variance between the studies' results was much smaller than reported. "It has been shown in this study that by cumulating across studies we can find consistent agreement that education and police performance are moderately related" (57). The authors further argue that inconsistent findings in this case and possibly in the general literature on police education are possibly due to artifactual errors in the data.

## Behaviors

**Job Performance.** Assumptions of several management reforms suggest that increased education of the police will affect job performance in several ways. Under community- and problem-oriented policing, higher education is assumed to improve problem-solving skills and provide police with a wider range of solutions available to them besides simply responding to a call for service and arresting individuals involved in illegal activity. Under the model of professionalism, higher education, (alongside training), is assumed to improve actual skills involved in the daily activities of policing such as communication with the public, diffusing potentially dangerous situations, and skills necessary to effectively solve crimes or prevent them from occurring.

> In sum, it is argued that a college-educated officer has a broader comprehension of civil rights issues from legal, social, historical, and political perspectives. Moreover, these officers have a broader view of policing tasks and a greater professional ethos, thus their actions and decisions tend to be driven by conscience and values, consequently lessening the chance of erroneous decisions. If these arguments are valid, the logical conclusion is that the college-educated officer would be less likely to place the department in a liability situation (Carter and Sapp 1989, 162).

Typical performance measures in empirical studies have included: arrests, tenure, citizen evaluations, and composite performance measures (Hayeslip 1989). Cohen and Chaiken (1973) found that police officers with higher education received fewer complaints and subsequent disciplinary actions. Several studies have concluded that police officers with higher education have higher corresponding arrest rates (Bozza 1973; Glasgow, Green, and Knowles 1973) which in the era of community-oriented policing may not necessarily be a positive advancement.

Wilson (1975) suggests that the relationship between education and police performance is curvilinear in that college education beyond two years may place a law enforcement officer at a disadvantage. He suggests that police officers possessing college beyond two years are more reluctant to perform certain tasks, are more resistant to authority, and are less likely to protect themselves in dangerous situations than are police officers with less than two years of college. Other studies completed by Smith (1978b) and Sherman and Blumberg (1981) refute these claims. Cascio (1977) found that higher educated officers had fewer preventable accidents and took less sick time away from work, and Lester (1979) concluded that officers with more education performed better in police training.

Several studies have identified strong positive relationships between education and specific police performance measures (Cohen and Chaiken 1972; Finnegan 1976; Sanderson 1978; Saunders 1970). Others have only reported moderate relationships between education and aggregate performance ratings (Cascio 1977; Roberg 1978; Spencer and Nichols 1971; Weirman 1978), or weak (Hayeslip 1989) to no relationship at all (Griffin 1980; Kedia 1985; Marsh 1962; Worden 1990). Furthermore, some studies have actually found an inverse relationship between higher education and overall performance (Gottlieb 1974; Smith and Ostrom 1974).

Krimmel (1996), in his self-report study, found that "in a number of categories, the college-educated police officers (those possessing a bachelor's degree) rated themselves higher on a self-report performance instrument than did police officers without bachelor's degrees." These categories included the ability to utilize employee contacts, knowledge of the law, preparedness for court, quality of work assignments, level of problem-solving ability, level of arrest analysis, level of confidence with supervisors, quality of written work, quality of oral presentations, self-image, arrest report quality, investigative report quality, and interpersonal relationships.

Kakar (1998) echoed these results in a study of patrol officers in Dade County, Florida. Kakar concluded that "the police officers with college education rated themselves significantly higher on several performance categories as compared to the officers without any college education and officers with a college degree rated themselves higher than the other two groups." These categories included attitudes and behaviors regarding change, stressful situations, extra work, and criticism. Overall, more highly educated officers rated themselves higher in their ability to deal with criticism, change, workload, and stress. In addition, college-educated officers rated themselves higher on knowledge of the law, use of mediation and conflict resolution, investigation and report-writing skills, leadership, responsibility, and problem-solving skills. However, it is interesting to note that Kakar found no significant differences in an officer's attitude toward their job, office, or department. Kakar also found that those officers with higher levels of education reported themselves lower on scores of job satisfaction and fulfillment and indicated more overall frustration.

The less than harmonious findings of Kakar's study and others may serve well to point out that higher levels of education may be "relevant to many aspects of police work but should not be assumed to predict all areas of job performance" (Truxillo et al. 1998, 269). For example, Truxillo et al. found that while college education was statistically significant for a variety of performance measures, it was not important in reducing disciplinary problems—a key variable in much of the literature on higher levels of education in policing. Thus it may be important to identify a wider variety of performance measures within policing and test the strength of relationship between them and college education individually.

**Communication Skills.** Education is assumed to improve police officers' communication in two distinct ways. First, under reforms of community-oriented policing, police officers are encouraged to keep open lines of communication between themselves and the community they patrol. Because community problems are not always dealing with law violations, police officers must have a greater knowledge base from which they draw available solutions. Second, it is assumed that the process of a college education strengthens written and oral skills necessary to improve police officers' report writing, and communication with a variety of different people throughout the day.

Empirical research suggests overall that education does indeed have a positive impact on communication. Vodicka (1994) concluded that police officers with more education had better communication skills and had a greater openness to change. Both Vodicka and Carter and Sapp (1992) found that college-educated police candidates, for the most part, have better verbal and written communication skills, make better discretionary decisions, and have more empathy and tolerance for people with different attitudes and lifestyles. Worden (1990) concluded that according to citizen reports, police officers who were college graduates were overall better problem-solvers, but were less courteous than their less educated counterparts. In addition, Worden found that there was no relationship between education and citizen evaluations of officer performance in police–citizen encounters. Hooper's (1988) research a few years earlier suggests that college graduates were also better at report writing and received fewer citizen complaints. Other studies have made similar conclusions regarding lower levels of citizen complaints and higher levels of education (Carter and Sapp 1989; Kappeler, Sapp, and Carter 1992; Shernock 1992; and Tyre and Braunstein 1992) and fewer disciplinary problems and college education (Carter and Sapp 1989).

## Attitudes/Demeanor

The demeanor in which a police officer conducts his/her job duties and the attitudes he/she holds about policing is important in understanding both job performance and citizen encounters. Because police officers work with a variety of people who differ in their attitudes, culture, and lifestyles, it is important for police officers to have a more tolerant and understanding demeanor, especially in community-oriented policing. Bayley (1986) asserts that "for disturbances, the manner in which contact was initiated had consequences for both processing and exit." He continues by stating that the demeanor of police has "substantial" explanatory usefulness for both disturbances and traffic stops—routine occurrences during daily patrol. Research examining police demeanor and attitudes has also suggested that college-educated officers are less authoritarian, less conservative, less rigid and legalistic, and less likely to invoke the criminal justice process (Dalley 1975; Finckenauer 1975; Smith et al. 1967; 1970; Taylor 1983). In addition, they tend to be less cynical, more open-minded and have a broader conception of the police role and have more positive attitudes toward legal restrictions on police powers (Niederhoffer 1967; Parker et al. 1976; Powell 1980; Roberg 1978; Worden 1990). Furthermore, college-educated police officers also have a more holistic attitude towards police work, place a higher value on ethical conduct, are more creative, and are more tolerant of people of different lifestyles, race and ethnicity (Carter and Sapp 1989; Lynch 1976; Shernock 1992; Smith et al. 1970; Trojanowicz and Nicholson 1976; Wycoff 1987).

Other studies suggest that there is no relationship between higher education and attitudes, specifically cynicism (Lotz and Regoli 1977; Regoli 1976; Weiner 1976; Wycoff and Susmilch 1979). Smith (1978b) and Sherman and Blumberg (1981) in their respective reviews of the relevant literature suggest that, overall, findings on the relationship between education and attitude are mixed. **Test-Taking Skills and Job Satisfaction.** The link between higher education and test-taking is more important when one also looks at the relationship between education, job satisfaction, and promotion. Patterson (1991) identified a specific and positive relationship between test-taking and oral interviewing skills and higher levels of education.

If reforms giving more autonomy in decision making and making problem solving an important job function coincide with increased levels of education, it can be hypothesized that job satisfaction will also increase. Empirical research on this area indicates that this may not always be the case. Dantzker (1993) identified a curvilinear relationship between job satisfaction and higher education. Specifically, he found that job satisfaction for college-educated officers was only evident during the first five years of experience:

> If a hypothesis were to have been offered based on the premise of the research, I would have suggested that college-educated patrol officers become less satisfied with their jobs the longer they remain in patrol while their high-school-only-educated colleagues remain more satisfied. The data appears to support this suggestion (106).

Dantzker suggested that the drop in job satisfaction after 5 years came from both the realization that education was not a predictive factor for promotion, and that there existed a significant difference between what college-educated officers were capable of doing and what they actually could do when attempting to solve problems in the community. In another study conducted by Dantzker (1994), he again concluded that "while findings from a national sample have indicated a strong correlation with education and perceived job satisfaction, in this department education had very little impact." In a more recent study, Dantzker (1998) found the relationship between education and job satisfaction to be dependent upon the amount of education the officer has. Cascio (1977) produced findings inconsistent with Dantzker in that he found higher-educated officers to be more highly job motivated.

In separate studies completed in Oakland and Detroit, Buzawa (1984) and Buzawa, Austin, and Bannon (1994) found mixed results:

> *The role of education as a predictor of higher levels of job satisfaction was not clearly demonstrated in the earlier study. Higher levels of education were found to be predictive of increased job satisfaction in one department—Oakland, California. On the other hand, education had virtually no effect on job satisfaction among Detroit officers* (1994, 53).

Charles Sherwood (2000) argued that the level of education did not make a significant difference on officer's feelings about job characteristics. In his study, what was more important was the notion of job enrichment. Similarly, in a survey of the Spokane Police Department in Washington state, Zhao, Thurman, and He (1999) found that "skill variety, task identity, and autonomy contribute most to the variation in officers' work satisfaction." Autonomy was especially important. Worden's (1990) work backs up these findings by suggesting that the dissatisfaction experienced by college-educated officers most likely due to a rigid work environment and an inability for officers to exercise their ideas (Worden 1990).

Job satisfaction is inherently linked to attrition and turnover rates within law enforcement. Numerous studies have found a positive and significant relationship between higher levels of education and higher levels of attrition in policing (Burbeck and Furnham 1985; Daniel 1982; Weirman 1978). Other studies have found no relationship (Marsh 1962), and still even others have found an inverse relationship (Sanderson 1978).

**Promotion.** The notion of job satisfaction has been linked not only to police officers' overall satisfaction with their job functions but also to whether or not higher education is a predictive factor in promotion. The literature suggests that higher education is not necessarily a straight shot to job promotion. Carter, Sapp, and Stephens (1989) suggest that education might be a consideration in some promotions, but there are few guarantees.

Penegor and Peak (1992) in their study of hiring practices of police chiefs concluded that education may be more of a predictive factor when outside hiring is conducted, but not when chiefs are hired from within their own department. Buckley, McGinnis, and Petrunik (1992) found that education was more related to the "perception" of promotion practices in that officers with higher education placed a higher value on education as a promotional factor. In addition, those with university degrees expected to retire at a higher rank than those without degrees. Furthermore, they found that the primary motivation for taking college courses was for promotion.

Truxillo et al. (1998) found statistical relationships between college education and promotion; and college education and supervisory ratings of job knowledge. They suggest that education and promotion could be related in several possible ways. First, the individual "motivation for educational achievement may be the same as for promotions." Second, skills such as studying and test-taking may be more finely-tuned in officers with a college background. These skills are certainly necessary in the process of promotion. Third, the authors argue that "college education instills a higher degree of professionalism and maturity that is needed and valued at higher organizational levels." What is more interesting in their study is that there was very little relationship found between job performance measures and how many college credits were criminal-justice focused. The authors suggest this may be a result of extensive training given to all police officers that mitigates any advantage offered by college-level criminal justice courses, or that due to the broad role and function of law enforcement officers, having a general education may be more important than having a criminal justice orientation.

When looking at careers within criminal justice in general, Carlan (1999) found that those holding a master's degree earn significantly more than those with a bachelor's degree. When examining law enforcement specifically, Polk and Armstrong (2001) state that:

> findings show that higher education reduces time required for movement in rank and assignment to specialized positions and was positively correlated to promotion into supervisory and administrative posts. Implications are that higher education will enhance an officer's probability of rising to the top regardless of whether the agency requires a college degree as a precondition of employment (78).

David Carter, Allen Sapp, and Darrel Stephens published what is quite possibly the "most comprehensive study of police education to date" in 1989. Their report, entitled *The State of Police Education: Policy Direction for the 21st Century*, reviewed significant findings from previous literature, and discussed findings from their three-phased study of police departments across the country. Significant findings suggest that college-educated officers perform policing tasks better, are better communicators, are more flexible in dealing with difficult situations, are more professional, adapt better to organizational change, and have fewer administrative and personal problems than their less-educated counterparts.

## Combining Training and Education

For the most part, police training and college education still operate "separately and distinctly" from each other. Only recently have the two begun to merge in selected programs or areas in the United States. One of the largest mergers occurred in the state of Minnesota in 1977 with the creation of the Peace Officer Standards and Training Board to replace the older Peace Officer Training Board. It was the first state to establish "licensing" requirements. The "Minnesota Model" was initiated to decentralize the training of recruits by making fuller use of the state's college and vocational school system. Also, requirements for continuing education for license renewal were implemented.

In Minnesota, there is an alternative to the traditional route of securing employment with a police agency first and then attending the recruit training. A person can complete a POST-certified law enforcement program at a 2- or 4-year academic institution and then sit for the academic portion of the licensing exam.

Upon successful completion of the exam, the person can enroll in a law enforcement skills course (of approximately 8 weeks in length). Then, after passing the skills training, the person takes the skills portion of the licensing exam. If both portions of the licensing exam are successfully completed, the candidate can then seek employment anywhere in the state as a police officer. Following a successful one-year probationary period, the new officer is granted a license. The academic portion of the program consists of the following subject areas (Minnesota State Statutes, §§ 626.843 and 626.845):

a. Administration of Justice

b. Minnesota Statutes

c. Criminal Law

d. Human Behavior

e. Juvenile Justice

f. Law Enforcement Operation and Procedures

The skills training consists of the following subject areas:

a. Techniques in Criminal Investigation and Testifying

b. Patrol Functions

c. Traffic Law Enforcement

d. Firearms

e. Defensive Tactics

f. Emergency Vehicle Driving

g. Criminal Justice Information Systems

h. First Aid

Another recent development in the training and education merger is exemplified by the West Virginia State Police Training Program and the Maryland Articulation Agreement. In conjunction with Marshall University's Community and Technical College, the completion of the 960-hour, 28-week, training course leads to an associate degree in addition to certification as a state police officer. This venture began in 1985 and as of this writing is still in effect. Cadets earn up to 72 semester hours of credit and take a number of regular college courses taught by Marshall University professors. In Maryland, in March of 1999, 18 participating colleges and universities approved an Articulation Agreement that will permit any graduate of a certified recruit program to receive 15 undergraduate credits toward a degree. The process varies somewhat among the colleges, but the credits are fully transferable.

During the late 1980s, developments in Ohio also led to a greater merger of education and training requirements at selected institutions. It is now possible for students to complete the total requirements for peace officer certification at state-approved "**college academies**" and sit for the mandated state exam. Students attending the college academies essentially complete the requirements for training as they complete their college degree program. Originally, most of the college academies "blended" academic material with training curriculum requirements over a two-year course of study. Recently, however, most of the college academies in the Ohio system have gone to a "caboose" delivery system—the mandatory training curriculum material is taught at the end of the associate degree program. Examples such as these are common in many states, especially in California and Florida, but most merger arrangements are associated with community colleges. Much of the debate against such programs has come from baccalaureate granting institutions/programs that emphasize the traditional differences between education and training and criticize narrow vocationally-oriented programs. However, it is not uncommon for advanced training academies or programs to affiliate themselves with colleges and universities that allow the granting of limited college credit or continuing education units for advanced or specialty courses. Nevertheless, today's trend is toward a greater merger of training and educational endeavors.

## ■ Three Major Emerging Factors

There are three emerging factors that will greatly impact the current aspects of police training and education: the evolving utilization of technology to enhance the learning process, the Violent Crime Control and Law Enforcement Act of 1994, and problem-oriented training. Greater use of technology, especially computer-based police training, is appearing in the academies in Florida, Illinois, California, Michigan, Ohio, and other states. Programs for basic, in-service, and advanced training are being developed and becoming cost-effective. A 1994 study (Hughes et al.) of 64 of the largest agencies in the United States found that 50.9% used computers in weapons training, 21.1% in police procedure, and 5% each in driver training and law. Multimedia and virtual reality programs are emerging in course work beyond firearms training, where many such programs were originally applied. The University of Illinois Police Training Institute has been a leader in developing course work for police training programs.

The future of police training will be closely tied to computerization for several reasons. First is because of the sheer volume of information and material that needs to be mastered by police recruits. Second is because of the individual attention that a computer can give to and demand of the user. Third is because of documentation on individual police officers relating to their mastery of concepts and material and that must be maintained. Fourth is because of the realism that will be available through virtual reality and artificial intelligence programming. A 1997 survey of state training commissions found 16 respondents indicating that computer-based training was part of their officer training programs. However, only two states had developed their own computer-based training courses. In the opinions of the respondents, the topics considered more useful than others for computer-based presentations were (Flink 1997, 111):

| | |
|---|---|
| Report Writing | Radar |
| First Aid/CPR | Insurance Fraud |
| Firearms | Arrest and Control |
| Driving | Computer Crime |
| Legal Areas | Narcotics Investigation |
| DUI Training | Domestic Violence |
| Bloodborne Pathogens | Traffic Accident Investigation |
| Cultural Diversity | |
| Use of Force | Crime Prevention Through Environmental Design |
| Sexual Assault | |
| Hazmat | |

The second major factor influencing police training and education is the Violent Crime Control and Law Enforcement Act of 1994, signed by President Clinton, which contained provisions for several programs. The act provided for the establishment of the Office on Community Policing, which approves funding to local communities for the hiring of additional officers for community policing activities. This was part of the president's initiative to add 100,000 officers to the policing community nationwide. Another initiative under the act has been the establishment of "regional community policing institutes" (RCPI) around the country. The national network of RCPIs has trained more than 210,000 officers, community members, and government leaders in innovative approaches to community policing. (For the location of the RCPIs in the nation, visit the Web site: http://www.cops. usdoj.gov/Default.asp?Item=229.) These institutes have assisted in bringing a wide range of training topics and programs to local and state agencies. These have included state-of-the-art courses that focus on improving training as well as the content of training materials. The police corps portion of the act established the Office of the Police Corps and Law Enforcement Education, which administer scholarships of up to $3,750 a year to participants who agree to work in a state or local police force for at least four years after graduating from an educational institution. As of the writing of this book, there are currently 27 states that participate in this program. (For additional information, see the Web site: http://www.ojp.usdoj.gov/ opclee/home.html.) Another portion of the Violent Crime Control and Law Enforcement Act of 1994 established law enforcement scholarships for in-service law enforcement personnel to further their education and for college students to work in law enforcement agencies full-time during the summer or part-time for a period not to exceed one year. Both of these programs will attract persons to criminal justice programs across the country if they are fully funded. (Congress has not fully funded either program to date.) One part of the police corps legislation also provided scholarships to dependents of law enforcement officers killed on duty. It is expected that the programs developed from the Violent Crime Control and Law Enforcement Act of 1994 will encourage and enhance cooperative working relationships among federal, state, and local agencies.

Some agencies simply require that a higher level of education be achieved prior to hire. Other states have developed their own strategies and policies to recruit better educated officers. Massachusetts in the early 1970s, for example, enacted legislation known as the Quinn Bill. The Quinn Bill guarantees a certain percentage raise in their salaries to police officers who have earned college degrees in criminal justice (from specified colleges). An associate's degree will earn an officer a 10% raise. Bachelor and graduate degrees will earn officers 20% and 25% raises in their salaries, respectively.

A third emerging force that will greatly impact law enforcement training is the trend toward problem-oriented training. This trend has several names or derivatives. Some describe it as "problem-based" or "scenario-based" training; others refer to it as "facilitated training." Traditional training methods have emphasized the cognitive knowledge and psychomotor skills of policing. Problem-based training attempts to move learning to the higher domains (refer to the previous section on learning domains) of analysis, synthesis, and application. The method generally flows like this: The cadet is expected to learn the cognitive aspects of policing early in the training process. This is followed by a development of psychomotor skills. Then, the cadet is immersed in a series of scenarios or problem-based situations where he or she must draw upon learned knowledge and skills and apply them to the situation encountered. Traditionally, this is what has been called role-playing situations. However, instead of just a few role-playing situations, a significant amount of time is spent with these scenarios. Cadets work individually and in groups in responding to these situations. Roles are carefully scripted to achieve maximum learning, and the review and the evaluation process assists the cadet in developing the critical thinking skills necessary to become decision-makers on the street. The problem-based training method has emerged under several so-called "models." The SARA Problem Solving Model (described in Chapter 10) is the foundation for these models.

Why is this approach significant as an emerging force in the training arena? We believe that if this trend continues across the United States it will enhance the professionalization of the policing function. In part, it will demonstrate the need for recruiting persons who can learn cognitive material quickly and early in the process—this may mean that some college education may become a "de facto" minimum expectation for entry into the academy environment. The trend is also significant because it will better prepare cadets for the critical thinking necessary in today's society.

## ■ Socialization into the Culture of Law Enforcement

As mentioned in the beginning of this chapter, some of the purposes of police training include job orientation, indoctrination, safety/survival, and morale. As such, training is a key feature in the **socialization process**. Simply stated, socialization is the process whereby individuals learn and internalize the attitudes, values, and behaviors appropriate to persons functioning as social beings and responsive, participating members of their society. Socialization ensures that the individual will develop an identity, or self-concept, and also the motivation and requisite knowledge to perform adequately in the social roles he or she is called upon to enact throughout his or her lifetime (Socialization 1974). Although this topic is often discussed separately from the training process, it includes a learning and internalizing process similar to any training program.

### The Police Culture

Socialization plays a vital role in any culture and prepares its people to function in society according to its norms and values. In an occupational aspect, every employment field has its own unique culture; in law enforcement, it is often referred to as the **police subculture**. Goldstein (1977, 10) describes it as "that intricate web of relationships among peers that shapes and perpetuates the pattern of behavior, values, isolation, and secrecy that distinguish the police." The police subculture has been referred to by numerous terms in the literature, including: police social system, police ethos, occupational personality, the cop personality, and the police mystique (Conser 1980).

Decades ago, James Sterling (1968) wrote about the relationship of training to the socialization process in these terms:

*Socialization for the police recruit includes both the adoption of normative modes of police behavior and the extinction of certain other behaviors, which were appropriate for his previous civilian roles. In learning the new role, the police recruit undertakes a complex process of learning, which includes more than just knowledge and skills. He will also learn a system of attitudes, beliefs, perceptions, and values. The most important learning related to perception concerns the identification of role relevant reference groups and a sensitivity to their expectations and evaluations* (112).

Police culture continues to be a topic of lively and vital discussions. Culture, in its broadest sense, is a shared sense of values, goals, and expectations about an organization or profession amongst its members. Police culture, then, is the sum total of the values, goals, and expectations that law enforcement officers share. There are many ways in which police culture has been viewed, and one recent effort attempted to integrate prior perspectives by searching for common themes that tie police together (Crank 1998). Crank argued that police culture reproduces itself in similar ways in different locations. Similarly, it results from a shared application of practical skills while facing similar problems and environments, and engaging in similar daily routines. These similarities produce shared themes that Crank identifies as coercive territorial control, the unknown, solidarity with other officers, death, and a collection of "loosely coupled" themes (e.g., deception, outsiders). Crank's view—that the nature of the work in a particular environment produces culture—conflicts with other recent views of policing organizations as being influenced by external political factors (Zhao 1996), while beat style is influenced by the nature of the beat (Klinger 1997). Recently, conflict between the new chief of police in Spokane, Washington and the police unions in that department was blamed on the different style of policing that the new chief brought from the East Coast. If the impression of the patrol officers is true, it is suggestive that cultural differences exist between agencies. Little empirical work has been conducted in this area, partially because of the vagueness of the term "organizational culture," but the notion is intriguing and important for officers and citizens alike to consider.

Conceptually, the police subculture can be viewed as containing four dimensions (Goldsmith and Goldsmith 1974). The **occupational dimension** considers the uniquely job-related factors that affect and condition the police to behave in selected ways. The **psychological dimension** focuses of police self-identity and personality development. The **political dimension** considers the relationship between the police community and the policy-making authorities of the agency and society at large. The **social dimension** addresses the police officers' social organization, subculture norms, and the nature of police solidarity. It must be noted that although these dimensions permit a nontechnical framework for viewing the police subculture, the variables and affects found in each are not isolated to that dimension. The variables are dynamic and can influence the factors or variables in other dimensions.

## The Occupational Dimension

Research associated with this dimension focuses on the unique characteristics of the job of policing and how it impacts officers. Studies have concluded that policing often leads to collectively supported secrecy among officers. Such secrecy is considered so important that officers may break the law or their ethical code to support it (Westley 1956). Role conflict, development of police styles, isolationism, and negative perceptions of citizens have been issues discussed in much of the research, which reflects occupational variables (Manning 1997; Bayley 1994; Bittner 1990; White 1972; Wilson 1968; Banton 1964; and Goldstein 1963).

The work of Jerome Skolnick regarding the "working personality" of police officers has become a classic in the scholarship of policing. His findings state that the variables of danger and authority, when viewed in the context of a prevailing pressure to be efficient, are fundamental to the development of an officer's occupational personality. This preoccupation with potential violence also fosters the development of a **symbolic assailant**, which is a person who uses "gesture, language, and attire that the police have come to recognize as a prelude to violence" (Skolnick 1994, 44). Police are trained to be suspicious, partly because that suspicion may mean the difference between injury and non-injury, between survival and death. Unfortunately, this suspicion may be generalized toward the public at large, which results in increased isolation from citizens and increased police solidarity.

## The Psychological Dimension

This dimension emphasizes the self-concept and personality development of officers and attempts to answer the question: "Do officers' personalities change because of the job, independently of the job—or do they change at all?" There is no definitive answer to this question, and studies can be found that are contradictory and inconclusive. The variables that are usually addressed in this dimension concern conservatism, authoritarianism, stereotyping, cynicism, aggressiveness, mental strength and toughness (machoism), and sexism.

Professor William Doerner (1985) has written about his experience of going from professor to police officer and the changes he perceived as a result of the transition. "Changes, which I though were subtle and only partially visible to others, have altered me to such a degree that I am an entirely different person with a completely different set of values, beliefs, and attitudes." Doerner's description of his transition is similar to Professor Kirkham's of the early 1970s. Both reflect the "reality shock" of working the street and how it affected their outlook on things. Their accounts and others discuss how personalities of individuals who have become officers appear to turn callous, less trusting, more cold and cynical, and frustrated. Nonetheless, the research is mixed concerning possible personality changes brought on by becoming a police officer.

## The Political Dimension

This dimension attempts to analyze policing in light of community power structures and internal/external influences upon the officer. The police have been discussed in terms of political styles, decision makers, and deviant groups (Wilson 1975; Skolnick 1969). Louis A. Radelet (1973) pointed out four distinguishable types of police-political relationships:

1. Partisan, which refers to playing politics in a partisan manner, meaning the influence of the political party in power, the political ma-

chine. The history of partisan politics in policing generally has been one of the spoils system and corrupt practices.

**2.** Cultural political forms of policing from a cultural perspective are when the police enforce local mores and expectations even when they may not be lawful. Priorities are given to local parochial interests, and "outsiders" are at a disadvantage.

**3.** Fraternalistic, where the political power and influence emanates from within the police organization itself, usually through lobbying and/or union efforts.

**4.** Administrative, which pertains to the relationships of the department's chief executive officer to decision makers in government, such as the mayor, city manager, city councils, and so on. It relates to influencing public opinion, budget decisions, and department goals. It encompasses the leadership role, which is integral to effective public administration.

Radelet stated that administrative political policing is the only legitimate form, and that the others are questionable at best and often have resulted in improper, sometimes even illegal actions by police. However, contemporary developments involving community policing create a different perspective or set of problems. Consider these comments from Carter (Carter and Radelet 1999):

> *And now community policing adds yet another dimension to the politics and structure of administration. Traditionally, police activities have been dictated by a complete "top-down" approach. That is, police administrators would define programs, the types of crimes that would be addressed, and assorted activities of officers, usually based on a crime analysis that balanced trends with efficiency. Sometimes, this would be even more "top directed" when elected officials asked (or instructed) the police department to focus on specific issues— violent crimes and the illicit drug trade serve as recent examples (426).*

## The Social Dimension

The role of the police officer is of major concern here, primarily in terms of role conflict, group behavior, and the socialization process. In many ways, the social dimension is the culmination and integration phase of the entire police subculture. Generally speaking, the operation of police units demands a strong sense of loyalty, comradeship, solidarity, and secrecy. The perceptions of the police as an occupational group strongly influence their behavior and how they indoctrinate (socialize) and accept new members. According to Harris (1973), the most significant consequence of police training is the cultivation of solidarity—the subjective feeling of belonging, moral support, and depersonalization (toward other non-officers).

Other aspects of the social dimension have focused on such things as divorce, alcoholism, and suicide rates of police as compared to other groups and other health issues related to stress. The empirical evidence on these matters varies from place to place and from study to study. We cannot conclude that officers suffer from higher rates of divorce, heart disease, ulcers, alcoholism, and so on because the empirical evidence is mixed.

In the midst of all this confusion, one thing is certain: a police subculture exists, although we may not agree as to its universal characteristics, codes, and behavior. The police themselves perceive it, and as long as they do, it is real to them. Barbara Bennett (1978) referred to it as the "police mystique"—". . . a body of ideas and attitudes that has become associated with a group of people or an institution . . . often more imagined than real."

There are of course studies that refute the importance of the police subculture and the impact of police socialization on officers. Some of the more recent developments, such as community policing and emphasis on crime prevention and social service roles, may reverse or impede some of the negative aspects of the police subculture. Also, since more educated persons are being attracted to the field, their backgrounds may modify the traditional negative impact of some of the socialization process. Students of policing are being taught about the negative aspects of the police subculture in academic and even academy programs today. This is often coupled with greater emphasis on ethics and integrity and how the police subculture can become a positive force for change and integrity maintenance. Conser (1980) has suggested the following policy recommendations in order to reduce or lessen some of the perceived negative aspects of the police subculture and the socialization process:

1. *A commitment to a more open system organization that, in part, reduces the secretiveness that often permeates the structure.*
2. *A greater understanding of the role of the officer in policing the community, particularly regarding norm violations and minor misdemeanors.*
3. *A greater emphasis at training academies on the police subculture; its positive and negative effects—possibly taught by non-police personnel or in a cooperative effort with selected non-police trainers.*
4. *A greater care and emphasis on the selection and training of Field Training Officers in order to overcome aspects of the **detraining syndrome**—the process of transforming the highly motivated, idealistic recruit to one that is disillusioned and distrustful.*
5. *A greater commitment and recognition of individual integrity and ethical standards in order to reduce conformity pressures.*
6. *A commitment to excellence in supervision; developing educated, well trained and enlightened supervisors who understand principles of leadership, motivation, accountability, and integrity (52–53).*

If the police subculture is the result of the learning process, then that process can be utilized to reduce the negative attributes usually associated with the subculture.

## ■ Summary

Training and education in the law enforcement field have evolved from on-the-job training to a merger of the traditional training academy with an academic curriculum. Variations, of course, do exist because the United States is a very large and diverse country of multiple jurisdictions, and there simply are no nationally accepted standards. Training and education should be viewed as a compound phrase and not two individual and different terms. Education is the more global learning outcome desired for today's officers who must police a complex world. Training is only one method of acquiring the knowledge and skills necessary for the task.

Although national commissions have recognized the importance of and recommended higher education as a condition of employment for local police officers, few departments require it. The majority of police officers, however, do have some college education according to recent surveys. This trend is an important one, since most officers can remain on the job for 20–30 years. Departments must ensure that continued education and training occur or their officers will begin to lag behind the average educational levels of society.

The formal training process is considered a major aspect of the socialization of the law enforcement officer. This socialization plays a key role in modifying or developing an officer's attitudes, values, and beliefs. Researchers have been investigating the socialization of police and the resulting occupational subculture. Although studies are sometimes contradictory, the findings have brought a greater understanding of the job and those who perform it.

The issues and controversies related to training and education are diverse and complex. This chapter has addressed only the major ones. Issues related to certification versus licensure, reciprocity of training, the granting of college credit for training (both recruit and advanced), the merger of training and education, mandated continuing education credits/hours, and minimum education requirements as conditions for employment and promotion, have been debated for over 25 years, and no consensus or national standard has been reached yet. With the recent interest in national crime legislation, it is possible that an influx of research and programming funds may assist in reaching closure on some of these issues in the near future.

## QUESTIONS FOR REVIEW AND DISCUSSION

1. What is the relationship of learning, learning domains, and teaching to the concept of education?
2. What are the seven reasons for or purposes of training?
3. What are five types of training commonly found in law enforcement? Give examples of each.
4. What did the National Advisory Commission on Criminal Justice Standards and Goals recommend regarding educational levels as conditions of employment for police officers?
5. What are three major emerging influences on police education and training?
6. What is meant by the police culture?
7. What are the negative and positive characteristics of the police culture as summarized in this chapter?
8. How does training impact the socialization of law enforcement officers?

## SUGGESTED ACTIVITIES

1. Using available library resources or the World Wide Web, locate the state POST for selected states, then compare and contrast their provisions regarding peace officer training. Focus on the certification and minimum training standards for peace officers. If a law library is available, this would be an excellent source for such research; however, the state codes of most states can be found on the Internet.
2. Contact your local police department and inquire about where and how new recruits are trained; ask a local training academy commander to speak to your class about state rules, regulations, and matters of reciprocity of certification.
3. Have police officers appear as guest speakers in your class and ask them about the police culture. Do they believe they have "changed" since becoming a police officer? If so, how?
4. On the World Wide Web, use the Infoseek search engine and enter the words: "peace officer training." Review the results and visit several of the POST sites.
5. Log on to the World Wide Web, and conduct a search of the phrase "citizen police academy." Write a brief report on your findings, including a description of two or three of the most interesting sites located.

## ■ Chapter Glossary

**advanced** or **specialized training**   refers to those sessions that address specialty topics or material that is an extension or a more enhanced version of what was taught at basic academies.

**citizen police academy** an informative program containing many of the subjects taught in a basic police academy but meant for members of the local community so they can learn more about the typical duties, policies, and procedures related to policing in their local communities.

**college academies** a state-approved recruit training program incorporated into the academic curriculum of an institution of higher education.

**continuing education credit** formal recognition of additional training received following recruit training; it may be required by state law to remain in your position.

**detraining syndrome** the process of transforming the highly motivated, idealistic recruit to one that is disillusioned and distrustful.

**education** that which is learned.

**executive and managerial training** focuses on administrative decision making or supervision issues and skills. Courses in this type of training address subjects such as leadership, motivation, budgeting, first line supervision, FTO program development and administration, media relations, public speaking, and communication skills.

**field training** consists of "formalized, on-the-job instruction by specially selected and trained personnel called Field Training Officers (FTOs)."

**in-service training** refers to training received by officers following their recruit training.

**learning** a process that changes a person's behavior or attitude.

**learning domains** various levels of learning that include the cognitive, motor skills, and affective domains.

**mandatory minimum training standards** the minimum training requirements usually established by statutory or regulatory mandates.

**occupational dimension** the uniquely job-related factors that affect and condition the police to behave in selected ways.

**on-the-job training** (OJT) the lessons learned by actually doing the job without any preservice instruction; includes methods and techniques taught by coworkers and supervisors.

**police subculture** an intricate web of relationships among peers that shapes and perpetuates the pattern of behavior, values, isolation, and secrecy that distinguish the police.

**political dimension** the relationship between the police community and the policy-making authorities of the agency and society at large.

**psychological dimension** the self-identity and personality development aspects of the police subculture.

**social dimension** the police officers' social organization, subculture norms, and the nature of police solidarity.

**socialization process** the process whereby individuals learn and internalize the attitudes, values, and behaviors appropriate to persons functioning as social beings and responsive, participating members of their society.

**symbolic assailant**   a person who uses gesture, language, and attire that the police have come to recognize as a prelude to violence.

# ■ Chapter References

Ayers, Richard M. (1990). *Preventing Law Enforcement Stress: The Organization's Role*. Alexandria, VA: National Sheriffs' Association.

Banton, Michael (1964). *The Policeman and the Community*. London: Taviatock.

Bayley, David H. (1994). *Police for the Future*. New York, NY: Oxford University Press, Inc.

Bayley, David H. (1986). The Tactical Choices of Police Patrol Officers. *Journal of Criminal Justice*. 14.

Bennett, Barbara (1978). The Police Mystique. *The Police Chief*, April:46.

Bittner, Egon (1990). *Aspects of Police Work*. Boston, MA: Northeastern University Press.

Bloom, Benjamin Samuel (ed.) (1956). *Taxonomy of Educational Objectives: Cognitive Domain*. New York: David McKay Company, Inc.

Bozza, C.M. (1973). Motivations Guiding Policemen in the Arrest Process. *Journal of Police Science and Administration*, 1(4):468–476.

Buckley, Leslie B., James H. McGinnis, and Michael G. Petrunik (1992). Police Perceptions of Education as an Entitlement to Promotion: An Equity Theory Perspective. *American Journal of Police*, 12(2):77–99.

Burbeck, E. and A. Furnham (1985). Police Officer Selection: A Critical Review of the Literature. *Journal of Police Science and Administration*, 13:58–69.

Buzawa, E.S. (1984). Determining Patrol Officer Job Satisfaction: The Role of Selected Demographic and Job-Specific Attitudes. *Criminology*, 22:61–81.

Buzawa, Eve, Thomas Austin, and James Bannon (1994). The Role of Selected Sociodemographic and Job-Specific Variables in Predicting Patrol Officer Job Satisfaction: A Reexamination Ten Years Later. *American Journal of Police*, 13(2):51–75.

California, State of, Commission on Peace Officer Standards and Training (1994). *The California Law Enforcement Command College*. Sacramento, CA: Commission on Peace Officer Standards and Training.

California, State of, Commission on Peace Officer Standards and Training (May 29, 1998). http://www.post.ca.gov/ and http://www2.4dcomm.com/comdcoll/.

Carlan, Philip E. (1999). Occupational Outcomes of Criminal Justice Graduates: Is the Master's Degree a Wise Investment? *Journal of Criminal Justice Education* 10(1):39–55.

Carter, David L. and Allen D. Sapp (1989). The Effect of Higher Education on Police Liability: Implications for Police Personnel Policy. *American Journal of Police*, 8(1):153–166.

Carter, David L. and Allen D. Sapp (1992). College Education and Policing: Coming of Age. *FBI Law Enforcement Bulletin*, January:11.

Carter, David L., Allen D. Sapp, and Darrel W. Stephens (1989). *The State of Police Education: Policy Direction for the 21st Century*. Washington, DC: Police Executive Research Forum.

Carter, David L. and Louis A. Radelet (1999). *The Police and the Community*, 6th Ed. Upper Saddle River, NJ: Prentice-Hall, Inc.

Cascio, W.F. (1977). Formal Education and Police Officer Performance. *Journal of Police Science and Administration*, 5:89–96.

Center for Leadership Development, State of California Commission on Peace Officer Standards and Training (2000). *The Law Enforcement Command College*. Sacramento, CA: Commission on Peace Officer Standards and Training.

Colorado, State of, Peace Officers Standards and Training Board (May 29, 1998). http://www.state.co.us/gov_dir/dol/post96mv2/96m/pa.htm.

Cohen, B. and J.M. Chaiken (1973). *Police Background Characteristics and Performance*. Lexington, MA: Lexington Press.

Cohen, B. and J.M. Chaiken (1972). *Police Background Characteristics and Performance: Summary*. New York: Rand Institute.

Conser, James A. (1981). The Training and Education Cosmos. *The Police Chief*, July:42, 64.

Conser, James A. (1980). A Literary Review of the Police Subculture: Its Characteristics, Impact and Policy Implications. *Police Studies*, 2(4):46–54.

Crank, John P. (1998). *Understanding Police Culture.* Cincinnati: Anderson Publishing Co.

Dalley, A. (1975). University vs. Non-University Graduated Policemen: A Study of Police Attitudes. *Journal of Police Science and Administration,* 3:458–468.

Daniel, E. (1982). The Effects of a College Degree on Police Absenteeism. *Police Chief,* September:70–71.

Dantzker, M.L. (1998). Police Education and Job Satisfaction: Educational Incentives and Recruit Educational Requirements. *Police Forum,* 8:1–3.

Dantzker, M.L. (1994). Measuring Job Satisfaction in Police Departments and Policy Implications: An Examination of a Mid-Size, Southern Police Department. *American Journal of Police,* 13(2):77–101.

Dantzker, M.L. (1993). Issue for Policing: Educational Level and Job Satisfaction: A Research Note. *American Journal of Police,* 12(2):101–119.

Doerner, William G. (1985). I'm Not the Man I Used to Be: Reflection on the Transition from Prof to Cop in Blumberg, Abraham and Elaine Niederhoffer (eds.), *The Ambivalent Force.* Hinsdale, IL: Dryden Press.

Eson, Morris E. (1972). *Psychological Foundations of Education,* 2nd Edition. New York: Holt, Rinehart and Winston, Inc.

Fielding, N., and J. Fielding (1987). A Study of Resignation During British Police Training. *Journal of Police Science and Administration* 15:24–36.

Finckenauer, J.O. (1975). Higher Education and Police Discretion. *Journal of Police Science and Administration,* December: 450–457.

Finnegan, J. (1976). A Study of the Relationship Between College Education and Police Performance in Baltimore, Maryland. *The Police Chief,* August: 60–62.

Flink, William L. and the International Association of Directors of Law Enforcement Standards and Training (1997). *Sourcebook: Executive Summary.* Richmond, VA: CJ Data/Flink and Associates.

Gaines, Larry K. and William Forester (1983). Recruit Training Processes and Issues in Swank, Calvin J. and James A. Conser (1983). *The Police Personnel System.* New York: John Wiley and Sons, Inc.

Gammage, Allen Z. (1963). *Police Training in the United States.* Springfield, IL: Charles C. Thomasand Project STAR, Police Officer Role Training Program (1974). Santa Cruz, CA: Davis Publishing Company, Inc.

Glasgow, E.H., R.R. Green, and L. Knowles (1973). Arrest Performance Among Patrolmen in Relation to Job Satisfaction and Personal Variables. *The Police Chief,* April:28–34.

Goldsmith, Jack and Sharon Goldsmith (eds.) (1974). *The Police Community.* Pacific Palisades, CA: Palisades Publishing Company.

Goldstein, Herman (1977). *Policing a Free Society.* Cambridge, MA: Ballinger Publishing Company.

Goldstein, Herman (1963). Police Discretion: The Ideal vs. the Real. *Public Administration Review,* 23:140–148.

Gottlieb, M.C. and C.F. Baker (1974). Predicting Police Officer Effectiveness. *Journal of Forensic Psychology,* December: 35–46.

Griffin, G.R. (1980). *A Study of Relationships Between Level of College Education and Police Patrolmen's Performance.* Saratoga, CA: Century Twenty-One.

Gronlund, Norman E. (1970). *Stating Behavioral Objectives for Classroom Instruction.* New York: The Macmillan Company.

Harris, Richard (1973). *The Police Academy: An Inside View.* New York: John Wiley and Sons, Inc.

Hayeslip, David W., Jr. (1989). Higher Education and Police Performance Revisited: The Evidence Examined through Meta-Analysis. *American Journal of Police ,* 8(2):49–63.

Hooper, M.K. (1988). The Relationship of College Education to Police Officer Job Performance. Doctoral Dissertation, Claremont Graduate School.

Hoover, Larry T. (1983). The Educational Criteria: Dilemmas and Debate in Swank, Calvin and James A. Conser (1983). *The Police Personnel System.* New York: John Wiley and Sons, Inc.

Hughes, Thomas, Beth Sanders, and Robert Langworthy (1996). *Police Forum,* (6)2:18–20.

Hunter, J.E., F.L. Schmidt, and G.E. Jackson (1982). *Meta-Analysis: Cumulating Research Findings Across Studies.* Beverly Hills: Sage Publications.

Kakar, Suman (1998). Self-Evaluations of Police Performance: An Analysis of the Relationship between Police Officers' Education Level and Job Performance. *Policing,* 21(4):632.

Kappeler, V.E., A.D. Sapp, and D.L. Carter (1992). Police Officer Higher Education, Citizen Complaints, and Departmental Rule Violations. *American Journal of Police,* 11(2):37–55.

Kedia, P.R. (1985). Assessing the Effect of College Education on Police Performance. Doctoral Dissertation, University of Southern Mississippi.

Kenney, Dennis J., and Gary W. Cordner (1996). *Managing Police Personnel*. Cincinnati, OH: Anderson Publishing.

Klinger, David A. (1997). Negotiating Order in Patrol Work: An Ecological Theory of Police Response to Deviance. *Criminology*, 35(2):277–306.

Krimmel, John T. (1996). The Performance of College-Educated Police: A Study of Self-Rated Police Performance Measures. *American Journal of Police*, 15(1):85–95.

Krimmel, John T., and Paul Lindenmouth (2001). Police Chief Performance and Leadership Styles. *Police Quarterly*, 4(4):469–483.

Lester, D. (1979). Predictors of Graduation From a Police Training Academy. *Psychological Reports*, 44:362–368.

Lotz, R. and R. Regoli (1977). Police Cynicism and Professionalism. *Human Relations*, 30:175–181.

Lynch, G.W. (1976). The Contributions of Higher Education to Ethical Behavior in Law Enforcement. *Journal of Criminal Justice*, 4(4):285–290.

Manning, Peter K. (1997). *Police Work: The Social Organization of Policing*, 2nd Edition. Prospects Heights, IL: Waveland Press, Inc.

Marsh, S. (1962). Validating the Selection of Deputy Sheriffs. *Public Personnel Review*, January: 41–44.

McCampbell, Michael S. (1986). Field Training for Police Officers: State of the Art. *Research in Brief*. Washington, DC: National Institute of Justice.

"Men & Women of Letters" (1997). *Law Enforcement News*, November 30:1.

Minnesota, State of, (1978), *Minnesota Code of Agency Rules: Peace Officer Standards and Training Board*. St. Paul, MN: Office of the State Register.

Minnesota State Statutes (1998), §§ 626.843 and 626.845.

National Advisory Commission on Criminal Justice Standards and Goals (1973). *Report on Police*. Washington, DC: US Government Printing Office.

Niederhoffer, A. (1967). *Behind the Shield: The Police in Urban Society*. New York: Doubleday.

O'Brien, Kenneth (1999). *Mini Report*. International Association of Directors of Law Enforcement Standards and Training, Conference Manual. Orlando, FL: (June 8):271.

Parker, L. Jr., D. Donnelly, J. Gerwitz, J. Marcus, and V. Kowalewski (1976). Higher Education: Its Impact on Police Attitudes. *The Police Chief*, 43:33–35.

Patterson, D.E. (1991). College Educated Police Officers: Some Impacts on the Internal Organization. *Law and Order*, 39(11):68–71.

Penegor, Janice K., and Ken Peak (1992). Police Chief Acquisitions: A Comparison of Internal and External Selections. *American Journal of Police*, 11(1):17–32.

Polk, O Elmer, and David A. Armstrong (2001). Higher Education and Law Enforcement Career Paths: Is the Road to Success Paved by Degree? *Journal of Criminal Justice Education*, 12(1):77–99.

Powell, D.D. (1980). A Study of Police Supervisors, Criminal Justice Educators, Non-Criminal Justice Educators, and Citizen's Attitudes in Michigan Concerning the Need for Higher Education in Michigan. Doctoral Dissertation, Michigan State University.

President's Crime Commission Law Enforcement and Administration of Justice (1967). *Task Force Report: The Police*. Washington, DC: US Government Printing Office.

President's Commission on Law Enforcement and Administration of Justice (1967). *The Challenge of Crime in a Free Society*. Washington, DC: US Government Printing Office.

Project STAR (1974). *Police Officer Role Training Program*. Santa Cruz, CA: Davis Publishing Company, Inc.

Radelet, Louis A. (1973). *The Police and the Community*. Beverly Hills, CA: Glencoe Press.

Reaves, Brian and Matthew J. Hickman (2004). *Law Enforcement Management and Administrative Statistics, 2000: Data for Individual State and Local Agencies with 100 or More Officers*. Washington, DC: US Department of Justice.

Regoli, R. (1976). The Effects of College Education on the Maintenance of Police Cynicism. *Journal of Police Science and Administration*, 4:340–345.

Roberg, R.R. (1978). An Analysis of the Relationships Among Higher Education, Belief Systems, and Job Performance of Patrol Officers. *Journal of Police Science and Administration*, 6(3):336–344.

Sanderson, B. (1978). Police Officers: The Relationship of College Education to Job Performance. *The Police Chief*, 44 (August):62–63.

Saunders, Charles B., Jr. (1970). *Upgrading the American Police: Education and Training for Better Law Enforcement*. Washington, DC: The Brookings Institution.

Sherman, L. and M. Blumberg (1981). Higher Education and Police Use of Deadly Force. *Journal of Criminal Justice,* 9(4):317–331.

Shernock, S. (1992). The Effects of College Education on Professional Attitudes Among Police. *Journal of Criminal Justice Education,* 3 (1):71–92.

Sherwood, Charles W. (2000). Job Design, Community Policing, and Higher Education: A Tale of Two Cities. *Police Quarterly,* 3(2):191–212.

Skolnick, Jerome (1994). *Justice Without Trail: Law Enforcement in Democratic Society,* 3rd Edition. New York: Macmillan College Publishing Company, Inc.

Skolnick, Jerome (1969). *The Politics of Protest.* New York: Simon and Schuster.

Smith, A.B., B. Locke, and W.F. Walker (1967). Authoritarianism in College and Non-College Oriented Police. *Journal of Criminal Law, Criminology and Police Science,* 58:128–132.

Smith, A.B., B. Locke, and B. Fenster (1970). Authoritarianism in Policemen Who Are College Graduates and Non-College Graduates. *Journal of Criminal Law, Criminology and Police Science,* 61:313–315.

Smith, D.C. (1978a). Dangers of Police Professionalization: An Empirical Analysis. *Journal of Criminal Justice,* 6(3):199–216.

Smith, D.C. (1978b). *Empirical Studies of Higher Education and Police Performance.* Washington, DC: Police Foundation.

Smith, D., and E. Ostrom. The Effects of Training and Education on Police Attitudes and Performance: A Preliminary Analysis in H. Jacob (ed) (1974). *The Potential for Reform in Criminal Justice.* Beverly Hills, CA: Sage Publications.

Socialization (1974). *Encyclopedia of Sociology.* Guilford, CT: The Dushkin Publishing Group.

Spencer, G., and R. Nichols (1971). A Study of Chicago Police Recruits. *The Police Chief,* June:50–55.

Sterling, James (1968). *Changes in Role Concepts of Police Officers during Recruit Training.* Gaithersburg, MD: International Association of Chiefs of Police as cited in Louis A. Radelet, *The Police and the Community,* Beverly Hills, CA: Glencoe Press, 1973, p. 112.

Taylor, M. (1983). Police Training: Towards a New Model. *The Police Journal,* 56:124–133.

Trojanowicz, Robert, and T. Nicholson (1976). A Comparison of Behavioral Styles of College Graduate Police Officers v. Non-College Going Police Officers. *The Police Chief,* August:56–59.

Truxillo, Donald M., Suzanne R. Bennett, and Michelle L. Collins (1998). College Education and Police Job Performance: A Ten-Year Study. *Public Personnel Management,* 27(2):269–280.

Tyre, M. and S. Braunstein (1992). Higher Education and Ethical Policing. *FBI Law Enforcement Bulletin,* 61(6):1–5.

Vodicka, A.T. (1994). Educational Requirements for Police Recruits. *Law and Order,* 420:91–94.

Weiner, N. (1976). The Educated Policeman. *Journal of Police Science and Administration,* 4:450–458.

Weirman, C. (1978). Variances of Ability Measurement Scores Obtained by College and Non-College Educated Troopers. *The Police Chief,* August:34–36.

Westley, William A. (1956). Secrecy and the Police. *Social Forces,* 34:254–257.

White, Susan (1972). A Perspective on Police Professionalization. *Law and Society Review,* 7:61–85.

Wilson, James Q. (1968). *Varieties of Police Behavior.* Cambridge, MA: Harvard University Press.

Wilson, James Q. (1975). *Thinking About Crime.* New York: Basic Books.

Wilson, James Q. (1983). *Crime and Public Policy.* San Francisco: ICS Press.

Withal, D. (1985). *The American Law Enforcement Chief Executive: A Management Profile.* Washington, DC: Police Executive Research Forum.

Worden, R.E. (1990). A Badge and a Baccalaureate: Policies, Hypotheses, and Further Evidence. *Justice Quarterly,* 7(3):565–592.

Wycoff, M. (1987). New 'Yes Person' Managers. *Police Manager: Newsletter of the Police Management Association,* June: 18.

Wycoff, M., and C. Susmilch. The Relevance of College Education for Policing: Continuing the Dialoguein D. Peterson (ed) (1979). *Police Work: Strategies and Outcomes in Law Enforcement.* Beverly Hills, CA: Sage Publications.

Xavier University (2004). Learning Styles. Cincinnati, OH: The Learning Assistance Center. http://www.xu.edu/lac/learning_styles.htm

Zhao, Jihong (1996). *Why Police Organizations Change.* Washington, DC: Police Executive Research Forum.

Zhao, Jihong, Quint Thurman, and Ni He (1999). Sources of Job Satisfaction Among Police Officers: A Test of Demographic and Work Environment Models. *Justice Quarterly,* 16(1):153–173.1

# Personnel Issues

**9**

## Learning Objectives

The major tasks of policing are accomplished through the efforts of people—policing is a very labor-intensive service. Personnel policies, procedures, and practices are described in this chapter, and upon its completion you will be able to:

- Identify and describe the major stages of personnel recruitment and selection functions in police agencies.
- Describe the legal prerequisites and limitations of personnel functions.
- Explain at least four different methods utilized in policing for promoting persons to higher rank and responsibility.
- Distinguish between the concepts of "labor relations" and "collective bargaining."

## Chapter Outline

## Key Terms Used in This Chapter

promotion
career development
selection process
recruitment
active recruitment
passive recruitment
pre-application conference
ride-along
self-selection
structured interview
unstructured interview
background check
conditional offer of employment
polygraph
psychometric exam
psychological interview
appointing authority
civil service
bonus points
eligibility list
rule of three
probationary status
permanent employee status

Civil Rights Act of 1964
protected classes
adverse impact
Equal Employment Opportunity
  Commission (EEOC)
*Griggs v. Duke Power Company*
job analysis
remedies
consent decree
affirmative action
reverse discrimination
bona fide occupational
  qualification
assessment center
lateral entry
labor relations
collective bargaining
benevolent associations
police crime
occupational deviance
corruption
abuse of authority
civilian review

# ■ The Importance Of Human Resource Considerations

Of all the available resources, people are the greatest asset to the policing function. Granted, the United States is a very advanced technological society, but the services provided by law enforcement agencies are performed by humans. It takes many people working together to carry out the functions performed by policing agencies. Although "robocops" may one day assist in this function, people will continue to be the mainstay for the next several decades. (Issues related to technology in policing are discussed in Chapter 11.)

Individuals preparing to enter the criminal justice field today often are misinformed or have misinterpreted many aspects of personnel selection, **promotion**, and **career development**. It is not difficult to meet someone working in the field that may be bitter, frustrated, or disillusioned about his/her job. Others with a criminal justice education may be frustrated because they have not been successful in obtaining employment. In conversations with those employed in the field, negative statements may be made when asked about job openings and career advancement:

- "It all depends on who you know—it's all politics."
- "Merit has little to do with getting ahead in this department."
- "It doesn't matter how much education or ability you have, you have to play their political games to get ahead."
- "You'll never make it, you're the wrong color (or sex, or religion, or ethnic group)."

Statements such as these may cause some highly qualified applicants to pursue other careers or agencies. Although there may be some truth to these statements in some agencies, for the most part, they are exaggerated and based on emotion rather than fact and understanding of the personnel process. The motive behind such statements also may be suspect. For example, if I am a police officer who knows that the competition for jobs in my agency is very rigorous, might I *discourage* someone from applying if I am trying to support a friend or relative who also is applying (thus reducing the competitive pool)? Or, am I upset with my employer and trying to keep highly qualified persons from applying? Or maybe I do not want a person to join the department because of the potential competition for promotion slots in the future.

The "bottom line" is do not believe everything someone tells you about the personnel function of an agency! The personnel function in policing is highly complex and becoming very legalistic. By understanding the legal, political, and social framework of the personnel function, one has a greater likelihood of successfully passing through its stages. One potential outcome is a highly rewarding career in law enforcement.

## Personnel and Expenditures

As mentioned in Chapter 4, the policing function in the United States consists of over one million persons employed in about 18,000 agencies. Sworn officers account for about 800,000 of these persons. Annual expenditures, in payroll, amount to over $69.8 billion. When reduced to the local level of policing, police personnel is usually one of the largest, if not the largest, units of employees in a jurisdiction. Generally speaking, the public safety function (police and fire fighting) is the largest expenditure in jurisdictions regarding personnel costs. Within the individual agencies, personnel costs usually consume 75–95% of the budget.

Personnel expenditures include salaries and fringe benefits (health/life/disability/liability insurance, clothing allowances, vacation and holiday pay, etc.). There are also operating costs for agencies, which include furniture, heat, light, communications systems, etc. **Figure 9-1** depicts the entrance salary and the per-officer operating costs for selected agencies. Agencies were selected to show some of the geographical differences (city versus county, suburban versus rural).

## Qualities and Attributes

The day-to-day street policing functions have not yet been computerized; it takes thinking people to analyze crime scenes, to interview victims and witnesses, to locate and apprehend suspects, and to prepare cases for prosecution. These aspects of the police function can be assisted with technology, but people carry out these tasks associated with bringing offenders to justice. This is no small point. Do we want a machine to do the police function for us? Think of all the ramifications of this question before answering it because the technology exists today to almost completely "automate" the criminal justice system. Of course, it would mean transforming our society, our Constitution, and our current sense of privacy. Stop reading for just a moment and answer this question: "What qualities and attributes do you want in the police officers that protect you and your fam-

| Agency | Entry Level Salary* | Annual Operating Cost* |
| --- | --- | --- |
| Gadsden Police, AL | $27,914 | $ 76,205 |
| Anchorage Police, AK | $38,064 | $129,032 |
| Riverside Police, CA | $40,488 | $142,953 |
| Phoenix Police, AZ | $33,093 | $ 82,871 |
| Denver Police, CO | $33,660 | $ 82,819 |
| Hartford Police, CT | $32,000 | $ 79,566 |
| Miami-Dade Police, FL | $28,891 | $116,916 |
| Boston Police, MA | $42,717 | $ 94,270 |
| Duluth Police, MN | $38,000 | $ 82,770 |
| Billings Police, MT | $30,347 | $ 78,942 |
| Wayne Police, NJ | $49,632 | $ 87,571 |
| Lucus County Sheriff, OH | $18,930 | $ 94,238 |
| Spartanburg Police, SC | $12,280 | $ 57,746 |
| San Mateo County Sheriff, CA | $63,000 | $260,163 |

*Salaries and costs are based on 2000 data. Operating costs are per officer and they include salary and fringe benefits, supplies, and contractual services. Capital expenditures such as equipment and construction costs are not included.
*Source:* B.A. Reaves and M.J. Hickman (2004). *Law enforcement management and administrative statistics, 2000: Data for individual state and local agencies with 100 or more officers,* Tables 5a and 6a. Washington, DC: US Department of Justice, Bureau of Justice Statistics.

**Figure 9-1** Personnel costs of employing an officer in selected agencies.

ily?" August Vollmer is credited for making the following statement concerning police officers:

> *The citizen expects police officers to have the wisdom of Solomon, the courage of David, the strength of Samson, the patience of Job, the leadership of Moses, the kindness of the Good Samaritan, the strategical training of Alexander, the faith of Daniel, the diplomacy of Lincoln, the tolerance of the Carpenter of Nazareth, and finally, an intimate knowledge of every branch of the natural, biological, and social sciences. If he had all these, he* might *be a good policeman* (1969, 222).

As a society and as individuals, we expect a great deal from our law enforcement personnel. We expect integrity, honesty, self-control, tolerance, intelligence, objectiveness, courtesy, courage, concern for others, fairness, maturity, commitment, dedication, a strong character, physical and emotional strength, and insight. Few will argue against such qualities, but take another look at these expectations. How can they be identified in the **selection process**? How are these measured? How can they be "trained" into an individual? In short, how are such expectations turned into realities? There are no easy solutions to this quest; however, it does take commitment from administrators to strive toward the goal of selecting promising candidates.

## ■ The Recruiting and Selection Process

Not everyone who wants to become a law enforcement official will become one. Some who enter law school never become attorneys; some who enter medical school never become doctors. It is important to understand that there are many variables that go into the hiring of law enforcement personnel. Everyone simply cannot be hired; there are not enough positions in agencies for that to occur. Of course, "wanting" to be an agent or officer is usually a prerequisite to selection, but it alone is not sufficient.

### Recruitment

**Recruitment** is the development and maintenance of an adequate supply of qualified persons interested in being employed by a specific agency. In reality, there are two types of recruiting efforts: active and passive. **Active recruitment** occurs when an agency makes a concerted effort to attract candidates to it. This may entail the deployment of existing personnel, either sworn or civilian, as recruiters and sending them into the community to generate interest among potential applicants. This task can be done by personnel specifically assigned to that function or by personnel as part of their regular assignments. **Passive recruitment** is when the agency has openings and takes applications from those who come to the agency. No outreach or concerted effort is made to attract candidates; it is a "sit back, wait, and see" approach.

Some departments spend considerable resources attempting to attract qualified applicants. Recruiting brochures are printed; officers are sent out of town on recruiting trips to colleges, universities, and job fairs; and public announcements are placed in local public media (newspapers, public service announcements on radio, television, and even the Internet). Recruitment material can contain a generous amount of information about the hiring process and the opportunities with the agency or may contain only the basics with telephone numbers and an address to pick up the application. The Columbus (Ohio) Police Department's Web site on employment information contains considerable detail about the department, such as the selection process, salary, and fringe benefits. As a recruiting tool, it attempts to answer many basic questions. **Figure 9-2** depicts the salary schedule and **Figure 9-3** lists the fringe benefit package reported on the Web pages of the Columbus (Ohio) Police Department (Columbus Division of Police 2004, http://www.columbuspolice.org/).

The major objective of the recruiting process is to ensure an adequate supply of interested applicants from which selection will occur. The underlying premise is that the larger the pool of applicants, the greater the likelihood of obtaining enough qualified candidates to process through the selection procedures. Although the recruiting phase is an attempt to increase the number of candidates available for hire, there is a need to attract serious and qualified applicants. Sheer numbers alone are not sufficient; some agencies attract thousands of applicants every time they offer the entrance exam, even if there are no current openings! The recruiting phase should present an accurate portrayal of the job and the responsibilities it carries. Being an officer is not all red lights and sirens, and those who are attracted because of that image may be some of the first to be disqualified. Likewise, some potential and needed candidates, such as women and members of minority groups, may have an image of not being wanted. These groups have not always been treated well by some law enforcement personnel, or the image of abuse or perceptions and reputations of mistreatment may be prevalent in their immediate environments. If the reputation of an agency is a negative one, attempting to recruit highly qualified candidates from any segment of the community may be difficult. An active recruitment program is often the best approach to overcoming negative perceptions. Of course, an agency's administrators must be responsive to any known negative perceptions on the part of the community and should be investigating the source of them.

## The Selection Process

The selection process includes the various techniques, devices, and procedures used to identify candidates to whom offers of employment may be made. It is often viewed as a series of events linked together and through which an applicant must pass in order to be hired. Most perceive the application form as the beginning of the process and a job offer as the conclusion of the process; however, that is not totally accurate. The selection process actually begins

| Pay Steps | Seniority | 6/5/05 |
|-----------|-----------|--------|
| A-Step | hire date–12 months | $ 18.19/hr $37,835.20/yr |
| B-Step | 12–24 months | $19.09/hr $39,707.20/yr |
| C-Step | 24–36 months | $20.05/hr $41,704.00/yr |
| D-Step | 36–48 months | $23.95/hr $49,816.00/yr |
| E-Step | over 48 months | $27.86/hr $57,948.80/yr |

*Source:* Columbus, Ohio Division of Police, 2004, http://www.columbuspolice.org/.

**Figure 9-2** Columbus Police Department recruiting information—salary schedule.

*Shift differential pay*—If the majority of work hours are between the hours of 2:00 pm and 7:00 am, $.85 per hour shift differential is paid.

*Health insurance*—The health insurance plan covers the officer and family and is provided at a cost of $27.45 per month for single coverage and $71.40 for family coverage (effective 8/1/2005).

*Life insurance*—Will pay to officer's estate one hundred thousand dollars ($100,000).

*Paid holidays*—Eleven paid holidays per year, including the officer's birthday.

*Paid sick leave*—15 days per year. Officers using 8 or less sick hours per calendar year will receive an additional 16 vacation hours.

*Paid vacation leave*—2.4 weeks each year for the first 3 years. It then advances in stages up to 6.3 weeks after 20 years of service.

*Clothing and equipment allowance*—Uniforms and equipment at no cost to the officer plus a uniform maintenance of $850 per year for uniformed officers and $1200 per year for non-uniformed officers.

*Prescription drugs*—The deductible is $5 per prescription with the remainder at 100%.

*Dental plan*—After 1 year of service.

*Personal liability insurance*—Fully furnished by the city of Columbus.

*Retirement*—After 25 years of service and age 48.

*College tuition reimbursement*—After 1 year of service.

*Annual service credit*—Paid yearly starting with your 6th year of service.

*Family leave*—After 1 year of service.

*Military leave*—When called to service in armed forces of the United States.

*Deferred compensation program*—Defer up to $13,000 yearly for additional retirement benefits.

*Credit union*—After 90 days employment.

*Promotions*—Eligible to take Sergeant's Exam after 3 years. Pay differential is 18% between ranks.

*Source:* Columbus Ohio Division of Police, 2004, http://www.columbuspolice.org/.

**Figure 9-3** Fringe benefit package—Columbus Police Department.

during the recruiting phase or announcement of job openings. Would-be applicants then begin assessing their true desires and aspirations about applying (some would call this "soul-searching"). Some agencies also require a **pre-application conference** with a ranking field officer. This meeting is for the conveyance of information about the job, the required training, and the agency's expectations of its personnel. It may include watching a videotape and obtaining information about the academy training and probationary periods.

The primary objective of the pre-application conference is to supply accurate, realistic information and to clarify any misperceptions of the future applicant. Some departments encourage possible applicants to meet with officers to discuss the realities of police work before applying. Some departments offer **ride-along** opportunities with uniformed patrol officers for any member of the public and especially for potential applicants. By obtaining accurate information about the position and agency, future applicants can better assess their desire and willingness to work for that jurisdiction. This is sometimes referred to as **self-selection** in the sense that the applicant is making an informed and more objective decision to continue in the selection process.

**Figure 9-4** depicts the typical phases of the selection process for a medium to large agency. The sequence may vary somewhat among agencies, and some agencies may omit certain phases. Smaller agencies may have a somewhat shorter process. Each of the phases is described in this section in an overview manner. It must be understood that detailed information about each phase is beyond the scope of this text, but the reader should consult the references at the end of this chapter for additional information.

## The Application

The application form varies greatly from one agency to the next; there is no universally applied standard form. It may be a simple one-page format to a ten-page (or more) document. The information requested may range from basic identification-type inquiries to a complete educational and employment history coupled with questions about drug use. Usually, those agencies that utilize a longer, more detailed application use it as part of the background investigation, whereas the shorter formats are used to contact the applicant and to identify him/her at the next phase of the process.

## Written Exam

Written exams are very common in today's selection process. They have changed some over the years because of certain technical and legal requirements (discussed

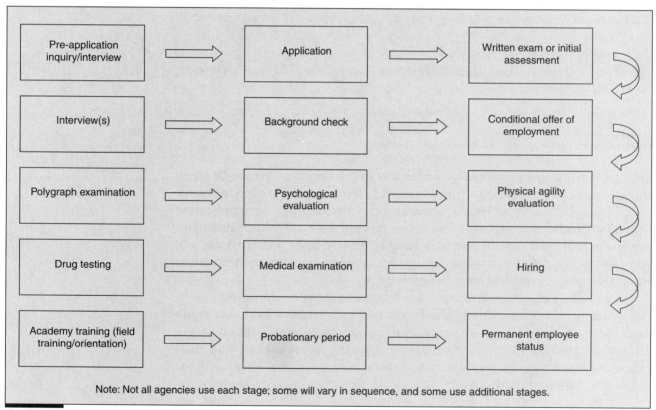

Figure 9-4 Typical stages in a selection process.

in the next major section of this chapter). Some exams are developed by the local jurisdiction while others may be developed by private companies or public entities that specialize in testing. The examination itself usually consists of several sections, which may include a selected number of the following:

— English grammar, spelling, punctuation, and sentence structure
— English comprehension, vocabulary, and word usage
— Basic mathematics, percentages, and thought problems
— Essay or writing samples, printing samplers
— Memorization of facts, numbers, and/or photos and descriptions
— Reasoning/judgment based on scenarios or situational analyses
— Interpretation/application of law/code sections to situations
— Questions about material distributed before the examination that applicants were told to study

## Interview(s)

Of all the phases of the selection process, the interview is the most universal regardless of the size of the agency. There may be one, two, or even three interviews. They may be conducted by an individual or by a group (sometimes referred to as an interview or selection board), by civilians (e.g., personnel officials, elected officials), and/or police personnel. They may be conducted at the police department, in the applicant's home, or at another agency location (e.g., personnel office, mayor's office).

There are two types of interviews: **structured** and **unstructured**. The structured interview usually consists of specifically compiled questions that focus on various aspects of the job or the applicant's abilities and background. Some follow-up questions may also be asked, many of which are also of a structured nature. The unstructured interview consists of general areas of focus, but the questions are not specifically spelled out. There is greater potential for the unstructured interview to wander off-course during follow-up questions to initial responses, which could be problematic in legal challenges to the selection process.

Candidates for positions sometimes believe that there are right and wrong responses to the questions asked during the interview. In the majority of interviews, it is less a matter of specific responses than it is the reasoning, directness, and appropriateness of what is said as well as the manner in which statements are made; interviewers often evaluate oral communication skills, poise, composure, responsiveness, and appearance rather than the content or accuracy of the specific responses.

## Background Check

As the phrase implies, a **background check** is a formal review and verification of the candidate's formal education, current and previous residences, current and prior employment, traffic and criminal citations and convictions (if any), reported drug history, and credit rating. This usually includes interviews with neighbors, named references, teachers and/or professors, employers, and possibly relatives. In some jurisdictions, background checks are done in person by investigators of the agency to which one has applied; in others they are conducted by mail and over the phone. If an applicant is from another town, the agency may request certain background information from the police in the candidate's local jurisdiction. An applicant will be required to sign certain release forms that grant the background investigators the authority to gain access to records that would otherwise be confidential.

## Conditional Offer of Employment

Because of certain potential liabilities and allegations, this phase of the selection process has become an important stage in public agencies. A **conditional offer of employment** means that the candidate is suitable and eligible for hire at that point in the selection process. It means that the candidate will be employed if certain other factors related to physical ability, medical, and mental conditions are within job-related limits. Ultimately, if physical, mental, and/or medical conditions are identified that are not within the standards for the position, the offer of employment will be withdrawn.

## Polygraph Examination

While sometimes considered part of the background check, polygraph testing should be considered a separate phase of the selection process. The **polygraph** is a scientifically calibrated instrument that records physiological changes in respiration (pneumograph), electrical resistance of the skin (galvanograph), and changes in blood pressure and pulse rate (cardiosphygmograph). These three measurements are recorded independently of each other by three pen-like devices on graph paper in the instrument. It operates by the existence of a direct relationship between a person's state of mind and their physiological condition (Territo 1974). The purpose of polygraph testing is to verify a person's truthfulness or the detection of deception regarding an area of inquiry. The central premises upon which the polygraph is based are that: (a) lying leads to conflict, (b) conflict causes fear and anxiety, and (c) these mental states are the direct cause of measurable physiological changes (Shattuch 1973, 5–6).

## Psychological Evaluation

The Strawbridge (1990) survey of 72 major police departments in 1990 found 66 (91.6%) agencies included either a **psychometric exam** or **psychological interview** as part of the selection process. This is in stark contrast to surveys done in 1972 and 1976, where the rates were 39% and 20%, respectively, for the agencies surveyed (Eisenberg et al. 1973; Conser and Thompson 1976). A 1994 survey of 59 departments found 91.5% utilizing psychological interviews (Langworthy et al. 1994). Generally speaking, the larger the department, the greater the likelihood of having some form of psychological evaluation. Some state regulatory commissions require this type of evaluation as a condition for certification and/or employment of officers throughout the state.

Psychometric examinations, as used here, refer to written instruments used to measure various psychological characteristics such as intelligence, interests/preferences, and personality traits/characteristics. There is a wide variety of such instruments, but the most common to the police selection process include the MMPI (Minnesota Multiphasic Personality Inventory), the CPI (California Personality Inventory), the IPI (Inwald Personality Inventory), Rorschach Psychodiagnostic Inkblots, Human Figure Drawing, and the Wonderlic Personnel

Test. Some departments utilize more than one test and may combine the process with exams that measure reading levels, attitudes, opinions, and ethical values. Some of these tests can be machine scored and interpreted while others may require interpretation by a trained psychologist/psychiatrist. The most appropriate approach and use of these tests is when the results are normed against police officer samples. The Law Enforcement Assessment and Development Report (LEADR) and the Minnesota Personnel Interpretive Report (MPIR) are attempts to do just that (Moriarty and Field 1994, 212–215).

Where utilized, psychological interviews are conducted by trained psychologists or psychiatrists. Such interviews may be conducted privately or in group sessions. While many of the psychometric tests have specific, more objective scoring schemes, the psychological interview is considered more subjective and interpretive and, of course, is dependent on the specialist's ability and experience. Both techniques attempt to accomplish the same objective: to select a psychologically stable person who is free of psychopathic (mental illnesses) tendencies. However, psychological evaluation is not an exact science; the process usually results in "screening-out" candidates with known or suspected unacceptable traits or "selecting-in" candidates with acceptable or predictable traits believed to make a good police officer.

## Physical Ability Test

Historically, the physical ability test in selection processes often consisted of completing a specific number of sit-ups, push-ups, and/or chin-ups and performing certain events that included climbing, pushing, running, or crawling. Today, because of adverse court decisions and law-related expectations, the physical ability testing has undergone considerable change. Such testing must be related to job tasks and functions performed by police officers. The test now often consists of some type of obstacle course that simulates what an officer may experience in the field, a 150–170 pound "dummy drag," and a combination of running and sprinting. It may also include other routines such as dry-firing a service weapon and/or making a simulated arrest. **Figure 9-5** reports the recommendations of a national conference held on the matter of physical fitness testing in law enforcement by the Major City Chiefs Association, the National Executive Institute Associates, and the Federal Bureau of Investigation (Major City Chiefs Association 1993).

However, there is still great controversy over physical fitness standards because of the Americans with Disabilities Act (ADA) and the Civil Rights Act of 1991. Litigation continues on these matters and the Supreme Court has yet to rule definitively on physical fitness standards. The issues appear to be whether an agency should establish validated *job-related standards* or *fitness standards*. If they establish job-related standards, the standards must be the same for all ages and for both men and women. If the agency establishes *fitness standards,* they may be gender-and age-based. The New Hampshire legislature in 1998 enacted statutory law that, effective January 1, 2001, required every full-time police, state, corrections, and probation/parole officer hired by a state, county, or local law enforcement agency in the state to pass the same medical exam and physical fitness test that the state training council prescribed for new recruits, on an ongoing basis at three-year intervals throughout their careers, as a condition of

1. The person taking the test must complete a 1/4 mile course consisting of a series of 20- to 40-yard runs/sprints interspersed with the events listed below.

2. The course includes a 5- to 6-foot wall climb, 4-foot horizontal jump (may be done while running), a stair climb (six steps up, six steps down), the drag of a 160–170 pound dummy for 50 feet, and another run/sprint in different directions. No specific order or frequency of events was established, but all events should appear at least once.

3. At the conclusion of the course, the applicant must dry fire the service weapon five times with both strong and weak hands.

> NOTE: The addition of a 1.5 mile run may be legally defensible for agencies that can demonstrate extended endurance is a needed physical ability, that it is job-related and consistent with business necessity.

The passing time for completion of this test is to be determined by each agency based on the levels of performance required of its employees. The passing times should not be age or gender adjusted.

Since all physical abilities needed to perform as a law enforcement officer are not tested in this recommended task test, a department may choose to separately test such areas as vision, speech, hearing, reading, writing, manual dexterity, flexibility, sitting, standing, reflexes, and weight/body composition.

*Source:* Major City Chiefs Association, et. al. (1993). *Physical fitness testing in law enforcement: An analysis of the impact of the Americans with Disabilities Act, The Civil Rights Act of 1991, and the Age Discrimination in Employment Act. A Conference Report, pp. i-ii.* Washington, DC: *Federal Bureau of Investigation.*

**Figure 9-5** Recommended physical abilities test.

maintaining their police certification. The tests are based on the Cooper Aerobics standards at the 35th percentile for the applicant's age and sex to enter the academy and the 50th percentile as an exit standard (Sweeney 1999). The State of Ohio instituted an exit standard at the 50th percentile for peace officer academy cadets in 2002. Other states have academy exit standards but the percentile scores for successful completion can vary.

## Drug Testing

Employers have the right to prohibit all employees from using or being under the influence of alcohol or illegal drugs at the workplace. Of the 72 major law enforcement agencies surveyed by the Strawbridge in 1990, 55 (76%) conducted drug tests as part of the selection process (Strawbridge 1990). Because law enforcement agencies have the responsibility of enforcing the country's drug laws and because of possible impairment while under the influence of drugs (a safety hazard to others), police agencies are justified in conducting such exams. The major precaution that must be taken is to grant appeals and second tests to those who test positive for drug use when they claim the test is inaccurate and has unfairly disqualified them from employment consideration.

## Medical Examination

Medical fitness for police officer candidates is an obvious expectation on the part of an employer. The hiring of an unfit/unhealthy candidate could cost the employer (and taxpayer) large sums of money should the person have to retire early on disability or other abnormality that renders them unfit for duty. The focus of concern here is the detection of respiratory, circulatory, or skeletal conditions that are early signs of existing or degenerative diseases or conditions that would interfere with the performance of required tasks and functions. During the late 1980s, some departments began not hiring persons who smoked because of the likelihood of developing respiratory and circulatory diseases (which are covered under some retirement systems). Some agencies still have such restrictions in their hiring process; however, since 1989, at least 29 states and the District of Columbia have enacted legislation prohibiting employers from requiring, as a condition of employment, that employees or prospective employees abstain from the use of tobacco products outside the course of employment (Bureau of National Affairs 1993). In 2003, an officer in Fall River, Massachusetts became the third public safety officer in the state in 10 years to loose his job because of smoking. A state statute prohibits public safety workers hired after January 1, 1988 from smoking either on or off duty. Virgina Beach public safety officers also are prohibited from smoking off duty (*Law Enforcement News* 2003). Today, departments that emphasize greater health consciousness or physical health maintenance in their personnel processes have the added benefit of reducing or slowing the rising cost of their health insurance premiums.

## Hiring

In every jurisdiction there is an **appointing authority** that officially hires the successful applicant according to law. The title of the appointing authority may vary according to the type of jurisdiction. It may be the mayor of a city, the sheriff of a county, a board of supervisors or trustees of a township, the department head of a state agency, a personnel official, or some other official granted such authority by law. It often is believed that the administrative head of the law enforcement agency (the chief, superintendent, commissioner, etc.) is the one who appoints new candidates; however, it is more accurate to say that the chief administrator "recommends" the candidates to the appointing authority.

The hiring process may include the involvement of a central personnel office of a jurisdiction. This office is usually separate from any personnel unit found in the law enforcement agency. For example, some jurisdictions are covered under **civil service** law or regulations. These vary from state to state, so general statements are difficult. Where civil service law exists, strict adherence to the regulations is required. The regulations may relate to written examinations, medical exams, residency, citizenship, **bonus points**, eligibility lists, appeals, grievances, promotions, layoffs, dismissals, and so on.

A civil service or central personnel agency may actually conduct the initial phases of the selection process and develop a list of qualified candidates; this is known as an **eligibility list** in some jurisdictions. It is from this list of qualified candidates that the law enforcement agency must select its employees. Certain requirements of the law may also apply in considering candidates from such a list. For example, in Ohio, statutory civil service law prior to 1995 required consideration of the top three candidates on a ranked eligibility list for every open entry-level position. This is known as the **rule of three** in personnel practices. This allows the appointing (and recommending) authority some discretion in hiring. In 1995, the statutory law was modified to allow the rule of ten, so now the top ten candidates can be considered for the open position.

The ranking of candidates on the eligibility list is based on the raw score of written examinations or assessment procedures and any bonus points awarded for certain factors or job-related criteria such as previous police experience, state peace officer certification, college education, military experience (veteran), and residency.

Any person interested in employment with a particular agency is encouraged to inquire about the details of its selection process. One needs to develop a full understanding of the process in order to know what to expect and to appreciate the complexity of the process. Some agencies are bound by very rigid civil service or merit system procedures while others offer continuous hiring opportunities.

### Academy Training

Once appointed to a law enforcement position, some form of academy training is normally required (unless the person has been a practicing police officer elsewhere, in which case minimal refresher or indoctrination training may be all that is required). Chapter 8 described this process in detail and is not elaborated upon here. The basic training of a new recruit may take from 6 to 36 weeks and could extend up to a year or more if field training is counted. In medium and larger departments, newly hired persons are paid a regular salary during the basic training period; in smaller departments, officers may have to attend classes on their own time and at their own cost before being considered for the job.

### Probationary Period

At the time candidates are hired, they are placed on **probationary status**, which means that their employment is conditional. Not only must their performance meet acceptable standards, their attitudes toward others, willingness to follow orders, ability to be a team player, and so on are also under evaluation. Probationary periods vary in length with the norm being from 6 months to 24 months; one year is the average length of probation. During the probationary period in most jurisdictions, the new officer may be dismissed without cause or a reason being given. The rights and limitations of probationers are usually controlled by law and department policy. In some agencies, probationers receive lower rates of pay, are not permitted to patrol solo, may not be allowed to join an officer's union, and have limited appeal rights if dismissed.

### Permanent Employee Status

Once a candidate has successfully passed through the probationary phase of employment, the officer then achieves **permanent employee status**, which brings with it additional rights and privileges. This status often includes a pay raise; the right to join the union, officer's association, or credit union; additional grievance and appeal rights; and the inclusion of selected personnel benefits such as educational benefits, leave, and certain types of insurance. Once officers reach this phase, the selection process has been completed.

## ■ The Law and Personnel Practices

Chapter 3 described the evolution of policing in the United States in broad terms and generalities. It was mentioned that in the early years of policing, particularly in municipalities, the selection and other personnel practices were highly political. Following the passage of the Pendleton Act in 1883, the concepts and procedures of civil service (or merit system) were introduced and adopted in many states throughout the country. Civil service and other personnel related statutes became the guiding influence upon personnel practices until the 1970s. However, events occurred in the 1960s that set the stage for a decade that would see great challenges to the personnel practices of agencies at all levels across the United States.

## The Civil Rights Act of 1964

Although two other major civil rights acts had been enacted by Congress in the 1800s (the Civil Rights Acts of 1866 and 1871), neither had focused its attention specifically on the employment process. In 1964, Congress enacted the **Civil Rights Act of 1964** because of its concern over the reported and documented racial discrimination in employment throughout the country. Specifically, Title VII of the act stated, in part:

> *It shall be an unlawful employment practice for an employer . . . to fail or refuse to hire or to discharge any individual, or otherwise to discriminate against any individual with respect to his compensation, terms, conditions, or privileges of employment, because of such individual's race, color, religion, sex, or national origin . . .* (Public Law 92-261, Section 703).

The concept of **protected classes** can be used to describe one of the outcomes of this legislation. Persons who are discriminated against in employment because of their race, color, religion, sex, or national origin are "protected" by law and may have a right to sue that employer. (The list of who is protected has been extended to other "classes" of persons by other federal and state statutes and now includes the military veteran, persons over age 40, the handicapped, the disabled, pregnant women, and, in some jurisdictions, homosexuals.) One method that is used to determine violations of Title VII is whether the practice in question has an **adverse impact** (also called disparate impact) on a protected class. A procedure or qualification that appears neutral on its face can actually impact negatively one group more than another. For example, a height requirement of 5'9" may appear reasonable, but it excludes about 95% of the females in the United States; therefore, it has an adverse impact on women. Unless the requirement can be substantiated as being required to do the job (job relatedness), the requirement is discriminatory. Another problem dealing with job requirements and descriptions becomes apparent when examining the American Disabilities Act (ADA) and the Fair Labor Standards Act (FLSA). For example, a common practice in many departments is to assign light duty to officers who acquire permanent health conditions, which preclude them from performing previously held positions within the department. Risher (2003) uses the hypothetical example of "Sergeant Smith" who suffered a major heart attack and was granted a light duty assignment, answering calls at the switchboard to illustrate this point. Given that Sergeant Smith no longer fulfills his supervisory job description at the switchboard, he is no longer exempt from the FLSA (which poses issues with payroll). In addition, given that the switchboard position does not require a person to be able to withstand the physical requirements necessary to perform the duties of a police officer, the hypothetical Jones who applies for Smith's job after his retirement, and who is denied employment based on his disability, may file suit for violating the ADA. The most common method used to allege adverse impact is statistical comparison of hiring rates, promotion rates, and passing rates of protected classes to majority rates (Sauls 1991).

The Civil Rights Act of 1964 also created the **Equal Employment Opportunity Commission** (EEOC), which is authorized to enforce the legislation and to develop guidelines for its implementation. The 1964 act did not apply to public employers and, therefore, had no immediate impact on their practices. However, some agencies did begin a review of their personnel practices to address possible discrimination.

In 1971, the landmark case of *Griggs v. Duke Power Company* (401 US 424) was decided by the US Supreme Court. It was the first interpretation of the Civil Rights Act of 1964 by the court, and as such its decision became precedent and guiding. The court said that, ". . . good intent or absence of discriminatory intent does not redeem employment procedures or testing mechanisms that operate as 'built-in headwinds' for minority groups and are unrelated to measuring job capability" (Griggs 1971, 432). The court ruled that Griggs and other employees had been discriminated against because the requirements (a high school diploma and passing a standard intelligence test), imposed for promotional opportunities were not adequate measures to determine suitability for the job. The court concluded: "If an employment practice which operates to exclude Negroes [a protected class] cannot be shown to be related to job performance, the practice is forbidden" (Griggs 1971, 431). The court's decision in *Griggs* essentially established that job qualifications and selection devices must be related to job performance criteria, and that artificial, arbitrary, and unnecessary barriers to employment be removed.

## The Equal Employment Opportunity Act of 1972

Congress amended the Civil Rights Act of 1964 with the Equal Employment Opportunity Act of 1972, which extended the provisions of the 1964 law to public employers with 25 or more employees. The EEO Act also granted authority to the EEOC to sue public agencies when necessary to redress the effects of discrimination in employment. Following the passage of this act, public agencies (especially police and fire departments) were sued by members of protected classes, often because their selection processes were inadequate and sometimes indefensible.

The essence of Title VII, as amended (and other anti-discrimination in employment law), is that employers must determine what job skills, knowledge, and abilities (SKAs) are required for proper job performance in a particular position. Determining these SKAs is usually done through a **job analysis** (or task analysis) of the position in question (police officer, supervisor, commander, etc.). The results of the job analysis then are used to develop the criteria that will be used for selection, promotion, transfer, and other personnel actions. The details of conducting job analysis are beyond the scope of this text; however, the intent of it is to determine such things as minimum qualifications for employment, the necessary content for training curriculums, and required criteria for promotion and/or transfer. However, one can observe the outcome of job analysis in the job description and listing of qualifications for an announced opening.

## Other Legislative Mandates

Besides the Civil Rights Act of 1964 and the Equal Employment Opportunity Act of 1972, several other pieces of federal legislation have been enacted that impact on the personnel practices of law enforcement agencies. The following is a selected listing with only a brief description of each as to the personnel practices affected.

- Equal Pay Act of 1963—Made applicable to public agencies by 1974 amendments, it provides equal pay for equal positions regardless of one's gender. Bona fide seniority plans are exempt from the act.
- Age Discrimination in Employment Act of 1967—Amended in 1974 to apply to the public sector, it protects persons over the age of 40 from discrimination based on age.
- Civil Rights Act of 1968—Provides criminal penalties for the interference with any person applying for or enjoying employment or related privileges, or interference with a person's use of hiring halls, labor organizations, or employment agencies.
- Rehabilitation Act of 1973—Protects individuals from discrimination based on mental or physical disabilities (originally referred to as "handicapped"). State and local governments are impacted if receiving federal assistance.
- Americans with Disabilities Act of 1990—This legislation modified and extended aspects of the Rehabilitation Act of 1973 but applies to all public employers with 15 or more employees. Agencies cannot discriminate against otherwise qualified individuals with a disability.
- Civil Rights Act of 1991—Reestablished and reaffirmed some of the provisions and judicial interpretation of earlier legislation. It does prohibit punitive damages in lawsuits against public agencies.

Other state and local legislation in addition to those listed above may impact the personnel practices of law enforcement agencies. The total picture adds up to a very legalistic quagmire with which police administrators must cope every day.

## Remedies

One segment of the law is referred to as **remedies**, and it is usually defined in terms of making a person who has been wronged "whole again." In grievances and lawsuits regarding personnel practices, the following remedies are commonly sought through the legal system:

*Injunction*—A court order prohibiting certain actions by an agency or person.

*Writ of Mandamus*—A petition to a court seeking an order that compels certain actions by an agency or person (orders that it be done).

*Back Pay*—If a complaint is found to be justified, the court could order back pay (the amount that would have been earned) to the injured party.

*Back Seniority*—The injured party can receive seniority from the time of the original action that injured him or her.

*Attorney Fees*—The injured party is awarded monetary fees to cover the expense of the litigation against the party that wronged him or her.

*Quotas*—The setting of fixed ratios of protected group members to receive preference in certain personnel functions. For example, this may lead to an agency hiring two minority members for every majority member hired or the hiring of one woman for every two males hired.

*Goals/Time Tables*—Unlike quotas, this is the setting of percentage or numerical targets to be achieved within certain time limits. It does not require the specific ratios of quotas.

Any one or a combination of these remedies may be ordered by the court or agreed to by the parties to a lawsuit. An out of court agreement is called a **consent decree**, and it often includes conditions (such as quotas, or revisions of personnel policies and practices) that cause hardships or morale problems for law enforcement agencies. Of course, it can also modernize personnel practices and sometimes bring needed resources to the personnel function of an agency or jurisdiction.

## Affirmative Action and Reverse Discrimination

One concept that has become broadly debated is that of **affirmative action**. The concept itself refers to taking a more aggressive position at recruiting and hiring protected classes that are underrepresented in an agency's workforce. It is sometimes interpreted by many to mean that members of protected classes are given preference in personnel actions. This belief occasionally leads to allegations of **reverse discrimination** by majority members. It is these allegations and beliefs that cause tension and frustration among many officers already employed and many of those who apply for positions and are not hired. The concept of affirmative action is not illegal; however, showing preference during hiring and other personnel practices is. Consider the words of the United States Supreme Court:

> . . . *In short, the Act does not command that any person be hired simply because he was formerly the subject of discrimination, or because he is a member of a minority group. Discriminatory preference for any group, minority or majority, is precisely and only what Congress has proscribed* (Griggs 1971, 430–431).

The Court was referring to Section 703 (j) of the Civil Rights Act of 1964 which reads:

> *Nothing contained in this title shall be interpreted to require any employer . . . subject to this title to grant preferential treatment to any individual or to any group because of the race, color, religion, sex, or national origin of such individual or group on account of an imbalance which may exist with respect to the total number or percentage of persons of any race, color, religion, sex, or national origin employed by any employer . . . in comparison with the total number or percentage of [such] persons . . . in any community, state, section, or other area, or in the available work force. . . .*

In 2003, the US Supreme Court reviewed two cases involving affirmative action in admissions policies of the University of Michigan. In *Grutter v. Bollinger*,

539 US 306 (2003), the admissions process of the law school of the University of Michigan was upheld because it used race in admissions decisions in a narrowly tailored way. The university was attempting "to further a compelling interest in obtaining the educational benefits that flow from a diverse student body." The court stated that such a policy is not prohibited by the Equal Protection Clause, Title VI, or §1981 (USC). In the second University of Michigan case, *Gratz v. Bollinger*, 539 US 244 (2003), the court ruled that the university's current policy, which automatically distributed 20 points to every "underrepresented minority" applicant solely because of race, was not narrowly tailored to achieve educational diversity, and therefore, violated the Equal Protection Clause, Title VI, and §1981. In short, the court ruled that the concept of affirmative action does not violate the Constitution and discrimination statutes, but race can be considered only when narrowly tailored to achieve diversity.

Other court decisions over the years indicate that the anti-discrimination laws apply to all persons, not just minorities. The significance of all this is that agencies must have justifications for their personnel qualifications and practices. They cannot do things simply out of tradition or by intuition and whim. If challenged, they may have to justify their actions to a court or to an investigative agency. In recent years some jurisdictions (most notably California's adoption of Proposition 209) have rescinded or modified state affirmative action statutes that permitted preferential treatment of protected groups. The United States Supreme Court refused on November 3, 1997, to interfere with the enforcement of the 1996 ballot initiative prohibiting preferential treatment (Savage 1997).

## Bona fide Occupational Qualification

The personnel law enacted to date allows for some discrimination if based on a **bona fide occupational qualification** (BFOQ). This is a form of "legal discrimination" in that it allows the establishment of certain criteria if they are shown to be necessary for the operation of the business (or agency). There are limitations that restrict BFOQs to religion, sex, or national origin, meaning that they cannot discriminate on the basis of race or color. In 1985, the city of Dallas, Texas successfully defended its college education requirement (45 hours of credit) for police officers by using a BFOQ-based justification (see *Davis v. City of Dallas*, 777 F.2d 205, 1985). Appeal of the case to the US Supreme Court was denied, thus allowing the appellate decision supporting the requirement to stand. The Appellate Court found that the characteristics of professionalism, unusual degree of risk, and unique public responsibility were part of the position of police officer and were not capable of specific identification and quantification (see Carter et al. 1988).

## The Recruitment and Retention of Women in Law Enforcement

There are several complex and hotly debated issues when examining women in law enforcement. Lonsway et al. paint a rather discouraging picture of women's representation in law enforcement:

> *In 2001, women accounted for only 12.7% of all sworn law enforcement positions in large agencies (with 100 or more sworn personnel)—*

*a figure that is less than 4% higher than in 1990, when women comprised 9% of sworn officers. In small and rural agencies (fewer than 100 sworn personnel), women comprise an even smaller percentage (8.1%) of all sworn personnel. When these figures are combined in a weighted estimate, they indicate that women represent only 11.2% of all sworn law enforcement personnel in the United States—dramatically less than the participation of women in the whole of the labor force at 46.5% (2002, 2).*

However, it appears that this grim picture of female representation in policing may be getting worse. Lonsway et al. furthers our understanding of the problem:

*Although women gained approximately half a percentage point per year in their representation within large police agencies from 1972 to 1999, there is mounting evidence that this trend has now stalled or even reversed. In 2000 and 2001, the representation of women in large police agencies actually declined from the year before—from 14.3% in 1999 and 13.0% in 2000 to 12.7% in 2001. At the present rate, women will not achieve equality in large police agencies for several generations, if at all (2002, 2).*

Why is there such a dramatic underrepresentation of women in law enforcement? Lonsway et al. argue that, "Despite overwhelming evidence that women and men are equally capable of police work, widespread bias in police hiring, selection practices and recruitment policies keeps the numbers of women in law enforcement artificially low" (Lonsway et al. 2002, 2).

Consent decrees beginning in the 1970s mandated many agencies to hire and promote qualified female applicants. While in place, these decrees have been highly successful in increasing the percentage of female representation in police departments. For example, prior to an imposed court order (from 1975 to 1991), only 1% of Pittsburgh's Police Department was female. In 1990, female representation on the force was at 27.2% (Lonsway et al. 2003a). However, once these decrees are lifted, the recruitment and retention of female officers can drop dramatically. In 2001, Pittsburgh's Police Department reported that only 22% of their officers were female, and the percentage of women hired dropped from the mandated 50% to 8.5% shortly after the decree expired (Lonsway et al. 2003a). Unfortunately, Pittsburgh Police Department is not alone in this trend.

Physical entrance exams may also be an impediment to female entry into the field of policing. A recent study funded by the *National Center for Women and Policing* found that agencies that did not employ physical agility testing employed 45% more sworn female officers than those agencies that did utilize them (Lonsway et al. 2003b). Lonsway and her colleagues suggested possible alternatives for physical agility testing that include no physical testing, health-based screening, job simulation tests, and post-academy training.

Future research into this area is much needed. In today's society, such a low representation of women in law enforcement is unacceptable and undesirable. Research suggests that women make excellent police officers and bring with them invaluable skills. Seklecki and Paynich found that:

> *When looking at the dispersion of the data, it appears that for the categories of responding to calls for service, interviewing witnesses and victims, writing reports, investigating crime scenes, gathering evidence, and dispute resolution, a significant percentage (at least 30%) felt that they performed these duties better in quality than their male counterparts. In fact, 61.8% of female officers felt that they wrote better or far better reports than male officers (2004, 28).*

Additionally, research suggests that the majority of female police officers love their jobs, feel they are making a difference in the community, and do not intend on leaving their career in law enforcement (Seklecki and Paynich 2004). Therefore, it is important that attention is focused on the recruitment and retention of women in policing.

## ■ Promotion and Career Development

Persons entering the law enforcement field look forward to a long and satisfying career. Many or most remain with the same agency in which they start. They look forward to promotion and/or career development and growth, which may also include a specialized assignment. Promotion generally refers to a positive change in rank status. A patrol officer is promoted to sergeant; a sergeant is promoted to lieutenant and so on. Career development refers to a desired change in work assignment that is accompanied by increased responsibility and may involve additional training and/or education. Career development may include a promotion; however, it is not necessary. For example, officers may prefer to continue working in a particular assignment, such as patrol or investigation, and not want promotion into positions that may be more supervisory or managerial in nature. The officers' growth will then be directed at becoming more knowledgeable about patrol work and investigation. Their career development will include skill development and training/education in those areas.

Modern departments recognize the fact that not everyone wants to be promoted in rank and are therefore developing compensation schemes that reward officers who pursue excellence in the critical areas of patrol and investigation. Also, some departments are streamlining their rank structures and eliminating middle management positions. As this movement continues, the opportunities for promotion will decrease. The challenge in such departments is how to increase the incentives of career development in those ranks that continue to exist.

### Promotion

There are several methods by which officers are promoted within the law enforcement community. Agency policies differ, and these are often contingent upon the personnel system adopted and state law. The most prevalent models include: political, seniority, past achievements, appointment on merit, testing (under civil service or central personnel office policies), **assessment center**, and hybrid, or a combination of the above. Each of these is discussed here in an overview manner.

## Political

As one would expect, this is the concept of who you know. It is based on influence and power; it does not necessarily consider merit or ability. Power brokers and political leaders influence the promotion of officers; promotion is a reward for devoted and loyal service to those individuals. Such systems are much less common today, but they still exist in some areas. Modern professional policing rejects this method of promotion.

## Seniority

In this type of promotion system, the officer with the longest tenure or length of service with the agency gets the promotion when there is an opening. One is rewarded for putting in the time or for surviving. Promotion is viewed as a reward for years of service. This system too is rejected by modern professional departments when used as the sole criterion for promotion.

## Past Achievements

Some promotion schemes are rewards for past performance. If officers do an excellent job in one rank, they are promoted to the next rank. The premise here is that if they did well in one position, they will do well in the next, and it is a reward for their efforts to date. Of course, and unfortunately, the premise is faulty as to the belief that the officers will perform well at the next level. Just because one is a good patrol officer, it does not follow that he or she will make a good supervisor.

## Appointment on Merit

This system refers to promotion based on ability to perform at the next level. It will involve the evaluation of candidates and the talents, skills, and knowledge needed for the promoted position. All candidates may have been excellent performers in their current rank, but which ones have the leadership, communication, and interaction skills needed in the promoted position? Assessment of candidates focuses on skills and abilities that will be used in the new position; the process is forward-looking and not based merely on past performance. (Of course, it is recognized that some past performance measures may indicate certain skills and abilities needed in the promoted position, but they should be identified as such through job analysis.)

## Testing

In order to be more objective (and less political) in the promotion of candidates, many jurisdictions administer written exams for promotion. Some use highly rigid procedures and do not allow for input from supervisors or administrators; the results of the test dictate the promotional rankings. The rule of one is used often in such systems, meaning that the person with the highest test score is the next person promoted. While there are benefits to this approach, it relies heavily on book knowledge and test-taking ability. It does not necessarily measure interpersonal communications and other leadership qualities. Nor does it adequately simulate field conditions under which this person must make decisions.

## Assessment Center

As someone once said, "It is a process or technique, not a place." The assessment center approach to promotion involves observation and measurement of what a candidate does and how well it is done in simulated job situations or scenarios that would be encountered in the promoted position. It may involve interviews, oral presentations, psychological testing, writing memos, and role playing. The "assessors" in this approach may be top-level managers/administrators inside the department and/or individuals (with policing expertise) from outside the department. The objective is to analyze the candidate's ability to perform in situations that are common to the promoted position. Elements of stress and confrontation are usually part of this assessment. The entire process may take several days or be conducted intermittently over several weeks.

### Hybrid

A hybrid model of promotion may involve two or more of the above approaches. For example, a civil service promotion system may involve a written exam, a supervisory rating, and seniority points. Or an appointment system may involve past performance ratings, ratings of supervisors, and an oral board. Even a primarily political system can involve some assessment of ability and skills so that the appointing authority can defend the choice made.

Whichever system of promotion is used, one must remember that the law of personnel practices discussed above applies, and therefore (if challenged), the agency must be able to show that the criteria for promotion were job-related and relevant. Just as many agencies found themselves in court over selection procedures, many have had their promotional procedures examined and thrown out.

## Career Development

Career development is closely associated with various types of training that are discussed in detail in Chapter 8. However, besides the training component, career development involves increasing levels of responsibility and personal growth. Some departments allow for growth within a given rank by establishing sub-ranks or classifications within ranks such as Police Officer I, II, and III, or Sergeant I, II, and III. This allows an officer to remain within a specific rank or job category and still pursue an increase in responsibility and a change of assignment.

Some departments allow for personal growth and assignment change through **lateral entry**. It usually refers to conditions where an officer at the patrol, investigative, or supervisory level can transfer to another agency without any loss of seniority, rank, and salary. Lateral entry is not as common in municipal departments or state agencies as it is in sheriff's departments. Most seniority systems and central personnel system policies protect officers within agencies from the lateral transfer of officers outside the agency (which is a form of protectionism).

## ■ Labor Relations in Law Enforcement

The concept of **labor relations** refers to the sum total of all interaction between the administration of an agency and its employees. One area of concern under the topic of labor relations is the involuntary termination of a sworn police officer. As public safety employees, police officers can be fired for exhibiting inappropriate behavior that might reflect upon the integrity of the department. For example, while all citizens are guaranteed the right to free expression under the First Amendment, officers can be terminated for expressing disparaging remarks, which are deemed a matter of "private concern" about the department (for example, stating that the chief is a complete jerk). However, if the remarks expressed are a matter of "public concern" (stating that many of the officers are frequently drunk on duty), the remarks may be protected under the US Constitution. The court utilizes a two-step approach. First, determining whether or not the officer's speech was a matter of public concern and second, whether or not the individual's interests outweigh the employer's "in promoting the efficiency of the public services it performs through its employees" (Newbold 2003, 10).

A second issue of concern involves name-clearing hearings. Essentially, when an employee has a "liberty interest," which is "when his or her good name, reputation, honor, or integrity is at stake because of what the government is doing to that employee" (Unkelbach 2003, 13), they have the right to a predetermination name-clearing hearing. However, there are certain restrictions placed on the eligibility for these hearings:

> *The Circuit Court for the Tenth Circuit has set forth a four-part test which must be met before a claim of deprivation of liberty interests is actionable: (1) the statements at issue must impugn the good name, reputation, honor, or integrity of the employee; (2) these statements must be false; (3) these statements must occur in the course of terminating the employee or must foreclose other employment opportunities; and (4) these statements must be published* (Unkelbach, 2003, 13).

Some form of labor relations occurs in all law enforcement agencies; some of these are formal while others are informal. The most formal means of labor relations is referred to as **collective bargaining**, in which a representative of an employee group (often a union) negotiates the terms and conditions of employment with the representative of the employer. The negotiated document that results from this process is usually called "the contract," or "the agreement." In a 1990 survey of 72 major departments in the United States, 56 (77.7%) permitted union membership, 9 compelled it, and 5 forbade it (3 agencies gave no response to the question) (Strawbridge 1990). In the 2000 LEMAS study of state and local agencies with 100 or more officers, 72% of municipal agencies and 51% of state agencies authorized collective bargaining for sworn officers (Reaves and Hickman 2004). However, formal collective bargaining varies from state to state. For example, in the survey of local agencies mentioned above, no agencies in the states of Georgia (local level), North Carolina, South Carolina, and Virginia authorize collective bargaining for sworn officers.

## History of the Police Union Movement

The unionization movement in the public sector can be traced to the 1830s when mechanics, carpenters, and other craftsmen employed by the federal government joined existing unions made up of private sector employees. Some of the early issues addressed by public sector employees at that time included the desire for a shorter (10-hour) workday and better wages. But most of the gains made in the public sector up through the 1880s came after such work conditions were considered a standard in the private sector (Public Sector Unionism 1972).

Police officers, too, in the late 1880s began to organize. Initially their organizations were **benevolent associations,** which focused on improving the working conditions and providing assistance (in the form of funeral expenses and widows and orphans funds) to its members who suffered losses. These early associations were often controlled by high ranking officers, and they did not generally interfere with the operation of the department. In addition to benevolent purposes, these associations often served the fraternal and social aspects of the officers. Although not unions in the formal sense, these associations were early forms of employee organizations.

By the early 1900s, associations were common in most major cities. Some agencies had even encountered more organized officer groups: Ithaca, New York experienced a walk-out in 1889 because officers' pay had been reduced from $12 to $9 per week, and Cincinnati, Ohio experienced a strike by 450 officers in 1918 over issues of union organization. By 1919, the American Federation of Labor (AFL) had changed its position on granting formal charters to police locals. It was immediately swamped with 65 applications which, by the end of summer, resulted in 37 locals (with a total of over 4,000 officers) being officially recognized (see Smith 1975 and Gammage and Sachs 1977 for details of early police unionism).

## The Boston Police Strike of 1919

One of those locals chartered (August 8, 1919) included the Boston Police Social Club. The officers of Boston had been at odds with the city administration over a pay raise and working conditions for almost a year. The pay raise offered by the city had been deemed insufficient by the social club, which had acted as a representative of the officers in conferring with the city. Eventually, the city yielded by granting higher wages; however, with the soaring costs and the delayed increase, the amounts were still inadequate. **Figure 9-6** describes the working conditions found in the Boston Police Department in 1919.

Two days after the Boston Police Social Club received its charter (as the Boston Policemen's Union), Police Commissioner Curtis issued the following order, which in essence prohibited officers from joining a union affiliated with any national organization:

> *No member of the force shall join or belong to any organization, club or body composed of present or present and past members of the force which is affiliated with or a part of any organization, club or body outside the department, except that a post of the Grand Army of the Republic, the United Spanish War Veterans, and the American Legion of World War Veterans may be formed within the department* (Spero 1977, 384).

A "war of words" raged for weeks. On August 26, the commissioner filed charges against eight police officers who had been elected to positions in the union; shortly thereafter, 11 more were charged. Although discussions between the union and members of a select citizens' committee (appointed

— 78–90 hour workweek depending on assignment

— $21 a week salary

— Officers had to purchase own uniforms

— Political promotion

— Graft at command levels

— Unsanitary, rodent infested station houses

— Unanswered grievances

*Source:* Data from J.D. Smith (1975), Police unions: An historical perspective of causes and organizations. *Police Chief.* November: 24.

**Figure 9-6** Working conditions in the Boston Police Department in 1919.

by Mayor Peters) attempted to resolve the conflict and were making progress, the commissioner insisted on pursuing the charges against the officers. On September 8, after refusing a settlement proposed by the citizen's committee, the commissioner found the officers guilty and suspended them from service.

The reaction of the stunned union came quickly. Later that same day, the union membership voted 1,134 to 2 to strike at 5:45 PM on September 9, 1919. For days, Mayor Peters attempted to engage the assistance of Governor Calvin Coolidge, but he refused to become involved; even a meeting of the citizen's committee with the Governor on the night of September 8th proved fruitless. At noon on the 9th, the Governor issued a letter explaining why he would not interfere in the developments in the department. At 5:45 PM, 1,117 of 1,544 patrol officers left their posts.

Although the commissioner had promised the mayor and the governor that he had planned for continued protection of the city, general rioting, looting, disorder, and individual robberies occurred. By morning, the commissioner said his resources were inadequate and asked the mayor to activate the troops stationed in the city. The mayor did this but also assumed command of the department under statutory authority and restored order to the city. Then, not to be outdone, Governor Coolidge activated the state militia throughout the state and sent it to Boston; he then assumed control of the department. It appeared as though every politician was going to make political points out of the situation. Some reports indicate that 100 people were injured, 7 were killed, and over one million dollars' worth of property damage was done during the four-day strike.

Overnight the opinion of the public had turned against the officers; where sympathy for their cause had once existed, condemnation was universal. Over 1,100 striking officers were dismissed from the Boston police force and the AFL dissolved all charters to police organizations. For the next 20–30 years, the police unionization movement reverted back to local fraternal associations.

Governor Coolidge became nationally recognized because of the Boston police strike and his famous statement, "There is no right to strike against the public safety, by anyone, anywhere, anytime." It helped propel him to the vice presidency and then, following the death of President Harding, to the presidency in 1923. Did the strike have any benefits for the Boston police officers? Yes, working conditions improved after the strike, not only in Boston but in other cities as well, but none of the striking officers were rehired.

## Labor Legislation and Growth of Public Sector Unionization

From the early 1900s through the 1950s, police associations at the local level increased significantly in number. While the law in many states did not permit formal collective bargaining, it was not prohibited in most. Municipalities at the local level began to recognize local associations as representing the local department's rank and file. This led to formal dialogue (but not necessarily binding negotiated contracts) between the association and the administration of agencies. The efforts of national associations such as the Fraternal Order of Police; the International Conference of Police Associations; the American Federation of State, County, and Municipal Employees, and other groups kept the issue of formal labor relations and the rights of employees in the forefront of personnel discussions. In 1959, Wisconsin enacted a collective bargaining statute for the public sector; President Kennedy issued Executive Order 10988 in 1962, granting bargaining rights to federal employees; and in 1967, New York State enacted the Taylor Law, which permitted collective bargaining in the public sector. By 1974, there were 35 states with legislation granting collective bargaining rights to public employees (only 27 of these allowed it for police officers, however). By 1985, 40 states had passed some form of legislation dealing with public employees (Gaines et al. 1991, 313).

It was the decade of the 1960s that experienced the largest growth in formal unionization efforts. Four general factors have been identified as contributing to that growth during those chaotic years: (1) the perception of increased public hostility, (2) rising crime rates and public demand for law and order, (3) salaries and benefits that were lower than those for other public employees and the private sector, and (4) poor personnel practices of police agencies (Juris and Feuille 1974). These factors and conditions related to them brought about a police militancy never experienced before in the United States. Work stoppages, slow downs, sick-outs (known as the "blue flu"), ticket blitzes, and strikes occurred frequently during labor disputes in the late 1960s and through the mid-1970s. However, because of major strikes in the cities of Albuquerque, New Mexico, Oklahoma City, Oklahoma, and San Francisco, California, in 1975, unions came under heavy criticism by the public, press, and politicians (Ayres 1977, 431).

## Contemporary Unionism

Some of the labor dispute practices mentioned above are still used today by employee organizations. For example, during one two-year contract dispute, the Los Angeles police utilized blue flu, job slowdown, and massive demonstration tactics to move negotiations forward. Consider the following report:

> *California—The Los Angeles Police Department was struck this month [June 94] by an outbreak of "blue flu" in a continuous battle with the city over a new contract. Nearly half the department's night shift failed to show up one day this month, forcing day-shift officers to work overtime to fill in. While the next day's overnight shift was normal, half the force again took off during the day shift. The absences could cost the city as much as $1 million a day in overtime costs. A 6% raise over 2 years was rejected by the union earlier in the month (Law Enforcement News 1994a, 2).*

The union even rented 22 billboards throughout the city showing a masked gunman menacing a young woman as she gets into her car; the signs read, "Warning: This Can Be You Without the Police Department." Following a threat to call a job action during the World Cup soccer tournament in June–July of 1994, Mayor Richard Riordan stepped in to make a new offer, which was accepted by the union. During the late 1990s, many law enforcement bargaining units and their national affiliated associations were active in obtaining proper compensation for overtime pay, defending the rights of officers during grievances, pushing for broader carrying-concealed-weapons laws, and advocating national legislation for an officers' bill of rights. Lately, the focus of collective bargaining issues has centered on fringe benefits, especially health insurance and the matter the co-pay of premiums.

Police unions today are more organized and sophisticated than they have ever been. They have access to excellent legal representation, and they are powerful forces in political lobbying. They have matured greatly in the last three decades. There are many more unionized forces than before, and many departments have to negotiate with more than one union because state laws often allow different unions to represent officers in supervisory ranks. Unions and formal collective bargaining are the norm, which means that personnel practices for the most part are controlled through negotiated agreements. In essence, if an officer believes that he or she has been mistreated by management, the contract is the first document consulted. In many departments, this document (the contract) is as important to the officers as the state criminal code book.

# ■ Police Misconduct and Departmental Responses

Maintaining discipline and high morale in law enforcement agencies is not an easy task. As discussed in earlier chapters, the use of discretion often opens an officer or agent to criticism. Officers who use force, including deadly force, are placed under scrutiny not only by the department but also by the news media and public. And, while the use of this discretion and force may have been appropriate and proper, the department must investigate alleged misconduct in order to assure the public that the integrity of the force is intact.

## Traditional Terms and Newer Categories

Police misconduct is used here as a general phrase to describe various forms of behavior that the public and the police themselves consider inappropriate for officers of the law. In 1999, the Gallup News Service released its findings of a poll related to the public's perception of police brutality:

> *The poll, conducted March 5–7, shows that 38% of Americans believe there have been incidents of police brutality in their area, while 57% disagree. That compares with a similar Gallup poll conducted in March, 1991, in which roughly the same number, 35%, said police brutality existed in their area. The poll also underscores perceptions that minorities feel unfairly targeted by police officers. Fifty-eight percent of non-whites believe police brutality takes place in their area, compared to only 35% of whites. When asked, "Have you personally ever felt treated unfairly by the police or by a police officer?" twenty-seven percent of Americans said yes. Again, the answers differ along racial lines, with 39% of non-whites saying yes, compared to just 24% of whites. Police brutality is also more likely to be reported in urban areas (57%, compared to 35% in rural areas)*

*and in the West and the South (43% and 41% respectively)* (Gillespie 1999).

An extensive study of law enforcement nationwide found seemingly widespread appearance of intentional use of excessive force (Skolnick and Fyfe 1993). According to a special report by Human Rights Watch:

> *Police abuse remains one of the most serious and divisive human rights violations in the United States. The excessive use of force by police officers, including unjustified shootings, severe beatings, fatal chokings, and rough treatment, persists because overwhelming barriers to accountability make it possible for officers who commit human rights violations to escape due punishment and often to repeat their offenses* (1998).

It is beyond the scope of this section, however, to examine this problem in detail. Many scholarly sources have reported on the typical types of behavior associated with police misconduct. **Figure 9-7** contains a listing of some of the more common terms associated with the various forms of police misconduct.

Recent research into police misconduct by Professors Kappeler, Sluder, and Alpert is reported in their text, *Forces of Deviance*, Second Edition (1998), which

---

*Booming doors*—the practice of confiscating from drug dealers keys of apartments where drugs and guns are hidden and then going there to steal drugs, guns, and money.

*Bribery*—payments of cash or gifts for past or future assistance to avoid prosecution; usually higher in value than in "mooching."

*Chiseling/badging in*—police demands for discounts or free admission to entertainment whether on duty or not.

*Extortion*—demands by officers for advertisements in police magazines or for the purchase of tickets to police sponsored events through the use of compulsion, force, or fear. Also could involve sums of cash to avoid arrest or for "protection."

*Favoritism*—granting immunity from traffic arrest or citation or from a summons for minor offenses because of relationship to officer or because of display of window sticker or license plate emblem.

*Grass-eaters*—officers who take advantage of opportunities for graft that might arise but do not aggressively initiate them.

*Meat-eaters*—officers who aggressively seek opportunities for graft and other forms of misconduct.

*Mooching*—receiving free coffee, cigarettes, liquor, food, or other items either as a consequence of being in an underpaid occupation or for future acts of favoritism which might be expected or received by the donor.

*Pad*—refers to a shadow organization (group) within the department that receives shares of regular bribe payments from citizens; amounts of share depend on rank.

*Shakedown*—practice of appropriating expensive items for personal use from crime scenes (and may include money, gifts, or favors from citizens).

*Shopping*—practice of picking up small items (candy, food, etc.) at a store where the door has been accidentally left unlocked after business hours.

*Testilying*—the making of false arrests, tampering with evidence, and then committing perjury on the witness stand.

*Source:* Adapted from Stoddard, E., Organizational norms and police discretion: An observational study of police work with traffic violators (1979). *Criminology* 17(2):159–71; Langworthy, R.H., F. Travis III (1994). *Policing in America: A balance of forces.* New York: Macmillan Publishing Company; and NYPD corruption woes bring more bad news (1994b). *Law Enforcement News*, March 15:13.

**Figure 9-7** Terms and phrases associated with police misconduct.

examines this issue in detail. They categorize deviant police behaviors into four types: **police crime**, **occupational deviance**, **corruption**, and **abuse of authority**. Police crime includes those acts where the officer's authority and powers as a police officer assisted or facilitated the commission of crime(s). Occupational deviance is akin to police crime, but in these situations the acts (ticket fixing, strip searching females in custody, abusing a prisoner) probably could not have been committed by anyone not employed in the police occupation. Corruption, as defined in this categorization, "involves the potential for personal gain and the use of police power and authority to further that gain." The emphasis and distinction here is the element of personal gain, and it is usually tied to economic gain. Abuse of authority refers to the mistreatment and/or violation of human and legal rights, regardless of motive or intention, by officials possessing police authority. Such abuse may be physical, psychological, or legal (Kappeler et al. 1998, 20–25). **Figure 9-8** identifies sample behavior of each of the above-mentioned categories of police misconduct.

## Major Scandals since the Early 1990s

The evolution and history of policing in the United States is fraught with incidents of police misconduct. Media attention to the subject appears to have reached an all-time high. The decade of the '90s did not start off to be very favorable for the police occupation. Some of the nation's largest police departments were spotlighted because of police misconduct. In March of 1991, the Rodney King incident occurred; it resulted in over 3 years of litigation, disturbances at the end of the criminal trial on state charges where officers were found not guilty, two officers being sentenced to prison for violating the civil rights of King, and a civil suit award of $6 million to King. Only a portion of the videotape that captured the incident was shown (over and over again) on all major television networks, but it left an indelible impression in the minds of all who saw it. The findings of the Christopher Commission, which was appointed to investigate the conditions within the LA Police Department following the King incident, led some to conclude that, "[w]hat emerges from such statistics is a department where the use of force against citizens is not considered a matter of great concern" (Alpert et al. 1992, 476).

| Police Crime | Occupational Deviance | Corruption | Abuse of Authority |
|---|---|---|---|
| Off-duty burglary | Theft of evidence | Accepting bribes | Perjury |
| Off-duty robbery | Tampering with evidence | Selling drugs | Illegal wire taps |
| Domestic abuse | Prisoner abuse | Selling "protection" | Forced confessions |
| Child abuse | Ticket fixing | Accepting sexual favors | Physically beating suspects/prisoners |
| Prostitution | Improper strip searches | Extortion | Humiliating witnesses |
| Gambling | Driving impounded vehicles | | |

*Source:* Compiled from Kappeler, Victor E., Richard D. Sluder, and Geoffrey P. Alpert (1998). *Forces of deviance: Understanding the dark side of policing*, Second Edition. Prospect Heights, IL: Waveland Press, Inc. All rights reserved.

**Figure 9-8** Examples of police misconduct by category.

At the other end of the country, a major drug-related scandal which took years of persistent investigation by a determined internal affairs investigator (Sgt. Joseph Trimboli) began to surface in mid-1992. "The Loser's Club" was a group of rogue cops led by Michael Dowd that engaged in wholesale drug racketeering. (See **Figure 9-9** for additional details about the Dowd investigation.) By the end of 1992, there were 101 police officers of the NYPD who had been arrested for misconduct in that one year.

The Mollen Commission was established to hear testimony and to investigate corruption within the NYPD. (The scandal brought back memories of the Knapp Commission of the early 1970s and the testimony of Detective Frank Serpico.) The Mollen Commission heard testimony about robberies, thefts, on-duty drug abuse, excessive use of force, and scams. In 1994 a series of arrests and internal actions occurred:

March 15   While off duty, an officer was arrested and charged with beating a man in a convenience store. He pled guilty, and he and two other officers who were with him (all had been drinking heavily) were suspended from the department.

March 18   Three officers were arrested after a police sting videotaped them breaking into an apartment, ransacking it, and beating an undercover officer.

March 30   A community police officer was arraigned on 14 counts of grand larceny ("shake downs" of several local merchants).

April 14   Fourteen officers (from the 30th Precinct) were arrested on charges of stealing drugs, money, and guns from narcotics dealers and criminals.

April 15   Twelve more officers were arrested on similar charges from the same precinct.

May 4   Eleven more officers at the 30th Precinct had service weapons and badges confiscated and were assigned to

In the same auditorium where Frank Serpico testified 21 years earlier, Michael Dowd told the Mollen Commission his story. He described his indoctrination into petty crime and brutality by his superiors and how he went from $200/week scores of drug money to an $8,000/week payoff from a major drug dealer. He spoke of pervasive corruption in the force and how accepted it was.

Former officer Dowd, of the 75th Precinct, had plead guilty to corruption charges before testifying before the commission. He admitted to sniffing lines of cocaine off the dashboard of his police car in the company of his partner. Dowd was eventually arrested by Suffolk County, NY police for operating a drug ring.

Dowd indicated that he was introduced to corruption at the police academy since it promoted an "us" against "them" (the public) attitude; then drinking on the job helped to continue his illegal activity. He spoke about the "rendezvous at the pool" where virtually the entire 75th would go for drinks, laughs, shooting off their guns and other immature behavior. He and fellow officers would plan their illicit drug raids there as well. He said his supervisors helped promote a corrupt attitude by implying "do whatever you wish" but have an answer if asked.

*Source:* Extracted and paraphrased from Frankel, Bruce (1993). "Ex-NYC officer tells stark tale of cops gone bad." *USA Today*, September 28:A3.

**Figure 9-9** Cops gone bad in New York City.

"administrative duty." (*Law Enforcement News* 1994b; *Law Enforcement News* 1994c).

New York and Los Angeles were not alone in the problem of controlling police misconduct. Washington, DC, as of December 1993, had 113 officers under indictment or with charges pending. A group of 12 officers was arrested in mid-December of 1993 after "bragging" about misdeeds to an undercover FBI agent posing as a drug dealer. The chief of the department was quoted as saying that during 1989 and 1990, "mistakes" were made in an intensive recruiting effort; most of the officers arrested had been hired during that time (Fields 1993, 3A). In July of 1995, the City's Civilian Complaint Review Board closed its doors because of a budget cut. The backlog of 770 pending cases of police misconduct was transferred to the Police Department for further action. By the middle of 1998, it was reported that 500 officers were under charges of wrongdoing in the Washington, DC Police Department (*Law Enforcement News* 1998a).

In November of 1992, Malice Green was reportedly pulled from his car and beaten by two officers with their hands and flashlights. A total of seven officers were present before the incident ended. Two of the officers were convicted of second degree murder, initially, but after appeals and new trials, convictions for involuntary manslaughter were rendered in 2000 (Brand-Williams 2000). In the Atlanta area, three officers were arrested in 1993 for murder; two others for robbery. All were thought to be part of a burglary and robbery ring (Edmonds 1993, 2A; Kappeler et al. 1998, 276). In New Orleans, between 1992 and 1996, 40 officers were arrested on charges including auto theft, robbery, rape, aggravated assault and even murder (Kappeler et al. 1998, 57). One female officer killed three people as she attempted to rob a restaurant; she's now on death row in Louisiana.

The allegations and revelations of the O.J. Simpson trial of 1995 prompted a number of internal investigations and created an atmosphere of great suspicion of the police in that city and elsewhere. Also during 1995, it was revealed that over 20 officers in the city of Philadelphia were charged with various counts of perjury, civil rights violations, and engaging in drug trafficking. Many of the cases handled by those officers were reopened, and wrongfully convicted subjects were released from prison. The FBI came under great scrutiny during 1995 as well because of its involvement in the Waco incident, the shooting of a wife and daughter of a Montana fugitive (several years earlier), and allegations that the forensics experts from the crime lab routinely doctored evidence and lied in court.

As the decade of the 1990s closed, the problem of police misconduct and allegations of abuse continued to plague the law enforcement community. Such issues also receive much media attention. New York City again was the site of controversy when, on February 4, 1999, an African immigrant, Amadou Diallo, was hit 19 times by four officers who shot 41 rounds at the 22-year-old man. The man was apparently unarmed and the four officers were indicted (*Law Enforcement News* 1999). As this matter was being investigated, another high profile allegation of police abuse in August of 1997 was going to trial in New York City. The broomstick torture case of Haitian immigrant Abner Louima went to trial in May of 1999. Five officers were indicted for the alleged station house bathroom beating of Louima; two were charged with using a broom handle to sodomize him (Hays 1999). During the trial, one officer changed his plea to guilty. Of the other four, one was found guilty and three not guilty. Also in May of 1999, the survivors of Tyisha Miller, 19, filed a federal civil rights lawsuit against five officers and the city of Riverside, California. In December of 1998, officers found Miller in a locked car. She appeared unconscious but a handgun was seen on her lap. The officers broke the window and tried to remove the handgun. When they did, Ms. Miller reached for the weapon and the officers shot her 12 times. The District Attorney's investigation cleared the officers of criminal charges, although he criticized their judgment (*USA Today* 1999). In each of these incidents, the subject involved was a person of color and most of the officers were white, which heightened the tensions and allegations of racial unrest. In 1999 Attorney General Janet Reno called for a national commission to investigate police integrity in light of several incidents involving allegations of police abuse and the high levels of public mistrust of the police, especially among minority segments of the nation (Johnson 1999).

Corruption and scandal do not just hit the large cities. For example, during 1998:

- The entire command structure of two departments in Cicero, IL and West New York, NJ, was replaced because of systematic corruption.
- A sheriff in Starr County, Texas was indicted for kickbacks.
- A three-year corruption scandal in North Carolina resulted in the firing of two highway patrol supervisors and the demotion of another.
- Fifty-five officers in Suffolk County, NY faced dismissal related to fraudulent actions in a hiring entrance exam scandal.
- Officers in Dallas; Philadelphia; Erie County, NY; and Pioneer Village, KY face charges in shootings or deaths of others, not related to on-duty incidents.
- Federal authorities charged 44 persons in a corruption probe, many of them police and corrections officers in the Cleveland, Ohio area.
- In Mahoning County, Ohio, six officers from local departments and the sheriff's office were indicted on charges ranging from felony theft in office and complicity to commit theft to dereliction of duty; other law enforcement officials were under investigation in a large corrupt practices probe in northeast Ohio; by early 1999, the Mahoning County Sheriff had been indicted, and three former officers, including the retired chief of police of Campbell, Ohio, were imprisoned.
- A former police captain in Akron, Ohio was sentenced to life for the killing of his ex-wife outside her medical office.

(*Law Enforcement News* 1998a; *Law Enforcement News* 1998b; Meade and Niquette 1998; Associated Press 1998.)

Police abuse and corruption has continued in the new millennium. The city of Los Angeles is still suffering the aftermath of the Rampart scandal that began in 1999. By March of 2003, the city had paid out over $40 million in settlements and had about 100 cases where either convictions were overturned or charges canceled. Of 70 officers investigated, nine have gone to prison (Associated Press 2003). Chief of Police William J. Bratton called for an independent Blue Ribbon

Rampart Review Panel, which was convened in July of 2003, to investigate and review the response by the city and others to the Rampart Area scandal in order to determine the extent to which the underlying causes for the scandal have been identified and addressed. In November of 2004, an assistant police chief was disciplined for her supervisory role in the 2001 scandal, "in which dozens of people, mostly Mexican immigrants, were wrongly jailed on drug charges based on fake evidence" (Associated Press 2004). A deputy chief announced his retirement, as well. In April of 2004, three Miami police officers were convicted for their part in a scheme in which guns were planted near the bodies of two fleeing robbers shot to death by police. The incidents occurred between 1995–1997. A total of 11 officers were tried on various charges. Three had been convicted earlier, four were acquitted, and juries were deadlocked on four others. Of the three convicted in 2004, one officer was convicted for planting the weapon; two others were convicted for conspiracy, perjury and obstructing justice (Wilson 2004).

Unfortunately, we could list even more examples of law enforcement officer misconduct, but you get the picture. There is an excellent source of additional material regarding police corruption and integrity maintained by the Michigan State University Library at http://www.lib.msu.edu/harris23/crimjust/polcorr.htm. The site contains links to over 40 Web sites. You are encouraged to visit this site and review the related material.

## Department Efforts to Control Misconduct

It must be understood that misconduct is not controlled with one simple technique or program. Establishing an internal affairs unit does not ensure control. Control of misconduct (the goal) is achieved through the use of multifaceted control mechanisms (the means). These include professional selection standards, in-depth background investigations, training, corporate values, codes of ethics, written policies and expectations, managerial/supervisory training, citizen complaint procedures, internal investigations systems, complaint monitoring, and civilian review processes. Administrative and elected officials and the public also need to demand accountability. Police errors and intentional wrongdoing can and do lead to substantial penalties from civil litigation. These errors can include everything from the handling of an accident scene to intentional infliction of physical injury (Kappeler 1997). The costs can add another burden to the tax payers and to government budgets.

A.C. Germann once stated the following regarding traditional policing. The words have a unique relevance to this discussion of misconduct:

> *There are far too many police whose values are selfish and individualistic, and who make the position work for them in many ways— free coffee, newspapers, foods, liquor, unnecessary overtime—a plethora of freebies that can lead all the way to theft of property, resale of drugs. . . . Unprofessional police misuse their power and authority against anyone they choose to and, particularly against anyone who does not show deference. . . . Traditional internal discipline is more harsh and punitive with respect to violations of policy and*

*procedure involving facilities and equipment than it is with respect to violations of human rights. . . . The traditional police academy seems to have as its goal the preparation of brutal hit-squad members, rather than community helpers and non-violent conflict resolvers. . . . The traditional police union or employee organization resists any and all attempts to eliminate unsavory customs and traditions. . . . The majority of traditional officers support their colleagues with a code of silence, cover-up, and sophisticated political pressure that often results in the dismissal or resignation of professionally-oriented administrators (1994, 6, 10).*

On the other side of the coin, Germann recognizes that there are:

*. . . police administrators, supervisors and officers who are very professional, very honorable, very truthful, and who are truly the unsung heroes of our age. . . . People like these—professional, well-educated, highly motivated, with keen minds, social sensitivity, strength of character, and the courage to tell the king that he is naked—are the pride of the American police service. They need to be encouraged, supported, and given the access to the authority and power that are needed for immediate implementation of necessary changes of policy and procedure (1994, 6).*

While it is recognized that the negative aspects of the police subculture are prevalent, it can been argued that the subculture itself can be an agent for change in agencies. Not only can enlightened administrators and supervisors encourage proper behavior, the subculture can be used by professional officers to support and maintain a highly professional atmosphere (Conser 1980). Good, honest, dedicated officers need to take a stand and tell recalcitrant officers that "we won't tolerate that (misconduct) here!"

Because of the attention given to police misconduct in recent years, many jurisdictions have turned to **civilian review** of police misconduct complaints and allegations. In a 1991 study of the nation's 50 largest city police departments, Walker and Bumphus found that 30 had some form of civilian review procedures. (Ten of these had been established in just three years, indicating an upward trend.) They categorized the review procedures into three types:

Class I: (a) Initial investigation and fact-finding by non-sworn personnel; (b) Review of investigative report and recommendation for action by non-sworn personnel or board consisting of a majority of non-sworn persons.

Class II: (a) Initial investigation and fact-finding by sworn police officers; (b) Review of investigative report and recommendation for action by non-sworn personnel or board which consists of a majority of non-sworn persons.

Class III: (a) Initial investigation and fact-finding by sworn officers; (b) Review of investigative report and recommendation for action by sworn officers; (c) opportunity for the citizen who is dissatisfied with the final disposition of the complaint to appeal to a board which includes non-sworn persons (Walker and Bumphus 1991, 3).

Of the 30 civilian review programs, 12 were Class I; 14 were Class II; and 4 were Class III. Historically, police officer unions and employee associations have resisted the establishment and operation of civilian review boards because they do not believe that civilians can adequately judge their actions. Officers often have demonstrated over such proposals. In August of 1992, New York City officers demonstrated at city hall to protest the proposal of an all-civilian review board. It polarized the various groups of police officers, with the Grand Council of Guardians (a Black officers' group) denouncing the protest (*USA Today* 1992). By 1991, over 66% of the 50 largest cities in the United States had created some form of civilian review (Walker and Bumphus 1992). Kappeler, Sluder, and Alpert summarize this trend by stating, "The boards are viewed by many as important vehicles for making the police more democratic and accountable. Although some boards have achieved a measure of success, many of the efforts at civilian oversight have met with failure" (1998, 250).

## ■ Summary

Personnel are the lifeblood of law enforcement agencies. The quality of service rendered by these persons is dependent on the thoroughness of the selection process, the effectiveness of the training process, the commitment to promote capable people, and the accountability demanded by supervisors and administrators. Human resource operations in police agencies are extremely complex and riddled with legal proscriptions and potential pitfalls. Numerous legislative, administrative, judicial, and contractual issues must be considered in personnel decisions today. Lawsuits are costly, and allegations of misconduct erode public confidence and trust.

The purpose of this chapter has been to present an overview of the issues impacting the human resource (personnel) function of law enforcement agencies. It reviewed the basic aspects of the recruiting and selections functions, highlighted many of the legal issues related to personnel management, and described the evolution of unionism in US policing. We concluded by outlining the primary aspects of police deviance and the need for department initiatives to control misconduct. It is hoped that persons committed to a career in policing will achieve an understanding and an appreciation for the matters discussed here.

# QUESTIONS FOR REVIEW

1. What are the major stages of the police selection process, and why are they more complex in some departments than in others?
2. Define the concept of "protected class," and describe how it relates to personnel functions such as selection and promotion.
3. What is the significance of the legal concept of "remedies," and what are the typical ones often implemented in cases alleging job discrimination in law enforcement agencies?
4. What are the seven different methods by which an officer can be promoted to higher rank and responsibility?
5. What are the differences between the concepts of "labor relations" and "collective bargaining"?
6. What was the significance of the Boston Police Strike of 1919 in terms of its impact on police unionism?
7. What are four types of police misconduct? Describe each.

# SUGGESTED ACTIVITIES

1. Contact local law enforcement agencies in your area and ask for a recruitment packet or information about entry positions.
2. At the library, read the landmark US Supreme Court decision of *Griggs v. Duke Power Company*, 401 US 424 (1971); then read the Appellate decision of *Davis v. City of Dallas*, 777 F.2d 205 (1985). What are the implications of each of these decisions?
3. Attend a job fair where law enforcement agencies are represented, and talk to recruiters about the stages of the selection process for their agencies.
4. Browse the Internet for the state required physical fitness standards for peace officers in at least five states. How do they differ?
5. Log on to the World Wide Web and conduct a search on two of the following words or phrases: "personnel selection," "job discrimination," "affirmative action," "police union," or "police corruption." Write a brief report of the types of sites found.
6. Log on to the URL http://www.eeoc.gov and review the legal information available at this site.

## ■ Chapter Glossary

**abuse of authority**   refers to the mistreatment and/or violation of human and legal rights, regardless of motive or intention, by officials possessing police authority; may be physical, psychological, or legal.

**active recruitment** occurs when an agency makes a concerted effort to attract desired candidates to it; includes using existing personnel, either sworn or civilian, as recruiters and sending them into the community to generate interest among potential applicants.

**adverse impact** one form of proving job discrimination; the procedure or qualification affects a protected class more negatively than the majority group.

**affirmative action** the taking of a more aggressive position at recruiting and hiring protected classes that are underrepresented in an agency's workforce.

**appointing authority** an official who hires a person for a particular job according to established law and procedures.

**assessment center** a process/procedure involving observation and measurement of a candidate for promotion; it normally includes simulated job situations or scenarios that would be encountered in the promoted position.

**background check** the formal review and verification of the candidate's application information and general suitability for employment; usually addresses formal education, current and previous residences, current and prior employment, traffic and criminal citations and convictions (if any), reported drug history, and credit rating.

**benevolent associations** one form of employee association; early associations attempted to provide employees with benefits that employers did not; were also fraternal and social in nature. Today, a police benevolent association (PBA) may also be a union for purposes of collective bargaining.

**bona fide occupational qualification** certain criteria deemed required or necessary for the operation of the business (or agency) and which may have adverse impact on some protected classes.

**bonus points** the awarding of additional credit (beyond written exam scores) for certain factors or job-related criteria such as previous police experience, state peace officer certification, college education, military experience (veteran), and residency.

**career development** refers to a desired change in work assignment that is accompanied by increased responsibility and may involve additional training and/or education; career development may include a promotion.

**Civil Rights Act of 1964** federal legislation that addressed the equal rights of persons; one part, Title VII, prohibited discrimination in employment in the private sector on grounds of race, color, religion, sex, and national origin.

**civil service** a term referring to non-military government employment or to a specific personnel system established by state or local law.

**civilian review** the review of police misconduct complaints and allegations by non-police persons.

**collective bargaining** the most formal means of labor relations, in which a representative of an employee group (often a union) negotiates the terms and conditions of employment with the representative of the employer.

**conditional offer of employment** the candidate is suitable and eligible for hire at a particular point in the selection process and will be employed if certain other factors related to one's physical ability and medical and mental conditions are within job-related limits.

**consent decree**   an out-of-court settlement by parties to a lawsuit where each agrees to do specified things (remedies) under certain conditions.

**corruption**   actions that involve the potential for personal gain and the use of police power and authority to further that gain.

**eligibility list**   a list of qualified candidates from which the law enforcement agency must select its employees; usually associated with state and local civil service systems.

**Equal Employment Opportunity Commission**   (EEOC) the federal agency authorized to enforce the anti-discrimination in employment legislation and to develop guidelines for employers.

*Griggs v. Duke Power Company*   the landmark decision by the US Supreme Court in 1971 which interpreted the Civil Rights Act of 1964.

**job analysis**   the process of examining and evaluating the required performances of a particular job to determine what job skills, knowledge, and abilities (SKAs) are required.

**labor relations**   the sum total of all interaction between the administration of an agency and its employees.

**lateral entry**   the transferring to another agency without any loss of seniority, rank, and salary.

**occupational deviance**   akin to police crime, but are acts which probably could not have been committed by anyone unless employed in the police occupation.

**passive recruitment**   when the agency has openings and takes applications from those who come to the agency; it is a 'sit back, wait, and see' approach.

**permanent employee status**   achieved after successful completion of probation; it grants additional rights and privileges related to position.

**police crime**   those acts where the officer's authority and powers as a police officer assisted or facilitated the commission of crime(s).

**polygraph**   a scientifically calibrated instrument that records physiological changes in respiration, electrical resistance of the skin, and changes in blood pressure and pulse rate; sometimes called a lie detector.

**pre-application conference**   usually a meeting with a ranking field officer for the conveyance of information about the job, the required training, and the agency's expectations of its personnel.

**probationary status**   conditional employment during which time the person's performance must meet acceptable standards, their attitudes toward others, willingness to follow orders, ability to be a team player, and so on also are under evaluation.

**promotion**   usually refers to a positive change in rank status.

**protected classes**   individuals and/or groups against which discrimination in employment is prohibited by federal, state, or local law.

**psychological interview**   discussion conducted by trained psychologists or psychiatrists, one-on-one or in group sessions, in an attempt to determine suitability, stability, and any psychopathic diseases or illnesses.

**psychometric exam**   written instruments used to measure various psychological characteristics such as intelligence, interests/preferences, and personality traits/characteristics.

**recruitment**   the development and maintenance of an adequate supply of qualified persons interested in being employed by a specific agency.

**remedies**   that portion of law consisting of various actions or conditions that can be implemented or ordered to make a person "whole" again when wronged.

**reverse discrimination**   allegation by majority members claiming that their rights have been violated by an employer who is showing unlawful preferences to minorities or women.

**ride-along**   the opportunity to accompany a uniformed patrol officer while on-duty for purposes of observation and learning more about what the job is like.

**rule of three**   the practice of considering the top three candidates on a ranked eligibility list for every open entry-level position.

**selection process**   includes the various techniques, devices, and procedures used to identify candidates to employ; it is often a series of events linked together and through which an applicant must pass in order to be hired.

**self-selection**   the concept of providing accurate, in-depth information to potential applicants so they can make an informed and more objective decision about entering the selection process.

**structured interview**   usually consists of specifically compiled questions that focus on various aspects of the job or of the applicant's abilities and background; some follow-up questions also may be asked.

**unstructured interview**   consists of general areas of focus, but the questions are not specifically spelled out.

## ■ Chapter References

Alpert, Geoffrey, W.C. Smith, and D. Watters (1992). Implications of the Rodney King beating. *Criminal Law Bulletin*, 28(5):476.

Associated Press (1998). Cop gets life in ex-wife's killing. *The Vindicator* (24 August):B4.

Associated Press (2003). Los Angeles police review big scandal. March 1, *NYTimes on the Web* as reported at http://www.truthinjustice.org/rampart-redux.htm.

Associated Press (2004). Dallas police shake-up continues. November 23, http://www.chron.com/cs/CDA/ssistory.mpl/metropolitan/2916435.

Ayres, Richard M. (1977). "Police strikes: Are we treating the symptom rather than the problem?" in Ayres and Wheelen.

Brand-Williams, Oralandar (2000). Nevers gets no break in 2nd Green sentence. *The Detroit News*. May 17, http://www.detnews.com/2000/metro/0005/17/c01-57902.htm.

Bureau of National Affairs (1993). *Individual employment rights manual*. Washington, DC: Bureau of National Affairs.

Carter, David L., Allen D. Sapp, and Darrel W. Stephens (1988). Higher education as a bona fide occupational qualification (BFOQ) for police: A blueprint. *American Journal of Police*, VIII(2):1–27.

Columbus Division of Police (2004). Pay and Benefits of a Columbus Police Officer. http://www.columbuspolice.org

Conser, James A. and Roger D. Thompson (1976). *Police selection standards and processes in Ohio: An assessment.* Youngstown, Ohio: Youngstown State University.

Conser, James A. (1980). A literary review of the police subculture: Its characteristics, impact, and policy implications. *Police Studies,* 2(4):46–54.

*Davis v. City of Dallas,* 777 F.2d 205 (1985).

Edmonds, Patricia (1993). Detroit calm for officers' beating trial. *USA Today,* June 2:2A.

Eisenberg, Terry, Deborah Kent, and Charles Wall (1973). *Police personnel practices in state and local government.* Washington, DC: Police Foundation.

Fields, Gary (1993). Indictment: DC cops bragged about crimes. *USA Today,* December 16:3A.

Gaines, Larry K., Mittie D. Southerland, and John E. Angell (1991). *Police Administration.* New York: McGraw-Hill, Inc.

Gammage, Allen Z. and Stanley L. Sachs (1977). Development of public employee/police unions in Ayres and Wheelen.

Germann, A.C. (1994). Changing the police: An impossible dream? *Law Enforcement News,* June 30:6, 10.

Gillespie, Mark (1999). One third of Americans believe police brutality exists in their area. *The Gallup News Service,* March 22. Princeton, NJ: The Gallup Organization.

*Gratz v. Bollinger,* 539 US 244 (2003)

*Griggs v. Duke Power Company,* 401 US 424 (1971).

*Grutter v. Bollinger,* 539 US 306 (2003)

Hays, Tom (1999). Brutality case testimony: Officer showed off stick used in torture. *USA Today,* May 21:5A.

Human Rights Watch (1998). Shielded from Justice: Police Brutality and Accountability in the United States, http://www.hrw.org/press98/july/polic707.htm.

Johnson, Kevin (1999). Too many believe they can't trust police, Reno says. *USA Today,* April 16:8A.

Juris, Henry A. and Peter Feuille (1974). Employee Organizations, in O. Glenn Stahl and Richard A. Staufenberger (eds.), *Police Personnel Administration.* Washington, DC: Police Foundation.

Kappeler, Victor E. (1997). *Critical issues in police civil liability.* Prospect Heights, IL: Waveland Press.

Kappeler, Victor E., Richard D. Sluder, and Geoffrey P. Alpert (1998). *Forces of deviance: Understanding the dark side of policing,* Second Edition. Prospect Heights, IL: Waveland Press, Inc.

Langworthy, R.H. and L. F. Travis III (1994). *Policing in America: A balance of forces.* New York: Macmillan Publishing Co.

*Law Enforcement News* (1994a). Around the Nation. June 15:2.

*Law Enforcement News* (1994b). NY corruption woes bring more bad news. May 15:13.

*Law Enforcement News* (1994c). Bountiful harvest of bad apples. March 31:4.

*Law Enforcement News* (1998a). Justice by the numbers. XXIV (501, 502) December 15/31:19.

*Law Enforcement News* (1998b). On the side of the law—or are they? XXIV (501, 502) December 15/31:17.

*Law Enforcement News* (1999). NYPD under fire over killing of unarmed man. XXV (507) March 15:1, 10.

*Law Enforcement News* (2003). Where there's smoke, there's fired. August 31:1, 10.

Lonsway, K.A., Patricia Aguirre, Nicole Gilliams, and Ashley Lukens (2003a). *Under scrutiny: The effect of consent decrees on the representation of women in sworn law enforcement.* Research report prepared and distributed by the National Center for Women and Policing, a division of the Feminist Majority Foundation. Available from www.womenandpolicing.org.

Lonsway, K.A., Patricia Aguirre, and Hannah Dupes (2003b). *Tearing down the wall: Problems with consistency, validity, and adverse impact of physical agility testing in police selection.* Research report prepared and distributed by the National Center for Women and Policing, a division of the Feminist Majority Foundation. Available from www.womenandpolicing.org.

Lonsway, K.A., Susan Carrington, Patricia Aguirre, and Michelle Wood (2002). *Equality denied: Status of women in policing.* Annual report of the National Center for Women and Policing, a division of the Feminist Majority Foundation. Available from www.womenandpolicing.org.

Los Angeles Police Department (2003). The blue ribbon Rampart review panel moves forward in its quest. Press Release, November 18, http://www.lapdonline.org/portal/generic.php?page=/press_releases/press_releases.htm.

Major City Chiefs Association, National Executive Institute Associates, and Federal Bureau of Investigation (1993). *Physical fitness testing in law enforcement: An analysis of the impact of the*

*Americans with Disabilities Act, The Civil Rights Act of 1991, and the Age Discrimination in Employment Act, A Conference Report*. Washington, DC: Federal Bureau of Investigation.

Meade, Patricia and Mark Niquette (1998). Six charged with taking cash, drugs. *The Vindicator*, September 2:A1.

Moriarty, Anthony R. and Mark W. Field (1989). Police psychological screening: The third generation. *The Police Chief*, February:36–40.

Moriarty, Anthony R. and Mark W. Field (1994). *Police officer selection: A handbook for law enforcement administrators*. Springfield, IL: Charles C. Thomas.

Newbold, Mark (2003). Free expression and the public safety employees. *The Police Chief*, March: 10-11.

Public Law 92-261, Section 703(a) (Civil Rights Act of 1964, Title VII).

Public sector unionism—origins and perspective—part I: historical summary (1972). *UCLA Law Review* 19(6): 893–894, in Richard M. Ayres and Thomas L. Wheelen (eds.).

Reaves, Brian and Matthew J. Hickman (2004). *Law enforcement management and administrative statistics, 2000: Data for individual state and local agencies with 100 or more officers*. Washington, DC: US Department of Justice.

Risher, Julie (2003). A chief's conundrums: Light duty, ADA, FLSA. *The Police Chief*, May:12–13.

Sauls, John Gales (1991). Employment discrimination: A title VII primer. *FBI Law Enforcement Bulletin*, December: 8–24.

Savage, David G. (1997). High court allows prop 209's repeal of affirmative action. *Los Angeles Times*. November 4:1.

Seklecki, Richard and Rebecca Paynich. (2004). A national survey of female police officers: An overview of findings. Paper presented at the national ACJS conference in Las Vegas, March. Paper has been conditionally accepted for publication by *Police Practice and Research: An International Journal*.

Shattuch, John (1973). *The lie detector as a surveillance device*. New York: American Civil Liberties Union.

Skolnick, Jerome H. and James J. Fyfe (1993). *Above the law: Police and the excessive use of force*. New York: Free Press.

Smith, Joseph D. (1975). Police unions: An historical perspective of causes and organizations. *The Police Chief*, November:24.

Spero, Sterling D. (1977). The Boston police strike in Ayers and Wheelen (eds).

Stoddard, E. (1979). Organizational norms and police discretion: An observational study of police work with traffic violators. *Criminology* 17(2):159–71.

Strawbridge, Peter and Deirdre (1990). *A networking guide to recruitment, selection and probationary training of police officers in major police departments of the United States of America*. New York: John Jay College of Criminal Justice.

Sweeney, Earl M. (1999). New Hampshire's Ongoing Fitness Assessment Program. *Annual Conference Manual*, International Association of Directors of Law Enforcement Standards and Training, Orlando, FL: June 8.

*USA Today* (1992). Police protest, August 21:3A.

*USA Today* (1999). Suit filed against California officers in fatal shooting, July 1.

Territo, Leonard (1974). The use of the polygraph in the pre-employment screening process. *The Police Chief*, July:51.

Unkelbach, L. Cary (2003). Name-clearing hearings. *The Police Chief*, July:13–16.

Vollmer, August (1969). *The police and modern society*. College Park, MD: McGrath Publishing Company. Reprint of the 1936 publication, Regents of the University of California.

Walker, Samuel and Vic W. Bumphus (1991). *Civilian review of the police: A national survey of the 50 largest cities*. Omaha, NE: University of Nebraska at Omaha.

Walker, Samuel and Vic W. Bumphus (1992). The effectiveness of civilian review: Observations on recent trends and new issues regarding the civilian review of the police. *American Journal of Police* XI (4):1–21.

Wilson, Catherine (2004). 3 Miami officers convicted in gun cover-up. Associated Press, http://www.montereyherald.com/mld/montereyherald/8330467.htm.

## 10

# Crime and Theory: Applying Values and Strategies

### Learning Objectives

Policing officials need to understand the basic aspects of crime causation and victimization. Police officers need to understand how crime impacts the local community and national policy. This chapter's focus is on crime in the United States. After studying this chapter, you should be able to:

- Describe the role of patrol officers in gathering and interpreting information.
- Identify the major methods by which we count and track crime.
- Describe the impacts of crime on communities and policy making.
- Define the major theories of crime causation.
- Identify the trends in five major areas of crime that may impact future discussions of crime causation theory.
- Compare and contrast the four major strategies of policing.
- Describe the relationship of role to policing strategy selection.
- Define the purpose of a code of ethics and explain the basic tenets of the police code of conduct.

## Chapter Outline

## Key Terms Used in This Chapter

Uniform Crime Report or UCR
Part 1 Offenses
Index Crimes
victimless crime
National Crime Victimization Survey (NCVS)
lost opportunity costs
Drug Abuse Resistance Education (DARE)
public policy
street level bureaucrats
cause of crime
utilitarian principle
pleasure-pain
rationalism
deterrence
associate
learn
differential association

Chicago School
Ecological School
subculture
labeling
social control
socialization
hackers
recidivism
strategies of policing
professional crime-fighting policing
reactive policing
preventive patrol
strategic policing
problem-solving policing
community policing
code of ethics
morality
moral behavior (or right conduct)

## ■ The Need to Understand Crime

Why must a patrol officer or field agent understand the causes of crime or how it is measured? Why should these same officers concern themselves with emerging trends in crime? Because patrol officers are the front line in the continuing struggle to control antisocial activity, and because they are the eyes and ears of law enforcement management. Patrol officers are the primary sources of community information. In order for managers to properly plan, they need to understand developing trends. Contemporary law enforcement management techniques require patrol officers to gather information and assist in its interpretation. Information on individual offenders is also important for sentencing, probation, parole, and corrections assessment. Finally, policy makers in legislative and administrative agencies rely upon data and information collected by officers to project trends and develop policy.

Often, patrol officers do not even realize they perform an information-gathering role outside of investigations. They may give statements in court or write various reports (e.g., investigative reports, supplemental reports, administrative reports, or offense reports) but usually do not think of themselves as "researchers." Officers may be the subject of opinion surveys or observation by academic researchers, and they may give policy testimony before legislative, policy-making, or other investigative boards. Finally, they may serve on a departmental team or task force reporting to the command staff on community problems and likely solutions. In each of these cases, information either gathered by officers or interpreted by officers goes beyond investigations of an individual case and can be of the utmost importance to the department and other policy-making actors.

Understanding the various theories of crime causation is one task of the professional law enforcement official. Data on crime may not match the personal experience of each officer in a given jurisdiction, nor may crime in that jurisdiction fully reflect accepted explanations on the causes of crime. General theories and approaches are just that—general. They give us a view of how things seem overall. We expect locations to differ slightly, or even in major ways, from the general trends of data. But that, too, is important for patrol officers to know. If other jurisdictions seem to have one general sort of experience, why, based upon their own experience, is their jurisdiction different? Do trends in criminal behavior in that jurisdiction differ in ways that might give officers a better understanding of the causes of criminality in their community and therefore an ability to find at least partial solutions? These questions are important and set the tone for emerging expectations of the contemporary law enforcement officer.

## Counting Crime

There are three primary sources of data on the amount of crime in the United States.

### Self-Reported Crime

The first source of crime data is self-reporting of criminal activity by offenders. This is obviously problematic and not very reliable in many instances, though it may be useful for academic research. It is also limited in scope, as it captures only a picture of one type of offense, some characteristics of some types of offenders, or types of offenders in one area. An example is data that is collected on drug and alcohol use by offenders in some cities (see **Table 10-1**). This sort of data is important for theory building, but it has less significance for community problem

## Table 10-1  Drug Test Results, By Drug By Site—Adult Arrestees, 2000

### (Percent Testing Positive)

| City | Any drug* | Cocaine | Marijuana | Opiates | Meth | PCP | Multiple drugs* |
|---|---|---|---|---|---|---|---|
| *Male* | | | | | | | |
| Albany/Capital Area, NY | 64.9% | 24.6% | 44.7% | 6.5% | 0.0% | 0.3% | 10.4% |
| Albuquerque, NM | 64.9 | 34.8 | 47.3 | 11.7 | 4.7 | 0.0 | 28.2 |
| Anchorage, AK | 52.2 | 22.1 | 37.7 | 3.5 | 0.2 | 0.0 | 10.3 |
| Atlanta, GA | 70.4 | 48.5 | 38.2 | 2.8 | 0.5 | 0.0 | 19.2 |
| Birmingham, AL | 64.8 | 33.0 | 45.3 | 10.2 | 0.2 | 0.0 | 21.8 |
| Charlotte-Metro, NC | 68.2 | 43.5 | 44.2 | 1.9 | 1.4 | 0.0 | 22.9 |
| Chicago, IL | 75.9 | 37.1 | 45.7 | 27.0 | 0.0 | 3.7 | 34.4 |
| Cleveland, OH | 72.0 | 38.4 | 49.2 | 3.7 | 0.1 | 8.1 | 25.6 |
| Dallas, TX | 54.5 | 27.7 | 35.8 | 3.0 | 2.1 | 3.9 | 14.8 |
| Denver, CO | 63.7 | 35.4 | 40.9 | 3.4 | 2.6 | 0.4 | 18.1 |
| Des Moines, IA | 55.3 | 11.0 | 41.4 | 2.7 | 18.6 | 1.7 | 19.1 |
| Detroit, MI | 69.5 | 24.4 | 49.8 | 7.8 | 0.0 | 0.0 | 11.7 |
| Fort Lauderdale, FL | 61.8 | 30.9 | 43.3 | 2.1 | 0.0 | 0.0 | 14.5 |
| Honolulu, HI | 62.9 | 15.8 | 30.4 | 6.8 | 35.9 | 0.2 | 22.6 |
| Houston, TX | 57.2 | 31.5 | 35.8 | 7.4 | 0.5 | 4.8 | 18.0 |
| Indianapolis, IN | 64.1 | 31.1 | 48.9 | 3.4 | 0.7 | 0.6 | 20.0 |
| Laredo, TX | 59.0 | 45.0 | 28.5 | 9.9 | 0.0 | 0.0 | 20.8 |
| Las Vegas, NV | 58.5 | 22.5 | 33.3 | 4.8 | 17.8 | 3.0 | 19.6 |
| Miami, FL | 62.8 | 43.5 | 38.5 | 4.0 | 0.0 | 0.0 | 22.5 |
| Minneapolis, MN | 66.7 | 25.7 | 54.2 | 3.0 | 1.6 | 1.8 | 18.5 |
| New Orleans, LA | 69.4 | 34.8 | 46.6 | 15.5 | 0.2 | 0.3 | 22.8 |
| New York, NY | 79.9 | 48.8 | 40.6 | 20.5 | 0.0 | 0.7 | 27.7 |
| Omaha, NE | 63.4 | 18.0 | 48.1 | 2.0 | 11.0 | 0.0 | 14.9 |
| Oklahoma City, OK | 74.1 | 22.4 | 57.0 | 3.2 | 11.3 | 5.2 | 24.8 |
| Philadelphia, PA | 71.9 | 30.9 | 49.4 | 11.8 | 0.0 | 2.5 | 17.8 |
| Phoenix, AZ | 65.5 | 31.9 | 33.7 | 6.6 | 19.1 | 1.7 | 24.1 |
| Portland, OR | 64.3 | 21.9 | 35.6 | 14.1 | 21.4 | 0.3 | 24.6 |
| Sacramento, CA | 73.5 | 18.4 | 50.0 | 3.3 | 29.3 | 0.3 | 25.3 |
| Salt Lake City, UT | 54.1 | 18.0 | 33.5 | 6.6 | 17.1 | 0.0 | 17.9 |
| San Antonio, TX | 52.9 | 20.4 | 40.7 | 10.2 | 0.2 | 0.0 | 17.6 |
| San Diego, CA | 65.3 | 14.8 | 38.6 | 6.0 | 26.3 | 0.1 | 20.2 |
| San Jose, CA | 52.9 | 12.1 | 35.9 | 5.9 | 21.5 | 3.6 | 21.0 |
| Seattle, WA | 64.2 | 31.3 | 37.8 | 9.9 | 9.2 | 1.4 | 21.5 |
| Spokane, WA | 57.9 | 15.1 | 40.2 | 7.9 | 20.4 | 0.8 | 21.4 |
| Tucson, AZ | 69.4 | 40.8 | 45.1 | 8.8 | 6.9 | 0.1 | 28.7 |

## Table 10-1 Drug Test Results, By Drug By Site—Adult Arrestees, 2000, continued

### (Percent Testing Positive)

| City | Any drug* | Cocaine | Marijuana | Opiates | Meth | PCP | Multiple drugs* |
|---|---|---|---|---|---|---|---|
| *Female* | | | | | | | |
| Albany/Capital Area, NY | 50.0% | 52.5% | 7.5% | 30.0% | 0.0% | 0.0% | 10.0% |
| Albuquerque, NM | 57.5 | 41.4 | 13.8 | 18.4 | 5.7 | 0.0 | 19.5 |
| Anchorage, AK | 46.2 | 23.5 | 8.4 | 27.7 | 0.8 | 0.0 | 11.8 |
| Atlanta, GA | 71.7 | 57.6 | 3.4 | 26.3 | 0.0 | 0.0 | 15.1 |
| Birmingham, AL | 53.3 | 42.2 | 4.4 | 17.8 | 2.2 | 0.0 | 13.3 |
| Chicago, IL | 79.5 | 59.2 | 40.0 | 26.4 | 0.3 | 3.2 | 41.1 |
| Cleveland, OH | 68.1 | 52.0 | 6.6 | 24.0 | 0.0 | 4.5 | 17.4 |
| Dallas, TX | 38.8 | 23.9 | 4.5 | 20.9 | 3.0 | 1.5 | 13.4 |
| Denver, CO | 70.5 | 46.9 | 5.8 | 33.8 | 5.3 | 0.0 | 19.4 |
| Des Moines, IA | 59.1 | 18.2 | 6.8 | 36.4 | 20.5 | 2.3 | 22.7 |
| Detroit, MI | 69.7 | 42.4 | 24.2 | 24.2 | 0.0 | 0.0 | 21.2 |
| Fort Lauderdale, FL | 61.3 | 44.8 | 7.2 | 28.2 | 0.0 | 0.0 | 18.2 |
| Honolulu, HI | 62.5 | 18.9 | 8.1 | 18.9 | 47.2 | 0.0 | 22.0 |
| Houston, TX | 51.7 | 31.7 | 3.3 | 26.7 | 1.7 | 1.7 | 10.0 |
| Indianapolis, IN | 72.3 | 45.4 | 6.4 | 38.3 | 0.7 | 0.0 | 18.4 |
| Laredo, TX | 31.0 | 22.4 | 6.9 | 17.2 | 0.0 | 0.0 | 12.2 |
| Las Vegas, NV | 60.9 | 27.4 | 4.8 | 25.3 | 20.6 | 1.3 | 16.0 |
| Los Angeles, CA | 64.6 | 33.1 | 7.7 | 31.5 | 12.3 | 1.5 | 19.2 |
| New Orleans, LA | 56.5 | 41.1 | 8.5 | 28.0 | 0.4 | 0.4 | 19.5 |
| New York, NY | 74.9 | 53.0 | 19.1 | 28.2 | 0.0 | 1.3 | 23.5 |
| Omaha, NE | 52.6 | 22.4 | 1.3 | 32.9 | 13.2 | 0.0 | 13.2 |
| Oklahoma City, OK | 67.2 | 27.2 | 4.6 | 44.7 | 16.2 | 4.3 | 25.8 |
| Philadelphia, PA | 59.3 | 40.7 | 11.1 | 22.2 | 0.0 | 3.7 | 16.7 |
| Phoenix, AZ | 66.3 | 35.0 | 6.4 | 23.1 | 24.1 | 1.0 | 21.2 |
| Portland, OR | 69.2 | 29.9 | 22.2 | 26.2 | 23.5 | 0.0 | 28.1 |
| Salt Lake City, UT | 59.2 | 14.5 | 9.2 | 25.0 | 28.9 | 0.0 | 14.5 |
| San Diego, CA | 66.4 | 26.1 | 7.5 | 27.2 | 28.7 | 0.4 | 21.3 |
| San Jose, CA | 68.0 | 7.8 | 3.9 | 29.4 | 40.0 | 2.0 | 14.0 |
| Tucson, AZ | 70.7 | 49.6 | 17.9 | 28.5 | 9.0 | 0.0 | 32.0 |

Note: These data are from the Arrestee Drug Abuse Monitoring (ADAM) program sponsored by the National Institute of Justice. ADAM data are collected in booking facilities in participating cities throughout the United States.

Note that several cities did not test or interview female arrestees.

* Includes NIDA-5 drugs (cocaine, opiates, marijuana, methamphetamines, and phencyclidine (PCP).

*Source:* Reprinted from National Institute of Justice (2003). *Annual Report 2000: Arrestee Drug Abuse Monitoring.* US Department of Justice, p. 21 and 108.

- Arson
- Assault
- Burglary
- Forcible rape
- Larceny-theft
- Motor vehicle theft
- Murder and non-negligent manslaughter
- Robbery

*Source*: Federal Bureau of Investigation (2002).

**Figure 10-1** Part 1 offenses/index crimes.

solving. Therefore, we tend to rely upon other sources of major crime data.

## Reported Crime

The second and most commonly known data source is taken from offenses reported to police and is counted at the level of the local law enforcement agency. Collected and presented in the **Uniform Crime Report** or **UCR**, it is published annually by the FBI under the title *Crime in the United States*. Participating law enforcement agencies keep monthly records of offenses reported to or discovered by police. Monthly totals are then forwarded to the Federal Bureau of Investigation. Monthly reports have two parts. **Part 1 Offenses** are called **Index Crimes** and are those from which the FBI tracks the "Crime Index," which it reports to the nation through the media (see **Figure 10-1**). If you read or hear a story in the media that crime was reported going up or down, it is likely based upon this data. These offenses are used to gauge the crime "index," or its rate of decrease or increase.

**Table 10-2** shows the total reported numbers of Index offenses for the past two decades. In 2002 there were 11,877,218 Index (Part 1) offenses reported to law enforcement agencies. Of that, 1,426,325 were violent offenses. This is expressed, however, as the rate of Index offenses per 100,000 people. We express it as a rate in order to compare periods and take into consideration population growth. The index is shown for the past two decades in **Table 10-3** (Maguire and Pastore 2004). The 1993 Crime Index fell 3% from 1992, with similar drops up through 1995. The crime rate fell between 1991and 2000, and then a slight increase occurred in 2001. In 2002, the crime rate again slightly decreased. Early figures from 2003 show a slight decrease from 2002.

There are some problems with this method of counting, however. First, it covers only crime reported to law enforcement, and much of the crime committed in the United States is not reported. Hence, if victims change their behavior and report more crimes, the result may leave the impression that crime is increasing. This may not be true and is a significant problem. Second, if law enforcement agencies become more effective in discovering crimes, the rate will seem to increase because more crime was discovered. Third, the definitions of crimes are not the same from state to state and, in some cases, from year to year. For example, an offense such as entering an outbuilding (storage shed) might be a criminal trespass in Ohio, but a burglary in Georgia. One is a minor offense, while the other is more serious. A fourth problem with the UCR is that it does not account for **victimless crime**, which is behavior defined as criminal but engaged in by many who think it should not be. Generally, this includes prostitution, gambling, drug abuse, pornography, and others. The fifth problem with the UCR is that it relies on victims to report crimes. If victims do not trust police or the criminal justice system, or fear retaliation or humiliation, they may never report victimization. For all of these reasons and more, the UCR alone is not sufficient for us to grasp the true rate of crime. **Figure 10-2** summarizes the problems with the UCR discussed here.

## Table 10-2 Estimated Number of Offenses Known to Police, 1976–2002

| Number of offenses for year | Total crime index[a] | Violent crime[b] | Property crime[b] | Murder and non-negligent manslaughter | Forcible rape | Robbery | Aggravated assault | Burglary | Larceny-theft | Motor vehicle theft |
|---|---|---|---|---|---|---|---|---|---|---|
| 1976 | 11,349,700 | 1,004,210 | 10,345,500 | 18,780 | 57,080 | 427,810 | 500,530 | 3,108,700 | 6,270,800 | 966,000 |
| 1977 | 10,984,500 | 1,029,580 | 9,955,000 | 19,120 | 63,500 | 412,610 | 534,350 | 3,071,500 | 5,905,700 | 977,700 |
| 1978 | 11,209,000 | 1,085,550 | 10,123,400 | 19,560 | 67,610 | 426,930 | 571,460 | 3,128,300 | 5,991,000 | 1,004,100 |
| 1979 | 12,249,500 | 1,208,030 | 11,401,500 | 21,460 | 76,390 | 480,700 | 629,480 | 3,327,700 | 6,601,000 | 1,112,800 |
| 1980 | 13,408,300 | 1,344,520 | 12,063,700 | 23,040 | 82,990 | 565,840 | 672,650 | 3,795,200 | 7,136,900 | 1,131,700 |
| 1981 | 13,423,800 | 1,361,820 | 12,061,900 | 22,520 | 82,500 | 592,910 | 663,900 | 3,779,700 | 7,194,400 | 1,087,800 |
| 1982 | 12,974,400 | 1,322,390 | 11,652,000 | 21,010 | 78,770 | 553,130 | 669,480 | 3,447,100 | 7,142,500 | 1,062,400 |
| 1983 | 12,108,630 | 1,258,087 | 10,850,543 | 19,308 | 78,918 | 506,567 | 653,294 | 3,129,851 | 6,712,759 | 1,007,933 |
| 1984 | 11,881,755 | 1,273,282 | 10,608,473 | 18,692 | 84,233 | 485,008 | 685,349 | 2,984,434 | 6,591,874 | 1,032,165 |
| 1985 | 12,430,357 | 1,327,767 | 11,102,590 | 18,976 | 88,671 | 497,874 | 723,246 | 3,073,348 | 6,926,380 | 1,102,862 |
| 1986 | 13,211,869 | 1,489,169 | 11,722,700 | 20,613 | 91,459 | 542,775 | 834,322 | 3,241,410 | 7,257,153 | 1,224,137 |
| 1987 | 13,508,708 | 1,483,999 | 12,024,709 | 20,096 | 91,111 | 517,704 | 855,088 | 3,236,184 | 7,499,851 | 1,288,674 |
| 1988 | 13,923,086 | 1,566,221 | 12,356,865 | 20,675 | 92,486 | 542,968 | 910,092 | 3,218,077 | 7,705,872 | 1,432,916 |
| 1989 | 14,251,449 | 1,646,037 | 12,605,412 | 21,500 | 94,504 | 578,326 | 951,707 | 3,168,170 | 7,872,442 | 1,564,800 |
| 1990 | 14,475,613 | 1,820,127 | 12,655,486 | 23,438 | 102,555 | 639,271 | 1,054,863 | 3,073,909 | 7,945,670 | 1,635,907 |
| 1991 | 14,872,883 | 1,911,767 | 12,961,116 | 24,703 | 106,593 | 687,732 | 1,092,739 | 3,157,150 | 8,142,228 | 1,661,738 |
| 1992 | 14,438,191 | 1,932,274 | 12,505,917 | 23,760 | 109,062 | 672,478 | 1,126,974 | 2,979,884 | 7,915,199 | 1,610,834 |
| 1993 | 14,144,794 | 1,926,017 | 12,218,777 | 24,526 | 106,014 | 659,870 | 1,135,607 | 2,834,808 | 7,820,909 | 1,563,060 |

continued

**Table 10-2  Estimated Number of Offenses Known to Police, 1976–2002, continued**

| Number of offenses for year | Total crime index[a] | Violent crime[b] | Property crime[b] | Murder and non-negligent manslaughter | Forcible rape | Robbery | Aggravated assault | Burglary | Larceny-theft | Motor vehicle theft |
|---|---|---|---|---|---|---|---|---|---|---|
| 1994 | 13,989,543 | 1,857,670 | 12,131,873 | 23,326 | 102,216 | 618,949 | 1,113,179 | 2,712,774 | 7,879,812 | 1,539,287 |
| 1995 | 13,867,727 | 1,798,792 | 12,063,935 | 21,606 | 97,470 | 580,509 | 1,099,207 | 2,593,784 | 7,997,710 | 1,472,441 |
| 1996 | 13,493,863 | 1,688,540 | 11,805,323 | 19,645 | 96,252 | 535,594 | 1,037,049 | 2,506,400 | 7,904,685 | 1,394,238 |
| 1997 | 13,194,571 | 1,636,096 | 11,558,475 | 18,208 | 96,153 | 498,534 | 1,023,201 | 2,460,526 | 7,743,760 | 1,354,189 |
| 1998 | 12,485,714 | 1,533,887 | 10,951,827 | 16,974 | 93,144 | 447,186 | 976,583 | 2,332,735 | 7,376,311 | 1,242,781 |
| 1999 | 11,634,378 | 1,426,044 | 10,208,334 | 15,522 | 89,411 | 409,371 | 911,740 | 2,100,739 | 6,955,520 | 1,152,075 |
| 2000 | 11,608,070 | 1,425,486 | 10,182,584 | 15,586 | 90,178 | 408,016 | 911,706 | 2,050,992 | 6,971,590 | 1,160,002 |
| 2001 | 11,876,669 | 1,439,480 | 10,437,189 | 16,037[c] | 90,863 | 423,557 | 909,023 | 2,116,531 | 7,092,267 | 1,228,391 |
| 2002 | 11,877,218 | 1,426,325 | 10,450,893 | 16,204 | 95,136 | 420,637 | 894,348 | 2,151,875 | 7,052,922 | 1,246,096 |

[a]Because of rounding, the offenses may not add to totals.

[b]Violent crimes are offenses of murder and non-negligent manslaughter, forcible rape, robbery, and aggravated assault. Property crimes are offenses of burglary, larceny-theft, and motor vehicle theft. Data are not included for the property crime of arson.

[c]The murders and non-negligent manslaughters that occurred as a result of the events of September 11, 2001 are not included in this table.

*Source:* Compiled from Maguire, Kathleen and Ann L. Pastore (eds.) (2003). *Sourcebook of Criminal Justice Statistics 2002* [Online]. Available online: http://www.albany.edu/sourcebook/ [12/14/04]; *Sourcebook of Criminal Justice Statistics, 1996,* p. 309, US Department of Justice, Bureau of Justice Statistics, 1997; *Crime in the United States, 2002,* p. 66; and *1995,* p. 58, US Department of Justice, Federal Bureau of Investigation (Washington, DC: US Government Printing Office).

**Table 10-3   Estimated Rate Per 100,000 Inhabitants of Offenses Known to Police, 1976–2002**

| Year | Total crime index[a] | Violent crime[b] | Property crime[b] | Murder and non-negligent manslaughter[c] | Forcible rape | Robbery | Aggravated assault | Burglary | Larceny-theft | Motor vehicle theft |
|---|---|---|---|---|---|---|---|---|---|---|
| 1976 | 5,287.3 | 467.8 | 4,819.5 | 8.8 | 26.6 | 199.3 | 233.2 | 1,448.2 | 2,921.3 | 450.0 |
| 1977 | 5,077.6 | 475.9 | 4,601.7 | 8.8 | 29.4 | 190.7 | 240.0 | 1,419.8 | 2,729.9 | 451.9 |
| 1978 | 5,140.3 | 497.8 | 4,642.6 | 9.0 | 31.0 | 195.8 | 262.1 | 1,434.6 | 2,747.4 | 460.5 |
| 1979 | 5,565.5 | 548.9 | 5,016.6 | 9.7 | 34.7 | 218.4 | 286.0 | 1,511.9 | 2,999.1 | 505.6 |
| 1980 | 5,950.0 | 596.6 | 5,353.3 | 10.2 | 36.8 | 251.1 | 298.5 | 1,684.1 | 3,167.0 | 502.2 |
| 1981 | 5,850.0 | 593.5 | 5,256.5 | 9.8 | 36.0 | 258.4 | 289.3 | 1,647.2 | 3,135.3 | 474.1 |
| 1982 | 5,600.5 | 570.8 | 5,029.7 | 9.1 | 34.0 | 238.8 | 289.0 | 1,488.0 | 3,083.1 | 458.8 |
| 1983 | 5,179.2 | 538.1 | 4,641.1 | 8.3 | 33.8 | 216.7 | 279.4 | 1,338.7 | 2,871.3 | 431.1 |
| 1984 | 5,038.4 | 539.9 | 4,498.5 | 7.9 | 35.7 | 205.7 | 290.6 | 1,265.5 | 2,795.2 | 437.7 |
| 1985 | 5,224.5 | 558.1 | 4,666.4 | 8.0 | 36.8 | 209.3 | 304.0 | 1,291.7 | 2,911.2 | 463.5 |
| 1986 | 5,501.9 | 620.1 | 4,881.8 | 8.6 | 38.1 | 226.0 | 347.4 | 1,349.8 | 3,022.1 | 509.8 |
| 1987 | 5,575.5 | 612.5 | 4,963.0 | 8.3 | 37.6 | 213.7 | 352.9 | 1,335.7 | 3,095.4 | 531.9 |
| 1988 | 5,694.5 | 640.6 | 5,054.0 | 8.5 | 37.8 | 222.1 | 372.2 | 1,316.2 | 3,151.7 | 586.1 |
| 1989 | 5,774.0 | 669.9 | 5,107.1 | 8.7 | 38.3 | 234.3 | 385.6 | 1,283.6 | 3,189.6 | 634.0 |
| 1990 | 5,802.7 | 729.6 | 5,073.1 | 9.4 | 41.1 | 256.3 | 422.9 | 1,232.2 | 3,185.1 | 655.8 |
| 1991 | 5,898.4 | 758.2 | 5,140.2 | 9.8 | 42.3 | 272.7 | 433.4 | 1,252.1 | 3,229.1 | 659.0 |
| 1992 | 5,661.4 | 757.7 | 4,903.7 | 9.3 | 42.8 | 263.7 | 441.9 | 1,168.4 | 3,103.6 | 631.6 |
| 1993 | 5,487.1 | 747.1 | 4,740.0 | 9.5 | 41.1 | 256.0 | 440.5 | 1,099.7 | 3,033.9 | 606.3 |

continued

## Table 10-3 Estimated Rate Per 100,000 Inhabitants of Offenses Known to Police, 1976–2002, continued

| Year | Total crime index[a] | Violent crime[b] | Property crime[b] | Murder and non-negligent manslaughter[c] | Forcible rape | Robbery | Aggravated assault | Burglary | Larceny-theft | Motor vehicle theft |
|---|---|---|---|---|---|---|---|---|---|---|
| 1994 | 5,373.8 | 713.6 | 4,660.2 | 9.0 | 39.3 | 237.8 | 427.6 | 1,042.1 | 3,026.9 | 591.3 |
| 1995 | 5,274.9 | 684.5 | 4,590.5 | 8.2 | 37.1 | 220.9 | 418.3 | 987.0 | 3,043.2 | 560.3 |
| 1996 | 5,087.6 | 636.6 | 4,451.0 | 7.4 | 36.6 | 201.9 | 391.0 | 945.0 | 2,980.3 | 525.7 |
| 1997 | 4,927.3 | 611.0 | 4,316.3 | 6.8 | 35.9 | 186.2 | 382.1 | 918.8 | 2,891.8 | 505.7 |
| 1998 | 4,620.1 | 567.6 | 4,052.5 | 6.3 | 34.5 | 165.5 | 361.4 | 863.2 | 2,729.5 | 459.9 |
| 1999 | 4,266.5 | 523.0 | 3,743.6 | 5.7 | 32.8 | 150.1 | 334.3 | 770.4 | 2,550.7 | 422.5 |
| 2000 | 4,124.8 | 506.5 | 3,618.3 | 5.5 | 32.0 | 145.0 | 324.0 | 728.8 | 2,477.3 | 412.2 |
| 2001 | 4,162.6 | 504.5 | 3,658.1 | 5.6[c] | 31.8 | 148.5 | 318.6 | 741.8 | 2,485.7 | 430.5 |
| 2002 | 4,118.8 | 494.6 | 3,624.1 | 5.6 | 33.0 | 145.9 | 310.1 | 746.2 | 2,445.8 | 432.1 |

[a]Because of rounding, the offenses may not add to totals.

[b]Violent crimes are offenses of murder and non-negligent manslaughter, forcible rape, robbery, and aggravated assault. Property crimes are offenses of burglary, larceny-theft, and motor-vehicle theft. Data are not included for the property crime of arson.

[c]The murders and non-negligent manslaughters that occurred as a result of the events of Sept. 11, 2001 are not included in this table.

Note: All rates were calculated on the number of offenses before rounding.

Source: Compiled from Maguire, Kathleen and Ann L. Pastore (eds.) (2003). Sourcebook of Criminal Justice Statistics 2002 [Online]. Available online: http://www.albany.edu/sourcebook/ [12/14/04]; Sourcebook of Criminal Justice Statistics, 1996, p. 309, US Department of Justice, Bureau of Justice Statistics, 1997; Crime in the United States, 2002, p. 66; and 1995, p. 58, US Department of Justice, Federal Bureau of Investigation (Washington, DC: US Government Printing Office).

## Victim Studies

A third means of measuring crime derives from the **National Crime Victimization Survey (NCVS)**. This is a survey of thousands of households conducted for the Bureau of Justice Statistics (US Department of Justice) by the Federal Bureau of the Census. Essentially, this survey measures crimes that were committed against households, residents, and businesses. In conducting the survey, people are asked if they have been the victim of a crime in the past year and, if so, to describe it. Detailed information is acquired for each victimization. On the basis of this broad survey, estimates are generated for the nation as a whole. The NCVS provides interesting information, such as the fact that the rate of victimization is generally going down, not up. However, as much as 65% of all crime is not reported. For example, of the 167,550 rapes that were estimated to have occurred in 1994, only 102,100 were reported to police.

- Crime increases in Index may reflect changed enforcement, not crime
- Only includes crimes actually reported to law enforcement agencies
- Same actions are given different names in different states
- Cannot provide accurate count for victimless crimes
- Depends largely upon victim reporting behavior

**Figure 10-2** Problems with UCR data.

Still, victimization surveys are limited. Self-reported recollections, as noted above, are not reliable, and each respondent is going to interpret events from his or her own perspective. She or he may see a situation as an assault when it was not. Another limitation of the NCVS, like that of the UCR, is its inability to capture information regarding white collar crime and fraud, or information about crimes in which the respondent may have been involved. Respondents must be relied upon to report offender characteristics, and frequently this information is not known to the victim at all. Information from the NCVS is important, but it is limited as well, and we need to keep that in mind while interpreting it.

## Impact of Crime

The rate of crime and the impression it leaves has very clear effects in society. First, this can affect policy decisions. In late 1993, Congress passed a crime bill that, among other things, provided for the addition of 100,000 police officers on the streets of the United States. This major policy shift resulted from the perception of increased crime. But was crime increasing? As **Figure 10-3** graphically illustrates, general victimization rates were falling overall, and, while violent crime increased in the period from 1990 to 1994, it decreased in 1995 and continued falling through 2001. Violence, of course, is what most people fear, and many people believe violence is increasing, but Figure 10-3 depicts a downward trend. **Table 10-4** presents the estimated number, percent distribution, and rate of victimizations for both personal and property crimes for 2002 according to National Crime Victimization Survey data. The important thing for law enforcement departments to make clear is the status of offending in their own community. Use of national data can cause erroneous perceptions.

The sense of increasing crime produced demands, beginning in the 1980s, for stiffer penalties and longer sentences, and for a greater portion of the sentence to actually be served. Hence, while victimization studies consistently showed a general decrease in offenses against persons and households between 1980 and 1995, the rate of imprisonment increased dramatically. As **Table 10-5** demonstrates, the rate

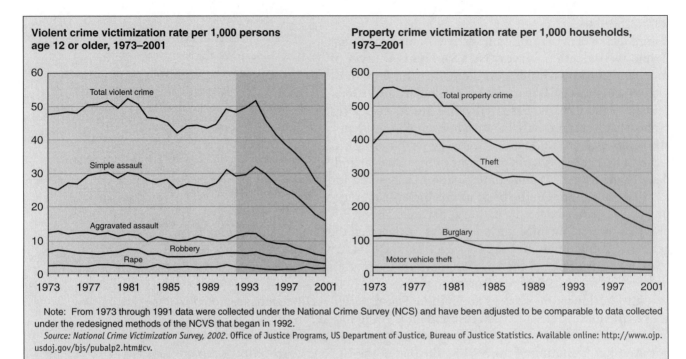

**Figure 10-3** Crime victimization rates 1973–2001.

with which people were placed in prison escalated quickly between 1980 and 2003—a rate of increase far greater than the drop in the crime rate over the same period.

Other impacts can be less immediate but no less clear. There are social and economic costs associated with each offense, including loss of income and property, as well as increased medical costs and insurance. Families of both victim and perpetrator are damaged, and there are costs to society as well (see **Figure 10-4**). Policing, prosecution, and incarceration costs, loss of productivity, and distribution of medical costs by way of insurance premiums or taxes are only some of these costs. **Lost opportunity costs** are also tangible. These losses represent the things that society and victims could have done with the money otherwise wasted on crime. Other losses are community pride and attractiveness. In the wake of the riots associated with the Rodney King case, community groups tried to rebuild South-Central Los Angeles, but they found few investors who wanted to risk their money in an area that was thought to be crime- and gang-ridden. The net result is a general and steady decline in the standard of living in the area. This affects the social fabric of the community, the schools, and overall patterns of crime. In effect, it is a spiral of decline. Research has consistently demonstrated that if people in an area feel safe, they behave differently. Investing, spending, and communication increase, even if the crime rate is stable. Therefore, one of the major impacts of crime prevention and community policing programs has been the elevation of a sense of community security (Skogan 1990).

## Changing Patterns of Crime

In the latest edition of his book *Sense and Nonsense about Crime and Drugs*, Samuel Walker argues that the patterns of crime have changed in the past decade for

## Table 10-4   Number, Percent Distribution, and Rate of Victimizations by Type of Crime, 2002

| Type of Crime | Number of victimizations | Percent of all victimizations | Rate per 1,000 persons or households |
|---|---|---|---|
| All crimes | 23,036,030 | 100% | NA |
| | | | |
| **Personal crimes** | **5,496,810** | **23.9** | **23.7** |
| Crimes of violence | 5,341,410 | 23.2 | 50.8 |
| Completed violence | 1,753,090 | 7.6 | 7.6 |
| Attempted/threatened violence | 3,588,320 | 15.6 | 15.5 |
| Rape/sexual assault | 247,730 | 1.1 | 1.1 |
| Rape/attempted rape | 167,860 | 0.7 | 0.7 |
| Rape | 90,390 | 0.4 | 0.4 |
| Attempted rape | 77,470 | 0.3 | 0.3 |
| Sexual assault | 79,870 | 0.3 | 0.3 |
| Robbery | 512,490 | 2.2 | 2.2 |
| Completed/property taken | 385,880 | 1.7 | 1.7 |
| With injury | 169,980 | 0.7 | 0.7 |
| Without injury | 215,890 | 0.9 | 0.9 |
| Attempted to take property | 126,610 | 0.5 | 0.5 |
| With injury | 42,600 | 0.2 | 0.2 |
| Without injury | 84,020 | 0.4 | 0.4 |
| Assault | 4,581,190 | 19.9 | 19.8 |
| Aggravated | 990,110 | 4.3 | 4.3 |
| With injury | 316,260 | 1.4 | 1.4 |
| Threatened with weapon | 673,850 | 2.9 | 2.9 |
| Simple | 3,591,090 | 15.6 | 15.5 |
| With minor injury | 906,580 | 3.9 | 3.9 |
| Without injury | 2,684,510 | 11.7 | 11.6 |
| Purse snatching/ pocket picking | 155,400 | 0.7 | 0.7 |
| Completed purse snatching | 55,400 | 0.2 | 0.2 |
| Attempted purse snatching | 2,140* | 0.0* | 0.0* |
| Pocket picking | 97,860 | 0.4 | 0.4 |
| | | | |
| Total population age 12 and older | 231,589,260 | X | X |

*continued*

| Table 10-4 | Number, Percent Distribution, and Rate of Victimizations by Type of Crime, 2002, continued | | |
|---|---|---|---|

| Type of Crime | Number of victimizations | Percent of all victimizations | Rate per 1,000 persons or households |
|---|---|---|---|
| **Property crimes** | 17,539,220 | 76.1 | 159.0 |
| Household burglary | 3,055,720 | 13.3 | 27.7 |
| Completed | 2,597,310 | 11.3 | 23.5 |
| Forcible entry | 1,017,660 | 4.4 | 9.2 |
| Unlawful entry without force | 1,579,650 | 6.9 | 14.3 |
| Attempted forcible entry | 458,410 | 2.0 | 4.2 |
| Motor vehicle theft | 988,760 | 4.3 | 9.0 |
| Completed | 780,630 | 3.4 | 7.1 |
| Attempted | 208,120 | 0.9 | 1.9 |
| Theft | 13,494,750 | 58.6 | 122.3 |
| Completed | 13,039,920 | 58.6 | 118.2 |
| Less than $50 | 4,186,570 | 18.2 | 37.9 |
| $50 to $249 | 4,455,080 | 19.3 | 40.4 |
| $250 or more | 3,270,530 | 14.2 | 29.6 |
| Amount not available | 1,127,740 | 4.9 | 10.2 |
| Attempted | 454,830 | 2.0 | 4.1 |
| | | | |
| Total number of households | 110,323,840 | X | X |

Note: The National Crime Victimization Survey (NCVS) is conducted annually for the US Department of Justice, Bureau of Justice Statistics by the US Bureau of the Census. These estimates are based on data derived from a continuous survey of a representative sample of housing units in the United States. Readers should note that murder is not measured by the NCVS because of the inability to question the victim. The NCVS has undergone a redesign and all data presented are based on the redesigned survey. Detail may not add to total because of rounding.

*Estimate is based on about 10 or fewer sample cases.

*Source:* Reprinted from Maguire, Kathleen and Ann L. Pastore, eds. *Sourcebook of Criminal Justice Statistics* [Online]. Available online: http://www.albany.edu/sourcebook/ [12/14/04], citing Criminal Victimization in the United States, 2002, (US Government Printing Office), Table 1, 2002, US Department of Justice, Bureau of Justice Statistics.

several reasons. First, he argues that the "get tough" policies of the 1980s generally failed. Not that they failed in getting tough—rather, the whole idea of getting tougher did not produce an expected dramatic reduction in crime. Second, the appearance of crack cocaine altered the crime problem by changing the manner in which drugs were marketed. Crack was cheaper, more easily transported, and offered a higher profit potential than other drugs, including other forms of cocaine. The latter fact invited widespread violence as gangs fought over "turf" and market share. In behavior reminiscent of the bootleg days of the 1920s, murder escalated in the major cities of the United States.

A third change was also the result of drugs. In the 1980s, a new war on drugs emerged as middle-class white America brought political pressure to do something about drug use in the country. The result was a rapid tripling of the prison population nationwide, much of this coming in the form of drug convictions (Walker 1998). As prisons became overcrowded, conditions deteriorated,

| Table 10-5 | Adults On Probation, In Jail or Prison, and On Parole, 1980–2003 | | | | |
|---|---|---|---|---|---|
| Year | Total estimated correctional population[a] | Probation | Jail | Prison | Parole |
| 1980 | 1,840,400 | 1,118,097 | 182,288[b] | 319,598 | 220,438 |
| 1981 | 2,006,600 | 1,225,934 | 195,085[b] | 360,029 | 225,539 |
| 1982 | 2,192,600 | 1,357,264 | 207,853 | 402,914 | 224,604 |
| 1983 | 2,475,100 | 1,582,947 | 221,815 | 423,898 | 246,440 |
| 1984 | 2,689,200 | 1,740,948 | 233,018 | 448,264 | 266,992 |
| 1985 | 3,011,500 | 1,968,712 | 254,986 | 487,593 | 300,203 |
| 1986 | 3,239,400 | 2,114,621 | 272,735 | 526,436 | 325,638 |
| 1987 | 3,459,600 | 2,247,158 | 294,092 | 562,814 | 355,505 |
| 1988 | 3,714,100 | 2,356,483 | 341,893 | 607,766 | 407,977 |
| 1989 | 4,055,600 | 2,522,125 | 393,303 | 683,367 | 456,803 |
| 1990 | 4,350,300 | 2,670,234 | 405,320 | 743,382 | 531,407 |
| 1991 | 4,535,600 | 2,728,472 | 424,129[c] | 792,535 | 590,442 |
| 1992 | 4,762,600 | 2,811,611 | 441,781[c] | 850,566 | 658,601 |
| 1993 | 4,944,000 | 2,903,061 | 455,500[c] | 909,381 | 676,100 |
| 1994 | 5,141,300 | 2,981,022 | 479,800 | 990,147 | 690,371 |
| 1995 | 5,342,900 | 3,077,861 | 507,044 | 1,078,542 | 679,421 |
| 1996 | 5,490,700 | 3,164,996 | 518,492 | 1,127,528 | 679,733 |
| 1997[d] | 5,734,900 | 3,296,513 | 567,079 | 1,176,564 | 694,787 |
| 1998[d] | 6,134,200 | 3,670,441 | 592,462 | 1,224,469 | 696,385 |
| 1999[d] | 6,340,800 | 3,779,922 | 605,943 | 1,287,172 | 714,457 |
| 2000 | 6,445,100 | 3,826,209 | 621,149 | 1,316,333 | 723,898 |
| 2001 | 6,581,700 | 3,931,731 | 631,240 | 1,330,007 | 732,333 |
| 2002 | 6,759,100 | 6,759,100 | 665,475 | 1,367,856 | 750,934 |
| 2003 | 6,889,800 | 6,889,800 | 691,301 | 1,387,269[e] | 774,588 |

*continued*

| Table 10-5 | Adults On Probation, In Jail or Prison, and On Parole, 1980–2003, continued | | | | |
|---|---|---|---|---|---|
| Year | Total estimated correctional population[a] | Probation | Jail | Prison | Parole |
| *Percent change* | | | | | |
| 2002 to 2003 | 1.9% | 1.2% | 3.9% | 2.3% | 3.1% |
| 1995 to 2002 | 2.9 | 3.1 | 4.0 | 3.5 | 1.5 |
| 1985 to 1995 | 78.5 | 57.3 | 95.8 | 121.2 | 133.2 |

Note: Counts for probation, prison, and parole population are for December 31 of each year; jail population counts are for June 30 of each year. Counts of adults held in jail facilities for 1993 and 1994 were estimated and rounded to the nearest 100. Data for jail and prison are for inmates under custody and include those held in private facilities. Totals for 1998–2003 exclude probationers held in jail or prison. These data have been revised by the source based on the most recently reported counts and may differ from previous editions of *Sourcebook*.

[a]A small number of individuals may have multiple correctional statuses; the total number of persons under correctional supervision is an overestimate.

[b]Estimated.

[c]Includes an unknown number of persons supervised outside jail facilities.

[d]Coverage of probation agencies was expanded. For counts based on the same reporting agencies, use 3,266,837 in 1997 (to compare with 1996); 3,417,613 in 1998 (to compare with 1997); and 3,772,773 in 1999 (to compare with 1998).

[e]As of June 30, 2003.

*Source:* Reprinted from Maguire, Kathleen and Ann L. Pastore, eds. *Sourcebook of Criminal Justice Statistics* [Online]. Available online: http://www.albany.edu/sourcebook/ [12/14/04], citing Probation and Parole in the United States, 2003, (US Government Printing Office), Table 6.1, 2003, US Department of Justice, Bureau of Justice Statistics.

and rehabilitation took a back seat. The crush of cases also inundated the criminal justice system generally. Law enforcement allocated tremendous resources to this crime type, and the courts were overwhelmed by the increased case loads. This left less prison space for violent offenders and fewer law enforcement resources for other areas such as violent crime investigation and patrol activities. Coupled with budget cuts, law enforcement was left more overworked than before. Limited community services that might have helped many who could turn themselves around were further reduced. Despite clear evidence that most offenders can be directed away from crime without the potentially harmful effects of incarceration, incarceration rates increased. Those convicted of nonviolent offenses (e.g., drug offenses) were given priority thereby pushing more violent offenders onto probation and parole (Irwin 1994). During the late 1980s and continuing through the late 1990s we also have experienced

- Community pride and attractiveness
- Families damaged
- Incarceration costs
- Increased medical costs
- Increased insurance costs
- Loss and damage to property
- Loss of income
- Loss of productivity
- Lost opportunity costs
- Policing
- Prosecution
- Tax revenue loss

**Figure 10-4** The costs of crime.

a serious increase in the violence of juveniles, despite an overall decline in violent crime in the late 1990s.

For patrol officers in major cities, these changes meant an increased level of danger associated with the job. While the number of American police officers killed each year declined between 1980 and 2002 (104 to 56), the number assaulted remained relatively stable (57,847 to 58,066), despite a jump to more than 81,000 in 1992 (see **Table 10-6**). These conditions are bad enough to keep the level of stress for patrol officers high and reduce the degree of positive interaction with citizens, thereby hampering efforts to reduce crime.

These conditions also significantly altered the social conditions in cities. Earlier, we noted that crime was decreasing rather than increasing. Based upon victimization studies as opposed to crime indexes, this trend was relatively consistent for the 15 years preceding 1995. However, violent crime increased in some major cities in that same period. Drug arrests, which also dramatically increased, tended to cluster in the major cities. Hence, while the average American was less likely to be a victim of crime in 1995 than in 1978, the average poor citizen and the average African-American citizen were more likely to be a crime victim than had been the case only a decade earlier. The decreased level of safety felt by citizens, mixed with law enforcement's increased sense of community hostility and the clustering of arrests in particular areas in the cities, resulted in increased community resentment and fear. Patrol officers became less connected to the population, more reactive, more aggressive, and more hostile. These pervasive feelings contributed to the Rodney King incident. These same conditions ushered in the advent of Community Policing as a major initiative in law enforcement to reconnect law enforcement to the community it served. In many ways, changing crime patterns produced changes in community responses toward law enforcement and in law enforcement's approach to communities.

The lessons are clear for patrol officers. They must learn to see past the immediate incident, avoid stereotyping, and look for larger trends revealed by the big picture. Many of the problems encountered by patrol officers in cities are the result of a bad mix of poverty, drugs, and despair. Intervention in and interaction with the community are necessary both to reduce opportunities for crime and reduce tensions. Crime prevention approaches are as important as arrests. In order to make **Drug Abuse Resistance Education (DARE)**, Neighborhood Watch, or other community involvement approaches work, patrol officers must know the community and become connected to it. They are the eyes and the ears of policy creation and implementation.

## ■ Causes of Crime—Overview

**Public policy** is the sum total of what the government decides to do. Public policy is made by elected officials in a democracy and is carried out by administrative agents in executive agencies such as law enforcement agencies. Patrol officers are, in effect, administrative agents or **street level bureaucrats** with a tremendous amount of discretion (Lipsky 1980). Though they cannot decide what the law is, they can and do decide when to use the law. Policy makers identify problems

**Table 10-6** **Assaults on Law Enforcement Officers and Percent Receiving Personal Injury— By Type of Weapon Used, 1980–1995**

| | | Type of weapon used | | | |
|---|---|---|---|---|---|
| | Total victims | Firearm | Personal weapon | Knife or cutting instrument | Other dangerous weapon |
| **Total** | | | | | |
| 1980 | 57,847 | 3,295 | 47,484 | 1,653 | 5,415 |
| 1981 | 57,174 | 3,334 | 47,304 | 1,733 | 4,803 |
| 1982 | 55,775 | 2,642 | 46,802 | 1,452 | 4,879 |
| 1983 | 62,324 | 3,067 | 51,901 | 1,829 | 5,527 |
| 1984 | 60,153 | 2,654 | 50,689 | 1,662 | 5,148 |
| 1985 | 61,724 | 2,793 | 51,953 | 1,715 | 5,263 |
| 1986 | 64,259 | 2,852 | 54,072 | 1,614 | 5,721 |
| 1987 | 63,842 | 2,789 | 53,807 | 1,561 | 5,685 |
| 1988 | 58,916 | 2,760 | 49,209 | 1,368 | 5,579 |
| 1989 | 62,172 | 3,154 | 51,861 | 1,379 | 5,778 |
| 1990 | 72,091 | 3,651 | 59,370 | 1,647 | 7,423 |
| 1991 | 64,803 | 3,619 | 52,451 | 1,536 | 7,197 |
| 1992 | 81,150 | 4,445 | 66,013 | 2,093 | 8,599 |
| 1993 | 62,933 | 3,880 | 50,412 | 1,486 | 7,155 |
| 1994 | 64,967 | 3,174 | 53,086 | 1,510 | 7,197 |
| 1995 | 57,762 | 2,354 | 47,638 | 1,356 | 6,414 |
| 1996 | 46,608 | 1,878 | 38,790 | 871 | 5,069 |
| 1997 | 52,149 | 2,110 | 43,268 | 971 | 5,800 |
| 1998 | 60,673 | 2,126 | 50,034 | 1,098 | 7,415 |
| 1999 | 55,971 | 1,772 | 45,640 | 999 | 7,560 |
| 2000 | 58,398 | 1,749 | 47,502 | 1,015 | 8,132 |
| 2001 | 57,463 | 1,841 | 46,221 | 1,168 | 8,233 |
| 2002 | 58,066 | 1,889 | 46,795 | 1,056 | 8,326 |
| **Percent receiving personal injury** | | | | | |
| 1980 | 37.2% | 22.5% | 38.2% | 34.4% | 38.0% |
| 1981 | 35.5 | 18.3 | 36.2 | 34.3 | 40.6 |
| 1982 | 30.7 | 16.4 | 30.7 | 27.0 | 39.1 |
| 1983 | 33.4 | 21.8 | 33.4 | 31.4 | 40.2 |
| 1984 | 33.6 | 20.1 | 33.5 | 30.0 | 42.2 |

| Table 10-6 | Assaults on Law Enforcement Officers and Percent Receiving Personal Injury—By Type of Weapon Used, 1980–1995, continued | | | | |
|---|---|---|---|---|---|

| | | Type of weapon used | | | |
|---|---|---|---|---|---|
| | Total victims | Firearm | Personal weapon | Knife or cutting instrument | Other dangerous weapon |
| Percent receiving personal injury | | | | | |
| 1985 | 33.7 | 20.8 | 33.9 | 27.4 | 41.1 |
| 1986 | 33.7 | 22.3 | 33.9 | 29.9 | 38.3 |
| 1987 | 33.3 | 21.7 | 33.5 | 30.7 | 38.4 |
| 1988 | 35.8 | 27.3 | 35.6 | 32.4 | 42.1 |
| 1989 | 35.2 | 30.2 | 35.0 | 30.5 | 40.8 |
| 1990 | 36.3 | 29.4 | 36.2 | 29.6 | 42.6 |
| 1991 | 37.1 | 30.2 | 36.9 | 30.2 | 43.0 |
| 1992 | 36.5 | 25.5 | 36.9 | 30.3 | 40.9 |
| 1993 | 36.3 | 27.7 | 37.1 | 31.6 | 36.2 |
| 1994 | 35.8 | 26.6 | 36.4 | 29.3 | 36.7 |
| 1995 | 30.1 | 19.3 | 30.7 | 23.9 | 31.1 |
| 1996 | 32.1 | 24.8 | 31.5 | 30.7 | 39.4 |
| 1997 | 30.4 | 23.1 | 30.6 | 25.4 | 32.1 |
| 1998 | 30.7 | 20.7 | 31.3 | 23.7 | 30.2 |
| 1999 | 28.0 | 11.9 | 29.0 | 17.5 | 27.1 |
| 2000 | 28.1 | 11.4 | 29.2 | 15.2 | 26.9 |
| 2001 | 28.3 | 10.3 | 29.7 | 15.3 | 26.1 |
| 2002 | 28.4 | 12.2 | 29.8 | 17.1 | 25.7 |

Note: These data are based on agencies reporting assaults to the Federal Bureau of Investigation's Uniform Crime Reporting Program; the number of agencies reporting and percent of total population represented vary from year to year. Data for 2002 are based on 9,987 agencies covering approximately 75% of the total population. Data for previous years are from agencies covering from 63% to 85% of the total population. Some data have been revised by the source and may differ from previous editions of the *Sourcebook*.

Source: Reprinted from Maguire, Kathleen and Ann L.Pastore, eds. *Sourcebook of Criminal Justice Statistics* [Online]. Table 3.168 Available online: http://www.albany.edu/sourcebook/ [12/14/04], citing *Law Enforcement Officers Killed and Assaulted*, 1989, p. 55; 1999, p. 80; 2002, p. 79; FBI Uniform Crime Reports (Washington, DC: US Department of Justice).

in society and create public policy (law) in an attempt to respond to observed problems. In the area of crime and criminal justice, public policy initiatives are usually a response to the believed causes of crime.

Religious-based assumptions of crime (sin in church law) date to the dawn of civilized society. Typically, the rules based upon such principles sought to punish evil or influence from the devil. More recently, theorists and researchers focused rigorously on finding a **cause of crime** rooted in human behavior and environment. Modern efforts in this direction can be traced to at least the late

1700s. Jeremy Bentham (1748–1832), an English philosopher, suggested that the **utilitarian principle** of seeking pleasure and avoiding pain should guide policy responses to crime. Similarly, Cesare Beccaria (1738–1794) held that people will always seek to maximize their pleasure and minimize their pain. In their view, legal institutions could control conduct by increasing one or the other, with pain discouraging crime. These theorists believed that if an act is deemed illegal by society, then the society should only increase the "pain" of committing the act in order to prevent its occurrence. This **pleasure-pain** principle lies at the heart of early crime control ideas (Williams and McShane 1988).

The age in which these theories developed was very much caught up in **rationalism**, and this period produced another rational theory—capitalism. Bentham's early model of **deterrence** reasoning formed a basic set of theoretical principles around which much of our early criminal justice system evolved. However, despite the fact that England used the death penalty for nearly 200 offenses, including picking pockets, crime did not decrease. The simplicity of the pleasure-pain principle did not fully explain the causes of crime. Others tried different techniques, thought to be scientific approaches, to finding causes of crime. These included notions such as counting the bumps on the heads of those convicted of offenses (Williams and McShane 1988). Obviously, this and other similar methods left much to be desired in terms of science.

In the twentieth-century, social sciences including criminology, sociology, psychology, and anthropology improved society's ability to both accumulate and analyze evidence concerning crime causation. In the past 40 years or so, the social sciences have compiled an impressive array of partial explanations for the causes of crime. They are categorized here for discussion purposes into two groups. Some theories focus on the individual offender while others focus on society as a whole. This is an important distinction for the patrol officer to consider.

Persons associated with law enforcement frequently ask why a given defendant committed a particular crime. Usually, in any such discussion, several theories are commonly advanced. These theories tend to focus on background, family, and prior life experiences (drug use, child abuse, etc.). When a defendant is found guilty and a court contemplates the level of punishment, these same issues surface in the sentencing process. In both cases, the focus is on individual actions and history. Policy makers, however, look at large numbers of offenders in a given period of time and determine whether there are events in the society at large that explain some crime. Without debating the point, assume that drugs cause crime. If this were true, then a policy directed at limiting the availability of drugs would seem prudent if it could be achieved. Here we are not concerned with the individual. Rather, our focus is on social causes of crime. We assume that certain social conditions produce increased or decreased risks of crime. Both individual focused theory and societal level explanations are useful for patrol officers to know and understand.

A discussion of criminological theories in a policing textbook may seem at first glance unnecessary and more appropriate in a criminology textbook. However, we feel that not addressing theory produces a gap in understanding why police employ the strategies that they do. For example, resting on the assumption that criminals function to seek pleasure and avoid pain, as discussed above, an appropriate police strategy to reduce crime would be to patrol city streets increasing the risk of arrest. Of course, we know from the Kansas City patrol experiment in the 1970s that mere random patrol (e.g., the number of officers randomly driving around a city) is not associated with deterrence or crime prevention. However, we also know that in most cities a few addresses or locations generate the largest number of calls for service. Hence, targeted patrol is a strategy that employs theories of human behavior and problem solving to structure a focused response to observed problems. Individual-based theories may assist officers in solving a crime or in structuring a plausible motive. Social theories of crime call upon officers to be alert to changes in their environment that may signal changes in the nature and kind of crime they might expect. Some aspects of the theory of community policing address exactly these issues. If officers are alert, proper community intervention may actually prevent crime from occurring.

## ■ Individual Level Theories of Crime

While early theorists focused on offender physical attributes (by counting bumps on the head, or measuring body types, for example), others took note of obvious profiles of offenders. They found that offenders tended to be young males with relatively poor intellectual skills. This did not mean, of course, that youth, gender, or lack of intellect caused crime. Rather, it suggested that there might be things about society that influenced young, poorly educated males to commit crimes. Specifically, gender roles might influence males to become more aggressive. Similarly, young people tend be less cautious and are more easily influenced by peers. Finally, poor educational experiences may cause a person to believe that legal approaches to success are not possible (or will not produce benefits). Poor education also precludes skills development necessary to see future value to lawful pursuits. In a complex theory reminiscent of the pleasure-pain theory, James Q. Wilson and Richard J. Hernstein argued that much of the explanation for crime lies in the relationship between (1) human needs, (2) the anticipation that these needs will be fulfilled by lawful conduct, and (3) internalized prohibitions against unlawful conduct to fulfill needs (1985). In this view, criminals typically fail to learn internal controls that would prevent needs satisfaction by illegal conduct. Wilson and Hernstein maintain that offenders cannot see how lawful conduct will fulfill those needs.

Similarly, the idea of internalization of norms or values suggests that those who experience a very dysfunctional childhood will either internalize the wrong norms, or no norms at all. On the one hand, if children are exposed to alcohol, drug abuse, or violence, their norms may be very abnormal and at odds with those of society. Children may **associate** or **learn** approaches to satisfying their needs that are wholly illegal. **Differential association**, originally proposed by Edwin Sutherland in 1939, suggests that criminal behavior results when one is exposed to the "patterns" or "definitions" of others which are favorable to, or supportive of, antisocial behavior (Akers 1997, 61). This theory was expanded by Akers and others to include the notion of rewarding or punishing those definitions. This is frequently referred to as learning "theory" (Akers 1997; Gorman and White

1995; Braithwaite 1989). This may seem like "deterrence" theory combined with "hanging around with the wrong crowd," but it is not. These theories are complex suggestions about how we respond to examples in our environment and, as a general theory of deviance, apply to us all and to all forms of deviance, even police deviance. If neighborhoods and families present "definitions" to children that are contrary to social standards of lawfulness, and these children are rewarded for accepting those definitions, we should not be surprised that they adopt those behaviors. Hence, interventions with families of offenders my well produce a net reduction in the potential for future crime. On the other hand, if families, neighborhoods, and peers assist in internalizing proper values (including supporting educational performance) and teaching the value of future lawful rewards, crime as a path of conduct will be less likely for that person.

Both of these observations offer value for patrol officers. In one sense, officers can assume there is a good probability that offenders are young and male. It is not a good assumption, however, that all young males are likely offenders (see **Table 10-7**). A small number commit most Index offenses. While 30% to 40% of

| **Table 10-7** | **Percent Distribution of Total US Population and Persons Arrested For All Offenses By Age Group, United States, 2002** | |
|---|---|---|
| **Age** | **US resident population** | **Persons arrested** |
| 14 years and younger | 21.0% | 5.2% |
| 15 to 19 | 7.1 | 21.3 |
| 20 to 24 | 7.0 | 19.9 |
| 25 to 29 | 6.6 | 12.3 |
| 30 to 34 | 7.3 | 10.9 |
| 35 to 39 | 7.6 | 10.4 |
| 40 to 44 | 8.0 | 8.9 |
| 45 to 49 | 7.4 | 5.5 |
| 50 to 54 | 6.5 | 2.9 |
| 55 to 59 | 5.2 | 1.4 |
| 60 to 64 | 4.0 | 0.6 |
| Age 65 and older | 12.3 | 0.6 |

Note: This table presents data from all law enforcement agencies submitting complete reports for 12 months in 2002 (US Department of Justice, p. 452). Because of rounding, percents may not add to 100.

Source: Reprinted from Maguire, Kathleen and Ann L. Pastore, eds. *Sourcebook of Criminal Justice Statistics* [Online]. Table 4.4 Available online: http://www.albany.edu/sourcebook/ [12/14/04], citing US Department of Justice, Federal Bureau of Investigation, *Crime in the United States, 2002* (Washington, DC: USGPO, 2003), pp. 244, 245; and US Department of Commerce, US Census Bureau [Online] Available online: http://www.census.gov/popest/archives/2000s/vintage_2002/NA-EST2002-ASRO-D1.html [Sept. 10, 2004].

all males will be arrested once before their 18th birthday, only 6% of all young males account for 50% of the arrests (Greenwood 1995). However, this information also suggests a focus of patrol information gathering and departmental intervention. Most juvenile offenders can clearly be pointed in positive directions. For example, pursuing the possibility that a child has been abused or neglected, an officer may have a hand in preventing, possibly even reversing, damaging lessons. Participation in school activities such as sports programs, tutoring, DARE, police athletic leagues, and camp sponsorships can provide positive role models and experiences. In part, officers become role models as a big brother/big sister for children at risk.

# ■ Social Level Theories of Crime

While some theories focus on the specific attributes of individual offenders, learning environments to which they were exposed, and personal experiences they have had, social level theories choose a much broader perspective. These theories suggest that social structure impacts the prevention or creation of crime. Some of these theories attempt to bridge the distance between individual explanations and social explanations. These theories examine how individuals are exposed to the process of a social system. Hence, individual behavior is more or less directly influenced by social conditions. Not all people respond in the same way to the same social conditions, but overall, we can predict that many will. Hence, alteration of social conditions will also predictably have an effect, according to these theories.

## Chicago School

The **Chicago** or **Ecological School** examined the conditions in which people grow, live, and develop for an explanation of crime. These theorists argued that as an area of a city deteriorates, certain processes take place. A new culture develops with its own norms and values. These may and probably will differ from the norms of the larger society. For example, gangs may form as social support mechanisms. Gangs represent a local cultural response to conditions of conflict with other cultures. While gangs may turn to the manufacture and sale of drugs, or fencing stolen property, the reason for gang emergence is a sense of belonging, replacing structures that are missing in their lives (such as a stable family or strong scholastic support). In this respect, the law society seeks to enforce is not theirs because it is not from their culture. If law enforcement officers have difficulty accepting this interpretation, it is understandable. But, studies of gangs and the Mafia substantiate the claim that conflict over culture plays a large role in crime creation. Cultures are based upon values that are transmitted to members of that culture. The idea of **subculture** is based upon this theory. Conflict between the main culture, which creates the law and the culture of a given group or neighborhood (subculture), generates violations of norms from the main culture.

In many cultures, bribing and gambling are accepted, lawful behaviors. In ours, they are illegal. Some Native American tribes claim the right to use some parts of natural plants in their religious ceremonies, but society calls them drugs and bans them. In the 1800s, fistfighting in streets and bars rarely led to arrest and prosecution. In short, crime is very value laden. Of course, as we will discuss later, some actions strike us as patently wrong (robbery, murder, assault, and rape to name a few) and it is difficult to imagine a culture in which such conduct would be accepted.

## Differential Association

Closely related to the idea of subculture is the theory of differential association. This theory holds that crime is learned from close personal contacts with others, and accordingly, it bridges individual and social level theories. Hence, close contact with a given cultural perspective would lead one to learn those cultural values and act on them even though these actions were contrary to established law. Because this theory focuses on the process of "learning," it can be thought of as social theory, as well as an individually focused theory.

For law enforcement, these theories suggest that mere reaction to criminal events is insufficient to stop crime. Rather, breaking down cultural barriers seems to be a more responsive strategy to prevent crime. Reactive behavior assumes that crime is generated by a rational actor; that is, someone who thinks about the consequences of criminal acts. As discussed earlier, that rational model holds that if offenders know they will get caught and punished, they will not do the crime. But, if crime is partially created by culture, then rational models do not apply. For example, when prohibition came into being, very honest, dedicated citizens found themselves on the other side of the law because in their culture drinking was not only permitted, it was part of everyday life. This was particularly true for those of European descent.

In the same respect, today's problems of drugs, gambling, sex, gang-related violence, and theft suggest that some of the problem is more cultural than individual. To curb crime, then, law enforcement would need to address community concerns, listen to community interests, and develop a more positive, less conflict-oriented image in the community. These results are achieved by intervention in the culture and neighborhoods, not by traditional enforcement methods alone. Such intervention approaches do not mean lower levels of law enforcement. Rather, they mean more complex methods of enforcement and prevention mixed together. Law enforcement becomes not merely the response to criminal actions. It must involve the whole environment of the community including schools, community services, citizen organizations, and alternative outlets. In this respect, modern policing is partially concerned with introducing and positively reinforcing new values. This, in essence, is what community policing means.

## Labeling

Other explanations for crime attempted to bridge the gap between theories that focused on the individual and those that focused on the social structure. These theories focused on the processes by which people were exposed to different forces in society. **Labeling** theory was one prominent notion. There are a number of different perspectives in this approach, but essentially they argue that when an individual is "labeled" deviant, that person is more likely to continue being deviant. For some, this might seem either obvious or not very informative. However, this theory is supported by evidence that juveniles who are subjected to high levels of labeling (that is, repeatedly labeled from one event) are more likely to continue deviant patterns (Braithwaite 1989). **Table 10-8** reveals the formal reasons for which many juveniles are institutionalized.

| Table 10-8 | Juveniles in Public and Private Residential Custody Facilities, 1999[a] |
|---|---|
| **Most serious offense** | **Total** |
| Total juveniles | 108,931 |
| Male | 94,370 |
| Female | 14,561 |
| Delinquent offenses | 104,327 |
| Violent offenses | 38,055 |
| Index offenses[b] | 27,221 |
| Other violent | 10,784 |
| Property offenses | 31,817 |
| Index offenses[c] | 26,517 |
| Other Property | 5,300 |
| Drug-related offenses | 9,882 |
| Public-order offenses | 10,487 |
| Technical Offenses | 14,046 |
| Status offenses[d] | 4,694 |

Note: These data are from the *Census of Juveniles in Residential Placement*, conducted by the US Department of Justice, Office of Juvenile Justice and Delinquency Prevention. Public and private facilities, secure and nonsecure, that hold alleged or adjudicated juvenile delinquents or status offenders were asked to provide information on each juvenile in residence on the reference date of Oct. 27, 1999. A 100% response rate was achieved for the 1999 census and indicated that 108,931 juveniles under 21 years of age were assigned a bed in a public or private residential facility on the reference date as a result of being charged or court adjudicated for an offense.

[a]On October 27, 1999. Detail may not add to total because of rounding.

[b]Includes criminal homicide, violent sexual assault, robbery, and aggravated assault.

[c]Includes burglary, theft, auto theft, and arson.

[d]Status offenders include running away, underage drinking, truancy, curfew violations, and other offenses that are illegal for juveniles but not adults. Care should be exercised when interpreting status offense data because states differ in what they classify as an adjudicable status offense.

*Source:* Reprinted from Maguire, Kathleen and Ann L. Pastore, eds. *Sourcebook of Criminal Justice Statistics* [Online]. Table 6.9 Available online: http://www.albany.edu/sourcebook/ [12/14/04], citing Melissa Sickmund and Yi-chun Wan, "Census of Juveniles in Residential Placement Databook" [Online] Washington, DC: US Department of Justice, Office of Juvenile Justice and Delinquency Prevention, 2002. Available online: htpp://www.ojjdp.ncjrs.org/ojstatbb/cjrp [Aug. 7, 2002].

Evidence from a number of perspectives and studies suggests that non-index crime offenders, particularly juveniles, who pass through the criminal justice system display an increased rate of offending as a result of formal charge processing. In other words, for many offenders, arresting, charging, and formally pursuing a charge caused them to become more likely to offend, not less likely (Ludman 1993). This discovery led to the creation of large diversion programs for first offenders who committed relatively minor offenses. While recent research has called labeling theory into question, prior evidence of this effect has not been fully refuted.

For law enforcement, labeling theory suggests that the use of guided discretion in making arrests is effective in crime prevention. This system cannot work like that of the early days of this century, however, where unlimited discretion was typical. This approach requires departments to develop (in consultation with the prosecution function) a set of policy guidelines on the appropriate use of such methods. It also suggests that crime prevention will result from the application of carefully defined procedures for diversion. Patrol officers need to understand the theory behind this approach.

## Social Control

A final theoretical approach attempts to pull all of these diverse perspectives together. **Social control** theory suggests that internal controls (learned values) and restraining controls from other significant influences (family, peers, etc.) dramatically influence behavior. A breakdown of the appropriate controls is caused by, among other things, surrounding culture and life experiences.

**Socialization** is the process by which we learn the norms of society. The family, as the primary socializing agent of good effect, is central to developing internal restraints in individuals (also see social control discussions in Chapter 1). The breakdown of families makes this more difficult to achieve, though not impossible. Similarly, the breakdown of traditional neighborhoods reduces the reinforcing effects of other socializing agents such as extended families, schools, neighbors, and social organizations. Gangs play a role in replacing all of these missing agents of socialization.

This approach was echoed in one recent effort to create a "general theory of crime" (Gottfredson and Hirschi 1990). The authors of this theory argue that the absence of self-control (internal control) and the presence of opportunity account for most criminal behavior, that is either violent or theft-related. In this view, people with low self-control are likely to commit antisocial behavior given the opportunity. Self-control, in this theory, is developed early in childhood from all of the contacts which children experience. This theory may seem abstract and unrelated to the day-to-day activities on the streets and in the station houses, but closer examination may yield some benefits for law enforcement organizations. Other similar efforts to develop a "general theory" of crime attempt to integrate multiple theories but are complex enough to justify exploration in a course devoted to criminology (Tittle 1995; Braithwaite 1989).

Because young males produce much of the serious crime in the United States, a focus on youth is important. Preschool care for children, schools in general, sports (both scholastic and community organized), and family units are important socializing agents. In a similar fashion, the neighborhood is a powerful influence. By looking at these particular socializing agents, some general approaches for addressing the problem of crime can be sketched. For law enforcement officers specifically, this theory offers some obvious strategies that deviate from the reactive response model typical to law enforcement until recently.

Volatile patterns of youth crime make crime predictions difficult. For example, Cook and Laub (1998) note that homicide arrests for youth in the 10–17 age range peaked in 1993, but by 1995 they had declined by 23% (1998). Still, they argue, it is generally true that youth arrests in 1994 for violent crime were about the average for the previous 30 years (Cook and Laub 1998). Hence, the notion that there has been an "epidemic" of youth crime is not borne out by the evidence. Still, it is true that violent and property crime is committed disproportionately by young males, and this pattern is one that continues (Miethe and McCorkle 1998).

The evidence is clear that most juvenile offenders will stop offending relatively early in their lives. Therefore, law enforcement officers should look at youthful offenders not as lifetime troublemakers. Rather, officers should see them as people who are capable of being properly directed. This does not mean going easy on offenders. On the contrary, it means paying close attention to them but with the approach that help is being offered. Officers must show offenders that they do care about them as people. No one says this is easy or enjoyable, but one can be tough with offenders and still offer the human touch that may be, and most likely is, missing in their lives. Stopping by their homes, talking to friends and families, going out of the way to find work, or assisting programs to redirect the energies of offenders are all means to the same end: crime prevention. These approaches are also part of community policing. The community is not merely juveniles who are in school, or citizens who have not violated the law; the community is everyone.

Patrol officers must understand that they are the closest and most important law enforcement contacts with the community. They represent, in most respects, not just law enforcement, but the government and society in general. Messages sent by patrol officers are sent on behalf of the whole society. Patrol officers, therefore, are central to the prevention of crime by finding ways to draw young offenders away from offending patterns. This may be by arrest, patrol, and inquiry, or intervention in the schools, neighborhoods, or families. Patrol officers are the key to successful crime prevention and law enforcement. As Robert Sampson and John Laub argue in their life course theory, youth lives follow certain trajectories, and during that path experience good and bad events. The support of their environment, family, neighborhood, and peers will dictate how they respond and in what direction they may travel next. In short, how we assist youth who experience negative events is associated with future offending patterns (1993).

Routine Activities Theory (or RAT theory to some) suggests that much violence and property crime is the result of an interaction between motivated offenders, attractive targets, and levels of guardianship (Cohen and Felson 1979). Implications of this theory for law enforcement are significant. Guardianship can be conceived of in many ways. However, in its most broad conception, it would involve neighborhood groups providing surveillance, target-hardening efforts to make property less attractive (e.g., window locks), and police-community interactions to provide other means to increase guardianship and reduce target availability. In theory, community interventions should be able to succeed in reducing some patterns of crime. This theory has many critics (including your authors) and has not successfully been supported by research (Miethe and McCorkle 1998). Like all theories, however, it is important to test the theory against the real world in order to improve our understanding of human behavior as it relates to crime and, in doing so, revise our theories to give policy better direction. Law enforcement is essential in this effort. At the same time, situational crime prevention, which suggests focusing on particular conditions or environments, does seem to work if by working we mean reducing offending without displacing offending to another location (Felson 2002; Rosenbaum et al. 1998). On the other hand, recent research has called into question the viability of community policing as a one-size-fits-all answer to crime prevention (Skogan 2004).

## ■ Emerging Issues in Crime Causation

### Drugs

Surely one of the most significant changes in crime in the United States during the past two decades has been related to the use, importation, sale, and manufacture of drugs. While general discussion in the nation focused on the relationship between drugs and crime, those either working in the field or studying the subject examined the complex impact that drugs seemed to have on society. It must be noted that there are several different kinds of drugs in ready supply, each of which differs in several ways. Physical effects, profit potential, ease of transport, sources, and demand all differ from drug to drug. Complicating this is the way in which a legal drug, alcohol, impacts crime and general drug use.

A good place to start is by looking at the usage of drugs. By far the most widely used drugs are alcohol, marijuana, and cocaine (crack form or crystal powder form). Information consistently shows that drug use is high among those arrested for criminal offenses, running as high as 50% on average (see **Table 10-9**). The rate of drug use depends on the age and gender of the offender, as well as location and nature of the offense. Rates of drug use run as high as 78% and as low as 30% among offenders. Incidence of drug use is closely linked with incidence of violent crime, though drugs are not necessarily a cause of that violence (US Department of Justice 1992). It is just as likely that both violence and drug use are related to a set of conditions that are the core causative agents for both.

Interestingly, drug use rates have declined in the past decade except for marijuana, which increased from 1992 to 1996 after a sharp decline from high levels of usage in the mid-1980s (Walker 1998). The rates among the young are particularly important, as early use is generally highly related to their likelihood to be involved in crime. Because the rate of drug use among the young seems to be declining (except for marijuana) and because the young commit most offenses, it is no surprise that crime rates are declining slightly (see **Table 10-10**). However, as was noted earlier, violent crime is increasing, thereby suggesting that overall

| Table 10-9 | Reported Drug Use by Convicted Prison and Jail Inmates |||

| | Percent who used drugs at the time of the offense | | Percent who used drugs in the month before the offense | |
|---|---|---|---|---|
| | **1997** | **1991** | **1997** | **1991** |
| **Drug type** | State prison inmates ||||
| Any drug | 32.6% | 31.0% | 56.5% | 49.9% |
| Marijuana | 15.1 | 11.4 | 39.2 | 32.2 |
| Cocaine/crack | 14.8 | 14.5 | 25.0 | 25.2 |
| Heroin/opiates | 5.6 | 5.8 | 9.2 | 9.6 |
| Depressants | 1.8 | 1.0 | 5.1 | 3.8 |
| Stimulants | 4.2 | 2.9 | 9.0 | 7.4 |
| Hallucinogens | 1.8 | 1.6 | 4.0 | 3.7 |
| | **1996** | **1989** | **1996** | **1989** |
| **Drug type** | State prison inmates ||||
| Any drug | 35.6% | 27.0% | 55.0% | 43.8% |
| Marijuana | 18.5 | 9.0 | 36.8 | 28.0 |
| Cocaine/crack | 15.2 | 13.7 | 24.1 | 23.5 |
| Heroin/opiates | 5.6 | 4.9 | 8.8 | 7.2 |
| Depressants | 2.4 | 1.2 | 5.9 | 3.9 |
| Stimulants | 6.1 | 2.2 | 10.4 | 5.4 |
| Hallucinogens | 1.6 | 1.6 | 4.6 | 3.2 |
| | **1997** | **1991** | **1997** | **1991** |
| **Drug type** | Federal inmates ||||
| Any drug | 22.4% | 16.8% | 44.8% | 31.8% |
| Marijuana | 10.8 | 5.9 | 30.4 | 19.2 |
| Cocaine/crack | 9.3 | 7.7 | 20.0 | 15.4 |
| Heroin/opiates | 3.0 | 3.7 | 5.4 | 5.5 |
| Depressants | 1.0 | 0.3 | 3.2 | 1.4 |
| Stimulants | 4.1 | 1.8 | 7.6 | 3.9 |
| Hallucinogens | 0.8 | 0.5 | 1.7 | 1.2 |

*Source:* Reprinted from Bureau of Justice Statistics: *Drugs and Crime Facts*, (2004); *Substance Abuse and Treatment, State and Federal Prisoners*, (1997); *Profile of Jail Inmates*, (1996); Washington, DC: US Department of Justice. Available online: http://www.ojp.usdoj.gov/bjs/dcf/duc/htm.

drug use is not a primary cause of most violent crime (if by "cause" we mean doing drugs produces criminals). It is more reasonable to observe that doing drugs conditionally adds to the probability of criminal activity. Over the long term, drug use has remained relatively stable, as has that of alcohol, and has not fluctuated as widely as crime rates. This suggests a more conditional relationship.

| Table 10-10 | Percent of Inmates Who Committed Their Offenses for Money to Buy Drugs |||||||
|---|---|---|---|---|---|---|
| Most serious current offense | Federal prison inmates, 1991–1997 || State prison inmates, 1991–1997 || Jail inmates, 1991–1996 ||
| All offenses | 10% | 16% | 17% | 19% | 13% | 15.8% |
| Violent offenses | 18 | | 12 | | 12 | 8.8 |
| Homicide[a] | 3 | | 5 | | 3 | |
| Sexual assault[b] | 0 | | 2 | | 2 | |
| Robbery | 27 | | 27 | | 32 | |
| Assault | 2 | | 6 | | 3 | |
| Property offenses | 9 | | 26 | | 24 | 25.6 |
| Burglary | 32 | | 30 | | 31 | |
| Larceny/theft | 13 | | 31 | | 28 | |
| Motor vehicle theft | — | — | 7 | | | |
| Drug offenses | 9 | | 22 | | 14 | 23.5 |
| Possession | 7 | | 16 | | 10 | |
| Trafficking | 10 | 25 | 19 | | | |
| Public-order offenses | 6 | 5 | 3 | | 4.2 | |

[a]Includes murder, nonnegligent manslaughter, and negligent manslaughter.

[b]Includes rape.

— Not reported

*Source:* Reprinted from Bureau of Justice Statistics: *Drugs and Crime Facts, 1994 and 2004; Substance Abuse and Treatment, State and Federal Prisoners, 1997; Profile of Jail Inmates, 1996.* Washington, DC: US Department of Justice. Available online: http://www.ojp.usdoj.gov/bjs/dcf/duc/htm. Accessed December 20, 2004.

Still, the increase in the rate of violent crime more or less coincides with the appearance of crack cocaine (see **Table 10-11**). This drug is easy to manufacture and transport and offers a large profit margin. But there seems to be a declining market for this and other drugs. The result appears to be a concentrated market in which violence is both a product of the use of the drug and of competition over "turf" to sell the drug. While general use declines, use and sales become more concentrated in the central city. Much of the increase in violence may therefore be specifically related to the crack market. While there is widespread belief about this, there is insufficient evidence to be certain.

## Hate Crimes

Because it is difficult to determine if a crime was motivated by racial, religious, ethnic, or gender status hatred, there is very little data on the subject of hate crimes. However, the impression of most people in law enforcement is that crimes motivated by such attitudes are, in fact, on the increase. Hate crimes pose a particular problem for law enforcement since they tend to be random and spontaneous crimes, thereby leaving few traces of evidence from which to proceed.

| Table 10-11 | Drug-Related Homicides | |
|---|---|---|
| Year | Number of homicides | Percent drug-related |
| 1986 | 19,257 | 3.9% |
| 1987 | 17,963 | 4.9 |
| 1988 | 17,971 | 5.6 |
| 1989 | 18,954 | 7.4 |
| 1990 | 20,273 | 6.7 |
| 1991 | 21,676 | 6.2 |
| 1992 | 22,716 | 5.7 |
| 1993 | 23,180 | 5.5 |
| 1994 | 22,084 | 5.6 |
| 1995 | 20,232 | 5.1 |
| 1996 | 16,967 | 5.0 |
| 1997 | 15,837 | 5.1 |
| 1998 | 14,276 | 4.8 |
| 1999 | 13,011 | 4.5 |
| 2000 | 13,230 | 4.5 |
| 2001 | 14,061 | 4.1 |
| 2002 | 14,263 | 4.7 |
| 2003 | 14,408 | 4.6 |

*Source:* Reprinted from Bureau of Justice Statistics. *Drugs and Crime Facts* (2004), Washington, DC: US Department of Justice. Available online: http://www.ojp.usdoj.gov/bjs/dcf/duc/htm.

Enforcement is made more difficult by the fact that merely saying hateful things or making hateful signs is insufficient to overcome the constitutional protection of free speech. In 1992, the United States Supreme Court declared a municipal ordinance unconstitutional, which made it a crime to convey hateful messages (See **Figure 10-5**). The ordinance in question made the content of the message illegal. The court refused to permit this infringement of what it called "protected speech" (*RAV v. St. Paul*, 505 US 377). This leaves very little room for the prosecution of hate crimes by other than traditional means: prosecuting the action (assault, arson, criminal damaging, etc.). This issue will no doubt occupy a good deal of litigation as we define what the limits might be for language that is not protected, but rather, "fighting words" that can be prosecuted. In April of 1990, Congress passed the Hate Crime Statistics Act and mandated the collection of data on crimes motivated by religious, ethnic, racial, or sexual-orientation prejudices. Over time, this data will enhance our knowledge of the prevalence of such offenses. In most respects, the causes of these sorts of crimes are also found in the socialization of the perpetrators. This type of crime can be reduced by proper education and socialization of children in the community.

Decided June 22, 1992

JUSTICE SCALIA delivered the opinion of the Court.

In the predawn hours of June 21, 1990, petitioner and several other teenagers allegedly assembled a crudely made cross by taping together broken chair legs. They then allegedly burned the cross inside the fenced yard of a black family that lived across the street from the house where petitioner was staying. Although this conduct could have been punished under any of a number of laws, [fn1] one of the two provisions under which respondent city of St. Paul chose to charge petitioner (then a juvenile) was the St. Paul Bias-Motivated Crime Ordinance, St. Paul, Minn. Legis.Code § 292.02 (1990), which provides:

*Whoever places on public or private property a symbol, object, appellation, characterization or graffiti, including, but not limited to, a burning cross or Nazi swastika, which one knows or has reasonable grounds to know arouses anger, alarm or resentment in others on the basis of race, color, creed, religion or gender commits disorderly conduct and shall be guilty of a misdemeanor.*

. . . (W)e conclude that, even as narrowly construed by the Minnesota Supreme Court, the ordinance is facially unconstitutional. Although the phrase in the ordinance, "arouses anger, alarm or resentment in others," has been limited by the Minnesota Supreme Court's construction to reach only those symbols or displays that amount to "fighting words," the remaining, unmodified terms make clear that the ordinance applies only to "fighting words" that insult, or provoke violence, "on the basis of race, color, creed, religion or gender." *Displays containing abusive invective, no matter how vicious or severe, are permissible unless they are addressed to one of the specified disfavored topics. Those who wish to use "fighting words" in connection with other idea— to express hostility, for example, on the basis of political affiliation, union membership, or homosexuality— are not covered. The First Amendment does not permit St. Paul to impose special prohibitions on those speakers who express views on disfavored subjects.*

In its practical operation, moreover, the ordinance goes even beyond mere content discrimination to actual viewpoint discrimination. Displays containing some words—odious racial epithets, for example—would be prohibited to proponents of all views. But "fighting words" that do not themselves invoke race, color, creed, religion, or gender—aspersions upon a person's mother, for example—would seemingly be usable ad libitum in the placards of those arguing in favor of racial, color, etc. tolerance and equality, but could not be used by that speaker's opponents. One could hold up a sign saying, for example, that all "anti-Catholic bigots" are misbegotten; but not that all "papists" are, for that would insult and provoke violence "on the basis of religion." St. Paul has no such authority to license one side of a debate to fight freestyle, while requiring the other to follow Marquis of Queensbury Rules.

One must wholeheartedly agree with the Minnesota Supreme Court that "[i]t is the responsibility, even the obligation, of diverse communities to confront such notions in whatever form they appear," ibid., but the manner of that confrontation cannot consist of selective limitations upon speech. St. Paul's brief asserts that a general "fighting words" law would not meet the city's needs, because only a content-specific measure can communicate to minority groups that the "group hatred" aspect of such speech "is not condoned by the majority." The point of the First Amendment is that majority preferences must be expressed in some fashion other than silencing speech on the basis of its content.

. . . (T)he reason why fighting words are categorically excluded from the protection of the First Amendment is not that their content communicates any particular idea, but that their content embodies a particularly intolerable (and socially unnecessary) mode of expressing whatever idea the speaker wishes to convey. St. Paul has not singled out an especially offensive mode of expression. Rather, it has proscribed fighting words of whatever manner that communicate messages of racial, gender, or religious intolerance. Selectivity of this sort creates the possibility that the city is seeking to handicap the expression of particular ideas.

Let there be no mistake about our belief that burning a cross in someone's front yard is reprehensible. But St. Paul has sufficient means at its disposal to prevent such behavior without adding the First Amendment to the fire.

The judgment of the Minnesota Supreme Court is reversed, and the case is remanded for proceedings not inconsistent with this opinion.

It is so ordered.

**Figure 10-5** *RAV v. St. Paul,* 505 US 377 (1992).

# Computer Crime

One area of crime for which data is virtually nonexistent is computer crime. Once the domain of only federal law enforcement concerns, this complex and virtually transparent crime is now the concern of local enforcement. Recently, a computer consultant was arrested for intentionally implanting a virus (a program that kills stored information) in a computer sold to a customer. The consultant threatened to activate the virus if he did not receive full payment for his work. The proliferation of thousands of electronic bulletin board services (BBS) and World Wide Web pages opened avenues for illegal distribution of pornography, anonymous messages related to drug deals, and theft of software and other intellectual property (including company trade secrets). These crimes are in addition to embezzlement, illegal fund transfers, data alteration, and simple extensions of existing crime syndicates.

There is no national accounting of such crime, and the numbers of unreported (and undiscovered) events is no doubt very large. Accurate figures are difficult to obtain as businesses choose not to report them. While many might think that law enforcement agencies must react by creating special units to deal with such crime, for most departments, this is not an option. Instead, it is clear that law enforcement as a whole must become computer literate quickly. There are already substantial resources at the command of law enforcement for information retrieval about suspects, criminal histories, and fingerprints (see Chapter 11).

The causes of this form of crime seem to be rooted in two areas. The traditional causes such as greed or anger (related to the social control models and socialization) are certainly one realm. However, there is also a new characteristic not common in any crime committing group. Some computer-based crime is committed by highly capable specialists who commit the offenses solely as a test of their skills. Those who engage in such criminal invasions of computers via phone lines or Internet connections are commonly referred to in the media as **hackers**, and they commit computer crimes as a means to test their skills. The types of computer-based crime are identified in **Figure 10-6**.

Between the year 2000 and 2004 the number of viral attacks on the Web increased by an astounding 300%. The appearance of other forms of malicious software, often called malware, also increased in that period of time. Malware comes in many forms. Unlike most viral infections on computers which seek to destroy data or render your system inoperable, these are small programs that may be tracking cookies that report your Web behavior to another Web site, report your email address book contents to someone else, or prevent some programs from working properly. A number of free solutions to these sorts of parasites are available on the Web. Another form of computer crime has been the appearance of denial of service or DOS attacks. This occurs when a Web site is flooded with computer-generated "hits" causing the Web server to crash. Finally, another emerging problem is child pornography on the Web, and adults luring children into meeting them someplace through Internet chat rooms. Small law enforcement agencies are not equipped to handle these and related problems, but state police, the FBI,

- Information theft
- Illegal fund transfers
- Information destruction
- Fund transfers to assist other crimes

**Figure 10-6** Types of computer-based crime.

and groups of agencies pooling their resources can reduce the problem. For example, setting up dummy Web sites to lure perpetrators, or pretending to be a teenager in Web chats to lure offenders into capture have been effective.

## Gangs

An area of increasing concern to law enforcement is the continuing influence of youth and street gangs. The impression of most people in and out of law enforcement is that gangs are becoming more prevalent, more violent, and more involved in drugs. Research on gangs is relatively substantial, but one major problem that hampers good policy research is the definition of a gang: There is no generally accepted definition from which research, whether government or private, has proceeded. The result is a wide variation in definitions (Ball and Curry 1995; Winfree et al. 1992).

However, we can say that gangs seem to operate in the manner suggested earlier, as a social mechanism that replaces lost or dysfunctional family and community structures. As such, there is a long history, because we can find references to gang activity in England as early as the 1600s or earlier, should we choose to include the legend of Robin Hood. A reading of the Charles Dickens classic *Oliver Twist*, for example, details the exploits of Oliver Twist as a member of a young gang of orphaned thieves in nineteenth-century London.

This evidence of a long-term presence of gangs is useful because it seems that gangs appear to grow more active during times of social upheavals and instability. The evidence suggests that there is a wide variation of gang activity in the United States over the past 30 years. It has not been constant and seems to vary according to the year and the region. Overall, there is no real evidence of an increase in gang size or participation. In many specific areas, however, gang activity has reached the critical stage. These suggestions contradict the commonly held view that gangs are rampant everywhere. Part of this seeming contradiction is the difference between the highly organized gang and mere delinquent groups (so-called "wannabe" groups).

We do know that those who engage in gang membership tend to have a much higher rate of offending and much higher rates of violence than do nongang members (Esbensen and Huizinga 1993). As a general rule, it is clear that gang member crime patterns are more violent now than at any time in the past, but they are not consistent. However, this behavior does not persist if the member leaves a gang, which suggests the strong social influence of the group (Spergel 1990). For example, in Los Angeles 25.2% of the murders in 1987 were gang-related, but in Chicago in the same year, only 6.9% were related to gangs. Moreover, despite contrary public views, there is no strong, clear relationship between gangs, drug use, drug sales, and the commission of violent crimes (Klein, Maxson, and Cunningham 1991).

While the growth of crack sales in the 1980s was quite significant, street gang member involvement was low both in New York and Los Angeles. Gang members did not play a predominant role in crack distribution. Nor did they seem to elevate the level of violence and organization related to distribution (Thornberry et al. 1993). The sharp rise in 1993 of crack-related shootings in cities altered this perception, but there is no reason to believe that this level of violence will persist or that it is related to gang activity as opposed to temporary groups of delinquents.

For patrol officers, this evidence provides both useful and disturbing information. The increase in drive-by shootings suggests that extreme caution is needed regarding occupied vehicles. It also suggests that understanding the role of gang-related activity in a neighborhood is essential to understanding the community. In a way, gang activity becomes a barometer of the condition of the community. A perceived increase should send signals that the community itself is suffering. Community involvement and intervention plays a large role in controlling and reducing gang influence in a community that is declining and destabilizing. The fact that members of gangs who leave gangs will return to low levels of criminality offers incentive for officer involvement in community programs to reduce gang influence and provide alternatives for juveniles. The evidence is strong that gangs form when there are insufficient community and family structures to properly socialize young people.

## Domestic Violence

While juvenile problems frequently relate to family problems, another family-centered problem of concern to law enforcement is the area of domestic violence. Sometimes referred to as spousal abuse, this arena has taken on a larger meaning as the number of households involving unmarried couples has grown. Moreover, because of the levels of violence surrounding couples who are separated or divorced, the concept must include even those loosely connected to another person in a way that suggests a spousal type of relationship. One effect of the O.J. Simpson trial was to refocus attention on spousal abuse between separated or divorced adults.

Estimates of spousal abuse range greatly, from 2.1 million to more than 8 million per year, and there is a lifetime probability, according to some studies, that 25–30% of all couples will experience a violent incident (Hirschel et al. 1992a). It is a generally accepted estimate that only about half of those who are abused will report an incident to the police. But, for patrol officers it is important to understand that events that are likely to be reported are not typical of the events that occur. Victimization surveys demonstrated that those who do report events of violence are more likely to be poor and uneducated. Nonwhite lower income females are almost twice as likely to report an incident than other females. Moreover, the calls are more likely to involve more severe violence. Hence, calls that are made are not representative of all offenses that do occur (Hirschel et al. 1992a).

The traditional law enforcement response to such calls was to attempt to separate the parties and restore order. While there were many reasons advanced for this approach, that approach changed when an experiment addressed alternate approaches. The Minneapolis experiment seemed to suggest that arrest of the alleged offender was the most effective means of deterring subsequent events. The National Institute of Justice sought to conduct more controlled experiments of this approach to assess the effectiveness of arrest as a deterrent. The first two of these studies found that arrest may not be the most effective. Generally, three possible results were (1) arrest, (2) citation by the officer, or (3) separation and advice. In fact, there was no difference in the rate of **recidivism** (re-offending) regardless of which approach was used. Even more significant were findings from follow-up surveys that the true rates of re-offending were very high, though most subsequent violent events were not reported. Repeat incidents were the rule, not the exception, but were no less frequent for those arrested the first time (Hirschel et al. 1992b). Therefore, the actions of responding officers were not related to subsequent violence.

There could be many reasons for these results. In the one study, most of the offenders had criminal records and came from relationships in which abuse was common. Hence, it was likely to happen again, and a few hours in jail was not very significant to the outcome. Some studies suggest that as few as 10% of calls for domestic violence result in arrest despite the fact that as many as 50% of such cases have sufficient evidence for making arrests (Hirschel et al. 1992b). Because of the shortage of available jail and prison space, it is unlikely that priorities on incarceration will change in the near future. This may help explain, but not justify, the low arrest rate. Even if arrest does occur, past experience suggests few will be convicted unless the criminal justice system as a whole alters the manner in which domestic violence is addressed. In one study, only 35% of the cases produced a finding of guilty, and in only 1% of the cases was any jail time actually served (Gondolf and McFerron 1989). Clearly, research must continue in order to assist law enforcement and the courts in controlling and preventing domestic violence. Still, while there is no evidence that arrest prevents future events of violence, it may be inferred that arrest prevents escalation of current violence.

The evidence to date suggests some approaches for the patrol officer. First, it is likely that a domestic violence incident event is not the first such event in the household. Second, it is more likely to be a serious violent event. Third, a records check is in order where independent evidence of violence seems clear. Fourth, officers should assume that the likelihood of a subsequent offense is great and should endeavor to build trust with the victim in order to establish bridges rather than destroy communications. Fifth, examine the event in light of the neighborhood, and determine if there are any approaches that might be used to involve other services to interdict the situation. Last, a determination to arrest or not should be based upon the question of probable cause and legal authority to arrest since there is no social science evidence that arrest does harm to the situation.

The next section of this chapter examines the major strategies of policing. Given the above discussion of theory and current crime trends, it is important to discuss how both theory and an understanding of crime influence the strategy employed by an agency and the overall approach implemented to reduce crime.

# ■ Major Strategies of Policing

This portion of Chapter 10 discusses the major strategies of policing as analyzed and developed in the last decade within the Harvard University John F. Kennedy School of Government's Executive Session on Policing. The phrase **strategies of policing** as used here refers to the agency's definition of what the organization proposes to do and how. It describes the principal products, technologies, and methods used in striving for and achieving the agency's goals and objectives. An agency's strategy of policing helps managers maintain a consistent focus for performance and expectations. It helps identify what the agency values and has established as primary activities.

The following strategies of policing are not meant to be mutually exclusive or exhaustive—elements of more than one strategy may exist in an agency at the same time, and other formal strategies may emerge in the future. At the present time, these categories describe the primary philosophies toward policing utilized by agencies in the United States. It also must be stated that these strategies coexist throughout the policing community—no one strategy necessarily dominates the others, and it is not necessarily accurate to claim that one is "better" or "worse" than another.

## Professional Crime-Fighting Policing

**Professional crime-fighting policing** became the dominant approach to policing following the reform movements of the 1920s and 1930s. It is a strategy based on the legal authority of the police coupled with political independence for the purpose of achieving crime control through expert service. Kelling and Moore (1988) stated the following about the professional crime-fighting strategy: It carried them from a world of amateurism, lawlessness, and political vulnerability to a world of professionalism, integrity, and political independence.

This strategy is carried forth by a disciplined, technically sophisticated, quasi-military, well-trained crime-fighting force whose primary tactics are radio-equipped patrol vehicles responding quickly to calls for service, coupled with expert follow-up investigations utilizing modern criminalistic technology and techniques. Underlying this approach is an emphasis on accountability of officer actions that are impacted by centralized operations, written policies and procedures, and close supervision. One objective served by this strategy is to maintain a highly competent force that is free from corrupting political and criminal influence. This approach embodies the quest for professional status advocated by early and mid-twentieth-century reformers.

### Major Weaknesses

The professional crime-fighting strategy did much to bring policing into its own right during the 50 years that it dominated policing philosophy; however, it was not without weaknesses. The strategy is primarily **reactive policing** in that quick and competent response to calls for service occur after the incident; crime prevention primarily is premised on **preventive patrol** (the highly visible and random presence of the police).

Another weakness of the professional crime-fighting strategy is that the police become the experts at fighting crime and, therefore, should be allowed to solve the problems with little interaction with or involvement of the community. Incidents are handled according to legal authority and procedure. The community was not expected to get involved with crime fighting and crime control efforts.

A third weakness is that this strategy removes officers from close proximity of citizens. A highly mobilized force runs from one call to the next, not having time to interact with the normal, law-abiding citizen. The majority of an officer's contacts in this strategy involves victims, witnesses, and suspects. This often isolates the officer from knowing the concerns and needs of the citizens and gives the appearance and perception that the officers are less accessible.

A fourth weakness is the fact that this strategy fails to adequately control crime. While the department can be highly efficient with its use of resources, its effectiveness in controlling crime and the underlying social causes of criminal and anti-social behavior is limited at best.

### Research Findings

During the 1970s and 1980s, a number of research studies were conducted that tested the effectiveness and perceived benefits of several of the methods or tactics utilized in the professional crime-fighting approach. The concept of preventive patrol with its objectives of deterring crime and intercepting crimes in progress were some of the first tactics scrutinized. Preventive patrol tactics are associated with the uniformed officer's use of "uncommitted time" during a shift (or time between calls for service and other specific assignments). The options available to an officer during this time are varied as summarized by Cordner and Trojanowicz (1992):

> Patrolling can be stationary or mobile; slow-, medium- or high-speed; and oriented toward residential, commercial, recreational or other kinds of areas. Some patrol officers intervene frequently in peoples' lives by stopping cars and checking out suspicious circumstances; other officers seem more interested in inanimate matters such as parked cars and the security of closed businesses; still other officers rarely interrupt their continuous patrolling. Some officers devote all of their uncommitted time to police-related business, while others devote substantial time to loafing or personal affairs (5).

While the amount of uncommitted time varies greatly from department to department and from beat to beat within departments, until the 1970s departments rarely questioned the effectiveness of preventive patrol. In the early 1970s, a one-year study of the effects of preventive patrol was undertaken in the Kansas City, Missouri Police Department. A portion of the city was divided into 15 beats, and these beats were grouped according to similar characteristics and demographics. One of three patrolling tactics was used in each beat: (1) no preventive patrol activities—squad cars entered the area only to respond to specific calls for service, (2) customary patrol, including normal preventive patrol tactics, and (3) increased preventive patrol, using additional cars to double and triple the normal levels of preventive patrol. Citizen surveys and interviews were conducted before, during, and after the experiment concerning a number of factors, including reported crime, arrests, fear of crime, citizen satisfaction, and traffic accidents. An analysis of the findings yielded the following:

— The practice of having marked police cars conduct random patrol on pre-assigned beats does not necessarily prevent crime or reassure the citizens, even if the police strength is increased significantly.

— Police can stop routinely patrolling beats for up to a year without necessarily being missed by the residents, and without a rise in crime rates in the patrol area (Petersilia 1993).

The "Kansas City Preventive Patrol Experiment" neither went unnoticed nor without criticism; however, it was a landmark study because of its findings and because it ushered in an era of other major studies and experiments that focused on the widely held beliefs in police operations. It is not our purpose here to examine these in depth, but a listing of the major ones demonstrates the research efforts directed at police operations since the early 1970s and the various police practices that have been scrutinized:

*Response Time Studies*—From 1977 through 1982, beginning with Kansas City, Missouri and including the cities of Jacksonville, Florida; San Diego, California; Peoria, Illinois; and Rochester, New York; studies have concluded that police response time was unrelated to the probability of making an arrest or locating a witness. Also, neither dispatch nor travel time were strongly associated with citizen satisfaction. These studies concluded that because of the delay in reporting incidents by citizens, police response time has a negligible impact on crime outcomes (Petersilia 1993; Klockars and Mastrofski 1991).

*Alternative Patrol Strategies*—Following the preventive patrol and response time studies, several projects were undertaken during the mid-1970s to modify the traditional model of patrol. In San Diego, community-oriented policing (described in greater detail below) was initiated and allowed patrol officers greater flexibility to analyze police-related problems and to develop and implement measures to cope with them. In New Haven, Connecticut, the use of directed deterrent runs (D-runs) were initiated. The patrol activity was directed by detailed crime analysis of the times and places of criminal activity. Tactics such as saturation patrol (increased aggressive patrol of selected areas) were implemented to address the identified problems. In Wilmington, Delaware, the split patrol program was developed which allowed about one-third of the patrol force to engage in directed (or structured) patrol activities designed to increase criminal apprehensions. These various alternatives to traditional preventive patrol clearly demonstrated that other patrol utilization tactics could produce equal or better results (Gay et al. 1977; Schell et al. 1976; Petersilia 1993).

*Investigations Research*—During the mid-1970s, two major studies were undertaken regarding the criminal investigation process in policing. The RAND Corporation study was national in scope while the other, by the Stanford Research Institute, focused on Alameda County, California (Greenberg et al. 1975). Both studies plus the follow-up projects that followed yielded several conclusions:

— Many serious crimes are not and often cannot be solved.

— Patrol officers are responsible for most arrests because of either making on-scene apprehensions or obtaining identifications from victims or witnesses that lead to apprehensions.

— Only a small percentage of all Part I arrests result from detective investigations that require special organization, training, or skill.

— Investigators play a critical role in the post-arrest process, particularly in collecting evidence that will enable the prosecutor to file formal criminal charges (Petersilia 1993, 228).

## Strategic Policing

**Strategic Policing** refers to an attempt to expand the professional crime-fighting strategy through more sophisticated, analytical, and targeted crime control applications. In essence, this approach employs directed patrol, decoy and sting operations, drug task forces, violent crimes task forces, and special teams to address specific problems (ranging from street crime to sophisticated white-collar frauds). For example, the 1997 LEMAS study found that 79% of local agencies assigned officers on a full-time basis to a special unit for drug enforcement and 76% of the agencies participated in a multi-agency task force (Reaves and Smith 1999). This strategy of policing maintains centralized control of operations and problem identification. It hinges on greater intelligence gathering and information analysis efforts coupled with sophisticated forensic science methods. The principal value of strategic policing is improved crime control through proactive directed methods.

Police "crackdowns," as described by Lawrence Sherman (1990, 2), refer to a "sudden, usually proactive change in activity . . . intended to drastically increase either the communicated threat or actual certainty of apprehension." As such, the tactic of police crackdowns falls within the general strategy of strategic policing. Crackdown targets have included drug trafficking locations, loitering and disorder problems, subway station crimes, prostitution, drunk driving offenders, public housing fears, and street gang activities.

## Problem-Solving Policing

**Problem-solving policing**, also called problem-oriented policing (POP), is a strategy based on the assumption that crime is successfully controlled by discovering the underlying reasons or causes for offenses, which include frustrating relationships and a disorderly environment. Instead of treating criminal activity through the response to "incidents," the police respond to possible underlying causes, the community problems that foster or promote such activity. The police are trained to engage in the problem-solving approach by utilizing the following four-step process, usually referred to as SARA (Goldstein 1990):

> Scanning—*The identifying and clarifying of what the problem is; its specific location, who is involved, what behavior is occurring, and when it occurs.*

> Analysis—*Obtaining detailed information specifically about the perceived problem. It is an attempt to answer the appropriate who, what, when, how, and especially why questions that surface regarding the particular problem.*

> Response—*The development of alternative approaches to resolve the problem and selecting from among those alternatives the ones that are likely to significantly impact the problem.*

> Assessment—*The evaluation of the response(s) used in order to determine whether it (or they) worked.*

Problem identification in problem-oriented policing often involves more interaction with the community than the professional crime-fighting and strategic approaches. Additionally, data and information gathering takes a broader perspective since the range of agency responses is not limited to the traditional arrest and prosecution tactics. Since the ideas about the causes of crime and methods for controlling it are substantially widened, the data gathering and response to crime or disorder must be broadened as well. According to Goldstein, the "level of analysis" varies according to the problem being addressed. Some problems require a "top-level analysis," some "street-level analysis," while others require some "intermediate level of analysis" within the police organizational structure. For example, if a problem exists throughout the city, a top-level analysis would be appropriate. If the problem were very localized to a particular part of the jurisdiction or just a few neighborhoods, a street-level analysis would be appropriate. Goldstein (1990) adds that problems ought to be explored as close to the operating (local) level as possible.

In the strategy of problem-solving policing, there is a greater emphasis on crime prevention in that it is hoped that by resolving underlying problems, that specific criminal behavior will not surface or manifest itself again. This approach also attempts to mobilize the community residents to defend themselves and to practice prevention tactics. It also mobilizes other governmental agencies (such as parks and recreation, public works, housing and building inspection, etc.) when necessary to attack neighborhood problems. The total spectrum of police responses under this strategy is much broader than the previously discussed strategies and includes both formal and informal responses.

## Community Policing

It appears as though **community policing** was to the 1990s what the professional crime-fighting strategy was to the 1970s, at least in terms of prevailing thought and advocacy. Students of policing and practitioners have been hearing much about this strategy for the last decade. Community policing (also called community-oriented policing, COP) is the attempt by agencies to form a partnership with the residents of the area to reduce crime victimization and to improve the overall quality of life. It is an extension of problem-oriented policing, to a degree. Community policing utilizes the SARA methods of defining problems and devising potential responses, but the community residents play a more integral role in the process. Consider the following explanation:

> *In community policing, community institutions such as families, schools, neighborhood associations, and merchant groups are seen as key partners to the police in the creation of safe, secure communities. The success of the police depends not only on the development of their own skills and capabilities, but also on the creation of competent communities. Community policing acknowledges that police cannot succeed in achieving their basic goals without both the operational assistance and political support of the community. Conversely, the community cannot succeed in constructing decent, open, and orderly communities without a professional and responsive police force* (Moore and Trojanowicz 1988, 9).

In their acclaimed text *Community Policing*, Trojanowicz and Bucqueroux (1990) describe the major principles of community policing. The principles should be reviewed for a better understanding of the underlying premises of community policing. Of particular interest is their emphasis on police-resident interaction and communication, foot patrol, problem-solving techniques, proactiveness, and commitment to a more comprehensive form of policing. A slightly condensed version of the principles follow:

*The Ten Principles of Community Policing*

1. *Community Policing is both a philosophy and an organizational strategy that allows the police and community residents to work closely together in new ways to solve the problems of crime, fear of crime, physical and social disorder, and neighborhood decay . . .*

2. *Community Policing's organizational strategy first demands that everyone in the department, including both civilian and sworn personnel, must investigate ways to translate the philosophy into practice . . .*

3. *To implement true Community Policing, police departments must also create and develop a new breed of line officer, the Community Police Officer (CPO), who acts as the direct link between the police and people in the community. . . .*

4. *The CPO's broad role demands continuous, sustained contact with the law-abiding people in the community, so that together they can explore creative new solutions to local concerns involving crime, fear of crime, disorder, and decay, with private citizens serving as unpaid volunteers . . .*

5. *Community Policing implies a new contract between the police and the citizens they serve, one that offers the hope of overcoming widespread apathy, and at the same time restrains any impulse to vigilantism . . .*

6. *Community Policing adds a vital proactive element to the traditional reactive role of the police, resulting in full-spectrum police service . . .*

7. *Community Policing stresses exploring new ways to protect and enhance the lives of those who are most vulnerable—juveniles, the elderly, minorities, the poor, the disabled, and the homeless . . .*

8. *Community Policing promotes the judicious use of technology, but it also rests on the belief that nothing surpasses what dedicated human beings, talking and working together, can achieve . . .*

9. *Community Policing must be a fully integrated approach that involves everyone in the department, with the CPOs as specialists in bridging the gap between the police and the people they serve . . .*

10. *Community Policing provides decentralized, personalized police service to the community. It recognizes that the police cannot impose order on the community from outside, but that people must be encouraged to think of the police as a resource they can use in helping to solve contemporary community concerns . . . (xiii–xv).*

If police employ a broader definition of what police work really is, community problems, which are not necessarily criminal in nature, can be addressed by police resources. That is, police officers can instigate clean-up efforts within a community or direct teenagers to more constructive places to "hang out," such as neighborhood teen centers. Second, when police focus on increased and better contacts with the community, better police-community relations can be fostered. A benefit to improved relations is elevated levels of information gathering. That is, businesses and residents can relay community needs to police that the police may not have been able to identify otherwise. Third, greater attention to creative problem-solving can offer alternative solutions to problems instead of the traditional, and often ineffective, responsive approach. Police officers could identify why teens are loitering in particular districts and redirect them to other places instead of wasting time asking them to leave every day. Finally, decentralizing the police organization and giving line officers more autonomy in decision-making can, in theory, produce more effective solutions. That is, the community officer knows his/her beat better than his commanding officer. If he/she is practicing the aforementioned three elements, he/she maintains an intimate knowledge of community problems through community interaction. Also, the officer has observed and analyzed these problems and has developed strategies to deal with them. Therefore, it makes little sense not to give the line officer authority in implementing solutions.

As one can see, even though communities can have unique problems, the basic elements to community policing are starting blocks to effective implementation. Therefore, when asked how to effectively implement community-oriented policing, these basic building blocks can serve as the framework in which to develop a solution.

When comparing how traditional ("professional") and community-oriented approaches to policing differ, a few observations must be made. In traditional policing, there are a "manageable" number of problems (usually violations of the law) whereas in community policing there may be an overwhelming number of problems, encompassing both social and legal concerns. Next, in traditional policing, arrest is a primary tool, making the approach both numerically oriented and incident-driven. That is, the traditional approach for police was to respond to an incident call, make an arrest, if necessary, and count the arrest as an indicator of success. Community policing encompasses additional problem-solving tools, is results-oriented, and prescribes proactive problem-solving measures. That is, incidents are grouped together in an effort to detect similar characteristics, patterns and root causes of community problems and crime. Solutions seek to eliminate or reduce the problem and take a proactive rather than reactive stance. Finally, in traditional policing, the "us vs. them" mentality prevails by reinforcing the attitude that the police work for the community and should just simply respond to calls for service. Community policing forms police-community partnerships where problems are collaboratively identified and discussed and the police work with the community in solution-finding efforts.

In the literature, community-oriented policing is currently a very popular theory, gaining widespread attention and funding within the last decade. Eck and Rosenbaum (1994) discuss four traditional functions of policing and their goals:

First, police have typically been defined as "part of society's attempts to control crime." This is problematic because the police's day to day activities have very little to do with crime (Eck and Rosenbaum 1994) and because traditional "crime-related" functions have little impact on crime (Cordner and Williams 1996). Second, one of the traditional and current goals held by police is to provide immediate response. However, research shows that very few crimes are actually solved or interrupted by rapid police response (Spelman and Brown 1991). This is due, in large part, to citizen delay. Therefore, it makes little difference in most cases if the police respond immediately or if they hesitate in their response. Third, police have the authority to arrest and serve justice. This is true for both traditional and community-oriented approaches. Finally, the fourth traditional utility of police is the "delivery of a variety of non-emergency services".

Consider now how the goals of community-oriented policing goals differ from those of the traditional model of policing. The goals themselves are the same, however, they are arranged in different priorities. Traditional, reactive responses are replaced by a proactive, preventative approach. "In the process of applying community policing problem-solving strategies toward the 'root cause' of problems, police organizations are finding that they must address a host of non-crime-related actions" (Williams 1996, 309).

In summary, the goals for both approaches are similar, but prioritized differently. In traditional policing, increasing police presence, reducing crime rates and increasing response times were important. However, studies such as the Kansas City experiment found that increases in random or directed patrol had little impact on crime. Also, as noted earlier, studies have shown that very few crimes are solved or interrupted by rapid police response (Spelman and Brown 1991). This is due, in large part, to citizen delay. Therefore, it makes little difference in most cases if the police respond immediately or if their response is prolonged. This suggests a valuable resource which is not being tapped—line officer idle time. When the goals of policing are changed to decreasing fear of crime, improving police-community interactions and communications, and engaging in more effective problem-solving techniques, this idle time becomes much more valuable.

## ■ Relationship of Strategies to Roles

Chapter 7 discussed police roles and styles and explained why it is difficult to examine those concepts in a democratic society. It is not easy to reach a consensus on what the police should emphasize in carrying out their tasks and how they should engage the community. The current discussion of police strategies illustrates the conceptual and philosophical differences in the policing field. Each strategy has its strong advocates; each has its underlying assumptions and goals, and each has its advantages and disadvantages (see **Table 10-12**) for a comparison of key elements of each strategy). But, each strategy should not be viewed as an isolated approach within itself. As one can see, it would be difficult for strategic policing to exist by itself, and the same holds true with problem-solving policing and community policing, to an extent. The real challenge may be a question of "What mix of these strategies will work best in a particular community?"

| Table 10-12 | Corporate Strategies For Policing | |
|---|---|---|
| **Factor** | **Professional crime fighting** | **Strategic policing** |
| Aim: | Create a disciplined, technically sophisticated, quasi-military crime fighting force | Increased capacity through strategic operations and specialization |
| Principal operating strategies | High visibility patrol, rapid response, in-depth investigation; Centralized command | More sophisticated investigations, task forces, raids, use of technology; Centralized command |
| Authority: | Based solely on the law | Legalistic, professional, and non-political autonomy |
| Values | Crime-control<br>Investment in training<br>Enhanced status and autonomy<br>Elimination of corruption and bribery<br>Emphasizes accountability<br>- - - - - - - - - - - - - - - - - - - - -<br>Basically reactive<br>Little emphasis on mobilizing the community | Strategies and aggressiveness rather than purely reactive;<br>Community can assist the police in crime prevention;<br>Political independence and lawfulness |
| **Factor** | **Problem-solving policing** | **Community policing** |
| Aim: | Order maintenance, fear reduction and crime control through proactiveness and thoughtfulness | Crime control through an effective working partnership between police and the community |
| Principal operating strategies | Diagnosing and resolving underlying problems/causes related to crime; believes crime is caused by particular continuing problems in the community<br>Decentralized operation but specialized | More interaction with citizens builds trust, improves cooperation and information exchange<br>Decentralized geographical distribution and accountability |
| Authority: | Based on the law and the obligation to assist the community in resolving recurring problems | Authority of officers is validated through the community in the form of support |
| Values | Crime-control and prevention through actions other than traditional methods<br>Broader use of alternatives both civil and criminal; mobilizes the community when necessary; mobilizes other agencies | Community organizations and institutions seen as key partners in creating safe and secure communities<br>Police need the political support and operational assistance of community; community views/concerns given high priority<br>- - - - - - - - - - - - - - - - - - - - -<br>Increases risks of illegitimate political demands on officers because of closer relationships with community |

*Source:* Adapted from M.H. Moore and R.C. Trojanowicz, (1988). Corporate strategies for policing. *Perspectives on Policing.* Washington, DC: National Institute of Justice and Cambridge, MA: Harvard University.

One could argue that each of the above strategies has its place in policing today. Much will depend on the situation and environment found within a particular community. For example, some departments review the comments and literature on community policing and wonder why others are so excited by it, and why some are such strong proponents of it, because some departments have been doing community policing for decades without the fanfare or the notoriety! Small departments always have utilized community-policing principles, to some extent, in their daily operations because of their size. As some have tried to explain, community policing is an attempt for some larger communities to bring "small town policing" to their neighborhood or their "corner of the world."

The professional crime-fighting strategy in many larger cities has resulted in the police being isolated from the law-abiding citizenry—patrol officers go from one call to the next, never taking the time to build a more trusting and friendly relationship with the citizens they serve. As some ask, "Talk to citizens in your community; do they know the name of the officers that patrol their area?" Ask that question in a small town whose citizens may have never heard of community policing, and your answer may be: "Of course, we know everyone in the department!"

Community expectations as to what the local policing efforts should accomplish vary from place to place. The smaller the community, the greater the likelihood for consensus; the larger the community, the more diverse the opinions (since larger communities usually have more extensive and diverse crime-related problems). All the strategies discussed above are used by agencies of all sizes in an attempt to combat crime and to serve the people—it is largely a matter of priority, commitment, and role expectation that determines which ones are operational at a given time.

The challenge for police managers appears to be: How can the police respond effectively to the crime problem and calls for service within their jurisdiction and do it in such a way that they are sensitive to everyone's needs, responsive to victims, and protective of constitutional rights; and that they instill trust, reduce fear, and encourage self-defense and community vigilance; and do it all cost-efficiently and without partisan-political interference? We do not mean to imply that this challenge is an impossible one. We merely are pointing out that policing does not occur in a vacuum and that many pressures and issues interact in the selection of an agency's role and the implementation of a policing strategy. Only when the public and all police officers fully understand these issues, can a true dialogue and partnership in policing begin to blossom in a community.

Aside from the challenge of how the police can respond effectively, police managers must also grapple with how they can respond equally and efficiently. Police managers and patrol officers are often faced with decisions in which the values of effectiveness, equality, and efficiency are in conflict. The next section discusses ethics in decision making in law enforcement.

## ■ Ethics

The law enforcement community of the United States does have an established and published **code of ethics**; in fact, it has more than one. The International Association of Chiefs of Police (IACP) at its 64th Annual Conference in 1957 adopted a code of ethics for the occupation. Along with that code was developed The Canons of Police Ethics, containing 11 articles. In 1989, a new code of ethics was adopted by the Executive Committee of the IACP during its 96th Annual Conference. At the 98th Annual Conference, the most recently adopted (1989) code of ethics was renamed "The Police Code of Conduct" and the 1957 version of the code of ethics was resurrected, revised, and adopted as the (1991) Law Enforcement Code of Ethics. In 1998, at the 105th Annual Conference, IACP adopted the Law Enforcement Oath of Honor, which states:

> On my honor, I will never betray my badge, my integrity, my character, or the public trust. I will always have the courage to hold myself and others accountable for our actions. I will always uphold the Constitution and community I serve (Higginbotham 1999).

Internationally, countries may substitute the word "Constitution" with a monarchy or person or ideal. The IACP, as well as other professional associations, has been very concerned about ethics and integrity in the field. Several key documents such as the IACP's *Law Enforcement Code of Ethics* (**Figure 10-7**), *The Police Code of Conduct* (**Figure 10-8**), and the *Canons of Police Ethics* (**Figure 10-9**) are reprinted here, as well as the National Sheriffs' Association's *Code of Ethics for the Office of the Sheriff* (**Figure 10-10**).

But what is a code of ethics and why have one? A code of ethics is a basic set of guidelines, or set of standards of behavior, to which one should conform in the performance of his or her duty. The word "ethics" has several connotations, including the study of human conduct in light of **morality**; the science dealing with moral duty; and the science of doing the right thing, at the right time, in

As a law enforcement officer, my fundamental duty is to serve the community; to safeguard lives and property; to protect the innocent against deception, the weak against oppression or intimidation, and the peaceful against violence or disorder; and to respect the Constitutional rights of all to liberty, equality, and justice.

I will keep my private life unsullied as an example to all and will behave in a manner which does not bring discredit to me or my agency. I will maintain courageous calm in the face of danger, scorn, or ridicule; develop self-restraint; and be constantly mindful of the welfare of others. Honest in thought and deed in both my personal and official life, I will be exemplary in obeying the law and the regulations of my department. Whatever I see or hear of a confidential nature or that is confided to me in my official capacity will be kept ever secret unless revelation is necessary in the performance of my duty.

I will never act officiously or permit personal feelings, prejudices, political beliefs, aspirations, animosities, or friendships to influence my decisions. With no compromise for crime and with relentless prosecution of criminals, I will enforce the law courteously and appropriately without fear or favor, malice or ill will, never employing unnecessary force or violence and never accepting gratuities.

I recognize the badge of my office as a symbol of public faith, and I accept it as a public trust to be held so long as I am true to the ethics of police service. I will never engage in acts of bribery nor will I condone such acts by other police officers. I will cooperate with all legally authorized agencies and their representatives in the pursuit of justice.

I know that I alone am responsible for my own standard of professional performance and will take every opportunity to enhance and improve my level of knowledge and competence. I will constantly strive to achieve these objectives and ideals, dedicating myself before God to my chosen profession . . . law enforcement.

*Source*: International Association of Chiefs of Police. Adopted by resolution at the 98th Conference, October 1991. Modified version of the original Code of 1957, © 1991. International Association of Chiefs of Police.

**Figure 10-7** The Law Enforcement Code of Ethics.

All law enforcement officers must be fully aware of the ethical responsibilities of their position and must strive constantly to live up to the highest possible standards of professional policing.

The International Association of Chiefs of Police believes it is important that police officers have clear advice and counsel available to assist them in performing their duties consistent with their standards, and has adopted the following ethical mandates as guidelines to meet these ends.

### Primary Responsibilities of a Police Officer

A police officer acts as an official representative of government who is required and trusted to work within the law. The officer's powers and duties are conferred by statute. The fundamental duties of a police officer include serving the community; safeguarding lives and property; protecting the innocent; keeping the peace; and ensuring the rights of all to liberty, equality, and justice.

### Performance of the Duties of a Police Officer

A police officer shall perform all duties impartially, without favor of affection or ill will and without regard to status, sex, race, religion, political belief or aspiration. All citizens will be treated equally with courtesy, consideration, and dignity.

Officers will never allow personal feelings, animosities, or friendships to influence official conduct. Laws will be enforced appropriately and courteously and, in carrying out their responsibilities, officers will strive to obtain maximum cooperation from the public. They will conduct themselves in appearance and deportment in such a manner as to inspire confidence and respect for the position of public trust they hold.

### Discretion

A police officer will use responsibly the discretion vested in the position and exercise it within the law. The principle of reasonableness will guide the officer's determinations and the officer will consider all surrounding circumstances in determining whether any legal action shall be taken.

Consistent and wise use of discretion, based on professional policing competence, will do much to preserve good relationships and to retain the confidence of the public. There can be difficulty in choosing between conflicting courses of action. It is important to remember that a timely word of advice rather than arrest—which may be correct in appropriate circumstances—can be a more effective means of achieving a desired end.

### Use of Force

A police officer will never employ unnecessary force or violence and will use only such force in the discharge of duty as is reasonable in all circumstances. Force should be used only with the greatest restraint and only after discussion, negotiation and persuasion have been found to be inappropriate or ineffective. While the use of force is occasionally unavoidable, every police officer will refrain from applying the unnecessary infliction of pain or suffering and will never engage in cruel, degrading, or inhuman treatment of any person.

### Confidentiality

Whatever a police officer sees, hears, or learns of, which is of a confidential nature, will be kept secret unless the performance of duty or legal provision requires otherwise. Members of the public have a right to security and privacy, and information obtained about them must not be improperly divulged.

### Integrity

A police officer will not engage in acts of corruption or bribery, nor will an officer condone such acts by other police officers. The public demands that the integrity of police officers be above reproach. Police officers must, therefore, avoid any conduct that might compromise integrity and thus undercut the public confidence in a law enforcement agency. Officers will refuse to accept any gifts, presents, subscriptions, favors, gratuities, or promises that could be interpreted as seeking to

*continues*

**Figure 10-8** The Police Code of Conduct.

**Figure 10-8** continued

cause the officer to refrain from performing official responsibilities honestly and within the law. Police officers must not receive private or special advantage from their official status. Respect from the public cannot be bought; it can only be earned and cultivated.

*Cooperation with Other Officers and Agencies*

Police officers will cooperate with all legally authorized agencies and their representatives in the pursuit of justice. An officer or agency may be one among many organizations that may provide law enforcement services to a jurisdiction. It is imperative that a police officer assist colleagues fully and completely with respect and consideration at all times.

*Personal/Professional Capabilities*

Police officers will be responsible for their own standard of professional performance and will take every reasonable opportunity to enhance and improve their level of knowledge and competence. Through study and experience, a police officer can acquire the high level of knowledge and competence that is essential for efficient and effective performance of duty. The acquisition of knowledge is a never-ending process of personal and professional development that should be pursued constantly.

*Private Life*

Police officers will behave in a manner that does not bring discredit to their agencies or themselves. A police officer's character and conduct while off duty must always be exemplary, thus maintaining a position of respect in the community in which he or she lives and serves. The officer's personal behavior must be beyond reproach.

*Source*: International Association of Chiefs of Police. Adopted by resolution at the 98th Conference, October 1991. Modified version of the original Code of 1957, © 1991. International Association of Chiefs of Police.

the right way. Morality refers to the conformity to rules of **right conduct** and **moral behavior** and can be described as representing actions prescribed by the society for the welfare of the people and society as a whole. The interconnectedness of ethics, morality, and right conduct becomes evident upon review of these terms and their meanings. Thus, to act ethically is to act according to certain agreed-upon expectations of proper (right) conduct. The purpose of a code of ethics, then, is to guide the behavior of persons in that particular occupation (or profession). The code becomes the standards against which others will judge the actions of those in the occupation.

Developing a code designed to regulate behavior, however, does not make decision making in law enforcement any easier. As was discussed earlier in this chapter, police officers are value-based decision makers. In any given situation, officers must make decisions based on competing values such as equality versus efficiency; security versus liberty; and the individual good versus the collective good. Codes of ethics are simply guidelines for law enforcement to reflect upon when making difficult decisions. These codes do not, however, tell an officer which value to choose over another equally important and respected value. For example, some would argue that the overarching value in law enforcement is what is termed the "noble cause" (Caldero and Crank 2004). The noble cause is a moral commitment to make the world a safer place to live. Put simply, it is getting bad guys off the street. People are trained and armed to protect the innocent and:

## ARTICLE I. PRIMARY RESPONSIBILITY OF JOB

The primary responsibility of the police service, and of the individual officer, is the protection of the people of the United States through the upholding of their laws; chief among these is the Constitution of the United States and its amendments. The law enforcement officer always represents the whole of the community and its legally expressed will and is never the arm of any political party or clique.

## ARTICLE II. LIMITATIONS OF AUTHORITY

The first duty of a law enforcement officer, as upholder of the law, is to know its bounds upon him in enforcing it. Because he represents the legal will of the community, be it local, state, or federal, he must be aware of the limitations and pro-scriptions which the people, through the law, have placed upon him. He must recognize the genius of the American system of government which gives to no man, groups of men, or institution, absolute power, and he must insure that he, as a prime defender of that system, does not pervert its character.

## ARTICLE III. DUTY TO BE FAMILIAR WITH THE LAW AND WITH RESPONSIBILITIES OF SELF AND OTHER PUBLIC OFFICIALS

The law enforcement officer shall assiduously apply himself to the study of the principles of the laws which he is sworn to uphold. He will make certain of his responsibilities in the particulars of their enforcement, seeking aid from his superiors in matters of technicality or principle when these are not clear to him; he will make special effort to fully understand his rela-tionship to other public officials, including other law enforcement agencies, particularly on matters of jurisdiction, both geographically and substantively.

## ARTICLE IV. UTILIZATION OF PROPER MEANS TO GAIN PROPER ENDS

The law enforcement officer shall be mindful of his responsibility to pay strict heed to selection of means in discharging the duties of his office. Violations of law or disregard for public safety and property on the part of an officer are intrinsically wrong; they are self-defeating in that they instill in the public mind a like disposition. The employment of illegal means, no matter how worthy the end, is certain to encourage disrespect for the law and its officers. If the law is honored, it must be honored by those who enforce it.

## ARTICLE V. COOPERATION WITH PUBLIC OFFICIALS IN THE DISCHARGE OF THEIR AUTHORIZED DUTIES

The law enforcement officer shall cooperate fully with other public officials in the discharge of authorized duties, regard-less of party affiliation or personal prejudice. He shall be meticulous, however, in assuring himself of the propriety, under the law, of such actions and shall guard against the use of his office or person, whether knowingly or unknowingly, in any improper action. In any situation open to question, he shall seek authority from his superior officer, giving him a full report of the proposed service or action.

## ARTICLE VI. PRIVATE CONDUCT

The law enforcement officer shall be mindful of his special identification by the public as an upholder of the law. Laxity of conduct or manner in private life, expressing either disrespect for the law or seeking to gain special privilege , cannot but reflect upon the police officer ant the police service. The community and the service require that the law enforcement offi-cer lead the life of a decent and honorable man. Following the career of a policeman gives no man special privileges. It does give the satisfaction and pride of following and furthering an unbroken tradition of safeguarding the American republic. The officer who reflects upon this tradition will not degrade it. Rather, he will so conduct his private life that the public will re-gard him as an example of stability, fidelity, and morality.

## ARTICLE VII. CONDUCT TOWARD THE PUBLIC

The law enforcement officer, mindful of his responsibility to the whole community, shall deal with individuals of the com-munity in a manner calculated to instill respect for its laws and its police service. The law enforcement officer shall conduct

*continues*

**Figure 10-9** Canons of Police Ethics.

**Figure 10-9** continued

his official life in a manner such as will inspire confidence and trust. Thus, he will be neither overbearing nor subservient, as no individual citizen has an obligation to stand in awe of him nor a right to command him. The officer will give service where he can, and require compliance with the law. He will do neither from personal preference or prejudice but rather as a duly appointed officer of the law discharging his sworn obligation.

### ARTICLE VIII. CONDUCT IN ARRESTING AND DEALING WITH LAW VIOLATORS

The law enforcement officer shall use his power of arrest strictly in accordance with the law and with due regard to the rights of the citizen concerned. His office gives him no right to prosecute the violator nor to mete out punishment for the offense. He shall at all times, have a clear appreciation of his responsibilities and limitations regarding detention of the violator; he shall conduct himself in such a manner as will minimize the possibility of having to use force. To this end he shall cultivate a dedication to the service of the people and the equitable upholding of their laws whether in the handling of law violators or in dealing with the law-abiding.

### ARTICLE IX. GIFTS AND FAVORS

The law enforcement officer, representing government, bears the heavy responsibility of maintaining, in his conduct, the honor and integrity of all government institutions. He shall, therefore, guard against placing himself in a position in which any person can expect special consideration or in which the public can reasonably assume that special consideration is being given. Thus, he should be firm in refusing gifts, favors, or gratuities, large or small, which can, in the public mind, be interpreted as capable of influencing his judgment in the discharge of his duties.

### ARTICLE X. PRESENTATION OF EVIDENCE

The law enforcement officer shall be concerned equally in the prosecution of the wrong-doer and the defense of the innocent. He shall ascertain what constitutes evidence and shall present such evidence impartially and without malice. In so doing, he will ignore social, political, and all other distinctions among the persons involved, strengthening the tradition of the reliability and integrity of an officer's word.

The law enforcement officer shall take special pains to increase his perception and skill of observation, mindful that in many situations his is the sole impartial testimony to the facts of a case.

### ARTICLE XI. ATTITUDE TOWARD PROFESSION

The law enforcement officer shall regard the discharge of his duties as a public trust and recognize his responsibility as a public servant. By diligent study and sincere attention to self-improvement he shall strive to make the best possible application of science to the solution of crime and, in the field of human relationships, strive for effective leadership and public influence in matters affecting public safety. He shall appreciate the importance and responsibility of his office, hold police work to be an honorable profession rendering valuable service to his community and his country.

*Source*: Copyright © International Association of Chiefs of Police.

*. . . think about that goal in terms of 'keeping the scum off the streets.' It is not simply a verbal commitment, recited at graduation at the local Peace Officer Standards and Training (POST) academy. Nor is it something police have to learn. It's something to which they are morally committed. Those who don't feel it are not destined for police work and will be quickly liberated from the hazards of a career in blue* (29).

At face value, if the "noble cause" is indeed the overarching value of law enforcement, police officers then must simply make those decisions that make

As a constitutionally elected Sheriff, I recognize and accept that I am given a special trust and confidence by the citizens and employees whom I have been elected to serve, represent and manage. This trust and confidence is my bond to ensure that I shall behave and act according to the highest personal and professional standards. In furtherance of this pledge, I will abide by the following Code of Ethics.

I SHALL ENSURE that I and my employees, in the performance of our duties, will enforce and administer the law according to the standards of the US Constitution and applicable State Constitutions and statutes so that equal protection of the law is guaranteed to everyone. To that end I shall not permit personal opinions, party affiliations, or consideration of the status of others to alter or lessen this standard of treatment of others.

I SHALL ESTABLISH, PROMULGATE AND ENFORCE a set of standards of behavior of my employees which will govern the overall management and operation of the law enforcement functions, court related activities, and corrections operations of my agency.

I SHALL NOT TOLERATE NOR CONDONE brutal or inhumane treatment of others by my employees nor shall I permit or condone inhumane or brutal treatment of inmates in my care and custody.

I STRICTLY ADHERE to standards of fairness and integrity in the conduct of campaigns for election and I shall conform to all applicable statutory standards of election financing and reporting that the Office of the Sheriff is not harmed by the actions of myself or others.

I SHALL ROUTINELY CONDUCT or have conducted an internal and external audit of the public funds entrusted to my care and publish this information so that citizens can be informed about my stewardship of these funds.

I SHALL FOLLOW the accepted principles of efficient and effective administration and management as the principle criteria for my judgments and decisions in the allocation of resources and services in law enforcement, court related and corrections functions of my Office.

I SHALL HIRE AND PROMOTE only those employees or others who are the very best candidates for a position according to accepted standards of objectivity and merit. I shall not permit other factors to influence hiring or promotion practices.

I SHALL ENSURE that all employees are granted and receive relevant training supervision in the performance of their duties so that competent and excellent service is provided by the Office of the Sheriff.

I SHALL ENSURE that during my tenure as Sheriff, I shall not use the Office or Sheriff for private gain.

I ACCEPT AND WILL ADHERE TO THIS CODE OF ETHICS. In so doing, I accept responsibility for encouraging others in my profession to abide by this Code.

*Source:* Copyright © National Sheriffs' Association.

**Figure 10-10** Code of Ethics for the Office of the Sheriff

our streets safer. However, when taking a deeper look into the elements of daily police work, seemingly simple tenants of the noble cause become blurred. For example, "bad guys" are often victims themselves. Victims often precipitate their own victimization. Arresting the "bad guy" is not always possible nor is it always the most desirable or effective response. The "bad guy" is not always a criminal and "crime" in and of itself is not always the biggest problem in a community. In addition, value-based decisions in law enforcement are further complicated when looking at means and ends. Decisions made regarding the ends of policing (getting the bad guy off the street) may be ethical until one looks at the means of doing so (planting evidence or lying in a report). Furthermore, the ethical standards society holds police to is also situational. For example, society is much more accepting of unethical behavior by law enforcement if it results in the life of a child being saved versus if police acted unethically in investigating a tax fraud case.

## ■ Summary

In this chapter, we examined many suggested causes of crime (**Figure 10-11** summarizes these). In nearly each case, the theories are based upon the conditions of the community (or environment) in which people live, grow, learn, and work. People's families (or lack thereof), relationships, and experiences all influence behavior both criminal and noncriminal. Understanding the behavior of people is the key. It is related to determining who has committed an offense, as well as who might commit an offense and what might be done to prevent future crime. Understanding begins by identifying the underlying causal forces of crime. This very cursory view is intended only as an introduction to the more detailed aspects of criminological theory.

Similarly, this chapter addressed several emerging areas in which particular types of crime pose significant challenges for law enforcement and for patrol officers in particular. Because we are only now learning about many of these kinds of problems in sufficient detail to address corrective approaches, the new patrol officer must commit him or herself to learning about these as knowledge develops. They will form some of the most significant crime challenges of the next decade.

In addition, the major strategies of policing (professional crime-fighting, strategic, problem-solving, and community) that have been utilized during the last 30 years were presented and described in terms of underlying philosophies and operational tactics. It was pointed out that these strategies are interrelated to the degree that they can coexist in the same agency, and each strategy attempts to fulfill particular objectives. The relationship of role to the selection of a department's policing strategy was mentioned as an important factor in understanding the complexities of these issues.

Finally, the challenge for police appears to lie on three fronts: providing effective service, responding to emerging crime problems, and improving ethical decision making within the ranks. What policing personnel must understand is that their responses to these challenges will determine the likelihood of acquiring respect and satisfaction from the communities they serve.

Individual causes
- Pleasure-pain principle
- Internal control deficiency
- Poor education
- Dysfunctional childhood

Social causes
- Ecological conditions
- Differential association and learning labeling
- Social control and socialization

Emerging possible causes
- Drugs
- Technological ease
- Discriminatory attitudes
- Gang organization
- Domestic dysfunction

**Figure 10-11** Causes of crime.

## QUESTIONS FOR REVIEW

1. What are the underlying problems with UCR data?
2. What are the advantages of NCVS data over URC data?
3. Compare individual theories of crime to social theories of crime. Which theories offer us more direction in what law enforcement should do? Why?
4. Define, in one or two sentences, each of the major theories of crime.
5. What are the two primary motives of those who commit computer-based crime?
6. What is meant by "lost opportunity costs" of crime?
7. What are basic tenets of each of the four major strategies of policing?
8. What is the relationship of role to policing strategy selection?
9. What is the purpose or significance of a code of ethics?

## SUGGESTED ACTIVITIES

1. At the library, look up UCR data for your city, county, and state. How does it compare to other cities, counties, and states? To the national data?
2. Divide into teams. Prepare a debate concerning the usefulness of crime causation theory in policy making. What policies seem to be most suited to reducing crime?
3. Explain each of the major theories of crime. For each theory, list the kinds of data or information needed to test the theory. Examples might include the divorce rate, single parenthood rate, child abuse rate, unemployment rate, and the number of hours children watch television as opposed to spending time with parents.
4. With the data you developed in exercise 3, develop a debate surrounding each theory and what it means for law enforcement.
5. Go to the home page of the National Criminal Justice Reference Service (NCJRS) and locate at least one article and one graph depicting trends in crime patterns.
6. Interview a local police administrator about his/her department's policing strategy. Does the department utilize more than one strategy of the four discussed in this chapter?
7. Contact local crime prevention units or associations and ask a guest into your classroom for a discussion of their typical activities.
8. Log on to the World Wide Web and go to several of the following URLs and review the concepts and techniques associated with crime prevention:
   http://www.ncpc.org
   http://ncjrs.aspensys.com/
   http://www.weprevent.org
   http://www.nationaltownwatch.org/natw.html
   http://www.crimepreventcoalition.org/

http://ourworld.compuserve.com/homepages/iscpp/

http://www.tcpa.org/home/htm

http://www.c-s-i.org/index.htm

**9.** Contact a local police department and ask how the code of ethics is explained or distributed to its officers.

## ■ Chapter Glossary

**associate**   certain traits, norms, or behaviors are learned by close connections with others who act the same way.

**cause of crime**   if one thing happens another will follow; in this sense, each theory of the cause of crime states that if the conditions outlined in the theory occur, crime will follow.

**Chicago School**   the group of theorists who believed that one's surroundings account for subsequent behavior.

**code of ethics**   a basic set of guidelines, or set of standards of behavior.

**community policing**   an attempt by agencies to form a partnership with the residents of the area to reduce crime victimization and to improve the overall quality of life.

**deterrence**   a theory that suggests that people are rational and if threatened with potential punishment for doing certain things, they will not commit the acts.

**differential association**   a theory that holds that close contact with another culture will cause the subject to adopt that culture.

**Drug Abuse Resistance Education (DARE)**   a national educational program that places police officers in the elementary classrooms to teach children about drugs and the negative aspects of drug use.

**Ecological School**   *see* Chicago School.

**hackers**   common title used by the media to refer to computer specialists who seek ways to get into other computers and bypass the security systems to test their skills.

**Index Crimes** or **Crime Index**   the number of index crimes committed in each year per 100,000 population; the eight major crimes counted by the UCR.

**labeling**   a theory that suggests that juveniles who are repeatedly described as delinquent will come to act in exactly that manner.

**learn**   acquire norms or attitudes by observing others with whom there is some close connection.

**lost opportunity costs**   money lost due to crime and which cannot be used for other more beneficial things in society or individually.

**morality**   refers to the conformity to rules of right conduct.

**moral behavior** or **right conduct**   is described as representing actions prescribed by the society for the welfare of the people and society as a whole.

**National Crime Victimization Survey (NCVS)**    a survey of thousands of households and businesses regarding victimization during the last year; conducted for the Bureau of Justice Statistics (US Department of Justice) by the Bureau of the Census.

**Part 1 Offenses**    *see* index crimes.

**pleasure-pain**    the central aspect of the utilitarian theory.

**preventive patrol**    the highly visible and random presence of the police coupled with the belief that this deters and/or prevents crime from occurring.

**problem-solving policing**    also called problem-oriented policing; a strategy based on the assumption that crime is successfully controlled by discovering the underlying reasons or causes for offenses which include frustrating relationships and a disorderly environment.

**professional crime-fighting policing**    a strategy based on the legal authority of the police coupled with political independence for the purpose of achieving crime control through expert service.

**public policy**    anything that the government chooses to do or to not do.

**rationalism**    the school of thought associated with utilitarianism, which held that people make decisions after weighing the costs and benefits, choosing the course of action most likely to benefit them.

**reactive policing**    an orientation that involves a response to calls for service after the incident.

**recidivism**    committing crimes after once being punished.

**social control**    a theory which contends that family and other similar groups teach people internal controls (self-control) and exercise direct control over their behavior, thereby preventing antisocial actions.

**socialization**    the process of learning one's culture.

**strategic policing**    refers to an attempt to expand the professional crime-fighting strategy through more sophisticated, analytical, and targeted crime control applications.

**strategies of policing**    the phrase used to refer to the agency's definition of what the organization proposes to do and how. It describes the principal products, technologies, and methods used in striving for and achieving the agency's goals and objectives.

**street level bureaucrats**    term used to apply to government employees, including police, who make street level decisions that affect people's lives.

**subculture**    a set of norms and beliefs that are separate from the main culture and represent the beliefs of a small number of people.

**Uniform Crime Report** or **UCR**    reports made by participating law enforcement agencies which keep exact monthly records of offenses reported to them. Monthly totals are given to the FBI.

**utilitarian principle**    people attempt to maximize their self-interest (seek pleasure) and will avoid penalties (pain). If the cost of doing something exceeds the value of doing it, then the action will be avoided.

**victimless crime**  behavior defined as criminal but engaged in by many who think it should not be.

## Chapter References

Akers, Ronald L. (1997). *Criminological theories: Introduction and evaluation.* Los Angeles, CA: Roxbury Publishing.

Ball, Richard A. and G. David Curry (1995). The logic of definition in criminology: Purposes and methods for defining 'gangs.' *Criminology 33*(2):225–245.

Braithwaite, John (1989). *Crime, shame and reintegration.* Cambridge, UK: Cambridge University Press.

Bureau of Justice Statistics (1994). *Drugs and crime facts.* Washington, DC: US Department of Justice.

Bureau of Justice Statistics (1998). *Profile of jail inmates, 1996.* Washington, DC: US Department of Justice.

Bureau of Justice Statistics (1999). *Substance abuse and treatment, state and federal prisoners, 1997.* Washington, DC: US Department of Justice

Bureau of Justice Statistics (2002). *Criminal victimization, 2001.* Washington, DC: US Department of Justice.

Bureau of Justice Statistics (2002). National Crime Victimization Survey. US Department of Justice, Office of Justice Programs. Available online: http://www.ojp.usdoj.gov/bjs/pubalp2.htm#cv.

Bureau of Justice Statistics (2004). *Drugs and crime facts.* Washington, DC: US Department of Justice.

Caldero, Michael A. and John P. Crank (2004). *Police ethics: The corruption of noble cause.* Dayton, OH: LexisNexis/Anderson Publishing.

Cohen, Lawrence E. and Marcus Felson (1979). Social change and crime rate trends: A routine activity approach. *American Sociological Review 44*:588–608.

Cook, Philip J. and John H. Laub (1998). The unprecedented epidemic in youth violence. In *Youth Violence,* Michael Tonry and Mark H. Moore (eds.). Volume 24 of *Crime and Justice: A Review of Research.* Chicago, IL: University of Chicago Press.

Cordner, Gary and Robert C. Trojanowicz (1992). Patrol. In Cordner, Gary W. and Donna C. Hale (eds.), *What works in policing?* Cincinnati, OH: Anderson Publishing Co.

Cordner, G.W. and G.L. Williams (1996). *Community policing and accreditation: A content analysis of CALEA.* Washington, DC: Police Executive Research Forum.

Eck, John E. and Dennis P. Rosenbaum (1994). The new police order: Effectiveness, equity, and efficiency in community policing. In Dennis P. Rosenbaum (ed.), *The challenge of community policing: Testing the promises.* Thousand Oaks, CA: Sage Press, 3–23.

Esbensen, Finn-Aage and David Huizinga (1993). Gangs, drugs, and delinquency in a survey of urban youth. *Criminology 31*(4):565–586.

Federal Bureau of Investigation (2002). *Crime in the United States, 2002.* US Department of Justice, Washington, DC: US Government Printing Office.

Felson, Marcus (2002). *Crime and everyday life,* 3rd Edition. Thousand Oaks, CA: Sage Press.

Gay, William G., Theodore H. Schell, and Stephen Schack (1977). *Improving patrol productivity, Volume I, Routine patrol,* and *Improving patrol productivity, Volume II, Specialized Patrol.* Washington, DC: Law Enforcement Assistance Administration, pp. 220–226.

Goldstein, Herman (1990). *Problem-oriented policing.* New York: McGraw-Hill.

Gondolf, Edward W. and J. Richard McFerron (1989). Handling battering men: Police action in wife abuse cases. *Criminal Justice and Behavior 16*(4):429–439.

Gorman, Dennis M. and White, H.R. (1995). You can choose your friends, but do they choose your crime? Implications of differential association theories for crime prevention policy. In H.D. Barlow (ed.), *Crime and public policy: Putting theory to work,* pp. 131–155. Boulder, CO: Westview Press.

Gottfredson, Michael and Travis Hirschi (1990). *A general theory of crime.* Palo Alto, CA: Stanford University Press.

Greenberg, Bernard, et al. (1975). *Felony investigation decision model—An analysis of investigative elements of information.* Menlo Park, CA: Stanford Research Institute.

Greenwood, Peter (1995). Juvenile crime and juvenile justice. In James Q. Wilson and Joan Petersilia (eds.), *Crime,* pp. 91–117. San Francisco: ICS Press.

Higginbotham, Charles (1999). Law enforcement oath of honor. *Resolution adopted 21 October 1998.* Correspondence regarding action taken at the 105th Annual Conference of the International Association of Chiefs of Police, June 3, at Salt Lake City, Utah.

Hirschel, J. David, Ira W. Hutchinson, Charles W. Dean, and Anne-Marie Mills (1992a). Review essay on the law enforcement response to spouse abuse: Past, present and future. *Justice Quarterly* 9(2):247–283.

Hirschel, J. David, Ira W. Hutchison, Charles W. Dean, and Anne-Marie Mills (1992b). The failure of arrest to deter spouse abuse. *Journal of Research in Crime and Delinquency* 29(1):7–33.

International Association of Chiefs of Police (1991). *The law enforcement code of ethics.* Adopted by resolution at the 1998 Conference, October (modified version of the original Code of 1957).

International Association of Chiefs of Police (1991). *The police code of conduct.* Adopted by resolution at the 98 Conference, October (modified version of the original Code of 1957).

Irwin, John (1994). *It's about time: America's imprisonment binge.* Belmont, CA: Wadsworth Publishing.

Kelling, George and Mark H. Moore (1988). *The evolving strategy of policing.* Washington, DC: National Institute of Justice and Cambridge, MA: Harvard University.

Klein, Malcolm W., Cheryl L. Maxson, and Lea C. Cunningham (1991). Crack, street gangs and violence. *Criminology* 29(4):623–650.

Klockars, Carl B. and Stephen D. Matrofski (eds.) (1991). *Thinking about police: Contemporary readings,* 2nd Edition. New York: McGraw-Hill.

Lipsky, Michael (1980). *Street-level bureaucracy: Dilemmas of the individual in public service.* Newbury, CA: Russell Sage Foundation.

Ludman, R.J. (1993), *Prevention and Control of Juvenile Delinquency.* New York: Oxford University Press.

Maguire, Kathleen, Ann L. Pastore, and Timothy J. Flanagan (1993). *Sourcebook of criminal justice statistics, 1992.* Washington, DC: US Department of Justice.

Maguire, Kathleen and Ann L. Pastore (eds.) (2003). *Sourcebook of criminal justice statistics 2002* [Online]. Available: http://www.albany.edu/sourcebook/ [12/14/04].

Miethe, Terance D., and Richard McCorkle (1998). *Crime profiles: The anatomy of dangerous persons, places and situations.* Los Angeles, CA: Roxbury Publishing.

Moore, Mark H. and Robert C. Trojanowicz (1988). Corporate strategies for policing. *Perspectives on policing.* Washington, DC: National Institute of Justice and Cambridge, MA: Harvard University.

National Institute of Justice (2003). *Annual report 2000: Arrestee drug abuse monitoring.* Washington, DC: US Department of Justice.

National Sheriffs' Association (nd). *Code of ethics for the office of the sheriff.* Alexandria, VA.

Petersilia, Joan (1993). The influence of research on policing. In Dunham, Roger G. and Geoffrey P. Alpert (eds.), *Critical issues in policing: Contemporary readings.* Prospect Heights, IL: Waveland Press, Inc.

*RAV v. St. Paul,* 505 US 377 (1992).

Reaves, Brian and Andrew L. Smith (1999). *Law enforcement management and administrative statistics, 1997: Data for individual state and local agencies with 100 or more officers.* Washington, DC: US Department of Justice.

Rosenbaum, Dennis P., Arthur J. Lurigio, and Robert C. Davis (1998). *The Prevention of crime: Social and situational strategies.* Belmont, CA: Wadsworth Publishing.

Sampson, Robert J. and John H. Laub (1993). *Crime in the making: Pathways and turning points through life.* Cambridge, MA: Harvard University Press.

Schell, Theodore H., et al. (1976). *Traditional preventive patrol.* Washington, DC: Law Enforcement Assistance Administration.

Sherman, Lawrence W. (1990). Police crackdowns. *NIJ Reports.* Washington, DC: US Department of Justice.

Skogan, Wesley G. (1990). *Disorder and decline: Crime and the spiral of decay in American neighborhoods.* New York: Free Press.

Skogan, Wesley G. (2004). *Community policing: Can it work?* Belmont, CA: Thompson/Wadsworth Publishing,

Spelman, William G. and Dale K. Brown (1991). Response time. In Klockars, Carl B. and Stephen D. Mastrofski (eds.), *Thinking about police: Contemporary readings,* 2nd Edition, pp. 163–169. New York: McGraw-Hill.

Spergel, Irving A. (1990). Youth gangs: Continuity and change. In Michael Tonry and Norval Morris (eds.), *Crime and justice: A review of the research,* volume 12. Chicago: University of Chicago Press.

Thornberry, Terence P., Marvin D. Krohn, Alan J. Lizotte, and Deborah Chard-Wierschem. (1993). The role of juvenile gangs in facilitating delinquent behavior. *Journal of Research in Crime and Delinquency,* 30:55–87.

Tittle, Charles R. (1995). *Control balance: Toward a general theory of deviance.* Boulder, CO: Westview Press.

Trojanowicz, Robert, and Bonnie Bucqueroux (1990). *Community policing.* Cincinnati, OH: Anderson Publishing Co.

US Department of Justice (1992). *National center for the analysis of violent crime: Annual report, 1991.* Washington, DC: Federal Bureau of Investigation.

Walker, Samuel (1998). *Sense and nonsense about crime and drugs,* 4th edition. Belmont, CA: Wadsworth Publishing.

Williams, A. Kevin (1995). Community mobilization against urban crime: Guiding orientations and strategic choices in grassroots politics. *Urban Affairs Review* 30(3):407-431.

Williams, Emma Jean (1996). Enforcing social responsibility and the expanding domain of the police. *Crime & Delinquency,* 42(2):309–323.

Williams, Franklin P. and Marilyn D. McShane (1988). *Criminological theory.* Englewood Cliffs, NJ: Prentice Hall.

Wilson, James Q. and Richard J. Hernstein (1985). *Crime and human nature: The definitive study of the causes of crime.* New York: Touchstone/Simon and Schuster.

Winfree, L. Thomas, Jr., Kathy Fuller, Teresa Vigil, and G. Larry Mays (1992). The definitions and measurement of 'gang status': Policy implications for juvenile justice. *Juvenile and Family Court Journal* 43(1):29–38.

Wolfgang, M., Robert M. Figlio, and Thorsten Sellin (1972). *Delinquency in a birth cohort.* Chicago: University of Chicago Press.

# Technology in Law Enforcement

## 11

This chapter addresses technology's impact on crime and the use and application of technology in law enforcement. The common person uses the term technology in many ways; to many it is limited to the fields of the physical sciences, such as physics and engineering. Some include the natural sciences (e.g., biology and chemistry) in the discussion of technology. Still others include the methods and techniques developed from the social sciences (e.g., sociology and psychology) when referring to technology. We think of technology as the practical application of any science or tool to common endeavors. As such, this chapter's focus is threefold: it presents (1) the challenges posed by technologically enhanced criminal behavior, (2) the uses of technology in law enforcement operations, and (3) the future implications of technology on privacy rights. Upon completion of this chapter, you should be able to:

- Describe technology's general impact on criminal behavior by identifying two categories of technologically enhanced crime and give examples of each.
- Identify the three influencing factors since the early 1900s that led to establishing filing systems and the need for more documentation of law enforcement operations.
- Briefly describe the evolution and importance of the NCIC and other large databases to law enforcement's mission and operation at the different levels of government.
- Explain the concept of "data mining" and how it relates to the multiple databases used in law enforcement.
- Identify several reasons for the need of communications interoperability and information sharing among law enforcement agencies and how these concerns are being addressed.
- Identify at least five major applications of technology in the field of law enforcement.

■ Identify the major concerns related to the potential abuses of technology in the law enforcement field.

## Chapter Outline

## Key Terms Used in This Chapter

technologically enhanced crime
spyware
National Crime Information Center (NCIC)
NCIC 2000
CODIS
Secure Flight
FinCEN
US-VISIT
data mining
data warehouse
MATRIX
ECHELON
interoperability
regional information sharing systems (RISS)
computer-aided dispatch systems
automated vehicle locator system (AVLS)

global positioning system (GPS)
geographic information systems (GIS; also called computer mapping and geocoding)
crime analysis
Compstat
less-than-lethal technologies
automated fingerprint identification systems
teleforensics
personal video surveillance systems
personal vertical takeoff and landing aircraft (VTOL)
unmanned aerial vehicles (UAVs)
augmented reality
privacy rights paradigm

## ■ Technology and Crime

Americans have a love affair with technology! A major part of our economy is based on goods and services related to technology. Just look around. People everywhere are walking or driving with cellular phones up to their ears, some even wearing handless headphone varieties. We observe people using personal data assistants (PDAs) as appointment and address books and listening to music on portable devices. Digital cameras and camcorders have become commonplace and allow users to immediately view captured images, and, of course, the most modern and expensive cell phones combine all of these functions into one device. Wearable computers are emerging on the scene, and they will probably be one of the next waves of technological devices to capture the desires of the consuming public (see **Figure 11-1**).

We use technology for a variety of purposes: entertainment and leisure, business and commerce, public safety and order, and unfortunately, in criminal endeavors. As the technology evolves, so do the methods of operation of criminal perpetrators. **Technologically enhanced crime** can be classified into two categories: "traditional crimes" and "high-tech crimes." Traditional crimes include those that are committed with the use or aid of technology, such as counterfeiting, money laundering, forgery, theft of trade secrets, identity theft, credit card theft, the distribution of child pornography, the sale of illegal drugs, Internet fraud and scams, illegal gambling, and hate propaganda. Technology enhances the ability of perpetrators to lessen the time to commit such offenses, to enhance obtaining personal information from potential victims, to make detection more difficult, or to enhance the quality of materials or documents used in such offenses. High-tech crimes employ new technologies to shield, store, or communicate criminal activities. Such offenses and abuses include crimes directed against a computer itself or a computer network, including unauthorized use of computer systems (e.g., criminal hacking), denial of service attacks, and virus transmission.

One of the most common traditional crimes in the United States is fraud (a form of theft). In 2004, the Federal Trade Commission (FTC) estimated that some form of fraud victimizes 1 in 10 Americans annually. Of those victimized, 33% were lured into the fraud by printed media (newspapers, direct mail, posters, etc.), 17% were lured into the fraud by telemarketing, and 14% by the Internet or email. The latter two methods are related to technology. The FTC reports that the median loss for victims of fraud was $228 and that the median loss for victims of Internet-related fraud was $195 (Federal Trade Commission 2004a). For 2003, the most prevalent types of Internet fraud based on complaints and reports are listed in **Figure 11-2** (Federal Trade Commission 2004b).

In addition to the various types of fraud, the FTC also estimated that 13.9 million consumers were victims of telephone "slamming"—unauthorized and il-

For decades the talk has been "when will the Dick Tracy wristwatch get here?" The question referred to a cartoon strip where the key character, beginning in 1946, wore a wristwatch that served as a transmitting and receiving device. In January of 2004, *USA Today* ran an article about the availability of a wristwatch that could also display temperature, wind chill, humidity, stock quotes, news headlines, personal messages, and act as a calendar. The watch cost about $129 plus $59 per year for data service.

*Source:* Edward C. Baig (2004). A forearm forecast, and more. *USA Today*, January 8, p. 5B.

**Figure 11-1** The net wristwatch.

- Internet auctions
- Shop-at-home/catalog sales
- Internet services and computer complaints
- Prizes, sweepstakes, and lotteries
- Foreign money offers
- Advance fee loans and credit protection
- Telephone services
- Business opportunities and work-at-home plans
- Magazine buyers clubs
- Office supplies and services

*Source:* Federal Trade Commission, 2004.

**Figure 11-2** Top 10 forms of Internet fraud.

legal changes in long distance telephone service. Technology can be confusing to consumers or it can help to confuse people into becoming victims (Federal Trade Commission 2004a).

Identity theft is the fastest growing crime in the United States. In 2003, nearly 10 million persons were victims of identity theft. Some experts indicate the number of cases has doubled every year since 2000 (Fleck 2004). The FTC estimated that in 2003, identity theft cost individuals over $5 billion in uninsured expenses and cost businesses over $48 billion. It also indicated that about 38% of victims spend more than a month trying to figure out what happened to them. Identity theft can occur by several methods, from the simple theft of a wallet containing documents and credit cards to the sophisticated planting of "**spyware**" on one's computer to remotely capture and obtain personal information, bank account numbers, and passwords. Spyware is the general term used to describe a computer program that is surreptitiously downloaded to one's computer that permits others to obtain information from that computer when it is online (see **Figure 11-3**). Some have referred to the technique as the "virtual peeping Tom."

*Cookies*—Small pieces of state stored on individual clients' Web browsers on behalf of Web servers that can be retrieved by the Web site that initially stored them. They can potentially track the behavior of users across many Web sites; a passive form of spyware.

*Web bugs*—Invisible images embedded on pages; passive forms of spyware; they contain no code of their own, relying instead on existing Web browser functions.

*Browser hijackers*—Software that changes Web browser settings to modify home pages.

*Tracks*—A generic name for the recording of selected information by an operating system. Recently visited Web site lists are maintained by most browsers. Malicious programs can mine tracks.

*Keyloggers*—Software that records all keystrokes in order to capture passwords and account and credit card numbers.

*Malware*—A variety of malicious software, such as viruses, worms, and Trojan horses, that can freeze a computer or destroy files.

*Spybots*—Software that monitors users' behavior, collects logs of activity, and then transmits them to third parties without the users' knowledge.

*Adware*—A more benign variety of spybot; a program that displays advertisements tuned to the users' current activity, potentially reporting aggregate or anonymized browsing behavior to a third party.

*Source:* Saroiu, Stefan, Steven D. Gribble, and Henry M. Levy (2004). Measurement and Analysis of Spyware in a University Environment. Paper presented at the First Symposium on Networked Systems Design and Implementation. March 29–31, http://www.cs.washington.edu/homes/tzoompy/publications/nsdi/2004/spyware.html.

**Figure 11-3** Forms of spyware.

Other costs and statistics related to technologically enhanced crime are difficult to estimate because of reporting deficiencies; however, various groups have provided such estimates from time to time based on surveys and estimated losses:

- High-tech crimes are estimated to cost the world economy over $1 trillion a year in loss of business revenue and damage to computer equipment and data (Public Safety and Emergency Preparedness Canada 2003).
- Visa estimates annual losses due to fraud to be about $700 million (*The Sacramento Bee* 2003).
- ID theft costs banks $1 billion a year (Sullivan 2003).
- A 2003 survey of 530 security specialists working in US corporations and government agencies found that theft of proprietary information was reported as being responsible for the most financial loss, with the average reported loss pegged at about $2.7 million per incident (http://techrepublic.com.com/5100-6264-5054396.html).
- The Motion Picture Association of America estimates that studios lose more than $3 billion in potential revenue annually from piracy (http://sfgate.com/cgi-bin/article.cgi?f=/c/a/2003/04/28/BU269543.DTL).
- The Business Software Alliance (BSA) reported that in 2003 world software piracy losses climbed to $29 billion (http://www.cnn.com/2004/TECH/biztech/07/07/software.piracy.reut/).

Besides these reported losses, the Computer Emergency Response Team (CERT) Coordination Center of the Software Engineering Institute at Carnegie Mellon University tracks computer security incidents reported by public and private sector organizations. The CERT/CC has compiled the incidents since 1988. The reported incidents include attacks via the Internet. **Table 11-1** depicts the trend of these attacks.

The incidents cited above are only a portion of the technologically enhanced criminal behavior that could be presented here. Further examples emerge weekly and the future will undoubtedly reveal new ones. Law enforcement agencies are attempting to address such high-tech crime and some successes are noteworthy.

| **Table 11-1** | Computer Security Incidents 1988–2003 Reported to CERT | | |
|---|---|---|---|
| **Year** | **Incidents** | **Year** | **Incidents** |
| 1988 | 6 | 1996 | 2,573 |
| 1989 | 132 | 1997 | 2,134 |
| 1990 | 252 | 1998 | 3,734 |
| 1991 | 406 | 1999 | 9,859 |
| 1992 | 773 | 2000 | 21,756 |
| 1993 | 1,334 | 2001 | 52,658 |
| 1994 | 1,334 | 2002 | 82,094 |
| 1995 | 2,412 | 2003 | 137,529 |

*Source:* CERT Coordination Center (2004).

For example, Operation Web Snare ran from June 1 to August 26, 2004 and consisted of more than 160 investigations. The focus of the operation was a variety of online economic crimes including identity theft, fraud, counterfeit software, computer intrusions, and other intellectual property crimes. Investigators identified more than 150,000 victims with estimated losses of more than $215 million. More than 140 search and seizure warrants were executed as part of the operation, and prosecutors obtained 117 criminal complaints, informations, and indictments. By late August, the charges had led to more than 150 arrests or convictions. Operation Web Snare involved coordination among 36 US Attorneys' offices nationwide, the Criminal Division of the Department of Justice, 37 of the FBI's 56 field divisions, 13 of the Postal Inspection Service's 18 field divisions, the FTC, together with a variety of other federal, state, local, and foreign law enforcement agencies (US Department of Justice 2004).

In summary, as technology changes, so do the methods of committing crime. Traditional crimes still occur but with greater ease and a higher volume because of the assistance the technical advances provide. With some technology, especially computer technology, new types of crime emerge. The challenge of new and exciting technology is that it brings both positive benefits and negative consequences for society.

# ■ Information Technology

When the criminal justice system is officially invoked, one element of the process is universal: information has been the basis for action. Today, officers' observations and actions are recorded and may become the foundation for any subsequent initiation of arrest and prosecution. Historically, these actions took place with little documentation. An officer's word and testimony in early years were sufficient, and little was done in maintaining a record base or filing system. Incidents were not that frequent, so one's memory was not cluttered with other cases and field notes. The court system was not "backed up," and jails were not overcrowded. "Justice" was often swift and definite with few appeals. Extensive documentation simply was not necessary. Those days are long gone!

By the turn of the twentieth century, three influencing factors led to establishing filing systems and the need for more documentation. The first was the increasing level of crime (primarily in urban areas) and the need to keep information about each case in an accurate and detailed manner. One's memory simply could not keep all details readily available. The second influencing factor was the professionalization of policing, which emphasized the increased use of scientific tools and processes (such as fingerprinting, photography, and analysis of crime incidents) and extensive record-keeping systems to help identify suspects. The third influencing factor was the evolving legal requirements related to the rules of evidence and judicial review of cases. All of these factors led to greater emphasis on processing, storing, and retrieving information.

Today, there probably is not a law enforcement officer alive who goes to work without carrying a pen or pencil and some kind of notepad (unless working undercover). Of course, some carry handheld, laptop, and notebook computers. Information gathering and storage also includes the use of mobile digital terminals in patrol cars, audio recording devices, and video technology. The reason for much of this emphasis on information is obvious—it is the basis of operation for the criminal justice process. Another reason for the importance of technology is that society and the criminal justice system itself demand accountability; that information be accurate, detailed, verifiable, and readily accessible. The system has become so complex today that information technology is more important than ever.

## General History of Information Technology

One can argue that the history of information technology began with the evolution of language and writing. The first recordings of pictographic signs and symbols date back to the Sumerian clay tablets of 4000–3500 BC. Early uses of papyrus and inks have been dated at 2500 BC. The abacus, a device to assist in the computing of numbers, dates to 3000 BC. Although scrolls began to be replaced by an early form of "books" around 360 AD, and the use of lamp-black ink by Chinese artists about 650 AD led to the introduction of wood blocks for printing, the printing press was not perfected by Johann Gutenberg until the 1450s. And, the use of black-lead pencils was first used in England in 1500. Consequently, modern societies have been recording information routinely for only about 500 years (see Grun 1991 and Augarten 1984 for additional historical information about this evolution).

The use of mechanical devices to process information is a more recent endeavor. Appendix 11-A identifies the most significant developments from the years 1600 to 2000 in the ideas and devices related to the evolution of computerized information technology. Understanding this evolution leads to an appreciation of where society has been and how rapidly new advancements are occurring. In fact, there are so many significant changes and applications occurring that one cannot do justice to extending the timeline in our Appendices. Just as our grandparents and great-grandparents witnessed the transition from the horse and buggy to the automobile and space travel, today's generations are witnessing the transition from playing PacMan on TVs to simulating real situations through virtual reality on wearable computers. The question that remains is, "What will be our capabilities in the next 5 to 20 years?" Are Star Trek and Stargate SG-1 really far-fetched, or will many of us living today actually witness those possibilities?

The majority of adults today were born before computers became commercially available. Personal computers entered the school system only after the mid-1980s, so today's grade school, high school, and college students have grown up with personal computers, cellular phones, CD players, MP3 players, and/or other computerized devices at home and school. While young people today may take computing in stride (and for granted), some adults are still hesitant to learn about and use them. This situation also exists, to a lesser extent, in law enforcement agencies; older personnel may resist the increased use of technology while younger officers take it in stride, although some older officers are reportedly more adept at incorporating technology than younger officers. The reality is that no generalized comment can be made about generational acceptance of new technology. There is such diversity among agencies and personnel that it would be an error to generalize. One thing is certain, however: Acquisition of new technology requires resources, and most times the differences among agencies are differences in economic resources available for new technology.

## Information Technology in Law Enforcement

The evolution of information technology in law enforcement activities is a very interesting one and needs to be placed in context. Today in policing we take many things for granted, such as the telephone and portable radio. It must be remembered that it has been less than 100 years since officers had the means of communicating with headquarters and other officers. Appendix 11-B presents a timeline in order to appreciate the evolution of major applications in law enforcement from the mid-1800s to the year 2000. Persons entering the law enforcement field today may witness as much change or more than those who preceded them.

One of the most important milestones for US law enforcement regarding the application of information technology occurred in 1967 with the establishment of the FBI's **National Crime Information Center** (NCIC). It is the national repository for crime-related information on wanted persons and stolen property. Originally located in Washington, DC at FBI headquarters, the center's new national headquarters opened in July 1999 at Clarksburg, West Virginia. It provides computerized information to thousands of criminal justice agencies in the 50 states, the District of Columbia, Puerto Rico, the US Virgin Islands, and Canada on a 24-hour, 7-days-a-week basis. See **Figure 11-4** for an overview of the NCIC.

Initially established on January 27, 1967 following lobbying efforts from the law enforcement community at all levels of government, it had 16 terminals, 15 participating agencies, and a database of 23,000 records in five file categories: wanted persons, stolen vehicles, stolen plates, stolen firearms, and identifiable stolen items (Federal Bureau of Investigation 1984; FBI 1996–1997). Over the years, other file categories have been added. Of the automated files, the major ones now include:

| | |
|---|---|
| **1.** Stolen vehicle | **9.** Interstate identification index |
| **2.** Stolen license plate | **10.** Witness security program |
| **3.** Stolen boat | **11.** BATF violent felon |
| **4.** Stolen gun | **12.** Missing persons |
| **5.** Stolen article file | **13.** US Secret Service protective |
| **6.** Stolen securities | **14.** Violent gang |
| **7.** Securities file | **15.** Terrorist |
| **8.** Foreign fugitive | **16.** Unidentified person |

NCIC responds to over 2 million inquiries daily (over 1 trillion yearly). It provides access to over 80,000 criminal justice users through more than 110,000 terminals and maintains over 24 million criminal and missing person records (Pilant 1996 and Sessions 1993). Any record entered into NCIC must be associated with a document and must contain the identity of the agency entering the record as well as other specific data, depending on the file. Some files can be updated only by specifically authorized agencies. Local agency users must furnish the network system with a specific request and a specially NCIC-assigned code that identifies the agency. A standard code for various types of requests is en-

**Description:**

NCIC is the national repository for crime-related information. Located in Clarksburg, West Virginia, it provides computerized information to over 80,000 law enforcement and criminal justice agencies in the 50 states, the District of Columbia, Puerto Rico, the US Virgin Islands, and Canada on a 24-hour, seven-days-a-week basis.

**History:**

NCIC went online in January of 1967. Initially NCIC had 16 terminals, 15 participating agencies, and a database of 23,000 records in five file categories: wanted persons, stolen firearms, stolen vehicles, stolen plates, and identifiable stolen items. By the end of 1967, NCIC had handled a total of two million transactions. Some 38 years later, NCIC is handling over two million transactions—a day—or over one trillion a year. In 1992, the center became part of the newly structured Criminal Justice Information Service Division within the FBI. NCIC was relocated in July of 1999 to its new facility in Clarksburg, West Virginia. Artificial intelligence software capabilities and imaging technology has been incorporated. A recent survey on the benefits of NCIC found that during a one-year period: 81,750 "wanted" persons were found; 113,293 individuals were arrested; 39,268 missing juveniles and 8,549 missing adults were located; and 110,681 cars, together valued at over $570 million, were found. It can be—and has been—used for virtually any type of investigation. One of the most recent well-known cases involving NCIC was the Oklahoma City bombing. Federal investigators, after running Oklahoma City bombing suspect Timothy McVeigh's name through NCIC, discovered that an Oklahoma state trooper had stopped and run an NCIC search on an individual by the name of Timothy McVeigh a little more than an hour after (and about 88 miles away from the site of) the explosion. He was still in custody and was consequently held for further questioning.

**Access constraints:**

Data is restricted to duly authorized criminal justice agencies and personnel for criminal justice purposes. All records in NCIC are protected from unauthorized access through appropriate administrative, physical, and technical safeguards. These safeguards include restricting access to those with a need to know to perform their official duties, and using locks, alarm devices, passwords, and/or encrypting data communications.

**Recent developments:**

Its recent upgrade, known as NCIC 2000, permits the electronic transmission of photographs, mugshots, photographs of stolen property, and fingerprint data. It has an automated fingerprint matching system that identifies someone based on a right index fingerprint when the subject presents no identification or is suspected of presenting a false ID. A main feature of NCIC-2000 is that a mobile imaging unit can be installed inside police squad cars. This unit consists of a personal computer, a hand-held fingerprint scanner, a hand-held digital camera, and a small printer. NCIC 2000 capabilities add several features such as enhanced name searches using phonetically similar names, records of subjects under supervised release, a sex offender registry, and an index of persons incarcerated in the federal prison system; provides online manuals to users; and allows online ad-hoc inquiries (allows users to search the active databases and access the system's historical data).

*Sources:* Sessions, William S. (February 1993). Criminal justice information services: Gearing up for the future. *FBI Law Enforcement Bulletin*, pp. 1–3; and Federal Bureau of Investigation (June 1993). *Cooperation: The Backbone of Effective Law Enforcement*. Washington, DC: US Department of Justice. Federal Bureau of Investigation (December 1996/January 1997). National crime information center: 30 years on the beat. *The Investigator*. Washington, DC: Federal Bureau of Investigation; and Federation of American Scientists (2004). NCIC, http://www.fas.org/irp/ agency/doj/fbi/is/ncic.htm.

**Figure 11-4** The National Crime Information Center (NCIC).

tered and then processed. A response is transmitted back to the initiating agency. When an inquiry about a person or property matches data contained in one of the files, it is referred to as a "hit."

In 1992, the center became part of the newly structured Criminal Justice Information Service Division within the FBI. Artificial intelligence software capabilities have been incorporated into the system in an effort to detect related (linked) criminal activity in its early stages, and to detect misuse of information by helping to ensure accuracy and reliability of the data. Image technology has been incorporated in order to permit the improved transmission of mug shots and fingerprint images in response to inquiries. In all, over 60 planned upgrades have been incorporated into the revamped system called **NCIC 2000** (Buckler 1998 and Federation of American Scientists 2004).

The NCIC is only one of several major databases available to law enforcement agencies (or selected agencies). In recent years, because of greater computerization, networking, and the need to share information, a number of databases have been developed. Four examples of such databases include the following: (a) **CODIS**—a database containing the DNA signatures of convicted offenders; CODIS refers to COmbined DNA Indexing System. It enables federal, state, and local crime labs to exchange and compare DNA profiles electronically, thereby linking crimes to each other and to convicted offenders. Currently genetic samples from more than 1.8 million criminals are on file, with between 10,000 and 40,000 new samples being added monthly. At least 170 local crime labs across the country can run DNA samples through the database and find matches (Federal Bureau of Investigation 2004); (b) **Secure Flight**—a revamped version of the controversial *CAPPS II* (Computer Assisted Passenger Prescreening System II) program of the Transportation Security Administration (TSA). It is intended for the screening of airline passengers and is designed to identify known or suspected terrorists, not other law enforcement violators (Sternstein 2004); (c) **FinCEN**—the US Treasury Department's Financial Crimes Enforcement Network database identifies possible money laundering transactions. It is a neural network used to scan huge volumes of financial information for suspicious patterns in money movement in order to identify possible laundering operations. Federal agencies involved in FinCEN include US Customs, ATF, FBI, IRS, the US Postal Inspection Service, and others (US Department of Treasury 2004); (d) **US-VISIT**—operational since January of 2004, the database contains scanned fingerprints of the index fingers and a photograph of most foreign visitors traveling to the United States on a visa. This information is made available only to authorized officials and selected law enforcement agencies responsible for ensuring the safety and security of US citizens and foreign visitors (US Department of Homeland Security 2004c). See **Figure 11-5** for more examples of law enforcement databases.

Since the 9/11 attacks, there has been a growing concern and a need among law enforcement agencies not only to share information, but also to provide more effective means for searching that information. As databases grow in size and number, there is a need to tie them together in order to optimize their potential. However, databases are not always compatible with one another because of their internal programming code and structure. Because of this, sophisticated software that permits "super searches" of multiple databases has been and is being developed. **Data mining** is the technique that uses such software to search database(s) for hidden patterns in a group of data, which can then be used to predict future behavior or to link related data. The term **data warehouse** is sometimes used to describe large computer networks utilized for storing, retrieving, and managing large amounts of data.

Several such programs exist in the law enforcement field today and more are on the way. Examples of these include **MATRIX** and **ECHELON**. MATRIX—Multi-

*National Sex Offenders Registry* (NSOR)—Accessed through NCIC, the NSOR is a national database at the FBI that tracks the whereabouts and movements of each person who has been convicted of a criminal offense against a victim who is a minor, or has been convicted of a sexually violent offense, or is a sexually violent predator; it also registers and verifies the addresses of sex offenders who reside in states that do not have a "minimally sufficient" sex offender registry (SOR) program.

*National Integrated Ballistic Information Network* (NIBIN)—An ATF program that provides for the nationwide installation and networking of automated ballistic imaging equipment in partnership with state and local law enforcement agencies. Currently, about 228 law enforcement locations are making use of this valuable technology. In FY 2003, NIBIN equipment assisted law enforcement agencies in finding more than 2,500 links, or "hits." In each of these instances, evidence from two or more crime scenes was identified as being potentially linked.

*Bomb and Arson Tracking System* (BATS)—Allows state, local, and other federal law enforcement agencies to share information about bomb and arson cases and incidents. Participants receive a user ID and password from ATF and then can capture, store and exchange information such as the type of incident, target, date, and location.

*National Virtual Pointer System* (NVPS)—Proposed to expand the information sharing with the National Drug Pointer Index (NDPIX). The NVPS would reach state and local law enforcement agencies through linkages with High Intensity Drug Trafficking Area (HIDTA) Systems, the National Law Enforcement Telecommunications System (NLETS), and the Regional Information Sharing Systems (RISS). The NVPS will allow existing target deconfliction systems to exchange information concerning targets under investigation for all types of criminal activity.

*National Child Victim Identification System*—In a partnership with the National Center for Missing and Exploited Children, Immigration and Customs Enforcement (ICE), the FBI, the US Postal Inspection Service, the US Secret Service, and the Department of Justice are developing the National Child Victim Identification Card Program. Together with its partners in this important effort, ICE's CyberSmuggling Center is hosting the nation's only comprehensive, searchable system for identifying digital child pornography images. With its capacity to search and identify known images, the system is designed to help law enforcement agencies throughout the world identify and rescue children featured in the images. The system is also designed to facilitate prosecution of those who possess or distribute digital child pornography images in the wake of a 2002 Supreme Court decision (*Ashcroft v. Free Speech Coalition*) requiring proof that such images depict an actual child.

*Student and Exchange Visitor Information* (SEVIS)—A database that the Department of Homeland Security uses to track foreign students and scholars studying or researching in the United States. SEVIS will allow the United States to ensure that foreign students and exchange visitors who have entered our nation to study in our schools actually enroll in those schools. Congress required the Immigration and Naturalization Service (INS) to maintain updated information on the approximately one million non-immigrant foreign students and exchange visitors during the course of their stay in the United States each year. SEVIS implements section 641 of the Illegal Immigration Reform and Immigrant Responsibility Act (IIRIRA) of 1996.

*Sources:* Federal Bureau of Investigation, Bureau of Alcohol, Tobacco, and Firearms, Drug Enforcement Agency, Bureau of Immigration and Customs Enforcement, and Department of Homeland Security.

**Figure 11-5** FYI—Other law enforcement databases.

state Anti-TerRorism Information eXchange—is currently funded with federal money and administered by Florida law enforcement officials. It is a "super search" program, allowing data already available to law enforcement, possibly in multiple databases, to be accessed at one time and in one place. ECHELON is believed to be the code name for a portion of an automated global interception and relay system operated by the intelligence agencies in five nations: the United States, the United Kingdom, Canada, Australia, and New Zealand. Reportedly the system intercepts satellite-based communications. It has been suggested that ECHELON may intercept as many as 3 billion communications every day, including phone calls, email messages, Internet downloads, satellite transmissions, and so on (ACLU 2002).

The significance of the wide variety of databases and information available to law enforcement lies not in the fact that the data is stored somewhere, but most importantly that it shared and available. One of the challenges in today's technological world is the issues of compatibility and **interoperability**. Communications interoperability is the ability of public safety agencies to talk across disciplines and jurisdictions via radio communications systems, exchanging voice and/or data with one another on demand, in real time, when authorized (see **Figure 11-6**).

The sharing of data has been less of a problem than radio communication interoperability. There are a number of regional information sharing systems

---

The National Commission on Terrorist Attacks Upon the United States determined that the inability to communicate was a critical element during the 9/11 incidents where multiple agencies and multiple jurisdictions responded. One of the commission's recommendations addressed this problem:

*Congress should support pending legislation which provides for the expedited and increased assignment of radio spectrum for public safety purposes. Furthermore, high-risk urban areas . . . should establish signal corps units to ensure communications connectivity between and among civilian authorities, local first responders, and the National Guard. Federal funding of such units should be given high priority by Congress* (National Commission on Terrorist Attacks Upon the United States, 2004:397).

The Federal Communications Commission administers the nation's telecommunications policy and assigns frequencies to public safety agencies. There is considerable debate over these issues and the result is often the lack of interoperability among agencies at the federal, state, and local levels. The debate includes the assigning of sufficient radio spectrum bandwidth, funding, and cooperation across jurisdictions. Communications systems are extremely expensive and require considerable planning. The Department of Homeland Security initiated the SAFECOM program in August of 2004 to serve as the umbrella program within the federal government to help local, tribal, state, and federal public safety agencies improve public safety response through more effective and efficient interoperable wireless communications. In July of 2004, the department announced another project, RapidCom 9/30, to ensure that 10 high-threat urban areas have incident-level, interoperable emergency communications capability by September 30, 2004. The areas include: New York, NY; Chicago, IL; Washington, DC and the surrounding capital region; Los Angeles, CA; San Francisco, CA; Philadelphia, PA; Houston, TX; Jersey City, NJ; Miami, FL; and Boston, MA. However, this capability is not true interoperability since it uses existing equipment that is made interoperable by a patch-panel device, interconnecting various models of equipment that would otherwise not be compatible. See the following sources for additional information about this important topic.

*Sources:* National Commission on Terrorist Attacks Upon the United States (2004). The 9/11 Commission Report. Authorized Edition. New York: W.W. Norton & Co.; and Raymond E. Foster (2005). *Police Technology.* Upper Saddle River, New Jersey: Pearson Education, Inc.; http://www.safecomprogram.gov/; and http://www.dhs.gov/dhspublic/ display?content=3869.

**Figure 11-6** Nationwide interoperable communications.

that have emerged over the last two decades. They are generally referred to as "**regional information sharing systems**" (**RISS**). They consist of a network of computers linked together on a regional basis that are designed to serve multiple agencies by providing access to databases, analysis, and other services. The national Regional Information Sharing Systems (RISS) Program is composed of six regional intelligence centers operating in mutually exclusive geographic regions that include all 50 states, the District of Columbia, US territories, Australia, Canada, and England. The centers have the following names: The Middle Atlantic-Great Lakes Organized Crime Law Enforcement Network (MAGLOCLEN), the Mid-States Organized Crime Information Center (MOCIC), the New England State Police Information Network (NESPIN), the Regional Organized Crime Information Center (ROCIC), the Rocky Mountain Information Network (RMIN), and the Western States Information Network (WSIN). The six centers combined serve nearly 6,800 local, state, federal, and tribal law enforcement member agencies by facilitating and encouraging information sharing and communications. Typical targets of RISS activities are terrorism, drug trafficking, violent crime, cybercrime, gang activity, and organized criminal activities. The range of services varies among the centers. However, since September 11, 2001, increased emphasis has been placed on anti-terrorism activity, in addition to traditional law enforcement activities. RISS also operates RISSNET™—the RISS nationwide secure criminal intelligence network for communications and information sharing by law enforcement member agencies. An important service provided on RISSNET is the availability of secure email among participants. It also provides access to the Investigative Leads Bulletin Board (RISSLeads), the RISS Criminal Intelligence Databases (RISSIntel), the RISS National Gang Database (RISSGang), the RISS training Web site (RISSTraining), as well as access to each center's Web site for additional information and services, such as criminal activity bulletins and publications (US Department of Justice, Office of Justice Programs, Global Justice Information Sharing Initiative, Security Working Group). For additional information regarding the national RISS Program, please visit the Web site: http://www.rissinfo.com/.

## Emergency and Non-Emergency Telephone Numbers

Today, most people living in the United States take 911 for granted, using it as the local number to dial for emergency services of all kinds: police, fire, or medical. Generically, many of these systems are referred to as **computer-aided dispatch systems.** However, even in our highly technical and modern world, the 911 number does not work everywhere in the United States. It first appeared in January 1968 when AT&T announced the creation of 911. "Within a relatively few years, 911 systems were established in many urban areas. Within 10 years, police chiefs of large departments were beginning to complain that ever-increasing 911-generated calls for service were starting to distort and even overwhelm the balanced deployment of police resources" (Seaskate, Inc. 1998). The 911 systems are of two types: Basic 911 and Enhanced 911. The differences are that enhanced 911 has greater automated features, such as the ability to display and record the address and phone number of the caller. This allows for proper routing of the call and the dispatching of the proper jurisdictional personnel. Cellular phones have complicated the delivery of emergency services because the systems have not been compatible with the land-based systems. By May of 2004 cellular phone companies were required to have in place the necessary technology to permit the location tracking of a 911 call made from a cell phone. Unfortunately, even though this technology is in place, it is estimated that at least "one-third of all rural police agencies won't be able to use the information" (Charny 2004).

Because of the overwhelming use (and abuse) of the 911 system, many large urban areas have or are overhauling their systems (see **Figure 11-7**). New York City in 2004, for example, received about 12 million 911 calls a year—that is 23 calls per minute! New York City is undergoing a massive revamping of the 911 system to improve efficiency and reduce redundancy. In many cases, whether needed or not, multiple first responders (police, fire, and EMS) end up being dispatched to a 911 call (McKay 2004a).

Because of the overwhelming number of 911 calls in urban areas, many of which were not emergency service calls, cities have undertaken the establishing of a simple non-emergency number—311. The first 311 system was established in Baltimore, MD in 1997 (US Department of Justice, COPS 2004), following approval by the FCC in February of 1997 designating 311 as a national, non-toll, and voluntary non-emergency phone number. Other cities with 311 systems in operation or soon to be in operation include San José, CA; Birmingham Police Department, AL; Houston Police Department, TX; Los Angeles City Police Department, CA; Dukes County Sheriff's Office, MA; Miami City Police Department, FL; Rochester City Police Department, NY; New York City, NY(see **Figure 11-8**); Austin Police Department, TX; Framingham Police Department, MA; and Orange County Sheriff's Office, FL (US Department of Justice, COPS 2004).

## Other Information Technologies

During the last two decades, advancements in computer technology have led to great interest and implementation of systems beyond 911 and 311. The **automated vehicle locator system (AVLS)** permits electronic map displays of the lo-

---

By 1993, Chicago's 911 system consisted of three independent dispatch centers. Emergency calls to the centers were recorded by hand on cards and then keypunched into time-clock systems. The city undertook a massive consolidation of the system and in September of 1995, a new five-story emergency call center opened for police, fire, and EMS. Caller information could be located in 1.2 seconds of making the call. The consolidation effort cost $214 million over all phases, including construction, training, and working with multiple vendors.

The center today serves as a model for other cities contemplating upgrades to their emergency call systems. The system can send voice messages to 2,500 mobile police terminals and 490 fire stations. It tracks every fire vehicle by plotting coordinates on a geographical positioning system (GPS) map. The system is constantly being improved and is on its third evolutionary upgrade.

*Source:* Jim McKay (2004). Fixing 911. *Government Technology*, August: 22.

**Figure 11-7** Chicago's 911 upgrade.

In the last few years, New York City established a 311 system that consolidated over 40 call centers and 14 pages of telephone numbers. It has over 300 operators and handles more than 30,000 calls daily. Calls to the 311 system are routed through the regular phone system and do not require the data collection that the 911 system does.

*Source:* Jim McKay (2004). Fixing 911. *Government Technology.* August: 20, 22.

**Figure 11-8** Dial 311 in New York City.

cation of agency vehicles. It has recently been incorporated into some 911 systems. Vehicles equipped with **global positioning system (GPS)** transmitters can be identified by dispatchers as being the closest ones to respond to emergencies. Such technology permits dispatchers to know the direction of vehicle pursuits without the driver having to constantly verbalize a change. The AVLS system also improves officer safety (see **Figure 11-9**). Of course GPS technology can be used to track other vehicles as well, including suspect vehicles or ones carrying special cargo or hazardous materials through a jurisdiction (see **Figure 11-10**). GPS vehicle technology has become commercially available through the OnStar® system marketed through several automobile manufacturers.

Many progressive law enforcement agencies have placed their records of criminal incidents and calls for service online for quick access and retrieval. Such databases, when properly configured, can be utilized in conjunction with **geographic information systems** (**GIS**; also called **computer mapping** and **geocoding**). Such systems permit the displaying of jurisdictional maps along with any number of selected types of key structures (e.g., schools, hospitals, bridges, museums) and features (e.g., parks, rivers, closed roads). Crime-related information can be incorporated into any of these variables in order to conduct **crime analysis**—a systematic inquiry of incidents or occurrences within selected parameters of time and area.

An example of GIS technology being applied to crime analysis appears on the popular television show "The District," where the chief and his top command-

South Jordan, West Valley City, and Sandy, Utah Police Departments are using auto vehicle locator systems (AVLS) to track the position of active duty cars on a mapped computer screen. Digital displays permit commanding officers to observe locations of vehicles, and officers in their cars can see the same display as well.

The system tracks speed, location, direction, and time of day—information that can improve officer safety when assistance is needed and can help investigators review incidents, such as high-speed pursuits or allegations of officer misconduct.

The AVLS is just one facet of the Sandy, Utah Police Department's technology upgrade. It works off of the modem systems installed in officers' cars a year ago, at a cost of about $70,000. That equipment gave officers the ability to file reports directly to the system, look up criminal histories, and watch live dispatch entries in their cars.

*Source:* Michael N. Westley (2004). Utah computer system tracks its patrol cars on video display. *The Salt Lake Tribune,* April 23, http://www.policeone.com/police-technology/software/cad-rms/articles/85161/#.

**Figure 11-9** FYI—Utah agencies use AVLS.

Global positioning system technology is being used by selected departments from San Diego, California to Arlington, Virginia to detect and apprehend auto thieves. The concept is simple: Park a bait car equipped with a GPS transmitter and wait for the car to be stolen. Officers can then not only track and locate the vehicle, but the technology allows them to shut down the engine and lock suspects inside the vehicle until they arrive to make the apprehension. The technique can employ audio and video evidence to help insure a conviction.

By 2003, the technique was being used in 40 law enforcement agencies in the United States and Canada. One such system costs about $500 plus a $35 monthly fee, but costs can range as high as $3,000 or more. The insurance industry has taken interest in the program and some companies are working with law enforcement agencies to attack vehicle theft in certain high-theft areas.

*Source:* Bill Siuru (2003). Car thieves take the "Bait", *Police and Security News*, July/August, p. 40.

**Figure 11-10** GPS applied to auto theft.

ers are shown in a small auditorium viewing graphical displays of recent crimes or trends. This recent combining of crime analysis, computerization, GIS, and managerial accountability is called **Compstat**. The name is derived from the two words "computer" and "statistics." Most of the literature on Compstat traces its recent development to the program developed in New York City in the 1990s, where commanders and bureau chiefs were held accountable for crime and clearance rates in their respective precincts or areas of responsibility. The NYC model was based on four crime-reduction principles: accurate and timely intelligence, effective tactics, rapid deployment of personnel and resources, and relentless follow-up and assessment (Shane 2004). Compstat is a strategic management concept that is spreading across the country. As more and more cities utilize these principles successfully, others take notice and seek the same results (see **Figure 11-11** for more information on Compstat trends).

# ■ Major Applications of Technology in Law Enforcement Today

The previous section focused primarily on information technology and how it has evolved and affected law enforcement. Suffice it to say that any form of administrative and management processes (e.g., fiscal control/payroll, training records, personnel records, incident reports, etc.) can be automated with various kinds of information technology. While some agencies still use paper-based reporting and processing systems, some have incorporated field-based tablet computers and mobile digital technology that permits officers to file electronic reports. These are then processed through internal networks and databases. In this section, we move to other applications of technology that are being utilized in operational and investigational aspects of policing.

The uses and applications of technology in law enforcement are as broad as one's imagination and creativeness. (See **Figure 11-12** regarding the application

According to recent publications, the application of Compstat in policing is spreading across the nation. In a survey by the Police Foundation, of the 445 large police departments (100 sworn officers or more) that responded, 33% reported implementation of a Compstat-like program and 26% indicated that they were planning such a program. Of the 85 medium-size departments (50 to 99 sworn officers) that responded, 11% reported implementation of a Compstat-like program and 29% indicated that they were planning such a program. Even in cities hit by rough economic times such as Bridgeport, Connecticut and Chattanooga, Tennessee violent crime is dropping. Both are employing Compstat concepts to attack crime issues and both have experienced about a 32% drop in violent crime since 2000. Police chiefs in both cities attribute the drop to techniques that utilize the principles used in Compstat: Map every crime, put cops on the dots, address quality-of-life issues, clean the streets, and don't let crime spikes become trends. Both cities also hold police units accountable for crime and clearance rates. The focus is on results. Check it out on the Web, by using the search term Compstat.

*Sources:* Weisburd, David, Stephen D. Mastrofski, Rosann Greenspan, and James J. Willis (2004). The growth of compstat in American policing. *Police Foundation Reports*. Washington, DC: The Police Foundation, April; *Criminal Justice Newsletter* (2004). Compstat policing is spreading across the country, survey finds. *Criminal Justice Newsletter*, June 1: 1; and Apuzzo, Matt (2004). Police rethinking crime fighting. Associated Press, August 27, http://www.fortwayne.com/mld/journalgazette/news/nation/9512787.htm.

**Figure 11-11** Compstat—emerging trends.

of technology to the very time consuming task of locating lost individuals). Today, individual officers are developing new applications—the process is no longer one limited to the research and planning of communications sections of an agency. The advent of the personal computer in the 1980s has brought computing power to the individual level and has opened a new realm of applications. Greater interest in science and electronics has expanded the potential of applications to the law enforcement field. A detailed examination of the emerging applications of technology in law enforcement is not possible here. However, we do recommend the reader to a recent publication by Raymond E. Foster that examines the use of technology in policing; it is entitled *Police Technology* and is published by Prentice Hall. Other periodicals such as *The Police Chief*, *Law and Order*, *Law Enforcement Technology*, *Law Enforcement News*, and *Government Technology* contain numerous articles on this ever-changing technology.

What other areas of policing have been impacted by improved technology? With regard to weapons, the days of the simple pistol and rifle have given way to automatic weapons, laser-scoped rifles, and Tasers. Nighttime (low-light) vision devises, thermal imaging cameras, and high-tech surveillance equipment are now less costly and more readily available. Of course, the automobile has continued to be refined, streamlined, and equipped with low-profile light emitting diode (LED) lights and electronic sirens. Hand tools such as flashlights, batons, PR-24s, and even handcuffs have undergone redesign and improvements. Radar systems for detecting speeders on the highways have begun using lasers.

Since the terrorist attacks of 9/11, there has been greater interest in improving the technology transfer from military research and development to civilian law enforcement applications. A decade ago the Pentagon spent about $35 bil-

Technology can be used in many ways, but one way that has helped save considerable time and effort in locating and returning wandering adults and children to their families and caregivers is called Project Lifesaver. It is an innovative program that aids victims and families suffering from Alzheimer's disease and related disorders such as Down syndrome and autism. The program forms partnerships with local law enforcement and public safety organizations in order to acquire equipment and train officers. A personalized radio transmitter worn by vulnerable individuals can be used to track them should they become lost or disoriented. The technology used by the public safety organization is capable of tracking a signal up to a mile by ground and five to nine miles by air. These devices work by giving an audible signal that leads law enforcement to the victims. The devices transmit over special radio frequency equipment that is considered the most reliable and practical technology available in locating the missing and wandering. It is considered more reliable than GPS technology at this time. Project Lifesaver is being adopted by law enforcement agencies across the country.

*Source:* Project Lifesaver, http://www.projectlifesaver.org/aboutus.htm.

**Figure 11-12** Applied technology—Project Lifesaver.

lion a year on research and development, and the US Department of Justice spent only about $5 million (Komarow 1994). In a 1994 "Memorandum of Understanding," the Department of Defense and the Department of Justice agreed to work more closely in developing and sharing technology that could be applied to civilian law enforcement. The National Law Enforcement and Corrections Technology Center (NLECTC) was established in the Justice Department to coordinate and facilitate technological transfer to the civilian law enforcement sector. The Office of Law Enforcement Technology Commercialization (OLETC) is the primary unit in the NLECTC working on this effort. The Center is heavily involved in high-technology research to enhance the law enforcement function and to protect officers. One of the center's publications is called *TechBeat* and is available online at http://www.nlectc.org/techbeat/justnet.html. The next sections of this chapter will review some of the other technologies emerging within laboratories to be used in law enforcement.

## Less-than-Lethal Technologies

In the last fifteen years, greater scientific inquiry and research have been conducted into subduing individuals in ways that would lessen the chance of serious injury or death. Besides protecting officers from hostile individuals, a major impetus for this type of research has been an attempt to avoid lawsuits for wrongful death filed against police departments or allegations of excessive force in making arrests and controlling crowds. The major products being tested and used for less-than-lethal application include the following (Foster 2004; Hambling 2004; US Department of Justice, NIJ 2004; Pilant 1998; Boyd 1995):

> *Beanbag Shotgun*—this is primarily named for the ammunition that can be used with a standard shotgun. The ammunition can take several forms but usually contains rubber pellets. If not properly used, the ammunition can cause serious injury and death.

*Tactical 37mm Launcher*—a special less lethal control device that expels wooden or rubber bullets or chemical agents toward large crowds; they have a psychological effect as well because of the amount of smoke, noise, and flash that is produced. For examples of various types of less lethal ammunition and launchers visit the Web site of Combined Tactical Systems, Incorporated at http://www.less-lethal.com/.

*Taser*—this device is used by over 4,000 police departments in the United States; it is an electric shock gun that fires two darts that trail current-carrying wires. When the darts hit the intended target, the current causes involuntary muscle contractions, momentarily stunning and incapacitating the target.

*Other Stun Gun Technology*—currently under development and soon to be commercially available are other types of stun guns. One utilizes electrically conductive fibers shot through the air in a stream toward the target; it utilizes no wires. Another is the $9000 Close Quarters Shock Rifle that projects an ionized gas, or plasma, toward the target that receives an electrical shock; it is reported to interfere with electronic ignition systems of vehicles. Still another uses solid-state lasers that ionize the air, producing long, thread-like filaments of glowing plasma that deliver a shock to the target.

*Acoustical Weapons*—a variety of devices are available and under development that utilize low- and high-intensity sound and sonic pulses to target disruptive individuals and crowds. The impulse causes pain and physiological discomfort.

*Sticky Foam*—this is a taffy-colored, gel-like substance that turns into a glue that sticks on contact. It can be dispensed from a shoulder-slung apparatus that contains the material under pressure. When applied, it expands, becomes sticky, and trips-up subjects. At the present time, it takes a large amount of material to be effective, and clean-up is a problem.

*Strobe-and-Goggle Technology*—the purpose of this technology is to disorient subjects during raids or assaults on barricaded structures. It uses bright flashing light to blind subjects while officers wearing special goggles enter to apprehend subjects. During testing, the limitations have been that the subjects were not disoriented long enough, and the devices generated extreme amounts of light and heat.

*Backseat Airbag*—as the name implies, this is a backseat version of the airbags used in vehicles to protect the occupants during collisions. This version is placed in the backseat to control unruly subjects who often attempt to kick out windows or to damage partitioning screens.

*Remote-Controlled Barrier Strips*—in an attempt to limit the dangers of high-speed vehicular pursuits, barrier strips that would pop-up and puncture the tires of a vehicle are being researched. The strips would be activated by police as the vehicle being pursued approaches them.

*Fleeing Vehicle Tagging System*—also in an attempt to reduce the dangers from high speed pursuits, officers might one day be able to "tag" a vehicle with a miniature radio transmitter. The police could then track the vehicle at a safe distance without giving immediate chase and endangering the lives of others.

*Vehicle Disablers*—another future technological application may be a device that police could aim at a vehicle and disable its internal computer system, which would cause the engine to shut down. The vehicle would be useless, and the occupants could be trapped inside.

*People Netting*—as with fishnets, people nets could be used to control unruly persons or crowds. This netting would entangle the subjects, making movement difficult.

In 1997, the Pentagon created the Non-Lethal Weapons Program to research and develop new technologies. It is similar to the National Institute of Justice's program that began in 1986. In 1994, the NIJ created a working partnership with the Department of Defense. The goals of the NIJ program are the "identification and development of new or improved weapons and other technology that will minimize the risk of death and injury to officers, suspects, prisoners, and the public, and contribute to the reduction of civil and criminal liability suits against police, sheriff, and corrections departments" (Pilant 1998, 55). An example of NIJ's involvement in developing safety products for law enforcement is described in **Figure 11-13**. For more information about the NIJ's less lethal technologies, visit their Web site at http://www.ojp.usdoj.gov/nij/sciencetech/ltl.htm.

## Investigative Tools

The ongoing search for better detection equipment and identification technologies continues in both the research lab and the field. A fingerprint visualization system was recently developed by the Alaska Crime Laboratory in cooperation with a nationally known private firm. A device known as the "magic wand" can lift fingerprints from nonporous surfaces at the scene of the crime. When cou-

---

The technology used for soft body armor worn by police officers was initially developed for heavy-duty military truck tires that were bullet-resistant. In 1972, a researcher from the US Department of Justice's National Institute of Justice (NIJ) stumbled upon the fiber used in the tires, better known by its trade name Kevlar. Vests were subsequently developed, and NIJ conducted field tests in 15 cities. Since 1975, it is estimated that soft body armor has saved the lives of thousands of police officers.

Development continues today on vests and helmets that would offer greater protection to officers. In the near future, inserts made of titanium and ceramic that offer greater bullet protection may be available. The vests are designed to be more concealable and offer greater freedom of movement. Research is underway on a liquid body armor that becomes rigid when suddenly hit. The military and other agencies test new products using prototypes.

*Sources:* Boyd, David G. (July 1995). On the Cutting Edge: Law Enforcement Technology. *FBI Law Enforcement Bulletin*, 1–6; Pennella, John J. and Peter L Nacci (1997). Department of Justice and Department of Defense Joint Technology Program: Second Anniversary Report, February. Washington DC: US Department of Justice; and Miller, Christina M. (2004). Body Armor Update: 2004. *Police and Security News*, July/August: 31–36.

**Figure 11-13** How did soft body armor originate?

pled with **automated fingerprint identification systems** (AFIS), such technology increases the chances of identifying suspects and reduces the time to do so. As its name implies, AFIS systems use computer technology for the imaging, transmission, comparison, and storage of fingerprints. Systems are now in operation in many jurisdictions across the nation and some can be accessed even from patrol cars equipped with fingerprint scanners.

Some envision other devices that assist police in detecting weapons on subjects. It would be like a hand-held magnetometer but could be used some distance from the subject. It may be possible one day to stand outside a building and detect the person or persons inside through infrared technology. Some "smart-guns" are used today that cannot be fired unless being held by an authorized person. Subjects who steal such weapons or take guns from officers during a struggle would find them useless if attempting to fire them. They have been available for years, but are expensive and controversial.

Concealed weapons detection equipment is under development that may be able to prevent random firearm violence and protect criminal justice and military personnel as they perform their tasks. Programs initiated in 1995 are pursuing five technological approaches to detect concealed weapons on individuals: passive millimeter wave (MMW) sensors and infrared (IF) cameras, X-ray sensors, active low-frequency magnetic sensors, magnetometers, and a sensor system combining ultrasound and radar sensors. The hope is to create a portable system that can detect concealed weapons from up to 30 feet (Pennella and Nacci 1997). Such devices could be used in airports, prisons, courts, police stations, schools, and at large public gatherings. As the devices become more portable, they could become standard equipment on the uniform of officers.

Ballistics analysis technology also has evolved in recent years. At the federal level, the ATF and FBI have integrated their systems into the National Integrated Ballistic Information Network (NIBIN). The network utilizes Integrated Ballistics Identification System (IBIS) units to obtain firearm information from state and local law enforcement agencies for comparisons. These units allow technicians to acquire, digitize, and compare markings made by a firearm on bullets and cartridge casings. The network also permits the analysis to link offenses related to those bullets or casings (NIBIN). In 2003, NIBIN equipment assisted law enforcement agencies in finding more than 2,500 links, or "hits" (see **Figure 11-14**).

Digital imaging systems coupled with wireless technology now permit the sending of crime scene videos, street photos, mug shots, and so on, to and from central police stations. Video and digital imaging technology is revolutionizing crime scene investigation. One strategy called **teleforensics** permits the recording of crime scenes using a camcorder fitted with a wireless transmitter that sends images to remote monitors in real time. Concurrently, the recorder makes videotape for investigators. One teleforensic project has been tested by the El Paso, Texas Police Department, and another project that was tested by the New York State Police transmits video and data from a crime scene vehicle in real time. Another project is underway by NASA for developing nondestructive techniques for the analysis of physical evidence at crime scenes. Of particular interest is the use of a portable X-ray fluorescence analysis system to identify gunshot residues, primer residues, blood, and semen at the crime scene (NLECTC 2003).

**Week of 6/14:**

The Chicago, Illinois Police Department linked two homicides that occurred two months apart through ballistic imaging. Officers were called to check on the occupants of a vehicle parked on a street. Upon arrival the officers found the two occupants had been shot and killed. Police recovered cartridge casings and projectiles and submitted them to the Illinois State Police Laboratory for entry into NIBIN. Almost two months later police responded to a report of a man who was shot at a food store. Witnesses told police that two males entered the store and demanded money from the cashiers. A security guard who attempted to exit a security booth was shot and killed by the suspects. A fired projectile was recovered and imaged into NIBIN, which resulted in a link to the homicide two months earlier. The investigation is ongoing.

**Week of 6/21:**

The Boston, Massachusetts Police Department used the NIBIN system to link a handgun recovered during a vehicle stop to a shooting that occurred two weeks before. Boston police responded to a report of shots fired where a witness indicated he observed a suspect walk down the street and fire several shots into a group of males. The witness also saw another male get out of a car that was parked at the location and return gunfire. Both suspects ran from the location. Responding officers located spent shell casings and had them entered into NIBIN. Two weeks later, Boston police made a vehicle stop in an area known for high firearms activity. The three occupants of the vehicle were searched and police recovered a .45-caliber pistol with an obliterated serial number. The gun was test fired and entered into NIBIN resulting in the link to the shooting two weeks before.

*Source:* ATF NIBIN Program, Hits of the Week, June 14 to June 28, 2004, www.atf.gov/nibin/nb_success.htm.

**Figure 11-14** NIBIN—Hits of the week.

A Canadian company, MD Robotics, has developed a 3D computer model called instant Scene Modeler (iSM). It records a stereo video image of the crime scene. The concept creates a panoramic view of the crime scene. The technique can be used to reduce possible contamination of the scene and can even be extended into a scene on a pole or by a robot. Investigators can add notations directly to the recorded model of the crime scene and the recording also can be transmitted anywhere in the world, if necessary (Dotto 2004).

Other investigative technologies include automated versions of the composite sketch devices and software that has been available for years. One vendor now has a version that is Web-based, allowing access to five billion different facial composites (Smith & Wesson Advanced Technologies 2003).

A number of other electronic devices are making crime detection and investigation more technical. Ohio recently added license plate scanning equipment to selected locations on the Ohio Turnpike. The system scans vehicle license plates as they enter the state and processes them through NCIC's stolen license plate file. If there is a match, dispatchers are alerted; they verify the information and then notify troopers who intercept the vehicle. In 2003, without the use of scanners, more than 500 stolen vehicles were seized on the turnpike. A selected number of cruisers are also outfitted with the technology (Meade 2004). Cruisers also have been outfitted in many departments with in-car video cameras. About

72% of all state police and highway patrol vehicles have been equipped with video systems that record officer actions and serve as evidence of offenses committed by subjects. In a recent survey of 3,000 respondents, officers accused of wrong-doing were exonerated 96.2% of the time because of video evidence captured by in-car camera systems (Westphal 2004). The technology supporting in-car video systems is continuing to advance; the latest equipment is now digital and can record two cameras simultaneously. Although not that common yet, **personal video surveillance systems** consisting of a small camera and microphone attached to the shirt of an officer and a transmitter attached to the duty belt, which sends images and sounds to a receiver/recorder subsystem located in the officer's vehicle, could become standard equipment for officers in the near future.

Global positioning system (GPS) technology can now be applied to crime scene processing to aid in measuring the location of evidence and enhancing crime scene sketching. This technology is used for surveillance purposes, especially in tracking suspect vehicles or tracking valuable cargo or property shipments. For example, police used GPS technology to track the whereabouts of suspect Scott Peterson before he was charged in the death of his wife Laci and their unborn son (McKay 2004a).

Another advancement in technology includes the **personal vertical takeoff and landing aircraft (VTOL)** being developed for personal use. As opposed to **unmanned aerial vehicles (UAVs)**, the VTOLs of the future will be staffed with a single person. They will be potentially less costly to maintain and more maneuverable than helicopters. Prototypes are already being tested and some are envisioning their application to law enforcement situations. According to one manufacturer, by 2006 full production of a vertical takeoff and landing aircraft is expected. It will be able to carry one person up to 180 miles at speeds up to 113 mph (Cowper 2004). UAVs (also referred to as drones) have proven to be very effective in military surveillance operations. Some law enforcement agencies are contemplating their use, especially for border protection.

There simply is no end to the advancement and application of technology to the various law enforcement functions. As we contemplate what the future holds for this topic, one can only imagine how things might be. As we reflect on the changing world around us, we see subtle changes being made. Sometimes we don't realize how fast things are changing. Artificial intelligence in computing was quite new a decade ago, and now there are many software developments that utilize it. Virtual reality has now been employed in training systems and its continued applications will spread as the technology becomes less expensive; however, its applications beyond training may be limited. **Augmented reality**, though, is being discussed today in the law enforcement arena and it may be upon us before we know it. It is a technological application that combines the real and the virtual, displaying information in real time, in a way that enhances the individual abilities of people operating in the real world (Cowper 2004). The helmet technologies displayed in the movie *Robocop* may best illustrate this concept. Various types of information—pictures, diagrams, and instructions—were received by the helmet's sensors to augment the situation that Robocop experienced. This additional information assisted him in carrying out his mission. We may soon have that same ability (see **Figure 11-15** for a more detailed explanation).

According to one policing technology expert, augmented reality (AR) "uses wearable components to overlay virtual (computer-generated) information onto individuals' real-world view or into their real-world experiences in a way that improves and enhances their abilities to accomplish a wide variety of tasks and missions." It combines the real and the virtual, displaying information in real time, in a way that enhances the individual abilities of people operating in the real world.

Although still in its early stages of development and applications, it is being utilized in football broadcasting (the yellow first down line superimposed on the football field), race car broadcasting (the driver and speed information tagged to race cars), and in military operations (aircraft systems data superimposed on cockpit monitors along with enemy targets).

A fully interactive AR system may derive information from a multitude of sources. Data can be transmitted wirelessly from a computer network, accessed from the wearable computer carried by the AR user. By using virtual graphics, three-dimensional maps, textual annotations, auditory information, and haptic (touch) sensations in a coordinated real-time presentation, AR brings together a variety of technologies to display information to individuals in a way that instantly applies to a given task or situation. Future law enforcement applications could include real-time language translations coupled with data on cultural customs and traditions; real-time display of intelligence information or crime analysis information about a neighborhood situation; facial and biometric recognition data about known criminal offenders and wanted persons; integration of chemical, biological, and explosive sensors to improve officer safety; and accessibility to maps and building plans to enhance hostage negotiations and SWAT situations; enhanced surveillance operation by coordinating use of robots, unmanned aerial vehicles (UAVs), and satellite images.

*Source:* Thomas Cowper (2004). Improving the view of the world: Law enforcement and augmented reality technology. FBI Law Enforcement Bulletin, January, 12–18.

**Figure 11-15** What is augmented reality?

# Law Enforcement and Privacy

Since technology is at the heart of many privacy issue debates, and the use and abuse of that technology is often the focal point of debate in policing, it is appropriate to review some of the issues related to technology that reduce privacy and enhance possible detection. Included in this category are technologies that reduce privacy (liberty) rights of an individual by increasing the ability of others to identify, locate, and follow an individual. Examples are geographic information systems (GIS), global positioning systems (GPS), satellite imagery (SI), remote sensing, telephony interception (including wiretapping, pen registers, and dialed number recorders), concealed weapons detectors, electronic license plate readers, surveillance cameras, and listening devices (Conser 1997). Radio Frequency identification (RFID) technology today is used for inventorying commercial products, tracking animals, tracking selected drugs, hazardous materials, and even automobile tires (Page 2004). RFID tags can be extremely small and barely visible. Their use has sparked a debate regarding potential privacy issues.

Michael G. Curry (1997) authored an excellent article that examines the potential invasion of privacy capabilities of GIS, GPS, SI, and remote sensing technologies when coupled with geodemographics. The combination of satellite surveillance technology and personal demographic information (age, occupation, income, race, education, etc.) can be utilized to track and locate an individual. The inappropriate use of this technology, which has little or no regulation restricting its use, is of concern. These same technologies, however, also can provide valuable services to consumers such as assisting lost motorists, locating stolen vehicles, or locating a desired destination.

Telephony interception capabilities include wiretaps, pen registers, and dialed number recorders. The differences among these are: wiretaps refers to the interception of telecommunications conversations, verbal or digital, wire or wireless; pen registers record the phone numbers of incoming phone calls to a target phone; and dialed number recorders (DNRs) capture all numbers dialed from a target phone. Of course, this technology is not just for phone calls. Since computer networks and modems operate on phone lines, the same technology is used to monitor and trace those types of communications as well. Congress enacted the Communications Assistance for Law Enforcement Act (CALEA) in 1994, which requires telecommunications companies to protect the privacy and security of communications and call-identifying information unless a court order authorizes interception. It also requires that the companies ensure that law enforcement has the capability to conduct court-ordered surveillance (Anderson 1997). The Electronic Surveillance Technology Section (ESTS) of the FBI today serves as the agency that coordinates that capability. It works with the telecommunications industry to assure that lawful electronic surveillance by law enforcement agencies can be carried out efficiently and effectively (Clifford 2003).

Concealed weapons detectors, electronic license plate readers, surveillance cameras, and listening devices all reduce privacy and liberty in that they are used in the detection of criminal behavior. However, they are used usually to screen or observe all individuals in a particular area, which means they reduce the privacy of all who are in that area. Cities such as Redwood City (CA), Baltimore (MD), Camden (NJ), Philadelphia (PA), and Washington, DC have experimented with or are using surveillance cameras and hidden listening devices to "patrol high-crime areas" (Lewis 1996). In Britain, over 400 city centers have used cameras to monitor public streets where crime was expected, resulting in a 60% decrease in crime in some areas (Scanning 1997). In the workplace, it is common practice for employers to monitor email, voice mail, and phone calls and to log Internet transactions to detect improper employee behavior. Such monitoring has been upheld by the courts, especially when accompanied by prior stated policy (Sahlberg 1991; Wallace et al. 1995; Levin 1995).

Conser (2000) proposed what he called the "**privacy rights paradigm.**" It is premised upon the principles found in the Preamble to the Constitution and the concepts of ordered liberty, citizenship, and responsibility. It has a guiding philosophy of a social compact that attempts to balance individual rights with the rights of society and an embodiment of the idea of "for the greater good." The proposed paradigm (see **Figure 11-16**) is designed to provide the greater privacy rights to the individual at the personal and intimate relationship levels. As interactions increase with a larger society and begin to involve the type of relationships that are of governmental concerns, privacy rights are more limited and

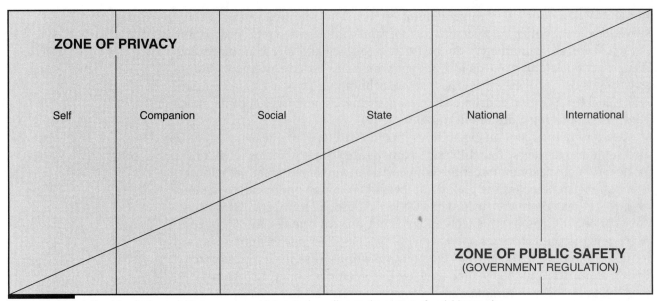

**Figure 11-16** Relationship of privacy rights to government interests depending on the context of social interaction.
*Source:* James A. Conser (2000). Privacy Rights and Public Safety in a Digital World. Futuristics and Law Enforcement: The Millennium Conference, FBI Academy, Quantico, VA, July 11.

subject to government control and determination (when government has a substantial interest).

The paradigm is not a panacea for the current privacy controversies and dilemmas facing society, but it is one approach to discussing the limits and parameters of proper government intrusion into our lives. It does require the recognition that the government has the right and authority to regulate morality to certain degrees, the right to protect national security interests, and the right to determine civil rights. The paradigm is a start; it is not meant to be a finished product. Some will not like it, since it does not correspond to their advocacy of total self-determination and unfettered behavior. The paradigm does adhere to the basic principles of communitarianism as presented by Amitai Etzioni.

Etzioni's (1999) communitarianism is based on a social philosophy that a good society seeks a carefully crafted balance between individual rights and social responsibilities, between liberty and the common good. He states "responsive communitarians seek to balance individual rights with social responsibilities, and individuality with community" (198). The approach advocated by Etzioni recognizes that rights and liberties are contingent on socio-historical contexts and that the balancing of individual and societal rights is necessary for the common good, which supports the social contract advocated in the Constitution's Preamble.

# ■ Summary

This chapter has reviewed the tremendous impact that technology is having on law enforcement today. Information and other technology may be one of law enforcement's most important tools in detecting and investigating crime. Information is the greatest asset to the law enforcement function—whether it is gained from incident reports, crime lab analysis findings, informants, intelligence operations, crime analysis matrices, or modus operandi files. Like any other tool, information technology systems can be used to streamline law enforcement processing of copious amounts of data and factual information. Resources can be better utilized, and the sharing of information should assist in detecting conspiracies, serial incidents, and trends. Since the terrorist attacks of 9/11, much emphasis and resources have been placed on intelligence gathering and sharing. Technology is at the heart of such efforts.

With the proper planning, organizing, and control, technology can become one of the most valuable tools used in law enforcement. As with any tool, abuses are possible, and one of the most controversial aspects of the use of information technology in policing today is the issue of privacy and the accuracy of information in the databases and systems used by law enforcement. Information is power in an information-based society. Power can be abused, and with abuses come oversight and restrictions. The greater the restrictions, the less effective the information system becomes, so it is incumbent upon the law enforcement community to ensure that progress in information technology does not restrict or impinge on the civil liberties of citizens unlawfully and unreasonably. This is one of the major debates surrounding civil liberties and homeland security.

Other technologies hold great promise for law enforcement. In the not-too-distant future, less-than-lethal restraining technology will lessen the need to use deadly force against aggressive subjects in the field. Likewise, improved investigative technologies will assist in evidence gathering and criminal prosecutions. Of course, all of this technology will be useless without adequately qualified and trained personnel to use it. So in many respects, technology may have an impact on increasing the hiring qualifications needed to enter the field. Future applicants should prepare themselves for this eventuality through the study of technology, science, and electronics. But how else can we learn to adjust to the changing technology? How can we better position ourselves for tomorrow's challenges? We offer a little advice and some resource tips in **Figure 11-17**.

Think about this for a few minutes: From the time you were a freshman in high school to the time you graduated from high school (normally a four-year period), what has changed in technology? How many different personal computers did you use? How many times did you upgrade software? Did your cell phone plan change? Did you purchase an MP3 player? Did you give up film cameras to make the move to digital? Did you change printers? Many of you in just four short years did all of these things and some of you did some of these more than once! Some of you did only a few of these things and some did none of these! Such is the diversity in the use of technology on the personal level. But the point here is that there will be significant changes in technology during the next four years! By the time you graduate from college, there will be faster computers, more people with cell phones, and more sophisticated digital cameras and printers. Some technology will become faster and smaller, while some technology will be completely new. How can we keep abreast of the changing technology trends and their applications to policing and public safety? The answer is to read technology-related magazines, browse selected Web sites using key terms in search engines, review specific technology-related URLs, and read the professional literature. A few suggestions appear below:

**Technology/professional periodicals:**

*Scientific American*
*Government Technology*
*Law Enforcement Technology*
*Police Chief Magazine*
*Police and Security News*
*Law and Order*
*SC Magazine*
*TechBeat*

**Key terms for search engines:**

"police technology"
"GIS"
"GPS tracking"
"surveillance"
"law enforcement technology
"comstat"
"compstat"
"crime analysis"; "crime mapping"

**Specific technology-related URLs:**

www.nlectc.org
www.ncjrs.org
www.iacptechnology.org/
www.hitechcj.com/index.html
www.nist.gov/srd/law.htm
www.ojp.usdoj.gov/nij/maps/
www.foresight.org/
www.cert.org
www.fcw.com
www.scmagazine.com
www.antiphishing.org
www.fas.org/main/home.jsp
www.kurzweilai.net/
www.lawtechnews
www.techweb.com/
http://news.com.com/
www.centerdigitalgov.com/
www.sciencedaily.com

**Figure 11-17** How to keep up with changing technology trends.

## QUESTIONS FOR REVIEW

1. What is the significance of information to the police function, and why is information technology important to the law enforcement community?

2. What are the major applications of information technology in the police field?

3. What is the NCIC, and why is it important? What are the concerns about such large databases in a democratic society?

4. What is meant by less-than-lethal technology, and what are some of the technologies that fit that category?

5. What are the technological innovations that are being applied to field procedures and crime investigation?

## SUGGESTED ACTIVITIES

1. Have members of the class ask their parents (and grandparents if possible) about their feelings and attitudes toward computers and about the impact of computers on their lives. Discuss their findings in class.

2. Ask the systems administrator or data processing manager of the largest law enforcement agency in your area to speak to your class about the ever-changing technology and what it means for the police occupation.

3. Have each member of the class be responsible for finding one article or detailed advertisement regarding an application of emerging technology in law enforcement. Discuss these in class.

4. Search the World Wide Web for articles and sites on "technology" and "privacy." What are the issues associated with policing discussed in some of the material found?

# ■ Chapter Glossary

**augmented reality**   a technological application that combines the real and the virtual, displaying information in real time, in a way that enhances the individual abilities of people operating in the real world.

**automated fingerprint identification systems**   a computerized process that scans a fingerprint and converts it into a digital image that is then analyzed and compared to other known images for matching purposes.

**automated vehicle locator system (AVLS)**   a system used to locate vehicles outfitted with a receiver/transmitter that picks up positioning signals from satellites. The information can be transmitted to a computer aided dispatch system capable of displaying a map showing the location.

**CODIS**   acronym for Combined DNA Indexing System; a database containing the DNA signatures of convicted offenders.

**Compstat**   a strategy and technique that combines crime analysis, computerization, GIS, and managerial accountability to crime investigation and solvability. The name is derived from the two words "computer" and "statistics."

**computer-aided dispatch systems**   an automated system that assists in prioritizing emergency situations and locating and guiding public safety personnel to incidents in the shortest time possible.

**crime analysis**   a systematic inquiry of criminal incidents or occurrences within selected parameters of time and area.

**data mining**   the process of conducting "super searches" of multiple databases using sophisticated software that detects patterns in a group of data.

**data warehouse**   phrase used to describe large computer networks utilized for storing, retrieving, and managing large amounts of any type of data.

**ECHELON**   believed to be the code name for a portion of an automated global interception and relay system operated by the intelligence agencies in five nations: the United States, the United Kingdom, Canada, Australia, and New Zealand; reportedly the system intercepts satellite-based communications.

**FinCEN**   The US Treasury Department's Financial Crimes Enforcement Network database that identifies possible money laundering transactions.

**geographic information systems (GIS)** or **computer mapping** and **geocoding**   a system for displaying and analyzing data. It can be used to display location, find patterns and model scenarios; also referred to as geocoding.

**global positioning system (GPS )**   a system that utilizes satellite technology, that receives signals from ground transmitters and then converts the exact longitude and latitude into locations on Earth.

**interoperability**   the ability of communications systems and computer networks to exchange voice/data across agencies and jurisdictions on demand, in real time.

**less-than-lethal technologies**   scientific inquiry and research that focuses on the subduing of individuals or controlling of crowds in ways that would lessen the chance of serious injury or death.

**MATRIX**   acronym for Multi-state Anti-Terrorism Information exchange; a "super search" program that allows data already available to law enforcement, possibly in multiple databases, to be accessed at one time and in one place.

**National Crime Information Center (NCIC)**   The national database maintained by the FBI which contains the names of missing and wanted persons and various stolen items. Accessible to officers throughout the country through a system of computer networks.

**NCIC 2000**   the planning and strategic effort underway by the FBI to upgrade the National Crime Information Center.

**personal vertical takeoff and landing aircraft (VTOL)**   a type of aircraft that permits individuals to take off and land in a vertical position; the types under development are smaller and meant for personal use.

**personal video surveillance systems**   a system consisting of a small camera and microphone attached to the shirt of an officer and a transmitter attached to the duty belt, which sends images and sounds to a receiver/recorder subsystem located in the officer's vehicle.

**privacy rights paradigm**   a proposed perspective based on the concepts of ordered liberty, citizenship, and responsibility; it is designed to provide the greater privacy rights to the individual at the personal and intimate relationship levels and fewer privacy rights when the type of relationships are of governmental concern.

**regional information sharing system (RISS)**   large computer systems servicing a regional geographical area and which usually serves as a gateway to the NCIC.

**secure flight**   a revamped version of the controversial CAPPS II (Computer Assisted Passenger Prescreening System II) program of the Transportation Security Administration (TSA). It is intended for the screening of airline passengers and will only look for known or suspected terrorists, not other law enforcement violators.

**spyware**   the general term used to describe a computer program that is surreptitiously downloaded to one's computer, which permits others to obtain information from that computer when it is online.

**technologically enhanced crime**   offenses in which scientific advances permit less time to commit offenses, make personal information from potential victims more readily available, make detection more difficult, or improve the quality of materials or documents used in offenses; can be classified into two categories: traditional crimes and high-tech crimes.

**teleforensics**   a strategy that permits the recording of crime scenes using a camcorder fitted with a wireless transmitter that sends images to remote monitors in real time.

**unmanned aerial vehicles (UAVs)**   remotely controlled small aircraft that are usually equipped with surveillance technology.

**US-VISIT**   The US Department of Homeland Security's database that contains scanned fingerprints of the index fingers and a photograph of most foreign visitors traveling to the United States on a visa.

## ■ Appendix 11-A    The Evolution of Information Technology

| | |
|---|---|
| 1600 | Galileo Galilei, the Italian mathematician, astronomer, and physicist who assisted in the renaissance of mathematics as a scientific language. He stated that the "*Book of Nature* is written in mathematical characters." |
| 1614 | The first publication of the discovery of logarithms (the exponent of a base number indicating to what power that base must be raised to produce another given number) by John Napier of Scotland. |
| 1620s | The slide rule was developed by William Oughtred and others to assist in the rapid calculation of numbers. |
| 1640 | Blaise Pascal developed an "adding machine" device, called the Pascaline, that remembered information and executed calculations by the use of wheels and interlocking gears. Its basic principle was used in adding machines for the next 300 years. |
| 1673 | Gottfried Wilhelm von Leibniz designed a machine that could process numbers beyond just addition. It was more like a calculator. Leibniz is better known, however, for his invention of calculus and the perfection of binary arithmetic. |
| 1800s | Charles Babbage, an English mathematician, proposed the "Difference Engine," and later the "Analytic Engine," which would have been a true computing device. Neither was ever perfected, and the latter was not completed because of problems in manufacturing the necessary parts. Augusta Ada Byron (daughter of Lord Byron, the poet) later assisted in translating and explaining Babbage's principles and theories. |
| 1804 | The first fully-automated loom was developed by Joseph Marie Jacquard. It was made possible by a memory device controlled by punched holes on a card and could weave very complicated patterns. |
| 1840s | George Boole devised a form of algebra (Boolean Algebra), which included the basic operators of AND, OR, and NOT. In 1867, Charles Sanders Pierce brought Boolean Algebra to the United States and continued to modify and extend it. |
| 1890 | Building on the punched card principle, Herman Hollerith devised a system of tabulating census forms. The machine counted the holes on the card. Hollerith went on to form the Tabulating Machine Company, which after several mergers and name changes came to be known as the International Business Machines Corporation (IBM). |
| 1930s | Vannevar Bush, an MIT professor, built a pioneering machine, capable of solving differential equations. Bush thought it could be improved. Ultimately, this led to one of his graduate students, Claude Shannon, applying Boolean Algebra to the design of electrical circuits. His work lies at the foundation of modern telephone systems. Other |

researchers such as John Atanasoff of Iowa State College, George Stibitz of Bell Telephone Laboratories, and Konrad Zuse of Germany were also independently advancing the "computer evolution" with their work in electronics.

1941    Konrad Zuse designed and built (in Germany) the first operational computer that was program-controlled and based on the binary system.

1943    IBM and Howard Aiken succeeded in building the Mark I, a machine using punched paper tape that could "crunch" numbers up to 23 digits long. It was used by the navy to solve difficult ballistic problems.

The British built an electro-mechanical machine called COLOSSUS, which was used to decipher German codes and messages. It used vacuum tubes, which was a breakthrough in the development of the computer.

1945    John W. Mauchly and J. Presper Echert successfully tested the first all-electric digital computer. This Electronic Numerical Integrator And Calculator (ENIAC) was introduced in 1944 at the University of Pennsylvania. It filled an entire room (occupying 3000 cubic feet), weighed 30 tons, had 17,468 vacuum tubes, and consumed 200 kilowatts of electricity (enough to light 70–80 homes).

1947    Howard Aiken advised officials of the National Bureau of Standards that "there will never be enough problems, enough work for more than one or two of these computers. . . ."

The transistor was invented at Bell Telephone Laboratories, but did not appear economically in computer components until 1959. It was initially applied to radio technology.

1948    The Cathode Ray Tube (CRT) was applied to the Mark I by F.C. Williams.

1950s   The cold war with the Soviet Union fueled the government's willingness to invest large sums of money into the development of larger and faster computers.

1951    The first commercial computer, UNIVAC (UNIVersal Automatic Computer), was built by Echert and Mauchly. UNIVAC could process words as well as numbers. It was placed on the market by the Remington Rand (Sperry) Corporation. UNIVAC and other subsequent computers were made practical because of two innovations advocated during the mid- to late-1940s by the collective work of John W. Mauchly, J. Presper Echert, and John von Neumann, who recommended use of (a) a binary number system—1s and 0s, coupled with Boolean algebra, and (b) a stored program concept of instructions.

1953    Jay W. Forrester conceived and first used magnetic core memory successfully in the WHIRLWIND Computer at MIT, which was part of a massive federally-funded project. This project let to others, such as SAGE.

| | |
|---|---|
| 1954 | The IBM 650 Computer was placed on the market as the first mass-produced computer. During the 50s and 60s, there were many advances in the computer industry, such as the development and refinement of various programming languages including FORTRAN, COBOL, ALGO, and BASIC. |
| 1958 | Texas Instrument engineer Jack Kilby created the first bona fide integrated circuit, which led to the miniaturization of computer parts. |
| 1960s | Many computers were built with integrated instead of transistor circuitry. This opened the era of the minicomputer as well. |
| 1961 | The first commercially produced electronic chips (silicon chips) containing integrated circuits became available, but were very expensive. |
| 1968 | The first 256-bit chip was introduced, followed by the 1024-bit chip a few months later. |
| 1970 | The first microprocessor chip, the Intel 4004 (4-bit chip), was manufactured after being invented by Ted Hoff. |
| 1972 | The first 8-bit microprocessor, the Intel 8008, was introduced, which opened the microcomputer era. |
| 1974 | The Intel 8080 became commercially available. |
| 1975 | The first personal computer, the Altair 8800, was sold through Micro Instrumentation and Telemetry Systems of Albuquerque, New Mexico, thus launching the personal computer industry. |
| 1976 | A microcomputer on a "board" 5″ × 8″ could out-perform the ENIAC.<br><br>The Z-80 microprocessor (an 8-bit chip) was introduced by Zilog Company.<br><br>The Intel 8086 (16-bit) chip was introduced. |
| 1977 | The Commodore PET, TRS-80 Model I, and Apple I personal computers became commercially available, as well as about 28 other brands. |
| 1978 | Zilog Z8000 (16-bit) microprocessor was introduced. |
| 1979 | Motorola 68000 (16-bit) microprocessor was introduced.<br><br>The Osborne I portable with built-in 5 1/4-inch diskette drives was introduced with a 5.5 inch CRT. |
| 1981 | IBM enters the personal computer field with the production of the IBM PC.<br><br>The 32-bit microprocessor chip introduced by Hewlett-Packard. |
| 1983 | The 80286 microprocessor chip became commercially available.<br><br>The Tandy Model 100 laptop was introduced. |
| 1984 | The first laptops with a built-in disk drive were marketed. |
| 1985 | Handheld and laptop computers begin to become economically attractive. |

1986    The 80386 microprocessor became commercially available.

1989    The 80486-based microcomputers are marketed.

1993    The first "Pentium" (80586) microcomputers become available.

1997    The first "Pentium II" microcomputers become available.

1997–2000    The processors become even faster and the field moves into the 32 MB and toward the 64 MB microprocessors. New devices such as DVDs, MP3 players, handheld devices, multi-function cellular phones, and satellite radio emerge and become readily available commercially.

## ■ Appendix 11-B    The Evolution of Information Technology in Policing, 1845–2000

1845    All precinct stations of the New York City Police Department were connected by telegraph.

1867    Telegraph police call boxes were first installed.

1878    The Washington, DC Police Department installed its first telephone and by 1880 Chicago had installed them in call boxes on officer's beats.

1881    Chicago installed the first emergency police telephone booths.

1900s    Telephotography was employed by several departments, which permitted the sending of photos from one city to another.

1902    An electric police alarm box system was installed in Kansas City, Missouri.

1920s    The teletypewriter became a workhorse for communication between departments.

1926    Radio-equipped patrol cars with "receive only" capability were introduced in Berkeley, California.

1928    The Detroit Police Department initiated mobile radio receivers after several years of development. The Police Department of Cleveland, Ohio went on the air in 1929.

1929    The first state-wide teletypewriter system was installed by the Pennsylvania State Police.

1933    Two-way police radio communications were initiated in Bayonne, New Jersey, followed by Indianapolis, Indiana.

1940s    Three-way communications capability was introduced.

1960s    Portable radios became less expensive and more popular.

1964    The St. Louis Police Department was the only one in the United States to have a computer system. Also, none were in use at the state or national levels.

1967    The FBI's National Crime Information Center (NCIC) began operation in January.

| | |
|---|---|
| 1968 | AT&T announced creation of 911 in January. |
| | At least 10 states and 50 cities had acquired computerized systems. |
| | Kansas City, Missouri began operation of ALERT I (Automated Law Enforcement Response Team). |
| | The Ohio Law Enforcement Automated Data System (LEADS) became operational after 2 1/2 years of planning; as a statewide system, it linked Ohio to the Criminal Justice Information System (CJIS) which tied into NCIC and was later connected to NLETS. |
| 1970s | A big push through LEAA grants allowed many other departments to computerize. |
| 1970 | New York City's Special Police Radio Inquiry Network (SPRINT) was implemented. |
| 1972 | National Law Enforcement Telecommunications System (NLETS) became operational linking all states except Alaska and Hawaii. |
| | Over 400 systems were in use in criminal justice agencies nationally, 46% of which were at the state level and 54% at the local level. An LEAA survey identified 39 functions being performed by computer—mostly record keeping related to police calls, personnel, and fiscal accounting. |
| | ALERT II in Kansas City, Missouri expanded and included mobile digital terminals (MDTs) in cruisers. |
| 1976 | Computer Aided Dispatch systems were added to several agencies such as Virginia Beach, Virginia, also with mobile digital terminals. |
| 1978 | The first Automated Fingerprint and Identification Systems (AFIS) were developed. The large expense for these systems resulted in only a few sales. |
| 1983 | Over 800 systems were in use in criminal justice agencies nationally, not counting microcomputer systems. |
| | Renewed interests in AFIS surfaced among larger departments. By 1987, at least 15 states and 20 cities and counties had or were about to acquire AFIS systems. |
| 1984 | Notebook-size computers were incorporated into the daily routine of St. Petersburg, Florida police officers. |
| 1985 | The use of microcomputers expanded into every aspect of law enforcement imaginable. Officers began purchasing their own for home and department use. |
| 1986 | Cellular telephones were incorporated into the police vehicles in St. Petersburg, Florida. |
| 1987 | Optical disk technology is coupled with microcomputers to offer several advantages and new applications. |
| 1990s | Handheld computers appeared in agencies for traffic ticket enforcement; pen-based systems appeared for report taking tasks; "pa- |

perless" and "near-paperless" police departments begin to emerge; vehicle-mounted video cameras document traffic stops; personal video surveillance systems used to record officer actions.

1995    Law Enforcement OnLine (LEO), the national interactive computer communications system and information service, was initiated in the FBI.

1997    FCC approved and designated 311 as a national, non-toll, voluntary non-emergency phone number in February.

The first 311 non-emergency number system becomes operational in Baltimore, Maryland.

The National Drug Pointer Index system became operational in the United States in October.

1999    NCIC relocated to Clarksburg, West Virginia.

The Integrated Automated Fingerprint Identification System goes online at the FBI.

2000    NIBIN integrated ballistics identification system, merges the existing systems of the FBI and the ATF and becomes part of the Firearms Programs Division of the ATF.

# ■ Chapter References

ACLU (2002). Answers to Frequently Asked Questions (FAQ) about Echelon, http://archive.aclu.org/echelonwatch/faq.html; Updated February 7, 2002.

Anderson, Teresa (1997). Legal Reporter. *Security Management*, May:86.

Augarten, Stan (1984). *Bit by Bit: An Illustrated History of Computers*. New York: Ticknor & Fields.

Baig, Edward C. (2004). A forearm forecast, and more. *USA Today*, January 8:5B.

Boyd, David G. (1995). On the Cutting Edge: Law Enforcement Technology. *FBI Law Enforcement Bulletin*, July:1–6.

Buckler, Marilyn (1998). NCIC 2000: More Than Just Images. *The Police Chief*, April 16:18–19.

Center for Digital Government (2004). http://www.centerdigitalgov.com/.

CERT® Coordination Center (2004). *2003 Annual Report*. Pittsburgh, PA: Carnegie Mellon University, http://www.cert.org/annual_rpts/cert_rpt_03.html#intruder

Charny, Ben (2004). Cops missing out on IP benefits. CNET News.com, March 29, http://news.com.com/2100-7352-5181099.html.

Clifford, Michael P. (2003). Electronic Surveillance Technology. *The Police Chief*, July:31–35.

Communications Assistance for Law Enforcement Act (1994). PL:103–414.

Conser, James A. (2000). Privacy Rights and Public Safety in a Digital World. *Futuristics and Law Enforcement: The Millennium Conference*. Quantico, VA: FBI Academy, July 11.

Conser, James A. (1997). *The Right to Privacy in Digital America*. Paper presented at the Annual Meeting of the Academy of Criminal Justice Sciences, Louisville, Kentucky, March 13.

Cowper, Thomas (2004). Vertical takeoff & landing aircraft for 21st century policing. *Law Enforcement Technology*, September:36–41.

Curry, Michael G. (1997). The Digital Individual and Private Realm. *Annals of the Association of American Geographers*, 87 (4):681–699.

Dotto, Lydia (2004). Cyber Sleuth. *Toronto Star*, August 23, http://www.thestar.com/.

Etzioni, Amitai (1999). *The Limits Of Privacy*. New York: Basic Books.

Federal Bureau of Investigation (2004). CODIS Program Overview, http://www.fbi.gov/hq/lab/codis/program.htm.

Federal Bureau of Investigation (1993). *Cooperation: The Backbone of Effective Law Enforcement*. Washington, DC: US Department of Justice.

Federal Bureau of Investigation (1996–1997). National Crime Information Center: 30 Years on The Beat. *The Investigator,* December/January.

Federal Bureau of Investigation (1984). *National Crime Information Center: An Investigative Tool.* Washington, DC: US Department of Justice.

Federal Trade Commission (2004a). FTC Releases Consumer Fraud Report. August 5, http://www.ftc.gov/opa/2004/08/fraudsurvey.htm.

Federal Trade Commission (2004b). FTC Releases Top 10 Consumer Complaint Categories in 2003. January 22, http://www.ftc.gov/opa/2004/01/top10.htm.

Federation of American Scientists (2004). NCIC, http://www.fas.org/irp/agency/doj/fbi/is/ncic.htm.

Fleck, Carole (2004). Stealing Your Life. *AARP Bulletin,* February:3–5.

Foster, Raymond E. (2004). *Police Technology.* New York: Prentice Hall.

Grun, Bernard (ed.) (1991). *The Timetables of History,* 3rd Revised Edition. New York: Simon and Schuster.

Hambling, David (2004). Sweeping stun guns to target crowds. *New Scientist,* June 16, http://www.newscientist.com/news/news.jsp?id=ns99996014.

Komarow, Steve (1994). Technology could tip scales in crime war. *USA Today,* March 23.

Levin, Robert B. (1995). The Virtual Fourth Amendment: Searches and Seizures in Cyberspace. *Maryland Bar Journal,* May/June11 VIII(3):2–5.

Lewis, Claude (1996). Will residents trade privacy for security? *The Vindicator,* February 15:A15.

McKay, Jim (2004a). Fixing 911. *Government Technology,* August:19–24.

McKay, Jim (2004b). Nowhere to Hide. *Mobile Government,* June:6–9.

Meade, Patricia (2004). Scanners target stolen cars. *The Vindicator,* August 11:A1.

Miller, Christina M. (2004). Body Armor Update: 2004. *Police and Security News,* July/August:31–36.

National Commission on Terrorist Attacks Upon the United States (2004). *The 9/11 Commission Report,* Authorized Edition. New York: W.W. Norton & Co.

NIBIN (2004). http://www.atf.gov/nibin/.

NIBIN (nd). The Missing Link: Ballistics Technology That Helps Solve Crimes. Washington, DC: Department of the Treasury, Bureau of Alcohol, Tobacco, and Firearms.

NLECTC (2003). Up Close from a Distance. *TechBeat,* Spring:1–2, 10.

Page, Douglas (2004). RFID tags: Big brother is a small device. *Law Enforcement Technology,* August:128–133.

Pennella, John J. and Peter L. Nacci (1997). Department of Justice and Department of Defense Joint Technology Program: Second Anniversary Report, February, Washington DC: US Department of Justice.

Pilant, Lois (1996). Imaging & Identification Systems. *The Police Chief,* August:63–68

Pilant, Lois (1998). Crime & War: An Analysis of Non-lethal Technologies and Weapons Development. *The Police Chief,* June:55–68.

Project Lifesaver (2004). http://www.projectlifesaver.org/aboutus.htm.

Public Safety and Emergency Preparedness Canada (2003). Fact Sheet: High-tech Crime. July 29, http://www.psepcsppcc.gc.ca/policing/organized_crime/FactSheets/high_tech_crime_e.asp.

*The Sacramento Bee* (2003). Credit-card fraud goes high-tech, causing alarm. *The Vindicator,* August 24:I3–I4.

Sahlberg, John (1991). *Employee Privacy and Investigations.* Paper presented at American Society for Industrial Security Annual Seminar, September 16.

Scanning (1997). *Police Futurist,* Winter:9.

Seaskate, Inc. (1998). The Evolution and Development Of Police Technology. Excerpts From A Technical Report prepared for The National Committee on Criminal Justice Technology National Institute of Justice, July 1, http://www.911dispatch.com/911_file/history/911history.html.

Sessions, William S. (1993). Criminal Justice Information Services: Gearing Up For the Future. *FBI Law Enforcement Bulletin,* February:1–3.

Shane, Jon M. (2004). Compstat Process. *FBI Law Enforcement Bulletin,* April:12–21.

Siuru, Bill (2003). Car Thieves take the "Bait". *Police and Security News,* July/August:40.

Smith & Wesson Advanced Technologies (2003). https://swat.smithandwesson.com.

Sternstein, Aliya (2004). TSA launches Secure Flight. August 27, http://www.fcw.com/fcw/articles/2004/0823/web-tsa-08-27-04.asp.

Sullivan, Bob (2003). ID theft costs banks $1 billion a year. MSNBC, March 26. http://msnbc.msn.com/id/3078480/

US Department of Homeland Security (2004a). Fact Sheet: RapidCom 9/30 and Interoperability Progress, http://www.dhs.gov/dhspublic/display?content=3869.

US Department of Homeland Security (2004b). SAFECOM Program, http://www.safecompro-gram.gov/.

US Department of Homeland Security (2004c). US-VISIT Program, http://www.dhs.gov/dhspublic/interapp/editorial/editorial_0333.xml.

US Department of Justice (2004). Justice Department Announces Operation Web Snare Targeting Online Fraud and Crime. August 26, http://www.usdoj.gov/opa/pr/2004/August/04_crm_583.htm.

US Department of Justice (1994). *Regional Information Sharing Systems*. Washington, DC: US Department of Justice.

US Department of Justice, COPS (2004). *311 Initiative Timeline*. Office of Community Oriented Policing Services, http://www.cops.usdoj.gov/default.asp?Item=509.

US Department of Justice, National Institute of Justice (2004). Less Lethal Technologies, http://www.ojp.usdoj.gov/nij/sciencetech/ltl.htm.

US Department of Justice, Office of Justice Programs, Global Justice Information Sharing Initiative, Security Working Group (2004). Applying Security Practices to Justice Information Sharing. March, http://it.ojp.gov/documents/asp/introduction/index.htm.

US Department of Treasury (2004). FinCEN, http://www.fincen.gov/af_overview.html.

Video Privacy Protection Act of 1988, 102 Statute 3195.

Wallace, Donald H. and Everett K. Woods (1995). Surveillance, Eavesdropping and Citizens' Rights. *Journal of Security Administration*, December:10–17.

Westphal, Lonnie J. (2004).The In-Car Camera: Value and Impact. *The Police Chief*, August:59–65.

# Future Issues in Law Enforcement and Recommendations

**12**

## Learning Objectives

The future—that which lies ahead. When the first edition of this text was published, the authors did not use terms and phrases such as "homeland security," "Transportation Security Agency," and "dirty bomb." What a difference a few years make! How well can you foresee the future? How predictable are events such as the terrorist attacks of September 11, 2001? Did those attacks affect law enforcement operations in the United States? Of course they did; they changed the focus of several key functions, many of which were discussed in previous chapters. This chapter's focus is twofold: (1) to identify many of the future issues that will affect law enforcement in the United States by reviewing past events and current trends and (2) to make recommendations about improving law enforcement agencies and personnel. After studying this chapter, you will be able to:

- Identify the global challenges affecting the law enforcement community today and in the near future.
- Recite several recommendations of the 9/11 Commission.
- Describe the cultural, societal, and demographic trends affecting the United States.
- Discuss several legal issues that will continue to affect law enforcement operations.
- State the challenges to law enforcement agencies in maintaining a competent workforce.
- Summarize several recommendations for improving law enforcement in the United States.

## Chapter Outline

I. Future Problems Affecting Law Enforcement
   A. Why Study the Future?
   B. How Does One Anticipate the Future?

II. Global Challenges and Social Changes
   A. Foreign Terrorist Threats and National Preparedness
   B. Free Trade and Border Protection
   C. Immigration Patterns
   D. World Trade and Economic Patterns
III. National Changes and Challenges
   A. Domestic Terror and Hate Advocates
   B. Demographic and Workforce Changes
   C. Disaster and Civil Unrest
   D. Medical Issues
   E. Gangs and Neighborhood Decay
IV. Legal Issues
   A. Interrogation
   B. Criminal Law
   C. Evidence
   D. Administrative Law and Liability
V. Agency Management Issues
VI. Local Law Enforcement Trends and Strategy Recommendations
VII. Summary

## Key Terms Used in This Chapter

foresight
NAFTA
RIF
local militias
hate crime
penalty enhancement
baby boom generation

baby bust generation
FEMA
blood borne pathogens
encryption
Nominal Group Technique
Delphi Technique

# ■ Future Problems Affecting Law Enforcement

Law enforcement faces the same changes impacting the economic, social, and governmental structures of our nation. Law enforcement also must respond to the call for changes from the justice system. In order to assess the nature of those changes, each organization must look to its own environment. This chapter is intended to stimulate the curiosity of the reader and to encourage exploration of emerging forces of change. These forces may be global, national, or local in character. In Chapters 1 and 6 we wrote about the systems approach to viewing environmental forces. The future challenges peculiar to law enforcement, and what they may mean for patrol officers, supervisors, and managers are examined here. We review the means by which all law enforcement personnel may scan for information, identify issues, and help develop solutions (or at least accommodations) to these various challenges.

It is obvious that problems and challenges on the horizon are important to managers in law enforcement. Indeed, the nationally acclaimed Command College of the California Commission on Peace Officer Standards and Training is specifically designed as a futures and strategic planning program for managers. But, why should front line personnel (patrol officers, agents, and investigators) or supervisors pay attention to such issues? As noted earlier in this text, line officers and their supervisors are the eyes and ears of law enforcement. They will frequently be the first to notice changes in neighborhoods with which they interact. They are closer to changes in the environment and, accordingly, they will be aware of information sooner and in greater depth than analysts sitting in either headquarters or in some distant agency or university. It is not that these analysts are not important; the authors would never take that position. Rather, both types of analysts are important. Field and supervisory personnel must learn to analyze changes within their environment. They also must learn to interact with the other type of analysts and planners in order to discuss the implications of such changes and to develop adjustment strategies or countermeasures.

## Why Study the Future?

To many, the answer to this question may appear obvious, but there are actually several reasons. An article in *The Futurist* (Wagner 2002) magazine described 10 reasons to watch for trends. The ones most applicable to our purpose in this chapter can be summarized and paraphrased as follows: to prepare yourself for the future, to be informed of the forces affecting your field, to be informed about forces affecting other fields, to understand the differences between a trend and a fad, to obtain confidence in decision making, and to be forewarned of possible crises. These are basic reasons to give serious attention to what is going on in the world and specifically to what is happening in your chosen career field.

**Foresight** is the ability to think and envision what may happen in the future. We are not talking about taking a wild guess, or trying to predict the date of an event. We are referring to the ability to first identify possibilities, then develop evidence of probabilities, and thirdly to evaluate what options are preferable. The "Possible—Probable—Preferable" approach to studying and evaluating the environmental forces assists in understanding the future.

## How Does One Anticipate the Future?

There are a number of techniques available that can be utilized to improve foresight. **Figure 12-1** identifies 12 techniques proposed by the World Future Society, an international association whose members are interested in future trends and developments. The association publishes a number of books, a research journal, and a professional magazine. You are encouraged to learn more about the organization at its Web site: www.wfs.org. Other organizations interested in the future can be found on the Internet by using search terms such as "futures research," "futurists," "foresight," and "trend analysis." There also is a professional association dedicated to studying and discussing issues affecting policing;

*Scanning*—a systematic survey of newspapers, magazines, Web sites, and other media for indications of changes with future implications.

*Trend analysis*—examinations that identify the nature, causes, and direction of developments and their impacts.

*Trend monitoring*—watching key trends and reporting to key decision makers.

*Trend projections*—the plotting of data related to identified trends in order to project future direction and impact.

*Scenario development and analysis*—descriptions based on perceived and projected possibilities; usually depicts one or more plausible ways in which the future may unfold.

*Consulting others (polling)/Delphi*—asking others, including experts, what they think about specific issues.

*Modeling*—an imitation or static representation of real events or possible future events.

*Simulations or gaming*—role playing and using simulated situations to determine possibilities or to experience life-like events.

*Computer simulations*—automated simulations including complex data and numerical analyses and projections.

*Historical analysis*—an analysis of past events and situations in order to detect trends and forecast possible future directions of selected factors.

*Brainstorming*—articulating new ideas through small groups assembled for creative thinking and problem solving.

*Visioning*—the systematic creation of visions of a desirable future.

*Source:* World Future Society (2004). The art of foresight: Preparing for a changing world. A Special Report, *The Futurist*, May–June: 4–5.

**Figure 12-1** Techniques for anticipating the future.

it is the Society of Police Futurists International (PFI). The URL for PFI is www.policefuturists.org. Members of these and other organizations believe that by studying the future, they can have a role in shaping it.

One important aspect of the future is that it is built on the past. For that reason much of this text has included an historical perspective of where law enforcement has been and is currently. We continue that theme by reviewing a number of international, national, legal, and managerial issues facing the law enforcement community. We have not included all the issues affecting the law enforcement environment, but we believe that you will be able to pursue others on your own.

## ■ Global Challenges and Social Changes

In 1985, then-Senator and later Vice President Albert Gore Jr. introduced a bill in the US Senate that would require the United States government to create a group whose special function would be to focus on world trends and events and to project changes in the future in order to address them (Gore 1990). It is difficult to assess how such a group, if started in 1985, might have helped the nation deal with the changes of the past 20 years. One thing is certain: We were not prepared to deal with these changes and they have had profound affects on law enforcement, not to mention all other aspects of society in the United States.

### Foreign Terrorist Threats and National Preparedness

While problems in international relations used to be much removed from day-to-day concerns of law enforcement, they are no longer. Over the past few years, the United States has been recovering from the devastating attacks of September 11, 2001 and the military operations in Afghanistan and Iraq. Additionally, the collapse of the Soviet Union into various entities, the continuing disputes in the Middle East between the Palestinians and Israelis, open trade with Central and South America, or even increasing illegal immigration rates are all issues affecting the global economy and international security. Local governments must recognize the threat of international terrorists, not because the next attack will occur in small-town USA, but because of the residual effects of such incidents. Those residual effects included diverting much needed resources to homeland security activities, protection of infrastructures, such as the power grid, transportation systems, shipping ports, railroads, schools, and so on.

On the matter of homeland security, communities must now consider themselves more vulnerable as a result of the 2001 terrorist attacks and their aftermath. Those attacks occurred over three sites and killed nearly 3,000 people. It was not the first terrorist attack on our soil and probably will not be the last. The causes of the attacks and the alleged failures of the intelligence community will be debated for years to come. What is known is that terrorists are willing to use violence to make a political statement of the most profound sort.

While few localities expect to witness events of the magnitude of September 11, all should anticipate the possibility of something happening and should prepare for it. Events in one part of the country now affect other parts because of our mobility and interconnectedness. The September 11 incidents grounded all aircraft throughout the United States and other parts of the world. There have been dozens of books and articles written since these attacks, but international terrorism is not a new phenomenon. However, it is the current prevailing justification for much of what national and state law enforcement agencies are doing. According to the US State Department, in 2003 there were 208 acts of international terrorism worldwide, a slight increase from the 198 attacks in 2002. In 2001, there were 355 attacks. There were 625 persons killed in the 2003 attacks. In 2002, 725 persons were killed in terrorist attacks. However a total of 3,646 persons were wounded in the 2003 attacks, a significant increase over the 2,013 persons wounded in 2002 (US Department of State 2004). **Figure 12-2** shows the number of international terrorist incidents from 1982 through 2003.

**Figure 12-3** depicts the type of facility, type of event, and total casualties (killed and injured) for the international terrorist attacks that occurred in 2003. Businesses tend to be the most predominate type of facility attacked, with government and diplomatic facilities being the next frequent targets. Bombing is the most preferred method of attack, followed by armed attack. In terms of total casualties, the "other" category implies that civilians tend to be injured or killed more than other victim categories, with government employees being next.

Obviously international terrorism can be classified as an ongoing future issue for local law enforcement; the difficulties this creates are immense. The language barriers involved where incidents are international in character are significant and often prevent adequate intelligence gathering. Further, the nature of the threat demands multi-agency involvement and increased liaisons between state and federal law enforcement. Managing a relationship between multiple agencies at two levels in the midst of serious threats or disasters requires substantial prior planning and attention *at all levels*. The involvement of foreign nationals makes information gathering difficult. But patrol officers who know the community can

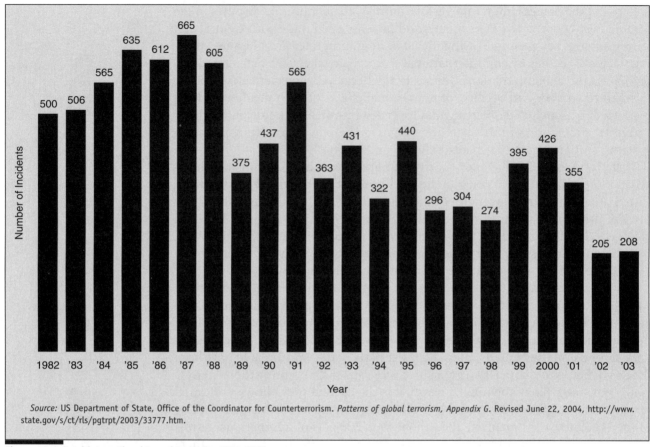

Source: US Department of State, Office of the Coordinator for Counterterrorism. *Patterns of global terrorism, Appendix G*. Revised June 22, 2004, http://www.state.gov/s/ct/rls/pgtrpt/2003/33777.htm.

**Figure 12-2** Total international terrorist attacks, 1982–2003.

interpret patterns of neighborhood events or individual behavior that are out of the norm. Such events are a cause for inquiry and are worthy of note. No officer can assume that information is unimportant merely because there is no crime of which they are aware. Well kept notes are very important in such conditions, since they may accumulate over a long period of time before patterns emerge.

While the attacks of September 11 were, in part, the result of Middle East tensions and disdain for US foreign policy, there are many places in the world equally volatile. Afghanistan, Bosnia, Pakistan, Indonesia, parts of Latin America and Africa, and certain areas of the former Soviet Union are only a few of the world regions with internal turmoil that have the potential to spread to the United States and to selected communities within our borders. Officers should be aware of world and national trends and events. They are frequently linked to local events (Cetron and Davies 1994).

Recent terrorist events have increased the heightened awareness of what could happen on US soil and to our way of life. Various scenarios are now examined regarding what could happen and how we should be better prepared for such incidents. One insightful author, Joseph Coates, has written about potential disasters and their policy implications. **Figure 12-4** lists some the key issues that Coates identifies.

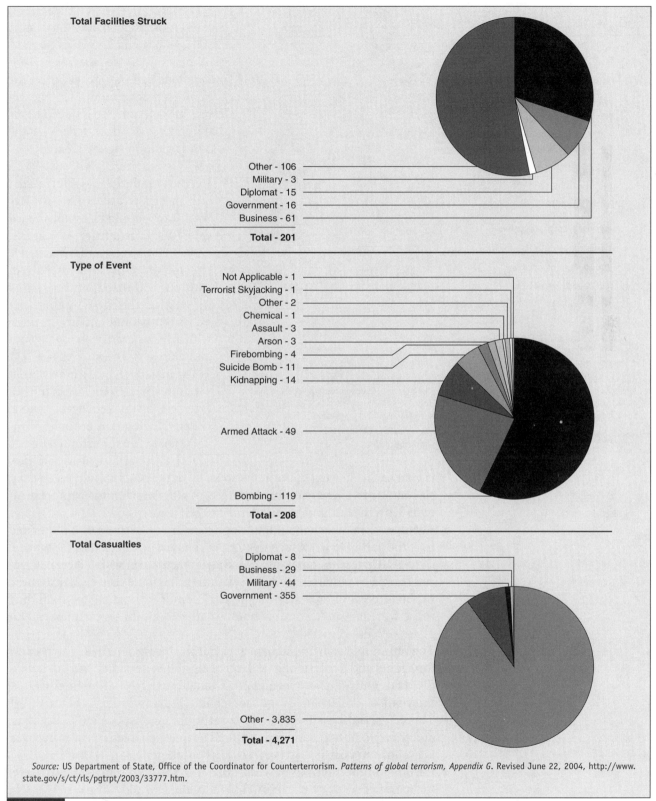

**Total Facilities Struck**

Other - 106
Military - 3
Diplomat - 15
Government - 16
Business - 61

**Total - 201**

**Type of Event**

Not Applicable - 1
Terrorist Skyjacking - 1
Other - 2
Chemical - 1
Assault - 3
Arson - 3
Firebombing - 4
Suicide Bomb - 11
Kidnapping - 14

Armed Attack - 49

Bombing - 119

**Total - 208**

**Total Casualties**

Diplomat - 8
Business - 29
Military - 44
Government - 355

Other - 3,835

**Total - 4,271**

*Source:* US Department of State, Office of the Coordinator for Counterterrorism. *Patterns of global terrorism, Appendix G.* Revised June 22, 2004, http://www.state.gov/s/ct/rls/pgtrpt/2003/33777.htm.

**Figure 12-3** Facilities struck, type of event, and total casualties, international terrorist incidents, 2003.

**Ten specific impending terrorist disasters:**

1. Disrupt global business
2. Initiate deadly panic
3. Deploy radioactive dust
4. Deploy dangerous chemicals
5. Poison the air
6. Silence telecommunications capabilities of Washington, DC
7. Put computer servers out of service
8. Infect pets
9. Target cruise ships
10. Miscellaneous

**Seven policy implications:**

1. Understand why they hate us
2. Abjure the use of "war"
3. Think like terrorists
4. Prepare the public to expect terrorist acts
5. Terrorist acts by good people
6. Understand Islamic cultures
7. Don't demonize

*Source:* Coates, Joseph F. (2002). *Were I Bin Laden.* Based on a presentation at a March 21, 2002, symposium, *Analysis . . . Where Do We Go From Here?* The Institute for Operations Research and the Management Sciences, The Washington Academy of Sciences, and the Washington, DC Chapter of The World Future Society, Commentary found at http://www.josephcoates.com/commentary1.html.

**Figure 12-4** Potential terrorist disasters and policy implications.

The National Commission on Terrorist Attacks Upon the United States (2004), commonly known as the 9/11 Commission, made several recommendations in its report that affect the law enforcement community. The following are verbatim recommendations that apply to, or affect, federal, state, and/or law enforcement agencies:

- ■ Recommendation: A specialized and integrated national security workforce should be established at the FBI consisting of agents, analysts, linguists, and surveillance specialists who are recruited, trained, rewarded, and retained to ensure the development of an in-stitutional culture imbued with a deep expertise in intelligence and national security (425–427).
  - The president, by executive order or directive, should direct the FBI to develop this intelligence cadre.
  - Recognizing that cross-fertilization between the criminal justice and national security disciplines is vital to the success of both missions, all new agents should receive basic training in both areas. Furthermore, new agents should begin their careers with meaningful assignments in both areas.
  - Agents and analysts should then specialize in one of these disciplines and have the option to work such matters for their entire career with the bureau. Certain advanced training courses and assignments to other intelligence agencies should be required to advance within the national security discipline.
  - In the interest of cross-fertilization, all senior FBI managers, including those working on law enforcement matters, should be certified intelligence officers.
  - The FBI should fully implement a recruiting, hiring, and selection process for agents and analysts that enhances its ability to target and attract individuals with educational and professional backgrounds in intelligence, international relations, language, technology, and other relevant skills.
  - The FBI should institute the integration of analysts, agents, linguists, and surveillance personnel in the field so that a dedicated team approach is brought to bear on national security intelligence operations.
  - Each field office should have an official at the field office's deputy level for national security matters. This individual would have management oversight and ensure that the national priorities are carried out in the field.

- The FBI should align its budget structure according to its four main programs—intelligence, counterterrorism and counterintelligence, criminal, and criminal justice services—to ensure better transparency on program costs, management of resources, and protection of the intelligence program.
- The FBI should report regularly to Congress in its semiannual program reviews designed to identify whether each field office is appropriately addressing FBI and national program priorities.
- The FBI should report regularly to Congress in detail on the qualifications, status, and roles of analysts in the field and at headquarters. Congress should ensure that analysts are afforded training and career opportunities on a par with those offered analysts in other intelligence community agencies.
- The Congress should make sure funding is available to accelerate the expansion of secure facilities in FBI field offices so as to increase their ability to use secure email systems and classified intelligence product exchanges. The Congress should monitor whether the FBI's information-sharing principles are implemented in practice.

■ Recommendation: The Department of Homeland Security and its oversight committees should regularly assess the types of threats the country faces to determine (a) the adequacy of the government's plans—and the progress against those plans—to protect America's critical infrastructure and (b) the readiness of the government to respond to the threats that the United States might face (428).

■ Recommendation: Targeting travel is at least as powerful a weapon against terrorists as targeting their money. The United States should combine terrorist travel intelligence, operations, and law enforcement in a strategy to intercept terrorists, find terrorist travel facilitators, and constrain terrorist mobility (385).

■ Recommendation: The US border security system should be integrated into a larger network of screening points that includes our transportation system and access to vital facilities, such as nuclear reactors. The president should direct the Department of Homeland Security to lead the effort to design a comprehensive screening system, addressing common problems and setting common standards with system-wide goals in mind. Extending those standards among other governments could dramatically strengthen America and the world's collective ability to intercept individuals who pose catastrophic threats (387–388).

- Americans should not be exempt from carrying biometric passports or otherwise enabling their identities to be securely verified when they enter the United States; nor should Canadians or Mexicans. Currently US persons are exempt from carrying passports when returning from Canada, Mexico, and the Caribbean. The current system enables non-US citizens to gain entry by showing minimal identification. The 9/11 experience shows that terrorists study and exploit America's vulnerabilities.
- To balance this measure, programs to speed known travelers should be a higher priority, permitting inspectors to focus on greater risks. The

daily commuter should not be subject to the same measures as first-time travelers. An individual should be able to pre-enroll, with his or her identity verified in passage. Updates of database information and other checks can ensure ongoing reliability. The solution, requiring more research and development, is likely to combine radio frequency technology with biometric identifiers.

- The current patchwork of border screening systems, including several frequent traveler programs, should be consolidated with the US VISIT system to enable the development of an integrated system, which in turn can become part of the wider screening plan we suggest.

- The program allowing individuals to travel from foreign countries through the United States to a third country, without having to obtain a US visa, has been suspended. Because "transit without visa" can be exploited by terrorists to enter the United States, the program should not be reinstated unless and until transit passage areas can be fully secured to prevent passengers from illegally exiting the airport.

■ Recommendation: The Department of Homeland Security, properly supported by the Congress, should complete, as quickly as possible, a biometric entry-exit screening system, including a single system for speeding qualified travelers. It should be integrated with the system that provides benefits to foreigners seeking to stay in the United States. Linking biometric passports to good data systems and decision making is a fundamental goal. No one can hide his or her debt by acquiring a credit card with a slightly different name. Yet today, a terrorist can defeat the link to electronic records by tossing away an old passport and slightly altering the name in the new one (389).

■ Recommendation: Secure identification should begin in the United States. The federal government should set standards for the issuance of birth certificates and sources of identification, such as drivers' licenses. Fraud in identification documents is no longer just a problem of theft. At many entry points to vulnerable facilities, including gates for boarding aircraft, sources of identification are the last opportunity to ensure that people are who they say they are and to check whether they are terrorists (390–391).

■ Recommendation: Hard choices must be made in allocating limited resources. The US government should identify and evaluate the transportation assets that need to be protected, set risk-based priorities for defending them, select the most practical and cost-effective ways of doing so, and then develop a plan, budget, and funding to implement the effort. The plan should assign roles and missions to the relevant authorities (federal, state, regional, and local) and to private stakeholders. In measuring effectiveness, perfection is unattainable. But terrorists should perceive that potential targets are defended. They may be deterred by a significant chance of failure (391).

- Major vulnerabilities still exist in cargo and general aviation security. These, together with inadequate screening and access controls, continue to present aviation security challenges.

- While commercial aviation remains a possible target, terrorists may turn their attention to other modes. Opportunities to do harm are as great, or greater, in maritime or surface transportation. Initiatives to secure shipping containers have just begun. Surface transportation systems such as railroads and mass transit remain hard to protect because they are so accessible and extensive.

- Recommendation: As the president determines the guidelines for information sharing among government agencies and by those agencies with the private sector, he should safeguard the privacy of individuals about whom information is shared (394).

- Recommendation: Homeland security assistance should be based strictly on an assessment of risks and vulnerabilities. Now, in 2004, Washington, DC and New York City are certainly at the top of any such list. We understand the contention that every state and city needs to have some minimum infrastructure for emergency response. But federal homeland security assistance should not remain a program for general revenue sharing. It should supplement state and local resources based on the risks or vulnerabilities that merit additional support. Congress should not use this money as a pork barrel (396).

- Recommendation: Emergency response agencies nationwide should adopt the Incident Command System (ICS).When multiple agencies or multiple jurisdictions are involved, they should adopt a unified command. Both are proven frameworks for emergency response. We strongly support the decision that federal homeland security funding will be contingent, as of October 1, 2004, upon the adoption and regular use of ICS and unified command procedures. In the future, the Department of Homeland Security should consider making funding contingent on aggressive and realistic training in accordance with ICS and unified command procedures (397).

- Recommendation: Congress should support pending legislation which provides for the expedited and increased assignment of radio spectrum for public safety purposes. Furthermore, high-risk urban areas such as New York City and Washington, DC should establish signal corps units to ensure communications connectivity between and among civilian authorities, local first responders, and the National Guard. Federal funding of such units should be given high priority by Congress (397).

- Recommendation: We endorse the American National Standards Institute's recommended standard for private preparedness. We were encouraged by Secretary Tom Ridge's praise of the standard, and urge the Department of Homeland Security to promote its adoption. We also encourage the insurance and credit-rating industries to look closely at a company's compliance with the ANSI standard in assessing its insurability and creditworthiness. We believe that compliance with the standard should define the standard of care owed by a company to its employees and the public for legal purposes. Private-sector preparedness is not a luxury; it is a cost of doing business in the post-9/11 world. It is ignored at a tremendous potential cost in lives, money, and national security (398).

## Free Trade and Border Protection

Other international concerns are free trade and open borders. The notion of free trade will most likely help the general economy in the long run, which can only be good for law enforcement of all levels. However, it also poses interesting and complex problems (Cornish 1990). The increase in truck and other vehicular traffic that followed the **North American Free Trade Agreement (NAFTA)** has increased smuggling dramatically. Freedom of travel across borders offers commercial opportunities for transport. Of course, it will not only be cocaine and marijuana. The possibilities for illegal alcohol, drugs (which have not yet been approved by the Federal Food and Drug Administration for the treatment of illnesses), and even banned items, such as ivory and other products related to endangered species, potentially will have new entry points. Paradoxically, the desire by some to have increased trade contradicts the desire by others to tighten the borders for purposes of homeland security.

Law enforcement problems are most likely to be apparent in locations with close proximity to seaports or international highway access. However, that includes most of the continental United States. Even the states along the Great Lakes have international seaports. Examine the map of the United States in **Figure 12-5** that shows the 317 official ports of entry in the country. A port of entry is an officially designated location (seaports, airports, and/or land border locations) where federal officers or employees are assigned to accept entries of merchandise, clear passengers, collect duties, and enforce the various provisions of related laws. If you are within 500 miles (a one-day drive) from such an entry point, consider your location to be impacted. Obviously very little of the nation is excluded. Recently a number of US Customs and Border Protection (CBP) efforts have been implemented to improve border protection (US Department of Homeland Security 2004):

- Augmented Integrated Surveillance Intelligence System (ISIS), that uses remotely monitored night–day camera and sensing systems to better detect, monitor, and respond to illegal crossings, on both the northern and southern borders.
- Deployed radiation detection technology, including Personal Radiation Detectors (PRDs), to more than 10,400 CBP officers and agents, and Radiation Isotope Identification Detection System (RIIDS) to over 60 border patrol field locations.
- Increased the number of Remote Video Surveillance Systems (RVSS), which are pole-mounted cameras that provide coverage 24 hours a day/7 days a week to detect illegal crossings, on both our northern and southern borders.
- Deployed two Unmanned Aerial Vehicles (UAV) to support the Arizona Border Control Initiative. UAVs are equipped with sophisticated onboard sensors that provide long-range surveillance and are useful for monitoring remote land border areas where patrols cannot easily travel and infrastructure is difficult or impossible to build.
- Increased use of radiation portal monitors. These detection devices provide CBP with a passive, nonintrusive means to screen trucks and other conveyances for the presence of nuclear and radiological materials.
- Tripled the number of border patrol agents on the northern border before 9/11, bringing the total number of agents to 1,000 assigned to the US border with Canada. Currently, there are about 11,200 border patrol agents nationwide.

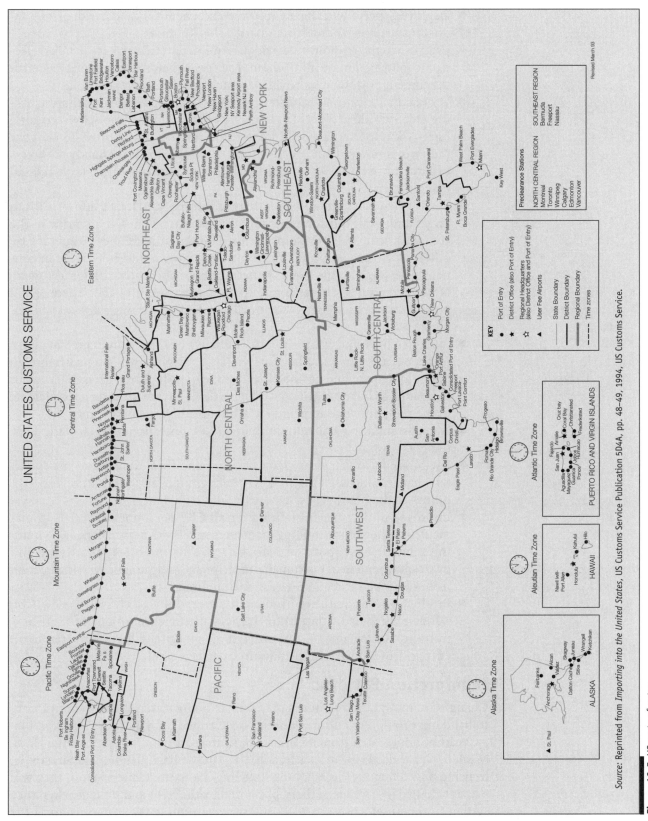

*Source:* Reprinted from *Importing into the United States,* US Customs Service Publication 504A, pp. 48–49, 1994, US Customs Service.

**Figure 12-5** US ports of entry.

- Deployed specially trained explosive and chemical detector dogs to conduct inspections at our border patrol checkpoints.
- Established the 24-hour rule, which requires that CBP receive detailed electronic information on all US-bound sea cargo before the cargo is loaded at the foreign port, which provides for improved targeting capability.
- US Food and Drug Administration (FDA) and CBP personnel are working side by side at the NTC to protect the US food supply by screening high-risk imported food shipments and implementing provisions of the Bioterrorism Act of 2002. CBP and FDA are able to react quickly to threats of bioterrorist attacks on the US food supply or to other food-related emergencies.
- Established the Container Security Initiative (CSI). CSI allows CBP to target and, with our foreign counterparts, screen containers prior to the container being laded on ships destined for the United States. Teams of CBP officers have been assigned to 25 overseas ports to target and screen containers destined for the United States that pose a potential risk for terrorism. Nineteen countries have committed to participation in CSI. There are 37 ports within those nineteen countries that are in various stages of CSI implementation.
- Instituted the Immigration Security Initiative (ISI) pilot program that places teams of CBP officers at key foreign "hub" airports working with foreign law enforcement and airline officials to inspect high-risk passengers prior to boarding US-bound aircraft. The first two foreign airports to participate in the program were Amsterdam, Holland and Warsaw, Poland.
- Named a single port director for unified CBP operations at each of the more than 300 ports of entry.
- Established a short, clear chain of command from the field to headquarters that encompassed the customs, immigration, and agriculture responsibilities of the new agency.
- Improved antiterrorism training for all CBP personnel. CBP has implemented antiterrorism training for all personnel with a special focus on training related to weapons of mass effect. This includes identifying and intercepting potential instruments of terrorism using nonintrusive inspection technology and radiation detection equipment.
- Produced an agriculture fundamentals module for classes of new CBP Officers as their initiation to the agriculture component of their new training. A new agriculture procedures module will be delivered to all current CBP Officers at the nation's ports of entry.

## Immigration Patterns

Changes in immigration patterns may impact many things other than just contraband importation or culture conflict. Accelerated immigration (legal and illegal) can be anticipated from a number of sources in the future, including Haiti, Mexico, Cuba, Eastern Europe, Russia, the Middle East, China, and Singapore, to name only a few. As these populations migrate to the United States, they will present challenges similar to those presented by the Irish and Italians when they settled in the nineteenth century. One recent example is the explosion of the

"Russian Mafia" and its activities in the United States. According to the US Bureau of the Census, there will be about 820,000 immigrants per year added to the US population. Of these, 42% will be of Hispanic origin, 27% will be Asian, 23% will be non-Hispanic whites, and 7% will be non-Hispanic blacks. By 2050, it is expected that 25% of the US population—about 80 million people—will be post-1994 immigrants or their descendants. Bouvier and Grant (1994) estimate that by the year 2100 45% of the US population will be immigrants or their descendants, using the year 2000 as a baseline. **Table 12-1** shows the percentage of the population by race and ethnic background from 1990 through 2050. Note that for the year 2050, the lowest and highest series projections are included. The middle series is thought to be the most likely to occur; however, the others are possibilities.

Immigration patterns will have other impacts. Tightly knit families with their own language will not be open to law enforcement. To them, US law enforcement may represent negative governmental forces from which they fled. If their experience taught them that uniformed personnel were not on their side, there is little chance that they will be comfortable calling upon or assisting police officials. Language barriers will pose their own particular difficulty. Departments will need to find new ways to acquire diverse language skills, or they will not be able to do their jobs, even in regards to investigating traffic accidents or reading *Miranda* warnings. Languages needed by officers include Spanish, Russian, Chinese, Japanese, Vietnamese, Thai, Hmong, Korean, and even French Caribbean to name but a few.

## World Trade and Economic Patterns

World trade and economic patterns will also affect localities. As economic patterns shift, so will the tax base upon which government rests. Rapid changes in world trade patterns resulted in US steel and auto industry decline and consolidation in the 1970s, which negatively impacted US cities in profound ways. Now small industrial firms are closing, in part, because companies are outsourcing work to other countries where labor costs are significantly less. While the federal government, and many state governments, can shift resources and draw upon a much more diverse tax base for income, local governments have few options. Traditionally, planning in law enforcement was predicated upon reasonably stable municipal and county budgets. In the past two decades, however, stability has given way to widely fluctuating budget resources. Projected budget needs will continue to outpace available resources for some time to come.

Budget impacts may require the reliance upon obsolete equipment, pay cutbacks, reduced training opportunities, and reductions in force (**RIF**), meaning layoffs and terminations. Turnover may increase as officers pursue other career options. Finally, the quality and quantity of recruits will fall precipitously as those with higher skill and knowledge levels seek safety and economic security in another location or career. The most highly educated officers may be the most recently hired—if RIFs occur, they generally will be the first to go because of seniority.

As local economic experience produces change and workers are displaced, unemployment will produce predictable outcomes. The population base will grow increasingly poor. Poverty and social problems related to poverty will increase.

**Table 12-1  Percent Distribution of the Population by Race and Hispanic Origin: 1990 to 2050**

| Year | Total | Race | | | | | Not of Hispanic origin | | | |
|---|---|---|---|---|---|---|---|---|---|---|
| | | White | Black | American Indian[1] | Asian[2] | Hispanic origin[3] | White | Black | American Indian[1] | Asian[2] |
| Estimate | | | | | | | | | | |
| 1990 | 100.0 | 83.9 | 12.3 | 0.8 | 3.0 | 9.0 | 75.6 | 11.8 | 0.7 | 2.8 |
| Projections | | | | | | | | | | |
| *Middle Series* | | | | | | | | | | |
| 1995 | 100.0 | 83.0 | 12.6 | 0.9 | 3.6 | 10.2 | 73.6 | 12.0 | 0.7 | 3.3 |
| 2000 | 100.0 | 82.1 | 12.9 | 0.9 | 4.1 | 11.4 | 71.8 | 12.2 | 0.7 | 3.9 |
| 2005 | 100.0 | 81.3 | 13.2 | 0.9 | 4.6 | 12.6 | 69.9 | 12.4 | 0.8 | 4.4 |
| 2010 | 100.0 | 80.5 | 13.5 | 0.9 | 5.1 | 13.8 | 68.0 | 12.6 | 0.8 | 4.8 |
| 2020 | 100.0 | 79.0 | 14.0 | 1.0 | 6.1 | 16.3 | 64.3 | 12.9 | 0.8 | 5.7 |
| 2030 | 100.0 | 77.6 | 14.4 | 1.0 | 7.0 | 18.9 | 50.5 | 13.1 | 0.8 | 6.6 |
| 2040 | 100.0 | 76.2 | 14.9 | 1.1 | 7.9 | 21.7 | 56.7 | 13.3 | 0.9 | 7.5 |
| 2050 | 100.0 | 74.8 | 15.4 | 1.1 | 8.7 | 24.5 | 52.8 | 13.6 | 0.9 | 8.2 |
| *Lowest Series* | | | | | | | | | | |
| 2050 | 100.0 | 75.7 | 15.7 | 1.2 | 7.4 | 22.0 | 55.8 | 14.2 | 1.0 | 7.0 |
| *Highest Series* | | | | | | | | | | |
| 2050 | 100.0 | 73.5 | 15.8 | 1.0 | 9.7 | 25.7 | 50.5 | 13.8 | 0.8 | 0.2 |

[1] American Indian represents American Indian, Eskimo, and Aleut.

[2] Asian represents Asian and Pacific Islander.

[3] Persons of Hispanic origin may be of any race. The information on the total and Hispanic population shown in this report was collected in the 50 States and the District of Columbia and, therefore, does not include residents of Puerto Rico.

*Source:* Reprinted from Day, J.C. (1996). Population Projections of the United States by Age, Sex, Race, and Hispanic Origin: 1995–2050. US Bureau of Census, *Current Population Reports*, P25–1130, p. 13, US Government Printing Office.

These effects are associated with emotional problems, frustration, alcohol and drug abuse, physical assaults, and domestic violence. Consequently, service demands will increase for such things as random low-level violence and drug trafficking. Neighborhoods will fall into disrepair and the general feeling of security and safety will deteriorate, thereby generating more crime opportunities (Wilson 1983).

Shifting economic patterns may also produce an economic stimulus in some areas, however. There also are problems associated with these changes. Large numbers of new people will pose problems. Neighborhoods will grow increasingly transient in nature, which will provide widespread opportunity for household burglaries. Increased income in an area will generate a good deal of new property and new property generates theft (which is essentially an opportunity crime). These conditions create higher demands for police service as well.

Management, supervisors, and patrol officers all need to be aware of both patterns. Because patterns will vary from location to location, management will need a steady flow of good information from line and supervision in order to assess the implications for their particular agency. Peculiar patterns will develop for each geographical area. Policies and approaches that work in one may not work in another.

## ■ National Changes and Challenges

Obviously, many of the problems that impact law enforcement have international causes. However, many also have local causes and many international trends have multiple local implications. These changes relate to the kinds of crime that will occur in the future, and the processes of hiring, training, and assigning law enforcement personnel. National trends may not be noticed in all locations. They may be more pronounced in some places, and less so in others. However, the idea that they are observable trends implies that every area of the nation will eventually be impacted by these changes in some manner.

### Domestic Terror and Hate Advocates

On April 19, 1995, a bomb exploded in front of the Federal Building in Oklahoma City, killing 167 people, including several children, and injuring more than 500 others. The bomb was made of several thousand pounds of fertilizer-based explosives and was packed into a rental truck. Timothy McVeigh, a former member of the US Army and Gulf War veteran, was charged, convicted, and executed (on June 11, 2001) for the act. Terry Nichols, an accomplice of McVeigh's, was convicted in federal court in 1997 and in the state court of Oklahoma in 2004. Nichols is serving 161 life sentences consecutively. As the investigations and trials of these two men unfolded, national attention turned to the growing influence of so-called **local militias**, one of which McVeigh was said to be a member. The isolated location of Oklahoma City, in the so-called heartland of America, and its generally conservative culture combined to add to the shock of the event. People began to realize that such things could happen anywhere.

While the Oklahoma City bombing was shocking in and of itself, the specter of thousands of armed militia members produced serious concern for law enforcement planners. These groups of loosely organized, poorly disciplined armed citizens seem to represent a variety of radical antigovernment political groups. They are loosely allied nationally and are located in nearly every state in the union. The problem these organizations pose for law enforcement is substantial. They are secretive organizations, train in the use of combat weapons, and espouse anti-government rhetoric. They use the FBI shootout at Ruby Ridge (Idaho) and the Branch Davidians assault at Waco, Texas as evidence of a great government conspiracy to suppress fundamental rights of self-government.

Other forms of domestic terror exist. The killing spree of two snipers began October 2, 2002 in the Washington, DC suburban county of Montgomery. Within 15 hours, 5 fatal shootings occurred. The attacks kept the metropolitan area semi-paralyzed for days until the saga ended on October 24, when police arrested John Allen Muhammad and Lee Boyd Malvo at a highway rest area (after an observant citizen noticed the suspect's vehicle, a description of which had been made public). A total of 10 people were killed and three injured (see **Figure 12-6**). In March 2004, Muhammad was sentenced to death and Malvo to life imprisonment for the attacks (Nationmaster 2004). In 2003, another sniper case occurred on the I-270 beltway around Columbus, Ohio. It took police and the county sheriff's office some time to link the total of 24 shootings at moving vehicles, but eventually Charles A. McCoy Jr., 28, was identified and captured in Las Vegas while he was on the run. The shootings started in May of 2003 and he was caught in March of 2004, two days after being identified as the primary suspect in the shootings.

Although the DC Beltway attacks were solved in a relatively short time period, the Ohio shootings took about nine months. Some serial offenses take much longer to solve. Gary Leon Ridgway pleaded guilty to 48 murders on November 5, 2003, making him the worst known serial killer in the nation's history. Ridgway's killings go back to the 1980s when the remains of women, mainly runaways and prostitutes, turned up near ravines, rivers, airports, and freeways. He was dubbed the "Green River Killer" for the river near Seattle, Washington where the first bodies were found. Ridgway had been a suspect but it took over 13 years for the evolution of DNA technology to tie him to the victims. He struck a plea bargain that resulted in a sentence of life in prison without parole (CBSNews.com 2003).

One of the most singularly well known domestic terrorists in contemporary American experience was the unknown individual called the Unabomber, now known to be Ted Kaczynski, a former math professor. The name given to this domestic terrorist derives from the tendency of the terrorist in his earliest attacks to target university and airport settings. However, he also attacked non-university individuals. Between 1978 and 1996 he struck 16 times, killing 3 and injuring 23. He followed a 1995 bomb threat with a demand that his manifesto against technology be published. He threatened to kill more people with more bombs if the document was not published. It was published by the *Washington Post* in September, 1995, and it was generally a rambling denunciation of the role of technology in our society. Partially as a result of that publication, his brother David turned him in when he became suspicious of Ted Kaczynski's actions and the language used in the manifesto, resulting in an arrest in April of 1996. He also hoped to be able to spare his brother's life. He apparently succeeded, as Ted Kaczynski

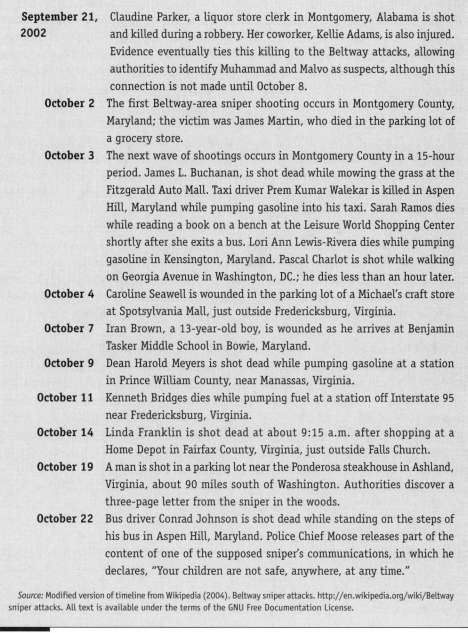

| September 21, 2002 | Claudine Parker, a liquor store clerk in Montgomery, Alabama is shot and killed during a robbery. Her coworker, Kellie Adams, is also injured. Evidence eventually ties this killing to the Beltway attacks, allowing authorities to identify Muhammad and Malvo as suspects, although this connection is not made until October 8. |
| --- | --- |
| October 2 | The first Beltway-area sniper shooting occurs in Montgomery County, Maryland; the victim was James Martin, who died in the parking lot of a grocery store. |
| October 3 | The next wave of shootings occurs in Montgomery County in a 15-hour period. James L. Buchanan, is shot dead while mowing the grass at the Fitzgerald Auto Mall. Taxi driver Prem Kumar Walekar is killed in Aspen Hill, Maryland while pumping gasoline into his taxi. Sarah Ramos dies while reading a book on a bench at the Leisure World Shopping Center shortly after she exits a bus. Lori Ann Lewis-Rivera dies while pumping gasoline in Kensington, Maryland. Pascal Charlot is shot while walking on Georgia Avenue in Washington, DC.; he dies less than an hour later. |
| October 4 | Caroline Seawell is wounded in the parking lot of a Michael's craft store at Spotsylvania Mall, just outside Fredericksburg, Virginia. |
| October 7 | Iran Brown, a 13-year-old boy, is wounded as he arrives at Benjamin Tasker Middle School in Bowie, Maryland. |
| October 9 | Dean Harold Meyers is shot dead while pumping gasoline at a station in Prince William County, near Manassas, Virginia. |
| October 11 | Kenneth Bridges dies while pumping fuel at a station off Interstate 95 near Fredericksburg, Virginia. |
| October 14 | Linda Franklin is shot dead at about 9:15 a.m. after shopping at a Home Depot in Fairfax County, Virginia, just outside Falls Church. |
| October 19 | A man is shot in a parking lot near the Ponderosa steakhouse in Ashland, Virginia, about 90 miles south of Washington. Authorities discover a three-page letter from the sniper in the woods. |
| October 22 | Bus driver Conrad Johnson is shot dead while standing on the steps of his bus in Aspen Hill, Maryland. Police Chief Moose releases part of the content of one of the supposed sniper's communications, in which he declares, "Your children are not safe, anywhere, at any time." |

*Source:* Modified version of timeline from Wikipedia (2004). Beltway sniper attacks. http://en.wikipedia.org/wiki/Beltway sniper attacks. All text is available under the terms of the GNU Free Documentation License.

**Figure 12-6** Timeline of the 2002 Beltway sniper killings.

was sentenced to four consecutive life terms plus 30 years with no option of parole in a federal court in Sacramento, California on May 4, 1998.

In July of 1996, at the summer Olympics in Atlanta, Georgia, a bomb exploded, killing one person and injuring more than 110 others. Later, in 1997 and 1998, bombs exploded at a building containing an abortion clinic (injuring seven), a gay and lesbian nightclub (injuring five), and another abortion clinic (killing one police officer and injuring a nurse). By May of 1998, the name of Eric Robert Rudolph was added to the FBI's Most Wanted list. For months federal agents combed the mountains of western North Carolina for Rudolph but did not find him. In late May of 2003, Rudolph was apprehended in Murphy, North Carolina by a 21-year-old officer, who found Rudolph foraging for food in garbage bins behind a grocery store at 4:30 in the morning (Seattle Times New Service 2003). In November of 2004 in Birmingham, Alabama, Rudolph began the first of possibly several trials. He is an example of another form of terror in the United States—hate.

Since the late 1980s, greater attention has been placed on **hate crimes**. A hate crime is defined generally as an offense committed against persons, property or society that is motivated, in whole or in part, by an offender's bias or anger against an individual's or a group's immutable characteristics (e.g., race, religion, ethnic/national origin, gender, age, disability, or sexual orientation). Most states have some sort of hate crime statute, usually in the form of a **penalty enhancement**—meaning that there is an increase in the standard criminal penalties when crimes target members of specified groups. Penalties are enhanced either through assigning a higher sentencing range for bias-motivated crimes or by increasing the level of the offense to a more serious category of crime. Hate crimes are not new, but this approach to punishing offenders for a bias-type motive is, and to some it is controversial because of the difficulty in proving motive (usually not an element of most offenses).

The FBI data for 2003 indicated a slight increase from 2002 in reported hate crime incidents. The total was 7,489 incidents involving 8,715 separate offenses, 9,100 victims, and 6,934 known offenders. The bureau has compiled annual statistics on hate crime since 1991 and now includes the data in its annual report *Crime in the United States* (see http://www.fbi.gov/ucr/03cius.htm). Of the 7,489 incidents, 4,511 were crimes against persons, 3,139 were crimes against property, and the remaining 59 were crimes against society. The focus of the bias motivation for the 2003 incidents were (Kelotra 2004):

> 51.3% Racial Bias
> 17.9% Religious Bias
> 16.5% Sexual Orientation Bias
> 13.7% Ethnicity Bias
> 0.4% Disability Bias

Other groups (e.g., Anti-Defamation League, Southern Poverty Law Center, and the Leadership Conference on Civil Rights) also maintain an emphasis on tracking hate crimes and informing law enforcement of hate activities. These groups also support law enforcement training programs. The Southern Poverty Law Center's Intelligence Project counted 751 active hate groups in the United States in their 2003 tabulations. The center maintains a unique interactive map of the United States on its Web site depicting the type and general location of hate groups (see http://www.splcenter.org/intel/map/hate.jsp). You can click on the map and have a listing of hate groups according to your choice of states. The center classifies the various groups as Black Separatist, Christian Identity, Ku Klux Klan, Neo-Confederate, Neo-Nazi, Racist Skinhead, and Other (see **Figure 12-7**). Of course it must be remembered that neither the center nor the authors of this

| Category | Approximate number | Brief description |
|---|---|---|
| Black separatist | 136 | Typically oppose integration and racial intermarriage; want separate institutions—or even a separate nation—for blacks. Most forms of black separatism are strongly anti-white and anti-Semitic, some religious versions assert that blacks—not Jews—are the biblical "chosen people" of God. |
| Christian identity | 31 | Religion that asserts that whites, not Jews, are the true Israelites favored by God in the Bible. In most of its forms, identity theology depicts Jews as biologically descended from Satan, while non-whites are seen as soulless "mud people" created with the other biblical "beasts of the field." |
| Ku Klux Klan | 158 | Founded in 1865, it is the most infamous—and oldest—of American hate groups and has a long history of violence. Although blacks have typically been the Klan's primary target, it also has attacked Jews, immigrants, homosexuals, and Catholics. |
| Neo-Confederate | 91 | Includes groups that celebrate traditional southern culture and the Civil War's dramatic conflict between the Union and the Confederacy. Embraces racist attitudes toward blacks and, in some cases, white separatism. |
| Neo-Nazi | 149 | Have a hatred for Jews and a love for Adolf Hitler and Nazi Germany. Often hate other minorities, homosexuals, and even sometimes Christians; they perceive "the Jew" as their cardinal enemy, and trace social problems to a Jewish conspiracy that supposedly controls governments, financial institutions, and the media. While some emphasize simple hatred, others are more focused on the revolutionary creation of a fascist political state. |
| Racist skinhead | 39 | A particularly violent element of the white supremacist movement; sometimes referred to as the "shock troops" of the hoped-for revolution. The classic skinhead look is a shaved head, black Doc Martens boots, jeans with suspenders, and an array of typically racist tattoos. |
| Other | 147 | Includes groups with a hodge-podge of doctrines. Some, like the National Association for the Advancement of White People, are white supremacist groups masquerading as mainstream groups with an interest in issues like black crime, busing, and affirmative action. Others embrace racist forms of neo-Pagan religions like Odinism, a pre-Christian theology that is largely focused on the virtues of the tribe or race. Includes groups like the Westboro Baptist Church, which hates homosexuals; the Council of Conservative Citizens (a reincarnation of the White Citizens' Councils of the 1950s and 1960s) oppose school desegregation primarily in the South. |

Source: Adapted from the Southern Poverty Law Center (2004). From http://www.splcenter.org/intel/map/hate.jsp.

**Figure 12-7** Classifications of bias motivated groups in the United States.

text are indicating that membership in any of these groups is a criminal offense. It is not against the law to hate others; it may not be healthy, but it is not against the law unless it is a motivating factor in the commission of a criminal offense against a specific class of victim.

From our presentation of domestic terror and hate, we simply want you to stop and think about what types of individuals our society will continue to experience in the future. What can be done to lessen the likelihood of serial killers either starting their activities or of being caught sooner? What are the limits of hate and the inciting of others because of that hate? How will investigative techniques improve across jurisdictions in order to detect serial killings?

## Demographic and Workforce Changes

From now until 2015, the US labor force is expected to undergo dramatic changes. These changes include the aging of the workforce as the average age of workers steadily increases. Other changes will be the continuing rise in the numbers of women, minorities, and legal immigrants entering professions and the attendant changes in the work place that must result to accommodate this trend. Finally, the labor force will also experience dramatic changes in racial, cultural, and language diversity. Such diversity is reflective of the trends in the population of the United States (see **Figure 12-8**).

### Age Distribution

One of the major concerns for organizations, both public and private, is the changing nature of the US workforce as it relates to the aging population. The members of the **baby boom generation** (those born between 1946 and 1964) now represent nearly one third of the population. The next generation after that, the so-called **baby bust generation** or generation X (1965–1975), is only half as large. This means that the labor pool will only grow at about 1% per year for the next decade, the slowest rate in nearly 70 years. Hence, there will be many older workers and fewer young workers. Since younger workers are the traditional source of entry-level employees for most organizations, including law enforcement, some are concerned about future staffing. Calls for service from the elderly population will probably increase as well because of their overall dependence on others.

Recruitment will be affected because older employees seek different job benefits. Training will change because older students learn in different ways than do younger students. Trainers also will need to appreciate the rich and diverse life experiences of older students. These differences will enhance actual job performance, but will complicate training, particularly where the age range in class is large. Promotion will also feel the affects of changing patterns as incoming cohorts of older students will seek promotion sooner and bring broader experiences to the promotion competition. The ever-increasing amount of technology being applied to law enforcement will demand that recruits be technologically literate beyond just being able to use cell phones and play computer games.

Discipline, too, will change as a result of aging. It will need to become more a teaching tool and less a punishing tool. Law enforcement is faced with more complex, less clear tasks and a candidate pool less able to respond to increased hiring demands. Accordingly, termination and replacement of officers will be less and less desirable as a disciplinary strategy. The desired strategy will be better training and management, and discipline will figure in this only to the degree it responds to these changes.

### Gender and Racial Changes

Other changes in the workforce will involve the influx of many more women and minorities. By the year 2000, women occupied about one half of the labor force. Indeed, nearly two thirds of those who do enter the workforce in the next

- Over four million babies are born each year in the United States.
- The US population is growing by about 2.5 million people each year. Of that, immigration contributes over one million people to the US population annually.
- The nation's Hispanic and Asian populations would triple over the next half century and non-Hispanic whites would represent about one-half of the total population by 2050.
- Overall, the country's population would continue to grow, increasing from 282.1 million in 2000 to 419.9 million in 2050. However, after 2030 the rate of increase might be the slowest since the Great Depression of the 1930s as the size of the "baby boom" population continues to decline.
- From 2000 to 2050, the non-Hispanic, white population would increase from 195.7 million to 210.3 million, an increase of 7%. This group is projected to actually lose population in the 2040s and would comprise just 50.1% of the total population in 2050, compared with 69.4% in 2000.
- The US fertility rate is currently 2.0 births per woman, an increase from 1.8 in 1988.
- Nearly 67 million people of Hispanic origin (who may be of any race) would be added to the nation's population between 2000 and 2050. Their numbers are projected to grow from 35.6 million to 102.6 million, an increase of 188%. Their share of the nation's population would nearly double, from 12.6 percent to 24.4%.
- The Asian population is projected to grow 213%, from 10.7 million to 33.4 million. Their share of the nation's population would double, from 3.8% to 8%.
- The black population is projected to rise from 35.8 million to 61.4 million in 2050, an increase of about 26 million, or 71%, raising their share of the country's population from 12.7% to 14.6%.
- The country's population is expected to become older. By 2030, about one in five people would be 65 or over.
- The female population is projected to continue to outnumber the male population, going from 143.7 million females and 138.4 million males in 2000 to 213.4 million females and 206.5 million males by mid-century.
- Along our coasts, where nearly half the population lives, the US is among the more densely populated countries in the world.
- 46% of the US population lives in coastal regions where ecosystems are the most fragile.
- California, Florida, and Texas account for one-quarter of the US population and were responsible for 38% of all US population growth between 1940 and 1990.

*Source:* US Census Bureau (2004). From http://www.census.gov/Press-Release/www/releases/archives/ population/001720.html and Negative Population Growth (2004). From Fast Facts About U.S. Population Growth. From http://about.com/.

**Figure 12-8** Selected facts and projections—population of the United States.

decade will be female. This change will force workplace redesign. Policies for parental leave, child care, and sexual harassment are only a few of the more obvious changes that will result. Although some benefits (e.g., parental leave, flexible hours, and child care) now exist in larger agencies, they will be necessary for smaller agencies in order to recruit and retain quality employees. The way in which teams work will change, too. Women tend to exhibit different management styles and are more comfortable with collaborative work approaches. Because collaboration and participatory management approaches dominate thinking in both public and private management literature and practice, males must learn to adopt these approaches. It is these approaches that will guide management for the next three decades. It is significant to note that Problem Oriented Policing, Community Oriented Policing, and Restorative Justice all rely upon collaborative decision-making models. In the year 2000, minorities made up nearly 25% of the national labor force. This will continue in future decades with more diverse cultures (including Asian, Hispanic, Middle Eastern, Caribbean, African, Native American, and African-American) entering traditional homogeneous workforces. Again, these changes will force some alterations in recruitment, training, and promotion strategies and policies.

## Educational Changes

Educational differences will continue to affect planning at all levels in law enforcement. Some of these problems arise from apparent contradictions in the landscape of education in the United States. By 2003, 85% of adults age 25 and over had completed at least high school, an all-time high according to the US Census Bureau. Also in 2003, 27% of adults age 25 and over had a college degree, another record. Yet, the number of functionally illiterate people increased. More people also attended college, but changes in funding for higher education coupled with a departure from affirmative action in university systems such as California's caused a decline in the number of minorities attending institutions of higher education. This information must be considered in light of increasing demands on the workforce for a higher degree of technical skill. One must also consider that more highly educated employees have elevated motivation needs and expect more responsibility and rewards (Jamieson and O'Mara 1991).

Given changes in the labor force and in the public clientele of law enforcement agencies, agencies will be under increased pressure to address training and educational needs of employees. Increased crime-solving complexity (cybercrime, cross-jurisdictional, transnational), emerging technological demands (crime analysis and computer mapping) in law enforcement, changing enforcement approaches (COP, POP), and competition with private industry for the same labor pool will combine to force law enforcement to address the training and education issues directly, including the provision of education (as distinguished from training). Many departments are adopting higher educational requirements as hiring criteria. While the number doing so has steadily increased, education does not necessarily solve department problems (Dantzker 1998).

## Disaster and Civil Unrest

Law enforcement must also concern itself with natural disasters and the increasing lethality of social unrest. In the case of natural disasters, the nation has seen several consecutive years of wildfires, floods, tornadoes, hurricanes, and earthquakes, which destroyed wide areas of territory and disrupted normal public service. The year 2004 witnessed very diverse weather patterns throughout the United States. Some sections experienced tornadoes, others suffered floods (including washed-out bridges), while others had draughts. The state of Florida experienced an unprecedented four hurricanes!

There are a wide range of matters that concern law enforcement in such emergencies, and a number of agencies must coordinate their emergency response. Fire services, emergency medical services (EMS), the state and federal Environmental Protection Agencies (EPA), search and rescue organizations, law enforcement agencies, National Guard units, corrections agencies, Departments of Transportation, and the **Federal Emergency Management Agency** (**FEMA**) are all likely to be involved in any major disaster. The coordination of these agencies is critical to success. Coordination requires predefined guidelines and protocols to which each agency agrees. It also requires practice and training in the implementation of emergency protocols. Such disasters also impact public safety personnel's personal lives. As agencies now prepare for coordinated efforts to respond to a terrorist threat or attack, the realization is that it is more likely that such plans would be put into operation for a natural disaster.

Natural disasters, however, may not be the most likely form of disaster, but rather only the most singularly damaging. Disasters that are the result of human actions are far more likely to cause industrial damage, for example. We can include in this list large vehicle accidents (train derailments and freeway chain reaction pile-ups for example), plane crashes, toxic chemical spills, riots, bombings, arsons, and major gas leaks. Each of these represents a unique challenge to law enforcement, and, again, a unique set of predefined response models. However, it is important to remember that contingency plans or standard operating procedures must be flexible enough to adapt to different conditions. Moreover, plans and procedures must be practiced and reviewed on a regular basis in order to ensure currency. The purpose of disaster drills is to be able to coordinate actions of all agencies into an effective response.

## Medical Issues

Until recently, law enforcement officers needed to concern themselves only with emergency aid to accident victims or getting those in custody to medical facilities if treatment was needed. Now, their environment is more complicated. While medical treatment for custodial individuals is still an issue, the need for adequate training to ensure the prompt delivery of treatment is critical. In a 1989 precedent-setting decision, the Supreme Court of the United States held a city liable for not getting proper care to a woman in custody (*Canton v. Harris*, 489 US 378). The failure to do so was traced to the lack of trained personnel present to assess the need for medical attention. Liability arose from a failure to observe that need.

Medical issues have arisen in other areas too, of course. Officers need to understand the fragile nature of evidence that requires forensic work. An error in the O.J. Simpson case arose when investigating officers carried a vial of Simpson's blood around Los Angeles for an entire day, exposing it to heat and light, rather than taking it quickly to the crime lab. Preserving evidence in a crime scene where victim assistance is required poses additional problems. While victim treatment is essential, care must be taken not to damage evidence. In some cases, there is a great need to deal directly with emergency personnel, and the medical community in general. In rape or driving while intoxicated cases, to name only two, officers must frequently deal directly with medical facility staff. Training is necessary in order to understand the needs and interests of the medical community.

Obviously, one of the largest problems is the threat of AIDS transmission. AIDS (Auto Immune Deficiency Syndrome) is a complex disease. Essentially it is a disease that destroys the body's ability to resist other diseases common to mankind. It is transmitted by bodily fluids, generally those such as blood or sexual fluids. Hence, contact with blood or sexual fluids of another person can provide the opportunity for transmission. Accidental exposure to blood or tissue is a major concern for law enforcement. Officers may make contact with either in the process of arresting a suspect or assisting a victim.

It is just this sort of risk that caused the Occupational Safety and Health Administration (OSHA) to issue its guidelines *Potentially Infectious Materials* (PIMs). These guidelines are applicable to all employers, including law enforcement agencies. They cover all **blood borne pathogens**, or pathogenic microorganisms, present in human blood. This includes not only AIDS-causing HIV (human immunodeficiency virus), but also hepatitis B virus (HBV), a pernicious and highly infectious blood disease. (A newer strain, hepatitis C, is now becoming a health and safety issue as well.) There are several serious illnesses, in fact, that can be contracted by contact with contaminated blood (CFR 1910.1030). The Code of Federal Regulations (CFR) details the diseases covered and the precautions necessary. It is incumbent on every agency to fulfill its mission to train law enforcement officers in the appropriate protective techniques to avoid exposure to blood and to maintain and periodically update policies related to blood borne pathogens.

AIDS and HBV are not the only medical problems looming, however. Law enforcement must concern itself with the possible exposure to a far more problematic disease. Tuberculosis (TB) is a disease that attacks all body tissue but primarily the lungs. It is spread primarily by sputum in either airborne droplets (from people spitting or sneezing) or on the ground. This disease was once thought to be conquered, but recently a new strain of the bacteria has emerged that is immune to the drugs previously used to kill the bacteria. There is no known cure for this current strain. Law enforcement will also need to concern itself with the problem of managing holding facilities and jails in ways that do not expose those in custody to disease. As smoking in the workplace becomes an issue we would expect that similar issues will invade the domain of law enforcement, not only for employees, but also for those in custody.

## Gangs and Neighborhood Decay

Another set of related social issues deals with the continuing decay of cities and the surrounding social fabric. Long before James Q. Wilson adopted the metaphor of "broken windows" to address the relationship between structural neglect and crime, social scientists noticed that as inhabited areas fell into general disrepair, crime and violence followed. There is no need here to detail why this theory is reasonably correct in suggesting such a relationship; it was discussed in detail in Chapter 10. The important questions deal with what this means for law enforcement.

In many ways, the overall condition of a neighborhood is related to both general criminal activity and gang activity. Indeed, addressing the issue of improving the way a neighborhood looks is central to combating gangs and crime

(California Department of Justice 1993). The importance to law enforcement is obvious. Officers must take a broader view of social conditions. Instead of merely responding to a criminal event, officers must also survey the neighborhood. If there is uncollected garbage, for example, they should call the appropriate authorities. In Marysville, California, officers used a public park clean-up as a "jump start" for reviving an entire neighborhood, rescuing it from drug dealing and prostitution. By organizing citizen groups and inviting businesses to donate materials, the park was revitalized and used as a focal point to attack other criminal activity in the neighborhood. In three years, the turnaround was clear.

Neighborhood deterioration may seem like someone else's problem, but it becomes a law enforcement problem if left alone. If an officer sees broken windows in a home that seems inhabited, inquiry should be made as to why they are not fixed. Maybe it is an elderly person too afraid to call for assistance, or someone with a landlord who refuses to act. In the first case, officers can do something directly. In the second case, officers can call city councils or service clubs for assistance. Someone will take action and help preserve the neighborhood if the problem is brought to the attention of appropriate agencies and pursued to resolution. If the department is fortunate enough to have community service officers, then this information should be reported to them. Follow-up should always be done.

Gangs and other outward evidence of decay cannot be addressed merely by dealing directly with those effects. The underlying conditions that give rise to such activity must be the primary focus. Because the interior regions of most cities are old and getting older, and because there are fewer and fewer government dollars for assistance in such projects, law enforcement officers should expect conditions to continue to get worse. Patrol and supervision officers can be the eyes and ears of the community as well as the department and they can coordinate a response.

Gangs are an ongoing problem in the United States for many cities and counties (see **Figure 12-9**). According to the 2002 National Youth Gang Survey, "All cities with a population of 250,000 or more reported youth gang problems in 2002, as did 87% of cities with a population between 100,000 and 249,999. Thirty-eight percent of responding suburban county agencies, 27% percent of responding smaller city agencies, and 12% of responding rural county agencies also reported youth gang problems in 2002" (Egley and Major 2004, 1). The National Youth Gang Survey also found:

> . . . it is estimated that, in 2002, youth gangs were active in more than 2,300 cities with a population of 2,500 or more and in more than 550 jurisdictions served by county law enforcement agencies. . . . It is also estimated that approximately 731,500 gang members and 21,500 gangs were active in the United States in 2002. The estimated number of gang members between 1996 and 2002 decreased 14% and the estimated number of jurisdictions experiencing gang problems decreased 32%. . . . Larger cities and suburban counties accounted for approximately 85% of the estimated number of gang members in 2002 (Egley and Major 2004, 1).

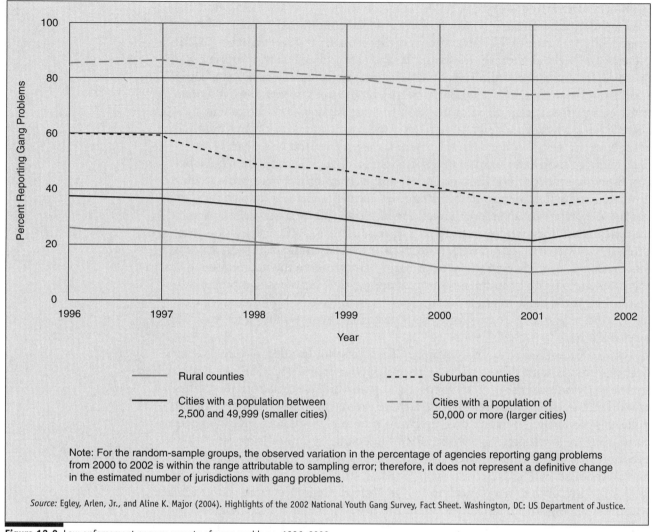

Note: For the random-sample groups, the observed variation in the percentage of agencies reporting gang problems from 2000 to 2002 is within the range attributable to sampling error; therefore, it does not represent a definitive change in the estimated number of jurisdictions with gang problems.

*Source:* Egley, Arlen, Jr., and Aline K. Major (2004). Highlights of the 2002 National Youth Gang Survey, Fact Sheet. Washington, DC: US Department of Justice.

**Figure 12-9** Law enforcement agency reports of gang problems, 1996–2002.

According to the National Survey, 42% of respondents indicated their youth gang problem was "getting worse" in 2002 compared with 2001, and 16% indicated it was "getting better" (Egley and Major 2004).

Most indications from the National Gang Survey were that gang activity would continue to be a problem in the near future, though it must be noted that there is little agreement in either academia or in law enforcement regarding a definition for gang activity. Research suggests that gang members are no more likely to engage in drug trafficking than non-gang members, but they are more likely to engage in violence (Decker and Van Winkle 1994; Esbensen and Huizinga 1993; Klein, Maxson, and Cunningham 1991). In the 2002 National Gang Survey, it was reported that 91 cities "reported one or more gang-related homicides, 89 (of them) reported a total of 577 gang-related homicides and two (Chicago and Los Angeles) reported a total of 655 gang-related homicides. When compared with the more than 1,300 total homicides recorded in Chicago and Los Angeles in 2002, these findings suggest that approximately half of the homicides in these two cities were gang related in that year" (Egley and Major 2004, 1).

# ■ Legal Issues

Any attempt at projecting the future is difficult business. But, much is known about the development of law and legal systems, especially in the United States. Accordingly, we can make some observations and predictions concerning future legal restrictions where we can expect to see the likely impact on law enforcement.

## Interrogation

One thing we should not expect to see is a fundamental change in the limits regarding interrogation. The current Supreme Court is not likely to broadly alter the current law regarding interrogation. The court is not inclined, in this era, to engage in activist policy making. There is little consensus by the court at the present time, and it takes consensus to create major policy shifts in the Supreme Court. Nor are they likely to reverse themselves, since the court has done this only 150 times in more than 200 years (and these reversals related to many issues besides criminal justice procedure). The next four years will probably see some new appointments to the Supreme Court because of the ages and length of service of current members. That fact, too, reduces the likelihood of any major reversals in criminal interrogation guidelines.

Still, the emergence of new means of interrogation might prove very challenging to the court. For example, as computer technology becomes more powerful and easier to use, three-dimensional animation programs with integrated sound offer interesting possibilities. Law enforcement investigators could program a scenario involving their depiction of events with the face of the suspect in the scenario depicting his or her role in the crime. A fully animated depiction of how the defendant acted, played for the defendant, would be a powerful tool to break a refusal to confess. Is this interrogation? Is it denial of counsel?

Other problems will arise as the population becomes more diverse. Multiple language demands have already complicated interrogation of suspects and witness interviewing. Even rendering *Miranda* warnings will be difficult. The problems will spread to areas of the United States not yet broadly impacted, and law enforcement will need to respond with sensitivity, training, and interagency agreements to share language resources. Interactive, real-time language interpretation technology is progressing significantly and will be part of the solution to this issue.

There is a movement by some to require videotaping of all interrogations of felony suspects to assure that inappropriate coercion or other techniques did not occur and that any statements were knowingly and voluntarily made. Such a requirement would definitely impact law enforcement agencies significantly. But some argue persuasively that it is of little inconvenience and cost when compared to the cost of one's liberty and to the price of maintaining trust in the criminal justice process.

## Criminal Law

The same problems are true of the criminal law, though there may be a shift in the policy focus on drugs. As noted elsewhere in this text, as drug arrests and incarcerations increased in the 1980s, incarcerations for violent offenses decreased while violent crime increased. Consequently, budget constraints and the resulting public outcry will likely alter the drug policy that is consuming large amounts of resources in criminal justice generally and law enforcement in particular. We can assume that some major transitions will occur on drug policy with either decriminalization or legalization and regulation replacing the current approach. While the relationship between crime and drugs is both complex and unclear, the mere cost of antidrug operations to the exclusion of other efforts directed at violent crime will force a change.

The trend in United States politics for harsher punishment will most likely continue for some time. Trends in attitudes about major public policy issues usually run a generation, and this is no exception. During the near future, demands for harsher punishment most likely will persist, especially for violent offenders. This will continue to push incarceration rates higher and higher. This will create long-term problems not only for corrections departments, but also for law enforcement. The only mitigating factor to alter this trend in past years has been the economic realities that affect local and state resources for jail and prison operations.

There will be a growing population of ex-cons in the cities. These individuals will have few employment skills to match a rapidly changing environment and will find, in any event, employment opportunities limited. These individuals will become increasingly hardened and networked from institutional contact. Further, absent effective social policy (i.e., reintegration efforts) to address employability problems for ex-cons, they will become a population growing in isolation from mainstream society. This will result in more criminal activity, possibly in organized structures.

New crimes should emerge from the wide variety of methods available to electronically steal both money and information. Criminal laws directed at such activities (cybercrime, identity theft, forged documents, financial fraud, etc.) will be very specific. Obtaining evidence regarding these types of offenses will demand highly specialized knowledge by officers. This includes the ability to detect and trace remote access to networks and knowledge of operating systems, computer programming, and storage techniques.

Theft of money and information by electronic means also poses interesting problems for search and seizure law. Development of probable cause will require significant amounts of data from indirect sources. In order to obtain permission for electronic transmission interception, you will need probable cause. This means relying upon data such as import-export information, local tax information, traffic (both human and vehicular) in and out of the location under suspicion, bank transfers, trap and trace data, and other related items.

Once you have permission for electronic interception, the problem does not end. Electronic transfer is done largely over telephone lines, satellite, and dedicated cable connections. For one thing, interception of data will be made extraordinarily difficult by emerging techniques of encryption. **Encryption** is the coding of data in such a manner that only a person who possesses the code can interpret the transmission. Just as significant is the hardware and software used to intercept this information. Compatibility is essential, yet this is hard to achieve even when you know what the sender is using.

# Evidence

There will be very interesting developments in evidence, thanks to technological advances. Officers will be able to obtain immediate confirmation of suspect identification from the scene of arrest via computer terminals in their patrol cars equipped with scanning, faxing, and data transmission abilities. Interactive fingerprint scanning will produce instant results because of computer links to state and national networks. Similarly, the ability to enhance any image will dramatically improve investigation. However, the burden on officers to preserve crime scenes will increase as modern, technologically sophisticated methods capture smaller and smaller bits of evidence. The evolution of DNA testing will similarly place burdens on officers securing a crime scene for protection without contaminating it. Each of these trends will require significant training and educational responses.

# Administrative Law and Liability

In the areas of administrative law, we expect the courts to become more and more involved in the day-to-day management of law enforcement agencies. Union issues, non-union labor issues, and procedural due process issues all will generate increased numbers of court cases that will test management's approaches to decision making. In those states where public employee unions are permitted, courts and law enforcement agencies will find themselves increasingly embroiled in issues concerning unfair labor practices and contract interpretations. These issues will significantly impact the ability to implement community policing, which requires role redefinition and reassignment. Some community policing and problem-oriented policing strategies may be seen as violating labor agreements or civil service laws.

For those states where unions exist but have no legal status, courts will play an increasing role in personnel decisions. These will include reverse discrimination suits for hiring and promotion and challenges to disciplinary actions on the basis of procedural due process flaws. These will tend to give the patrol officer greater power in the organization, but these trends will also interrupt the organizational flow (Hunt and Magenau 1993).

The liability exposure of individual officers will continue to grow. Jury damage awards are increasing although there is some evidence of legislatively establishing punitive limitations (financial "caps") on some types of lawsuits (part of the medical malpractice litigation debate). In communities where trust has disintegrated between officers and the people, the number of citizen complaints will continue to grow in number, absent some intervention by the department, and these will lead to more lawsuits. There will be an increase in the number of complaints filed by officers against their departments and other officers. While sexual and racial harassment claims will make up a portion of that total, so will other issues relating to employment, including the Americans with Disabilities Act (ADA). Finally, officers and their supervisors will come under increasing scrutiny regarding excessive use of force. Some of this scrutiny will come from probes by the US Department of Justice, Civil Rights Division. Some will come from local prosecutors and grand juries. Still more will come from citizen boards and commissions. All of these argue for a strategy by law enforcement to meet these challenges. That strategy is partially based on training and education, basic values of right and wrong in a democracy, community involvement, self-criticism, and self-examination. The tasks are daunting, but necessary!

## ■ Agency Management Issues

Most members of any organization tend to think in terms of daily routine. Patrol officers, investigators, and line supervisors in a law enforcement agency can identify with this statement. While the exact nature of daily demands and requests for service may be unplanned, there is a certain routine to the work (in terms of basic procedures and techniques). Each call can be both different and demanding, but over time the routine manner of handling situations becomes clear to new officers or agents and they settle into this routine. While routines may differ among agencies and assignments, a general similarity prevails (Bayley 1986). Part of these routines is taking orders, doing what is expected, and not making big decisions about department policy. Most training programs stress skills and following procedures or techniques. So, why should line officers who are not of command rank care about future problems that will affect their agency? Because change at every level is essential if law enforcement is to implement and accommodate societal expectations.

In order for law enforcement to meet the challenges of the next century, every officer must participate in decision-making processes. Information gathering is essential in order to meet these challenges. The function of planning in new models of management demands participation from all levels of an organization and COP and POP incorporate collaborative decision-making throughout the department. Therefore, all levels of an organization must participate in information acquisition and analysis, including line and supervisory personnel.

All personnel must acquire, evaluate, and share information. The key is being familiar with processes that are available for information acquisition and processing. Information is power within an organization. It is both personal power and organizational power. Information permits individuals and organizations to plan and achieve goals.

Generally speaking, information sources are of many types and varieties. They commonly take the form of articles, reports, documents, and computer analyses but they may also include people such as victims, witnesses, offenders, and other officers. The focus of this section concerns the types of documents available to law enforcement personnel for planning and analysis purposes. The "human" sources of information, however, should not be neglected and must be incorporated into the overall assessment in making decisions.

Planners in any organization begin by finding standard ways to locate, collect, and store information. In any organization, one can find valuable information from several sources for analyzing trends. Annual reports to legislative bodies such as city councils, county commissions, state legislatures, and Congress often provide good summaries of the past year, and an overview of plans for the next year. Compared to prior annual reports these documents offer a window into trends of an agency. These reports rely upon internal data summaries and analysis prepared by the chief administrative officers or staff officers (a Chief of Police, Sheriff, Agency Director, or their primary support personnel). Reports of interest include the crime statistical data (which details crime type, arrests, and clearance data), budget summaries, personnel allocation and assignments, organizational charts, major projects and program results, and possibly future planned initiatives. Other key internal documents are identified in **Figure 12-10**.

Information from such sources is organization-specific and will give you a good vision of where an organization has been in the past, how it has changed, and trends that seem to be developing. In many ways there is no better way to understand an organization than to read what it says about itself. Usually, the best and most accurate data are the numbers assembled by the agency itself. Look for budget trends, organizational impacts, staffing trends, equipment needs, and training needs. You must compare data from one reporting year to another in order to determine trends if trend charts are not included. In communities where controversies exist over critical incidents, you should also review newspaper accounts or external audits of the situation.

- Mission and agency values statements
- Annual reports
- Policy manual
- Budget reports
- Accreditation-related documents
- Press releases
- Internal data summaries and planning documents
- Crime reports and crime maps
- Project reports
- After action reports (agency internal investigative reports)
- Internal affairs reports
- Union/labor contracts or agreements

**Figure 12-10** Internal sources of information.

## Local Law Enforcement Trends and Strategy Recommendations

Knowledgeable and insightful managers, supervisors, and officers can use information more effectively by seeking answers to problems that confront their organization. One very useful and powerful way to encourage effective interaction and information sharing is to employ a method called the **Nominal Group Technique (NGT)**. NGT was developed in 1968 by Andre Delbecq (Delbecq and Van de Ven 1975; Moore 1987). This is a group process for using and sharing information, developing consensus on problems, and selecting solutions. Groups can employ this technique to make formal decisions or merely share information informally with fellow officers. **Figure 12-11** identifies the list of 10 trends that resulted from an NGT project made up of 26 individuals (a combination of students, faculty, city officials, and police practitioners) in 1996. It is relevant now for comparative purposes in that the list is about 10 years old. As you review the items, think about their current impact on law enforcement activities in the United States. Note that the items listed in Figure 12-11 are the trend issues and there is little, if any, description of what direction the trend item is moving. The important aspect of this exercise was the consensus about what trends were important. The group could then continue to discuss the impact of trend directionality and the possible agency strategies to address those trends.

Another approach to obtaining insight and to sharing information is called the **Delphi Technique**. Delphi is a method of soliciting and aggregating individ-

**Trend 1    Level of Cultural Diversity**

The change in the total diversity of the community. Includes all types such as ethnicity, sexual orientation, age, and gender.

**Trend 2    Change in Available Resources**

Level of funding will be a question. Local, regional, and global economic trends and their effects in law enforcement.

**Trend 3    Level of Economic Disparity Between Classes**

Collapse of society. Rich become richer and the poor become poorer. Demands of police executive to police both divisions of the community when one can pay for services and the other cannot.

**Trend 4    Court Interference with Management Decision Making**

Level of influence courts and judicial system will have on the police executive. How legal will every decision need to be?

**Trend 5    Change in Societal Values**

Back to the values of the past. The quality of life will become more important. Morals and ethics will play a critical role.

**Trend 6    Broader Leadership Responsibilities**

Role as a community leader. Consolidation of services under one director. The degree of regionalization.

**Trend 7    Technology Changing**

Understanding and staying on the edge of technology. Finding the necessary funding.

**Trend 8    Level of Public Expectations of Police Accountability**

Expectation of perfection. New system of board of review, level of community involvement, and amount of hands-on by city officials.

**Trend 9    Level of Ability to Communicate Effectively**

Qualification level of police executive candidates.

**Trend 10   Level of Public Confidence in Law Enforcement**

Public's trust and confidence in law enforcement officers to do the job.

*Source:* Gurrela, Ruban (January 1996). California POST Command College Futures Study, Class 21.

**Figure 12-11** Top 10 results to the question: "Name the trends affecting law enforcement executives in the next ten years."

ual opinions or judgments, typically of a group of experts, to arrive at consensus views concerning such things as what may happen in the future. It can be utilized to survey the professional opinions of knowledgeable individuals or experts and usually begins with a set of questions asked in round one, with ratings or rankings of agreement used in subsequent rounds. This technique has methodological variations and can be utilized when participants are geographically distant from one another. One recent example, using a modified Delphi technique, identified major issues and strategies for developing more effective law enforcement. The questions focused primarily on the next decade and were developed and worded by a panel of individuals who were members of the Society of Police Futurists International (www.policefuturists.org). The items focused on various aspects of policing, but were not mutually exclusive. It was expected that some responses would "overlap" and some issues would be perceived as related to more than one item. The questions asked were the following:

1. Please identify any changes to the mission of local policing that you believe will occur during the next decade.
2. What things must the police do, during the next decade, to ensure public safety and provide a high quality of service to the public?
3. What things must change in the police to meet the challenges of the future?
4. What pressure groups will have the greatest effect on the policing community during the next decade?
5. Do you believe that policing personnel should become more professional? If so, what things need to change to achieve this objective?
6. What are or will be the main ethical issues or problems facing officers/policing in the future?
7. What technologies do you think will have a significant impact on policing over the next decade, both in terms of new types of crime as well as the improvement of policing?

The responses to the questions were recorded and categorized, with similar responses being combined. Then lists of statements were compiled and submitted to respondents in round two with a request to rank them from highest or lowest value (the terminology varied according to the item. For example, some items said "most likely," others might state "highest priority," "most significant," "greatest effect," etc.). The statements were then assigned averaged (mean) scores from which further analysis and evaluation occurred. **Figure 12-12** contains the summary findings and the inferred strategies for more effective law enforcement in the future.

There are a number of tremendous challenges contained in the items identified in Figures 12-11 and 12-12. These need to be considered by every law enforcement executive and leader. There are some serious problems affecting the field as a whole today and if the future is to be manageable, they must be addressed in the near future. Students considering a career in law enforcement must learn to appreciate these many debates and controversies. Remember the adage, "You can be part of the solution or you can be part of the problem."

## ▪ Summary

This chapter addressed many of the challenges facing the future of law enforcement. Issues that are global or international in scope—such as civil wars in Africa, Bosnia, and the former Soviet Union, or NAFTA, immigration, and terrorism—may appear unrelated to local policing, but they are not. National problems such as racism, diversity, changing employment trends, gangs, AIDS, and hate groups may be visible daily but are difficult to deal with at the local level. It is

1. **The mission challenge**

   **During the next decade:** the demands for services and responsiveness will increase; the definition of "local" will become more blurred; mobility issues and technological crime will create "jurisdictional" problems. Particular to the short term will be the need to reduce fear of crime, terrorism, and religious fanaticism (homeland security issues). There will be personnel and resource shortages.

   **Strategy:** increase cooperation and interoperability between agencies (possibly mergers and regionalization of operations); and improve information analysis, surveillance, and intelligence gathering at all levels of government.

2. **What must be done to ensure public safety/quality service?**

   **The police must:** improve social competence; become managerially proactive; improve technological competence; and become more dedicated to upholding constitutional rights and liberties while working with citizens to improve safety and make communities more peaceful.

   Social competence: developing trust between community members and the police, realistic expectations through better communications with the public, more community-oriented, represent the community.

   Managerially proactive: developing futures orientation; becoming more knowledgeable about the future of policing and preparing organizations for the future; being more adaptable and proactive; becoming learning organizations; more innovative; more decentralized.

   Technological competence: understanding and applying technological advances, responding to technology-related crime, more proficient at database analysis, telecommunication systems, etc., to improve productivity and responsiveness.

   **Strategy:** move from the traditional paradigm to one of leadership, proactiveness, and community service.

3. **Things that must change**

   **The current police culture must change:** become more adaptable to change, less resistive, less reactive, more cooperative, less pseudo-militaristic to professional service-orientation; overcome generational differences, less competitive. Employ better caliber of officer: better educated, able to think outside the box, better interpersonal skills, higher integrity, positive attitude toward problem solving, less technophobic, less xenophobic, become service professionals; racist behavior must not be tolerated.

   **Strategy:** change the police culture from both the top (more insightful administrators) and from the bottom (better caliber recruits).

4. **Pressure groups' effect on policing**

   **Most significant groups:** organized community groups; some of whom will form around critical incidents of interest to the community. Elected Officials. Special interest groups (MADD, gun control groups, domestic violence advocates, victim rights advocates, etc.). Neighborhood residents and associations. Government/federal agencies/Homeland Security. Police unions.

   **Strategy:** recognize the power of the community and energize the leadership response of law enforcement officials.

5. **Changes to improve professionalism**

   **Current police culture must change:** it restricts attracting and retaining the right people in adequate numbers; it alienates cops from the people they serve; that culture must also accept "nontraditional" candidate profiles into the ranks. Greater adherence to the constitution/principles of government/rights/liberties and greater adulation and reward for behavior supportive of public service crime prevention, and protection. Police work must be viewed as a public service. Officers need to be more personable. Higher educational standards for entry; pay and benefit package comparable to teachers in public schools are recommended.

   *continues*

**Figure 12-12** The major strategies for more effective law enforcement.

**Figure 12-12** continued

**Strategy:** greater investment in selection and training techniques and standards.

### 6. Most likely ethical problems facing officers

**Predominant problems:** protecting constitutional liberties in light of powerful technologies to fight crime and thwart terrorists. Primary priority must not be "law enforcement." Immature behavior, conduct unbecoming, unprofessional demeanor. Breaking the "code of silence" or "veil of silence" of the "blue brotherhood" (or other similar labels); increased pressures on officers to report wrongdoing by other officers.

**Strategy:** establish accountability mechanisms/licensing and certification revocations.

### 7. Technological impacts on policing

**Technology challenges:** both veteran and new officers must be technologically savvy and embrace new approaches to policing. All the tools of the trade will change in the next decade and beyond: video and audio communications, weapons, investigations, forensics, vehicles, and so on will be different, improved, and more effective. Identity theft and fraud. Surveillance technology and recording and transmissions (including the use of UAVs, micro-robots and micro-cameras). Computer-related crime calls (particularly fraud and child enticement, child pornography; travelers, and harassment; eventually more commercial fraud; embezzlement calls requiring knowledge of computers).

**Strategy:** invest in and require technological competence of officers and the information technologies necessary for policing the modern world; convince funding sources and the private sector to partner in providing the technological tools necessary for public safety.

*Source:* Based on a survey of selected members of the Society of Police Futurists International, 2004. Conser, James A., et al, (2004). Strategies for more effective law enforcement in the future. Panel presentation, World Future Society Conference, Washington, DC, August 1.

much easier to recognize the impact or a consequence of these forces than it is to know how to change or prevent them. Additionally, social forces are always changing.

Your role in preparing for a career in law enforcement is to be alert to the social, political, environmental, and technological changes and challenges of the future. You must be aware that there are others we have not addressed here. All of these factors will impact the profession of law enforcement in profound ways. You are the future employee who will address these issues.

## QUESTIONS FOR REVIEW

1. How do international events impact law enforcement in the United States?
2. What are the recent trends in terrorism and how do they affect law enforcement in the United States?
3. How do economic trade and immigration patterns relate to law enforcement?
4. How will the population of the United States change by the year 2010?
5. What impact will the changes in the labor force have on law enforcement agencies?
6. What are the major diseases that threaten law enforcement officers on the streets, and why?
7. What are several recommendations for the future of the law enforcement community based on surveys of selected professionals?

## SUGGESTED ACTIVITIES

1. In groups of three to five students, discuss how you would project trends in any of the areas covered in this chapter. What evidence would you examine for hints about such trends? What methods would you use to gather evidence?
2. How can law enforcement respond to changes in the demographics of the United States? What are the demographics of your local community? Develop a list of approaches and discuss them in class, along with arguments for and against.
3. Search the Internet for pages concerning serial killers.

## ■ Chapter Glossary

**baby boom generation**   those born between 1946 and 1964; the largest generation in American history.

**baby bust generation**   those born between 1965 and 1975; a much smaller generation than the prior one.

**blood borne pathogens**   pathogenic microorganisms present in human blood.

**Delphi Technique**   a method of soliciting and aggregating individual opinions or judgments, typically of a group of experts, to arrive at consensus views concerning such things as what may happen in the future.

**encryption**   the coding of data in such a manner that only a person who possesses the code can interpret the transmission.

**FEMA**   the Federal Emergency Management Agency is charged with responding to major national disasters if requested by the state affected and approved by the president.

**foresight**  the ability to think and envision what may happen in the future.

**hate crime**  defined generally as an offense committed against persons, property or society that is motivated, in whole or in part, by an offender's bias or anger against an individual's or a group's immutable characteristics (e.g., race, religion, ethnic/national origin, gender, age, disability, or sexual orientation).

**local militias**  military-type groups of civilians organized locally for the protection, of their civil and constitutional rights; usually heavily armed and may practice defensive military maneuvers.

**NAFTA**  the North Atlantic Free Trade Agreement attempts to reduce the restrictions or tariffs on trade among the countries of Mexico, Canada, and the United States.

**Nominal Group Technique** (NGT)  a group decision-making approach used to identify multiple problems and multiple solutions.

**penalty enhancement**  an increase in the standard criminal penalties when crimes target members of specified groups; the penalties are enhanced either through assigning a higher sentencing range for bias-motivated crimes or by increasing the level of the offense to a more serious category of crime.

**RIF**  reduction in force; a clever name for permanent layoffs.

# ■ Chapter References

Bayley, David H. (1986). The tactical choices of police patrol officers. *Journal of Criminal Justice* 14:329–348.

Bouvier, Leon F. and Lindsey Grant (1994). *How many Americans?* San Francisco: Sierra Club Books.

California Department of Justice (1993). *Gangs 2000: A call to action*. Sacramento, CA: California Department of Justice.

*Canton v. Harris*, US 489:378, 1989.

CBSNews.com (2003). Gary Leon Ridgway: Green River killer. http://www.cbsnews.com/elements/2002/08/08/in_depth_us/whoswho518068_0_9_person.shtml.

Cetron, Marvin J. and Owen Davies (1994). The future face of terrorism. *The Futurist*, November–December: 10–16.

Coates, Joseph F. (2002). What's next? Foreseeable terrorist acts. *The Futurist*, September–October:23–26 and Were I Bin Laden (2004). World Future Society Web site, http://www.wfs.org/jcoates.htm.

Conser, James A., Alan Beckley, Tyree C. Blocker, Andreas Olligschlaeger, Jenny Gomery, and Shelby Williams (2004). Strategies for more effective law enforcement in the future. Panel presentation, World Future Society Conference, Washington, DC, August 1.

Cornish, Edward (1990). Issues of the nineties. *The Futurist*, January–February:29–36.

Dantzker, M.L. (1998). Police education and job satisfaction: Educational incentives and recruit educational requirements. *Police Forum* 8(3):1–4.

Day, J.C. (1996). Population projections of the United States by age, sex, race, and Hispanic origin: 1995–2050. US Bureau of Census, *Current Population Reports,* P25-1130, p.13, Washington, DC: US Government Printing Office.

Decker, Scott and Barrick Van Winkle (1994). Slinging dope: The role of gangs and gang members in drug sales. *Justice Quarterly* 11(4):583–604.

Delbecq, A.L., A.H. Van de Ven, and D.H. Gustafson (1975). *Group Techniques for Program Planning: A Guide to Nominal Group and Delphi Processes*. Glenview, IL: Scott Foresman.

Egley, Arlen, Jr., and Aline K. Major (2004). *Highlights of the 2002 National Youth Gang Survey*. Fact Sheet. Washington DC: US Department of Justice.

Esbensen, Finn-Aage and David Huizinga (1993). Gangs, drugs, and delinquency in a survey of urban youth. *Criminology* 31(4):565–86.

Federal Bureau of Investigation (2003). *Crime in the United States.* http://www.fbi.gov/ucr/03cius.htm.

Gore, Albert, Jr. (1990). The Critical Trends Assessment Act: Futurizing the United States government. *The Futurist*, March:22–24.

Gurrela, Ruban (1996). California POST command college futures study. Class 21, January.

Hunt, Raymond G. and John M. Magenau (1993). *Power and the Police Chief.* Newbury Park, CA: Sage Publications Inc.

Jamieson, D. and J. O'Mara (1991). *Managing workforce 2000: Gaining the diversity advantage.* San Francisco: Jossey-Bass Publishers.

Kelotra, Ritu (2004). New FBI data reports increase in hate crimes for 2003, www.civilrights.org.

Klein, Malcom W., Cheryl L. Maxson, and Lea C. Cunningham (1991). Crack, street gangs, and violence. *Criminology* 29(4):623–50.

Moore, Carl M. (1987). *Group Techniques for Idea Building.* Newbury Park, CA: Sage Publications.

National Commission on Terrorist Attacks Upon the United States (2004). *The 9/11 Commission report*, Authorized edition. New York: W.W. Norton & Co.

Seattle Times New Service (2003). Olympic bombing suspect captured. *The Seattle Times*, June 1:1,7.

Southern Poverty Law Center (2004). Active US hate groups in 2003. http://www.splcenter.org/intel/map/hate.jsp.

US Census Bureau (2004). http://www.census.gov/Press-Release/www/releases/archives/population/001720.html.

US Department of Homeland Security (2004). US customs and border protection actions taken since 9.11. Fact sheet. http://www.customs.ustreas.gov/xp/cgov/newsroom/fact_sheets/09172004.xml.

US Department of State, Office of the Coordinator for Counterterrorism (2004). *Patterns of global terrorism*, Appendix G. Revised June 22, 2004, http://www.state.gov/s/ct/rls/pgtrpt/2003/33777.htm.

Wikipedia (2004). Beltway sniper attacks. http://en.wikipedia.org/wiki/Beltway_sniper_attacks.

Wilson, James Q. (1983). *Thinking about crime.* New York: Basic Books.

World Future Society (2004). The art of foresight: Preparing for a changing world. A special report. *The Futurist*, May–June: 4–5.

# Constitution of the United States

I

WE THE PEOPLE of the United States, in Order to form a more perfect Union, establish Justice, insure domestic Tranquility, provide for the common defence, promote the general Welfare, and secure the Blessings of Liberty to ourselves and our Posterity, do ordain and establish this Constitution for the United States of America.[1]

## ARTICLE. I.

SECTION. 1.     All legislative Powers herein granted shall be vested in a Congress of the United States, which shall consist of a Senate and House of Representatives.

SECTION. 2.     [1]The House of Representatives shall be composed of Members chosen every second Year by the People of the several States, and the Electors in each State shall have the Qualifications requisite for Electors of the most numerous Branch of the State Legislature.

[2]No person shall be a Representative who shall not have attained to the Age of twenty five Years, and been seven Years a Citizen of the United States, and who shall not, when elected, be an Inhabitant of that State in which he shall be chosen.

[3][Representatives and direct Taxes shall be apportioned among the several States which may be included within this Union, according to their respective Numbers, which shall be determined by adding to the whole Number of free Persons, including those bound to service for a Term of Years, and excluding Indians not taxed, three fifths of all other Persons].[2]

---

[1]This text of the Constitution follows the engrossed copy signed by General Washington and the deputies from the 12 states. The superior number preceding the paragraphs designates the number of the clause; it was not in the original.

[2]The part included in heavy brackets was changed by section 2 of the Fourteenth Amendment.

The actual Enumeration shall be made within three years after the first Meeting of the Congress of the United States, and within every subsequent Term of ten Years, in such Manner as they shall by Law direct. The Number of Representatives shall not exceed one for every thirty Thousand, but each State shall have at Least one Representative; and until such enumeration shall be made, the State of New Hampshire shall be entitled to chuse three, Massachusetts eight, Rhode-Island and Providence Plantations one, Connecticut five, New-York six, New Jersey four, Pennsylvania eight, Delaware one, Maryland six, Virginia ten, North Carolina five, South Carolina five, and Georgia three.

[4]When vacancies happen in the Representation from any State, the Executive Authority thereof shall issue Writs of Election to fill such Vacancies.

[5]The House of Representatives shall chuse their Speaker and other Officers; and shall have the sole Power of Impeachment.

SECTION. 3.     [1]The Senate of the United States shall be composed of two Senators from each State, [chosen by the Legislature thereof,][3] for six Years; and each Senator shall have one Vote.

[2]Immediately after they shall be assembled in Consequence of the first Election, they shall be divided as equally as may be into three Classes. The Seats of the Senators of the first Classes. The Seats of the Senators of the first Class shall be vacated at the Expiration of the second Year, of the second Class at the Expiration of the fourth Year, and of the Third Class at the Expiration of the sixth year, so that one third may be chosen every second Year; [and if Vacancies happen by Resignation, or otherwise, during the Recess of the Legislature of any State, the Executive thereof may make Temporary Appointments until the next Meeting of the Legislature, which shall then fill such Vacancies].[4]

[3]No Person shall be a Senator who shall not have attained to the Age of thirty Years, and been nine Years a Citizen of the United States, and who shall not, when elected, be an Inhabitant of that State for which he shall be chosen.

[4]The Vice President of the United States shall be President of the Senate, but shall have no Vote, unless they be equally divided.

[5]The Senate shall chuse their other Officers, and also a President pro tempore, in the Absence of the Vice President, or when he shall exercise the Office of President of the United States.

[6]The Senate shall have the sole Power to try all Impeachments. When sitting for that Purpose, they shall be on Oath or Affirmation. When the President of the United States is tried, the Chief Justice shall preside: And no Person shall be convicted without the Concurrence of two thirds of the Members present.

Judgment in Cases of Impeachment shall not extend further than to removal from Office, and disqualification to hold and enjoy any Office of honor, Trust or Profit under the United States: but the party convicted shall nevertheless be liable and subject to Indictment, Trial, Judgment and Punishment, according to Law.

---

[3]The part included in heavy brackets was changed by section 1 of the Seventeenth Amendment.
[4]The part included in heavy brackets was changed by clause 2 of the Seventeenth Amendment.

SECTION. 4.     [1]The Times, Places and Manner of holding Elections for Senators and Representatives, shall be prescribed in each State by the Legislature thereof; but the Congress may at any time by Law make or alter such Regulations, except as to the Places of chusing Senators.

[2]The Congress shall assemble at least once in every Year, and such Meeting shall [be on the first Monday in December,][5] unless they shall by Law appoint a different Day.

SECTION. 5.     [1]Each House shall be the Judge of the Elections, Returns and Qualifications of its own Members, and a Majority of each shall constitute a Quorum to do Business; but a smaller Number may adjourn from day to day, and may be authorized to compel the Attendance of absent members, in such Manner, and under such Penalties as each House may provide.

[2]Each House may determine the Rules of its Proceedings, punish its Members for disorderly Behaviour, and, with the Concurrence of two thirds, expel a Member.

[3]Each House shall keep a Journal of its Proceedings, and from time to time publish the same, excepting such Parts as may in their Judgement require Secrecy; and the Yeas and Nays of the Members of either House on any questions shall, at the Desire of one fifth of those Present, be entered on the Journal.

[4]Neither House, during the Session of Congress, shall, without the Consent of the other, adjourn for more than three days, nor to any other Place than that in which the two Houses shall be sitting.

SECTION. 6.     [1]The Senators and Representatives shall receive a Compensation for their Services, to be ascertained by Law, and paid out of the Treasury of the United States. They shall in all Cases, except Treason, Felony and Breach of the Peace, be privileged from Arrest during their Attendance at the Session of their respective Houses, and in going to and returning from the same; and for any Speech or Debate in either House, they shall not be questioned in any other Place.

[2]No Senator or Representative shall, during the Time for which he was elected, be appointed to any civil Office under the Authority of the United States, which shall have been created, or the Emoluments whereof shall have been encreased during such time; and no Person holding any Office under the United States, shall be a Member of either House during his Continuance in Office.

SECTION. 7.     [1]All Bills for raising Revenue shall originate in the House of Representatives; but the Senate may propose or concur with Amendments as on other Bills.

[2]Every Bill which shall have passed the House of Representatives and the Senate, shall, before it become a Law, be presented to the President of the United States; If he approve he shall sign it, but if not he shall return it, with his Objections to that House in which it shall have originated, who shall enter the Objections at large on their Journal, and Proceed to reconsider it. If after such Reconsideration two thirds of that House shall agree to pass the Bill, it shall be sent, together with the Objections, to the other House, by which it shall likewise

---

[5]The part included in heavy brackets was changed by section 2 of the Twentieth Amendment.

be reconsidered, and if approved by two thirds of that House, it shall become a Law. But in all such Cases the Votes of both Houses shall be determined by yeas and nays, and the Names of the Persons voting for and against the Bill shall be entered on the Journal of each House respectively. If any Bill shall not be returned by the President within ten Days (Sundays excepted) after it shall have been presented to him, the Same shall be a Law, in like Manner as if he had signed it, unless the Congress by their Adjournment prevent its Return, in which Case it shall not be a Law.

[3]Every Order, Resolution, or Vote to which the Concurrence of the Senate and House of Representatives may be necessary (except on a question of Adjournment) shall be presented to the President of the United States; and before the Same shall take Effect, shall be approved by him, or being disapproved by him, shall be repassed by two thirds of the Senate and House of Representatives, according to the Rules and Limitations prescribed in the Case of a Bill.

SECTION. 8.     [1]The Congress shall have Power To lay and collect Taxes, Duties, Imposts and Excises, to pay the Debts and provide for the common Defence and general Welfare of the United States; but all Duties, Imposts and Excises shall be uniform throughout the United States;

[2]To borrow Money on the credit of the United States;

[3]To regulate Commerce with foreign Nations, and among the several States, and with the Indian Tribes;

[4]To establish an uniform Rule of Naturalization, and uniform Laws on the subject of Bankruptcies throughout the United States;

[5]To coin Money, regulate the Value thereof, and of foreign Coin, and fix the Standard of Weights and Measures;

[6]To provide for the Punishment of counterfeiting the Securities and current Coin of the United States;

[7]To establish Post Offices and post Roads;

[8]To promote the Progress of Science and useful Arts, by securing for limited Times to Authors and Inventors the exclusive Right to their respective Writings and Discoveries;

[9]To constitute Tribunals inferior to the Supreme Court;

[10]To define and punish Piracies and Felonies committed on the high Seas, and Offences against the Law of Nations;

[11]To declare War, grant Letters of Marque and Reprisal, and make Rules concerning Captures on Land and Water;

[12]To raise and support Armies, but no Appropriation of Money to that Use shall be for a longer Term than two Years;

[13]To provide and maintain a Navy:

[14]To make Rules for the Government and Regulation of the land and naval Forces;

[15]To provide for calling forth the Militia to execute the Laws of the Union, suppress Insurrections and repel Invasions;

[16]To provide for organizing, arming, and disciplining, the Militia, and for governing such Part of them as may be employed in the Service of the United States, reserving to the States respectively, the Appointment of the Officers, and the Authority of training the Militia according to the discipline prescribed by Congress;

[17]To exercise exclusive Legislation in all Cases whatsoever, over such District (not exceeding ten Miles square) as may, by Cession of particular States, and the Acceptance of Congress, become the Seat of the Government of the United States, and to exercise like Authority over all Places purchased by the Consent of the Legislature of the Sate in which the Same shall be, for the Erection of Forts, Magazines, Arsenals, dock-yards, and other needful Buildings;-And

[18]To make all Laws which shall be necessary and proper for carrying into Execution the foregoing Powers, and all other Powers vested by this Constitution in the Government of the United States, or in any Department or Officer thereof.

SECTION. 9.     [1]The Migration or Importation of such Persons as any of the States now existing shall think proper to admit, shall not be prohibited by the congress prior to the Year one thousand eight hundred and eight, but a Tax or duty may be imposed on such Importation, not exceeding ten dollars for each Person.

[2]The Privilege of the Writ of Habeas Corpus shall not be suspended, unless when in Cases of Rebellion or Invasion the public Safety may require it.

[3]No Bill of Attainder or ex post facto Law shall be passed.

[4]No Capitation, or other direct, Tax shall be laid, unless in Proportion to the Census or Enumeration herein before directed to be taken.

[5]No Tax or Duty shall be laid on Articles exported from any State.

[6]No Preference shall be given by any Regulation of Commerce or Revenue to the Ports of one State over those of another: nor shall Vessels bound to, or from, one State, be obliged to enter, clear, or pay Duties in another.

[7]No Money shall be drawn from the Treasury, but in Consequence of Appropriations made by Law; and a regular Statement and Account of the Receipts and Expenditures of all public Money shall be published from time to time.

[8]No Title of Nobility shall be granted by the United States: And no Person holding any Office of Profit or Trust under them, shall, without the Consent of the Congress, accept of any present, Emolument, Office, or Title, of any kind whatever, from any King, Prince, or foreign State.

SECTION. 10.     [1]No State shall enter into any Treaty, Alliance, or Confederation; grant Letters of Marque and Reprisal; coin Money; emit Bills of Credit; make any Thing but gold and silver Coin a Tender in Payment of Debts; pass any Bill of Attainder, ex post facto Law, or Law impairing the Obligation of Contracts, or grant any Title of Nobility.

[2]No State shall, without the Consent of the Congress, lay any Imposts or Duties on Imports or Exports, except what may be absolutely necessary for executing it's inspection Laws: and the net Produce of all Duties and Imposts, laid by any State on Imports or Exports, shall be for the Use of the Treasury of the United States; and all such Laws shall be subject to the Revision and Control of the Congress.

[3]No State shall, without the Consent of Congress, lay any Duty of Tonnage, keep Troops, or Ships of War in time of Peace, enter into any Agreement or Compact with another State, or with a foreign Power, or engage in War, unless actually invaded, or in such imminent Danger as will not admit of delay.

# ARTICLE. II.

SECTION. 1.    [1]The executive Power shall be vested in a President of the United States of America. He shall hold his Office during the Term of four Years, and, together with the Vice President, chosen for the same Term, be elected, as follows

[2]Each State shall appoint, in such Manner as the Legislature thereof may direct, a Number of Electors, equal to the whole Number of Senators and Representatives to which the State may be entitled in the Congress: but no Senator or Representative, or Person holding an Office of Trust or Profit under the United States, shall be appointed an Elector.

[The Electors shall meet in their respective States, and vote by Ballot for two Persons, of whom one at least shall not be an Inhabitant of the same State with themselves. And they shall make a List of all the Persons voted for, and of the Number of Votes for each; which List they shall sign and certify, and transmit sealed to the Seat of the Government of the United States, directed to the President of the Senate. The President of the United States shall, in the Presence of the Senate and House of Representatives, open all the Certificates, and the Votes shall then be counted. The Person having the greatest Number of Votes shall be the President, if such Number be a Majority of the whole Number of Electors appointed; and if there be more than one who have such Majority, and have an equal Number of Votes, then the House of Representatives shall immediately chuse by Ballot one of them for President; and if no Person have a Majority, then from the five highest on the List the said House shall in like Manner chuse the President. But in chusing the President, the Votes shall be taken by States, the Representation from each State having one Vote; A quorum for this Purpose shall consist of a Member or Members from two thirds of the States, and a Majority of all the States shall be necessary to a Choice. In every Case, after the Choice of the President, the Person having the greatest Number of Votes of the Electors shall be the Vice President. But if there should remain two or more who have equal Votes, the Senate shall chuse from them by Ballot the Vice President.][6]

[3]The Congress may determine the Time of Chusing the Electors, and the Day on which they shall give their Votes; which Day shall be the same throughout the United States.

[4]No Person except a natural born Citizen, or a Citizen of the United States, at the time of the Adoption of this Constitution, shall be eligible to the Office of President; neither shall any Person be eligible to that Office who shall not have attained to the Age of thirty five Years, and been fourteen Years a Resident within the United States.

[5]In Case of the Removal of the President from Office, or of his Death, Resignation, or Inability to discharge the Powers and Duties of the said Office,[7] the Same shall devolve on the Vice President, and the Congress may by Law provide for the Case of Removal, Death, Resignation or Inability, both of the President and Vice President, declaring what Officer shall then act as President, and such

---

[6]This paragraph has been superseded by the Twelfth Amendment.
[7]This provision has been affected by the Twenty-fifth Amendment.

Officer shall act accordingly, until the Disability be removed, or a President shall be elected.

[6]The President shall, at sated Times, receive for his Services, a Compensation, which shall neither be encreased nor diminished during the Period for which he shall have been elected, and he shall not receive within that Period any other Emolument from the United States, or any of them.

[7]Before he enter on the Execution of his Office, he shall take the following Oath or Affirmation:-"I do solemnly swear (or affirm) that I will faithfully execute the Office of President of the United States, and will to the best of my Ability, preserve, protect and defend the Constitution of the United States."

SECTION. 2.    [1]The President shall be Commander in Chief of the Army and Navy of the United States, and of the Militia of the several States, when called into the actual Service of the United States; he may require the Opinion, in writing, of the principal Officer in each of the executive Departments, upon any Subject relating to the Duties of their respective Offices, and he shall have Power to grant Reprieves and Pardons for Offences against the United States, except in Cases of Impeachment.

[2]He shall have Power, by and with the Advice and Consent of the Senate, to make Treaties, provided two thirds of the Senators present concur; and he shall nominate, and by and with the Advice and Consent of the Senate, shall appoint Ambassadors, other public Ministers and Consuls, Judges of the Supreme Court, and all other Officers of the United States, whose Appointments are not herein otherwise provided for, and which shall be established by Law: but the Congress may by Law vest the Appointment of such inferior Officers, as they think proper, in the President alone, in the Courts of Law, or in the Heads of Departments.

[3]The President shall have Power to fill up all Vacancies that may happen during the Recess of the Senate, by granting Commissions which shall expire at the End of their next Session.

SECTION. 3.    He shall from time to time give to the Congress Information of the State of the Union, and recommend to their Consideration such Measures as he shall judge necessary and expedient; he may, on extraordinary Occasions, convene both Houses, or either of them, and in Case of Disagreement between them, with Respect to the Time of Adjournment, he may adjourn them to such Time as he shall think proper; he shall receive Ambassadors and other public Ministers; he shall take Care that the Laws be faithfully executed, and shall Commission all the Officers of the United States.

SECTION. 4.    The President, Vice President and all civil Officers of the United States, shall be removed from Office on Impeachment for, and Conviction of, Treason, Bribery, or other high Crimes and Misdemeanors.

# ARTICLE. III.

SECTION. 1.    The judicial Power of the United States, shall be vested in one supreme Court, and in such inferior Courts as the Congress may from time to time ordain and establish. The Judges, both of the supreme and inferior Courts, shall hold their Offices during good Behaviour, and shall, at stated Times, receive for their Services, a Compensation, which shall not be diminished during their Continuance in Office.

SECTION. 2.    [1]The judicial Power shall extend to all Cases, in Law and Equity, arising under this Constitution, the Laws of the United States, and Treaties made, or which shall be made, under their Authority;-to all Cases affecting Ambassadors, other public Ministers and Consuls;[8]-to all Cases of admiralty and maritime Jurisdiction;-to Controversies to which the United States shall be a Party;-to Controversies between two or more States;-between a State and Citizens of another State;-between Citizens of different States,-between Citizens of the same State claiming Lands under Grants of different States, and between a State, or the Citizens thereof, and foreign States, Citizens or Subjects.

[2]In all Cases affecting Ambassadors, other public Ministers and Consuls, and those in which a State shall be Party, the supreme Court shall have original Jurisdiction. In all the other Cases before mentioned, the supreme Court shall have appellate Jurisdiction, both as to Law and Fact, with such Exceptions, and under such Regulations as the Congress shall make.

[3]The Trial of all Crimes, except in Cases of Impeachment, shall be by Jury; and such Trial shall be held in the State where the said Crimes shall have been committed; but when not committed within any State, the Trial shall be at such Place or Places as the Congress may be Law have directed.

SECTION. 3.    [1]Treason against the United States, shall consist only in levying War against them, or in adhering to their Enemies, giving them Aid and Comfort. No Person shall be convicted of Treason unless on the Testimony of two Witnesses to the same overt Act, or on confession in open Court.

[2]The Congress shall have Power to declare the Punishment of Treason, but no Attainder of Treason shall work Corruption of Blood, or Forfeiture except during the Life of the Person attainted.

# ARTICLE. IV.

SECTION.1.    Full Faith and Credit shall be given in each State to the public Acts, Records, and judicial Proceedings of every other State. And the Congress may be general Laws prescribe the Manner in which such Acts, Records, and Proceedings shall be proved, and the Effect thereof.

SECTION. 2.    [1]The Citizens of each State shall be entitled to all Privileges and Immunities of Citizens in the several States.

[2]A Person charged in any State with Treason, Felony, or other Crime, who shall flee from Justice, and be found in another State, shall on Demand of the executive Authority of the State from which he fled, be delivered up, to be removed to the State having Jurisdiction of the Crime.

[3][No Person held to Service or Labour in one State, under the Laws thereof, escaping into another, shall, in Consequence of any Law or Regulation therein,

---

[8]This clause has been affected by the Eleventh Amendment.

be discharged from such Service or Labour, but shall be delivered up on Claim of the Party to whom such Service or Labour may be due.][9]

SECTION. 3.     [1]New States may be admitted by the Congress into this Union; but no new State shall be formed or erected with in the Jurisdiction of any other State; nor any State be formed by the Junction of two or more States, or Parts of States, without the Consent of the Legislatures of the States concerned as well as of the Congress.

[2]The Congress shall have Power to dispose of and make all needful Rules and Regulations respecting the Territory or other Property belonging to the United States; and nothing in this Constitution shall be so constructed as to Prejudice any Claims of the United States, or of any particular State.

SECTION. 4.     The United States shall guarantee to every State in this Union a Republican Form of Government, and shall protect each of them against Invasion; and on Application of the Legislature, or of the Executive (when the Legislature cannot be convened) against domestic Violence.

## ARTICLE. V.

The Congress, whenever tow thirds of both Houses shall deem it necessary, shall propose Amendments to this Constitution, or, on the Application of the Legislatures of two thirds of the several States, shall call a Convention for proposing Amendments, which, in either Case, shall be valid to all Intents and Purposes, as Part of this Constitution, when ratified by the Legislatures of three fourths of the several States, or by Conventions in three fourths thereof, as the one or the other Mode of Ratification may be proposed by the Congress; Provided [that no Amendment which may be made prior to the Year One thousand eight hundred and eight shall in any Manner affect the first and fourth Clauses in the Ninth Section of the first Article; and][10] that no State, without its Consent, shall be deprived of its equal Suffrage in the Senate.

## ARTICLE. VI.

[1]All Debts contracted and Engagements entered into, before the Adoption of this Constitution, shall be as valid against the United States under this Constitution, as under the Confederation.

[2]This Constitution, and the Laws of the United States which shall be made in Pursuance thereof; and all Treaties made, or which shall be made, under the Authority of the United States, shall be the supreme Law of the Land; and the Judges in every State shall be bound thereby, any Thing in the Constitution or Laws of any State to the Contrary notwithstanding.

[3]The Senators and Representatives before mentioned, and the Members of the several State Legislatures, and all executive and judicial Officers, both of the United States and of the several States, shall be bound by Oath or Affirmation, to

---

[9]This paragraph has been superseded by the Thirteenth Amendment.
[10]Obsolete.

support this Constitution; but no religious Test shall ever be required as a Qualification to any Office or public Trust under the United States.

# ARTICLE. VII.

The Ratification of the Conventions of nine States, shall be sufficient for the Establishment of this Constitution between the States so ratifying the Same.

DONE in Convention by the Unanimous Consent of the States present the Seventeenth Day of September in the Year of our Lord one thousand seven hundred and eighty seven and of the Independence of the United States of America the Twelfth

IN WITNESS where of We have hereunto subscribed our Names.

Go. WASHINGTON—
President and deputy from Virginia.

NEW HAMPSHIRE.
    JOHN LANGDON,              NICHOLAS GILMAN.
MASSACHUSETTS.
    NATHANEIL GORHAM,     RUFUS KING.
CONNECTICUT.
    WM. SAML. JOHNSON,     ROGER SHERMAN.
NEW YORK.
    ALEXANDER HAMILTON.
NEW JERSEY.
    WILL: LIVINGSTON,       WM. PATERSON,
    DAVID BREARLEY,        JONA: DAYTON.
PENNSYLVANIA.
    B FRANKLIN,            THOMAS MIFFLIN,
    ROBT MORRIS,          GEO. CLYMER,
    THOS. FITZSIMONS,      JARED INGERSOLL,
    JAMES WILSON,         GOUV MORRIS.
DELAWARE.
    GEO: READ,             GUNNING BEDFORD, Jr,
    JOHN DICKINSON,       RICHARD BASSETT.
    JACO: BROOM,
MARYLAND.
    JAMES McHENRY,       DAN OF ST THOS. JENIFER,
    DANL CARROLL.
VIRGINIA.
    JOHN BLAIR—           JAMES MADISON Jr.
NORTH CAROLINA.
    WM. BLOUNT,          RICH'D DOBBS SPAIGHT,
    HU WILLIAMSON.
SOUTH CAROLINA.
    J. RUTLEDGE           CHARLES COTESWORTH PINCKNEY,
    CHARLES PINCKNEY,     PIERCE BUTLER.
GEORGIA.
    WILLIAM FEW,          ABR BALDWIN.
Attest: WILLIAM JACKSON, SECRETARY.

# RATIFICATION OF THE CONSTITUTION

The Constitution was adopted by a convention of the States on September 17, 1787, and was subsequently ratified by the several States, on the following dates: Delaware, December 7, 1787; Pennsylvania, December 12, 1787; Connecticut, January 9, 1788; Massachusetts, February 6, 1788; Maryland, April 28, 1788; South Carolina, May 23, 1788; new Hampshire, June 21, 1788. Ratification was completed on June 21, 1788.

The Constitution was subsequently ratified by Virginia, June 25, 1788; New York, July 26, 1788; North Carolina, November 21, 1789; Rhode Island, May 29, 1790; and Vermont, January 10, 1791.

# AMENDMENTS TO THE CONSTITUTION OF THE UNITED STATES

The ten original amendments — The Bill of Rights — proposed by Congress on September 25, 1789 and ratified December 15, 1791.

## AMENDMENT I

Congress shall make no law respecting an establishment of religion, or prohibiting the free exercise thereof; or abridging the freedom of speech, or of the press; or the right of the people peaceably to assemble, and to petition the Government for a redress of grievances.

## AMENDMENT II

A well-regulated militia, being necessary to the security of a free State, the right of the people to keep and bear arms, shall not be infringed.

## AMENDMENT III

No soldier shall, in time of peace be quartered in any house, without the consent of the owner, nor in time of war, but in a manner to be prescribed by law.

## AMENDMENT IV

The right of the people to be secure in their persons, houses, papers, and effects, against unreasonable searches and seizures, shall not be violated, and no warrants shall issue, but upon probable cause, supported by oath or affirmation, and particularly describing the place to be searched, and the persons or things to be seized.

## AMENDMENT V

No person shall be held to answer for a capital, or otherwise infamous crime, unless on a presentment or indictment of a Grand Jury, except in cases arising in the land or naval forces, or in the militia, when in actual service in time of war or public danger; nor shall any person be subject for the same offense to be twice put in jeopardy of life or limb; nor shall be compelled in any criminal case to be a witness against himself, nor be deprived of life, liberty, or property, without due process of law; nor shall private property be taken for public use without just compensation.

## AMENDMENT VI

In all criminal prosecutions, the accused shall enjoy the right to a speedy and public trial, by an impartial jury of the State and district wherein the crime shall have been committed, which district shall have been previously ascertained by law, and to be informed of the nature and cause of the accusation; to be confronted with the witnesses against him; to have compulsory process for obtaining witnesses in his favor, and to have the assistance of counsel for his defense.

## AMENDMENT VII

In suits at common law, where the value in controversy shall exceed twenty dollars, the right of trial by jury shall be preserved, and no fact tried by a jury shall be otherwise reexamined in any court of the United States, than according to the rules of the common law.

## AMENDMENT VIII

Excessive bail shall not be required, nor excessive fines imposed, nor cruel and unusual punishments inflicted.

## AMENDMENT IX

The enumeration in the Constitution, of certain rights, shall not be construed to deny or disparage others retained by the people.

## AMENDMENT X

The powers not delegated to the United States by the Constitution, nor prohibited by it to the States, are reserved to the States respectively, or to the people.

## AMENDMENT XI

The judicial power of the United States shall not be construed to extend to any suit in law or equity, commenced or prosecuted against one of the United States by citizens of another State, or by citizens or subjects of any foreign state (proposed by Congress March 4, 1794 and ratified February 7, 1795).

## AMENDMENT XII

The Electors shall meet in their respective States and vote by ballot for President and Vice-President, one of whom, at least, shall not be an inhabitant of the same State with themselves; they shall name in their ballots the person voted for as President, and in distinct ballots the person voted for as Vice-President, and of the number of votes for each, which lists they shall sign and certify, and transmit sealed to the seat of the Government of the United States, directed to the President of the Senate; the President of the Senate shall, in the presence of the Senate and House of Representatives, open all the certificates and the votes shall then be counted; The person having the greatest number of votes for President, shall be the President, if such number be a majority of the whole number of Electors appointed; and if no person have such majority, then from the persons having the highest numbers not exceeding three on the list of those voted for as President, the House of Representatives shall choose immediately, by ballot, the President. But in choosing the President, the votes shall be taken by States, the representation from each State having one vote; a quorum for this purpose shall consist of a member or members from two-thirds of the States, and a majority of all the States shall be necessary to a choice. And if the House of Representatives shall not choose a President whenever the right of choice shall devolve upon them, [before the fourth day of March next following,] Altered by 20th Amendment then the Vice-President shall act as President, as in case of the death or other constitutional disability of the President. The person having the greatest number of votes as Vice-President, shall be the Vice-President, if such numbers be a majority of the whole number of electors appointed, and if no person have a majority, then from the two highest numbers on the list, the Senate shall choose the Vice-President; a quorum for the purpose shall consist of two-thirds of the whole number of Senators, and a majority of the whole number shall be necessary to a choice. But no person constitutionally ineligible to the office of President shall be eligible to that of Vice-President of the United States (proposed by Congress December 9, 1803 and ratified July 27, 1804).

AMENDMENT XIII
Section 1. Neither slavery nor involuntary servitude, except as a punishment for crime whereof the party shall have been duly convicted, shall exist within the United States, or any place subject to their jurisdiction (proposed by Congress January 31, 1865 and ratified December 6, 1865).
Section 2. Congress shall have power to enforce this article by appropriate legislation.

AMENDMENT XIV
Section 1. All persons born or naturalized in the United States, and subject to the jurisdiction thereof, are citizens of the United States and of the State wherein they reside. No State shall make or enforce any law which shall abridge the privileges or immunities of citizens of the United States; nor shall any State deprive any person of life, liberty, or property, without due process of law; nor to deny to any person within its jurisdiction the equal protection of the laws.

Section 2. Representatives shall be apportioned among the several States according to their respective numbers, counting the whole number of persons in each State, excluding Indians not taxed. But when the right to vote at any election for the choice of Electors for President and Vice-President of the United States, Representatives in Congress, the executive and judicial officers of a State, or the members of the Legislature thereof, is denied to any of the male inhabitants of such State, being twenty-one years of age, and citizens of the United States, or in any way abridged, except for participation in rebellion, or other crime, the basis of representation therein shall be reduced in the proportion which the number of such male citizens shall bear to the whole number of male citizens twenty-one years of age in such State.

Section 3. No person shall be a Senator or Representative in Congress, or Elector of President and Vice-President, or hold any office, civil or military, under the United States, or under any State, who, having previously taken an oath, as a member of Congress, or as an officer of the United States, or as a member of any State Legislature, or as an executive or judicial officer of any State, to support the Constitution of the United States, shall have engaged in insurrection or rebellion against the same, or given aid or comfort to the enemies thereof. But Congress may by a vote of two-thirds of each House, remove such disability.

Section 4. The validity of the public debt of the United States, authorized by law, including debts incurred for payment of pensions and bounties for services in suppressing insurrection or rebellion, shall not be questioned. But neither the United States nor any State shall assume or pay any debt or obligation incurred in aid of insurrection or rebellion against the United States, or any claim for the loss or emancipation of any slave; but all such debts, obligations and claims shall be held illegal and void.

Section 5. The Congress shall have the power to enforce, by appropriate legislation, the provisions of this article (proposed by Congress June 13, 1866 and ratified July 9, 1868).

AMENDMENT XV
Section 1. The right of citizens of the United States to vote shall not be denied or abridged by the United States or by any State on account of race, color, or previous condition of servitude.

Section 2. The Congress shall have the power to enforce this article by appropriate legislation (proposed by Congress February 26, 1869 and ratified February 3, 1870.) .

AMENDMENT XVI
The Congress shall have power to lay and collect taxes on incomes, from whatever sources derived, without apportionment among the several States, and without regard to any census or enumeration (proposed by Congress July 2, 1909 and ratified February 3, 1913).

AMENDMENT XVII
The Senate of the United States shall be composed of two Senators from each State, elected by the people thereof, for six years; and each Senator shall have one vote. The electors in each State shall have the qualifications requisite for electors of the most numerous branch of the State Legislatures.

When vacancies happen in the representation of any State in the Senate, the executive authority of such State shall issue writs of election to fill such vacancies: Provided, That the Legislature of any State may empower the Executive thereof to make temporary appointments until the people fill the vacancies by election as the Legislature may direct.

This amendment shall not be so construed as to affect the election or term of any Senator chosen before it becomes valid as part of the Constitution (proposed by Congress May 13, 1912 and ratified April 8, 1913).

AMENDMENT XVIII
After one year from the ratification of this article the manufacture, sale, or transportation of intoxicating liquors within, the importation thereof into, or the exportation thereof from the United States and all territory subject to the jurisdiction thereof for beverage purposes is hereby prohibited.

The Congress and the several States shall have concurrent power to enforce this article by appropriate legislation.

This article shall be inoperative unless it shall have been ratified as an amendment to the Constitution by the Legislatures of the several States, as provided in the Constitution, within seven years from the date of the submission hereof to the States by the Congress (proposed by Congress December 18, 1917 and ratified January 16, 1919. Altered by Amendment 21).

## AMENDMENT XIX

The right of citizens of the United States to vote shall not be denied or abridged by the United States or by any State on account of sex. Congress shall have power to enforce this article by appropriate legislation (proposed by Congress June 4, 1919 and ratified August 18, 1920).

## AMENDMENT XX

Section 1. The terms of the President and the Vice-President shall end at noon on the 20th day of January, and the terms of Senators and Representatives at noon on the 3rd day of January, of the years in which such terms would have ended if this article had not been ratified; and the terms of their successors shall then begin.

Section 2. The Congress shall assemble at least once in every year, and such meeting shall begin at noon on the 3rd day of January, unless they shall by law appoint a different day.

Section 3. If, at the time fixed for the beginning of the term of the President, the President elect shall have died, the Vice-President elect shall become President. If a President shall not have been chosen before the time fixed for the beginning of his term, or if the President elect shall have failed to qualify, then the Vice-President elect shall act as President until a President shall have qualified; and the Congress may by law provide for the case wherein neither a President elect nor a Vice-President shall have qualified, declaring who shall then act as President, or the manner in which one who is to act shall be selected, and such person shall act accordingly until a President or Vice-President shall have qualified.

Section 4. The Congress may by law provide for the case of the death of any of the persons from whom the House of representatives may choose a President whenever the right of choice shall have devolved upon them, and for the case of the death of any of the persons from whom the Senate may choose a Vice-President whenever the right of choice shall have devolved upon them.

Section 5. Sections 1 and 2 shall take effect on the 15th day of October following the ratification of this article (October 1933).

Section 6. This article shall be inoperative unless it shall have been ratified as an amendment to the Constitution by the Legislatures of three-fourths of the several States within seven years from the date of its submission.

## AMENDMENT XXI

Section 1. The Eighteenth article of amendment to the Constitution of the United States is hereby repealed.

Section 2. The transportation or importation into any State, Territory, or Possession of the United States for delivery or use therein of intoxicating liquors, in violation of the laws thereof, is hereby prohibited.

Section 3. This article shall be inoperative unless it shall have been ratified as an amendment to the Constitution by conventions in the several States, as provided in the Constitution, within seven years from the date of the submission hereof to the States by the Congress (proposed by Congress February 20, 1933 and ratified December 5, 1933).

## AMENDMENT XXII

No person shall be elected to the office of the President more than twice, and no person who has held the office of President, or acted as President, for more that two years of a term to which some other person was elected President shall be elected to the office of President more that once.

But this Article shall not apply to any person holding the office of President when this Article was proposed by Congress, and shall not prevent any person who may be holding the office of President, or acting as President, during the term the term within which this Article becomes operative from holding the office of President or acting as President during the remainder of such term.

This article shall be inoperative unless it shall have been ratified as an amendment to the Constitution by the Legislatures of three-fourths of the several States within seven years from the date of its submission to the States by the Congress (proposed by Congress March 21, 1947 and ratified February 27, 1951).

## AMENDMENT XXIII

Section 1. The District constituting the seat of Government of the United States shall appoint in such manner as Congress may direct:

A number of electors of President and Vice President equal to the whole number of Senators and Representatives in Congress to which the District would be entitled if it were a State, but in no event more than the least populous State; they shall be in addition to those appointed by the States, but they shall be considered, for the purposes of the election of President and Vice President, to be electors appointed by a State; and they shall meet in the District and preform such duties as provided by the twelfth article of amendment.

Section 2. The Congress shall have power to enforce this article by appropriate legislation (proposed by Congress June 16, 1960 and ratified March 29, 1961).

## AMENDMENT XXIV

Section 1. The right of citizens of the United States to vote in any primary or other election for President or Vice President, for electors for President or Vice President, or for Senator or Representative in Congress, shall not be denied or abridged by the United States or any State by reason of failure to pay poll tax or any other tax.

Section 2. Congress shall have power to enforce this article by appropriate legislation (proposed by Congress August 27, 1962 and ratified January 23, 1964).

AMENDMENT XXV
Section 1. In case of the removal of the President from office or of his death or resignation, the Vice President shall become President.

Section 2. Whenever there is a vacancy in the office of the Vice President, the President shall nominate a Vice President who shall take the office upon confirmation by a majority vote of both houses of Congress.

Section 3. Whenever the President transmits to the President Pro tempore of the Senate and the Speaker of the House of Representatives his written declaration that he is unable to discharge the powers and duties of his office, and until he transmits to them a written declaration to the contrary, such powers and duties shall be discharged by the Vice President as Acting President.

Section 4. Whenever the Vice President and a majority of either the principal officers of the executive departments or of such other body as Congress may by law provide, transmits to the President Pro tempore of the Senate and the Speaker of the House of Representatives their written declaration that the President is unable to discharge the powers and duties of his office, the Vice President shall immediately assume the powers and duties of the office as Acting President.

Thereafter, when the President transmits to the President Pro tempore of the Senate and the Speaker of the House of Representatives his written declaration that no inability exists, he shall resume the powers and duties of his office unless the Vice President and a majority of either the principal officers of the executive departments or of such other body as Congress may by law provide, transmits within four days to the President Pro tempore of the Senate and the Speaker of the House of Representatives their written declaration that the President is unable to discharge the powers and duties of his office. Thereupon Congress shall decide the issue, assembling within forty-eight hours for that purpose if not in session. If the Congress, within twenty-one days after receipt of the latter written declaration, or, if Congress is not in session within twenty-one days after Congress is required to assemble, determines by two-thirds vote of both houses that the President is unable to discharge the powers and duties of his office, the Vice President shall continue to discharge the same as Acting President; otherwise, the President shall resume the powers and duties of his office (proposed by Congress July 6, 1965and ratified February 10, 1967).


AMENDMENT XXVI
Section 1. The right of citizens of the United States, who are 18 years of age or older, to vote shall not be denied or abridged by the United States or any state on account of age.

Section 2. The Congress shall have power to enforce this article by appropriate legislation (proposed by Congress March 23, 1971 and ratified June 30, 1971).


AMENDMENT XXVII
No law, varying the compensation for the services of the Senators and Representatives, shall take effect, until an election of Representatives shall have intervened (proposed by Congress September 25, 1789 and ratified May 8, 1992).

# Timelines

**II**

## ■ Major American Riots, Disorders, and Social Tensions, 1692–2004

Law enforcement and social control is influenced by the social, political, and economic, and cultural events of the day. Throughout American history, there have been a number of events and periods of social unrest that, in the final analysis, generally brought about changes in policing or in public policy.

| | |
|---|---|
| 1692 | Salem witchcraft episodes |
| 1765 | Stamp Act riots in Boston and New York (taxes on legal documents, newspapers, almanacs, playing cards and dice) |
| 1767 | The Regulators—South Carolina's "vigilante group" |
| 1772 | Burning of the *Gaspee*, a British ship, off the coast of Rhode Island by colonists |
| 1774 | Resistance to the Boston Port Bill, which required the Port to close until Boston paid restitution for the lost tea thrown overboard by colonists |
| 1776–1783 | American Revolutionary War |
| 1784 | Revolt against North Carolina—sections of the State claimed secession from to form a separate state and to look to Spain for possible affiliation |
| 1786 | Shay's Rebellion—over 2,000 western Massachusetts farmers, in armed rebellion over heavy taxation, high legal and court fees, and state government waste |
| 1794 | Whiskey Rebellion in Pennsylvania, over the federal tax on whiskey. |
| 1795 | Demonstrations against the Jay Treaty with England |

| | |
|---|---|
| 1798 | Virginia and Kentucky Resolutions declared the certain Federal Government actions could be declared "unconstitutional" by state legislation—particularly directed toward the Alien and Sedition Acts (which were anti-immigrant in nature) |
| 1799 | Fries Rebellion (John Fries led mob to free two tax-evaders from prison) |
| 1819 | Panic of 1819 followed by economic depression |
| 1829–1850 | Five major race riots in Philadelphia. |
| 1832 | Tariff Nullification by South Carolina brought a national crisis in federal/state relationships and authority |
| 1830s–1840s | Indian/Army skirmishes and small "wars" |
| 1834 | Boston convent burned (anti-Catholic sentiment) |
| 1837 | Irish immigrants clash with fire department—15,000 people involved |
| 1842 | Dorr Rebellion (over extension of suffrage to all males instead of property owners) |
| 1844 | Anti-Catholic riots in Philadelphia |
| 1849 | Astor Place riot in NYC; 31 killed, 150 wounded, 86 arrested |
| 1851 | San Francisco Committee of Vigilance (vigilantism forces) |
| 1850s | American Indians were "concentrated" to certain geographical areas (reservations). The struggle and debate continues for decades. |
| 1854 | Struggle and dissent over slavery in Kansas' application for statehood |
| 1855 | German tavern-keeper's revolt in Chicago, many killed, hundreds injured |
| 1859 | John Brown's raid at Harper's Ferry, Virginia |
| 1856 | The Dred Scott decision by the Supreme Court—ruled that Blacks could not be entitled to federal citizenship and Congress did not have authority to regulate slavery in the territories, nor did the territorial legislatures |
| 1861–1865 | Civil War in the United States |
| 1863 | Conscription (Draft) Riots in Boston and NYC—many killed, hundreds injured |
| 1865–1877 | KKK activity; founded in Pulaski, Tennessee |
| 1871 | Anti-Chinese riot in Los Angeles; 23 Chinese killed |
| 1871 | Orange Riots in NYC; 33 killed, 91 wounded |
| 1878s–1900s | Jim Crow laws (segregation of the races) |
| 1877 | Great labor strikes in West Virginia and Pittsburgh, PA; in two days, 16 soldiers and 50 strikers killed; 125 locomotives, 2,000 freight cars, and depot burned and destroyed; many killed and wounded in Chicago. |
| 1886 | Haymarket Riots in Chicago—labor disputes fueled tensions, a bomb killed a police officer and six others |

| | |
|---|---|
| 1913 | Ludlow Massacre, more than 30 killed |
| 1915 | The Ku Klux Klan officially organizes in Georgia (modeled after its predecessor) by William Joseph Simmons; lasted till WW II |
| 1917–1919 | World War I |
| 1919 | Chicago race riot; 38 killed, 537 injured |
| 1921 | Tulsa race riot; 30 killed, 700 injured |
| 1934 | Republic Steel plan in Chicago, union violence; police shot and killed 10 pickets; also called Memorial Day Massacre |
| 1930s | Nation of Islam (Black Nationalist) movement begins |
| 1941–1945 | World War II |
| 1943 | Detroit race riot; 34 killed, several hundred injured |
| 1943 | Zoot-Suit Riots in Los Angeles (anti-Mexican-American) |
| 1950s–1960s | Battle over desegregation leads to school integration and social tension |
| Early 1950s | The third Klan movement was revived by Dr. Samuel Green, an Atlanta dentist |
| 1954 | *Brown v. Board of Education of Topeka* (*Plessy v. Ferguson* reversed) segregation ruled illegal |
| 1955 | Montgomery, Alabama; boycott over segregated bus system; precipitated by Rosa Parks refusal to give up her bus seat to a white person |
| 1955 | Executive Order 10450 (Nov. 1) required the Attorney General of the United States to prepare a list of subversive or fascist groups in America |
| 1955–1956 | Segregationist groups called White Citizens' Councils spread throughout the South |
| 1956 | Clinton, Texas; racial violence |
| 1957 | Little Rock, Arkansas—Eisenhower orders in Federal troops |
| 1958 | John Birch Society formed in Indianapolis by Robert H.W. Welch, Jr. |
| 1960 | Racial violence in New Orleans |
| 1962 | President John F. Kennedy sends troops to University of Mississippi, Oxford, MS to protect James Meredith |
| 1963 | Birmingham, Alabama; racial confrontation with police—President Kennedy denounces Governor George Wallace's stand on segregation |
| | Medgar Evers assassinated |
| | Dr. Martin Luther King, Jr.'s march on Washington and "I Have a Dream" speech |
| | November 21, JFK assassinated in Dallas |
| 1964 | Race riots in NYC, Rochester, Philadelphia, Jersey City, Paterson, Elizabeth, and Chicago; 6 killed, 952 injured |

Civil Rights Act of 1964 passed; Title VII outlaws discrimination in employment on the basis of race, color, religion, national origin, or sex.

October 1; The Free Speech Movement was born at Berkeley California (Mario Savio and Joan Baez); the movement lasted about a year but received broad national attention and led to more "student movements"

1965     Los Angeles (Watts) race riot; 36 killed, 895 injured; violence spread to San Francisco where 200 were injured and 6 killed

In February, Malcolm X was assassinated by three gunmen as he began a speech in a Harlem ballroom; he was a major leader in the Nation of Islam movement

Students for a Democratic Society (SDS) experienced phenomenal growth; basically as an anti-Vietnam movement; Tom Hayden a leader of the movement

1967     George Lincoln Rockwell, Commander of the American Nazi Party, was killed from ambush in front of a laundromat in Arlington, Virginia

The Youth International Party (YIPPIE) is formed; Abbie Hoffman, Jerry Rubin, and Paul Krassner were primary leaders

150 U.S. cities experience racial disturbances

1968     Assassination of Martin Luther King, Jr.; over 168 cities in the United States experience demonstrations, riots, burnings, or protests

Assassination of Robert F. Kennedy; June 4

Black Panther Huey Newton convicted of voluntary manslaughter in killing an Oakland police officer

August 18–29; National Democratic Convention in Chicago becomes a "Police Riot"; over 24 "protest" organizations were represented in the crowded streets and demonstrations outside the convention; 192 officers injured, 49 hospitalized; 425 civilians treated at hospitals, 200 treated on the spot, and over 400 given first aid for tear gas or mace; 81 police vehicles damaged; 668 persons arrested; much of the confrontation was televised nationwide; 49 newsmen reported being hit, assaulted, or having cameras/recorders damaged by officers

Mid 1960s     Vietnam War protest movement gains momentum—Flower Power—SDS

1970     May 4; Four killed in Ohio; Kent State University; ROTC buildings burned.

Jackson State University violence, Jackson Mississippi

1971     Anti-war march in Washington, DC, 12,000 arrested

Voting age lowered to 18 (26th Amendment)

| | |
|---|---|
| 1972 | Presidential candidate, George Wallace shot in Laurel, MD |
| | Watergate |
| 1973 | US involvement in Vietnam ends |
| 1974 | Symbionese Liberation Army kidnapped Patricia Hearst |
| | President Ford escapes two assassination attempts |
| 1979 | Iranian militants seize US Embassy and take hostages |
| 1980 | Racial disturbances in Miami |
| 1981 | President Reagan shot by John W. Hinckley, Jr. |
| 1985 | Police storm/firebomb home of MOVE, fire spreads killing 11 and leaving 200 homeless. |
| 1991 | Rodney King incident in Los Angeles, California led to indictment of four officers |
| 1992 | On April 29, the officers charged in the King incident were found not guilty of all but one charge against one officer. Riots erupted and lasted for five days resulting in more than 40 deaths, 2,382 injuries, over 5000 buildings destroyed or damaged, an estimated 40,000 jobs lost and over $1 billion in property damage; 5633 people arrested. The riots spread to other cities across the country. |
| 1993 | Two of the four officers indicted in the King incident were convicted in federal court on civil rights charges and sentenced to 30 month in prison. |
| | February 26; bombing of the World Trade Center in New York City, six killed and over 1,000 injured |
| | April 19; following a 51-day standoff at Waco, Texas, compound of the Branch Davidians, headed by David Koresh burns to the ground after an assault by federal agents; 80 believed to have died in the incident, including women and children |
| 1994 | Nicole Simpson and Ronald Goldman murdered; O.J. Simpson accused but later found not criminally guilty |
| 1995 | Bombing (April 19) of the Murrah Federal Building in Oklahoma City, Oklahoma, 169 killed and over 800 injured |
| 1996 | National crime rate continues to drop, but juvenile violence increasing |
| | Bomb explodes at summer Olympics in Atlanta, Georgia killing one |
| | Theodore Kaczynski, the alleged Unabomber is arrested after 18 years of incidents |
| 1997 | Communications Decency Act ruled unconstitutional as an attempt to regulate the Internet |
| | Timothy McVeigh found guilty of the Oklahoma City Federal Building bombing |
| | Ramzi Ahmed Yousef and Eyad Ismoil were convicted of the NYC Trade Center Tower bombing |

O.J. Simpson found civilly responsible for the deaths of Nicole Simpson and Ronald Goldman

**1998**

A series of school violence incidents in several states where students and teachers were killed raises concerns about access to firearms by juveniles. Locations included Edinboro, Pennsylvania, Jonesboro, Arkansas, Springfield, Oregon; ages of the shooters range from 10–17.

Theodore Kaczynski, the Unabomber, is sentenced to life in prison.

Near Jasper, Texas, African American man was beaten, chained to a pickup truck, and dragged to his death by three white men with ties to hate groups.

Hate crimes statistics of the FBI reach 7,755 reported incidents involved a total of 9,235 offenses, 9,722 victims, and 7,489 known offenders.

**1999**

April 20; Columbine High School in Littleton, Colorado is site where two students open fire and explode bombs in the worst-ever school massacre in the U.S.; 12 students and one teacher are killed, 23 wounded before the two assailants commit suicide.

A student opens fire at Heritage High School, near Conyers, Georgia; six schoolmates were injured.

In July, a man in Atlanta kills his family and then fires at two office buildings, killing nine people and wounding 13 before killing himself.

Police shooting death of unarmed Amadou Diallo in New York heightens tensions between the community and the police.

A man blasts away with a gun at a church in Fort Worth, Texas, killing seven and wounding seven others; many of the victims are teenagers at the church for a special prayer rally.

A 12-year-old student shoots and kills a 13-year-old student in the lobby of Deming Middle School in Deming, New Mexico.

From November 30 through December 3, anti-globalization protesters attempt to disrupt the World Trade Organization meetings in Seattle, Washington. More than 600 protestors are arrested and dozens are injured as police use night sticks, pepper spray, tear gas, and rubber bullets.

A 13-year-old student wounds four other students Fort Gibson Middle School in Fort Gibson, Oklahoma.

Forty-year-old kills seven at Honolulu corporate office.

Forty-four-year-old kills his wife and two children, then nine persons in two brokerage offices; 12 injured at Atlanta, Georgia.

**2000**

A 19-year-old kills two students while leaving a dance sponsored by Beach High School, Savannah, Georgia.

Software tester kills seven coworkers after the government began garnishing his wages, Wakefield, MA.

Thirty-one year old man shoots four and wounds three the same day he was released from jail for assault and threatening to kill girlfriend, Baltimore, Maryland.

A man shot his estranged wife at work, a union hall where she was a secretary, in Chesterfield, Indiana and then kills himself.

Arsonist Jay Scott Ballenger was sentenced to 42 years in prison for an eight-state rampage of church burnings, primarily in the Midwest region.

An Indianapolis man shoots and kills his eight-year-old daughter and four-year-old son and kills himself.

**2001**    Fifteen-year-old student kills two students and wounds 13 others including security supervisor at Santana High School in Santee, California.

A police officer shoots an unarmed black male, 19 years old on April 7. The officer attempted to apprehend the subject who had 14 outstanding warrants for minor offenses. The incident set off many days of rioting, looting, and burning in the city of Cincinnati, Ohio. Heightened tensions continued for several months.

Hijackers crash two commercial jets into the twin towers of World Trade Center in New York City; another jet is crashed into the Pentagon and a fourth jet crashes in a field in rural Pennsylvania near Shanksville. Total dead and missing numbered 2,992: 2,749 in New York City, 184 at the Pentagon, 40 in PA, and 19 hijackers. Islamic al-Qaeda terrorist group is blamed.

Aftermath of the 9/11 attacks puts all of America and other countries on alert for more possible attacks. Homeland security becomes a national priority.

Disgruntled employee kills one, injures 6 coworkers and then commits suicide near Goshen, Indiana.

**2002**    Worker at plant in Southbend, Indiana kills four, wounds two police officers on a high-speed pursuit to Michigan, then kills himself.

Retired Sheriff kills daughter and three stepchildren, and then commits suicide.

Biker feud results in three killed and 15 injured during a cycle rally, Laughlin, Nevada.

Ohio State University students and fans riot following the OSU-Michigan football game; ten Ohio State students suspended on Monday, November 23.

**2003**    Post-Super Bowl Riots in Oakland.

A 15-year-old kills two students at Rocori High School in Cold Spring, Minnesota.

Columbus, Ohio area freeway sniper begins three-month shooting spree in November; one motorist dies.

Racial tensions and anti-police sentiment result in two days of rioting in Benton Harbor, Michigan following a high speed chase that ended with the fatal crash of the black cyclist being pursued. About 21 homes were torched, shots fired at police, vehicles set afire, and bystanders attacked. The incident heightened the problems of the community: high unemployment, poverty, and alleged segregation.

Gunman kills five and wounds nine, then commits suicide at Lockheed Martin Plant, Marion, Michigan.

Employee at manufacturing plant kills three and wounds five coworkers, Jefferson City, Missouri.

2004    In March, suspect kills nine family members in a residence in Fresno, California.

Disgruntled employee kills five in food plant, Kansas City, Kansas.

On December 8, a gunman, age 25, runs onstage at a Columbus, Ohio nightclub killing top heavy metal guitarist "Dimebag" Darrell Abbott and three other people before a police officer shots and kills the assailant; two others members of the band Damageplan are wounded and hospitalized.

## SELECTED PASSAGES DESCRIBING AMERICA'S RACE/ ETHNIC TOLERANCE

"Between 1790 and 1900, vigilantism prospered in the settlements of the American Frontier. The instability of settlements made social control almost impossible. Counterfeiting for example, became prevalent on the frontier because law enforcement agencies were almost totally nonexistent. . . Citizens saw vigilantism as a means of coping with social problems. They began to take the law into their own hands."

"The local law enforcement officer thus found that his methods of enforcing the law often conflicted with the mood of the community and the activities of the vigilantes. . . Vigilantism, however, was not just a phenomenon of the frontier or rural settlements. Law enforcement officers and the courts in larger cities were also criticized for their ineffectiveness by citizens' groups, newspaper editors, and popular opinion. . . When municipal law enforcement was ineffective, vigilante activities became commonplace."

"Rapid industrialization following the Civil War created new problems, especially for urban communities. Many conflicts existed between different socio-economic classes, as well as between races. Labor unions were still very weak and struggling to survive, and often violence erupted between labor and management." (Trojanowicz, Trojanowicz, and Moss, pp. 76–78.)

"Law and order means different things and yet the same thing—to an as yet undetermined number of the Black masses. It means historically the use of sadistic red-necked cops in the south to keep Blacks in their place, to keep them segregated, discriminated against, exploited, and brutalized. To Blacks it means police brutality, provocation and the epitome of all that is repressive in the history and operation of American Black-White relations."

"Mexican-Americans were perceived as vicious—they fought with lethal weapons such as knives, whereas other 'more acceptable ethnic groups' used their fists. This stereotyped perception of Mexican-Americans as lazy, dirty, and an undesirable contributed to a feeling of relief of any moral obligation by the community toward the Mexican-Americans who were exploited."

"The Broad Street riot of June 11, 1837 erupted when firemen returning from an alarm clashed with an Irish funeral procession [requiring a cavalry regiment to restore order]. Irish immigrants created problems for the police, especially in large cities. The Irish lived in poverty and misery and were involved in many types of criminal activities."

"'The Chickesters,' 'Roach Guards,' 'Plug Uglies,' 'Short Tails,' and 'Dead Rabbits,' were the names of some of the more notorious gangs [late 1920s]. Many battles raged between the gangs, and long-standing feuds culminated with killing and maiming, or both. The police were called into disperse gang activity but in larger disturbances, they almost always needed the assistance of the army."

"Time and again, lynching parties struck at Italians charged with murder. In 1891 a wild rumor that drunken Italian laborers had cut the throats of a whole American family in West Virginia set off further rumors of a pitched battle between the sheriff's posse and the assassins . . . The Italian immigrants not only had to bear the brunt of much hostility that was naturally directed at immigrants, they also had to 'live down' the stereotype of the Italian criminal that resulted from the problems police had with some immigrants from Sicily."

"Slavic and Polish immigrants were as exploited as any other ethnic group that ever set foot on this continent. Among other indignities, they were given the worst jobs, imprisoned for minor offenses, and forced to live like animals. Disturbances by Hungarian and Polish workers in the late 1800s were common."

"The Germans at one time were also recipients of much community hostility. In 1855, the arrest of saloon keepers touched off riots by Germans necessitating police intervention. . . Many Germans were injured in these confrontations, and increased hostility developed between the police and German immigrants because the police were perceived as agents of repression."

"Numerous complaints have been made in regard to the Hebrew immigrants who lounge about Battery Park, obstructing the walks and sitting on the chains . . . The police have had many battles with these newcomers, who are determined to have their own way. Jewish women were involved in disturbances in 1906 because of rumors that physicians were cutting the throats of children in the east-side schools."

"Orientals, especially the Japanese during the second world war, were also recipients of community hostility and the police force. The expression 'Yellow Peril' reflected the paranoiac feeling of many persons toward Asians." (Trojanowicz and Dixon, pp. 84–94)

*Source:* Alex, Nicholas (1969). *Black in Blue: A Study of Negro Policemen.* New York: Appleton-Century Crofts; Trojanowicz, Robert C., and Samuel Dixon (1974). *Criminal justice and the community.* Englewood Cliffs, NJ: Prentice Hall; Trojanowicz, Robert C., John M. Trojanowicz, and Forrest M. Moss (1975). *Community based crime prevention.* Englewood Cliffs, NJ: Prentice Hall.

## ■ TIMELINE OF CRIMINAL IDENTIFICATION IN THE UNITED STATES, 1854–1939

| | |
|---|---|
| 1854–1859 | Captain Lees of the San Francisco P.D. used a commercial photographer to make daguerreotypes (an early form of photograph using thin brass plate) of all arrested persons. |
| 1858 | New York City P.D. had collected over 450 photographs in its rogues' gallery. |
| 1884 | Chicago P.D. established its own police photograph gallery at police headquarters, believed to be the first city in the world to do so. |
| 1888 | Chicago P.D. became the first American city to adopt the Bertillon system of identification (which was developed by Alphonse Bertillon of the Paris Police in 1882—his "portrait parle" system was one that included a person's bodily measurements along with details about complexion, color of hair and eyes, shape of nose, ear and face, special marks and peculiarities, and photographs). |
| 1894 | The National Chiefs of Police Union (forerunner of the International Association of Chiefs of Police) petitioned Congress to establish a bureau of identification of criminals at the national level. |
| 1896 | The National Chiefs of Police Union created the National Bureau of Criminal Identification (on paper); it eventually opened in Chicago in 1897, staffed by George Porteous, an expert in the Bertillon system, as its superintendent. A single office could now receive and respond to police requests for "Identification Wanted." |
| 1902 | The National Bureau of Criminal Identification was relocated to the Washington, D.C. Police Department with Edward Evans as Superintendent. |
| 1904 | The World's Fair, held in St. Louis, MO, brought exhibitors from all over the world displaying and advocating criminal identification equipment and systems. Fingerprinting as a means of identification received great attention. The St. Louis P.D. begins using the Henry Finger Print System. |
| | Mrs. Mary E. Holland, assistant editor of *The Detective*, was trained in the Henry System and became competent to install and instruct the system as an expert. |
| | The US Army and Navy and federal prisons adopt the fingerprint system over the Bertillon system. |
| 1906 | The New York City P.D. inaugurates the use of the Henry Finger Print System. |
| 1921 | By this date, five state identification bureaus were in operation: California, Washington, Ohio, Wisconsin, and Iowa. |

| 1923 | Attorney General Harry M. Daugherty issued orders to transfer the IACP's National Bureau of Criminal Identification to the Justice Department's Division of Identification which became statutorily official on July 1, 1924. State Bureaus numbered 23. |
| 1935 | Eye Retina Pattern identification scheme developed and offered as an adjunct to the fingerprint system. |
| 1936 | The American Dental Association in conjunction with the US Department of Justice begins developing a system of identification for recording dental peculiarities and records. |
| 1939 | Colonel H. Norman Schwarzkopf of the New Jersey State Police demonstrated the uses of motion pictures in making a permanent record of criminals. |
| 1939 | First color photographs used in wanted circular, used by the Indiana State Police. |

*Source*: Donald C. Dilworth (ed.) (1977). *Identification Wanted: Development of the American Criminal Identification System, 1893–1943*. Gaithersburg, MD: International Association of Chiefs of Police.

# Selected Organizational Charts

The organizational arrangement within law enforcement agencies varies considerably. This appendix contains the organizational charts of selected agencies representing the federal, state, and local levels of government. They are presented to depict the similarities and differences among agencies. Many other charts can be found on agency Web sites, either as a standalone document or as part of an annual report. We encourage you to analyze these and other charts for examples of the various line and staff functions within law enforcement agencies.

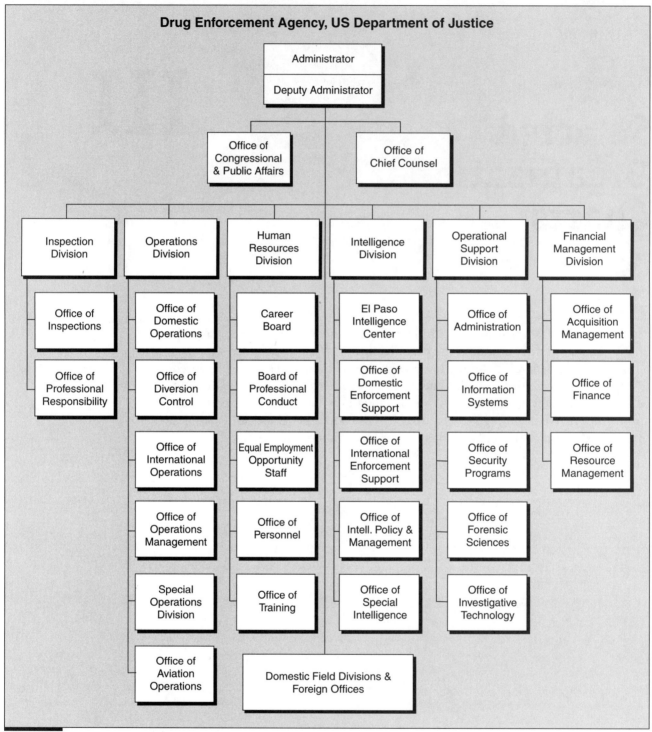

**Drug Enforcement Agency, US Department of Justice**

Administrator

Deputy Administrator

Office of Congressional & Public Affairs

Office of Chief Counsel

**Inspection Division**
- Office of Inspections
- Office of Professional Responsibility

**Operations Division**
- Office of Domestic Operations
- Office of Diversion Control
- Office of International Operations
- Office of Operations Management
- Special Operations Division
- Office of Aviation Operations

**Human Resources Division**
- Career Board
- Board of Professional Conduct
- Equal Employment Opportunity Staff
- Office of Personnel
- Office of Training

**Intelligence Division**
- El Paso Intelligence Center
- Office of Domestic Enforcement Support
- Office of International Enforcement Support
- Office of Intell. Policy & Management
- Office of Special Intelligence

**Operational Support Division**
- Office of Administration
- Office of Information Systems
- Office of Security Programs
- Office of Forensic Sciences
- Office of Investigative Technology

**Financial Management Division**
- Office of Acquisition Management
- Office of Finance
- Office of Resource Management

Domestic Field Divisions & Foreign Offices

*Source:* http://www.usdoj.gov/dea/agency/organizational.htm.

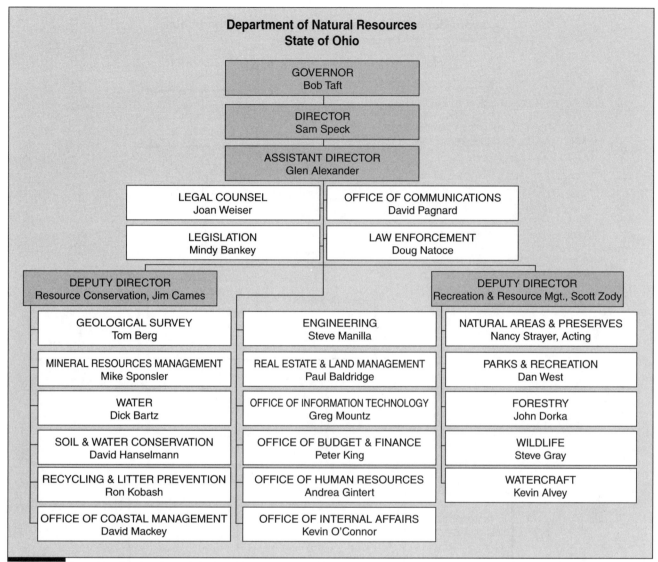

**Department of Natural Resources**
**State of Ohio**

GOVERNOR
Bob Taft

DIRECTOR
Sam Speck

ASSISTANT DIRECTOR
Glen Alexander

LEGAL COUNSEL
Joan Weiser

OFFICE OF COMMUNICATIONS
David Pagnard

LEGISLATION
Mindy Bankey

LAW ENFORCEMENT
Doug Natoce

DEPUTY DIRECTOR
Resource Conservation, Jim Cames

DEPUTY DIRECTOR
Recreation & Resource Mgt., Scott Zody

GEOLOGICAL SURVEY
Tom Berg

ENGINEERING
Steve Manilla

NATURAL AREAS & PRESERVES
Nancy Strayer, Acting

MINERAL RESOURCES MANAGEMENT
Mike Sponsler

REAL ESTATE & LAND MANAGEMENT
Paul Baldridge

PARKS & RECREATION
Dan West

WATER
Dick Bartz

OFFICE OF INFORMATION TECHNOLOGY
Greg Mountz

FORESTRY
John Dorka

SOIL & WATER CONSERVATION
David Hanselmann

OFFICE OF BUDGET & FINANCE
Peter King

WILDLIFE
Steve Gray

RECYCLING & LITTER PREVENTION
Ron Kobash

OFFICE OF HUMAN RESOURCES
Andrea Gintert

WATERCRAFT
Kevin Alvey

OFFICE OF COASTAL MANAGEMENT
David Mackey

OFFICE OF INTERNAL AFFAIRS
Kevin O'Connor

*Source:* http://www.dnr.state.oh.us/communications/torg.htm. (2004).

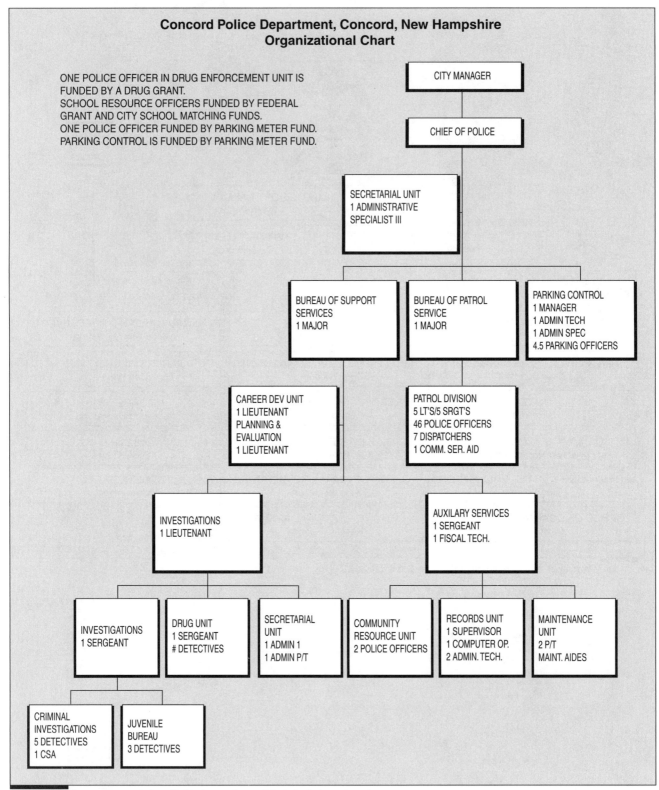

**Concord Police Department, Concord, New Hampshire**
**Organizational Chart**

ONE POLICE OFFICER IN DRUG ENFORCEMENT UNIT IS
FUNDED BY A DRUG GRANT.
SCHOOL RESOURCE OFFICERS FUNDED BY FEDERAL
GRANT AND CITY SCHOOL MATCHING FUNDS.
ONE POLICE OFFICER FUNDED BY PARKING METER FUND.
PARKING CONTROL IS FUNDED BY PARKING METER FUND.

CITY MANAGER

CHIEF OF POLICE

SECRETARIAL UNIT
1 ADMINISTRATIVE
SPECIALIST III

BUREAU OF SUPPORT
SERVICES
1 MAJOR

BUREAU OF PATROL
SERVICE
1 MAJOR

PARKING CONTROL
1 MANAGER
1 ADMIN TECH
1 ADMIN SPEC
4.5 PARKING OFFICERS

CAREER DEV UNIT
1 LIEUTENANT
PLANNING &
EVALUATION
1 LIEUTENANT

PATROL DIVISION
5 LT'S/5 SRGT'S
46 POLICE OFFICERS
7 DISPATCHERS
1 COMM. SER. AID

INVESTIGATIONS
1 LIEUTENANT

AUXILARY SERVICES
1 SERGEANT
1 FISCAL TECH.

INVESTIGATIONS
1 SERGEANT

DRUG UNIT
1 SERGEANT
# DETECTIVES

SECRETARIAL
UNIT
1 ADMIN 1
1 ADMIN P/T

COMMUNITY
RESOURCE UNIT
2 POLICE OFFICERS

RECORDS UNIT
1 SUPERVISOR
1 COMPUTER OP.
2 ADMIN. TECH.

MAINTENANCE
UNIT
2 P/T
MAINT. AIDES

CRIMINAL
INVESTIGATIONS
5 DETECTIVES
1 CSA

JUVENILE
BUREAU
3 DETECTIVES

Source: http://www.ci.concord.nh.us/Police/concordv2.asp?siteindx=P20,11. (2004).

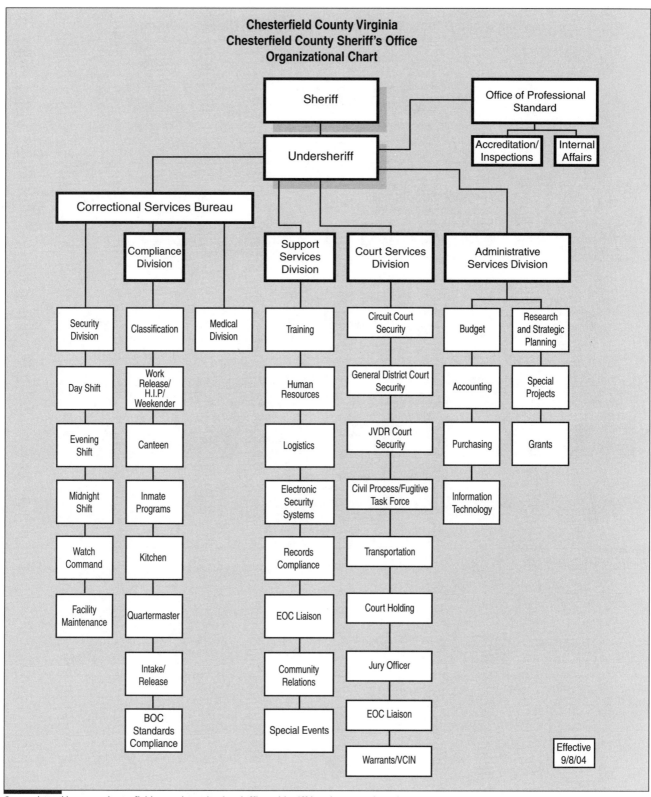

**Chesterfield County Virginia
Chesterfield County Sheriff's Office
Organizational Chart**

*Source:* http://www.co.chesterfield.va.us/constitutionalofficers/sheriff/orgchart.asp. (2004).

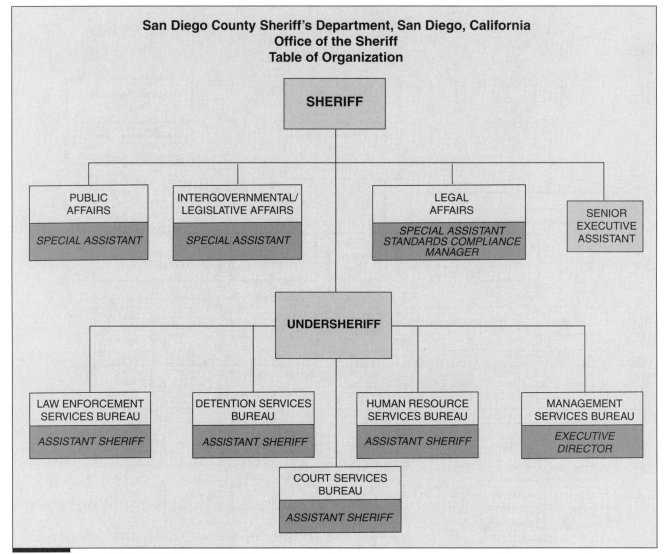

**San Diego County Sheriff's Department, San Diego, California**
**Office of the Sheriff**
**Table of Organization**

SHERIFF

PUBLIC AFFAIRS
*SPECIAL ASSISTANT*

INTERGOVERNMENTAL/ LEGISLATIVE AFFAIRS
*SPECIAL ASSISTANT*

LEGAL AFFAIRS
*SPECIAL ASSISTANT STANDARDS COMPLIANCE MANAGER*

SENIOR EXECUTIVE ASSISTANT

UNDERSHERIFF

LAW ENFORCEMENT SERVICES BUREAU
*ASSISTANT SHERIFF*

DETENTION SERVICES BUREAU
*ASSISTANT SHERIFF*

HUMAN RESOURCE SERVICES BUREAU
*ASSISTANT SHERIFF*

MANAGEMENT SERVICES BUREAU
*EXECUTIVE DIRECTOR*

COURT SERVICES BUREAU
*ASSISTANT SHERIFF*

*Source:* http://www.sdsheriff.net/org/org1.html. (2004).

## Palo Alto Police Department, Palo Alto, California

**POLICE CHIEF**
Lynne Johnson

**Police Personnel Services**
1.0-Police Lieutenant
1.0-Police Agent/Officer
1.0-Staff Secretary
1.0-Program Asst
0.5-Volunteer Coordinator

1.0-Administrative Services Manager
1.0-Administrative Assistant

**Technical Services**
1.0-Coordinator, Technical Serv
1.0-Business Analyst
1.0-Staff Secretary
1.0-Police Records Specialist
1.0-Crime Analyst
**Dispatching Services**
1.0-Supervisor, Police Services
4.0-Publ Safety Dispatcher, Chief
16.0-Public Safety Dispatcher
1.0-Community Service Officer
**Information Management**
1.0-Supervisor, Police Services
9.0-Police Records Specialist

**Field Services**
1.0-Police Captain
1.0-Police Agent/Officer
1.0-Staff Secretary
**Field Services (Patrol)**
4.0-Police Lieutenants
10.0-Police Sergeants
49.0-Police Agent/Officers
1.0-Supervisor, Police Services
1.75-Code Enforcement Officer
2.0- Community Service Officer
**Traffic/Parking Services**
1.0-Police Lieutenant
2.0-Police Sergeant
7.0-Police Agent/Officer
1.0-Community Serv Officer
1.0-Parking Enforcement Officer-Lead
7.0-Parking Enforcement Officer
0.5-Parking Examiner

**Investigative Services**
1.0-Police Captain
1.0-Staff Secretary
1.0-Office Specialist
1.0-Court Liaison
1.0-Community Serv Officer
2.0-Police Sergeant
12.0-Police Agent/Officer
3.0-Property/Evidence Technician
**Animal Services**
1.0-Superintendent, Animal Serv
1.0-Supervisor, Animal Serv
1.0-Veterinarian
4.5-Animal Control Officer
1.0-Animal Service Specialist
1.0-Animal Service Specialist II
2.0-Veterinarian Technician
0.5-Volunteer Coordinator

Fiscal Year 2004-05 Position Totals: 167.75 Full-time
4.62 Hourly

*Source:* http://www.cityofpaloalto.org/finance/documents/Police.pdf. (2004).

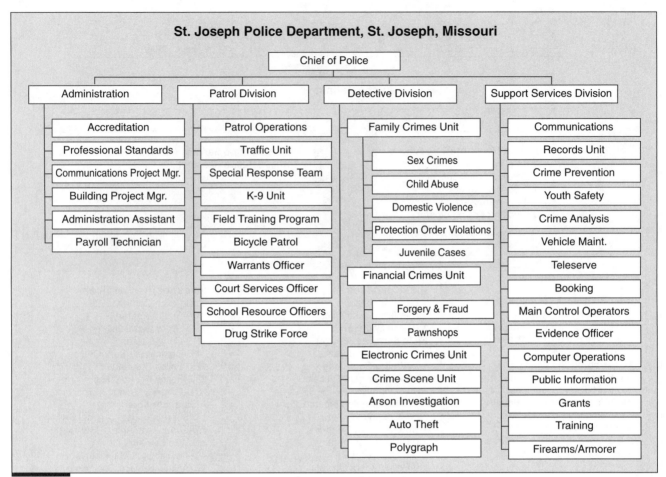

**St. Joseph Police Department, St. Joseph, Missouri**

Chief of Police

| Administration | Patrol Division | Detective Division | Support Services Division |
|---|---|---|---|
| Accreditation | Patrol Operations | Family Crimes Unit | Communications |
| Professional Standards | Traffic Unit | Sex Crimes | Records Unit |
| Communications Project Mgr. | Special Response Team | Child Abuse | Crime Prevention |
| Building Project Mgr. | K-9 Unit | Domestic Violence | Youth Safety |
| Administration Assistant | Field Training Program | Protection Order Violations | Crime Analysis |
| Payroll Technician | Bicycle Patrol | Juvenile Cases | Vehicle Maint. |
| | Warrants Officer | Financial Crimes Unit | Teleserve |
| | Court Services Officer | Forgery & Fraud | Booking |
| | School Resource Officers | Pawnshops | Main Control Operators |
| | Drug Strike Force | Electronic Crimes Unit | Evidence Officer |
| | | Crime Scene Unit | Computer Operations |
| | | Arson Investigation | Public Information |
| | | Auto Theft | Grants |
| | | Polygraph | Training |
| | | | Firearms/Armorer |

*Source:* http://www.ci.st-joseph.mo.us/police/orgcharts.asp. (2004).

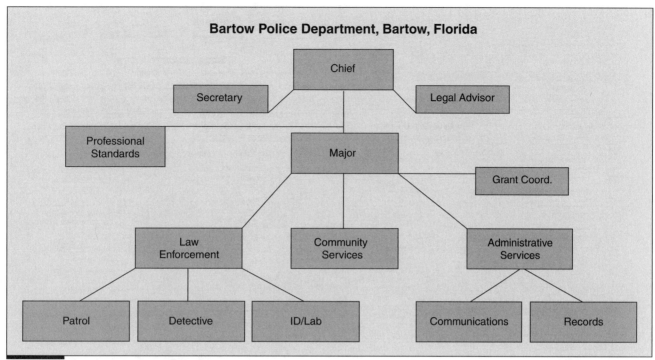

**Bartow Police Department, Bartow, Florida**

*Source:* http://bartowpd.usawebs.net/. (2004).

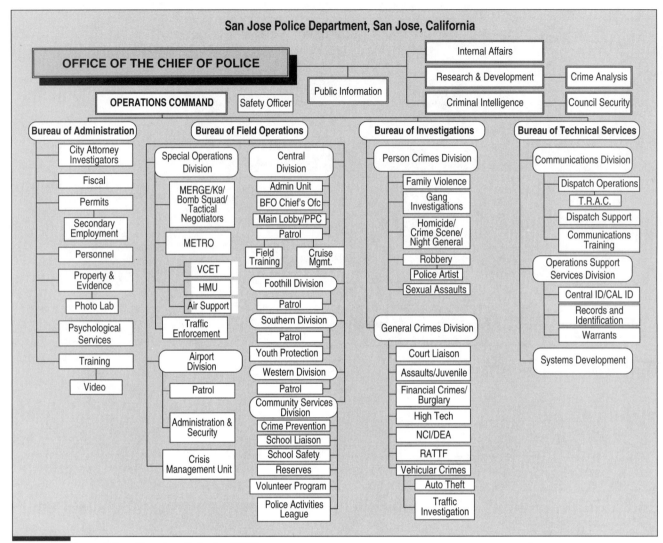

**San Jose Police Department, San Jose, California**

*Source:* http://www.sjpd.org/DepartmentInfo.cfm. (2003).

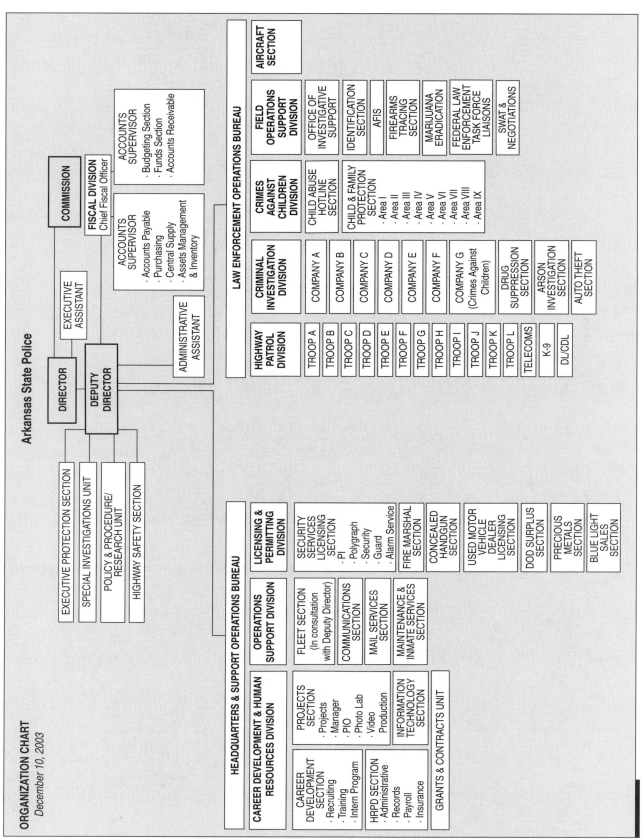

**ORGANIZATION CHART**
*December 10, 2003*

**Arkansas State Police**

# Minimum Hours of Basic Training for the States of New York, California, and Ohio

## NEW YORK STATE

**Basic Course for Police Officers Program Content**
**Part I Administrative Procedures**

A. Opening Ceremonies
   1. Registration
   2. Orientation and Introductions
   3. Distribution of Materials
B. Instruction in Study Habits, Note-Taking, Notebook Requirements
C. Quizzes and Examinations
D. Culmination and other Ceremonies

|  |  |  |
|---|---|---|
| **Total** | **(Set locally by academy)** | **Local** |

**Part II Administration of Justice**
   1. Introduction to Criminal Justice
   2. Jurisdiction and Responsibilities of Law Enforcement
   3. Adjudicatory Process and Court Structure - Criminal/Civil

|  |  |
|---|---|
| **Total for Part II** | 4 |

**Part III Basic Law**

| | |
|---|---|
| 4. Constitutional Law | 2 |
| 5. Discretionary Powers | 2 |
| 6. Penal Law—Offenses | 16 |
| 7. Justification—Use of Force/Deadly Physical Force (Penal Law - Article 35) | 7 |
| 8. Criminal Procedure Law    Total (a. through i.) | 21 |
|    a. Standards of Proof | |

**Part IV Procedures**

## Patrol Functions

## Traffic

## Investigations

35. Common Criminal Investigation Techniques     Total (a. through f.)     10
    a. Larceny
    b. Auto Theft
    c. Burglary
    d. Robbery
    e. Arson
    f. Electronic Media
36. Narcotics and Dangerous Drugs     3
37. Case Preparation and Demeanor in Official Proceedings     7
38. Organized Crime     2
39. Missing and Abducted Children/Missing Adult Cases     3

**Part V Proficiency Areas**
40. Interpersonal Skills/Arrest Techniques     Total (a. through f.)     40
    a. Communication/Interpersonal Skills
    b. Defensive Tactics
    c. Aerosol Devices
    d. Impact Devices
    e. Crowd and Riot Control Formations
    f. Rapid Deployment/Active Shooter
41. Firearms Training     40
42. Emergency Medical Services (First Responder)     40
43. Unusual Occurrences and Critical Incident Management
    (Includes Hazardous Materials Incidents and ICS100)     5
44. Emergency Vehicle Operation and Control     21

**Part VI Community Relations**
45. Community Resources - Victim/Witness Services     3
46. Crime Prevention and Crime Against the Elderly     4
47. Ethical Awareness     12
48. Cultural Diversity/Bias Related Incidents/Sexual Harassment     5
49. Community Oriented Policing and Problem Solving and
    Media Relations     2
50. Contemporary Police Problems     4

**Part VII Supervised Field Training Review and Orientation**
51. Supervised Field Training Review and Orientation     40

**Part VIII Physical Fitness/Wellness**
52. Physical Fitness/Wellness (Includes Officer Stress Awareness)     65

**Grand Total**     **510**

*Source:* New York State, Division of Criminal Justice Services, December 26, 2003.
http://criminaljustice.state.ny.us/ops/docs/training/pubs/basicpolice/bcpooutline.pdf.

# STATE OF CALIFORNIA

MINIMUM CONTENT AND HOURLY REQUIREMENTS
REGULAR BASIC COURSE (RBC) - STANDARD FORMAT

| DOMAIN NUMBER | DOMAIN DESCRIPTION | MINIMUM HOURS |
|---|---|---|
| 01 | Leadership, Professionalism & Ethics | 8 hours |
| 02 | Criminal Justice System | 4 hours |
| 03 | Policing in the Community | 12 hours |
| 04 | Victimology/Crisis Intervention | 6 hours |
| 05 | Introduction to Criminal Law | 6 hours |
| 06 | Property Crimes | 10 hours |
| 07 | Crimes Against Persons | 10 hours |
| 08 | General Criminal Statutes | 4 hours |
| 09 | Crimes Against Children | 6 hours |
| 10 | Sex Crimes | 6 hours |
| 11 | Juvenile Law and Procedure | 6 hours |
| 12 | Controlled Substances | 12 hours |
| 13 | ABC Law | 4 hours |
| 15 | Laws of Arrest | 12 hours |
| 16 | Search and Seizure | 12 hours |
| 17 | Presentation of Evidence | 8 hours |
| 18 | Investigative Report Writing | 40 hours |
| 19 | Vehicle Operations | 24 hours |
| 20 | Use of Force | 12 hours |
| 21 | Patrol Techniques | 12 hours |
| 22 | Vehicle Pullovers | 14 hours |
| 23 | Crimes in Progress | 16 hours |
| 24 | Handling Disputes/Crowd Control | 12 hours |
| 25 | Domestic Violence | 8 hours |
| 26 | Unusual Occurrences | 4 hours |
| 27 | Missing Persons | 4 hours |
| 28 | Traffic Enforcement | 22 hours |
| 29 | Traffic Accident Investigation | 12 hours |
| 30 | Preliminary Investigation | 42 hours |
| 31 | Custody | 4 hours |
| 32 | Lifetime Fitness | 40 hours |
| 33 | Arrest and Control/Baton | 60 hours |
| 34 | First Aid and CPR | 21 hours |
| 35 | Firearms/Chemical Agents | 72 hours |
| 36 | Information Systems | 4 hours |
| 37 | People with Disabilities | 6 hours |
| 38 | Gang Awareness | 8 hours |
| 39 | Crimes Against the Justice System | 4 hours |
| 40 | Weapons Violations | 4 hours |
| 41 | Hazardous Materials Awareness | 4 hours |
| 42 | Cultural Diversity/Discrimination | 24 hours |
| | Minimum Instructional Hours | 599 hours |

The minimum number of hours allocated to testing in the Regular Basic Course are shown below[1]

| TESTS | HOURS |
|---|---|
| Scenario Tests | 40 hours |
| POST-Constructed Pre-Course Test | 25 hours |
| (Non-scored test administered prior to instruction) | |
| POST-Constructed Tests | |
| POST-Constructed Knowledge Tests | |
| (LDs 2,3,5,6,7,8,9,10,11,12,13,15,16,17,19,20,25, 26,28,30,31,34,36,37,39,40 and 41) | |
| POST-Constructed Comprehensive Tests | |
| Mid-Course Proficiency Test | |
| (Assess domains 2,5,6,7,8,9,10,15,16,17,20, and 39) | |
| End-of-Course Proficiency Test | |
| (Assesses domains 2,5,6,7,8,9,10,11,12,13,15,16,17,19,20, 25,26,30,31,36,37,39,40 and 41) | |
| Total Minimum Required Hours | 664 hours |

*Source:* Peace Officer Standards and Training, State of California (2004). http://www.post.ca.gov/training/bt_bureau/TrainingSpecs/RBC_MINIMUM_HOURLY_ REQUIREMENTS.doc.

---

[1]Time required for exercise testing, instructional activities, and Physical Abilities Test Battery is included in instructional hours.

# OHIO PEACE OFFICER TRAINING COMMISSION

## BASIC TRAINING CURRICULUM (4/7/2003)

| UNIT | HOURS |
|---|---|
| 1. ADMINISTRATION | 21 TOTAL |
|   1. INTRODUCTION TO BASIC TRAINING | 1 |
|   2. ROLE OF AMERICAN PEACE OFFICER | 3 |
|   3. PHILOSOPHY & PRINCIPLES OF THE AMERICAN JUSTICE SYSTEM | 3 |
|   4. THE CRIMINAL JUSTICE SYSTEM & STRUCTURE OF THE AMERICAN COURTS | 3 |
|   5. ETHICS & PROFESSIONALISM | 3 |
|   6. COMMUNITY POLICING | 4 |
|   7. INTRODUCTION TO REPORT WRITING* | 4 |
| 2. LEGAL | 77 TOTAL |
|   1. GENERAL PROVISIONS | 2 |
|   2. OHIO REVISED CODE | |
|     A. HOMICIDE, ASSAULT, MENACING | 3 |
|     B. KIDNAPPING, EXTORTION | 1 |
|     C. SEXUAL ASSAULT | 2 |
|     D. PROSTITUTION, OBSCENITY | 2 |
|     E. ARSON & RELATED OFFENSES | 2 |
|     F. ROBBERY, BURGLARY, TRESPASS & RELATED OFFENSES | 2 |
|     G. THEFT, FRAUD & RELATED OFFENSES | 3 |
|     H. GAMBLING & RELATED OFFENSES | 2 |
|     I. LIQUOR CONTROL | 1 |
|     J. DRUG OFFENSES | 2 |
|     K. OFFENSES AGAINST PUBLIC PEACE | 2 |
|     L. SELECTED OFFENSES AGAINST THE FAMILY | 1 |
|     M. OFFENSES AGAINST JUSTICE AND PUBLIC ADMINISTRATION | 3 |
|     N. CONSPIRACY, ATTEMPT, COMPLICITY | 1 |
|     O. WEAPONS | 1 |
|   3. LAWS OF ARREST* | 16 |
|   4. SEARCH & SEIZURE* | 16 |
|   5. LEGAL ASPECTS OF INTERVIEW & INTERROGATION* | 4 |
|   6. CIVIL LIABILITY & USE OF FORCE* | 6 |
|   7. TESTIFYING IN COURT & RULES OF EVIDENCE | 5 |

*continues*

| UNIT | HOURS |
|---|---|
| 3. HUMAN RELATIONS | 76 TOTAL |
|    1. COMMUNICATING WITH THE PUBLIC & THE MEDIA | 2 |
|    2. HANDLING THE SPECIAL NEEDS POPULATION | 3 |
|    3. DOMESTIC VIOLENCE* | 15 |
|    4. CRISIS INTERVENTION* | 6 |
|    5. CHILD ABUSE & NEGLECT* | 6 |
|    6. MISSING CHILDREN INVESTIGATION* | 6 |
|    7. JUVENILE JUSTICE SYSTEM | 6 |
|    8. VICTIMS' RIGHTS | 2 |
|    9. CRIME PREVENTION | 6 |
|   10. UNDERSTANDING CULTURAL DIFFERENCES* | 24 |
| | |
| 4. FIREARMS | 60 TOTAL |
|    1. SAFETY PROCEDURES* | |
|    2. HANDGUN AND RELATED EQUIPMENT* | |
|    3. BASIC FUNDAMENTALS OF PISTOL CRAFT* | |
|    4. ONE HAND TECHNIQUE* | |
|    5. MULTIPLE TARGETS* | |
|    6. LOW LEVEL LIGHT CONDITIONS* | |
|    7. USE OF PROTECTIVE COVER* | |
|    8. MOVE AND SHOOT* | |
|    9. SHOTGUN TRAINING* | |
| | |
| 5. DRIVING | 24 TOTAL |
|    1. DEFENSIVE DRIVING* | 2 |
|    2. PURSUIT DRIVING* | 2 |
|    3. PRACTICAL EXERCISES* | 20 |
| | |
| 6. SUBJECT CONTROL TECHNIQUES* | 60 TOTAL |
| | |
| 7. FIRST AID* | 12 TOTAL |
| | |
| 8. PATROL | 48 TOTAL |
|    1. VEHICLE PATROL TECHNIQUES | 3 |
|    2. FOOT PATROL | 1 |
|    3. RESPONDING TO CRIMES IN PROGRESS | 2 |
|    4. BUILDING SEARCHES | 6 |
|    5. STOPS & APPROACHES* | 20 |
|    6. AUTO THEFT & V.I.N. RECONSTRUCTION | 2 |
|    7. GANG AWARENESS | 4 |
|    8. COMMUNICATIONS | |
|      A. RADIO PROCEDURES | 1 |
|      B. LEADS | 2 |
|    9. PRISONER BOOKING & HANDLING | 4 |
|   10. REPORT WRITING* | 3 |

*continues*

| UNIT | HOURS |
|---|---|
| 9.  CIVIL DISORDERS | 24 TOTAL |
|     1. CONTROL OF NONVIOLENT CROWDS, CONFRONTING HOSTILE CROWDS | 3 |
|     2. RIOT FORMATIONS | 3 |
|     3. CHEMICAL AGENTS | 2 |
|     4. BOMBS/EXPLOSIVES/WMD | 6 |
|     5. TERRORISM - DOMESTIC & INTERNATIONAL | 4 |
|     6. ICS/HAZARDOUS MATERIALS* | 6 |
| | |
| 10.  TRAFFIC | 72 TOTAL |
|     1. INTRODUCTION TO TRAFFIC | 1 |
|     2. MOTOR VEHICLE OFFENSES | 8 |
|     3. COMMERCIAL VEHICLE OFFENSES | 3 |
|     4. TRAFFIC CRASH INVESTIGATION | 15 |
|        A. TRAFFIC CRASH PLANNING, FACTORS & EVENTS | |
|        B. TRAFFIC CRASH REPORTING PROCEDURES | |
|        C. INTERVIEWING & FACT GATHERING | |
|        D. DIAGRAMMING & TEMPLATE | |
|        E. COLLECTION OF EVIDENCE | |
|        F. VEHICLE DAMAGE | |
|     5. UNIFORM TRAFFIC TICKET | 1 |
|     6. SPEED ENFORCEMENT | 5 |
|     7. TRAFFIC DIRECTION & CONTROL | 1 |
|     8. ALCOHOL DETECTION, APPREHENSION AND PROSECUTION | 32 |
|     9. EXERCISE FOR TRAFFIC INVESTIGATION | 6 |

*continues*

| UNIT | HOURS |
|---|---|
| **11. INVESTIGATION** | **54 TOTAL** |
| 1. CRIME SCENE SEARCH | 4 |
| 2. EVIDENCE COLLECTION TECHNIQUES | 16 |
| 3. CRIME SCENE SKETCHING & DETAILED DRAWING | 4 |
| 4. POLICE PHOTOGRAPHY | 3 |
| 5. TRACING STOLEN PROPERTY | 1 |
| 6. ARSON SCENE INVESTIGATION | 1 |
| 7. CONTROLLED SUBSTANCE & DRUG AWARENESS | 2 |
| 8. OHIO DRUG LAWS | 2 |
| 9. CONFIDENTIAL INFORMANTS | 2 |
| 10. OBSERVATION, PERCEPTION, & DESCRIPTION | 2 |
| 11. LINE-UPS | 2 |
| 12. GAMBLING & PROSTITUTION | 2 |
| 13. LIQUOR CONTROL & ENFORCEMENT | 2 |
| 14. SURVEILLANCE | 2 |
| 15. INTERVIEW & INTERROGATION TECHNIQUES* | 4 |
| 16. SEARCH WARRANTS* | 2 |
| 17. INVESTIGATIVE REPORT WRITING* | 3 |
| **12. PHYSICAL CONDITIONING** | **30 TOTAL** |
| | **558 TOTAL** |

*Source:* Attorney General's Office, State of Ohio, Ohio Peace Officer Training Commission (2004). Basic Training Curriculum. http://www.ag.state.oh.us/sections/pota/downloads/requirements_options.pdf.

---

*Denotes a topic requiring mandatory attendance.

# Index